John Martin Littlejohn,

A Clash of Three Cultures

By

Chris Campbell

Cover from drawing

By

Rosemary Taylor

John Martin Littlejohn, A Clash of Three Cultures

Copyright ©2020 by Chris Campbell

ISBN No. 978-1-912606-75-7

ALL RIGHTS RESERVED

Including the right of reproduction in whole or in part in any form. This edition printed and bound in the Republic of Ireland by:
Lettertec Publishing
Springhill House
Carrigtwohill
Co. Cork
Ireland.

No part of this publication may be reproduced or transmitted by any device, without the prior written permission of the copyright holder.

This book may not be circulated without a cover or in any cover other than the existing cover.

"I have given my life to osteopathy and have done what few have done for it. I have given my money and some of them who have been given the benefit of this have done more than the open enemies of osteopathy to hinder our progress and development"... the school owes its existence to myself and I have done for it what no one else could do." – September 17th, 1932

I had to borrow £4000 to keep the school as it is and provide our present building as our old building was not suitable. You know I don't get anything out of it beyond the satisfaction of being able to help you and others to keep up and carry on the work. That is my ambition to get men like you, and women too to keep up this work when I am laid aside. That is why instead of spending all my time doing practice for myself I try to teach others so that the work may expand and be carried on." (Letter to T. E. Hall April 11th, 1932)

A word needs to be said about references in general. Just because it is in print does not make it true or factual. Sometimes the wrong reference is put in by mistake; sometimes authors deliberately mislead by putting in an irrelevant reference, giving the impression of authenticity. My advice is to always check the references and decide for yourself.

One of the most reliable sources of information, my mentor J. Wernham, like most people, had many faults- for example, he did not reference his books and often did not give credit to those whose research he used. However, as a source of information about Littlejohn, he spoke of what he knew, stating his opinion as just that; when interviewed, he would not embellish, obfuscate or mischievously confuse. Unfortunately, his devotion to Littlejohn's teachings and his inclination not to reference his writings has left him open to the criticism that he is an unreliable if important source.

Newspaper reports, in particular, are prone to mistyping and printing; a prime example being Littlejohn's postnominal letters, appearing as FRS, FRSc, FSSc FRSL and other variations , usually only being correct when Littlejohn himself inserted them; many times he only used the post-nominal letters M.D., D.O., LL.D. with the occasional use of Ph.D. His use of FSSc., FRSL being the most misprinted.

Many people and libraries have help in the research for this work, too many to mention all. However, I would like to particularly thank Isaac Franco and Ben Adams for their comments and help on proof reading, many local libraries I have visited personally or a researcher has visited on my behalf, The Nodaway Valley Historical Museum, Clarinda, Iowa for the photographs of Amity College and College springs; The invaluable help from the archivists at The Glasgow University Archive, The British Library, The Wellcome Library, The A. T. Still museum for all their help over the years, The Chicago College of Osteopathy, The British School of Osteopathy (Now called University College of Osteopathy), The New York Academy of Medicine library and Jane Stark. Willie Siddall for bringing back to life some of the old photographs. Rosemary Taylor for her drawing of Littlejohn and the American school of Osteopathy. John Wernham without whom I would have known very little about Littlejohn, and of course, all the staff, officers and members of the Institute of Classical Osteopathy, UK, for their support and encouragement

As this research has been ongoing for more than 30 years many of the original sources have been lost. I was especially fortunate to have had access to many personal collections, including newspaper clippings over the years. While the original clippings are not available now, I have found that most newspapers can be viewed at the many digital sites, including Ancestry, newspaperarchive.com, find my past, ancestry.com, the British library, Chronicling America etc.

Apart from local libraries, many excellent digital research sources have been used including the Hathi Trust, Archive.org, Chronicling America, The British library, and other Familysearch.org, digitised newspaper archives including the commercial ones like Ancestry, newspaperarchive.com, find my past, etc.

The original source of many references has been lost in the mists of time, having collected this material over a period of more than 30 years. The research was done originally for my own education and only in later years was I made put it into book form. The purpose being to make it available to others and to try and correct much of the misinformation current about Littlejohn.

The old Osteopathic journals are available from the A T Still Museum of Osteopathy, The New York Academy of Medicine, The National Library of Medicine, Bethesda; some of the Journal of the Science of Osteopathy and the Osteopathic World are held in the British Library and also in the archives of the Mid-Western University,

Chicago (formerly the Chicago College of Osteopathy); Many of the old books and magazines can be found on the Hathi Trust and Archive.org web sites; The Christian Nation and other records of the Reformed Presbyterian Church can be found on the web site of Reformed Presbyterian church of North America, http://rparchives.org/; records of the congregations of the Reformed Presbyterian church of Ireland can be found at their Library at Knockbracken and The Public records office of Northern Ireland. Newspaper cuttings, some of which did not even have the name of the paper they came from proved difficult to find. However, For UK and Irish newspapers the British Library is the best source, some local papers are held in the local county libraries; For American papers Chronicling America website; newspaperarchive.com and local state libraries; The A T Still Museum of Osteopathy has a large collection of newspaper cuttings relevant to osteopathy.

Despite all the help the book will probably contain errors, omission, typing mistakes etc. I apologise if I have left out anyone or organisation that has helped in this research or mis-referenced or not credited a source. They are my responsibility; I have done my best to avoid them and apologise for any that remain. Many different spellings may be found, from UK English, American English as well as typographical errors. I felt it appropriate not to standardise the spelling. I hope this does not spoil your reading.

Chris Campbell D.O.
June 2020

Having and trying to live by lofty ideals and principles does not mean that he had lost the frailties of being human.

[1]

---

[1] LittleJohn had a full beard for a short time. From photos in the archives of the A. T. Still Museum of osteopathy this would seem to date from his time in Chicago until shortly after he first started in the ASO, and probably relates to throat irritation associated with his illnesses. Drawing by Rosemary Taylor

"If we have petty Jealousies and animosities, let us bury this forever. If we do not, these jealousies and strives may throw us back a century and retard us so as to allow us to become a reproach even to ourselves. Our colleges should be patterns of educational seminars in the true sense of the term; a professor should be men of commanding intelligence and learning in the fields of literature, science and therapeutics; our students and practitioners, students in natures realm of resources, neglectful of nothing that can add dignity to the truths of our system and careful of everything that throws light upon our theory and practice and gives us a better understand of our duty".
(The Osteopathic World May 1903 page 213-4)

"It is impossible for us to give rules for the observance of the Sabbatism. The religion of Jesus is not exactly a casuistical programme of precepts; it is a religion of principles which enter the mind, appeal to the conscience, and affect the heart and life. To lay down rigid regulation would be inconsistent with the spirt of Christianity"
(Essay on Sabbatism Glasgow university Archives ref. DC199/882)

Contents

Abbreviations 1

John Martin Littlejohn-**A Practical Covenanter** 3

Littlejohn's Vision 12

    Clash of Three Cultures 18

INTRODUCTION 22

BACKGROUND-1885 28

    THE REFORMED PRESBYTERIAN CHURCH 28

    FAMILY AND CHURCH BACKGROUND 35

Places of Interest in the early life of John Martin Littlejohn 42

    MOVE TO LORNE, SCOTLAND 43

    MOVE TO GARVAGH, County Londonderry, Ireland 46

        EDUCATION IN COLERAINE 47

        BOTH BROTHERS ATTEND GLASGOW UNIVERSITY 49

1885-1888 55

    RETURN TO GARVAGH 55

    CALL TO CREEVAGH 58

    CREEVAGH BACKGROUND 60

    BACKGROUND ON FINANCIAL MATTERS 63

    ORDINATION AND WORK IN CREEVAGH............................... 65

        The CREEVAGH MISSIONARY ASSOCIATION 70

    PROBLEMS ARISE IN CREEVAGH 73

        JANUARY 1888 - MAY 1888 75

Summary 82
MAY TO OCTOBER 1888 86
   LIFE IN THE US FROM OCTOBER 1888 UNTIL THE END OF SUMMER 1889 89
   1889, RETURNS TO GLASGOW UNIVERSITY 93
   A SERIOUS FALL, OUTCOME OF WHICH IS MOVE TO USA .. 100
   SEPTEMBER 1892, TRAVELS TO THE US 102
   1892, COLUMBIA COLLEGE 103
   WORK AS A MINISTER IN THE US 112
   SUMMER 1893, TRIP TO UK AND EUROPE 115
      Littlejohns D.D. degree 122
1894-1897 130
   1894, AMITY COLLEGE 132
   1895, TRIP TO ENGLAND 140
   An Ideal presented and history repeats itself 148
   The College Springs and Southwestern Railroad company. 152
   1895, FINALISES PHD THESIS WHILE AT AMITY 158
   LATE 1896, 1897, STARTS CONSIDERING MOVE FROM AMITY 164
1897- 1899 177
1897 – Chicago prior to Kirksville 177
   MOVE TO KIRKSVILLE 185
      Littlejohn, Still and Physiology 194
      Surgery and Osteopathy 199
      Tragic deaths of two students 204
      The Agreement 207

The Good Times 209

Graduating class commencement exercises February 1ST, 1899 214

Littlejohn's vision and work as Dean 217

The M.D. Osteopathic Idea 221

Dr William Smith 222

The Turning Tide 223

The Tornado 227

The A S O to Move from Kirksville 230

The M. D. O. question comes to a head 236

Summary 238

LITTLEJOHN'S RETURN FROM SUMMER IN ENGLAND 1899 ... 245

Hildreth the A.A.A.O, and Harry 245

C M T Hulett and the M.D.O. 246

Changes to the Journal of Osteopathy 254

"SOMETHING NEW OR NOTHING AT ALL" 256

Hildreth's Recall to the A. S. O. 265

Hildreth's Version of Events 267

JOURNAL OF OSTEOPATHY APRIL 1901 GRADUATING CLASS FEB 1901 CLASS POEM 277

The Seeds of Discontent 278

THE DISPUTE 288

SOME LEGAL MATTERS, DEPOSITIONS AND COURT CASES 307

Quotes from the Deposition 309

1900-1913 315

MOVE TO CHICAGO, FAMILY UPDATE 315

The American College of Osteopathic Medicine and Surgery 333
  THE ASSOCIATED COLLEGES 347
  THE ALABAMA DECISION AND MATERIA MEDICA 356
  Independent Boards 365
  A word about Hildreth the Politician 372
  THE 1906 AOA INSPECTION 375
  Change of Name to The Littlejohn College 384
  EXPERIMENTING ON ANIMALS 388
  DEFINITION OF OSTEOPATHY 394
  ISSUE OF TOXICOSIS 397
  Replenishing his Conscience 401
THE STATE BOARD OF HEALTH 403
  THE FLEXNER REPORT 412
FURTHER DETAIL ON THE A.O.A., THE A.C.O., THE M.D. DEGREE
AND DRUGS 420
  LAKE BLUFF 440
  THE PATH TO ENGLAND 445
  A REVIEW 449
  THE CASE OF THE MYSTERIOUS GROCERY BILL 457
THE CHICAGO COLLEGE OF OSTEOPATHY 459
  Littlejohn College Was a Non-Profit Institution 460
  Comment 462
JML'S CAREER IN ENGLAND 472
  Badger Hall 475
  Life in England 477
  Reverent Doctor William C. Minifie 482

Minifie's Canadian and USA fundraising trip 1916 489

Littlejohn and Minifie.. 498

Reverend Minifie, Littlejohn and the International Bible
Institute War Relief Fund 504

    The International Bible Institute Affair 505

1935 HOUSE OF LORDS SELECT COMMITTEE HEARING 527

    List of Degrees and Diplomas in Chronological Order 535

    The British Medical Associations approach 537

    Littlejohn's approach 546

        The Destruction of Littlejohn's Reputation 559

    Some Additional Context 564

        Jowitt's speech and the Looker Students 566

        Littlejohn and Hall... 573

    The Last Decade 578

A Footnote on the B.S.O. 590

    Littlejohn and his family.. 595

J M LITTLEJOHN'S LEGACY 600

APPENDICES 605

    National University of Chicago... 605

        Harkins defence of the National University 608

    The National Medical College. 612

    Dunham and Herring Colleges 620

THE SOCIETY OF SCIENCE, LETTERS AND ART 625

    What was the Society of Science, Letters and Art? 628

    How the Society recruited Members and Fellows 631

    Criticisms of the Society of Science, Letters and Art........... 633

An Interpretation and possible explanation 637
Hymns and Psalms for Littlejohn's Funeral 641
    Psalm 100 641
    Psalm 23 642
    Lead, Kindly Light 643
    Some final words about the man John Martin Littlejohn ... 645
        Wm. R. Dobbyn describing J. Martin Littlejohn 646

Abbreviations

AAO	American Academy of Osteopathy
AAAO	American Association for the Advancement of Osteopathy
AOA	American Osteopathic Association
ACOM&S	American College of Osteopathic Medicine and Surgery
AMA	American Medical Association
ASO	American School of Osteopathy
BSO	British School of Osteopathy
BMA	British Medical Association
BOA	British Osteopathic Association
IAO	Incorporated Association of Osteopaths
RPC	Reformed Presbyterian Church
RPCofNA	Reformed Presbyterian Church of North America
ICO	Institute of Classical Osteopathy
STILL	Andrew Taylor Still the founder of Osteopathy; other members of the Still family are mentioned by their full name or initials.
LITTLEJOHN	john Martin Littlejohn: other members of the Littlejohn family are mentioned by their full names or initials.

John Martin Littlejohn-**A Practical Covenanter**
(Rev Geoffrey Allen)

Growing up in the small Ulster town of Garvagh, I was familiar with the old Reformed Presbyterian church building which had been sold to another denomination in the early 1970s, yet I knew little of its history. When, many years later I became a minister in that same Covenanter denomination, my sister in law, who was training in osteopathy, studied the life of Rev John Martin Littlejohn the osteopathic pioneer. I could only offer some local knowledge and background having attended the same schools. However, through our church history committee, I was able to provide some information to John O'Brien for the book he was preparing about Littlejohn.

On further studying the history of the Garvagh Congregation, I became aware of the wider ministries of this Scottish family, father and sons in Scotland, Ireland and America. Therefore, when I was contacted by the present author, Chris Campbell, I was intrigued as he was looking more deeply into John Martin Littlejohn's background and beliefs. This investigation seeks to explain effectively, the principles which underpinned his life and work and at times brought him into conflict with others.

When approaching the study of a minister who has apparently moved out of ministry into other spheres of service, it can be tempting to dismiss them as having weakened in their positions or drifted from the sense of call. Certainly John Martin Littlejohn's brief ministry in the Irish Reformed Presbyterian church barely registers in the memory of the denomination, but having read through much of the research on his life, I found myself rebuked and in fact challenged in my opinions because of his tenacious application of theologically Reformed principles to every area of his life and in particular his steadfastness and willingness to engage in his contemporary world, yet maintain the overruling concept of his belief in the Kingship of Christ.

Chris Campbell in his research has thoroughly grasped and well explains Littlejohn's foundations in the Scottish Reformation and he is correct in seeing that this as the key to unlocking many aspects of John Martin Littlejohn's character and career.

The Biblical concept of the Kingship of Christ echoes from the closing address of Christ to his disciples before his ascension, that all authority was given him over heaven and earth. This has been historically applied in the realm of the church and of the civil state, which must also be seen as a divine institution and not the invention of men, both however separate in jurisdiction but united under Christ. When the Church of Scotland chose pragmatism over principle in the 1690's, the majority of the dissenting remnant, being the Reformed Presbyterian church, made the same choice in the 1860's to facilitate church union. John Martin Littlejohn's father remained with the minority group holding to the historical position. As a boy, John Martin would have been aware of the sacrifice made by his father in standing on principle and this central concept of Christ's kingship was the framework by which with his exceptional abilities, he was able to engage practically with his Covenanter beliefs in all his academic and theological pursuits.

Having preached in John Martin Littlejohn's congregation of Creevagh in County Monaghan several times, I have thought of him in the pulpit of that building, little changed in a century. As a preacher with considerable gifts, Littlejohn in his short ministry certainly turned the congregation's mind outward to the world of mission, then focused on Syria, but in practice an established congregation moves at a slower pace than the ideas of a zealous young pastor. Sadly circumstances led to his resignation and removal to the United States. There seems to have been little lasting discouragement and he did not become the object of pity or indeed self-pity as the 'stickit minister' of the Scots 'Kailyard school' of storytelling, rather he offered himself to the Reformed Presbyterian Church of North America, the daughter church of the Irish Covenanters. His energy was barely impeded by his troubling injury from a fall and while pursuing further studies he effectively revived a Reformed Presbyterian congregation in Brooklyn, New York.

His association with the Covenanter cause continued and he kept his ministerial credentials up to date. In his educational career he encouraged college links with local Reformed Presbyterian congregations where possible. In association with his brother and fellow minister William Littlejohn they established a Reformed Presbyterian congregation in College Springs, Iowa beside Amity College, of which he was president. He ambitiously proposed that the denomination receive Amity as sister college to Geneva College in Pittsburgh. This would have been a major achievement in moving it from the control of the larger United Presbyterian Church.

Although Reformed Presbyterianism was influential in the early days of pre- and post-Revolutionary North America, its views were becoming marginalised within American evangelicalism. Reformed Presbyterians historically found difficulty in applying their universal principles to a democratic and constitutional republic which rejected Christ as supreme authority. The Associate Reformed Presbyterian church was a union of early American Covenanters and Scottish Seceders in response to the American Constitution. However, it was the reconstituted Reformed Presbyterian Church of North America that were pioneers in the movement to abolish slavery. However, in post-bellum United States the A.R.P. and the Reformed Presbyterians were part of an ecumenical and Reformed movement called the National Reform Association which sought among other things a Christian amendment to the Constitution. This would fulfil the Covenanters goal of constituting the nation under the Kingship of Christ and allow them to fully participate in civil affairs. The periodical 'The Christian Nation' was the main outlet for this movement. For a time, Littlejohn was a department editor of this periodical and a frequent contributor. Among an amazing diversity of academic papers in many disciplines which Littlejohn produced he submitted a thesis entitled "Christian Sabbatism" In this he defended the observance of the Christian Sabbath, which was under attack even among conservative Protestants. This indicated the rigour that he applied to Biblical and philosophical apologetics while able to associate freely with those in his career in education, medicine and Osteopathy who did not share his religious or political opinions.

It is clear that his father and brothers were close partners in ministry and medicine and when he brought his parents to the United States his father assisted him on many occasions. Maintaining close links with his brothers one can feel his disappointment when his brother James, on the death of his father, was inaugurated into various oath bound societies to which the Reformed Presbyterians were strongly opposed, and all for the seeming advancement of his medical career.

James became an Elder in the 4th Presbyterian Church in Chicago. His brother William joined the larger United Presbyterian denomination and eventually in a process precipitated by the death of his father, became a Baptist. John at this point remained steadfast.

Education was an essential part of the Scottish and European Reformation, in this Littlejohn firmly believed that any discipline could be pursued to the glory of God as Christ the creative living word of God was the author of all that is true. The educational environment in the liberty of the United States was not as regulated as in the United Kingdom and he was attracted at times to some colleges and universities on the fringe. This caused some controversies later in his career where amalgamations meant that the original degree granting bodies had disappeared and some of his qualifications seemed unprovable. Littlejohn was concerned that the underprivileged would have every access to education and often personally paid the fees of financially struggling students. His involvement in the Chautauqua Movement, which to the observer had the vitality of a revivalist meeting, must have delighted him, where the dissemination of knowledge was free from the formal restraints of academia and college boards.

The late 19th Century in America was a period of non-mainstream medical practices, in a world of 'snake-oil' salesmen unregistered practitioners and religiously based sanatoriums such as Battle Creek, Littlejohn, probably through his own health problems and a belief that God heals though medicine as well as the miracle, was attracted to the emerging movement of Osteopathic treatments pioneered by Andrew Taylor Still. The holistic approach looking to the whole man and not merely the symptoms, would have appealed to his Biblical view of man and it was Osteopathy's emphasis on the application of healing hands, which, while not supernatural, was an extension of God's healing powers in a medical realm. Perhaps he appreciated the underlying and corresponding principle that God heals within in the natural laws of creation first before using the supernatural.

He believed that Osteopathy was compatible with his Christian faith but should be regularised and recognised as an orthodox medical discipline under the medical and civil authorities.

How the author describes Littlejohn's dealings with the personalities within the developing schools of Osteopathy, the college administrations and later the select committee of House of Lords, makes for griping reading. Attempts were made to undermine his character and remove him from his responsibilities, yet he would not press back with a vengeful spirit at the expense of exposing his opponents. This was perhaps to his cost, as he was side-lined in the history of American Osteopathy as an eccentric and idealist; nevertheless, his founding of the British School of Osteopathy has had lasting significance.

During research the author has uncovered the oath of allegiance taken but Littlejohn in 1924 when he was recovering his British citizenship[1]. This must have been overlooked and in Britain such an action binding by an oath to the Covenant breaking Monarchy, would have received censure as a denial of core principles. This perhaps reflects the gradual change in his stance on a matter he came to see as peripheral rather than foundational.

On his return to the United Kingdom he had no meaningful contact with Reformed Presbyterians who were not present in England and struggling in Scotland and transferred his credentials to the group nearest to the Reformed Presbyterian Church, the United Presbyterian church in England. Ironically this was the body that his father dissented from entering union with and a similar group to which his brother William joined. Without contact with Covenanter peers it is likely that his theological views broadened somewhat, yet he still was a man who loved the Bible and took any opportunity to promote Christian work

Littlejohn continued his teaching and his Christian work, establishing the British School of Osteopathy in 1917 and collaborating with his friend Rev. William C. Minifie, a Baptist evangelist whom he had known in America. Their association was unusual, Littlejohn would

---

[1] In taking his American Citizenship Littlejohn made a 'declaration of Intent ,"made and oath before H.M. Stonestreet, Clerk, on the Holy Evangelists of Almighty God, that it was BONA FIDE his intent to become a citizen of the UNITED STATES, and to renounce and abjure forever all allegiance and fidelity to every Foreign Power, prince, Potentiate, State and Sovereignty whatever"

have appreciated Minifie's training in Charles Spurgeon's college for pastors as being orthodox, however his methods became somewhat unorthodox and tended to revivalism. It seems that he also was a Freemason! Minifie had claimed that at one time he was assistant private secretary to Spurgeon and had preached in his church the Metropolitan Tabernacle. It is unclear whether this claim is accurate, but there is a temptation for a freelance evangelist, without accountability, to allow a certain amount of exaggeration. Littlejohn and he were drawn closer by Minifies interest in Osteopathy and also in their collaboration in Christian charitable work for the War effort.

For the admirer of Littlejohn, the matter of his involvement in the 'International Bible Institute War Relief Fund', calls into question the wisdom and for some the integrity those involved. The charity was a creation of Minifie and he raised funds in North America which were intended for soldiers' and prisoners' welfare and the provision of scriptures to European soldiers. Minifie travelled in the Sates wearing the uniform of an honorary chaplain of a London regiment, when had been mobilised into the regular army. His appeal was backed tenuously by letters from the respective charities stating only their willingness to receive such funds. The charity claimed various personalities for their board of reference who upon investigation denied any knowledge. Littlejohn, as treasurer, had embarrassingly little understanding of finances and limited power to administer the funds. This is strange from one who had been so effective as College President and administrator. Minifie and his daughter, under an assumed name, solely directed the donations. Minifie's integrity as an 'honorary chaplain' and the charity he founded were investigated and the work was closed having operated for a short time in 1918 being registered under the charities commission and then removed from the register. It is interesting that during the police investigation, which was undertaken into many War charities at the time, Littlejohn made nothing of his theological qualifications or his position as a minister. Minifie claimed to have raised large amounts of money but comparatively little was donated. Were his claims simply exaggerated or was money misappropriated, or spent on his expenses touring America? The matter was not pursued as no donations were derived from the United Kingdom.

Littlejohn moved in what were perceived as unorthodox circles, medically and ecclesiastically, his Covenanter views of society had been out of favour since the mid seventeenth century, so perhaps some of his associations with retrospect seemed ill advised. It would be hard to say that his intentions were not well meaning, but they certainly were not always well informed. The author sheds interesting light on this continuing friendship with the charismatic Minifie which lasted right to his death. Did Littlejohn place too much simple trust in him to keep his word? This had characterised his relationships with others over his career. His association with Minifie continued in pioneering Osteopathy in the United Kingdom, Littlejohn requesting him to take part in his funeral in 1947.

In 1935, Littlejohn appeared before the House of Lord's Select Committee, in what was a premature attempt to have Osteopathy recognised by the British medical establishment in law. The vision that Littlejohn had, involved the integration of the discipline within wider medical practices, a source of disagreement with Dr Still, the American founder of Osteopathy. His appearance before the committee met resistance from the medical establishment, Littlejohn's credentials were then open to scrutiny and he clearly wished the validity of Osteopathy to be self-authenticating rather than resting solely upon the record of his own career and qualifications. His failed effort had been undermined by the disunity among British Osteopaths and a wilful misunderstanding by British establishment of the lack of government regulation in the United States.

British Osteopathy owes so much to John Martin Littlejohn the son of a Scottish Covenanter, raised on an unfashionable but he believed Biblical and defendable view of the world. He sought to apply faithfully these principles to himself and career in which his abilities led him to pursue the knowledge of God's world. While he seemed far from his calling, I do not believe that that desire to serve Christ left him, seeking the best for Him and his fellow men.

Chris Campbell does not avoid the difficult aspects to his character and in presenting the arguments well, this is not a hagiography. We do have some serious issues to address, whether human weakness, a naïve trust in others integrity, or wilful deception?

He was always on the edge of theological and medical orthodoxy but surely he was raised in Christian world-view not fully endorsed by the wider church and although his opinions perhaps were shaped latterly by his experiences he is not an enigma rather a practical Covenanter.

Rev Geoffrey Allen

Member of Reformed Presbyterian Church of Ireland Church History Committee

2

"Dr A.T. Still needs no defence from our pen. We came in contact with him almost daily for over two years and formed our judgement of the man, of his character and of his work from our own personal observation and association. We heard the story of his life from those who had associated with him. It is true he went around in simple garb with staff in hand and indifferent to everything but the great subject of his lifework. Sincerity was always marked upon his countenance the investigators demeanour was the badge of his workmanship constant enquiry after something to corroborate his own investigations marked him as a deep student and the facility with which he delved into all the details of the machinery and workings of the human organism branded him as the master osteopath. The petty ribalding and contemptible ravings of such letter writing as the one on exhibit is no credit to any cause." (J. Martin Littlejohn, The osteopathic World July 1904 page 186)

---

[2] From a drawing by Rosemary Taylor

Littlejohn's Vision

*Littlejohn's Principled Approach
to Osteopathic Treatment*

Much of today's treatment approach in osteopathy is technique based. The American Association of colleges of Osteopathic Medicine lists 40 different Osteopathic Manipulative medicine techniques with more than 500 being mentioned in other publications[i] This can be very confusing when compared with Littlejohn's approach, which, like that of A T Still ,was based upon principle.

The principles of 'the Vital Force' 'adjustment' and 'articulation' dominated his approach to osteopathy. **"We must begin at the vital force, because there we find the secret of the patient"**.[ii]

"The trouble here is that the osteopaths do not understand the principle of Osteopathy. The principle of Osteopathy is not bone adjustment, but body adjustment. Hence, any maladjustment affecting the body, or any of its parts- structural, environmental or toxic - falls under the osteopathic aetiology, and any means of correction - manipulative, dietetic or surgical - that tend to correct the adjustment and thus elaborate the forces and fluids of the body so as to normalise the body, belong to the osteopathic system. Drugs are entirely eliminated because these represent elements foreign to the proximate principles[iii]

He came under the influence of the approach of James. Lorimer professor of public law in Edinburgh University[1] in the nineteen century who favoured an approach based on reasoning from 'cause to

---

[1] In the preface to his Ph.D. thesis he says "The topic was first selected and the original plan...was first formulated under the inspiration of the ideas of the late Professor Lorimer of Edinburgh university"

effect' rather than looking at and treating the effect.[2]. This fitted in with the Reformed Presbyterian background that he had of taking the principles in the teachings of Christ and the bible and working from that principle to the general aspect of how you lived your life. Littlejohn had a principled approach to life in general and to osteopathy specifically. His methodology was to explore the principle on which either life or osteopathy was based and then apply his vision to how this applied in general. Looking at Littlejohn's writings, it is found that his approach had some elements of the homeopathic approach of constitutional and specific treatments, coupled with his general approach to life which was always based on having a principle, elucidating that principle and working from it to form a vision to how you approach life and then trying to put that into practice. On speaking about A.T. Still, Littlejohn says, in the commencement address to the October class in August 1898 journal of osteopathy,

"... these views, history when it is written with a pen of iron on the mountains of time will tell the story of the wonderful life of Andrew Taylor Still, by whose patient labours for over a quarter of a century you and I have been enriched by receiving from him the principles of osteopathy".

In another article he wrote in the American Institute of Homeopathy in 1904 he states, *"We must begin at the vital force, because there we find the secret of the patient, and end at the tissues, where all sickness ultimates, because from one to the other we have the basis on which the body organism in health and disease is built".*

Its very easy to form the opinion that Littlejohn was dogmatic and to mistake his rigid application of principles to blind dogma. This is partly due to the fact that most of what we hear about Littlejohn comes from those who knew him in his later life. Wernham described Littlejohn as being "difficult at times," its easy to forget that in later life he had suffered many trials and was chronically ill, suffering from severe abdominal pain and neck pain and headaches quite often.

---

[2]" More influential in France and Germany than in Great Britain, Lorimer's theory held that the natural law was founded on divine authority and revealed in conscience and in history". Encyclopaedia Britannica

Therefore, it is important to go back to his early writings to find what his approach was.

From the educational point of view, he states *"In the field of education nature won a victory with the names of Rabelais, Rousseau, Montaigue, Pestallozzi and Froebel testify to the scientific power of nature in the hands of skilled educators under whose genius modern education has ceased to be a system of cramming and promises to be the stimulation of mental growth by the skilful communication of knowledge in nature's method."* (Journal of Osteopathy August 1898)

In the same article his advice to the new graduates is an indication of his approach in general to life and also into promoting the osteopathic philosophy. *"There is no virtue needed so much in the osteopathic field today as prudence……..prudence and consecrated loyalty to truth which osteopathy represents will change the order of things. As soon as osteopathy separates itself in the public mind, as it is in reality separated, from the faith cure or the spirit cure idea and establishes in the public esteem its nature cure method it will make rapid strides…………don't spend your time provoking your neighbours to a quarrel for that will only arouse bitter feelings. If you cannot make a friend, never imprudently make a foe, for every enemy you make adds to the difficulty of the task that osteopathy must perform".*[iv]

In his earlier writings in the Christian Nation he also espouses the same approach. That instead of bringing peoples' faults to the fore, try and put them on the path of 'righteousness'; he thought that the correct approach, the best approach, and the approach that would bring about the best results was to instil in peoples' hearts the path of truth, peace and understanding so that they would naturally give up the ways of robbery, corruption and addiction etc. In other words, he always took a positive approach not accentuating the negative but promoting the positive attributes.

While the debate raged about the general treatment versus specific treatment and about long treatments versus short treatments, Littlejohn again took a much more positive and pragmatic view. Quoting from the same article *"Do not be content to go out and give a general treatment. Remember that here is the danger of osteopathy as it has been the danger point of drugs"*[v]. He goes then to give the example of a famous physician and compounding chemist who kept a special jar in which he put a sample of all the prescriptions that he was ever called upon to make up. This jar then contained a complete mixture of all the prescriptions that he had ever prepared. So that when a case came that he couldn't diagnose, didn't know what to do with he simply made up a bottle of this general mixture in the hope that it would strike somewhere*[3]*. *"It may happen in our own profession the operator who simply gives general treatment in the hope of hitting the right spot is in the same box. Hence, we need specialists who know just where and how to treat".*

While addressing graduates for the October class in 1898, he put the other side of this to the recent graduates when he said *"In order that the vital force may be unobstructed the different parts of the machine must operate in harmony, the skeleton must be adjusted to every motion of bone, ligament and muscle; pure air must penetrate every minute cell of an unimpeded lung and every remote recess of healthy tissue; blood must circulate in every organ and tissue; and a perfect nervous system must animate every tissue and cavity of the body. To see that this is the condition of the body is your function as an osteopathic physician. You are not sent out with a set of formula to put down under the great R*[4]*, nor are you given a number of technical punches and movements like massage and fake osteopaths; you are sent out with principles and a correct knowledge of anatomy and physiology to apply these in the correction of diseases and disordered conditions".*[vi]

---

[3] This was an example he had used previously in regard to education in general: "education should be measured by quality not by quantity. One book well digested and well mastered is better than a hundred superficially studied. Our educational view may be illustrated by a story told by Dr. Smith of Bowdoin College. He had a large practice as a physician and had to make up his medicines. Too busy to return small quantities of medicine he had been using, to its proper jar, bottle, etc, he kept a large jar on his table, into which he dropped whatever was over in every prescription, powder, oil, essence, etc. When, he had a patient whose malady he could not diagnose, he used to give him a bottle of this mixture expecting it to hit somewhere. Our teaching is often very like this, the idea being that if the course is crowded with everything all cases will be met somehow"(Before the Southeastern Section of Page County Teacher's Association, College Springs, Iowa, Feb. 12, 1897, v by Dr. J. M. Littlejohn, published in the Clarinda Herald Feb. 23rd 1897)

[4] The great Rx = the short cut for 'prescription'

This leads to his approach, the application of a constitutional type treatment specific to that individual to allow the vital force to be unobstructed in the different part of the machine coupled with specific treatment to address the specific organs or lesions within the body. These always under the guidance of nature or that great principle within the body the vital force, that is so often do not talk about these days.

What others call the general treatment he would not use. Some advised using the general treatment as a means of making the patient feel as if they got their monies worth. Some that after doing a specific adjustment you give them a general rub down so that they felt they got their monies worth. Littlejohn would have none of this. In Class, Wernham would say that Littlejohn described giving only specific treatment as 'attacking the lesioned area, or the part that was in trouble, and leaving it to nature to sort out the resulting change', and he called it chiropractic and that he would have none of it. The general treatment that Littlejohn espoused was very specific in nature, specific to that patient. Minor differences in pressure, in angle of articulation, in depth of pressure etc made all the differences. We're deeply indebted to John Wernham for taking this approach and evolving it into the highly specific approach of the Body Adjustment.

Another aspect that Littlejohn emphasised was *"osteopathy sets aside medicines in the sense of drugs, but it cannot afford to set aside anything else. Osteopathy is certainly an independent school of medicine and need not fear to stand side by side with other schools, first to rival and finally to out rival them, if she adheres to anatomy, physiology, pathology, diagnosis, hygiene, surgery, obstetrics and chemistry, substituting osteopathic therapeutics and practice for the old school theory and practice of medicines"*[vii].

It's not possible to describe a technical approach in an article such as this only to give some clues as to the general principles involved. Regarding the specific treatment that Littlejohn taught it may be described, using his own words, as follows;

First, we make contact, we put our hand on the patient. *"There is a peculiar sacredness in the science and art of healing. You must face the most affecting scenes that mortals ever see and receive the great confidences that men can give. Can you tell from whence life comes, whether it goes and for what purpose it exists? When your hands are laid on the sick, lay them on reverently as if you were dealing with the master mechanism of earth and heaven, the body of man than which no more perfect embodiment of divine wisdom ever appeared......... what will you do with the treasures that lie in your hands? Become a spoiled child of science, or heroic champion of the latest truth. Do not let the 'auri sacra fames' eat out the vitals of your life; let you ambitions be to win in the race for fame not intoxicated by the desire for fame, as Milton says, 'fame is the spur which the clear spirit doth raise that last infirmity of noble mind, to scorn delights and live laborious days".*[viii]

There's no pushing or shoving or sudden impositions on the patient by jerking movements in this approach. This is not to say that he didn't use jerking movements or so-called thrusts when they were needed but they were only when they were needed. As Wernham use to say, 'gentle rhythm is the way'.

Moving back to his advice to new graduates we find again this gentle, kind, non-invasive, non-quarrelling approach of Littlejohn *"To one and all of you we would say, your primary duty is to heal the sick, to relieve the suffering, and to raise up the bowed down. Do not be carried away by assorted love or lust for money, ambition, for fame, pride or outranking others. Osteopathy asks no favours. Do not ask any for yourselves. She simply asks for an open field and you are to take possession of it, not in your own name but in the name of your science. Avoid the glitter and the pomposity of the self-importance. Be confident of your ability, unchangeable in your faith in the science, and leave to the hereafter the glory of your person. One of the menaces of your profession is quackery. This cannot be met by legislation, however honest and well meant, for legislation can never make men moral. We must educate the people in the principles of our science and teach them that the greatest consecration of manhood and womanhood is devoted to this great science. The grandest thing you can do to the prejudiced is to enable them to see clearly, for as John Ruskin says, 'To see clearly is poetry, prophecy and religion all in one'. As for the hypocritical element of society, these can only be aroused from their present condition by some seismic eruption belching them out of their own imaginatively formed hospitals in order to introduce them to the free breathing space in the parlours of nature where free oxygen is the medicine of nature".*[ix]

What a beautiful sentiment that he gives, as relevant if not more relevant today than it was in his time. Too often we try to make or correct the morality of people by legislation or by some other form of regulation within the profession, but this can never be so. That morality must come from within and our job is to educate people on the principles and to stick to those principles ourselves, and to remember as Littlejohn says *"osteopathy is an art, for 'knowledge is power', as Bacon says; and where knowledge is not power ,it is useless and worse than useless, because it becomes dangerous. Impart it to others for 'education is the generator of power".*[x] And this power we have we must not abuse. And to finish *"Learn to use your eyes and your ears. You must lie and wait for knowledge and for the opportunities of acquiring it. Pursue the science and keep your profession above the mere doggerel of duty. Do not regard it as a means only of gaining a livelihood or as a Klondike. Do not make it the avenue of personal fame or greatness nor as an instrument of practical beneficence, Emerson's ideal was a grand one; 'Tis nobleness to serve, help them who cannot help again; beware from right to swerve'."*[xi]

Clash of Three Cultures

To understand Littlejohn's journey, it is necessary to understand the three cultures that were involved. The first one is that of Littlejohn's upbringing itself. That is the Reformed Presbyterian background. It has to be said that the Reformed Presbyterians were a 'state within a state'. They did not acknowledge the authority of the state as it was considered to have broken its covenant with God and therefore was ungodly. They engaged in political descent, not voting, not taking oaths of allegiance, which involved foreswearing, and living by their own code of conduct, which was moral, honest, just with a particular emphasis on covenants or contracts. This would mean at one extreme that if people entered into a contract or gave their word for something and one reneged on that, the other would feel almost duty bound to see that the contract was fulfilled. To put it another way their word was their bond. They didn't engage in guile, deceit, manipulation or subterfuge. They spoke what they believed and expected others to do the same.

When Littlejohn went to America, he came in contact with the culture of the Midwestern American politician. This would have been almost the exact opposite of what Littlejohn was used to. The bread and butter of the politician was subterfuge and manipulation. They expected others to behave in the same manner. It would have been quite unusual for them to come across someone who not only spoke what they felt but stuck to their word and expected others to do the same.

The third culture involves the elite educational system that was in vogue in England in the early mid twentieth century and the late nineteenth century. This again would have been in contrast to Littlejohn's background where people would not take a degree if it involved taking an oath of allegiance to the crown or to the university. And even at the time when Littlejohn was in Glasgow the idea of going to university to get a degree was not yet in vogue[xii]. He went to university to get an education, the taking of the degree or conferring of the degree was secondary. The taking of the degree was a latter development and developed into the elite educational system that was in vogue in England on Littlejohn's return. We can trace his movement along these lines from the Halls of Glasgow and Columbia to the National university of Chicago, The Add-Ran university in Texas[5], Amity college and the Chautauqua movement and hence his career in Osteopathy with his support for those who had lesser good fortune. This journey was also a journey of discovery for Littlejohn of his true calling in the field of education. Education was an undercurrent in all of his studies and 'careers'. First in Glasgow university, then as a minister in the Reformed Presbyterian Church, through his experience in Columbia and then at Amity. While education was an undercurrent one can't help but feel that the final move came after he did his research into the fee system.[xiii] This research fitted into the realm of political Science but the subject would have shown such corruption that it could only have left Littlejohn struggling to come to terms with it, leaving the way open for him to move more into the true educational field.(In 1895 he

---

[5] Originating in 1869 and moving to Waco Texas in 1895 it has been called the Texas Christian University Since 1902 and today is a flourishing university. It owes its name to its founders the brothers **Add**ison and **Ran**dolph Clark, thus the name Add-Ran.

presented the first of his three papers on Education to the Society of Science, Letters and Art, London[xiv].) A good expose of the field is given by Thomas Urdahl in 1898:

"The Fee system and political corruption – very few people are so ignorant of politics as to not have heard, from rumor at least, of public offices the emoluments of which are so great as to enrich the occupant in a single year. No public office in the gift of the people is of such importance as to yield a regular legal salary of $100,000, even though it required the highest grade of ability which the country can furnish. This amount has been received more than once, however, by officers whose duties and abilities were of a comparatively low order........The income of the city clerk of Chicago was asserted to be $49,000 for two years, Chicago Times Herald Jan 16th 1896 page 1"

For Littlejohn to try and explain his allegiance to the less well-established universities, those that were connected with the so-called fundamentalists in America at the time, to those involved in higher education in England would have been impossible. We get a view of this from his association with the Chautauqua movement. He was *"a member of the executive committee in connection with what is called Chautauqua, and I(Littlejohn) lectured in practically all the centres in the middle west from Cleveland, Ohio, to Denver, Colorado and from the University of Minneapolis to Selma Alabama."*[xv]

This, originally the Chautauqua Lake Sunday School Assembly, was founded in 1874 as an educational experiment in out-of-school, vacation learning. It was successful and broadened almost immediately beyond courses for Sunday school teachers to include academic subjects, music, art and physical education.

While founders Lewis Miller and John Heyl Vincent were Methodists, other Protestant denominations participated from the first year onward.

"The Chautauqua Literary and Scientific Circle (CLSC) was started in 1878 to provide those who could not afford the time or money to attend college the opportunity of acquiring the skills and essential knowledge of a College education. The four-year, correspondence course was one of the first attempts at distance learning. Besides broadening access to education, the CLSC program was intended to

show people how best to use their leisure time and avoid the growing availability of idle pastimes, such as drinking, gambling, dancing and theater-going, that posed a threat both to good morals and to good health[6]. To share the cost of purchasing the publications and to take encouragement from others in the course, students were encouraged to form local CLSC reading circles. Soon these were established throughout the country and, in time, around the world. Among those who benefited most from the CLSC program were women, teachers, and those living in remote rural areas. At the end of their four years of study, students were invited to come to Chautauqua to receive their certificates in a ceremony, which is still held today during the first week in August.

"With the success of the CLSC, many new Chautauquas were created, known as "Daughter Chautauquas," giving rise to what was called the "Chautauqua Movement." Some years later, the talent agencies that provided speakers and entertainers for these platforms, put together shows of their own, which traveled to small towns across the United States and Canada. These were known as the 'circuit chautauquas" or "tent chautauquas."

"By 1880 the Chautauqua platform had established itself as a national forum for open discussion of public issues, international relations, literature and science. Approximately 100 lecturers appear at Chautauqua during a season." (CHQ.ORG The Chautauqua institute web site)

It was the difference in these cultures that had a direct influence on the outcome of his time in Kirksville and towards the end of his career in England particularly at the House of Lords Select Committee hearings in 1935. On the one hand his lack of guile and subterfuge allowing him to become a virtual scapegoat for the controversies around the curriculum development and the attempted move of the college from Kirksville together with the so-called 'M.D. Osteopathic' degree; and on the other hand in England left him vulnerable to his qualifications being questioned and his integrity brought into disrepute.

---

[6] This ideal seems to resonate with Littlejohn's gift to Blanche Still as mentioned in the introduction.

INTRODUCTION

I've often been asked why I got interested in John Martin Littlejohn and why it has taken me so long to write this book about his life. I was fortunate enough to be introduced to Littlejohn by John Wernham, an osteopath who had studied under Littlejohn and as a child and young adult knew the Littlejohn family, in the summer of 1984 and, subsequently, under Wernham's influence, I started to study osteopathy in that same year.

In the classroom, Wernham painted a picture of Littlejohn as a man of integrity, intellect and dedication to the principles and practice of osteopathy. In history books, however, I found that Littlejohn was rarely mentioned and, if he was, it was usually in connection with a supposed argument with A.T. Still, the founder of osteopathy, negative comments regarding his "degrees" or the quality of his testimony at the 1935 House of Lords select committee meetings. It is often reported that Littlejohn was sacked as Dean of the American School of Osteopathy by A.T. Still because of his introduction of too much physiology and drugs into the practice and the medicalisation of osteopathy. Wernham often said that, "Littlejohn took osteopathy and dipped it in a bath of physiology and, what's more, kept it there" giving credence to the suggestion that there was a disagreement between Littlejohn and Still on this subject.

These conflicting views on Littlejohn led me to research his life and his works to find out which was correct, or if there was a different view. In his writings on osteopathy, I found him always to be direct, simple to understand and his teachings to be consistent with the works of Still. I found no conflict between his writings and those of Still.

So, what was the truth? He was, as Wernham would say, 'written out of osteopathy history in America[7] and, subsequently, nearly written out of the history of osteopathy in England'. If it had not been for Wernham his works may have been totally forgotten.

Fortunately, Wernham was obstinate enough not to be influenced by others and to stick to the principles as he was taught by Littlejohn, and to pass them on and leave the legacy of the Institute of Classical Osteopathy as a vehicle for continuing adherence to osteopathy – the osteopathy of A.T. Still – as taught by John Wernham and by J.M. Littlejohn; osteopathy without the influence of drugs but not reduced to a mere manipulative science.

When I dug deeper into the reasons why Littlejohn was so treated, I found it had more to do with politics, family politics and institutional politics than with osteopathic philosophy. When I journeyed through his life, I found he was brought up in a culture which few people in the modern world would recognize. The Reformed Presbyterian Church at the time has been described as a 'state within a state'. They had their own view of life, they were involved in political dissent, not recognizing the state or government agencies as being above the headship of Christ, while at the same time obeying all the legitimate laws of the state that didn't conflict with their religious beliefs.

This meant, for example, that, while they attended university and took degrees, they were not allowed to graduate due to the conflict of

---

[7] A simple example of this is to be found in the two versions of Booths History of Osteopathy and twentieth century Medicine. In the 1905 version it says *"C. M. T. Hulett, J. M. Littlejohn, and Geo. M. Laughlin have rendered service as Dean of the Faculty"* (page 86): while in the 1924 revised version it says: *"The deans who have served the American School of Osteopathy are as follows:* **Dr. C. M. Turner Hulett, from the beginning to 1901**; *Dr. George M. Laughlin, 1901 to 1905; Dr. Wm. D. Dobson, 1905 to 1908; Dr. R. E. Hamilton, 1908 to 1912; Dr. George M. Laughlin, 1912 to 1919; Dr. C. C. Teall, 1919 to 1922; Mr. Fred W. Condit, 1922 to present time."*(Page 541) The bold emphasis is not in the original and is to demonstrate the difference.

[8] His attitude would have encompassed the ideals of the Chautauqua Literary and Scientific Circle –(CLSC) , "the CLSC program was intended to show people how best to use their leisure time and avoid the growing availability of idle pastimes, such as drinking, gambling, dancing and theater-going, that

taking an oath of allegiance either to the college or to the crown. However, this did not stop them from recognizing their educational attainments and using the letters B.A., M.A., etc after their names, even though they were not properly entitled to do so in the view of the universities or others in the educational field.

They also had a distinct attitude to oaths and loyalties. If a person gave their word to do something, then they respected that and accepted it. In fact, it went as far in some cases as having an obligation to try and make the person meet that commitment or ensure that the commitment was fulfilled. Education was viewed as something that should be available to all, not just to the elite or those that could afford it. Littlejohn began his journey in a poor background, progressed through what may be called the elite educational establishments of Glasgow and Columbia Universities and on to the world of teaching in Amity College, where the students were the sons and daughters of local farmers who had difficulty in keeping up their fees due to poor crops. This experience, along with his association with the Chautauqua movement, would have given him a view of education that had a real life meaning rather than just some philosophical words.

This journey also led Littlejohn into association with what some may call dubious educational establishments. While these establishments were dedicated to making education available to those who could not afford it or hadn't got the requisite background to enter the higher educational field, they were also susceptible to attracting people of poor reputation who may have used the institutions for their own financial gain.

These associations led to obvious conflict in England when the House of Lords Select Committee on the Regulation and Registration of Osteopaths was set up in 1935. This background was hard to explain to members of the House of Lords and, indeed, to those osteopaths who were now coming from America with what they considered to be a higher quality qualification in osteopathy and were associated with, or wanted to associate with, the higher echelons of the medical profession in the United Kingdom.

In America, Littlejohn's dedication to his upbringing and his faith led him into conflict with others who would have no problem in using somebody to gain a political advantage. Thus, for example, we find Charlie Still and Arthur Hildreth, Warren Hamilton and others who were engaged in the financial management of the America School of Osteopathy, trying to use Littlejohn to influence Still and the larger community in Kirksville so that they could move the school to a larger city. This led to Littlejohn giving an interview in which he announced that the school would be moving and, within one week,[xvi] having to make an announcement retracting that statement because he had been duped into making the first statement.

This was a common political ruse still in common use today; leaking information through somebody else to see how it floats and isolating yourself from any negative results. It could be said that Littlejohn was naïve in this respect, but that naivety was born out of strong belief in the innate honesty of man and a belief that a man's word was his bond and was to be taken seriously.

It became 'fashionable' for a time during the early part of this century for people to come to me when they found out that I had been studying his life with 'news' that they had found something untoward about Littlejohn (Thankfully this the tide has turned in regard to this tendency). With each of these events, when I investigated them, I found no truth in them. In fact, I discovered quite the opposite. This move to find fault with Littlejohn intrigued me and drove me on to further research his life.

We should remember that it is "normal" for us to apply our own experiences and biases when we examine someone else's life or actions. It is difficult to see it from their perspective and in the environment of the times. For example, the story is told of how Littlejohn attempted to "woe" Stills daughter, Blanche, by giving a gift of a set of encyclopaedias. To us this would seem to be a poor attempt at romance. However, if we remember than Still was deeply concerned about the introduction of hard liquor and other activities in the student body, especially in the Fraternities, and that his daughter was described as "a fun-loving girl" we may get a different picture. Littlejohn would have had similar views to his mentor and his approach was to show someone a better way rather than point out the "evils" of their actions[8]-this was not only in the field of alcohol but also included Fraternities and so-called secret societies. So, it would not be a surprise that given his mentors concerns (which no doubt would extent to his daughter) his actions would tend towards leading her to involving/ immersing herself in education so that she may see a better way of spending her time. That is not to say he did not have romantic inclinations towards her, just to put this "gift" into the context of the time instead of "our personal context/bias"; so that instead of it being told as a "negative" it shows his sensitivity to his mentors feeling, to Blanche as a human being and to his own beliefs.

There is little doubt that Littlejohn himself possessed this ability to set aside his own bias and experience and "invoke the historical sense" of the events he was investigating.

"Yet this modest Scotch-Huguenot, Littlejohn, was as familiar with the great characters of the great periods of this great span of time as if he had in some ante-natal capacity, ...Besides having a good memory, an unusual power of co-ordinating and co-relating, he is gifted with an imagination which enables him to transplant himself to any age and associate himself intimately with the characters whom he chooses. This power of invoking the historical sense is his most striking intellectual characteristic. It is this, fortified by those other intellectual qualities, which makes of him an inspiring teacher. It is this quality which more completely differentiates him from other men, than anything else about him"[xvii]

I claim no such ability. I never looked upon myself as a writer never mind a biographer but more of a researcher. I had always hoped that some "writer" would emerge who would take my research and produce an honest biography of Littlejohn. Unfortunately, no writer with such talents or interest has made my acquaintance and I am

---

[8] His attitude would have encompassed the ideals of the Chautauqua Literary and Scientific Circle –(CLSC) , "the CLSC program was intended to show people how best to use their leisure time and avoid the growing availability of idle pastimes, such as drinking, gambling, dancing and theater-going, that posed a threat both to good morals and to good health" and Blanche was , quoting Trowbridge, "in her early years she was a fun-loving, whist-playing, party-giving practical joker"(Andrew Taylor Still; Carol Trowbridge; page 214)

forced to put this attempt in print and ask you to forgive my shortcomings as a writer and look to the facts.

So I hope you understand that my aim, my objectives, if you like, were not only to research his life, but also to find the truth behind the man and to expose the untruths that have circulated about him; to restore faith in his character so that the modern students of osteopathy, when they look at his works, can see that they are worthy of research and are properly based on the osteopathic philosophy of A.T. Still and on the solid foundation of anatomy and physiology.

---

[i] A Brief Guide to Osteopathic Medicine For Students, By Students By Patrick Wu, DO, MPH and Jonathan Siu, DO; Second edition; AACOM
[ii] Journal of Homeopathics Volume 1; 1902-3 page 298.
[iii] J M Littlejohn; Principles of Osteopathy page 13)
[iv] Journal of Osteopathy August 1898
[v] Journal of Osteopathy August 1898
[vi] Journal of Osteopathy December 1898
[vii] Journal of Osteopathy December 1898 page 329.
[viii] Journal of osteopathy December 1898, address of Dr. J. Martin Littlejohn before the Graduating class, oct. 27, 1898. page 326
[ix] Journal of osteopathy August 1898 page 120
[x] Journal of osteopathy August 1898 page 116
[xi] Journal of osteopathy December 1898 page 326
[xii] Letter from University of Glasgow archives 18th October 1993
[xiii] Journal of osteopathy -BSO- June-august 1935
[xiv] The Osteopathic World, October 1903, page 476
[xv] house of Lords Select Committee minutes of evidence, 1935; paragraph 3393, page 226
[xvi] The Macon Citizen; Friday May 12, 1899
[xvii] W R Dobbyn Osteopathic world July 1905

BACKGROUND-1885

THE REFORMED PRESBYTERIAN CHURCH

Littlejohn was oft quoted as saying the environment must be understood and taken into account. This is equally true when we endeavour to understand a person, their actions and aspirations. So, to understand J Martin Littlejohn we must have more than a passing understanding of the origins, beliefs and ambitions of the Reformed Presbyterian Church. The following exploration of the Reformed Presbyterian Church is not definitive but sets out some historical events and theological beliefs central to the environment of John Martin Littlejohn's childhood and early adulthood.

Historically the first Irish Reformed Presbytery was established in 1763 but was dissolved in 1779 as a result of several factors, including the loss of ministers due to emigration to America and deaths. This led the church to transfer its official administration to the Scottish Reformed Presbytery and a standing committee took care of local matters in Ireland. Many congregations in Ireland resulted from migration from Scotland The Reformed Presbyterian Church in Ireland continued to grow as new congregations were founded and new ministers ordained. So, by the end of 1810 it was decided to divide the Reformed Presbyterian Church of Ireland into four presbyteries, called simply the Northern, Southern, Eastern and Western presbyteries, and to form a synod which would have oversight of the presbyteries. Ministers and congregations would regularly be in contact with their counter parts in Scotland and America. Emigration to America was the main driving force for the formation of the church there and led to close association between the three regions- Scotland, Ireland and America.[i]

In his book, The Theological Basis for Covenanting, F. S. Leahy gives a good summary of the covenanter's way of life.

"The Reformed Presbyterians ... have inherited the ideals and insights of the Scottish Covenanters of the Seventeenth Century and ... wish to remain the 'Church of the Covenants'."

Leahy advances two concepts of Covenant. The contract or treaty concept and the bond of loving loyalty concept. It is the second which is central to the religion to which Littlejohn belonged, Leahy defining Covenant as:

"Fidelity or loyalty confirmed by oath, resulting in a relationship characterized by love and heart-felt allegiance."

In essence it is seen that the human being enters a covenant with God, out of a response to God's Covenant, given in the Garden of Eden.

In practical terms, this is a devotional religion and one that must be adhered to in every act and relationship in life. The Covenant of Marriage may serve to illustrate the nature of the relationship of the Covenanter to God.

The life of a Minister would manifest this in daily works and habits. The day would begin with prayer which would be followed by study and/or visits to Congregation members. The purpose of the visits would be to minister to the suffering, to give encouragement to those in need, to oversee those succumbing to or in danger of temptation, to confront those falling by the wayside.

Each meal would be blessed, there would be afternoon visits or congregational work e.g. Assembly Hall, Schooling, Reports to the Synod, etc. Weekends would be a time for religious Assembly, and Congregation Members would also meet in groups of five to seven to discuss themes, meditations, etc. There would be Evening Prayers and preparations, and time with the family. This would have been the lifestyle that Littlejohn would have experienced as a child and one that he would have lived as a minister and throughout his life, with osteopathic work taking over from congregational duties as he moved in this direction.

Historically, the Covenanters were movers and shakers in their time, of that there can be no doubt. The roots of the reformed Presbyterian Church, to which Littlejohn belonged, are in the second Scottish

Reformation of 1683 to 1649. In simple terms, the question at issue was the relation of Church and State: more profoundly stated, it was the question of allegiance to the Crown, or to the Divine Order.

The Presbyterian system, which held sway in Scotland from the time of John Knox (died 1572) and Andrew Melville subsequently, favoured the Confessional state. In 1618, James 1 (James V1 of Scotland or James 1 of England and Ireland) overturned the Presbyterian system. In the National Covenant of 1638, the Presbyterians challenged Charles 1. This document summarised

i   The King's Confession, in which he subjected himself and his realm to the Divine Realm

ii Acts of Parliament establishing Presbyterianism

iii   Bonds adapted to the needs of time.

The signing of this Covenant, and the subsequent programme of reform, constituted the second Scottish Reformation. As time went on, the Scottish Presbyterians and the English Parliament formed an alliance against the despotism of the King. This resulted in a Solemn League and Covenant which was signed in 1643.

King Charles II swept away this work, and Presbyterianism was outlawed. The leaders, the Marquis of Argyll and James Guthrie were executed, and the Churches closed. The Presbyterians led by a Presbyterian minister by the name of Richard Cameron, on the June 22, 1680 nailed a declaration to the town cross in the town of Sanquhar, took arms against the King's authority.[1] The declaration stated:

"Therefore, although we be for government and governors, such as the Word of God and our covenant allows; yet we, for ourselves, and all that will adhere to us as the representative of the true Presbyterian

---

[1] Sanquhar is a small town, in the south west of Scotland and was the scene for no less than six "Declaration at Sanquhar" These were on 22 June 1680, (the Cameron Declaration); 28 May 1685 (the Renwick Declaration) and four after the Revolution by parties who were not satisfied by the existing state of things.

Kirk and covenanted nation of Scotland, considering the great hazard of lying under such a sin any longer, do, by these presents, disown Charles Stuart, that has been reigning, or rather tyrannizing, as we may say, on the throne of Britain these years begone, as having any right, title to, or interest in the said crown of Scotland for government."

And further, *"As also we being under the standard of our Lord Jesus Christ, Captain of salvation, and his cause and covenants, do declare war with such a tyrant and usurper, and all the men of his practices, as enemies to our Lord Jesus Christ, and his cause and covenants . . . ."*

Adam Loughridge, in 'The Covenanters in Ireland' says:

"It (the Declaration) expressed the conviction held by the minority of Scottish Presbyterians that the Scottish Nation had sinned in not resisting what they considered to be the tyranny and perjury of Charles II." (page 7)

Renwick was executed in 1688. Subsequently, under William of Orange, Presbyterianism was re-established in Scotland; however, the terms of its re-establishment were a big disappointment to the followers of Cameron and Renwick. This minority dissented from the new constitution and separated from the National Church and are the forbearers of Littlejohn's Congregation.

"Many attempts were made to "gain the loyalty" of the Non-Conformist, not least the so called Reginum Donum – a bounty paid to the ministers in return for their loyalty. A sister church of the Reformed Presbyterians, the Secession Church caused further problems when they asked for an increased grant in 1809 in return for swearing the oath of allegiance leading to many members in Ireland applying to join the Reformed Presbyterian Church giving as their reason the defection from its principles of their former Church 'for the sake of filthy lucre'. [ii]

This gives some idea of the principled approach to life the Reformed Presbyterian brethren had and how they were not prepared to sacrifice their beliefs for gain in worldly matters.

The tradition of strong adherence to principle did not diminish with time and we see examples of it in J Martin Littlejohn's life. For example, In 1863, his father was part of a dissenting minority who also separated off, this time because of the decision of Synod on the franchise (voting in the political sphere) Later still, in the U.S.A., in 1889, John Martin Littlejohn was one of a group dissenting from a proposed amendment, citing, among other reasons, that the proposed amendment would "...open(s) the way for voting indiscriminately at all political elections".[2]

This is not to say the Church was a static structure with no room for change. On the contrary it was very dynamic with changes in society being fiercely debated and a very liberal approach taken, provided it did not go against the basic tenets. For example, The Synod of 1888 in America approved the ordination of women to the diaconate, a bold move for the time and one which J Martin Littlejohn voted in favor of.
A flavor of the changes over time within the church can be gained from Nathaniel Pockras in his Forward to the 2015 edition of Glasgow's history of the reformed Presbyterian church of America; He says:

"Since 1888, the Reformed Presbyterian Church of North America has undergone many changes in its testimony to the nations. Primary among these is political dissent.
The Preface states, "Reformed Presbyterians have never voted at any of the elections, nor held office under the government." Today, Reformed Presbyterians routinely vote, and at least one Reformed Presbyterian holds state office. Likewise, there is no longer a prohibition against citizenship oaths, service on juries, or related acts.
Other matters, as well, have changed. While Glasgow says, "[I]t will be seen that this is a temperance Church," and while abstinence from the

---

[2] The resolution he dissented from was "The simple act of voting for amendments to State constitutions belongs to the class of political acts which are not inconsistent with the principles of the Reformed Presbyterian Church or with her position of political dissent" (The Reformed Presbyterian and Covenanter July & August 1889 page 265 and 284)

use of alcohol is still encouraged, members and officers are no longer required to refrain from beverage alcohol. Similar restrictions—for example, ones on the use of tobacco—have also been revised or removed....In 1888, if a Covenanter minister were asked to name the most distinctive principle of his church, the response would surely deal with political dissent—an issue about which many members know little today. If a similar question were asked of an RP minister today, the response would surely deal with worship—a matter relatively little debated then"

While the Reformed Presbyterian church originated in Scotland, with the Cromwellian and William of Orange era the plantation of Ulster its roots spread to the North of Ireland. One anomaly must be mentioned, that is the Liverpool congregation. It came under the domain of the Eastern Presbytery in Ireland for historical reasons and preaching appointments were made from the list of available ministers and licentiates from all four presbyteries in Ireland. This is why we see that James Littlejohn and both his sons, William and john Martin, all preached in Liverpool from time to time.

Another aspect of the association with William of Orange that needs special mention is the relationship with the Orange Order. It was regarded as a "Secret Society" and thus membership of it was a censorable offence.

"The fledgling Orange Order (and the Defenders) borrowed wholesale from Masonic practice and terminology. Orange 'lodges', 'masters', 'grand masters', 'oaths', 'signs', 'degrees', 'warrants' and 'brethren' all have a clear Masonic lineage"[iii]

The Reformed Presbyterian Church, because of their theological position on the Constitutional Settlement, is opposed to the Orange Institution. The *'Cameronians' disliked William of Orange because he had not signed the Covenant. Though some members of that denomination are members of the Order, none of their Ministers, to the best of my knowledge, were ever members or Chaplains"*[iv]

Membership of such societies involves taking an oath before being aware of the obligations involved, without a full knowledge of the extent of his undertaking and thus may find that it is in conflict with the "revealed Law of God" *"by secret societies we mean those voluntary, manmade associations that demand, as a condition of membership, an oath or promise, that the secrets of the order shall not be revealed to the uninitiates"*[v]

"among the devices of the Devil for maintaining and strengthening his hold upon mankind none is more effective than the secret-oath- bound societies"[vi]

This becomes important later in the Littlejohn family and influences many of their decisions.

In summary then, The Church to which the Littlejohns belonged was one which lived alongside the (relatively) secularised State, living by its own convictions, fiercely held and defended. They would, for instance, not take any oaths outside of their own religious context, such as oaths of allegiance to the Crown or to educational bodies. There was an argument against swearing testimony in Court[3]. It was a temperance church, preaching against the "evils" of alcohol, gambling and "secret societies". Within it we also find strong movements in favour of "animal rights and anti-vivisectionism" based upon a strong moral philosophical reasoning.[4]

---

[3] "that sitting upon juries in courts of law recognizes the immoral institutions against which we lift our testimony and is therefore, in direct opposition to that testimony" (The Reformed Presbyterian, Sept 1839, Vol3, No. 7, page 194)

[4] The following quote expresses the sentiments aptly; "Experimenting on live animals and birds in public schools in teaching physiology should be put away with, for it dulls the finer sensibilities of a child, aside from the cruelty practiced on the creatures themselves. We should have laws against vivisection." (The Christian Nation; January 20. 1892. Page 9)

FAMILY AND CHURCH BACKGROUND

> LITTLEJOHN, James — b. Bridgend, Kilwinning, Ayrshire, 29 May 1830; s. of Buchan L., collier, and Margaret Webster; ed.-GU. and R.P. Div. Hall; ord. to Lorn 22 Sep. 1870; inst. Garvagh Ire. 15 Jul. 1876; ret. 14 Feb. 1893; died 1598.
>
> He married 30 Jun. 1856, Elisabeth Walker, dau. of William Scott, handloom weaver, Glasgow, and had issue — Buchan, b. 13 Mar. 1857; Janet Alex., b. 17 Dec. 1855; Wm., R.P. min. at Lind Grove, Iowa 1889-93; Cedar Grove, Kansas 1893-96 ;joined U.P.C., b. 20 Aug. 1862; Elisabeth Walker, b .1863; John Martin, M.A., B.D. LL.B. (G.U.) R.P. min. Creevagh 1886-88, President of Amity Coll. Iowa 1895-98, teacher in Missouri and Chicago, b. 15 Feb. 1865 at27 Taylor St. Glasgow; James Buchan, M.B
>
> (CAMERONIAN FASTI MINISTERS AND MISSIONARIES of the Reformed Presbyterian Church of Scotland (1680 — 1929) compiled and edited by J. Robb)

In order to understand John Martin's life and influences it is important to look at the origin and roots of his family especially his father, James Littlejohn. He was born[5] on 29th May 1830 in Kilwinning, Ayrshire, Scotland, the third son of Buchan Littlejohn, a collier, and Margaret Webster. At the age of twenty-five James acceded from the Free Church and on the 5th June 1855 joined the Reformed Presbyterian Church. He had obviously found his vocation in life and enrolled in the Theological College of the Reformed Church which he attended for

---

[5] Family bible front pages and marriage certificate

four years from 1855 to 1859. He was duly licensed to preach on the 29th November 1859. Some idea of the strength of the man may be gained from the fact that he was the only probationary who sided with the minority synod in the division within the Church in 1863. This required courage as well as a deep conviction in his faith as it ultimately reduced his chances of earning a living as an ordained and settled Minister.

> "James Littlejohn, Glasgow, 1855-9, seceded from the Free Church on June 5, 1855. He was licensed on November 29, 1859 and was the only probationer who sided with the minority in 1863. For some years he was useful as supply. He was ultimately ordained over the remnant at Lorn on September 22, 1870, the ceremony taking place in the Free Church at Kilbrandon, as the building was still in the hands of the majority. He ultimately died as minister of Garvagh, Ulster" (the reformed Presbyterian church in Scotland its congregations ministers and students w. J. Gouper, M.A. the Scottish church history society 1925)

James married Elizabeth Walker Scott, whose father was a Glaswegian hand loom weaver, on the 30th June 1856. The ceremony was carried out at 5 Clyde Street, Portundas, Glasgow, under the rites of the Reformed Church.[vii] The timing of the marriage during his first year in the Theological College suggests that Elizabeth may have being influential in some measure at least in James's decision to seceded from the Free Church to the Reformed Church. At this time while studying at the Theological College, James earned his living as a city missionary assisting the regular preachers. The classes at that time were held in Great Hamilton Street Church, Glasgow, under the professorships of Dr. William Simmington and Dr.W.H. Goold.

On the 13th March 1857 their first son, Buchan was born followed by a daughter on the 17th December 1858(family bible) The children must have been a great source of joy to the Littlejohns and evidence that their union was blessed by God. It's hard to imagine the sorrow and tremendous test of faith that would have ensued from losing both children from scarlet fever in November 1863. The family bible has the following quotation beside their names *"they were lovely pleasant in their lives and in their death, they were not divided: to Jason 1:23"*.

His faith must have been further tested when in the same year, 1863, the great division occurred within the Reformed Church and James, who was still only a probationer, sided with the minority The minority synod consisted of the Rev. W. Anderson, two ministers and several elders of the church. They were later joined by another minister a total of four. For James to side with such a small group suggests that his faith and conviction in their stand must have being quite strong. The fact that he was the only probationer to do this is an indication of his strength of character. It would seem to say that no one or nothing could shake or uproot his faith and that his commitment would always be translated into action. (Further evidence of this is to be found in the statement that he made to his sons on his deathbed: *"One of the last things he said was that he had displeased many because he had remained the same, when he said I am the same, the same, the same and so is Jesus. He passed away glorying in those blessed palms he had loved and learned all his life."*[viii]

The division in the Church is described in the records as follow:

"Such a step as had now been taken was regarded by the members of the synod with pain and sorrow. There was no question as to the further conscientiousness of brethren who had withdrawn; whilst the attitude they had assumed was a matter of lamentation. Their personal worth and ability were fully recognised as well as the good work they had formally done for the church of our fathers. ... The withdrawal of four ministers with their congregations and a portion of several others, in consequence of a decision of synod on the franchise question could not fail to affect the church to some extent. It so far reduced its numbers and lessened its resources, but in a short time the loss in these respects was fully made up. The various departs work in which it was engaged were maintained in full efficiency and continue to expand"[ix]

The rationale for the disruption and division is well described by Keddie as follows.

"The RP Church had been agitated by two questions for several decades prior to 1863. These were the matter of the electoral franchise, already mentioned, and the pressure for ecclesiastical union. The former was, of course, the great obstacle to the latter, for the Covenanters' great practical 'distinctive' of the time was that they had banned the use of 'the vote' and made this a matter of discipline for their membership. This practice rested upon the doctrine of the perpetual obligation of the Covenants, National (1638) and Solemn League (1643), and the correlative theory that to involve oneself in an act that might imply the approval of the nation that had broken these Covenants was to become guilty of complicity in that nation's error. Taking oaths of allegiance, serving in the military or in political office and voting for anyone who might take political office (and have to swear to uphold the covenant-breaking British constitution) was therefore to be avoided as the sin of incorporation with an immoral government. Of all these, it was abstention from voting that was the visible, practical tip of the doctrinal iceberg - the whole covenanting corpus of doctrine - that separated the Covenanters from the rest of Scottish Presbyterianism.

"The non-voting position (with voting as a censurable offence) really came into play only with the extension of the franchise in the nineteenth century, most notably the Reform Act of 1832. Prior to that time, the focus of the distinctive principles of the RP Church had been more immediately upon the doctrinal ramifications of the Covenants as these were controverted between the different churches.

"After 1832, the option to vote became a reality for large numbers of the citizenry, to whom, formerly, it had been no more than a theory. The advance of political freedoms in Britain thus forced the issue upon the Covenanters in a fresh way." [x]

So the effect of the minority withdrawal from the church had no long lasting effect on the church itself in terms of its structure or operation and within a few years they were part of the Free Church.It did give rise and strength to the Reformed Presbyterian congregations and the growth of this within Ireland. Within this small base it became clear that James Littlejohn could hold out little hope of becoming an ordained minister over a settled congregation. This left him to serve the church as a missionary and as a supply preacher. He was obliged to travel great distances at times to deliver sermons and to service the outline districts particularly the remnants of some congregations who had joined the minority in this issue.

The loss of their two eldest children to scarlet fever can only have been seen as a trial sent by God and would no doubt have been faced with the resolute determination and faith in the righteousness of his actions that James Littlejohn displayed throughout his life. Even so, it would have placed considerable strain on the family, and it was into this environment that John Martin was born in 1865. (in the family bible it is recorded as 15th Feb. 1866 – and in his birth certificate as 15th feb 1865; many dates of births etc during this time were not recorded or given accurately.[6])

His elder brother, William, was born on 20th august 1862, a year prior to the loss of the two elder children.
His younger brother, James Buchan, was born in May 1867, followed by two daughters, Elizabeth Margaret Alexander and Mary Janet in 1869 and 1871 respectively: David the youngest being born in Sept 1874. Unfortunately, the family was to suffer the loss of Mary Janet in Feb 1873.
On the 15th February 1865 at eight in the evening John Martin[xi] Littlejohn was born, the fourth child of Elizabeth and James Littlejohn of 27 Taylor Street, Glasgow. James earned his living as a Probationary Preacher enrolled in the Theological College of the reformed church and working in the city and outlying areas. His mother, Elizabeth Walker Scott, was fully occupied with home and family. (Family Bible)

It was a difficult position as James had no regular congregation so acted as a supply preacher to outline and unserved congregations. Being a probationary preacher meant James had to leave his family for days or even weeks at a time while fulfilling his preaching obligations.

At the time of his birth there was little evidence to show the great things that lay in store for John Martin. He has been described as

---

[6] In Ireland it is well known that persons who emigrated during the nineteenth and early 20th centuries would often write home to ask, 'what age they were', not for their date of birth as this was not regarded as relevant.

rather sickly child at least in appearance. In later years he was likened in both looks and writing style to the American Pamphleteer Preacher William Ellery Channing.

"He looks like and writes like, William Elery Channing. Like the Boston Devine, his intellect always takes account of his sentiment, and his conclusions invariably represent the whole man"[xii]

Channing himself was described as being "Never a strong man physically, one hundred pounds being his normal weight...".

In fact, it is quite possible that the Littlejohns thought that they might lose John Martin as they had lost their two eldest children. Buchan and Janet Alexander, aged five and six respectively, died in November 1863 of scarlet fever just eighteen months before John Martin's birth.

Just a year previous to John Martin's birth their third child, William was born. Judging from later photographs, William seems to have been robust, especially when compared to John Martin. Perhaps the toll of losing her two eldest children in such unfortunate circumstances left Elizabeth both physically and mentally unprepared for another pregnancy, and John Martin's physical health and development were adversely affected as a result. Or he may have suffered from a childhood illness. His frailty of body was certainly not reflected in any frailty of mind and may even have been responsible in large measure for his major life developments and career.

We know too that the Littlejohns were a close-knit family, in a close-knit community. The effect of Buchan and Janet Alexandra's deaths in 1863 would most likely have been to deepen the parents' concern for the surviving children William and John Martin.

James Littlejohn's religious vocation and work in the Church would have governed his personal life and that of his family. Church teachings would have encouraged him and his wife to come to terms with the loss of their two children, and to turn towards life again with renewed strength and faith. In such a Congregation, the family life of the Minister would have been held at a slight remove from ordinary Congregation members while, at the same time, being an example to others.

The Reformed Presbyterian Church was by no means a wealthy Church: The Minister's family would have been outstanding by virtue of vocation and education, not due to great wealth. Economically, the Littlejohns lived in poor conditions in Glasgow, the city of John Martin's birth. Conditions improved with the move to Ardincaple on the island of Seil, and again with the move to Ireland, where Congregations and therefore Ministers were relatively better off.

The cornerstones, then, of John Martin Littlejohn's early life from which we may form an image of his character were a physically frail but mentally brilliant constitution; a family which having suffered grievous loss of young children, could only have cherished the remaining members more deeply; family membership of the Congregations of the Reformed Presbyterian Church, twinning fervently held religious beliefs with the intensity and earthiness of the Scots-Gael temperament. These forces, combined with modest economic circumstances, would have strongly nurtured and disciplined the young John Martin Littlejohn.

Another aspect that needs to be considered is a central tenet of the Reformed Presbyterian Church is that of "Divine predestination and providence and Man's creaturely role". This tenet would have raised the question of individual destiny. In particular, it would have supported the belief that God had a plan -a plan for which you were given particular skills and opportunities – and part of your duty was to follow that plan to the best of your ability. Support, moral and practical, particularly educational, was given to John Martin by his Church to fulfil his destiny, to employ his talents to the full and to value service and ministration to suffering, and apart from his own deeply held convictions and faith this would have fortified his loyalty to the Church of his Father.

Places of Interest in the early life of John Martin Littlejohn

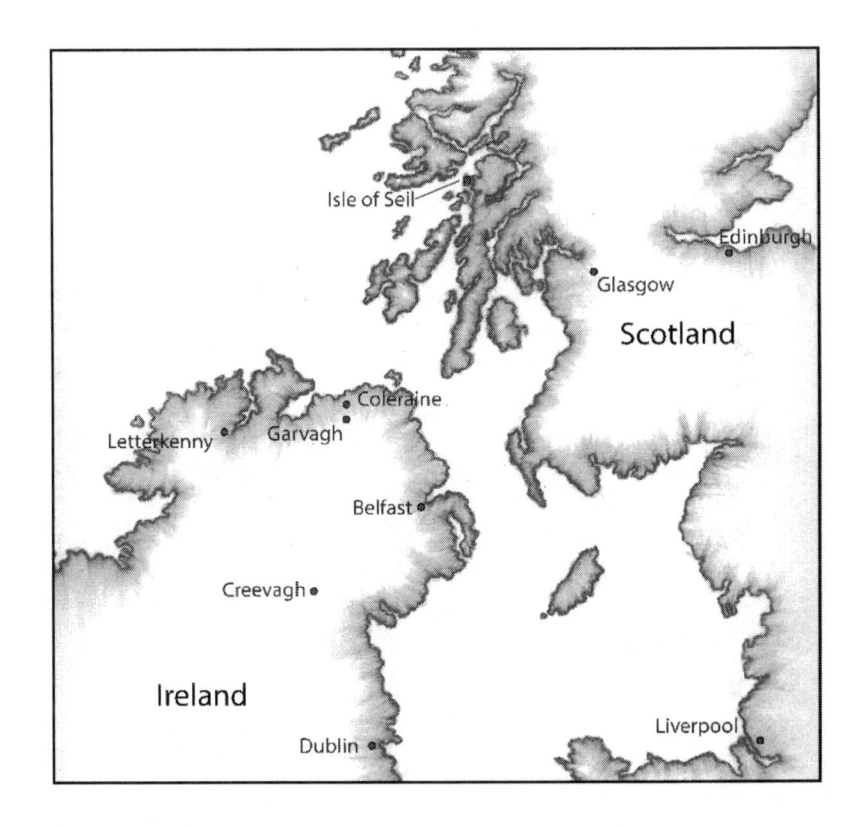

Born in Glasgow
Early life on the Isle of Seil
Early education at Garvagh Science Academy
 and Coleraine Academy
 Attended Glasgow University
Minister at Creevagh Reformed Presbyterian Congregation

MOVE TO LORNE, SCOTLAND

As time passed, James' commitment to the minority synod of the reformed church led to him being called to be settled as an ordained minister over the congregation at Lorne.

In 1870, the family moved to the Gaelic-speaking island of Seil in the West Highlands of Scotland, where James Littlejohn took up the post of Minister of the Congregation.

The Lorn congregation, situated on the island of Seil, Argyllshire, was the only Gaelic-speaking congregation in the Reformed Presbyterian Church, which was primarily found in the Covenanting areas of English-speaking central and south-west Scotland.

This congregation consisting mainly of the Islands of Luing and Seil[7] and the neighbouring mainland, as well as Lochgilphead had been struggling to find an ordained minister for some time. As a congregation of special significance to the Reformed Presbyterian Church, not only because of its origin and the fact that its members spoke Gaelic but also because of the number of ministers it provided for the church itself. In 1853 the congregation consisted of five elders and forty-five members. Finances were limited which made it difficult to attract a settled minister.

During the division in 1863 some members of the congregation sided with the minority synod and it was over these dissidents that James Littlejohn was ordained.[xiii] The ordination itself took place in the church of the regular minister which showed that while the division was real, cooperation and good feelings still existed.

This new ministry meant another move for the Littlejohns from urban Glasgow to a small island of Seil in the western highlands of Scotland. This was in 1870 and John Martin was only five years of age. The 1871

---

[7] Known as the slate island they lie off the west cost of Scotland and are accessed by crossing the 'Atlantic Ocean' over a bridge The main islands are Seil, Easdale, Luing, Lunga, Shuna, Torsa and Belnahua and are situated between Oban in the north and Jura in the south.

census places the Littlejohn as living at Ardincaple Cottage on the island of Seil, 'a comfortable dwelling with five rooms and a servant'.

During this time Littlejohn's scholastic ability began to shine, being built upon his earlier education in his native city of Glasgow.

"when 3 years old he went to one of the old parish schools in his native city afterwards completing his primary education in the public schools of the city"[xiv]

"The evidence of his (John Martin Littlejohn) scholarship and education attainment is abundant. When a boy of seven in the western highlands of Scotland, his native land, he was a student of classics, mathematics, and physics."[xv]

In modern times this may seem a little farfetched particularly as he was living in a remote part of the western highlands. Two things should be borne in mind. Firstly, we also find in the 1871 census that he also had access to a French national, Elizabet Hofer-Governess at Ardincaple House, as a teacher at this time, which goes some way to explain the prizes in French he gained in school and his later ability to teach French while in Amity College

Secondly, it is worth remembering that the ministers in the reformed church were highly educated and acted as teachers for their community and for their own children.

"Dr. Andrew Symington was far more moulding. In manner he was courtly and winning, in theology he seems to have read everything, and in his conversation in life he was experimental theology embodied".[xvi] Dr Symington was one of the professors that James Littlejohn would have studied under. On the subject of the syllabus for the course in the Theological College we find the following comment.

"The church in Ireland prepared an extensive academic course of study and included such subjects as English, mathematics, Philosophy, Logic and even Astronomy! Theological training was to be taken in Scotland"[xvii]

"For a considerable time no special arrangements were made for the training of students for the ministry. Candidates betook themselves to the usual classes at the Universities for Arts, and carried

on their studies in Divinity under the general care of the minister of the district in which they ordinarily resided (the Theological college itself being formed in the late 1780's)........

"....In 1854 the demands of the time were met by the appointment of two professors — Dr William Symington to the Chair of Systematic Theology, and Dr W. H. Goold to the Chair of Biblical Literature and Church History. The classes met in Great Hamilton Street Church, Glasgow."[xviii]

This gives some indication of the depth of study that a minister had to undergo before graduating from Theological College and put James in a good position to teach his young children, irrespective of the fact that they were living in a remote part of the western highlands.

The 1871 census also notes that Elizabeth Hofer, a French national and teacher was living in the Manor house (Ardincaple House) to which Ardincaple Cottage was the gate lodge. It is also probable that she was also available to the LittleJohn family as a teacher. It is fairly clear from this short quote that he was an avid student even at the age of seven and this is again borne out by the fact that he entered the University of Glasgow at the tender age of sixteen having gained distinction in school exams in Ireland.[xix]

However, the family was not destined to stay in the western highlands for very long. In 1872, the majority of those who had remained faithful to the Reformed Presbyterian Church united with the Free Church. By 1873, the membership stood only at only sixteen. To James Littlejohn this must have presented a further trial to his faith as he had left the Free Church to join the Reformed Church. Far from deserting his congregation in Seil, James and his family put up with considerable financial hardships. The fact that he stood by his dwindling congregation until the small number of remaining members joined the Free Church [8]in 1876[xx], demonstrated his conviction in the reformed principles and in the choices, he had made in life based on those principles.

---

[8] The congregation officially united with and was merged in the Free Church congregation of Kilbrandon

MOVE TO GARVAGH,
County Londonderry, Ireland

Because of the close ties between the churches in North of Ireland and in Scotland and James's renowned defence of the original covenant and loyalty to the Reformed Presbyterian Church, James received a call to the congregation in Garvagh in County Derry, in the North of Ireland. In April 1876[xxi] Ministers of the Reformed Church quite often preached in different congregations and travelled from Scotland to the North of Ireland and vice versa, and even across the Atlantic.

Garvagh in 1876 was a settled market town and a rural and predominately fertile agricultural part of County Londonderry. It would have represented quite a contrast to the life on the Island of Seil. We again get some indication of James's attitude towards his position as a preacher and missionary as he once again gave his full support to a small congregation which would not ordinarily find a settled minister and which could not afford to pay the stipend a minister would normally expect James is regularly in receipt of the lowest or nearly lowest stipend for ministers in the Ireland during his entire career. His salary in 1887 was listed as £50 and was the lowest in the church at that time.[xxii]

The report of the Northern Presbytery of the Reformed Church in 1877 gives the following quote:

"It is gratifying to the presbytery to be able to report that on the fifth day of July last the Rev. James Littlejohn was installed in the congregation of Garvagh with every prospect of success. The congregation has for a number of years without a fixed pastor and has been unsuccessful in many moderations. Settlement now affected will we confidently trust and by the blessing of the head of the church tend to advance the cause of a covenanted testimony in that interesting field"[xxiii].

While it is possible that the cause of this lack of a fixed minister was at least in part due to the low stipend, it is also likely that the congregation was looking for a minister of character who would defend the principles of the Reformed Church and apply these strictly in his preaching and spiritual guidance. In James Littlejohn they found such a man, one who viewed himself perhaps as a missionary preacher rather than a man holding a job. He accepted an annual stipend well below the average, one which would place hardship on any family.

EDUCATION IN COLERAINE

Although James joined a small congregation, he was a tireless worker on behalf of the church and served on the educational committee. This meant that his sons had the opportunity to pursue a good quality education in Northern Ireland, something which may have proved difficult for them if they had stayed in the western highlands of Scotland

In any event, both William and John Martin attended the upper school in Coleraine, an academic institution from February 3rd 1879[xxiv]. Even though there was a three year gap between the brothers they both entered the upper school and apparently graduated from it at the same time.

William Dobbyn, writing in the Osteopathic World in 1903, says:

"On the removal of his father to Ireland he (John Martin Littlejohn) attended the academy at Coleraine gaining prizes in the academic courses for three years and in competitive examination conducted by the National Government under Intermediate Education Board."[xxv]

In one of his early versions of his Ph.D. thesis he lists his early education as follows:

> SCHOOLS AND COLLEGE HONORS
>
> Public schools of Glasgow and Easdale, Scotland
> Garvagh Scientific Academy, Graduated 1st prize for first place Intermediate Education Board, Ireland, Examination, honors and prize 1879-80
> Coleraine Academical Institute, Three prizes with honors in classical, English and Scientific courses 1879-80-81

In this he gives credit to the schools in Glasgow, in the west of Scotland and to the 'Garvagh Scientific Academy'. We can get an idea of the strength of the education in this Academy by a later newspaper report. Here it says "Classes had been held in inorganic chemistry, animal physiology and principles of agriculture", all relevant to the local population of farmers. It would have been here that Littlejohn would have been introduced to physiology. During this period a common theme in lectures on temperance was "the Physiology of temperance". For example the lecture by the Rev. Richard Babington given in Castlerock, Co. Londonderry, on the 16th March 1883[xxvi] and the series the Rev. W. Patterson was to give in Fofar schools, on the east coast of Scotland.[xxvii] (the Reformed Presbyterian Synod of 1894 passed a motion that 'every congregation should had some organisation for promoting temperance" and Littlejohn's father, The Rev. James Littlejohn was appointed as president of the committee to promote temperance.[xxviii])

Confirmation of these prizes in school activity can be found in the newspaper accounts for that period., for example the Belfast News-Letter, Monday January 31st, 1881 lists Littlejohn, being awarded prizes in French and Latin while his brother William was awarded a prize in French.[xxix]

BOTH BROTHERS ATTEND GLASGOW UNIVERSITY

While James Littlejohn and his family had found a settlement in Garvagh in County Londonderry, John Martin was about to set off and find his own career and way in life. His first choice under the influence of his upbringing was to train for the ministry. In 1859, a plan of education sanctioned by the synod of the Reformed Church in Ireland required a degree of A.B or A.M[9] as necessary before students were allowed to enter into or complete the theological course in the theological hall [xxx](This law was not enforced until 1865).

They both entered Glasgow University in 1881- 82 term when John Martin was only sixteen.[xxxi]

> **John Martin Littlejohn**
>
> 1881-2 Aged 16, studied Humanity and Greek (matriculation no. 1915)

Both William and John Martin were inclined towards a career within the Reformed Church. This comes as no great surprise given their association with the Lorne congregation and the congregation in Argyllshire together with the fact that their father was a city missionary before becoming an ordained minister.

This background alone would give a tendency towards the church, but another aspect is worth considering. At this time ministers within the church were not only highly educated but were men of rare

---

[9] The more recognisable form today is B.A. and M.A.

intellect.[10] Somebody of John Martin's intellectual calibre would naturally have been drawn in this direction.

With this in mind, both William and John Martin entered an undergraduate programme in Arts in Glasgow University. And while studying there they were listed as under the care of the Northern Presbytery of the Reformed Presbyterian Church, which indicates their intention to attend Theological College upon completion of their undergraduate degrees. At the same time they attended the original sessions theological college in Glasgow.[xxxii] While J Martin was a "foundation scholar",[11] meaning he would have been in receipt of some form of a grant, both he and his brother's education would have been supported by the Church as they were going forward to the ministry.

At Glasgow University John Martin excellence in the field of study and research came to the fore. During sessions 1881 through to 1885 he took the art and theology degree and was eligible for graduation in 1885. A list of his achievements during this time shows the standard of his work.

1882-1883 Seventh in junior division of logic and rhetoric.

1883-1884 Fourth in junior class of oriental languages and second in examination vocabulary oriental languages and literature. [xxxiii]

This was no mean achievement for somebody entering university at the age of 16 and being eligible to graduate shortly after his twentieth birthday.

---

[10] "The leaders of the Irish Church wanted men for the ministry who had a broad education, were cultured, and above all were well grounded in biblical doctrine- men of sound learning and true piety" A School of the Prophets, F. S. Leahy, page 11

[11] "The Senate of Glasgow University have just awarded the Foundation Bursary, value £10, in Natural philosophy, to Mr. John M. Littlejohn, Son of the Rev. James Littlejohn of Garvagh. Mr. Littlejohn is a student of the fourth year in the above university, where he has distinguished himself in all the classed thorough which he has passed, especially in mathematics, natural philosophy, and mental philosophy" The Northern Whig, Wednesday January 14th, 1885; page 5

William followed the same course and was also eligible to graduate at this time. However, neither brother took the graduation ceremony. It has been suggested that one factor for this could have been the cost. It has also been suggested that the concept of graduation is a relatively late one. It would not have been unusual in the earlier nineteenth century for someone such as a doctor to practise medicine having attended the university but without graduating. His class tickets and testimonials would have been sufficient. However, in the case of John Martin and William it appears that the main reason for not graduating may have being due to their hard-line stance in the Reformed Presbyterian Church.[xxxiv]

There had been an earlier division in the Reformed Church in Scotland over the oath of allegiance to the established church that was required for any official job or capacity such as university graduation. Records do show that some non-conformists took a political stance upon this and it is quite feasible that the sons of James Martin would have being unlikely to do anything else.[xxxv] To take an oath of allegiance would have meant swearing to stand by the university even if it went against their beliefs in the future. This they could not do. In many areas the non-conformists would give "a declaration of intent" rather than swear an oath, thus avoid possible future conflicts with their conscience.

While attending Glasgow University, Littlejohn showed his interest in educational matters and developed a pattern that we will see he followed throughout his life. The student council obtained statutory recognition under the 1889 Act it had existed as a voluntary association among the students from 1886 and a University Union was instituted in 1885.[xxxvi]: he was there at the start of the council and later became involved as a representative of the law faculty, the student magazine, he was part of the editorial staff.[xxxvii]

So not only was J Martin fully engaged in his studies but also in student life. He was actively involved in the student body and politics. This may seem inconsistent to some as he was also engaged in "Political dissent" and not voting on principle. however, this can be easily understood by remembering the rational for not voting. It had to do with the government and not to do with political reform. The Reformed Presbyterians were actively involved in political reform but would not vote for someone or a government that did not recognise the Divine Order as being above that of the secular government.

Here we see the development of Littlejohn's approach to education in general - the foundation principles of having a governing body, a student representative body and a charter or Educational principle, as the three legs which he would see as essential to any educational establishment he became involved in.

Both brothers also spend time studying in the Original Sessions theological hall[xxxviii] during this time; thus, not only studying for their degree but also their religious studies for the ministry, with Littlejohn himself also engaging in tutoring[xxxix]

.

After finishing their studies both brothers returned to their family home in Garvagh and entered the Reformed Presbyterian Theological College in Belfast to finish their studies.

---

[i] From an article that was delivered as a short address at the 200th anniversary Synod held in Cullybackey, Co. Antrim, on 14 June 2011

[ii] . (From an article was delivered as a short address at the 200th anniversary Synod held in Cullybackey on 14 June 2011)

[iii] The Men of No Popery: The Origins of the Orange Order-Published in 18th-19th Century Social Perspectives, 18th–19th - Century History, Features, Issue 3 (Autumn 1995), Penal Laws, The United Irishmen, Volume 3
[iv] The Presbyterian Historical Society of Ireland Lecture March 2006 Rev Brian Kennaway

[v] minutes of the synod of the Reformed Presbyterian Church USA 1899; page 11,12

[vi] minutes of the synod of the Reformed Presbyterian Church USA 1897; page 17

[vii] Extract of an e n t r y in a REGISTER of MARRIAGES Registration of Births, Deaths and Marriages (Scotland) Act 1965
[viii] Christian Nation Vol. 30 8th March 1889.

[ix] The Reformed Presbyterian Church in Scotland; its origin and history 1680-1876; by Hutchison, Matthew 1893; Page 339
[x] THE REFORMED PRESBYTERIAN CHURCH OF SCOTLAND AND THE DISRUPTION OF 1863. I. DISRUPTION AND RECOVERY; GORDON J. KEDDIE, STATE COLLEGE, PENNSYLVANIA; http://www.biblicalstudies.org.uk/pdf/sbet/11-1_031.pdf

[xi] Birth Certificate for John Martin Littlejohn; Extract of an entry in a REGISTER of BIRTHS; Registration of Births, Deaths and Marriages (Scotland) Act 1965
[xii] The Osteopathic World, March 1903, Volume 10, NO. 3, page 128: Biography of Littlejohn by Wm. R. Dobbyn
[xiii] The Reformed Presbyterian Church in Scotland, its congregations, ministers and students by Couper, W. J;;.1925: page 63
[xiv] Journal of osteopathy, Kirksville; March 1898; page 489
[xv] Journal of Osteopathy, BSO, June-August 1935 of which J. Martin Littlejohn was the editor. This article was written after the failed attempt at legislation in 1935
[xvi] Reference: A School for Prophets, The History of the Reformed Theological College, Belfast, 1854 – 2004 by F.S. Leahy; page 12
[xvii] A School for Prophets, The History of the Reformed Theological College, Belfast, 1854 – 2004 by F. S. Leahy; page 11
[xviii] The Reformed Presbyterian Church in Scotland, its congregations, ministers and students by Couper, W. J.; 1925: page 161
[xix] 1881 - 2 Age 16, studied Humanity and Greek (matriculation no. 1915) Son of James, Clergyman. Address: c/o John Wilson, 15, Dowanhill St, Partick. Home: Garvagh, Co. Londonderry, via Belfast; source Glasgow University Archives.
[xx] The Reformed Presbyterian Church in Scotland, its congregations, ministers and students by Couper, W. J;;.1925: page 63
[xxi] Coleraine Chronicle - Saturday 08 April 1876
[xxii] Minutes of the Reformed Presbyterian, 1887 etc Synod of Ireland June 1886
[xxiii] report of the Northern Presbytery of the Reformed Church in 1877; held in the Public Records Office in Belfast
[xxiv] The exact reference for this could not be checked prior to printing due to the Covid 19 Lockdown. However, I am confident of the date.
[xxv] report of the Northern Presbytery of the Reformed Church in 1877; held in the Public Records Office in Belfast

[xxvi] Coleraine Chronicle - Saturday 24 March 1883; British newspaper archive at the British library
[xxvii] Dundee Evening Telegraph - Thursday 05 November 1891; British newspaper archive at the British library
[xxviii] Reported in the Belfast Newsletter, Friday June 14th 1884
[xxix] British newspaper archive at the British library
[xxx] A School of the Prophets; F. S. Leahy; page 19
[xxxi] University of Glasgow Archives
[xxxii] Commission of Synod of Reformed Presbyterian Church of Ireland; minutes of meeting 11th November 1885
[xxxiii] University of Glasgow Archives
[xxxiv] "It is possible that he did not graduate at the end of his sessions of study, although qualified to do so, because the ceremony of graduation was very much associated with the Established Church. At about this date, there were some non-conformists who took a political stance upon this, and it could be that J.M. Littlejohn was one of these. It did also cost money to graduate, and this could be another factor. The concept of going to university to graduate is a relatively late one, and it would not have been unusual in the earlier 19th century for someone such as a doctor, to practice medicine after having attended the University but not graduated. As long as he had class tickets or testimonials this would be sufficient." Email from University of Glasgow archives 18th October 1998
[xxxv] Ibid
[xxxvi] A Short Account of the University of Glasgow Prepared in Connection the celebration of the ninth jubilee in June; by James Coutts 1901
[xxxvii] Glasgow University archives, Glasgow university magazine; Ref dc198-1-2- pages 16&38
[xxxviii] Minutes of the Synod of the Reformed Presbyterian Church of Ireland, Wednesday 11th November 1885; Public Record Office of Northern Ireland.
[xxxix] List of degrees in chronological order as attached to letter from Hall and Canning to graduates of the BSO after the 1935 House of Lords select committee testimony by Littlejohn: Also the Biography of John M Littlejohn in Historical review of Chicago and cook county Volume ii, Munsell publishing company 1926 page 396

1885-1888
RETURN TO GARVAGH[1]

Their church and family welcomed them back and would have looked forward to them having an active role in the church and community life.

The church at the time was still short of ministers and some congregations were having difficulty in supplying a liveable salary and living accommodation. The Synod was trying to raise the annual stipend for ministers to a minimum of £110 per year, so that ministers could attend to their duties and look after their families.

Adam Loughridge, in his book 'The Covenanters in Ireland', gives a good description of the struggle the congregations had in paying their ministers and the efforts to raise their living conditions. *"Those whose incomes were on the minimum level had small farms, but in spite of that a low ministerial income continued to be a handicap to the well-being and progress of the Church"* Littlejohn's father fell into that category and he had a small holding to supplement his low stipend, which he was able to sell on his retirement[i] for £300, a good sum to help with his retirement due to illness[ii].

---

[1] When looking at his return to his family home after completing his studies in Glasgow it struck me that Littlejohn would have little to show for his attainments- perhaps class prize notices and letters of recommendation from his Professors. No certificate or parchment or Degree. His reputation would depend upon "letters of Good Standing or Credentials" from his Presbytery. It would then seem quite natural for him to keep a "portfolio" of his achievements so that he could produce it when needed to further his education or career. This would become important latter, particularly in relation to the 1935 House of Lords select committee and its consequences

SCHOLASTIC DISTINCTION

At the close of the classes in the Divinity Hall, in connection with the University of Glasgow, Mr John M. Littlejohn, son of the Rev. J. Littlejohn, Garvagh, was awarded a place of honourable distinction, gaining a prize for general excellence and proficiency during the session in the class of Oriental Languages; he also obtained a special prize for an examination at the close of the session in Hebrew Vocables, and in the Hebrew language generally; also, Mr Littlejohn passed the final examinations in Philosophy and Mathematics for the degree of M.A. These, together with the special recognition by the Senate of the attainments of Mr. Littlejohn in awarding him a prize of £10, give him a place of credit and honour among the successful candidates in the famous university in the sister country. He returns, after spending four years within the walls of a Scotch University, which has, as Principal Caird said, "the advantages of a systematised course, which, with all its defects, is the matured product of the experience of ages," and where the student experiences "the incalculable but most potent influence on his intellectual and moral development, which arises from the corporate life of a great university."

(The Coleraine Chronicle, Saturday, May 9th, 1885)

On completion of their degree both William and John Martin returned to Garvagh and registered as students in the Reformed Presbyterian Theological Hall in Belfast and were duly licensed to preach in May 1886. The commission of the synod of the Reformed Presbyterian Church for Wednesday 11th November 1885 held in Belfast noted the following:

"The clerk also reported respecting the opening of the sessions of the Theological Hall on the previous day. There were thirteen students in attendance, five of the third year, two of second year and four for the first. Besides these two were enrolled, the Messrs John Martin Littlejohn and William Littlejohn, who are attended sessions of the original session Theological Hall in Glasgow. Their statures as students of theology was left to be determined by the synod."[iii]

The minutes of the reformed synod of Ireland for the Northern Presbytery (which includes Garvagh) for the year ending 1886 note;

"At meetings of the court held recently three students Mr William Littlejohn, Mr John Martin Littlejohn and John Ramsey L.L.B. were licensed to preach the gospel. Presbytery heartily rejoices at the accession to the ranks of those who take part with us in this ministry. They are all young men of superior attainments and of good promise and are labouring with acceptance throughout the church."[iv]

> "At a Meeting of the Northern Presbytery of the R. P. Church, which was held at Ballymoney, on Wednesday, the 5th inst., Messrs. William and John Martin Littlejohn, sons of the Rev. James Littlejohn, of Garvagh, delivered their final pieces of trial, and were duly licensed to preach the Gospel".
>
> The Coleraine Chronicle; Saturday May 15th, 1886, page 8

CALL TO CREEVAGH

It wasn't long before John Martin's eloquence of speech and education brought him to the attention of the elders of the Creevagh congregation. Less than a year after returning to Northern Ireland John Martin received a call from the congregation at Creevagh. The congregation, who knew his Father[2] and through him Littlejohn himself as a child, had probably followed his career in Glasgow university and his preaching through his trials and after he was licensed. The call being made within a month of him being Licensed, they were taking no chances in him being called to another congregation.

> The Congregation of Creevagh, Ballybay county Monaghan, held a meeting on Saturday 5th inst., for the purpose of electing a minister, when a cordial and unanimous call was made in favour of Mr. John M. Littlejohn, recently licensed by the Northern Presbytery. Mr. Littlejohn, who has already distinguished himself as a forcible preacher, is the younger son of the Rev. James Littlejohn of Garvagh."
>
> The Coleraine Chronicle, Saturday, June 12th, 1886

"At the meeting of the Southern Presbytery of the Reformed Presbyterian Church in Derry in June 18th, 1886 a special presbytery meeting was to present the call from Ballybay to J.M. Littlejohn. The

---

[2] In speaking to Elders of the Creevagh Congregation in the early 1990's, I was surprised that they were able to recall, favourably and speaking highly of, both the Reverent James Littlejohn and John Martin Littlejohn. Both had made such an impression on the community.

members present having spoken, the moderator presented the call to Mr Littlejohn. Mr Littlejohn asked for a few weeks to consider before making a reply, and this was granted to him. It was agreed that the presbytery do not meet until its usual time in August but that Mr Littlejohn intimate to it the clerk his decision as early in July as possible"[v]

This was a tendency that he exhibited throughout his life, no decisions without a careful thought process, he did not jump into things without thinking.

It was also noted then at the next meeting in August 3rd, 1886 that *"the clerk announced that Mr Littlejohn had intimated to him the acceptance of the call presented to him by the congregation of Ballybay. Trial for ordination was then made up for him, hearing on the 21st.*

"The ordination of Mr Littlejohn was fixed for the 7th September"[vi] In the meantime it is worth noting that his brother William was preaching as a visiting minister on the 5th August in Ballybay.

So, having completed his university education and his education in the Theological Hall in Belfast it did not take John Martin Littlejohn long to find a congregation to be settled over. And it looked as if his career as a minister was set to take off.

CREEVAGH BACKGROUND[vii]

Although Littlejohn's time in Creevagh was very short, it lays the foundation for his later life. So, it is important to have an understanding of the social history of the area and the forces which would have moulded the members of his congregation. We are fortunate in having a wonderful history of the area in the book, "At the Ford of the Birches – History of Ballybay its People and Vicinity", By James H. Murnane and Peadar Murnane. From this we get a very clear picture of what Ulster was like in the hundred years before Littlejohn came to Creevagh. What follows is based upon their writings with specific quotes as indicated.

In the seventeen hundreds the so-called dissenters or Presbyterians had a terrible time being mainly tenant farmers. They suffered from increased rent, being barred from many occupations and government positions, the imposition of the established church (Anglican) rights for burial and while they may have been poor they still had to pay a tithe towards the salaries of the Anglican Clergy and supply labour for the maintenance of roads, while they were almost unable to pay their own ministers. These hardships led to several rebellions including the Hearts of Oak and the Hearts of Steel, rebellions in the seventeen hundreds.

This was also then followed by unusually stormy weather and drought which led to famine and disease in the mid eighteen hundreds. An inkling of how these dissenters were regarded is contained in a quote from the correspondence of the Rev Charles Humble, a vicar in County Tyrone (who maintained that the rebellious insurrection called Hearts of Oak originated in this parish; "nor is it to be wondered at when the Dissenters here shall be known for what they really are – a spawn of Scottish Covenanters, avowed enemies of all civil and religious establishments".)

The Murnanes go on to say that:

"His sentiments regarding Presbyterians were not unusual amongst what were known as 'Horse Protestants' (generally members of the Anglican Church of Ireland – also a term derived from Oliver Cromwell's supposed comment about someone who had less discernment than his horse in the moot points of the Protestant controversy- hence 'as good a Protestant as Oliver Cromwell's horse')at the time."

From the same source, we find an indication that Presbyterian Ministers were regularly regarded as being "great encouragers and promotions of sedition". And this was not confined to the regular Presbyterians as we find: "an itinerant Presbyterian Minister, William Gibson, a Covenanter, roamed to Antrim to preach sedition and the word, sometimes he even forgot himself and made untoward illusion to the Whore of Babylon" (a derogatory term used at times for the Roman Catholic Church). Again, this was in the late eighteenth century. Many of those ministers involved were hanged or imprisoned or forced to emigrate to the U.S.A. So, from the political point of view we find that the Presbyterians and particularly the Reformed Presbyterians were regarded as seditious and were barred from many occupations and suffered greatly at the hands of corrupt laws and taxes. Another point to remember is that they could not build their house of worship within a distance of one mile from the town centre and this is one reason we find the church at Creevagh in such an apparently isolated area.

Another influence at the time was the famine. Between 1841 and 1851 the population of the parishes of Ballybay and Tullycorbet had being reduced by 24%. Social conditions had been deteriorating with the collapse of the linen trade and the depression which came following the end of the Napoleonic wars. This led to a great increase in poverty and when in 1845 the potato crop was attacked by blight it was estimated that up to 55% of the potato crop in County Monaghan was affected by the disease making it one of the worse affected counties in the whole of Ireland.

"A report of the Castleblayney Union (in the same region as Creevagh and Ballybay, County Monaghan) in 1872 voted in for the small farmers in the union area. It stated that not for many years has the potato crop being so bad – not one quarter of the early crop was sound. The later crops had not reached maturity when the blight had set in and consequently were not only very small but were soft and unfit for table use, less than one half of them were sound. In many instances in Ballybay area the crop was so rotten that it was not

harvested, consequently prices had risen to six pence half penny and seven pence per stone."

(Potatoes had cost three pence per stone in 1846 as a result of the blight). And again, we find that in 1879 following three years of bad harvests the output of the main agricultural crops also failed. It is noted that:

"In the second and third quarters of 1879 it rained on two out of three days on average. Crops like hay and turf were ruined. Rich and poor farmers alike had difficulty in meeting their obligations. The winter of 1879 – 1880 was a time of near starvation for small holders, cottagers and labourers."

The spring and summer of 1880 were fine, and crops seemed to prosper. Gradually the hardship and distress were alleviated, and the various relief agencies and committees closed down.

Regarding alcohol the authors say:

"The abuse of alcohol was prevalent throughout town and county. Every possible celebratory occasion was used as an excuse for over-indulgence. Weddings and funerals were traditional excuses for excess and clerics who officiated on such occasions were often encouraged to take part. Fair days and market days or other occasions of temptation to excessive drinking many bargains being struck in public houses. Not all publicans were concerned to dispense good quality spirits. The legal, expensive whiskey was often adulterated with poitin and sold at the higher price. (There were twenty-two public houses in the town of Ballybay in 1824 when the population was only fifteen hundred). Rows and fights were commonplace on market days. It became customary for farmers to dispense drink to men and women even youngsters when they helped out at a meitheal (working party) for flax pulling or spreading. It was said that many a young man or woman was introduced to alcohol on occasions like these."

The reformed Presbyterians did not drink and were ardent promoters of the temperance movement, so tended to be more isolated.

BACKGROUND ON FINANCIAL MATTERS

Littlejohn was coming to Monaghan region at the end of a very trying period for the people financially in relation to failed crops and with the history in the previous century of political unrest. Added to this there was there was some controversy between the synod and the local congregations in the Reformed Presbyterian Church regarding how to pay the ministers.

The synod was finding great difficulty in raising the annual stipend given to a minister to a liveable wage and the history that they had of ministers being unable to clothe, or feed or educate their children. They recommended minimum of £110 per year and many congregations found or complained that they could not afford this. It was with great difficulty that the synod was trying to raise the stipend for ministers and provide a livelihood for them so that they could give their lives to their vocation without fear of not being able to feed or raise their families.

We find further background to these conditions in the minutes of the Reformed Presbyterian Synod of Ireland. The statistics of the congregation shows that Ballybay at the time had eleven elders, ten deacons and the number of communicants was about two hundred and thirty and the average attendance was one hundred and eighty with three Sabbath schools with no teachers. At the time the stipend was said to be £110 and a manse but the manse rent had to be repaid and the manse had to be maintained by the incumbent. [viii]

Looking down through the list of other congregations, it is found that some with a smaller number of communicants paid £120 per year plus a manse (free of rent). Another, with one hundred and forty members, paid a stipend of £140 plus a manse again free from rent. Two of the larger ones would pay £150 and £140 respectively but without a manse.

Garvagh, Littlejohn's father's congregation had six elders, four on the committee and seventy communicants and average attendance of eighty, paid a stipend of only £55 so his father was not a wealthy man as such[ix]. This gives an idea of the discrepancy between the different congregations and the difficulty the synod was having in securing their aim that all congregations should supply comfortable manse for their minister and pay a reasonable stipend.

In the June 1887 annual meeting of the synod, it's noted that the congregational aid scheme (to subsidies the low stipend some congregations could afford) was not being fully supported by the congregations. They decided that the congregations should contribute at the rate of four shillings per member per year and this would not be burdensome and much less an impossible amount if the contributions were proportioned to each member's according to their means.[x]

The statistics of what people actually paid, show that Creevagh was one of the lowest paying towards this scheme, with three and a quarter pence per person. And in the minutes it notes that some congregations were ignoring the synods orders about having two collections in the year and that the salaries of ministers who were in aid from this fund were still far too small and as a result the missions or preaching stations did not receive more than occasional supplies of preaching.[xi]

There is a history within Creevagh of having come from a troubled times in the previous century through famine and hardship with the burden of not only trying to support their own ministers but having to pay a tithe towards the established church and a law forbidding them to have built any places of worship within a mile of the town centre and now having to almost resist the additional burden from their own synod in trying to raise the standard of living of their ministers. And in Creevagh, in order to attract a minister this time, they had to raise their stipend to the minimum of £110 per year and supply a manse. In short, they had come from difficult times and times were still hard.

ORDINATION AND WORK IN CREEVAGH

Understanding all of this, the Rev John Martin Littlejohn, after due consideration, accepted the call and was settled over the congregation as minister with nine elders, ten deacons, two hundred and ten communicants and Sabbath school scholars numbering sixty over which he was the single teacher[xii]. It was a notable position for somebody so young and so relatively inexperienced and it could be speculated that the elders in choosing to put a call to the young John Martin Littlejohn, thought that in someone so young they could mould them after their own liking. They were soon to find that this was as far from the truth as it could be.

This summary is the net result of having met and personally spoken to some of the elders at Creevagh and gone through the records of the Creevagh congregation session book and the session books of the Southern Northern and Eastern Presbyteries and the synod of the Reformed Presbyterian Church. The following gives my interpretation of the events which led to Rev. John Martin Littlejohn's resignation and his departure for America in September of 1888. In order to get a clear picture of how things unfolded a timeline of the important events is useful.

TIMELINE of EVENTS relating to CREEVAGH

1885 November: J.M. and William enrolled in Theological Hall, Belfast

18th June 1886: Call to Creevagh

7th Sept 1886: Ordination at Creevagh

14th Oct 1886: Littlejohn set up Missionary Society at Creevagh

30th Oct 1886: Rev James Littlejohn assisted his son, John Martin, at Communion in Creevagh

22nd March 1887: Congregation affirms desire to clear the Manse debt by November

14th April 1887: William Littlejohn gave lecture at missionary Society

21st June 1887: Rev James Littlejohn gave talk at Creevagh Missionary Society. Praising it for having raised £210 for the Missionary effort

11th July 1887: Littlejohn is given permission by the congregation to raise funds for new Manse

2nd Aug 1887: Littlejohn is given approval from Southern Presbytery to collect funds for new manse

5th Oct 1887: Rev William Littlejohn assigned to minister in Liverpool for November 1887

23rd Oct 1887: Rev James Littlejohn assisted his son, John Martin, at Communion in Creevagh

6th Jan 1888: The Eastern Presbytery appoints Littlejohn to minister to the Liverpool congregation for all of Feb 1888. At the same meeting they were trying to find a minister to preach in Liverpool for March 1888

24th Jan 1888: Congregation rescinds decision of 11th July and to refuse to pay for assistants at communion

29th Jan 1888: John C Carlisle appointed by congregation to go to Presbytery to ask for advice concerning the financial state of the congregation

31st Jan 1888: Miss Cunningham of Antioch from the Syrian Mission gave talk to the Creevagh Missionary Society, on the Syrian mission. Littlejohn was present at this meeting and must have left soon after for Liverpool

7th Feb 1888: Representatives from Creevagh ask Presbytery if they had sent their pastor to Liverpool or given him permission to raise funds. *"The Clerk replied on behalf of the Court[3] that they had nothing to do with him going to Liverpool and that on his own application and on behalf of the congregation the presbytery had given him a recommendation in relation to a new manse. The Clerk here read the minute bearing on this latter subject from the records of the August meeting."*[xiii] It was approved by Presbytery at the meeting of 2nd August

6th March 1888: Special meeting of Synod at Creevagh to look at the problems between Littlejohn and the congregation

24th April 1888: Congregational meeting made the decision to petition Presbytery for a dissolution of the relationship between them and their pastor

1st May 1888: The petition for dissolution of the Congregations contract with their minister, J M Littlejohn, was presented to Presbytery

John Martin and his brother William had both graduated from the Theological College Belfast and were licensed by the Northern Presbytery to preach the gospel as probationaries. At this time the Creevagh congregation which had been trying find a settled a minister had borrowed money from the Fairview congregation at a 5% interest and looked to increasing their stipend offered to a minister to one hundred and ten pounds plus a manse. They secured a manse which they had then tried to bring up to a liveable standard, it needed a new thatch and various other maintenance works carried out on it, Having put this in motion they put out a call to John Martin Littlejohn who after consideration decided to accept. He was ordained on the 7th September 1886 and took up residence in the manse.

A meeting of the Southern Presbytery was held in Creevagh/Ballybay on the 7th September 1886 by special appointment for the purpose of ordaining to the work of the gospel ministry Mr J.M. Littlejohn.

---

[3] The term 'Court' is used to describe the meeting of the Presbytery and not in any legalistic manner.

The Rev. Thomas Madill of Garvagh, a minister of the regular Presbyterian Church, had the following comments to make about John Martin and his ordination.

"It is with the deepest regret that I find myself unable to be present at the ordination of my young friend Mr John Martin Littlejohn, over the congregation of Creevagh, Ballybay. I regret it all the more because being my native county and to some extent my native neighbourhood I could have bespoke for him something of that sympathy and encouragement so necessary for a young man in his position and which I'm sure will not be wanting in the Presbyterians of Ballybay. He goes to you with an unblemished reputation and a high character for industry and perseverance and success and carries with him the best wishes of this village and neighbourhood for his future welfare and prosperity in his master's service in Creevagh ... No better neighbour or more faithful friend could be found anywhere than his father and I'm sure the son won't be one whit behind him. And every work or movement which has for its object the good of society or the ingathering of souls and thereby the glory of our common master Mr Littlejohn will I am certain be found at his post co-operating with his brethren around him in the advancement of the Redeemer's kingdom. With every wish for Mr Littlejohn success in his new sphere in the master's vineyard I am very truly yours Thomas Madill." – The Moderator, Southern Presbyterian[xiv]. "

This quote gives some idea of the standing of both father and son in the community of Garvagh and in Northern Ireland in general. It was a reputation achieved over a short period and that, taken with his ordination at Creevagh, one of the strongest congregations within the Reformed Church, there would have being a burden of responsibility and pressure on the shoulders of the young John Martin Littlejohn.

The ordination service of John Martin Littlejohn took place in Creevagh on Tuesday 7th September 1886. The Northern Standard in Monaghan of Saturday 11th September 1886 gives a detailed account of the ordination service.[xv] It's interesting that Littlejohn was described as J.M. Littlejohn M.A. even though he had not taken the graduation service. This would be typical of the Reformed Church in that he had completed his education and therefore he was entitled to use the term M.A. even though from the so-called orthodox point of view he hadn't graduated and therefore hadn't received the degree.

It's clear from this that Littlejohn was well regarded not only within the community, but also within the ranks of the experienced ministers and theologians within the Reformed church. Littlejohn then threw himself into his work with the same vigour zeal determination and pattern that we have seen when he was in Glasgow and which would prove to be his pattern no matter what work he undertook.

Firstly, taking up teaching at the Sunday schools and teaching theology to his congregation, then giving a renewed purpose to the congregation by taking up the cause of missions, forming a missionary society and writing extensively in the Covenanter magazine. At the same time, he attended to the organisational activities of the Church attending and fully participating in the Presbytery and Synod meetings. All this within the first few months of his ministry.

Having become involved in student activities as an undergraduate in Glasgow he was no stranger to what was needed in order to pull a community together. He worked tirelessly as a minister for a congregation tending to their needs also at the same time put effort into the hierarchy within the church by attending and contributing to the synod meetings acting as moderator in November 1886. He acted as teacher and lecturer to the community at the Ballybay Union Hall, lecturing in theology to the Sabbath schools and to the congregation in general. He also paid attention to the Covenanter Magazine and wrote a series of articles on the church and the missions.[xvi][4]

---

[4] The sketch of John Martin Littlejohn in the Osteopathic World states that he taught Theology during the winter session of 1886 through 1887. This would have been to the congregation and in the Sunday schools associated with the congregations in Ballybay, being called the 'Ballybay Theological College or Hall or School'. He may also have taught at the Theological College in Belfast but the listing of active teachers there does not include his name and he was not a permanent member of the staff.

The CREEVAGH MISSIONARY ASSOCIATION

The Covenanter magazine Jan–Dec 1886 reports that:

"On Thursday evening October 14th (1886) an interesting missionary meeting was held in the R.P. Church Creevagh for the purpose of considering the subject of missions and its claim upon the sympathy and support of Christian people. The Rev J.M. Littlejohn delivered a lecture of considerable length on the subject Missions. In the introduction he contrasted the positions occupied by the ancient Jewish Church and the Christian Church under the New Testament dispensation, referring to the bearing of missions upon the work of Christ, and the activity of the Christian Church. This work, he said, was founded upon the resurrection of our Lord and supported by the mediatorial headship of Christ – so becoming the primary work of a Christian church. He said missions ought not to be considered a branch of Christian philanthropy in general, but ought to be taken up by the whole church as part of her divine commission; ought to be entered upon by the church united in sympathy, prayers and efforts for the common end of extending the borders of Christ's Kingdom. After referring to the obligation resting upon the church, arising from Christ's command, the need of the work itself, and the fact that it is the church's chief work, he referred to what was required of those who would engage in such work, how Christian people might lend a helping hand, and the high reward conferred upon such as sacrificed themselves and their own interest for the sake of such a noble cause. ... He concluded by showing the advantage to be derived from engaging in such a noble work, and the disadvantage following the neglect of a divine commission, showing itself in the prevalence of the spirit of selfishness, apathy and carelessness and in the losing hold of the bond of sympathy and love which should unite a common humanity bond by the same chains of sin and corruption."

At the close of the lecture it was proposed by Mr T. Henry and seconded by Mr T. Carson (an Elder of the Creevagh congregation) that:

"The meeting heartily approves of the work carried on in our name in the foreign field, and that a missionary association be formed in connection with the congregation for the purpose of exciting a livelier

interest in this worthy object and of doing something for the support of our missions."

A committee was then appointed and collecting cards handed to a number of young ladies who volunteered their services after which the meeting was brought to a close. [5]

Littlejohn was only a month into his ministry when he had already made a considerable change in challenging not only the congregation but the church itself in their attitude towards the missions and in setting up a missionary society associated with his congregation. Any idea the congregation had or might have had of moulding Littlejohn was seen to be misplaced. He continued to hold monthly meetings of the missionary society and invite lectures from other notable people including the Rev Thompson L.L.D. from whose lecture we have the following quote:

"There is a standing law of heaven that unless energy goes forth and develops itself energy cannot be brought in." [xvii] - a principle that would have appealed to Littlejohn and could be applied to how he lived his life.

On April 14th meeting of the Creevagh Missionary Association (1887) the guest lecturer was John Martin's brother William Littlejohn. He gave a talk on the subject *"I Live not Wholly for Myself"*. At the meeting on Tuesday 21st June, Littlejohn's father, the Rev James Littlejohn of Garvagh addressed the meeting and referred to the encouraging report presented of financial success attending the efforts of the lady collectors.

---

[5] Note: His ideas on the missions may at first sight seem to be a long way from his career in osteopathy, however if look upon in the light of education, it is a thought provoking appeal to make education – religious theology in the case of the missions- available to all, especially those in deprived areas or conditions. This is a theme in his approach to education in general that we see throughout his career and his actions, in endeavouring to make education available to all was often was the source of criticism and conflict

It was noted that the financial position of the association was good and that the young ladies of the congregation had during the last eight years (sic.) collected over £220 for the Syrian mission.[xviii] This seems like a misprint and should be the last eight months as the association was only formed eight months prior. And this is an important point because £220 would have been an incredible amount of money for the association to have collected over 8 months. But even if it were over the period of 8 years it still was a considerable sum!.

The whole idea of the missions was of great importance to Littlejohn and he devoted considerable energy to the society and in writing articles for the Covenanter magazine. Some idea of how he felt can be deemed from the following quote from his article:

"Seldom if ever has any great movement made rapid progress in its development. Every great cause presents itself as a new idea to the minds of a few; from small beginnings it advances to something great until it is an enterprise commanding sympathy and support of the vast majority. Such has been the history of missions ... Man's mind would be barren and unproductive of such noble points were it not for the operating influence of the spirit of inspiration. ... It is an imperative must, as the binding obligation of duty incumbent on the church, is she shall stand in God's sight as faithful. ... Times change most wonderfully, and with them change also the sentiments of the people."[xix]

Littlejohn put his heart and mind into the work in Creevagh by following a pattern which would development as he progressed in his career. To pull a community together he needed a teacher, a leader, an educator (in this case a minister); he needed a cause and a magazine to promulgate that cause (the cause of the Missions and the Covenanter magazine), and regular meetings with other experts brought in to support the issue.

PROBLEMS ARISE IN CREEVAGH[6]

Unfortunately in Creevagh, given the times that they were in, having come from considerable hardship during the famines and the imposition of unfair taxes on the Presbyterian communities, for them to find themselves now with a minister who put further burdens, financial, practical and philosophical, on them was going to prove troublesome, to say the least.

A compounding factor in this was from the congregation's point of view they had provided a 'comfortable manse' for their minister and they find their minister complaining about the state of the manse. At a special meeting of the congregation held on July 11th, 1887 with the Rev John Martin Littlejohn in the chair.

"The principle business of the meeting was to have the mind of the congregation if Mr Littlejohn would collect funds would it be appropriate to paying the manse debt or rebuilding the manse. From the condition that Mr Littlejohn stated the manse was in from damp, the meeting came to the conclusion that the manse was most urgent. Rev John Martin Littlejohn closed the meeting"[xx]

When looking at the references to the Creevagh Missionary Associations meetings in the Covenanter Magazine we find an interesting article just above the report on the meeting of 21st June 1887. This carries a report of the efforts of the minister from the Dromara congregations' efforts to raise money in America to help with their debts. He raised about £700 which was almost enough to meet all the congregation's liabilities. This must have been in Littlejohn's mind when he looked for permission to raise money to put the manse in order.

---

[6] I feel a particular duty to present the events around Littlejohn's time in Creevagh. This is because I gave my early research in this area freely to those interested and was astonished at how the "facts" became distorted and came back to me as "whispers" in a very negative fashion. No one had taken the time or put in the effort to investigate matters, particularly the "story of the three ladies" and the "his resignation as minister in Creevagh." So, I would ask you to be patient with me as I delve into the detail around this time of his life.

The Creevagh congregation had two previous meetings where the deficient fence had to be made right around the manse and a new thatch had to be put on the manse. At a previous meeting on Tuesday March 22nd, 1887 it was recommended that a final effort be made before November to clear off all the debt, and on the 11th July 1887 Littlejohn obtained permission that if he collected funds they would be used to pay off the debt on the manse or rebuilding the manse

This is important because at a later date, date 24th January 1888 at another meeting when Littlejohn was absent, the trustees of the manse got the congregation to pass a motion rescinding that authority as it was an infringement on the rights of the trustees. The wording was:

"They were also unanimous that the action of the meeting held on the 11th July last was an infringement on the rights of the trustees and they rescinded it but deferred acting upon it for some time."

It was at the same meeting, on the 24th January 1888, that we see another aspect of the problems arising between John Martin Littlejohn and the trustees of the manse. It was at this time that they agreed to pay for the straw previously mentioned. This is in January and this was for the thatch on the roof. (The terms of his "employment" were £110 plus a manse which he was to pay rent on and maintain.) You can imagine the condition of the manse if Littlejohn considered its repair to be outside of his contractual obligations

Littlejohn, having obtained sanction from the congregation to raise funds for the manse, also obtained permission from the synod for the same. It was noted on the meeting of the Southern Presbytery on August 2nd 1887 that John Martin Littlejohn intimated that his congregation had resolved to build a new manse and asked presbytery to recommend their claim to the church generally and the clerk was appointed to article a minute with that affect and send it to Mr Littlejohn. In July he got permission from his congregation and in August he got that sanctioned again by synod.

JANUARY 1888 - MAY 1888

All of this together paints a picture of Littlejohn trying his best to come to terms with a congregation that had almost reluctantly, due to past and present financial conditions, provided a manse for their pastor and raised the stipend to a reasonable level, finding that more action was need in terms of making the manse liveable.

True to his character, he put forward a solution that would solve the problem without putting extra financial burden upon his congregation. He proposed that he try and collect funds from various sources, provided it was put towards the manse. He followed the correct procedure, having got approval from his congregation he put this to presbytery in August and they approved it and gave him letters of credentials to collect money on behalf of the congregation. However, this led to some of the trustees of the Manse feeling that they had been slighted in the performance of their duties.[7]

Another indication of underlying disagreements over the running of congregational affairs is seen at the meeting of the congregation on 24th January 1888 when it was passed unanimously that *"we cease to pay an assistant at communion given to the fact that the time and choice was taken out of the sessions and congregations hand"* (They also change to half-yearly collections rather than quarterly due to the extra labour involved.) Littlejohn had used his father on a number of occasions as an assistant at communion and congregation were now saying that this had done this without their approval, even though it was normally the choice of the minister as to who would assist at communion

---

[7] As noted above it was at that meeting on the 24th January 1888 it was "unanimous that the action of the meeting held on the 11th July last was an infringement on the right of the trustees and they rescinded it". This was quite a strong statement and it comes five months after the time when Littlejohn got permission to raise funds (at the meeting of 11th July) and was taken at a time when Littlejohn himself was preparing for the visit of the noted missionary, Miss. Cunningham to Ballybay and preparing for his preaching appointment to the Liverpool congregation in February 1888.

Littlejohn had attended the congregation meeting on 20th December 1887 at which some disagreement about the monies paid to him arouse – his call, as was mentioned above, was for £110 plus a manse; At this stage it was stated that he had already been given £125. The discrepancy seemed to be related to bringing the manse into a liveable condition and it was noted that they needed to balance *"neglect on the one side, over generosity on the other"*. It was shortly after this that Littlejohn give his indication to the Eastern Presbytery of his willingness to serve in Liverpool[8] for the month of February 1888, this being noted in at the January 6th meeting of the Eastern Presbytery. Why did he decide to take the preaching appointment in Liverpool for month of February? Perhaps to put the additional earnings (and perhaps possible extra collections) towards the manse, as he had got permission to do so from both his congregation and their presbytery. Possible to get away from the tension in his congregation and allow things to settle; maybe he had even been advised do so by his family, to take this opportunity, as no other minister seemed to be available to cover February and the Eastern presbytery seemed to be having difficulty in finding someone to cover March. Maybe, the Liverpool congregation wanted to see if he or his brother William might be interested in looking favourably to a call to a ministerial position in Liverpool.[9] Or maybe a combination of the above. In any event it seemed like a poorly thought out response to the growing tensions in the congregation. Especially as Littlejohn did not attend the Congregational meeting on 24th January, at which, as we noted above, further discord was voiced, and then presided over the Missionary meeting with Miss Cunningham and other guests on Tues 31st January 1888. This would have involved quite some expense.

---

[8] It was common practice for settled ministers to take preaching appointments in other congregations when needed. Littlejohn having preached in the neighbouring congregation on occasion. Liverpool being an exception because it came under the Eastern Presbytery and being quite a distance, it would mean the minister being absent for a full month rather than just one Sabbath.

[9] His brother William attended as a minister to the Liverpool congregation in October 1887 and the congregation in Liverpool put a Call for a minister in August 1888

He would have had to leave quite soon after this meeting to be in Liverpool for the following Sabbath. The response from the elders of his congregation can be judged by the actions at the meeting on the 24th January and the subsequent Presbytery meeting on the 7th February.[10]

When he was then in Liverpool for the month of February 1888 ministering to the congregation there, the faction that was against him made their move to presbytery and to the congregation. From the congregations point of view they had done more than they could bear financially; providing a manse, increasing the stipend, then the added burden of the missionary Association; In January they had the expense of providing facilities for Miss Cunningham of Antioch, who was touring all the congregations at that time, to give a lecture that was attended by a large group including ministers from other congregations.

A meeting on February 7th in Newry of the Southern Presbytery the elders from Ballybay enquired of the presbytery if they had sent their minister to Liverpool and if they had given him a recommendation to collect money for a new manse. The clerk replied on behalf of the court that *'they had nothing to do with him going to Liverpool*[11] *and that on his own application and on behalf of the congregation the presbytery had given him a recommendation in relation to a new manse. The clerk read the relevant minutes bearing on the subject from the record of the August meeting'.*

LittleJohn was aware of this meeting and what would happen at it and had prepared his side of the argument in a letter which was presented on his behalf.

---

[10] I make these points because they start to indicate a problem arising not only over finances but also over the organisation within the congregation.

[11] The appointments for preaching in Liverpool were made by the Eastern Presbytery, not the Southern presbytery, hence the statement that "they had nothing to do with him going to Liverpool". The Eastern Presbytery were always looking for Ministers to take on this duty, no matter what Presbytery they belonged to. His brother William attended as a minister to the Liverpool congregation in October 1887

"At this stage a letter was handed in from Mr Littlejohn, part of which read in court; after some consideration on the theme of this letter and the questioning of the elders from Ballybay the Rev Savage moved and Mr Lyons seconded the presbytery to hold a special meeting at Creevagh, Ballybay on the 6th day of March at 11 O'C."

On March 6th the Presbytery met in Creevagh and the congregation made their case and Rev Littlejohn made his reply. It was then proposed by the Rev Lyons, seconded by the Rev Savage, that as far *"as the court has heard and is able to discern no insurmountable difficulties have arisen in this congregation and presbytery earnestly recommend the members of the congregation to remember their pastor's youth and inexperience and exercise towards him all Christian charity and the court would affectionately and urgently counsel their brother Rev Mr Littlejohn to give all diligence to the visitation of the afflicted of the congregation and such as fail to wait regularly on the public means of grace to consult with and to seek co-operation of his brethren in all matters congregational and to seek the appropriation and esteem of his flock in the discharge of his ministerial duties.*[xxi]*"*

This would have been standard advice when no fault was found with either side; that is for both parties to attend to their duties and does not reflect or give any indication that Littlejohn had in any way neglected his duties. The only additional advice to Littlejohn seems to have been that when members of the congregation stopped attending services, he should visit them and take advice to see if he could ascertain the reasons and remedy the situation. This seems to indicate that his fault was not to engage early enough and that instead of taking the preaching appointment in Liverpool, while seemingly good intentioned, his duty would have been to stay and engage with the dissenting members of his congregation.

At the April 24th, 1888 congregational meeting the sad condition of the congregation was mentioned, and it was agreed by a large majority to memorial presbytery for dissolution of the relationship with their pastor as the only remedy to save the life of the congregation. A number of Elders of the Congregation were appointed to draw up the memorial and have it signed by those desiring to do so. And they were appointed to go to Presbytery to support the memorial on the 1st May 1888[12]. From the notes of the numbers attending regularly and the members within the congregation who signed the petition it looks as if it was less than half of regular attendees openly applying for a dissolution of the relationship of the congregation with Mr Littlejohn. [xxii]

Another point that needs to be taken into consideration is the "scandal of the three women[13]. It was never elaborated upon it has often been a matter for speculation since it came to light in the 1990. Ongoing through the history it becomes relatively clear that this was probably related to the Creevagh Missionary Association.

Given that the young ladies who did the collection managed to raise a considerable sum at the time and the amount of time and energy that Littlejohn put in to that association and the fact that the average age for marriage of men was nineteen years and seventeen years for women[xxiii], it becomes reasonable to assume that the three women concerned were part of the collectors for the Missionary Association and that because Littlejohn was a young, eligible bachelor that there may have been a competition for his attention. If this was the case, then it is likely that at least one, if not all of the young ladies (and their family) were disappointed by Littlejohn's lack of emotional response. He was focused on his duties alone.

This, taken with stepping on the toes of the trustees by inferring that they were not doing a good enough job with regard to the manse, the nature of the dispute is aptly summed up in the minutes of the Congregational meeting chaired by Littlejohn on 20th December 1887; it is recorded *"They had now given him(Rev J M Littlejohn) £125. Mr Henry said £110+ a Manse was in the call and*

---

[12] 82 members signed the petition. The total number in the congregation was just over 200 with approximately 180 as regular attendees. This means that less than half of the regular attendees put their names to the petition to dissolve their relationship with littlejohn.

[13] This was first mentioned to me, in private conversation by one of the senior members of the congregation in Creevagh when I met her in the early 1990's. No further information was available only that there was some negative story around Littlejohn and three women in the congregation.

that whoever occupied the Manse was to refund the rent and other taxes to the Trustees ;**given the neglect on one side and over generosity on the other** they were undecided as to who should pay for the straw(for the thatch on the Manse)" The congregation found itself divided between their neglect (of the manse in particular and by inference their pastors health) and over generosity (in giving Littlejohn too much support financially)

The conditions were then right for a dispute, financial pressure, competition for the attention of the young pastor, the strict theological teachings as proposed by the young pastor and the strong hand by which he ran the affairs of the congregation.

One of Littlejohn's characteristics that has been so often spoken about by his student, John Wernham, was that when he felt he was right and had done nothing wrong he would not be moved. So, it's not surprising then that he stood his ground. Several meetings of presbytery and congregation took place to try and bring together the two sides of the congregation. While 82 members of the 200 strong congregation signed the petition against Littlejohn, the exact number that signed a memorial expressing their attachment and satisfaction with LittleJohn as their Minister is not known, many of the congregation stood firm in their support of Littlejohn. In the end the only solution that did not mean the break-up of the congregation was that Littlejohn resigned.[xxiv]

This is recorded in the minutes of the Southern presbytery meeting on the 30th May 1888 as follows:

"1st Resolution. Presbytery having heard both parties in relation to the disturbed state of the Creevagh congregation and also the full report of the (Minister) who visited the congregation in the name of the Presbytery resolves to place on record both their deep sympathy with their young brother and their anxious concern for the wellbeing of this large and influential congregation in their present divided condition.

"2nd Resolution. Seeing that all their efforts to secure a peaceable settlement have been unsuccessful and that neither the usefulness and comfort of the pastor nor the peace and prosperity of the congregation can possibly be maintained while the present

disaffection continues Presbytery agrees to recommend the Rev. Mr. Littlejohn to place his resignation in the hands of the Presbytery.

"3rd Resolution. While making this recommendation **Presbytery would have it distinctly understood that they do not recognise any charge or make any reflection in the least affecting the standing or ministerial efficiency of Mr. Littlejohn**[14] and would express the hope that he may soon be settled in another sphere where his undoubted ability will be deeply appreciated.

"4th Resolution. **Presbytery while refraining from any expression that would cast reflection on the actions of the congregation**[15] would most affectionately urge them not to allow the present disturbed state of feeling to weaken and scatter them, but in brotherly love to unite their energies in preserving the peace and prosperity of the congregation.

"5th Resolution. Presbytery would heartily recommend the congregation in settling accounts with and taking leave of their pastor to manifest towards him a very liberal and generous spirit. "

"Having heard the recommendation of the Presbytery, "Mr. Littlejohn in a few touching words complied with the recommendation of the court and resigned the congregation." The resignation was accepted, and the pastoral relationship was dissolved. "Mr. Littlejohn requested that his name be retained on the roll of the Southern Presbytery and that his name be not put on the probationers list.""

Littlejohn remained in good standing in the Southern presbytery and accepted preaching appointments in June and September, asking for and receiving his credentials in September[xxv]. It is also worth noting that he accepted a preaching appointment in Belfast in Sunday July 13^{th,} 1890[xxvi], so continued to be not only in good standing but also a respected and sort after preacher.

---

[14] Bold emphasis by the author
[15] Bold emphasis by the author

Summary

Littlejohn acted in good faith with approval of his congregation and approval of the presbytery to collect funds to help improve or bring the manse up to standard it being in a very damp and desolate condition. This upset some of the elders who were trustees of the manse and they took umbrage at it and found that it infringed upon their rights and got congregation to rescind this permission. This was done at a meeting when Littlejohn was absent and had already decided to accept a preaching appointment in Liverpool for February 1888 and perhaps even trying to raise funds on behalf of the congregation and the manse.[16]

The congregation then was then split in two with a sizable minority following the line of the elders who had felt their rights had been infringed upon by Littlejohn's actions and once this line or divide was drawn no way back could be found. Littlejohn, not having done anything wrong, in fact, having acted out of principle and best judgement on his part, resigned and moved to America.

As a final note on his relationship with the Creevagh congregation when Presbytery decided that the congregation should be liberal and generous in their settlement when disassociating themselves from their pastor it can be assumed, Littlejohn would take note of the fact that they only discharged their absolute legal minimum obligation to him[17]. Given his deep Covenanter convictions especially in the area of contracts, it comes as no surprise that he would then write a letter of complaint to presbytery about this. He had left for Philadelphia at this stage and Presbytery would see no advantage in pursuing this and

---

[16] This is a very different story to what some people have said that it was all about money and that the actions were that he took an all-expenses paid trip to Liverpool possibly to see his brother who was resident close to Liverpool - even though his brother was not to move to this area for several years yet. And that this was at the expense of the congregation. This is an example of the 'whispers' I mentioned earlier and could not be further from the truth.

[17] This was a suggestion, albeit a strong one, from the Presbytery, it left it open to the conflicting interpretations of Littlejohn and the Creevagh congregation

risking further conflict within the Creevagh congregation. Thus, the response of Presbytery was that

"A letter was read from Rev. J M Littlejohn complaining the congregation of Creevagh for not paying him anything beyond the legal debts. The presbytery after considering the whole case passed a resolution by which the congregation was exonerated from all further liability to their late pastor – The Rev. J M Littlejohn. The clerk was directed to write to Mr Littlejohn and to inform him that presbytery was satisfied with the actions of the Creevagh congregation and considered that they had left him no ground for complaint"[xxvii]

It is worth remembering that **"presbytery would have it distinctly understood that they do not recognise any charge, or make any reflection in the least, affecting the standing or ministerial efficiency of Mr. Littlejohn"**[xxviii] and this is reflected in his continuing to hold preaching post until he left Ireland in September 1888.

To try and put this conflict into a context within the reformed church we give two examples. One concerning the problem which arose within the Liverpool congregation. And it demonstrates just how easy it was for a congregation to get upset on a point of principle or through jealousy or some other aspect and for this to cause a rift or split within a congregation.

One example of this happened in the Liverpool congregation. To save money and make efficient use of their premises the congregation rented their building to the Knights Templar. While the Templars had similar ideals regarding temperance and morality, they were an 'oath-bound' society, a 'secret society'. Membership of it would be incompatible to being a Reformed Presbyterian. This split the congregation in Liverpool and Presbytery and Synod had to intervene.

Even when presbytery, having investigated the situation, decided that the way that it was done didn't contradict or infringe on the principles of the Reformed Presbyterian Church it so divided the congregation that the presbytery decided that it was best that they got out of the contract, if they could, rather than risking splitting the congregation into two factions. This reflects the fact that the life and integrity of the congregation was foremost in the approach of the Presbytery and Synod.

Another example was of a congregation which got very upset and split again concerning the wife of the minister just being seen with Christmas cards, not even sending them. (she was a convert from Catholicism and many relations would have sent her cards at Christmas)[xxix] This may seem strange to those who have no real knowledge of the Reformed Presbyterian Church. They don't celebrate Christmas as a commercial holiday. They celebrate the Sabbath and they celebrate Christmas as the birthday of Christ and not as something that should be commercialised in any way. So, the mere act of sending Christmas Cards or being seen with Christmas Cards could be seen as something not to be associated with and in this instance a petition to be drawn and brought to other members of the congregation to sign and show their disapproval. This story has a particular relevance to Littlejohn. It has been said he was not one to celebrate family holidays and the example was given that after his death several unopened Christmas presents were to be found in his study[xxx]. This may simply have been a reflection of his faith and attitude to Christmas as a religious occasion and not one for the exchange of gifts.

---

[i] The Coleraine Chronicle, Saturday February 25th, 1893.

[ii] The Coleraine Constitution, March 11th, 1893

[iii] Congregational, synod and other records of the Reformed Presbyterian Church; Some have been copied by Public Records Office Northern Ireland and can be found under the reference codes MIC1C and CR5; Others are held in the Reformed Presbyterian library of the Reformed Theological College Knockbracken, County Down

[iv] Ibid

[v] ibid

[vi] ibid

[vii] "At the Ford of the Birches – History of Ballybay its People and Vicinity", By James H. Murnane and Peadar Murnane.

[viii] Congregational, synod and other records of the Reformed Presbyterian Church; Some have been copied by Public Records Office Northern Ireland and can be found under the reference codes MIC1C and CR5; Others are held in the Reformed Presbyterian library of the Reformed Theological College Knockbracken, County Down

[ix] Ibid, Minutes of annual meeting in Londonderry, June 1886 and June 1887 in Belfast page 54-55

[x] Ibid, 1887, page 16

[xi] ibid
[xii] Ibid page 54-55
[xiii] Minutes of the Synod of the Southern presbytery of the Reformed Presbyterian Church of Ireland, February 7th, 1888
[xiv] The Northern Standard – Monaghan Saturday September 11th, 1886
[xv] ibid
[xvi] The Covenanter; a magazine of the Reformed Presbyterian Church of Ireland, 1886-1888; library of the Reformed Theological College Knockbracken, County Down
[xvii] ibid
[xviii] ibid
[xix] ibid
[xx] Congregational, synod and other records of the Reformed Presbyterian Church; Some have been copied by Public Records Office Northern Ireland and can be found under the reference codes MIC1C and CR5; Others are held in the Reformed Presbyterian library of the Reformed Theological College Knockbracken, County Down.
[xxi] Ibid
[xxii] Minutes of Southern Presbytery 1st May 1888
[xxiii] At the Ford of the Birches; History of Ballybay its People and Vicinity", By James H. Murnane and Peadar Murnane.
[xxiv] Minutes of Southern Presbytery 1st May 1888
[xxv] Minutes of the proceedings of the Reformed Presbyterian Synod of Ireland June 1889, page 200
[xxvi] Belfast evening telegraph, Saturday July 12th, 1890
[xxvii] Minutes of Southern Presbytery 6th November 1888
[xxviii] Minutes of Southern Presbytery of Reformed Presbyterian church of Ireland, 30th May 1888
[xxix] Personal conversation with members of a congregation who wished to remain anonymous.
[xxx] Letter to M Collins August 10th, 2000, from Littlejohn's granddaughter, Mary Elizabeth Lindsay.; Held in the National Osteopathic Archives at the Wellcome Libraries archives

MAY TO OCTOBER 1888

Having resigned his ministry at Creevagh on 30th May 1888 Littlejohn continued to be in good standing in the Reformed Presbyterian church in Ireland and received regular preaching appointments, especially in the Southern presbytery.[1] This continued until Sept 1888 when he asked for and was given his credentials[2i] and sailed to America where he was received by the Philadelphia presbytery on Oct 23rd, 1888.[ii]

William, also moved to America at this time being certified to the Pittsburgh Presbytery as a licentiate by the Northern Presbytery of the Reformed Presbyterian Church, Ireland and expecting to be in the country by the 1st June 1889 and wanted preaching appointments from the synod.[iii]

Prior to leaving for America William Littlejohn participated in the distribution of prizes in connection with the Science and Art Department, South Kensington[3] at the Garvagh Science School, on the 8th January 1889.

William's stay in the Pittsburgh Presbytery was short lived and he was on the 8th October 1889 granted certificate to the Ohio Presbytery to be settled over the Lind Grove congregation.

---

[1] Preaching appointments 1888 June 4th sabbath and July 2nd sabbath Fairview; July 1st sabbath, Sept 3rd Sabbath Dromore- all in Southern Presbytery- recorded in the minutes of the Southern Presbytery.

[2] 11 Sept 1888. Noted in the records of the Southern Presbytery of Ireland that he had asked for by letter, and received his credentials

[3] This was a government department promoting education in science and art with payments to teachers being linked to results in the Departments exams. Some have suggested that the Society of Science, Letters and Art styling their exams as 'Kensington locals' were implying that they were connected with the Government department (some Quasi medical institutions – American medical association, Chicago 1916)

Littlejohn himself states that he had a serious fall in 1888 and this led to him going to USA in 1889 on health grounds.[iv] The timing of this event is rather hard to pinpoint as in his testimony he associates it with his journey to America in 1890.

It's quite possible that it happened in the fall of 1888 and that his reason for being in Glasgow at the time was that his brother James Buchan was about to embark on his undergraduate studies for the degree on M.D.[4]

It would appear that between May 1888 when he resigned from Creevagh and October 1888 when he was received in Philadelphia that this would be the only time that he could have had an accident of such a nature as he describes in the report of the House of Lords Select Committee meeting. Dr Martin Collins in his book Osteopathy in Britain the First Hundred Years states:

"It must have been shortly after his return to Glasgow in 1888 that he had a serious fall down a flight of concrete steps at the Faraday laboratory and lay unconscious for four hours with concussion and a fractured cranium. Shortly after that he started having haemorrhages from his throat requiring periods of covalence. On account of his ill health he visited the U.S. in 1889, as recommended by Dr Matthew Charteris of Glasgow and Sir Morell Mackenzie of London and stayed at a sanatorium on Long Island."[v]

According to Wernham, Littlejohn was wont to say that: "Mackenzie said that I would be dead in six months, but it was Mackenzie who was dead in six months and not John Martin."[vi]

Sir Morell Mackenzie died on the 3rd February 1892[vii] this would place Littlejohn's consultation with him in the middle of the year 1891.

Matthew Charteris (1840-1897) was Regius Professor of Materia Medica at the University from 1880 until 1897.[viii]

---

[4] "1888- 9 Age 20, son of James, Clergyman, Studied Medicine: Chemistry, Junior Anatomy Address: Garvagh, Co. Londonderry, Ireland" Glasgow University Archives email

If the quote about Sir Morell Mackenzie is correct it would be at this time in 1891 that he consulted Sir Morell Mackenzie and made arrangements, then to go back to New York to study at Columbia University.[5]

Another reason for John Martin returning to Glasgow during this time would be to see how he might further his career. Perhaps he had even considered studying medicine at this time. It's interesting to note the covenanter's group to which John Martin was closely associated with, had many ardent anti-vivisectionists within it. And it may be that this put him off studying medicine (Natural philosophy) and led him into moral philosophy. This is of course speculation.

It would then seem that he left Creevagh, continued to work as a minister in the church, perhaps spent some time with his family before visiting Glasgow with his brother to prepare for his move to Glasgow to study. While there possibly had the accident and consulted Dr Charteris and was advised to move to America for health reasons. Arriving in Philadelphia in Oct 1888, he probably would have found that he needed his "degree" to pursue further study and thus returned to Scotland to take his degree M.A. that he had earned previously - graduating *"with an ordinary degree[6] in April 1889"* (at that time it would not have involved taking an oath of allegiance to the University but would have involved a fee and then returning to the USA with his brother William in June 1889[ix]. It is also possible, and in fact given the timeline, probable that it was during this visit to Glasgow that he had his accident.

"John Martin Littlejohn graduated with an ordinary degree in April 1889. It is possible that he did not graduate at the end of his sessions

---

[5] If I am correct in my reasoning, he would have consulted Dr. Charteris in 1888 and Sir Morel Mackenzie in late 1891 before his final move the America.

[6] At Glasgow University the M.A. was the ordinary degree. It seems puzzling that he did not go forward for an M.A. with honours, until you read the university regulations. Having not gone forward for the M.A. in 1888 and having "ceased to be a matriculated student in attendance on a class or classes in the University for more than one winter session", he would, in 1889, been ineligible for the 'with honours' degree. (see Glasgow University Calendars for 1888, 1889)

of study, although qualified to do so, because the ceremony of graduation was very much associated with the Established Church. At about this date, there were some non-conformists who took a political stance upon this, and it could be that J.M. Littlejohn was one of these.

It did also cost money to graduate, and this could be another factor. The concept of going to university to graduate is a relatively late one, and it would not have been unusual in the earlier 19th century for someone such as a doctor, to practice medicine after having attended the University but not graduated. As long as he had class tickets or testimonials this would be sufficient."[x]

LIFE IN THE US FROM OCTOBER 1888 UNTIL THE END OF SUMMER 1889

This may have been a short period of time but a difficult one to be exact about what happened and his whereabouts, but it is important in terms of the formation of his character and his career. It was at this time that he developed a relationship with the Brooklyn congregation in New York and with the colleges there including Columbia.

On arrival in America he was received on October 23rd, 1888 by the Philadelphia Presbytery and later attended the Reformed Presbyterian Synod in Ohio on June 5th, 1889 as a registered Minister of the Philadelphia Presbytery. At that meeting it was noted that from January until the synod in Ohio he was allocated to New York as a supply preacher, with an address at 326 West 48 Street, New York City.

He went to America in October '88 and stayed there through to the end of the summer '89 with perhaps a short return to Glasgow to finish his M.A. degree in April '89. He had completed all the studies and examinations necessary for graduation between '81 and '85 but did not take the graduation at the time as it was not necessary for him other than to have his class tickets to attend the Theological College in Belfast. So, the amount of work he'd have had to have done for graduating in April 1889 would have being minimal and perhaps only paying a fee and attending a graduation ceremony or collecting his certificate. He and his brother William are recorded as arriving in New York on the State of Nebraska from Glasgow and Larne – the ships passenger list and manifest are signed and dated as 5th June 1889 (by the ships Mate R S CAMPBELL, and not the Master of the Vessel; apparently this was not unusual and it was also not unusual for the manifest to be signed and lodged with the authorities sometime after the vessel docked[xi]). This means that the ship arrived sometime, perhaps up to two or more weeks prior to this. This would give them time to attend the Ohio Synod on 5th June at which they acted as stenographers for the speeches which were to be printed in the Christian nation. Further detail of this time can be gained from the Christian Nation. In the June 19th, 1889 it states that:

"The next issue of the Christian Nation will contain a verbatim report of the discussion which preceded the action of the synod with reference to voting on amendments to state constitutions. Appreciating the importance of preserving to the church, in exact language, a debate that must become historical, we engaged the excellent services of two expert stenographers, the Rev William and John Littlejohn, members of our own synod, to report the speeches."[xii]

So not only did he attend the synod in Ohio in June 1889 he also took the important work of a stenographer along with his brother William. This is a talent which along with dictation he would have gained in school and according to the quote was an expert in. The Christian Nation goes on to state that the two Littlejohns "did the work well"[7] and prints the entire debate verbatim. Anyone who knows anything about stenography knows that this is quite a talent.

The one confusing point during this time is that he received his ordinary degree in Glasgow University in April 1889 but was also listed as being allocated to New York as a supply preacher. This would seem to indicate that he took only a few months off back in Glasgow to get his M.A. in April before returning with his brother in June 1889.

---

[7] In view of the vast importance of this debate, or rather of the importance of the question debated, we felt that a full and accurate report of it should be taken and preserved, and so we engaged the expert services of the Revs. Wm. and John Littlejohn, to stenographically report the speeches. They did the work well." Christian Nation June 26th, 1889

Following the synod in June '89 he was allocated to Ohio in July/August/September, to Pittsburgh and October, November and December to Rochester[xiii]. These allocations would not have automatically been followed by preaching appointments. We find it clearly stated in the minutes of the Synod of 5th June that; -

> "ORDINATION OF MR. Wm. LITTLEJOHN. The Commission of Iowa Presbytery to ordain and install Mr. William Littlejohn, pastor of Lind Grove congregation, met for that purpose, Tuesday, Dec. 3d, 1889, at 10 A. m. …. Lind Grove congregation was organized Sept. 14,1856. Since that time, they have had three pastors, who have resigned to enter on other work. The congregation has been somewhat reduced in numbers, but the members who remain are earnest and spirited and still resolved to hold aloft " the old blue banner." We trust that under Mr. Littlejohn's ministrations the congregation will be greatly blessed and that the young pastor may be greatly cheered by reaping the fruits of his labors." (The Christian Nation Dec 25th, 1889)

"The Committee on Supplies present the following report: "Owing to the small amount of preaching asked for by the different Presbyteries, and the comparatively large number of unsettled ministers and licentiates, your committee find great difficulty in providing employment for all our laborers."

So, it may be that Littlejohn decided to further his education and defer to his brother the opportunity to have preaching appointments. From Williams point of view this seemed to work out well as he received a call from Lynd grove[8] congregation in Iowa, on October 21st, 1889 and was ordained and installed as minister on the first Tuesday in December[xiv]. John Martin was not noted as being present at his ordination.

---

[8] "Lately Lind Grove congregation, Ohio, has put on new life. They have secured the ministerial services of the Rev. Wm. Littlejohn, a devoted and earnest minister. They are repairing their house of worship, and although a somewhat scattered congregation, are making an earnest effort to carry on their Sabbath school." The Christian Nation October 22, 1890 page 7

Littlejohn was then said to have returned to Scotland by Jan 1890[xv]. He is also listed as attending Glasgow University during the session 1889/90 studying theology[9]. He would have registered for his studies at Glasgow university for the 1889-1890 session which would have started in Oct 1889. This means he would have had to leave America before his brother received the call from the congregation in Iowa and before the marriage of his brother William on October 22nd, 1890 at the residence of the bride's father in Mediapolis, Ohio.[xvi]

"Married. Oct. 22, 1890, at the residence of the bride's father, Mr. Wm. M. Orr, of Mediapolis, Iowa, by Rev. C. D. Trumbull, assisted by Revs. T. P. Robb, D. T. Campbell and J. A. Black: The Rev. William Littlejohn, pastor of Lind Grove congregation, and Miss Maggie A. Orr."[xvii]

Another factor may have been his Father's health which had been poor. In November 1891 it was noted in the Irish Covenanter that his father, the Rev James Littlejohn who had been ill for some time was again fit enough to attend the presbytery meeting in Ireland[xviii]

---

[9] "John Martin Littlejohn, MA; 1889 – 90, Age 23, studied Theology: Hebrew, Biblical Criticism, Ecclesiastical History,
Divinity (matric. no. 1857); Address: 86 Abingdon St, Glasgow" (Glasgow university matriculation albums)

1889, RETURNS TO GLASGOW UNIVERSITY

On returning to Glasgow he took courses for the Licentiate in Arts[xix], which is a lesser degree that the M.A. The reason for this is not quite clear, but probably to give him excess to library facilities, perhaps to allow him to take the graduation ceremony.

for the M.A. He duly graduated with an M.A. in 1889 and took courses for Bachelor of Divinity, which he received in 1890. In 1892 he became a Bachelor of Laws.

During this period, he excelled in his studies taking prizes as follows:[xx]

1889 – 90; fourth in senior division Divinity and Biblical riticism, fifth is senior class of Hebrew, fourth (proxime accesserunt) in senior class of church history.

1890 – 91; Ninth is class of Scots Law, third equal in examination for prizes in faculty of procurators in Glasgow. Third in class of constitutional law and history, first-class honours and first place in class of public law.

1891 – 92; received the Henderson Prize of twenty guineas for the best essay on 'The Sabbathism of Hebrews iv. 9' Second in class of civil law, second equal in class of conveyancing, ninth in eminently distinguished in examinations for prizes of faculty of procurators in Glasgow, the William Hunter Medal in forensic medicine[10].

It has been assumed that it was here that John Martin got his first taste of medicine and physiology. However, as mentioned above, his attendance at the Garvagh Science Academy, in his early teens included studies in Physiology. Winning this medal showed that he had an obvious predilection for this subject, particularly from the investigatory side.

His energy must have been boundless, not only did he attend to his studies but also maintained an active role in the Church, giving

---

[10] Forensic medicine was and still is part of a law degree.

services in the Milton Free Church Garnethill, Glasgow, in July 1892 and the Darvel Original Secession Church in March 1892 to mention two examples[xxi]. At the same time, he develops an interest in studying law and supplements his income by teaching at Rosemount College, a girl's school, in Glasgow at which he was Principal from 1890-1892;[11]

It is likely that during his time teaching at Rosemount he would have used the 'Science and Arts department South Kensington', or even the Society of Science, Letters and Art for some exams. We know his bother William had a connection with the 'Science and Arts department South Kensington', that was, some say confused with the Society of Science, Letters and Art and their involvement in school examinations as far back as 1889.[12] The Harvard College Library version of his Thesis on the Schoolmen and Grotius lists his attendance at the Garvagh Science academy graduating with first prize for first place in 1878.[xxii]

Some idea of his standing as a student may be gained from comments by R.T. Younger, M.A. L.L.B. Advocate, his teacher in constitutional law and history. On recommending John Martin to Columbia University for his Fellowship he wrote:

"Mr Littlejohn was a most distinguished student. In his examination for his degree of L.L.B. he acquitted himself with great distinction. Mr Littlejohn's work as a student was characterised not only by ability but also by great thoroughness. He worked hard and well. In the domain of political philosophy, he displayed exceptional ability. I have no hesitation is saying that he will be an ornament to any university with which he becomes connected."[xxiii]

---

[11] This appears to be the school established in connection with the Townhead established Church in 1872 and inspected in august 1892 with an address at 168 Garngad Hill Glasgow, and also used as a Sabbath School. Its principle as of 30th May 1892 was John Clanachan with an average attendance of 240 scholars over the previous 6 months. (Glasgow City Archives, Mitchell Library North Street G3 7DN

[12] A report in the Belfast Telegraph of 10th Jan 1889 mentions the distribution of prizes gained at the examination the previous May in connection with the "science and Art Department, South Kensington" took place at the upper school in Garvagh. The Rev. William Littlejohn was present in connection with the school committee.

Another indication of his industry is shown by the claim that he studied in three different seminaries in Europe while taking his B.D. degree[xxiv]. Probably after completing his B.D., in the summer of 1890, he could have taken the time to do this. This would be no mean feat as the time required for B.D. degree is quite substantial, and the time off would not allow extensive travel or study[xxv].

It could be said he had 'wanderlust' in his youth and travelled extensively when he could, especially during the summer when free from his formal studies. He gives some details of the countries he visited in his application to renew his British citizenship in 1924[xxvi] he states " ***I travelled abroad in search of health. France, Italy, Germany, Switzerland, Egypt, Palestine, India, Australia, Canada and US, Settling in USA in 1894.***"

During his time at Glasgow he also served on the magazine committee of the Student representative Council. (This council was officially set up in 1886[13] and it is reasonable to assume that Littlejohn involved himself in it from its inception, given his inclination to political reform at all levels. We see that in all teaching positions he set up or supported the existence of such councils) He also served as the law member of the Student representative council 1891-2[xxvii].

Given the acknowledgments he enumerates in the preface to his Ph.D. Thesis, 'The political theory of Grotius and the Schoolmen' it would appear that he may have been considering following up on his studies in Scotland by following a Ph.D. Course either at Glasgow or Edinburgh.

"The topic was first selected and the original plan, which has been adhered to throughout, was first formulated under the inspiration of the ideas of the late Professor Lorimer of Edinburgh University. Valuable suggestions were received from Advocate W.G. Miller, lecturer on Political Philosophy and International Law in my Alma Mater, Glasgow University."[xxviii]

---

[13] Glasgow University Students' Representative Council was founded on 9 March 1886 and recognised as the legal representative body for students of the University of Glasgow by the Universities (Scotland) Act 1889 (Glasgow University Archive Services)

Lorimer[14] was known for his approach "*that of constructing a system of reasoning from cause to effect*" and we find that throughout his studies and career Littlejohn also approach his subjects in this manner. Osteopathy as promulgated by A.T. Still would sit well with this method.

So, it is not surprising we find that even at this stage of his career he had the concept of the whole organism being more important than the parts; the parts must always be viewed in the context of their relationship not only with each other but also in relationship to the whole organism. We get a glimpse of this in his prize essay for his Bachelor of Divinity degree, when he says in relation to the Bible

"At the same time, while remembering our duty to interpret each passage on its own merits, we must not forget that Sacred Scripture forms an organic whole. Each part may be a perfect organism, yet when all the parts are put together, they form a complete unity"[xxix].

His brother, James Buchan, was also studying in Glasgow at this time and completed his studies graduating in 1892 M.B., C.M. (Bachelor of Medicine and Master of Surgery)[xxx]. The third medical degree of Doctor of Medicine required 2 years as a M.B. and aged not less than 24 years.

During his testimony at the House of Lords select committee hearing in 1935 he stated that he "was also at the Anderson's Medical College" where he got both anatomy and physiology[xxxi]. While there are no direct records to substantiate his claim, given the position and history of the Anderson's Medical college it is more than plausible. The College buildings were situated from 1889 in Dumbarton Road, within five minutes' walk of the Western Infirmary and Glasgow University. It held many extra mural classes in the medical field, including anatomy and physiology. In fact, *"The Medical School long*

---

[14] Lorimer's theory held that the natural law was founded on divine authority and revealed in conscience and in history. He was particularly concerned with the application of natural law to international relations. He was admitted to the Scottish bar in 1845, and in 1865 he became professor of public law at Edinburgh (https://www.britannica.com/biography/James-Lorimer)

held a foremost position as an extra-mural school, and provided a medical education at a cost suited to the circumstances of many who would not otherwise have been able to prosecute the study of medicine"[xxxii] In a letter reasoning why the new buildings for the Anderson College were built in close proximity to Glasgow university, Dr. Buchanan said " *The extraordinary success of the Extra-Mural Medical School in Edinburgh – a success admitted by all to be mainly due to the close proximity of the School to the University buildings allowing a free interchange of students. …. The recognition by Glasgow University of Extra-Mural Lecturers would allow attendance at the Anderson School on four courses of lectures, or for two winter sessions.*[xxxiii]*"*

Posters announcing details summer and winter session of Lectures at the Anderson Medical School advertised a series of lecture in Anatomy, practical, anatomy, Physiology, medical jurisprudence and other subjects, all of which would have been available to Littlejohn[xxxiv]

Given that he won the William Hunter Medal in Forensic Medicine in the summer session of 1891, it would seem he studied the subject intensely. So, while Littlejohn, unlike his brother David[15], was not a matriculant of The Anderson's Medical College, it is quite plausible that he did attend anatomy and physiology extra mural classes to supplement his forensic medicine course.

---

[15] David was registered at Anderson's College in session 1895-6 (Glasgow university archives ref. DC 244/9/2). He is listed as being in his third year, and as being a student at Glasgow University. He enrolled in classes in Practical Anatomy and Surgery. Unfortunately, there is a gap in the Anderson's College student records from 1884-1930 so the archives did not find any records of his attendance, exams or qualifications. (Email communication from duty archivist at Glasgow university)

ANDERSON'S COLLEGE
MEDICAL SCHOOL,
GLASGOW.
NEW BUILDINGS SITUATED in DUMBARTON ROAD,

Immediately to the West of the Entrance to the Western Infirmary, and within four minutes' walk of the University.

The WINTER SESSION will be opened on
TUESDAY, 20th OCTOBER, 1891, at TWO o'Clock,
WITH AN ADDRESS BY
Prof. J. ROBERTSON WATSON, M.A.

Junior Anatomy, ... 4 p.m.	Prof. A. M. BUCHANAN, M.A., M.D., Assisted by Three Demonstrators and Three Assistant Demonstrators.
Senior Anatomy, ... 11 a.m.	
Practical Anatomy, ... 9 a.m. till 5 p.m	
Chemistry, ... 10 a.m.	Prof. J. ROBERTSON WATSON, M.A., and Assistants.
Chemical Laboratory, ... 10 a.m. till 5 p.m	
Materia Medica and Therapeutics, .. 2 p.m.	Prof. ALEX. NAPIER, M.D., and Assistant.
Physiology, ... 12 Noon.	Prof. D. CAMPBELL BLACK, M.D., & Assistant.
Practice of Medicine, ... 4 p.m.	Prof. SAMSON GEMMELL, M.D., & Assistant.
Diseases of Women (Monday, Wednesday & Friday), 12 Noon	
Midwifery and Diseases of Children, (In Summer,) .... 12 Noon	Prof. WM. L. REID, M.D., and Assistant.
Surgery, ... 1 p.m.	Prof. JAMES DUNLOP, M.D.
Operative Surgery, ... (In Summer) 1 p.m.	
Medical Jurisprudence .... (In Summer) 11 a.m.	Prof. T. KENNEDY DALZIEL, M.B.
Botany, ... (In Summer), as may be arranged.	Prof. THOMAS KING.
Ophthalmic Surgery, ... Fridays, 8 p.m.	T. SPENCE MEIGHAN, M.D.
Hygiene and Public Health (Winter or Summer)	JAMES CHRISTIE, M.A. M.D.
Aural Surgery, ... (In Summer), 4 p.m.	THOMAS BARR, M.D.
Diseases of Throat and Nose, ...	JOHN MACINTYRE, M.B.
Hospital Practice and Clinical Lectures in Royal or Western Infirmary, ... 9 a.m.	PHYSICIANS and SURGEONS of ROYAL or WESTERN INFIRMARY.
Dispensary Practice in Royal or Western Infirmary Dispensary, ... 2 p.m.	

DEGREES AND DIPLOMAS.

Certificates of Attendance on the Lectures at Anderson's College Medical School are received by the Universities of London and Durham, by the Royal University of Ireland, and by all the Royal Colleges and Licensing Boards in the United Kingdom. They are also recognised by the Universities of Glasgow and Edinburgh under certain conditions.

Students entering at Anderson's College Medical School with a view to graduate in the University of Glasgow or Edinburgh or the Royal University of Ireland will obtain full particulars in the Calendar as to the conditions under which the Lectures are recognised.

CLASS FEES.

For each of the above Courses of Lectures (Anatomy excepted), First Session, £2 2s.; Second Session, £1 1s.; afterwards free. Anatomy Class Fees—First Session (including Practical Anatomy), £4 4s.; Second Session (including Practical Anatomy), £4 4s.; Third Session, £1 1s.

Students who have attended classes at other schools, but who desire to pursue their studies at Anderson's College Medical School, will be admitted to such classes as they may have attended elsewhere at the reduced fees.

Matriculation Fee—10s. to those taking out two or more classes; 5s. to those taking out one class only. The Matriculation Fee of 10s. represents a combined fee for the Winter and Summer Sessions.

ROYAL OR WESTERN INFIRMARY. Fees—Hospital Practice and Clinical Instruction, First Year, £10 10s.; Second Year, £10 10s.; afterwards free. Six Months £6 6s. at Royal Infirmary; £7 7s. at Western Infirmary; Three Months £4 4s. Vaccination Fee, £1 1s.

The Fees for all the Lectures and Hospital Practice required of Candidates for the Qualifications in Medicine and in Surgery granted conjointly by the Royal Colleges of Physicians and Surgeons of Edinburgh, and the Faculty of Physicians and Surgeons of Glasgow, amount to about £48. The Total Fees for the Triple Qualification amount to £59 5s.

A CALENDAR and all information relating to the Medical School, may be obtained from Prof. J. Robertson Watson, M.A., Parkhead Cross, Glasgow, Dean of the Medical Faculty of Anderson's College Medical School.

GLASGOW UNIVERSITY ARCHIVES

(courtesy of Glasgow University Archives)

During this time their father had being quite ill and must have been considering retiring which he eventually did on 14th February 1893[xxxv] and moved to Shropshire to live with James Buchan, who had taken a position there as the local Doctor[xxxvi].

> "The Rev J. Littlejohn of Garvagh, who had been for a considerable time in feeble health and unable to attend presbytery was able to be present and on recognition of this there was put on the minutes an expression of the presbytery's gratitude to God for Mr John Littlejohn's partial recovery and hope for his perfect restoration to health."
>
> (Christian Nation Dec 30th, 1891 quoting The Irish Covenanter for Dec 1891)

A SERIOUS FALL, OUTCOME OF WHICH IS MOVE TO USA

In his evidence before the House of Lords Select Committee meeting, Littlejohn states:

"The chief reason I went to America was that I was not able to continue living in this country. I had a severe accident in 1888, in connection with which I had concussion of the brain and a fracture of the cranium. This is still visible if your Lordships want to investigate it. It was on account of my health that I went to America in 1889 on the advice of two of the most distinguished physicians in this country Dr Matthew Charteris of Glasgow and Sir Morel Mackenzie of London. I went away with the express object of regaining my health. While I was in Columbia University I stayed in a sanatorium on Long Island and came in periodically. I was not required to attend daily because I was doing research work, and I came in periodically to Columbia College. As I pointed out, I went through the various line of work that I've outlined up to 1897"[xxxvii]

As outlined above it would have been during the summer of 1891 that he consulted Sir Morell Mackenzie and made arrangements, then to go back to New York to study at Columbia University.[16]

We find in the Journal of Osteopathy June-August 1935 the following quote:

"After a student career of distinction in three departments of his alma mater, no less an authority than Sir Morell Mackenzie told him that he could only survive seven months in the climatic conditions of his native land. As with tears in his eyes Sir Morell told him his verdict, he added this, which he afterwards confirmed in a letter to his father, 'May God make it possible for your student life to be prolonged in the summer climes of a new world'. Sunshine, diet and A.T. Still osteopathy

---

[16] It was at a meeting on 12th April 1892 that the University Council of Columbia College recommended Littlejohn as a Fellow for the year 1892-3; (Columbia College university Bulletin of No 3 July 1892, page 4)

prolonged the 'lengthened shadows' of seven months to over forty years."

This last quote seems to confirm that it was at this stage, 1891, that he saw Sir Morell Mackenzie and not in 1888, so it may be correct to assume that it was Mr Charteris that he saw in 1888 if he had the fall in that year. It seems to make more sense than any other analysis of this situation.

Given this verdict on his health, Littlejohn started to make arrangements for following his career in America. This may have been during the summer of 1891.

He had spent months studying in seminaries across Europe for his B.D. degree in Glasgow and presumably this would have been towards the end of his B.D. during the summer months of 1890., attaining his B.D. in Nov 1890.

it is likely that this study tour across Europe placed a considerable strain on his health and may have being the reason why he needed to consult with someone as eminent as Sir Morell Mackenzie. Another source of strain to the young Littlejohn during this time was that his father had been seriously ill during 1891.

In the meantime, his brother James Buchan finished his studies and return to live in Garvagh with his father, mother, brother David and sister Elizabeth. He would then find employment in Shropshire as a medical officer and public vaccination officer for the Munslow district. His other brother, David started his medical studies in Glasgow[xxxviii] in the 1893/4 session. Not long after this his father retired and moved to live with James Buchan in Munslow, taking with him his wife and their only surviving daughter Elizabeth Margaret A., now aged 23.[xxxix]

SEPTEMBER 1892, TRAVELS TO THE US

When the young Littlejohn set sail for New York in the fall of 1892[17][xl], even though his health was failing, he must surely have felt he was setting out on a new beginning. The new world beckoned before him, he had in his pocket testimonials from his teachers in Glasgow and was secure in the knowledge that he would be studying a subject close to his heart in one of the foremost universities in America, Columbia College, New York.

When he left Glasgow to attend Columbia University, he had already spent some time in the United States with his brother William and made useful contacts within the Reformed Presbyterian Covenanters with North America.

On arrival, he carried on as he had previously in all his endeavours, and put all his energies to use his intellectual gifts to the fullest extent in both his studies and whatever endeavour he took part in, following the Covenanter and Presbyterian ideal that gifts that we have been given by God had to be used to their full for the betterment of mankind and that the idea of preordination played a significant part. This does not mean that he viewed his life as being laid out by a higher power, but that the gifts given to him were to be used for a particular purpose during life. In his case, this was to be in the educational field and particularly in the area of moral philosophy and political science. He also continued his association with the Christian Nation working as a departmental editor and contributor[xli].

---

[17] John M. Littlejohn arrived on the 9th September 1892 on the ship City of New York and his occupation is listed as a minister. While the timeframe looks correct the age is listed as twenty. However, on the original document it looks more like 26 years than 20, which would be more correct. He is listed in the Ellis Island records as arriving on the 9th Sep 1892

1892, COLUMBIA COLLEGE

The September 14th, 1892 edition of the Christian Nation carries a note which state:

"Rev J.M. Littlejohn, B.D., L.L.B., will assist with the communions in Wyman and Lind Grove on the last two Sabbaths of September…. On account of the serious illness of Mrs Littlejohn, the Reverend William Littlejohn was only able to fulfil brother Acheson's pulpit on the fourth Sabbath of August."

Littlejohn, having just arrived in the United States in early September 1892 went straight to work undertaking duties in the Lind Grove congregation on the 18th and 25th September[xlii], giving some assistance to his brother whose wife was ill. Quickly after this he took up his studies in Columbia and continued to work as a minister, mostly in Brooklyn.

"The Reverend John M. Littlejohn, B.D., L.L.B., of our church has being made a fellow of Columbia College, this city and entered upon the duties of an associate professorship this week. He will reside in Brooklyn and help our struggling congregation there."[xliii]

> The Rev. John Martin Littlejohn, BD., LL.B., has been appointed University Fellow in Political Philosophy in Columbia University. His recent honours in Jurisprudence, Divinity and Philosophy at Glasgow should make him a credit to this time-honoured university. We offer him our congratulations on this well-deserved mark of distinction.
> (The Coleraine Chronicle, Saturday, July 16th, 1892)

While he was starting his studies, he was also maintaining his connection with the church and with preaching. This was to be his pattern throughout his life; he was both a dedicated minister and a dedicated scholar.

He started the term in Columbia in 1892 as a student studying political philosophy, political economy and finance. Special work was the political theory of the Schoolmen and Grotius.[xliv] The topic itself having been selected and formulated under the inspiration of Professor Lorimer of Edinburgh University.

This again suggests that it may have being his original intention to have studied at Edinburgh. Only his failing health forcing him again to move to the new world. However, when he returned to Glasgow from America in 1889, he didn't transfer his registration with the Reformed Presbyterian Church from America to Scotland during this time. He may have been conflicted about whether he wanted to stay in Scotland or would be forced to return to the States. From his future pattern of returning to the British Isles and Europe regularly during the rest of his stay in America it would appear he always hankered after a return to his homeland.

One of the testimonials, by way of introduction to Columbia University for his fellowship was from R.T. Younger.

"Mr Littlejohn was a most distinguished student. In his examination for the degree of L.L.B., he acquitted himself with great distinguish. Mr Littlejohn's work as a student was characterised not only by his ability, but also by great thoroughness. He worked hard and well. In the domain of political philosophy, he displayed exceptional ability. I have no hesitation is saying that he will be an ornament to any university with which he becomes connected." [xlv]

The evidence is that he was held in high regard by the faculty not only in Glasgow but also at Columbia. Doctor W.A. Dunning, head of the department of political philosophy in Columbia, speaks of him (J.M. Littlejohn) and his work:

"I have been most deeply impressed by the extent and accuracy of Mr Littlejohn's acquaintance with the field of general philosophy and with the scholarly character of the work that he has done therein. From his researches from the political theories of the middle ages, especially from Aquinas to Grotius, in which he has now being engaged in both sides of the ocean for a long time, I confidently anticipate a distinct and valuable contribution to our scientific knowledge and appreciation of those thinkers. Mr Littlejohn's erudition requires recognition from some higher

institution of learning, and I am profoundly grateful that the possibility of such recognition[18] has opened up."[xlvi]

Further detail on his life during this time is gained from the Christian Nation. In the October 1892 edition we find that:

"The Reverend J.M. Littlejohn B.D., LL.B., delivered the inaugural lecture in connection with the Mediapolis, Ohio, lecture association, at the opening of the session in 1892/93. It was really a university extension lecture, the subject being, 'How to keep pace with advancing intelligence'. The lecturer pleaded for an enlargement of the field of popular education commensurate with the advancement of knowledge in every department; in the maxim of Pestalozzi, 'Education is the generator of power'. This advance, he showed, could be made by receiving an inspirate of nature, identifying oneself with the brotherhood of man, opening up the treasures of antiquity, and especially by the exhaustive study of individual personality and placing oneself under the influence of the Christian ideal in private and public life".

His brother William had been the chairperson of the association and the two brothers obviously had been associated with the Mediapolis Lecture Association in the past years.[xlvii]

One thing we can gain from this which will become evident in his future life, is his commitment to popular education. This tends to confirm the influence that the ideas of Professor Lorimer had on him and the ideas that he himself expressed in his early writings on the Missions in Covenantor magazine. That education shouldn't be confined to those privileged few. This together with his background in the Reformed Church as we shall see later gave him a tendency towards the so-called lesser or fringe universities, those which would be opening their door to the education of the general population rather than securing it for those privileged by birth or their financial position. His association with the Chautauqua movement with its emphasis on popular education

---

[18] This seems to have been written after the end of his time in Columbia when again due to failing health he had being unable to finish the requirements for his Ph.D. in that university, and seems to refer to the degree of Doctor of Philosophy being conferred on him by the Chicago National University in 1895

through night and evening classes, individual tuition etc, would probably have started during this period.

His reputation in the field of political philosophy was growing and it may have seemed that he had found his vocation.

"We made reference last week to the fully equipped departments for the teaching of political philosophy in Johns Hopkins and in Columbia. The institution whose political philosophy department ranks next in the number of branches taught, is that at Ann Arbor, Michigan, where there are at present close to half a hundred students working for degrees in this line of study. The new University of Chicago also contemplates eventually covering possibly all the branches, although at this writing they have but two professors in this department and are seeking a third. The desire to teach this science of growing importance has reached Canada too, and Professor J.M. Littlejohn has received an invitation to inaugurate a school of political science in connection with one of the Canadian Universities that wishes to come into line with modern political philosophy. A large subsidy is offered as a foundation."[xlviii]

It's worth spending a little time looking at Littlejohn's reputation within the church itself and his social life as recorded again in the Christian Nation.

"The following letter has been received for publication from the Rev William Littlejohn, Mediapolis, Ohio, September 26th; we have just passed through another communion season and have had an exceptionally profitable and enjoyable time. We cannot doubt the presence of the Lord at our feast. My brother, the Rev John M. Littlejohn, B.D., LL.B., fellow of Columbia College, was my assistant and greatly refreshed and cheered us by the words which he spake in Christ's name. His pulpit power and eloquence as well as the power of the gospel truth was fitted to captivate and instruct[xlix]*."* (October 5th, 1892 edition.

"The preaching by Prof. Littlejohn was remarkably comforting and strengthening" (February 22nd 1893, page 6)

This gives an idea of the power of John Martin Littlejohn's preaching or lecturing. The word eloquent isn't something we hear much of from his time in England, however it is a comment that has being made more than once about his preaching ability. Many sermons would last over an hour and without the aid of 'power point', microphones or other aids, he would hold an audience captivated by his logic, eloquence and power of speech. And if we read his sermons and the works that he published within the Christian Nation and the Covenanter and other magazines we find it beautifully composed and eloquent isn't too strong a word to use. Further evidence of his work and reputation is given in the following:

"Prof Littlejohn of Columbia College and Rev William Littlejohn of Mediapolis, Ohio spent Thanksgiving at the home of the writer, and we had a pleasantly orthodox time, theologically and turkey logically. Prof. Littlejohn, of the department of Civil Government in Columbia, is doing a work for the spread of the knowledge of the principles of Christian civil government, the importance of which no man can measure. From his versatile pen also drop the items classified as 'the week' being regularly on page six, the Rev William Littlejohn has consented to assume charge of the helpful corner a valuable department attempted by the writer several months but dropped for want of time and inability to secure a suitable person to give it attention." (November 30th, 1892, page 8))

Looking again at the social side of things we find a note from his brother William in the December 21st, 1892 edition when his brother visited and spent some time with him in New York:

"I have also been privileged to make a general survey of the beauties and attractions of New York and Brooklyn. Friends both outside and inside the covenanter church done their utmost to make my visit to New York a pleasant one. My brother's time is mostly taken up with his college work and of course I could not have him much around with me. However, Thanksgiving was a college holiday and he and I at the kind invitation of editor Pritchard and his estimable wife, eat turkey at 28 Decatur Street, Brooklyn[19]. Thanksgiving evening, we received through our kind host and hostess an invitation to a temperance banquet in Brooklyn where we enjoyed ourselves. I only lacked one thing to make my visit supremely enjoyable, that was Mrs Littlejohn and my little daughter who were just one year old on Thanksgiving Day. I go back to

---

[19] Littlejohn was listed as living at 58 Decauter Street, Brooklyn, in the register of students 1892/3

my home in the west with many fresh ideas and pleasant memories formed during my visit to New York and hope to profit by them. William Littlejohn"

By the end of the 1892/start of 1893 academic year, Littlejohn's reputation in this field was growing and it seemed that all he had to do

> Prof. J. M. Littlejohn receives next week the degree of D. D. from Chicago. He has been elected an Honorary Fellow of the University. He was to have received the degree of Ph. D. from Columbia at its commencement in June, but at his own request it has been deferred until the Fall as he wishes to spend some time in Europe for the purpose of visiting the university Libraries to complete a work on Political Philosophy he is preparing to present as his Doctor's Dissertation. He will sail for Europe on his return from the West. (The Christian Nation, May 31st, 1893, page 8)

was hand in his thesis collect his doctorate and his career path was set. However, he decided to postpone his thesis until he had completed further studies in Europe during the summer of 1893. This was similar to what he had done for his B.D. degree in Glasgow. Then he had spent the summer of 1890 summer studying in seminaries in Europe before taking his final exams in November 1890.

During this time Littlejohn developed his interest in the Chautauqua movement and its approach to education[20]. As part of his study program at Columbia he also had to play an active part in the Academy of political science.

It's often being a source of puzzlement to people as to why Littlejohn didn't finish his Doctorate at Columbia. As we shall see later, on his return to America after his summer excursion to Europe in 1893, he was seriously ill, requiring not one but two serious operations on his throat and months of rehabilitation in three different sanitaria. This alone would be enough to account for his failure to finish his doctorate. However, there is another factor. According to university regulations, once the thesis was approved one hundred and fifty (150) bound copies had to be submitted prior to undertaking a defence or any other requirements. Given his loss of the bursary associated with his Fellowship and the meagre income he might have gotten from preaching, together with the cost of rehabilitation in the various sanatoria, the cost of printing and biding 150 copies of his thesis could have been prohibitive.[21]

---

[20] The Institution, originally the Chautauqua Lake Sunday School Assembly, was founded in 1874 as an educational experiment in out-of-school, vacation learning. It was successful and broadened almost immediately beyond courses for Sunday school teachers to include academic subjects, music, art and physical education….The Chautauqua Literary and Scientific Circle (CLSC) was started in 1878 to provide those who could not afford the time or money to attend college the opportunity of acquiring the skills and essential knowledge of a College education. The four-year, correspondence course was one of the first attempts at distance learning. Besides broadening access to education, the CLSC program was intended to show people how best to use their leisure time and avoid the growing availability of idle pastimes, such as drinking, gambling, dancing and theater-going, that posed a threat both to good morals and to good health.(The Chautauqua Institute web page history chq.org)

[21] "the administrative requirement of a publication requirement in later years (early 20th century) often tripped up would-be PhD recipients who either never officially received the degree or received it years after they officially completed the work. They just didn't have the funds to print the 100 required published copies of the dissertation at the time of completion."(email correspondence with the Columbia university archives)- Note in Littlejohns time the number was 150 copies according to the regulations at that time.

On examining the cover pages of his thesis, the earliest versions carry the date "College Springs, Current press, 1894" and it is noted in Clarinda Herald 12th February 1895 that the Current press (a publishing house in College springs) is publishing a book by Littlejohn on political economy which is intended as a text book in Amity College. This indicates that he had finished his thesis in 1894 but didn't get it published until 1896 as this is the date on the copies submitted as part of his requirements for the Doctor of Philosophy in Columbia college.

The copy of Littlejohn's thesis which came into possession of T. E. Hall, has the following inscription on it

J. Martin Littlejohn, A.M., J.U.B., S.T.B., D.D.,
F.N.U., F.C.C., Ph.D.
President of Amity College, Iowa

The Rev. John Heron, on reading Hall's Littlejohn memorial lecture had the following comments
"On page 104 of the Osteopathic Quarterly Vol. 5 No. 4
at the foot of the third paragraph you quote the letters
used by LittleJohn on the cover of his published thesis,
viz, A.M., J.U.B., S.T.B., F.N.U., F.C.C. You then go on
to comment "Apart from the A.D., which is the American
form of his M.A., the whole list is meaningless".
I have no idea what F.N.U., or F.C.C. mean, but I do
know that S.T.B. is IN SCIENTIA THEOLOGICA BACGALAUREUS.
In other words, it is a form of the Degree we know as B.D.
(Bachelor of Divinity) . There are still some Seminaries
in the U.S.A. which give an S.T.B. Degree instead of a B.D.
Being a Theologian and not a legal pundit I am not
quite sure whether the J.U.B. should be Ju.B. or J.U.B.,
but I am pretty certain that it is a form of the degree LL.B.
(Bachelor of Laws). It should not be difficult to verify
this from any reputable American University[li]."
This made sense of the letters, with F.N.U. being Fellow of the National University, and F.C.C. being Fellow of Columbia University.

It would seem that this copy was Littlejohn's personal copy printer by the Current Press in Amity as a textbook and not as a thesis for submission to Columbia University. Unlike other versions it did not have the inscription

"Submitted in partial fulfilment of the requirements for the degree of Doctor of Philosophy, in the University Faculty of Political Science, Columbia University, N.Y,"

These other versions had no post nominal letters after Littlejohn's name.[lii]

Thus, the use of the letters Ph.D., from the National University, was not an anomaly on a thesis presentation as has been suggested. This suggestion seems to have been a simple misunderstanding of which version of the book that was being viewed[liii]

WORK AS A MINISTER IN THE US

At the same time as his academic reputation was growing, so was his appeal as a minister in the Reformed Presbyterian Church. His work in the Brooklyn congregation as well as his commitment to the original principles of the Covenanters together with his academic prowess would make him an ideal candidate for a ministry

He had been preaching in New York and particularly with the Brooklyn congregation. In the Christian Nation we find acknowledgement of the good work that he had being doing here and that the Brooklyn congregation, which had been in a poor condition, was not only holding steady but growing under his ministration.

"It will be good news to the church at large that the Brooklyn congregation is holding steadily together and growing. Communion services were held on Sabbath, conducted by the Rev. Prof. J.M. Littlejohn ... The preaching by Prof Littlejohn was remarkable comforting and strengthening and the joyfulness of all hearts was heightened by the confident anticipation of soon having a church building of their own"[liv]

It comes as no surprise that he received another call, this time from the Penpont congregation in Scotland, one of the original secession congregations in Scotland [lv]. While it must have been very tempting to return to his native land, he declined in April 1893[lvi].

The strain of the travel together with the stress of his brothers and father's illness would take a toll. Towards the end of 1892/93 academic year his brother's family had suffered some serious illness, with his daughter being very ill that August and his mother in law in September 1893[lvii]. His father who had being ill for some time in 1892 finally resigned his position as minister[22] over the congregation at Garvagh on the 14th Feb 1893.

Even though he had health problems he was not a person to waste time, whatever energy he had he used not only in attending to his studies or attending to his preaching (particularly in Brooklyn) but also given time to being one of the editors of the Christian Nation. With all of this he did not neglect his family.

His brother moved to Kansas in response to the call from the church in Denison and was installed on 27th June 1893 with Littlejohn being present on June 14th to help him and his family settle in and also to attend and assist at the installation service[lviii].

The Wednesday evening of June 14th when his brother and wife were moving into their new home in Denison was quite an occasion, and gives us some idea of how sociable Littlejohn and his friends and relations were; again, quoting from the Christian Nation:

"The ladies of the congregation had kindly fitted up the house for their reception. On stepping of the train, they were met by a deputation of the congregation and driven straight to the house. On approaching the house, the situation revealed the surprise that had being prepared for the homecoming of the new pastor. The young people's Christian Endeavour of the congregation planned the welcome. The members of the congregation and their friends in the neighbourhood all turned out and manifested their hearty rejoicing at the appearance among them of their minister. An address of welcome was given to Mr Littlejohn on behalf of the young people and the congregation by Mr Jos Torrens, after which the welcome was beautifully rendered in song. After greetings were exchanged the YPSCE invited all present to participate of

---

[22] "At a meeting of the northern presbytery of the RP Church, Ireland 14th February the Rev James Littlejohn, the father of the Rev William and J.M. Littlejohn resigned his charge of the congregation of Garvagh ... He has preached in Ireland for seventeen years. Prior to a settlement in Ireland he preached for sixteen years in Scotland and is the only living Minister of the church who took part in the famous disruption of 1863".(1st May 1893 edition of the Christian Nation)

a magnificent ice cream supper which they had served on the lawn in front of the minister's resident. Reverends Doctors H.P. McClurkin and Prof J.M. Littlejohn were present during the evening and joined in the jubilations. After an enjoyable time spent in social conversation the company separated."[lix]

This indicates that Littlejohn was in the west, in Kansas to accompany his brother in his move and to assist at the installation just prior to his trip to Europe. Like all ministers from a missionary background he was not afraid to travel.

Shortly after this LittleJohn, on Saturday 8th July, sailed for Europe on the Umbria for a proposed three month stay to continue his studies in Europe and visit family.[lx]

SUMMER 1893, TRIP TO UK AND EUROPE

The whole time at the end of his first academic year was fraught with difficulty and family difficulties[23]. So, it is not surprising then that Littlejohn took the opportunity to return to Europe to complete his studies and to visit his family, particularly his parents who at this time due to the ill health of his father had retired and were now living with James Buchan Littlejohn in Shropshire.

J.M. Littlejohn sailed on Saturday July 8th on board the Umbria for a three month stay. He spent the summer travelling in Europe researching for his thesis. While there he spent some time in his native land and went on a 'pilgrimage' to Moniaive (Hill of Streams) Dumfries to preach a memorial service. We find an interesting snapshot of his time towards the beginning of this trip by a letter that he wrote to his friends concerning his time at Moniaive. This is taken from the Christian Nation September 6th, 1893. It was titled 'Prof. J.M. Littlejohn, D.D., at Moniaive'.

"I have had a very pleasant holiday so far. My trip across the ocean was delightful. Reunion with parents, brothers, sister, and friends has increased the pleasure of revisiting the land of my birth. Britain has not changed very much since I left it. At present harvest is coming on, promising abundance for man and beast. On Sabbath evening, August 6th, I was privileged to preach a memorial service in Moniaive, Dumfriesshire. It is beside this beautiful little village in Glencairn, that the monument of our martyred brother, James Renwick, marks the place of his birth. The glens that are around and the high hills that look down upon the vales with the smile of heaven are sacred to the memory of martyr lives and deaths, lives that were spent in hiding in caves and cairns in sweet fellowship with Christ, and deaths that took place upon the open plain and by the hillside, instigated by the malice of enemies of Christ's covenant people. I was permitted to lay a fresh wreath of immortelles, wrought by the spirit of inspiration, upon the monument of Renwick, in the words from which I spoke, 'Your fathers, where are

---

[23] Rev. Wm. Littlejohn has been suffering with a threatened attack of nervous prostration. He has been able to preach, but altogether unable to attend to other duties. (The Christian Nation July 19th, 1893 page 8)

they? The prophets, do they live forever? ... The God of our fathers raised up Jesus ... a Prince and a Saviour....

"Redemption in the key-note of history, and in the counsels of eternity, in the researches of angels, in the prophetic dispensation and in the gospel age of Christ and his representatives. Martyr lives and memories lay under fresh obligations, not to worship them or their lives, but to copy their example, to breathe their spirit, and to stand where they stood, so that inspired by the same spirit of fidelity, courage and intrepidity, we may work the 'greater works' of Him that sent us, to transmit the spiritual succession of prophets, apostles and disciples to the very end of time."[lxi]

This was a difficult time for Littlejohn. His Brother William having taken up a new appointment became ill with nervous exhaustion, his father was too ill to continue to work and had retired, his brother David[lxii] about to start studying medicine in Glasgow while his other brother James Buchan starting out on his career as a Doctor was getting involved in 'secret' albeit benevolent societies[24]. This would have caused some conflict with his father in particular. On top of all this he reaffirmed his relationship with the roots of his church in Moniaive and with his native country of Scotland. This was in addition to the research purpose of his trip. Under these circumstances it would not be unexpected for a healthy individual to become ill. But Littlejohn was far from healthy, having had a serious fracture of his skull in 1888 and been advised to move to America on health grounds in 1891/2.

He was so ill that it seems he had to postpone his return to America and stayed with his Brother and family in Shropshire until he was fit to travel in December 1893. This is based upon the fact that he preached in Liverpool[lxiii] on 5th November 1893, and the notice in The Christian Nation of December 13th, 1893 which said

"Prof. J. M. Littlejohn, D. D., has returned to Brooklyn, and is worshiping with the congregation there. He has been quite ill for a long time but is recovering. The Council of the University of Glasgow has nominated him

---

[24] The Medical directory for 1894 lists him as member of the 'Odd Fellows'. A benevolent society which may have been looked upon as a 'secret society' by the Reformed Presbyterian Church.

to the chair of Moral Philosophy, as we are informed by a private letter from the Secretary of the Council, He is also offered a Professorship in the University of the City of New York".

> Rev. prof. J. M. Littlejohn, A.M., LL.B., D.D., Columbia college, New York, conducted Devine service in the Reformed Church, Hall Lane, Liverpool on Sunday. At the forenoon service he preached on Sabbath Observance, by request of the Working Men's Day Rest Association, London. In the evening he lectured upon 'Christian companionship' Prof. Littlejohn has been visiting for some time at his brother's Dr. Littlejohn, Munslow.
> The Wellington journal and Shrewsbury news
> November 11, 1893

This is corroborated by his listing as a Fellow in the February 1894 Bulletin of Columbia university which gives him credit for studying both the summer and autumn

"Mr. John M. Littlejohn, University Fellow in Political Philosophy, has been nominated to the professorship of Philosophy in the University of Glasgow. Mr. Littlejohn spent the summer and the autumn in consulting the great University and Cathedral libraries in connection with his researches on Aquinas and Grotius."[lxiv]

And the final piece is found in Ellis island passenger records which lists a John M Littlejohn as arriving in New York on December 2nd, 1893 on board the Lucania from Liverpool[lxv]. [25]

He was so ill on returning from his trip to Europe that he hadn't been able to complete his thesis, missed the opportunity to extend his Fellowship into a second year, he had to turn down a professorship in the city of New York University and at the same time try and maintain his association with the Brooklyn congregation having done so much

---

[25] The listing says he is 'English' rather than Scottish, but otherwise it fits with all the other facts.

work there to bring it back and to maintain it in good condition. In his own words:

"While I was in Columbia University I stayed in a sanatorium on Long Island and came in periodically. I was not required to attend daily, because I was doing research work, and I came in periodically to Columbia College"[lxvi]

This sentence from his testimony to the House of Lords Select Committee in 1935 would appear to refer to his second year at Columbia. During his first year he was a Fellow of the College. This carried with it a bursary of $500 and a prohibition of engaging in remunerative employment without express permission and would have meant attending regularly, researching and performing those duties allotted to him including university extension lectures.[lxvii]

Another interesting event happened at this time. The Chair of Moral Philosophy at Glasgow University became vacant when Edward Caird left the post in Nov 1893 to take up the appointment of Master of Balliol College, Oxford. The post was advertised in Specified Newspapers at the end of April1894.

Littlejohn apparently became aware of it very early on as noted above ' *The Council of the University of Glasgow has nominated him to the chair of Moral Philosophy, as we are informed by a private letter from the Secretary of the Council*' (Christian Nation 13th Dec 1893) This 'private letter' could be a simple acknowledgment of his application. However, the timing of it, being well before the official advertising and just after Caird's resignation, as well as it being from the 'secretary of the university council' tends to indicate that he was asked to apply. The university council is the body of graduates of the university and not a governing body,as such being asked by some members in it may be an honour but does not carry any weight with the university court who make the appointments. It could be speculated that, LittleJohn who was well known and published within the Reformed Presbyterian Church in Scotland and Ireland, would make an ideal candidate for members of that church to put forward to fill the important and influential position of Chair of Moral Philosophy. The university council was made up of graduates of the university and all or most ministers of the reformed Presbyterian and allied churches would had graduated from Glasgow university. Thus, making it plausible that this was the group who 'nominated' or encourage Littlejohn to apply. In the University court minutes Littlejohn is listed as M.A., LL.B., Ph.D. which would also indicate that the application was made before he returned to America in Dec 1893 and the title Ph.D. added in anticipation of his graduation on his return to Columbia.

It turns out that LittleJohn then also applied for the new position of 'professor of History' [lxviii] which was advertised in March 1894. These events support the idea that he was thinking of returning to Scotland. Unfortunately, even if he had been successful in his applications, he would have been unable to take the position as his illness took a severe turn for the worst.

The seriousness of this illness is conveyed in the next two items from the 3rd January edition of the Christian Nation 1894 when it says that:

"*Prof. J. M. Littlejohn, D. D., accepted a professorship in the Postgraduate Department of the University of the City of New York, and was to have begun work two weeks ago, but was prevented by an affliction of the throat. A dangerous operation was successfully performed last week, and he is rapidly recovering*"[lxix].

This would have put the date of the operation in late December 1893, shortly after his arrival from England. His recovery was seemingly quite good as he was able to preach in Brooklyn for the opening of the new Reformed Presbyterian church in Monroe St, near Throop avenue on 14th January 1894[lxx]. However, as this was the opening of the new church, he would have made a special effort to be there with his congregation. However, he again had to give up preaching in May 1894 and undergo another operation.[lxxi]

"*Dr, J. M. Littlejohn, who has been supplying the Brooklyn pulpit, has been compelled, because of an affliction of the throat to give up preaching for the present as he expects to undergo an operation in Philadelphia next week. He has recommended the Brooklyn congregation to Call a pastor*"[lxxii]

We know from other writings that he claims that he suffered from hemorrhages of the throat and this may have been associated with the fall he had in and around 1888 with the fracture of the skull. Over the succeeding months we find that Littlejohn continued to supply the

Brooklyn congregation, until he finally came to the conclusion, he could not continue preaching in May 1894

The operation went ahead on Tuesday 29th May 1894 and was reported as being 'eminently successful' and he expected to resume preaching in a 'short time'[lxxiii] He had been accompanied by his physician to Philadelphia were the operation was performed by a specialist from the University of Pennsylvania[lxxiv]

It can be only imagine how dangerous an operation would be on the throat even today but back in 1894 to describe it as dangerous would be an understatement. It certainly would require a considerable length of time to recover from it. And the condition that would have led to the undertaking of such an operation must have being quite serious. In his testimony to the House of Lords in 1935 Littlejohn tells of his stays in various sanatorium during his recovery and how this led to his association with the Add-Ran Christian university of Texas.

> "I went into a sanatorium first in Waukesha, Wisconsin. Then in Denver, Colorado and then in Waco, Texas. That is where I first met Dr. Lowber, the Chancellor of the university that gave me the degree of LL.D. That was in 1893 and 1894".
> Report and minutes of House of Lords
> select Committee 1935 paragraph 3491

It wasn't until September of 1894 that his brother was to be able to say *"On Sabbath, the 9th September, the Lord's supper was dispensed. Valuable service was rendered by Dr Trumbull, of Morning Sunday, Ohio and my brother J.M. Littlejohn, made all the more enjoyable by my brother's recovery so far as to be able to take part"*[lxxv,26]

---

[26] Another important family occasion happened at this time. On September 7th, 1894 his sister was married to Thomas J Anthony in the presence of their brother James Buchan and Father James in Munslow, Shropshire England. (Wedding certificate, MXH 423303 register of marriages in the district of Ludlow England)

During this time Littlejohn continued to work on his thesis, operate as department editor of the Christian Nation and to preach when he was able and to contribute articles to the magazine. While he eventually had leave Brooklyn the work he had done there did not go unnoticed. On the occasion of the installation of their new pastor, the Brooklyn congregation paid him tribute saying

" It would have afforded the congregation much pleasure to have had with them Dr. Littlejohn, who worked so long, so patiently, so generously, and under such trying circumstances, to hold the congregation (in Brooklyn New York) together during the time it had no regular place of worship. A letter was received from him with congratulations and brotherly love"[lxxvi]

Littlejohns D.D. degree

His D.D. Degrees was for a work on 'Christian Sabbatism'. A work some have said was a "recycled" version[lxxvii] of his earlier prize-winning essay for his B.D. in Glasgow, on 'The Sabbatism of the Hebrews'. This does not do him justice. In any system of higher education, it is not unusual to take a theme at Master's level and expand on that theme for your Doctorate. However, the Doctor of Divinity is generally an honorary degree, awarded for work done and services performed in the field of Divinity. Littlejohn was a student in the Post Graduate School of Theology and a Fellow of the National University of Chicago in 1893 being awarded the degree of Doctor of Divinity (D.D.) and later the Ph.D. in 1895.[lxxviii]

The background on this subject is important in gaining an understanding of why his work would merit the award of Doctor of Divinity.

It wasn't awarded just for the thesis but also for his work in the congregations and possibly on the Chautauqua circuit.

"Brother Littlejohn came from your locality and ranks with us in the editorial staff of the (Christian) Nation. The honour conferred on him will be regarded with interest by those who knew him in his father's neighbourhood as well as by us with whom he is associated so honourably in work The Following is an extract from the Nation;- ' the university of Chicago, USA, has conferred upon the Rev. J. M. littlejohn, B.D., LL.B., the degree of D.D. Dr. Littlejohn holds an important official position in Columbia College, N.Y., and has attracted considerable attention since he entered upon his work by some very able lectures and contributions to the periodical literature of America. His latest defence of the Sabbath and exposition of the Political Philosophy of a Christian State have gained for him unique recognition from the great University of the west. He is called young to wear the laurels of a doctor's degree, being only twenty-six years of age, but, if spared in life, we trust that he

may adorn the University that has enrolled him among its honorary graduates' (The Coleraine Chronicle, Saturday, January 28th 1893)[27]

We get some idea of his preaching and work in defence of the Sabbath and the Christian State from the lectures he was asked to give in Liverpool in November 1893, mentioned above, and his work for Brooklyn Congregation[lxxix].

When he went to America, he would have found a controversy and debate on the subject of the Sabbath, this is put into context by comments on his essay 'The Sabbatism of the Hebrews' by Rev. G.D.

---

[27] It is sometimes hard to remember how connected the communities in the Reformed Presbyterian Church were, even across the Atlantic. One example may serve to illustrate this. Rev. John Lynd was brought up in the Ballylaggan Sabbath School, near Garvagh in the North of Ireland, emigrating to the USA in 1873, where he held a number of posts, both ministerial and teaching, in New York, Philadelphia and Ohio before returning to Ballylaggan in 1885. He would have known the Littlejohn's whose father served in Garvagh, a neighboring congregation to Ballylaggan.

While the above quote mentions 'the university of Chicago', it was in fact the National University of Chicago, the similarity of the two names being confused in the Newspaper article. It was sent to the Coleraine Chronicle by the editor of the Christian Nation, J Pritchard, who may have intended putting it in the next issue. However, it does not appear in the December 1892 or January 1893 issues. It may have been left out due to space or because Littlejohn himself did not approve of it, especially as the degree was not awarded until May/June 1893 and the notice may only have been to do with his submission of his thesis on Christian Sabbatism. A later announcement only said, 'Prof. J. M. Littlejohn receives next week the degree of D. D. from Chicago.' He received his D.D. at the commencement in June 1893. (the Christian Nation 31 May 1893). In the list of degrees on his thesis Littlejohn made it clear his D.D. was from the National University. O'Brien, in his book on Littlejohn, makes an issue of this and even goes as far as calling the national university the 'National Night University', even though the 'Chicago Night University' did not come into existence until 1905. (John Martin Littlejohn, an enigma of Osteopathy, page 53); see also appendix on The National Medical University and Littlejohns' Thesis 'The Political theory of the Schoolmen and Grotius

Allen[28]. (we unfortunately don't have a copy of his work 'Christian Sabbatism', published in 1893)

"Littlejohn explained and defended the principle of the Old Testament Sabbath as it has been transferred to the first day of the week by Christ. He argued against the decline in Sabbath observance in the American church which had seen the increase in the use of part of the day for recreation and business. In context it indicates that Littlejohn thought deeply about the theological topics of the day and as his interests broadened, he applied orthodox Reformed Presbyterianism to all that he engaged with.

"The main point he is arguing against, which is still current, is whether the change of the Jewish sabbath from the Saturday, the seventh day as in the Creation ordinance, is valid in the transfer of the fourth commandment to the Christian sabbath day, the first day of the week the Sunday.'

"There are two discussions

"1. The change of the Sabbath day of rest that Christ implied the change from the old 7th day observance to the first day observance. This argument has been generally accepted by the Christian Church only Seventh Day Adventists have returned to the Saturday seventh day and they also have re-implemented some of the Old Testament food laws. But their view is a minority and not what Littlejohn would have been discussing.

"2. The discussion of whether the commandment to keep the Sabbath day holy, because it has transferred to the first day, still applies the same as in the Old Testament Sabbath. This is the angle of Littlejohn's article. In this he was arguing against the decline in Sabbath keeping in the American Church. Sabbath keeping means the whole day set aside not church "and then recreation and shopping etc. The deeper part of the article discusses the matter of the Sabbath rest being compared to the rest of Israel in entering the Promised Land.

---

[28] 'Rev G.D. Allen is Reformed Presbyterian minister in Ireland at the time of writing

"What I would say about the article that may be helpful in the context of your topic is that it shows that Littlejohn was still engaged in the theological topics of the day and also maintained his orthodox reformed Presbyterian credentials. I would then comment that this is a good indicator along with the opposition to the Masonic order etc, that JML did not change his views. As his interests broadened, he applied the foundational principles to all that he engaged with."

A Glimpse of The Future

"At the same time, while remembering our duty to interpret each passage on its own merits, we must not forget that Sacred Scripture forms an organic whole. Each part may be a perfect organism, yet when all the parts are put together they form a complete unity".

J M Littlejohn; Sabbatism of the Hebrews page 1-2 (3)

THIS SHOWS THAT EVEN AT THIS STAGE OF HIS CAREER HE HAD THE CONCEPT OF THE WHOLE ORGANISM BEING MORE IMPORTANT THAN THE PARTS; THE PARTS MUST ALWAYS BE VIEWED IN THE CONTEXT OF THEIR RELATIONSHIP NOT ONLY WITH EACH OTHER BUT ALSO IN RELATIONSHIP TO THE WHOLE ORGANISM.

[i] Minutes of the Southern presbytery of the reformed Presbyterian church; Courtesy of the Library of the Reformed Theological College and Library, Knockbracken Road, Belfast, Northern Ireland

[ii] sketches of ministers from 1888 to 1930 by Rev Owen Thompson. Also, The Reformed Presbyterian and Covenanter, July & August 1889, Minutes of the Synod of the Reformed Presbyterian Church USA, page 253.

[iii] report of Pittsburgh presbytery at the June 1889 minutes of synod

[iv] Minutes of Testimony to House of lords select committee HMSO 1935, paragraph 3497 page 230

[v] Osteopathy in Britain, The First Hundred years; Dr. Martin Collins

[vi] Personal communications

[vii] https://www.britannica.com/biography/Morell-Mackenzie

[viii] https://www.universitystory.gla.ac.uk/biography

[ix] Passenger lists of arrivals on board of State of Nebraska: The Statue of Liberty - Ellis Island Foundation: "New York Passenger Lists, 1820-1891," database with images, FamilySearch (https://familysearch.org/ark:/61903/1:1:QVPN-B3QP : 11 March 2018), John M Littlejohn, 1889; citing Immigration, New York City, New York, United States, NARA microfilm publication M237 (Washington, D.C.: National Archives and Records Administration, n.d.), FHL microfilm 1,027,770

[x] Correspondence with Glasgow University archives; 18th October 1993

[xi] Passenger lists of arrivals on board of State of Nebraska: "New York Passenger Lists, 1820-1891," database with images, FamilySearch (https://familysearch.org/ark:/61903/3:1:939V-R7SL-: image 243FY?cc=1849782&wc=MX6L-RNL%3A165921401 : 26 November 2014), 534 - 3 Jun 1889-22 Jun 1889 > image 243 of 933; citing NARA microfilm publication M237 (Washington D.C.: National Archives and Records Administration, n.d.)
Passenger lists 3 Jun 1889-22 Jun 1889 (NARA Series M237, Roll 534)

[xii] the Christian Nation. In the June 19th, 1889 Volume 10, number 244, page 376

[xiii] The Reformed Presbyterian and Covenanter, July & August 1889, Minutes of the Synod of the Reformed Presbyterian Church USA

[xiv] The Reformed Presbyterian and Covenanter, July & August 1890, Minutes of the Synod of the Reformed Presbyterian Church USA, Page 247

[xv] The Christian nation, Volume 12, No 270, January 1, 1890 page 10

[xvi] The Christian Nation, November 5th, 1890, Vol. 13 Number 314, page 295

[xvii] Ibid

[xviii] The Christian Nation Volume 15 No 374 December 30, 1891 page 10

[xix] Glasgow university archives. The exact reference could not be verified due to restrictions during the Covid 19 Lockdown. However, I am confident of the accuracy of the information

[xx] Letter to T E Hall from the Secretary of the University of Glasgow, 19th August 1952 (held in National Osteopathic Archives, The Wellcome Library) and University Calendars for the respective years
[xxi] Glasgow Herald Thu Mar 24th, 1892: Glasgow Herald Sat Jul 16th, 1892.
[xxii] The political theory of the schoolmen and Grotius [by] J. Martin Littlejohn. pt.1-3 Archive.org
[xxiii] The Journal of Osteopathy (British School of Osteopath) Vol V1, June - August 1935
[xxiv] Journal of Osteopath (Kirksville) March 1898 page 489
[xxv] Glasgow University archives email communication 18th October 1993
[xxvi] Memorial of Certificate of Naturalization as a British Subject- 3rd March 1924 370.747 The National archives of UK reference H.O.144/ 4540
[xxvii] Glasgow university magazine 1892 and minutes of Student representative council March 3rd, 1892
[xxviii] The political theory of the schoolmen and Grotius [by] J. Martin Littlejohn. pt.1-3 Archive.org
[xxix] J M Littlejohn; Sabbatism of the Hebrews page 1-2, University of Glasgow archives, prize essays.
[xxx] Addison's Graduates of the University of Glasgow, 1727 -1897, (Glasgow, 1898)
[xxxi] Minutes of Testimony to House of lords select committee HMSO 1935, paragraph 3496 page 230
[xxxii] https://archiveshub.jisc.ac.uk/search/archives/4780e7fb-8931-3993-b3b4-b10a343359dc records of Anderson college of medicine, Glasgow.
[xxxiii] Glasgow university archives, letter dated 1884 by A M Buchanan concerning the new buildings of the Anderson School in the vicinity of the University of Glasgow and western infirmary
[xxxiv] Poster advertising the Anderson's College Medical School, University of Glasgow archives, reference 7812(a)
[xxxv] The Christian Nation, March 1st, 1893, page 7
[xxxvi] Medical Officers &; Public Vaccinators... Munslow district, James Buchan Littlejohn M.R, C.M. Miller house, Munslow; (Kelly's Directory 1895 page 123&292; Also, The Medical directory for 1894)
[xxxvii] Minutes of Testimony to House of lords select committee HMSO 1935, paragraph 3497 page 230
[xxxviii] 1893&94 medical registers for England
[xxxix] The Christian Nation, March 29th, 1899, page 15 & 1st March 1893
[xl] Year: 1892 Arrival: New York, New York; Microfilm Serial: M237, 1820-1897; Microfilm Roll: Roll 597; Line: 18; Page number 10; Source Information; Ancestry.com. New York, Passenger Lists, 1820-1957 [database on-line]. Provo, UT, USA: Ancestry.com Operations, Inc., 2010.
[xli] The Christian Nation November 30th, 1892, page 8.

[xlii] The Christian Nation, October 5th, 1892 and 14th September, page 9
[xliii] Christian Nation of October 5th, 1892
[xliv] Bulletin No.5, April 1893, Columbia College in the city of New York.
[xlv] The Journal of Osteopathy, British School of Osteopathy June/ August 1935.
[xlvi] Ibid
[xlvii] Christian Nation April 10th, 1892, page 10
[xlviii] Christian Nation February 1st, 1893, page 6.
[xlix] The Christian Nation October 5th, 1892
[l] Columbia college bulletin no 1 Page 6
[li] Letter to T. E. Hall from the Rev. John Heron, 23rd February 1953; copies of the original, letters of enquiry and information received relative to the inaugural john martin littlejohn memorial lecture delivered to the faculty of the British school of osteopathy at the Mayfair hotel, London, on the 3rd October, 1952 . Edward hall, D.O., Copies now held in the National Osteopathic Archive at the Wellcome Library
[lii] From Copies originally held in Columbia University Archives, University of California archives, Harvard College Library, University of Toronto library
[liii] Jane Stark lecture at the VOD-Congress October 2018 in Bad Nauheim
[liv] The Christian Nation Vol 18 February 22nd, 1893
[lv] Glasgow Herald Mon Dec 26, 1892.
[lvi] The Christian Nation, Wednesday 12th April 1893 page 8.
[lvii] The Christian Nation August 1893 page 8, Sept 27th, 1893 page 10.
[lviii] The Christian Nation June 21st, & July 12th & July 26th page 8 1893 Vol 18,
[lix] The Christian nation Vol 18 June 28th, 1893 Page 8
[lx] The Christian Nation Wednesday July 12th page 7
[lxi] Christian Nation September 6th, 1893
[lxii] Glasgow university archives
[lxiii] The Wellington journal and Shrewsbury news, November 11, 1893
[lxiv] "(Columbia university Bulletin No 7 February 1894 page 35)
[lxv] https://www.libertyellisfoundation.org/passenger-details
[lxvi] Minutes of Testimony to House of lords select committee HMSO 1935, paragraph 3497 page 230
[lxvii] Columbia College School of Political Science Circular of information 1893-4 page 30: the same rules applied for 1892/3
[lxviii] University of Glasgow archives communications, emails
[lxix] The Christian Nation, Vol. 20, 3rd January 1894, page 11.
[lxx] New York Daily Tribune, Monday January 15th page 10
[lxxi] The Christian Nation, Volume 20, 23rd May 1894, page 11
[lxxii] Ibid.
[lxxiii] The Brooklyn Daily eagle, Saturday 2nd June 1894
[lxxiv] The Brooklyn Daily eagle, Tuesday 29th May 1894
[lxxv] Christian nation Vol 21 26th sept 1894, page 10

[lxxvi] Christian Nation Vol 22 Jan 23, 1895, page 10
[lxxvii] John Martin Littlejohn, an enigma of osteopathy, page 113; John O'Brien; ISBN 978 1 848291 386
[lxxviii] List of degrees and honours, "Political theory of the Schoolmen and Grotius" J Martin Littlejohn, Submitted in partial fulfilment of the requirements for the Degree of Doctor of Philosophy in the Faculty of Political Science, Columbia University N.Y. 1896; List of Degrees and diplomas in chronological order, attached to Letter from Hall and Canning to BSO graduates in 1935, Welcome Library holdings
[lxxix] The Brooklyn Daily Eagle Mon Mar 12 1894

1894-1897

College Springs and Amity College

      A good description of Amity College is found in the Minutes of the Reformed Presbyterian Church of North America for the year 1896: -
"College Springs, the seat of Amity College, is comparatively a small place, yet can boast of the high order of its citizens.

An academy was founded there in 1857, which developed into a college in 1872. There are five buildings in the town—three used for educational purposes and two as dormitories—which belong to the institution.

"The old college building is of brick, 40x50 feet, and two stories high, with two wings, each 23x30 feet, also two stories high.

"The new college building is also of brick, 40x60 feet, with two wings, 21x33 feet, all two stories high, with a basement for boiler for steam heater. There is also a frame building, 22x56 feet, two stories high above a stone basement. This building is used for the Commercial and Art departments.

"The ladies' dormitory is a two-story frame building, 30x50 feet, divided into sixteen rooms above a stone basement, in which is the kitchen and dining hall. The gentlemen's dormitory is a cottage frame building of four rooms. These buildings and grounds, with furniture, library, and apparatus are valued by the Board at $34,300. There are interest-bearing notes, secured by mortgage, which amount to nearly $27,000, and other land and property which bring the total valuation to $66,477.16. The Board proposes to transfer all to the Reformed Presbyterian Church on the following conditions"

1894, AMITY COLLEGE

After a couple of bad seasons in the farming community the then president of Amity College Dr T.J. Kennedy went missing. This came about a week before the fall term of the college was due to open and the disappearance caused much apprehension. It was feared that the doctor had met with foul play or become partial deranged[i]. It turned out that he, being of an "almost morbid sensitiveness" recently had been concerned about the ability of the families to pay the fees of the college due to poor crops over the past few years. On top of this he had relatives and their children staying with him and "insisted on having some disciplinary rights "over the children and this led to more "friction" than the doctor could handle. He then had a nervous breakdown and disappeared. (People were so concerned about his wellbeing that funds were raised, and the Pinkerton Detective agency engaged to try and find him[ii]. It was reported that he was found several months later alive and well in Utah Pittsburgh Post-Gazette Jan 23rd, 1895). A separate report in the New York times of May 9th, 1898 reported him as being found in Australia[iii] and that "he refused to return to America and will not tell why he left the country"[iv]. The reward of $500 for information probably helped produce these reports.

However, this tragedy caused an opportunity for Littlejohn. He was well known in the Presbyterian community and in the 14th November 1894 issue of the Christian Nation the following article gives an idea of not only Littlejohns' standing but also of how important his appointment was viewed by the Covenanter community.

"On our front page we give a life picture of the President-elect of Amity College, Iowa. It is a personal pleasure for us to present our congratulations to the new president, and also to the board of trustees upon the appointment. The honour comes not to one but to all of us, for Prof Littlejohn is one of our number, on our editorial staff, and we are proud that one of our editors is deemed worthy of being raised to the head of a great institution of learning such as Amity College. The first tidings came as a surprise to us, being received at our office by telegram last Thursday. Rev. J.A. Thompson, an esteemed brother in our covenanter church, who is one of the directors of Amity College, was appointed by the board to write to brother Littlejohn

relative to his election. He writes: 'You were elected by an unanimous standing vote, although there were a number of applications before us. Covenanters stand high here. Last March's National Reform Convention did much good in this place. I was truly surprised to see the enthusiasm manifested by the members of our board to elect a covenanter minister as president of our college'.

"That Covenanters stand high in Amity College is not only manifest from the recent election of a President, but also from the fact that Brother Thompson represents them upon the Board, and that there is in the Faculty another of our Covenanter brethren, Professor I.A. Blackwood, who is a graduate of Geneva College. We hope that under the Presidency of our dear Brother, Amity will take high rank as an educational institution, and also as a centre of reform influence and education. Prof. Littlejohn's record as a scholar is well known to the church...

"From the time when he began his studies in his native city of Glasgow, at a remarkably early age, till the present time his career has been one of high standing in some of the oldest schools and Universities of Europe and America. Languages, Philosophy, Mathematical Science, Theology and Law, and last, though not least, Political Science have found in him an apt and distinguished graduate. In recent years his chief aim has been to investigate the whole domain of Politics and Political Science. He entered this field through the avenue of Law after having studied thoroughly Theological Science.

"When he came to this country, the present Moderator of the Church of Scotland, Rev. Prof. E. H. Story, D.D., LL.D., testified that he exhibited 'marked ability and acquirement' as a graduate in the School of Theology at Glasgow University, adding 'from my observations of your character and attainments while you studied here I should expect your future career to be useful and distinguished'.

"Advocate W.G. Miller, with whom he first studied Political Philosophy and Law says, 'I was impressed with his capacity for work, the extent of his knowledge and his power of exposition. I know he has since continued to prosecute his studies in these subjects with great zeal'.

"His Examiner for the LL.B. degree in commending him to Columbia, said: 'In his examination for the degree of LL.B. he acquitted himself with great distinction. In the domain of Political Philosophy, he displayed exceptional ability. I have no hesitation in saying that he will be an ornament to any University with which he becomes connected'.[1]

"Columbia College speaks of his work there in no measured terms. Dr. Dunning with whom he has been most intimately associated in his researches in Political Philosophy declares that 'his work has proved him to be very thoroughly equipped in all that pertains to Politics and Philosophy." This testimony we have taken from the pens of others lest our personal friendship should seem to overstate the truth'.[v]

In the past it was his own illness that caused change in Littlejohn's life and now we find tragedy in another place together with his illness moving Littlejohn in another direction. It's no surprise that he would accept the post when he was nominated to the position of Dean/President of Amity College when it came vacant. It was expected then that he would take charge of the college at the beginning of the winter term in 1894[vi], leaving the college with only one term without a president at its helm.

He arrived in Amity of Friday 7th December to take charge from the beginning of the winter term on Tuesday 11th, giving the inaugural address that evening.[vii]

Speaking at the House of Lords Select Committee in 1935, Littlejohn shows his adherence to the Christian ideal when he says:

"For example, according to our custom here in the universities they had chapel exercises. The universities that were supposed to be non-sectarian abolished these chapel exercises. This university (the Add-Ran) amongst others, adhere strictly to idea of opening the day in the university work by a short chapel exercise of ten minutes. When I was

---

[1] The quotes from his professors in Scotland most likely from the references he would have obtained before coming to America

President of Amity College in the State of Ohio, we followed the same rule."[viii]

There was a growing movement towards secularisation of educational establishments, affecting some professors' career. So, when the opportunity to work in a specific Reformed Presbyterian college arose, it would seem to the young Littlejohn as too good an opportunity to turn down.

The college movement at Amity was originally non-denominational, all the Christian religions and denominations were represented. However, the majority of the trustees of Amity College were United Presbyterians and they therefore held control over it.

This was until J.M. Littlejohn came along and the covenanters then tended to be in control. At the same time there was a growing congregation in College Springs connected to the covenanter church (It should be noted that the village and College Springs were the same, the residents at the founding of the village tending to call it Amity and the Post Office calling it College Springs).[2]

In the 'college yearbook and athletic record' for the academic year 1896/97 we find Amity described as:

"The college founded by Silas Thomas in 1853 was incorporated in 1855 and became a college in 1872. ... It has eleven acres of land, the degrees are B.A., B.S., B.L., M.A., and B.Ph. There are three literary societies the Athenian, the Aeolian and the Ionian: an athletic association and two Christian associations. 'The Amitonian' is the name of the monthly journal published by the college. Since the foundation of the school one hundred and twenty-one students have being graduated, one hundred and seventeen of whom are living. Of these James Anderson, 1879, of Omaha is the oldest. The academic year is from September 1st to June 12th."[ix]

The same source states that the total yearly income as $6,000, the number of students as two hundred and forty-six, twelve instructors,

---

[2] Amity was later changed to College springs after the discovery of a never failing spring in June 1856, (history of page county, By W.L. Kershaw Vol 1 , The S,. J. Clarke publishing co., 1909)

five buildings and two and a half thousand books in its library. It was a co-educational Christian college. J.M. Littlejohn A.M., L.L.B., D.D., is listed as president and mental, moral and political science professor. It had been a thriving college and had a good reputation. However, during the past few years (prior to 1894) there was some financial difficulties due to the poor crops that the local farmers had and their subsequent inability to keep up with the fees.

> "The year 1894 was one of disaster to the farming community around it (Amity college). There was destructive drought, and other circumstances placed the farmers in a bad position financially. It was from this class that the college drew the greater portion of its students and the outlook was dark"
>
> (Pittsburgh Post-Gazette Wed Jan 23, 1895)

Littlejohn came in the winter term of 1894, the college being without a president for one term due to the disappearance of the previous president as mentioned above. Littlejohn came to Amity when it was in the midst of a crisis and scandals[3]. He took a firm hold of the reins, steadied the institution restoring order and plotting a way forward for the College.

A further sign that he was fully committed to his stay at Amity was that he purchased a house in May 1895[x].

---

[3] There had been financial irregularities found but this was rectified when two letters were received from Dr. Kennedy saying were the money was to be found (The Inter Ocean Thu Sep 6 1894 & Pittsburgh Post-Gazette Wed Jan 23 1895)

It well worth noting that he and his brother William were instrumental in the formation of a new congregation at College Springs on 8th May 1895.

"A new congregation was organized at College Springs on May 8, of fourteen members. They expect more in the near future. There were three elders and two deacons elected, ordained and installed by the commission. The commission consisted of Rev. W. S. Fulton, Dr. J, M. Littlejohn, Rev. Wm. Littlejohn, Rev. J. A. Thompson, Elders D. G. McKee, J. O. Glasgow and Dr. R. C. Dodds. The new officers are: Elders, J: S. Bell, I. A. Blackwood, J, M. Caskey; and Deacons: Morton S. Bell and Maggie Thompson"[xi].

Littlejohn went about his business at Amity College with the same vigour, enthusiasm and single-mindedness as he did in every endeavour that he undertook. He set about reforming the college, its syllabus and recognition.[4] He put a proposal to Columbia College to have its degrees recognised by that college and also put a proposal to the Reformed Presbyterian Church that they should take the college under its wing, as a western sister college of Geneva College[5] in Pennsylvania.[xii] (Nov. 19th, 1895 minutes of council of Columbia university)[xiii]

---

[4] The Catalogue for Amity College for 1896-97 gives details of a proposed post-graduate department leading up to the degrees of B.D., Ph.D., D.Sc., and Lett.D. (The Nodaway Valley historical Museum)

[5] Geneva College was founded in 1848 and today (2018) is the only undergraduate institution affiliated with the Reformed Presbyterian Church of North America. In 1896 it 237 students and 12 instructors with "attendance at chapel being compulsory, but not so gymnastic drill" (college yearbook 1896-7)

> "The request of the Rev. Dr. J. M. Littlejohn, President of Amity College, College Springs, Iowa, asking that the courses at Amity College be recognized by the University Council as qualifying for post-graduate work and that Amity College be placed on the list of colleges whose graduates are admitted to post-graduate work at Columbia, was laid before the Council, and, on motion, the letter of the Rev. Dr. Littlejohn, of Amity College, the accompanying catalogue of Amity College, was referred to the committee on Higher Degrees"
>
> (Nov. 19th, 1895 minutes of council of Columbia university)

A report in the Clarinda herald of 26th March 1895 also gives an indication of the progress of Amity College under Littlejohn.

"The spring term at Amity opened Tuesday with a much larger attendance than was expected. Amity college is on a firmer basis and is doing better work than ever before. In regard to the length and thoroughness of its courses it has no equal within radius of one hundred miles Its grades are taken at Yale and Harvard and the other large educational institutions-of America without discount it is an institution, of which the Blue Grass region of Iowa, may well be proud, and deserves the undivided support of all those who desire to see southwest Iowa remain at the front".

"President Littlejohn is to be congratulated over a prosperous year for the college ... President Littlejohn, of Amity College, Ia., is spending the summer in Great Britain and on the continent and will return to his post early September."[xiv]. This would provide him with an opportunity to catch up with his sister whose wedding on 7th Sept 1894, he had missed. At that time, he was recovering from his throat operation. He sailed on 26th June on board the St. Louis[xv]

During this trip he delivered his first address for presentation to the Society of Science, Letters and Art on education.[6]

An interesting recollection of Littlejohn's time at Amity is to be found in an unusual place. At the first biennial conference of the World Federation of Educations Associations held in Edinburgh in 1925. Dr. Augustus O. Thomas president of the world federation of education associations gave the following unsolicited commendation of Littlejohn

"I took some of my work, in sociology and education, under Dr. J. Martin Littlejohn, a Minister and a Professor in the city and a very wonderful man. I have his name attached to the diploma which I have in my home. I remember what a very delightful character he was, and I often said: 'if all the people of Scotland are like him, the country must be all right'. I can remember when I took the Diploma from his hand and thanked him, as the grateful student will, I said: 'Dr. Martin(Sic), it seems to me that all I know I owe to you,' for he had opened up the new vision to me of education, and very sympathetically he said, 'Oh, my good friend, please don't mention such a trifle'."[xvi]

---

[6]"The first week in August (1903) we visited the hall and offices of the Society of Science, Letters and Art. They were making preparations for the annual meeting in September and gave us a very pressing invitation to remain to that meeting and meet the friends of Science Literature and Art that we have known for the last nine years. In that hall our papers on "education" were read in 1895, 1896 and 1897" (The Osteopathic world Oct 1903 page 476).

1895, TRIP TO ENGLAND

In the summer of 1895 Littlejohn returned to England.[7] Just prior to this trip he purchased a property in College Springs (Amity)

While there he met with his family and his father who

> "We learn that Dr. Lymer has sold his present residence to Dr. Littlejohn "We are happy to learn that Dr. Littlejohn Intends making this his permanent home"
> (Page 1 of The Clarinda Herald, Friday, May 10th, 1895)

returned with him in September 1895. His brothers, James Buchan and David Littlejohn (along with their mother) came to Amity in March 1896 [xvii], James becoming the assistant to the president of Amity and their father residing with them in College Springs. Their father had been ill for quite some time and while he had made enough of a recovery to travel, he was still not in full health but was on 13th May 1896 able to assist his son William at Denison, Kansas at the spring communion[xviii].

"It was the 29th March 1896 that their mother Mrs Littlejohn and her sons James and David arrived on the Umbria and they stayed in New York for a few days before they left for College Springs, Ohio, where their father the Rev. James Littlejohn had been visiting and staying with John Martin Littlejohn since the previous summer".[xix]

David attended Glasgow University for three years 1893/4 to 1895/6 but does not appear to have graduated.[xx] Some have speculated as to why his family removed him from college before completing his studies; one theory is that he was not a good student,

---

[7]"Dr. Littlejohn, president of Amity College, was in Clarinda Tuesday. He left at six o'clock for Pennsylvania, where he will make a short visit, and then proceed to Scotland, Germany, and other places in Europe, to spend the summer. (The Clarinda Herald, Page5, 1895 June-21)

and this has some support by comments from the Glasgow university archives. *"Our records show that David Littlejohn matriculated with the University of Glasgow between 1893 and 1895 (our refs: R8/5/14/5, R8/5/15/5, R8/5/16/5). During this period, he enrolled to study Chemistry in his first year, Anatomy, Practical Anatomy, and Physiology in his second year, and Materia Medica in his third. The University Calendars for this period (SEN10/38) note that Materia Medica would usually be taken by second year students, so for David to be taking it in his third year may suggest that he had to re-sit the year or take extra classes to qualify for the next session. Unfortunately, the student records for this period are incomplete, and there are few records for students who did not graduate"*

"David's name also appears in the Anderson College records for this period (DC244/9/2), showing that he enrolled to study Medicine there in 1895, taking Practical Anatomy and Surgery. Taking classes in a number of colleges and universities was common practice during this period, and was used by many students to gain a Medical Degree through the 'Triple Qualification'"[xxi]

On Thursday, June 11th 1896[xxii], David gained his Ph.B. (Bachelor of Philosophy) from Amity [xxiii]; this was one of the degrees that Amity was credited with awarding. He then attended the Central Medical College graduating in April 1897 and giving the Valedictory address[xxiv]

"David Littlejohn has been spending a few days at home. He graduates from the Central Medical college at
"St. Joe, this spring and as he stands at the head of his class got a vacation in which to write his oration."[xxv]

An interesting side note was given by David[xxvi] when he said that he was a member of the class, at the St. Joe Medical College, that recently dissected the body of the famous Missouri outlaw, Poke Wells[8]

---

[8] Charles Knox Polk Wells   He was born in Missouri in 1852; was an outlaw and murderer, He robbed banks and trains and allegedly killed over thirty men; was convicted of murder in May, 1882, received a life sentence and died in an Iowa prison in 1896. (https://www.legendsofamerica.com/outlaw-list)

David's qualifications have attracted some criticism. In the Freeport Daily Journal September 26th, 1907, we find the following which was written by William R. Dobbyn and reprinted from the Osteopathic World of January 1905. This was written in response to a letter in the same newspaper in which it was insinuated that David Littlejohn who graduated from the Central medical College in 1897 was not the same Dr. Littlejohn who had 'obtained his medical education in the university of Glasgow, Scotland' and belittling the Central medical college simply because it was a new College. [xxvii]

"Born in Glasgow, a staid University Town, at a time when theology and science confronted each other with half defined positions of distrust, the boy was carefully trained at home and is carefully taught at school. His love for the sciences caused him to specialise and we find the boy bearing away at the end of term special certificates in chemistry, physiology and hygiene. From the public school to the scientific academy and thence to the medical department of the University of Glasgow, Scotland mark the register of the boy's advance to young manhood and his rise to a distinguished position among his fellows of the university. He had unusual advantages in his alma mater. At the time of his attendance Sirs William S. Gairdner, T. McCall Anderson and William McEwen were adding lustre to their own and the university's name and the young Littlejohn by his brilliant scholarship received special consideration at their hands. Graduating at Glasgow did not satisfy his ambition along academic lines, and he enthusiastically began a course of study which lead to the degree of Ph.B., and M.E.(sic)[9] and eventually by reason of his merit was conferred upon him the honor of a fellow of the Society of Science, Letters and Art, London, England. Coming to America he became professor in Electro therapeutics and hygiene in the Central Medical College, St Josephs, MO., and while a student at the Western Medical School was assistant to the chair of chemistry. Becoming interested in osteopathy accepted a chair in the American School of Osteopathy. While there he had charge of the Department of X-ray, E-radiance and sanitary science, also of the laboratory work in histology and pathology and continued his studies in science to the degree of Doctor of Osteopathy."

---

[9] Possibly a misprint and meant to be M.D.

So even though this credits him with graduating from Glasgow University this may be excused on the grounds mentioned above and again coming from the family that he did graduating was not a pre-requisite for receiving recognition for his attainments and his studies[10].

Another factor was cost. In a letter from the acting deputy the archivist at Glasgow University, on the 18th October 1993 we find the following note:

"It did also cost money to graduate and this could be another factor. The concept of going to university graduate in a relatively late one, and it would not have been unusual in the early nineteenth century for someone such as a doctor to practice medicine after attending the university but not graduated. As long as he had class tickets or testimonial this would be sufficient."

Not only did David continue his medical studies in the States but was the class valedictorian speaking on the subject of 'medical education and medical progress' and became a lecturer in the School.

Family politics is always a funny thing and hard to fathom its effects. When James Buchan took his position as medical officer in Munslow he was attracted to the independent Order of Odd Fellows which he joined in 1893, possibly being introduce by the local schoolteacher, Thomas j Anthony (who was later to marry Littlejohn's sister.)

---

[10] The accuracy of newspaper reports always needs checking – for instance the local papers in Iowa credit J M L with being a graduate of Edinburgh or Oxford or Glasgow, depending upon which you read, when he arrived at Amity

While this society did a lot of good work and had many ideals that would have found a place in the heart of Littlejohn and his father, it was an "oath bound" society[11]. The Reformed Presbyterian Church has always avoided "secret societies" which are bound by an oath of allegiance.

> "by secret societies we mean those voluntary, man-made associations that demand, as a condition of membership, an oath or promise, that the secrets of the order shall not be revealed to the uninitiated; and this oath or pledge to be given before the so called secrets of the order are made known to the person taking the obligation"
>
> 1899 minutes of synod of R P Church USA page 11

Littlejohn's father would not have been happy with this and, together with his poor health, would probably have contributed to his leaving to go to America with John Martin in 1895. By 1896 James Buchan was not only a member of the Order of Odd Fellows but also a member of the Ancient Order of Foresters and the Free Gardeners[xxviii]. It seems logical that this train of events had an impact on the family and that it influenced them to take David out of college, possible on top of David not doing so well in his studies, and to move the whole family,(excluding their Daughter, who had married Thomas J Anthony in 1894), to College Springs. How attractive the idea of the

---

[11] The Independent Order of Odd Fellows (I.O.O.F.) is not affiliated with Freemasonry. However, the two Fraternities have similar symbolism, values and origins. They use many of the same symbols--the "All Seeing Eye," the sun and moon, the Holy Bible, and the beehive for example they also have an initiation and degree system much like Masonry.(Are the Odd Fellows a part of Free Masonry, by by Midnight Freemasons Contributor Todd E. Creason: http://www.midnightfreemasons.org/2015/01/are-odd-fellows-part-of-freemasonry.html

community of College Springs would have been for Littlejohn's Father can be gleaned from the following:

"A writer in the Midland grows enthusiastic over the new life, the influx of new citizens, and the bright prospects of the town of College Springs in S. W. Iowa. He says, " We challenge any place west of Ohio to compare with this community for its intelligence, morality and good order. It is a solid, churchgoing community. There are no secret society people here, no atheists nor infidels, no Sabbath-breakers, no disorderly class of any kind or name." Is this a new Eden? The geographical limits above given are rather hard on Indiana and Illinois, but very favorable to us of Ohio and Pennsylvania. Be it known that Revs. Wm. Johnston and T. J. Kennedy, and a big United Presbyterian Church, rule College Springs" (Christian Nation Jan 16th, 1889)

On his arrival in College Springs, James Buchan was appointed as assistant to the president of the Amity College and Professor of Philosophy and Civics.

That Littlejohn was happy with the arrival of his family could be said to be an understatement. He seemed to relish the reunion.

"Dr. Littlejohn's' mother and two brothers arrived from Scotland. Of course, the Dr. never gets homesick, but he does look real cheerful since the completion of the family circle. One of his brothers will assist him in conducting his classes".[xxix]

> Amity College. -Dr. James Buchan Littlejohn has been appointed Professor of Philosophy and Civics at Amity College, College Springs, Iowa. Dr. Littlejohn was born on May 18, 1867, at Glasgow, Scotland. He attended the Ballylaggan Male Institution at Coleraine, Ireland, and he entered the University of Glasgow in 1888, graduating in 1892, with the degrees of M. B. and C. M.
>
> He completed his studies for the higher degrees at the University of Chicago, receiving from that institution the M. A. and M. D. degrees.
>
> He has held various medical positions abroad, including that of Lecturer under the County Council of Shropshire in the Technical Education Department.
>
> Dr. Littlejohn is a member of the British Medical Association, of London. His thesis for his degree was entitled "Etiology of Pneumonia," Glasgow, 1895.
>
> (Annals of the American Academy of Political and Social Science Vol 8 July -December 1896 page 350)

If you consider that when he took on the position Littlejohn was recovering from serious bouts of illness and two operations on his throat and had intermittent crisis haemorrhages from the throat, and the plans he had for the development of the College, the arrival of his brother to help in the running of the College must have been seen as a welcome blessing.; even if it was tempered by the family circumstances around his involvement in "secret societies"

When he brought his father back with him from England in the Autumn of 1895, his father also was recovering from illness. The burden of running the college and particularly with no one fit to take over in his absence would have being too much. We know that there was nobody fit to take over in the staff because when the previous president went missing there was a crisis, there was no one there to step into the position to fill his shoes even on a temporary basis.

With all of this in mind and when James Buchan, David and their mother came back in 1896 it was an easy decision to appoint James, a graduate in medicine, well-educated and from a good solid background as his assistant. Even if this was a temporary measure with the benefit for James that he could settle into the country and find his feet.

However, this was not to last long. James Buchan was a surgeon and soon registered in Chicago as a physician, receiving his certificate on Jan 12th, 1897[xxx] and is listed as an instructor in the Chicago Clinical School for 1898. (David registered in Chicago on March 29th, 1898)[xxxi]. Both are listed as being resident in Chicago in Polk's 1898 directory[xxxii]

"Prof. J. B. Littlejohn, M.D., has resigned his position as. assistant to Pres. Littlejohn and is practising medicine in Chicago...about 30 friends of J. B. Littlejohn dropped in on him and completely surprised him last Friday. It was the evening before he went away and was a happy occasion" [xxxiii]

With everything apparently going well why did Littlejohn seemingly suddenly announce his intention to resign and move to Chicago?

In December 1896, Littlejohn notified the trustees of Amity College of his intention to resign and that he and his brother, Dr. James Littlejohn, intended to locate in the east[xxxiv]. He did, however, maintain his close relationship with College Springs (Amity) up until he sold his house at the beginning of 1898[12], lecturing at the Clarinda Chautauqua in June 1897, regularly preaching and staying on as President until the position was filled.

---

[12] J. W. Hewitt of Nodaway has purchased the Littlejohn property and will make this place his borne in the near
future ... (The Clarinda Journal, Page 5, Jan 28th 1898);J. M. Littlejohn to J. W . Hewitt blocks 3 and 4, College Springs. Consideration, $1,800. (The Clarinda Journal, Page 3, Feb 4th, 1898)

An Ideal presented and history repeats itself

There is no doubt that there was some conflict and differences of opinion in the running of Amity College. Some of this is related to the Board of trustees' decision to pass *"a resolution disapproving of but not prohibiting football. This caused quite a commotion on all sides and brought down upon the bald and grey heads of the board very strong criticism, not only from the students, but from a majority of the town. It seems to be the general opinion that the college has suffered from the opposition of this board to a gymnasium or to athletics of any kind. The Board's reason for passing the resolution was the roughness of the game, but many claim that football has saved ten men and given others health and stronger constitutions where It has killed or hurt one, for statistics say that 1/3 of the university students die from lack of physical development, and it is argued from this that physical development is man's duty. The question is being thoroughly discussed, but It is the almost universal opinion that it would hurt the college to prohibit the game"*[xxxv]. The football team did fall in line [13].

> *The football season is ended at last and although the game is said to be very brutal, some of the players still live at least, and notwithstanding the time spent in physical development, some of them did obtain passing grades in College. During all the games that have been played on Amity's grid iron this fall no one has been injured. And there have been no fights. We may then safely draw the conclusion that the game has been a help to the students.*
>
> The Clarinda Herald, 26th November 1895, page 1

---

[13] Amity's football men attended church Thanksgiving Day, this year, like ordinary mortals. They have pulled the cleats off their shoes, have shingled their hair and sold it to the plasterers, have taken their shin guards to patch their blankets and have put their suits to various domestic uses. They intend to be excellent citizens for the next nine months and live on good terms with the board of trustees. The footballs are in cold storage. (Clarinda herald 3rd Dec 1895 page 4)

It is doubtful that Littlejohn agreed wholeheartedly with the football resolution – we know he was on the athletics committee when he was in Kirksville[xxxvi] . However, he favoured fresh air and the physiological exercise rather than strong sports.[14]

Another aspect was the proposal to the Reformed Presbyterian Synod to take over the College. While this was strongly supported within College Springs and the College, it did emphasise the change of control from the United Presbyterians to the Reformed Presbyterians with the almost inevitable backlash of feeling when the proposal was eventually turned down.

The early history of Amity or College Springs shows that this type of conflict was almost inevitable when one group has an ascendency, no matter how well meaning

"The history of Amity affords an example of the inutility of pushing organic union, where there is not intelligent union of heart. At first all worshiped together, but as numbers increased, the preferences of the different denominations, while attracting those who were of the same mind to each other, at the same time drew them away from the common multitude, until Amity has become noted for the number of its churches in proportion to its population.

"The college movement at Amity was originally undenominational, but even a Christian college seems to flourish best under the patronage and support of some particular denomination. The majority of the trustees of Amity college has for many years been United Presbyterians, and they, therefore, hold the control of it".[xxxvii]

So, when Kennedy disappeared, and Littlejohn took over Amity College in 1894 the control as such passed from the United Presbyterians to the Reformed Presbyterians. This 'control', manifested itself in more ways than one – the formation of the new congregation in College springs, the employment of Reformed

---

[14] The difficulty with most active exercises is that they are developed by those who have no knowledge of physiology. Physical culturist's teach systems which are anti-physiological...It is not physical exercise we need but physiological exercise. (Principles of Osteopathy Page 374)

Presbyterians as college professors and the proposal to establish Amity College as 'the Western College of the Reformed Presbyterian church, a 'sister college' to Geneva College in the East. Littlejohn's heart may have been in the right place, but the lack of ' *intelligent union of heart*' between different groups he would try to unite would always undermine his efforts, even within Osteopathy and in England in later years.

The idea of a 'western college' had been floating around for some time without any definitive action. We even find Littlejohn's brother, William, making reference to it in early 1893; - "*It would certainly repay the efforts of our church to maintain a church home m Kansas City. It is the great railroad centre of the west. If we had the numbers and the means, I would be largely in favor of not only building a church but establishing a western college*"[xxxviii].

So what was the proposal? It is well summarised as follows: -

"*Dr. Littlejohn attended the Presbytery of the Reformed Presbyterian church which met at Olathe, Kan., last week, and presented to them the proposition of the Board of Amity College, i.e. to let the R. P. Church have control of Amity College, provided that they endow the college $50,000, and* **maintain the school and keep it at College Springs**. *The Presbytery accepted the proposition favourably and decided that active steps should be taken at once to transfer the institution at their Church. The proposition will be presented to the Synod which meets in Denver, Colo., June 6th, and if accepted there the Institution will be put under the control of that church. This proposition is in accordance with* **the petition signed by almost every citizen and patron of school in this community**. *Not that the people were dissatisfied with the management of the school, but the College needs an endowment and would be for the good of the community.*"[xxxix]

This show's it was not done on a whim, but after deep consideration and consultation with the community at large. However, while Littlejohn may have expected some opposition from the United Presbyterian community who had 'lost control' of Amity College, what he did not foresee was that neighbouring congregation of the Reformed Presbyterian Church would want the 'Western College' for their own community and therefore not back the College Springs proposal. The Congregations of Clarinda, Iowa and at La Junta,

Colorado, put competing proposals to the Reformed Presbyterian Synod.

As part of the process of assessing the merits of the proposals the Synod set up a committee which enquired of all the western congregations *"with reference to the establishment of a western college. All congregations in Illinois, Iowa, Kansas and Colorado Presbyteries are earnestly requested to take action, at their earliest convenience, on this subject, and especially on the proposition of the Board of Amity College, and to report promptly to the chairman of the committee"*[xl].. This was in December 1896, at this time the proposal from Clarinda was withdrawn and La Junta had not responded to further inquiries. This left the Amity proposal as the only viable one.

As would be expected, when asked about the proposals, the congregation associated with Colorado would favour the La junta proposition. For example, the Evans congregation in Colorado reported in February 1897; -

"Resolved that we, the Evans congregation of the R. P. church, deem it unwise for Synod to accept the proposition made by the trustees of Amity College. That we believe the obligations too great to be assumed at a time when the cause of reforms and missions are in urgent need of assistance, Resolved, that we recommend a favorable consideration of La Junta's advantages for a Western college." Let it be understood that La Junta's offer will require comparatively little expense of the church."[xli]

All in all, in December 1896 when Littlejohn handed in his notice to the Board of Amity College it looked as if not only was his proposal for Amity the only one on the table, but it had every chance of success. So, the failure of this was probably not the reason for his resignation.

"At the meeting of Synod on Friday 28th May 1897 the committee on a Western College, through Dr. Trumbull, reported adversely to accepting the offer of Amity College. Rev. T. H. Acheson reported that an effort is being made to get a Covenanter college at La Junta, Colorado. Money has already been subscribed, and he felt confident that it would be advisable to hold the matter open. Revs. B. M. Sharp and T. J. Allen seemed to have reason to believe that Amity college trustees would make more favorable terms than were originally offered. Rev. J. A. Thompson spoke strongly in favor of

College Springs. The report was adopted, and the committee continued for farther negotiations. (The Christian Nation volume 26, 9th June 1987, page 4)

The Synod didn't finally reject the proposal until the June 2nd, 1898 meeting [xlii]

They had been considering several offers for colleges in the west, the one from Amity seemed to be the best but due to continuing financial difficulties within the church it was decided that they would concentrate solely on Geneva College.

" The stringency of the times, the many schemes of the Church demanding increased aid, and the overburdened state of our treasuries. Only one congregation pledged itself to raise its proportion of the amount. In view of the above facts, your committee recommend that the proposition of the Board of Trustees of Amity College be respectfully declined. [xliii]

Alongside the college project was another venture – the "College Springs and Southwestern Railroad company"

The College Springs and Southwestern Railroad company

To many the advent of a railroad meant increase in prosperity to the local community, with access to travel, goods and services being increased. Others saw the negative aspects, and increase in saloons, alcohol and vice as the result.

College Springs itself, did not have a railroad stop of its own- people had to find their way from the nearby Clarinda Station a distance of about 13 miles. Many felt that a railroad would bring increased prosperity to the town.
As College Springs regarded itself as a 'temperance town' many viewed the lack of a railroad as a means of preserving their values.

A writer, in 1889, described College springs in the following glowing terms. *"There are no secret society people here, no atheists, nor infidels, no Sabbath-breakers, no disorderly class of any kind or name. Is this a new Eden?"*[xliv]

The Reformed Presbyterians in particular supported the movement towards a "Temperance Society" and the national reform movement of which Littlejohn was an advocate[15].
"young man, when you go to Clarinda to get married don't do like the young man who got so full of-what do you call it? Of course, it wasn't whisky, for Clarinda is a temperance town, you know"[xlv]
Littlejohn's attitude was strictly in line with the Reformed Presbyterian ethics:

"If we would make temperance men and Prohibitionist, we must convert them from sin and error. If we would win men from the idolatrous of the lodge room (Masonic and other Lodges) we must convert them by preaching Jesus as Saviour and Lord. We must so preach the truth that if any truly seek Jesus under our ministration they will be as sure to give up the lodge as they are to give up theft, profanity, adultery, or any other sin."[xlvi]

In the same article, he further says that we *"should be large enough of heart and mind to hold to the old and receive the new…. avoid one-sidedness and faddism."*; showing that while his principles were strict, he did not apply them to others in bigoted or sectarian manner.

His approach was to preach the positive aspects of the reformed Presbyterian theology rather than attacking or focusing on the negative aspects of sin or the secret societies. This approach may have been a possible point or conflict with some who spent their time preaching against secret societies, whiskey etc. These remarks were made when he was settling into his position as president of Amity College

---

[15] Dr. Littlejohn, Prof. Black and Rev Thompson attended the National Reform convention in Blanchard Friday. (The Clarinda Herald, 28th February 1894, Page 2)

The "railroad question, like many issues had promotors who saw nothing but benefits and those that saw problems. Littlejohn, in a fashion that was typical of him, saw the benefits and tried to steer a path that might heal the differences between factions.

Early in 1895, a company[xlvii] was set up to promote the cause, 'College Springs and Southwestern Railroad company', and Littlejohn was co-opted onto the board.

"At a recent meeting of the board of directors of the College Springs and Southwestern Railroad company, Dr. Littlejohn was chosen president; William Pollock, vice president; J. R. Prest, secretary; J. L. McLean, treasurer. An executive committee was appointed consisting of Dr. Littlejohn Dr. George and S. L. Sherman, we can rest assured that with these officers and this committee everything will be done for our best interest[xlviii]*."*[16]

Almost inevitably the progress of Amity College and the railroad proposals got entangled and were seen as not just complimentary but necessary for each other.

"it is expected that College Springs will take a boom in the spring as we are going to have a railroad this time without a doubt. Everybody is willing to help, and it is within our reach to obtain one in which we will have a direct communication with Clarinda. Hurrah for Amity College and College Springs"[xlix]

During the next year things looked as if they were proceeding well

"Everything still looks favorable for C.S (College Springs). to have a railroad within another year. With the college under the control of the Reformed Presbyterian church and a good railroad, things are sure to boom. (*The Clarinda Herald, 26th March 1895*)

---

[16] "At the railroad meeting Monday evening articles of incorporation were adopted and Dr. J. M. Littlejohn, Rev H. M. Burr, J. R. Prest, C. B. McClelland, A. B. Milner, W H. Pollock, W. S. McLean, E. F. Badger, S. L. Sherman, Dr. M. R. George were elected Directors". (The Clarinda Herald, 26th March 1895, Page 1,)

It wasn't long until the railroad proposal seemed to become dependent upon the Reformed Presbyterian Synod accepting the proposal to take over Amity college.

> "It is a pleasure to note that the steady growth our town has enjoyed for several years will continue during the next year or two at least. Fifteen thousand dollars will be invested in the new United Presbyterian church alone. Brickmakers were in town recently to examine the soil but owing to the frost were unable to tell much about what could be done. We know from experience that good bricks can be burned here if the right men do the work. **The time is drawing near when it will be decided whether or not the college will be taken charge of by the covenanters, then railroad talk is in order again.**[17] The railroad, the new church, and the several new business houses that are to be built, besides the dwelling houses contemplated, will serve to give employment to many workmen and will give a wonderful impetus to the business of our town. (college springs) Let us all work for the proposed improvements"[l]

> "The work for raising means to build a railroad is progressing better than was expected. We seem to realize that if we do not get this one there is forever no hope".[li]

As would be expected not everyone would be in favour of a railroad. We find evidence of this in the results of a debate in one of the societies in Amity College itself

*A representative of the HERALD had the pleasure of visiting Amity college Friday and meeting with a good part of the faculty. Under the management of the new president, Prof. Littlejohn, the college is doing as well as it ever did, and from the outlook we are induced to say that it has taken a new impetus. Among the notable features of the visit was a call at the young ladies' Literary society...The program was carried out and, in the debate, it was decided that **College Springs should not have a railroad.**"[18] [lii]

---

[17] Bold emphasis by the author
[18] Bold emphasis by the author

One is reminded of a story that J. Wernham used to tell regarding Maidstone in Kent where he had his college. That when the railroad from London to the south coast was being built the best route would have been through Maidstone but the "town Fathers" did not want the "riff-raff" of London coming to their town. So, they refused permission. Hence the rather long circuitous journey by rail from Maidstone to London.

The railroad was not to be but even in 1899 they were still "hopeful"

"New Railroad Through Iowa.
RED OAK, Ia., Oct. 17. Of late railroad promoters have been in this locality studying the lay of the country, with a view of building a new line south to Atlantic, thence to Red Oak and on south to Clarinda, or Page Center and College Springs, and on to St. Joseph, Mo. The parties interested have with them a civil engineer and are making a survey of the country, driving the entire distance by team[liii]."

While College springs did not get its sought after railroad it can boast having the first "railroad" in Page County, Iowa, but it was not what you might think!

"College Springs was the first town in Page county to have a railroad; it was called the Missouri Northern[19]. The peculiarity of this road was that the operating employees were all white folks, while the passengers were colored people. No fare was collected by the grumbling conductors, but on the other hand the passengers were tenderly cared for by the railroad company. The road did a good

---

[19] "Underground Railroad "Stations" Iowa shares a southern border with Missouri, which was a slave state. In the 1840s and 1850s, abolitionists (those who wanted to abolish slavery) developed a system of "stations" that could move runaways toward the Mississippi River to Illinois on their way to freedom. Members of two religious' groups, the Congregationalists and Quakers, played leading roles in abolitionist activities. They were also active in the Underground Railroad in the state." (State historical society of Iowa)

business until Abraham Lincoln, by the proclamation of emancipation, virtually declared the charter of the Missouri Northern, with all its underground branches, null and void. Since then College Springs has been without a railroad, but a prominent merchant of the place told us Saturday that they were going to have one sure now; it is to run from Tarkio, Mo., to Bedford. We hope it is true, but we are skeptical; guess he was talking with his mouth the way some folks farm, as Mr. Lisle says".[liv]

As a final note on the railroad question at the beginning of the twentieth century College Springs felt aggrieved that they were allegedly the largest town in Iowa without a railroad and that their "pride", the then struggling Amity College, thought that improved travel opportunities would attract more students.[lv] They finally got a line from Clarinda in 1912 only for it to go bankrupt in 1916.[lvi]

All the talk and possible controversy around the proposed railway again does not appear to give a reason for Littlejohn's declaration of intent, given in December 1896, to leave Amity college'

This leaves us with his and his father's health as the probable factors in his decision.

1895, FINALISES PHD THESIS WHILE AT AMITY

During this time, he also put together his thesis on the Political Theory on Schoolmen and Grotius which he published and presented to Columbia College as part of his thesis and PhD., requirements [lvii] It is probable that as he had been unable to finish and present the work within the required time and the other requirements for his Ph.D., at Columbia he did not graduate from this college. Columbia College had, in 1896[20], changed its PH.D. requirements to include the condition that the thesis must be submitted in less than three years from the commencement of studies. – He had written his thesis parts 1-3 in May 1895[lviii] and expected to have the final part done in the autumn of that year. The thesis cover that was presented to Columbia is dated 1896[lix]

This meant he would have been examined no earlier than April 1896 meaning it would have been 4 years since he started and thus outside the required timescale. Another factor was that he had "retired" from his Fellowship in 1893[lx], as mention earlier, due to ill health and hence he probably would not have had his registration books[21] in order. It is unfortunate that his illness coincided with the continued move of Columbia towards being a "first class university".

---

[20] "As of May 19, 1896, a regulation limiting students to 3 years for completion of a PhD dissertation was adopted by the University Council." Columbia University archives by email
"Applications to be examined for the degrees of Master of Arts or Doctor of Philosophy must be made on or before April 1st of the academic year in which the examination is desired" (Columbia university School of Political Science regulations 1893/4).

[21] "At the time of filing his application to be examined for the degrees of Master of Arts and Doctor of Philosophy, or either of them, every candidate must present to the dean his registration book properly signed and dated, as above prescribed, by the professors or instructors in charge of the several courses which he may have attended, as evidence that he is properly entitled to examination for a degree" (Columbia university School of Political Science regulations 1893/4).

> "I went out in 1891 and took up my fellowship at Columbia College, now Columbia University. I was in Columbia College in 1892 and 1893. In 1893 I had to give up work altogether. I went into a sanatorium first in Waukesha, Wisconsin then in Denver Colorado and then at Waco in Texas. That is where I first met Dr. Lowber, the Chancellor of the University that gave me the degree of LL.D. That was in 1893 and 1894" (House of Lords Select committee hearing 1935, paragraph 3491)
>
> ....."While I was in Columbia University I stayed in a sanatorium on Long Island and came in periodically. I was not required to attend daily, because I was doing research work, and I came in periodically to Columbia College."
>
> House of Lords Select committee hearing 1935 paragraph 3497

Under these circumstances it would have been highly unlikely that the college regulations would have been relaxed on his behalf even though he had permission not to attend daily during his second year.

According to the preface in his thesis, he had written the text in March 1894. He received his Ph.D. from the National University of Chicago in 1895, possibly with an endorsement from Dr. Dunning of Columbia[22]. As already mentioned, the cost of producing 150 copies of his thesis to submit to Columbia may have been prohibitive in 1894, as he was recovering from his operations and illness.

---

[22] In the Journal of Osteopathy 1935 from the British School of Osteopathy we find an article in which Dr. Dunning suggested the J.M. Littlejohn's work "required recognition from some higher institution and that he was profoundly grateful that the possibility of such recognition has opened up". This would suggest he was supporting a nomination for a Ph.D. degree from a college other than Columbia.

"In the summer and fall of 1893 he visited Europe for the purpose of investigating the field of Medieval Literature with the result that early in 1894 he presented to Columbia a Doctoral Thesis entitled "The Political Theory of the Schoolmen and Grotius".[lxi]

The Thesis was evidently accepted, as he said in answer to Lord Dawson's question:

> *"Dr. Littlejohn has Just received, from the Chancellor of his Alma Mater (The Chicago National University), the following letter: "I take pleasure in Informing you that the honorary degree of LL D will be conferred upon you by this university at the November graduation by a unanimous vote of its council, as an evidence of their appreciation of your success both pedagogical and literary, and a token of the high esteem in which you are held as a man and scholar." This is the second university which has conferred this honor upon Dr Littlejohn within the past year"*
> (The Clarinda Herald, Page 4, Oct 22nd, 1895)

"Was that an accepted and completed Thesis? —That was accepted:"[lxii]

In the event of having missed out on receiving his Doctorate from Columbia on technical grounds and especially having received recognition for his work from the National University in Chicago, it would have fitted in with his previous experiences and Political stance in Glasgow to use the title Ph.D. and give himself the credit for his work at Columbia.[23]

---

[23] Having completed the course requirement for M.A., he did not graduate for political reasons he and his Church used the letters M.A. See Introduction, "1895, Finalises Ph.D. Thesis While at Amity" And "May to October 1888"

The 'biography' of Littlejohn in the announcement of his appointment as Chair of Physiology at the American School of Osteopathy, Kirksville in 1898, does not say he gained a Ph.D. from Columbia, only that he attended and submitted his thesis. Even though this is technically quite correct it does give the reader the impression that he received the degree from Columbia and the prospectus for 1898/9 does list him as "J. Martin Littlejohn, Ph.D., LL.D".[lxiii]

In 1895, His brother William, who had just received his M.A. from the National University in Chicago was following this up with studying for his Ph.D. in the same university[lxiv] Littlejohn himself was a student in the postgraduate school of the National university in 1893 and 1894[lxv].

"Student in post graduate School of Theology, national University: Fellow, 1893; D.D. (Thesis, 'The Christian Sabbatism.') 1894"[lxvi]

This may have been instrumental in prompting Littlejohn to apply for and accept a Ph.D. from this university. (The controversy regarding the Nation University of Chicago didn't reached the pages of the Christian Nation in Oct 1897)

We don't know for sure what the Ph.D. from the National University of Chicago, in 1895, was for. It seems reasonable to assume that it was in connection with the work he had already done, either in the field of education[24] or, on Political philosophy, this is much less likely especially given that he went on to submit his thesis on Grotius to Columbia university in 1894.

This failure due to his illness must have hit him hard as he never produced the final part as far as we know. Another view of this can be obtained from the listing of the "school and college honors" listed in the different versions of his thesis. In the edition printed by "college Press, College Springs 1894" and probably submitted for approval, he lists the public schools of Glasgow and Easdale, Scotland,

---

[24] He gave three papers to the Society of Science, Letters and Art on education in 1895,1896 and 1897 (The Osteopathic World, October 1903, page 475.

and Garvagh Scientific Academy with the same pride of place as other more 'recognisable and mainstream' centres of learning as Coleraine Academical and Glasgow university. The later edition in 1896, possible presented as part of the official 150 copies needed to be submitted to Columbia University, leaves these schools out. This may seem of little importance. However, the Reformed Presbyterians would have looked upon their own schools as being at least on par with any other educational institution, even though they may be small, have a limited staff etc. (remember how well-educated Ministers of the Reformed Presbyterian Church were). The change may well have been suggested by his thesis supervisor, but to make the change would have gone against his beliefs and culture. Having the thesis then rejected for such a non academical reason as being outside the acceptable time limit/attendance regulations could be taken as "Gods Will" for such a lack of faith.

He was awarded two degrees of Doctor of Laws, one by Nation University in Chicago, the other by the Add-Ran University in Texas.

He has listed[lxvii] his PH.D. as being from 'Chicago National University 1895' and his LL.D. as being from the 'Add-Ran Christian University, Texas 1895'.[25] This tallies with other sources, including lectures given by J Wernham and the Kirksville Journal of osteopathy (March 1898), when it was said Littlejohn was twice the recipient of Doctor of Laws and Doctor of Divinity[lxviii]. To put this into context his background in relation to graduation and his earlier acceptance of the title M.A. even though he had not "graduated" from Glasgow at the time should be remember. He had done the work, received recognition from the National university of Chicago in the form of the degree Ph.D. in 1895.; so, in his mind and those of his background, he would be properly entitled to use the designation Ph.D.

---

[25] The Add-Ran Christian University, is listed in the 1896/97 college year book as having been founded in 1873; a reputable college with an income of over ten thousand dollars, two hundred and eighty-six students, fifteen instructors and James W. Lobber Ph.D. LL.D., as the chancellor ... and "no secret societies allowed". It is still a thriving Christian University - Texas Christian university.

It is also probable, that at this time, given his association with the Chautauqua Movement and its emphasis on popular education by correspondence, night and irregular lectures, and the difficulty the students in Amity were having with fees, together with the movement of Columbia University in the direction of becoming more secular and "exclusive"[26], he moved closer to those establishments that supported the less privileged student; and especially those establishments that had an emphasis on "Christian Education"- like the Add-Ran Christian University which did not allow "secret Societies.."

---

[26] "During the last half of the nineteenth century, Columbia rapidly assumed the shape of a modern university. The development of graduate faculties in political science, philosophy, and pure science established Columbia as one of the nation's earliest centers for graduate education. In 1896, the trustees officially authorized the use of yet another new name, Columbia University, and today the institution is officially known as Columbia University in the City of New York"
(Columbia university web site https://www.columbia.edu/content/history). This may not be seen as "exclusive", but it did mean stricter entrance and examination regulations and fees which would put it beyond many people.

LATE 1896, 1897, STARTS CONSIDERING MOVE FROM AMITY

His brother James, a medical doctor, would not seem to be content lecturing in Amity College. To further his career in medicine and particular in his chosen speciality of surgery a move towards Chicago where he could pursue this career would seem to be appropriate. On top of that given James Buchan's past association with so-called secret societies and future association with the Masonic order and the strict "anti-secrecy" movement within College Springs it would have been hard to see him settling in that region.

He did advertise as a physician in the local papers during November and December 1896 with a final announcement on 12th January 1897, that he had resigned his position as assistant to 'President Littlejohn and was practising medicine in Chicago [lxix]

Littlejohn's father had retired his ministry in Ireland due to ill health

```
J. B. LITTLEJOHN, A. M. M. D.
COLLEGE SPRINGS, IA
"PHYSICIAN AND SURGEON'
Office and residence
northeast part of town
```

and was inclined to have a prolonged sickness every Winter and Spring since then.[lxx]

This, together with his own health issue and his father's continual illness and the search for treatment would have tended to push Littlejohn in another direction.

It was noted in the Clarinda herald Nov 11th, 1954 that: -

"After Dr Littlejohn's four years at College Springs, his health caused him to give up" his teaching, and he went to Kirksville, Mo, to receive treatments from Dr A. T. Still. He had been going" there during his final, year as president. The success which followed correction of his neck so impressed him that he determined to make the newly discovered' Osteopathy his own life's work".

Today we might be inclined to think of College Springs as being remote from Kirksville and the chances of Littlejohn hearing of Still's osteopathy being unlikely. However, the local papers carried many reports of local people going to Kirksville for treatment[lxxi] and often having what seemed like miraculous results. In fact, one story tells of 5 young men from college Springs going to Kirksville to study osteopathy in 1897

> *Five of College Springs' best-known young men start today for Kirksville, Missouri, to go through the osteopathic institute. Page county is furnishing more than her quota to the ranks of the new school.*
>
> The Clarinda Herald, 2nd April 1897, Page 5

> **M.A. ENGLISH, M. D.**
> **HOMEOPATHIC PHYSICIAN AND SURGEON.**
> Special attention given to Chronic Diseases and Diseases of Children. Office over Pedersen's jewelry store Residence two and one-half blocks west of Page county bank
> (Clarinda Herald, Page 7, 1896-12-18)

Littlejohn would have been aware of osteopathy's growing reputation. The Reverent Mason Pressly was a renown Presbyterian preacher at the time and Littlejohn would have heard of him, if not known him personally. They were both in Philadelphia at the same time in the early 1890's and Pressly was also pastor of the Cumberland Presbyterian Church[lxxii] in Kirksville during his stay in that city.[27] His recent illness[lxxiii] was carried in the Christian Nation[lxxiv]. Pressly was to become the first Chair of Physiology at Kirksville, a

---

[27] M W Pressly was pastor from 1896 to 1897 (History of Adair County, E M Violette, The Denslow History Company, 1911, page 139-140)

position he was unable to take up due to personable problems, leaving it to Littlejohn to take that position in 1898.

Littlejohn's connection to Kirksville goes deep during 1896/7. The question then becomes, 'why did he not go directly to Kirksville to study osteopathy? and instead went to Chicago to study Medicine at a homeopathy college, Dunham college.

His brother had secured a position with The Chicago Clinical School[lxxv], which was associated with the College of Physicians and Surgeons in Chicago[lxxvi], one of the more reputable orthodox colleges. James Buchan was granted an Illinois Medical License on 21st Jan 1897 while still living in Page County Iowa (Amity).[lxxvii]

Dunham college had, as recently as 1895[lxxviii], opened up a new College building with much publicity, and had on a number of occasions exchanged lectures with the College of Physicians and Surgeons[lxxix].

It is also interesting to note that Dunham received endorsement from leading members of the Disciples of Christ in Chicago. This was the same group that Dr. Lowber of the Add-Ran college in Texas was associated with; Littlejohn received his LL.D. from Dr. Lowber[28] in 1895.(Lowber had also been associated with the National University of Chicago and Harkins through his position as an examiner in the National University in the early 1890's.[lxxx] ; but he had no known association with the National Medical University)

"Those interested in pure Homeopathic education will do well to look to the advantages-the marvellous advantages offered by Dunham Medical College, of Chicago.

---

[28] LOWBER, JAMES WILLIAM (1847–1930) Disciples of Christ minister and university chancellor, born in Chaplin, Kentucky, 1847...A.B. and A.M. degrees in 1871 and 1874 from Butler College. In 1868, he was ordained a minister in the Disciples of Christ Church. ..Ph.D. degree from Syracuse University in 1880 and Doctor of Political Science from Wooster University in 1897.... He was chancellor of Add-Ran Christian University from 1892 to 1897... He served as pastor of the Central Christian Church of Austin in 1897. (Handbook of Texas Online, Ida Tobin Hopper, "LOWBER, JAMES WILLIAM," accessed January 05, 2020, http://www.tshaonline.org/handbook/online/articles/flo40.).

Geo. W. Sweeney, D.D., L.L.D., Christian Church (Disciples of Christ) Chicago, July 11, 1899."[lxxxi]

It is known that he attended Dunham College in 1897.[lxxxii] While Dunham College was really only just in existence, it had by far the best collection of homeopathic books and magazines in Chicago due to a bequeathment by Dr Charles J. Watts whose death occurred in November 18th, 1895.[lxxxiii]

It has been suggested that it was the national medical College that he attended during this time and again in 1900/01[lxxxiv]. However, this can be discounted as a speculative theory as Littlejohn is not listed as a matriculant for these years, or any other years for which records exist, in the Annual Announcements of the National Medical College[lxxxv]. He is however, listed as a matriculant in Dunham for the year 1901/2 and graduating in 1902[lxxxvi]. Also, it was during or after the end of the 1896/7 year that the Dean of the National Medical College, J. J. Thompson, left with a number of other lecturers and some students to join the Hering College. It would beg the question as to why any serious student would want to enrol in a college that the Dean, some lecturers and students had abandoned.[lxxxvii]

> **Opposite medical schools will exchange courtesies**
>
> There will be today two meetings notable in the welfare of opposing medical schools. Dr. William E. Quine, the president of the College of Physicians and Surgeons, will deliver a lecture to the student of a homeopathic college at the county hospital, the chemical amphitheatre of which has been secured for the occasion. After the address the faculty of the Dunham Medical College will tender an informal reception to the faculty of the College of Physicians and Surgeons at the fine new building of the former on Wood Street.
>
> The Dunham medical College recognizes Hahnemann as the greatest medical philosopher, but it moved to the West Side and erected a splendid edifice near the county hospital, where its students could see and hear the great lights of the opposing school…
>
> The homeopathic students and their 'regular' neighbours are on very friendly terms. They room together, eat at the same table, attend clinics together and visit each other's lectures, but the spectacle of a great light of one school lecturing to the faculty and students of another school is something unusual in medical circles. In fact, Chicago can claim great credit for the fraternal gathering of this evening. In no other city would such an event meet with favour. That the faculty of one big regular college should pay a social visit to the new home of its homeopathic neighbour is without precedent…
>
> Their action sets a precedent which neither school has anything to lose by following
>
> The Daily Inter ocean
> Saturday 23rd November 1895, Page 7.

Osteopathy was relatively new and still very controversial, even in local newspaper, while Homeopathy was well established and had established local physicians that Littlejohn would at least have been aware off. A move to Chicago would have meant support from his brother and the possibility of local college work, good hospitals should his father need it as well as the chance to study medicine.

On the other hand, while Kirksville might offer a miraculous cure, there would be little opportunity for work and the prospects of local hospital care would seem unlikely. Coming into the winter of 1896/7, when he would have been expecting his father to have another bout of illness, and his own health not being great, Chicago would seem like the best move, while using the prospect of treatment from Still as something to be explored rather than depended upon.

Littlejohn always had an interest in medicine, he studied forensic medicine in Glasgow as part of his Law degree, and physiology when a boy in the Garvagh Science academy. It is also likely that he was attracted to Dunham College in Chicago, as this was an homeopathic college rather than a regular medical college and tended to fit in with his philosophical approach to life and of reasoning from cause to effect rather than dealing with effects.

The prime mover behind all of this I suspect was their father's illness and that he thought treatment in Chicago particularly at Dunham College would help. It was reported on 9th Dec 1896 that Littlejohn notified the trustees of his intention to resign and that he and his brother intended to locate in the east[lxxxviii] (Chicago) This would give the Trustees plenty of time to find a replacement, as he was not intending to leave until the end of the academic year.

It would seem reasonable to assume that Littlejohn considered Amity to be in a strong position and that he had done the job needed in steadying its position after the disappearance of the previous Dean, improving its relationships with other colleges (getting its degrees recognised by Columbia[lxxxix], Harvard[xc] and other universities) and, at this time, being hopeful that it would be taken under the patronage of the R P Church (even though this was to be turned down the follow June)

Apart from proposal to the R P Synod not being accepted and the subsequent appointment of a United Presbyterian to take charge of the college, there does not seem to be any major controversy following Littlejohn's departure form Amity[29]. It could even be said some in College Springs may have felt that the failure of the proposal to the Reformed Presbyterian Synod was linked to Littlejohn declaring his intention to leave Amity in December 1896 and perhaps the Synod and neighbouring congregations did not have faith in the Board to find a suitable successor – especially when the proposed railroad was linked to this proposal.

Events moved fast; in Dec 1896 LittleJohn announces his intention to resign (giving ample time for the trustees to find a replacement); the proposal for the college to be taken over by the Reformed Presbyterian Church was turned down in May 1897 with negotiations prior to that seemingly going well, yet only one congregation had

> *Prof. J. M. Littlejohn, of Amity College, is visiting in Chicago, where his father and mother have taken up their abode and where his two younger brothers are practicing medicine. They are located at corner of Polk Street and California ave.*
>
> (Christian Nation vol 26 June 30th, 1897 page 12)

definitely pledged financial support;

William left the Reformed Church, joining the United Presbyterians in Dec 1896[xci] and the College Springs congregation was in serious difficulties at the end of 1897[xcii].[30]

---

[29] Charlie Still searched long and hard for such evidence, writing as he did to anyone connected to the area, but came up with nothing - see chapter on Kirksville.

[30] The Congregation was officially dissolved on April 13th, 1899, one month after the death of Rev. J. A. Thompson who was for several years on the Board of Amity and the Leading Reformed Presbyterian associated with College Springs. (Minutes of the R. P. Synod 1899). It had been maintaining preaching from one third to one half of the time in 1896/7 which dropped to less than one third in 1897/8 (Minutes of R. P. Synod for 1897 & 1898)

The congregation had been "very anxious in regard to Amity College, Hoping the Church will take hold of it and make it such an institution as is needed in the west".[xciii]

Littlejohn's brother James Buchan, got his license to practice medicine in Chicago in Jan 1897; David, after graduating in Medicine in April 1897 moved to Chicago to work; Both James B. and David were listed in the 1897 street directory for Chicago as living at 408 South California[xciv]

Littlejohn's position and reputation at Amity was sound and well recognized even though he had tendered his resignation. For example, in March 1897 Rev Stevenson spent time in College Springs and reports that everything seems to be progressing prosperously with Dr. J.M. Littlejohn as the head of the institution[xcv].

And again, we find trustees of Amity held him in very high regard; -

"On tendering his resignation of the Presidency of Amity College last summer the directors adopted the following minute:
"We recognize in Dr. J. M. Littlejohn one of the ablest ministers and ripest of scholars, and as an educator he has no superior. A refined gentleman, a true Christian, his influence has always been on the side of right and the best interest of education, his aim in life being to lift up and stimulate the educational interests of the whole community."[xcvi][31]

There are very many references to Littlejohn's time at Amity in the Christian Nation and local newspapers, all of which go to credit him with work that he was doing there

---

[31] The entire faculty of Amity College was reorganized this week by the board of trustees. The presidential chair is not yet filled, but Pres. Littlejohn has not applied for re-election. (The Clarinda Herald, Page 7 18th June 1897)

> *"when music again filled the air and an increased audience listened to the able formal opening speech of Dr. Littlejohn, of College Springs, and talks by other leading workers."* (Page County Democrat, 17th June Page 8, 1897)
>
> *"Rev. J. W. Dill, assisted by J. M. Littlejohn will begin a series of meetings at the Covenanter church next Monday"*
>
> (The Clarinda Journal, Page 5, 31st Dec 1897)

There can be no doubt that Littlejohn remained a popular figure in the area. He was a leading speaker at the Clarinda Chautauqua in June 1897 when he gave the opening speech and is mentioned as continuing to preach in the area throughout 1897/8.

"The entire faculty of Amity College was reorganized this week by the board of trustees. The presidential chair is not yet filled, but Pres. Littlejohn has not applied for re-election". (The Clarinda Herald, Page 7 18th June 1897)

A new president of Amity was finally appointed in the summer of 1897. Amity, prior to Littlejohns time, had been 'under the control' of United Presbyterian brethren and now was returned to the control of that congregation

*"The trustees of Amity; college met Monday afternoon. and elected Rev. Mr. Calhoun - of Viola, Illinois, **president of** Amity college. He is a minister of the United Presbyterian church, a graduate of Monmouth college, and-comes very highly recommended for the position by his ministerial brethren, and we hope everyone will try to push Amity college to the front and that all past differences of opinion will be forgotten. Let all citizens of College Springs especially work for the best interest of the college for in doing so we can also better our own condition."* [xcvii]

The driving force behind Littlejohn was his solid spiritual belief that his gifts, in the fields of research, education, teaching particularly in the life sciences were given to him for a purpose. As each avenue closed, he tended to look for another one that he could continue to use his gifts to the fullest.

During the time he was in College Springs the congregation tended to flourish. After his time there, the congregation was dwindling with members leaving to join other branches of the Presbyterian Church including his brother William who was one of the founding members of the College Springs R P Congregation. William made application to be received into the fellowship of the United Presbyterian Church in December 1896 (Christian Nation 23rd Dec 1896).

---

[i] The New Era Wed Sep 12, 1894
[ii] Pittsburgh Post-Gazette Wed Jan 23, 1895
[iii] Xenia Daily Gazette Thu May 12, 1898
[iv] The New York Times Mon May 9, 1898
[v] Christian Nation Vol 21 Nov 14, 1894 page 4
[vi] The Christian Nation 5 Dec 1894
[vii] The Clarinda Herald, Page 1, Tuesday 11th December 1894
[viii] Minutes of Testimony to House of lords select committee HMSO 1935, paragraph 3393 page 226
[ix] The College Yearbook and Athletic Record 1896-7; New York, Sone and Kimball. University press at Cambridge Massachusetts
[x] The Clarinda Herald, May 10th Page 1, 1895
[xi] Christian nation vol 22 May 22nd, 1895 page 10
[xii] The Clarinda Herald, Page 1, 1895-04-26
[xiii] Email correspondence from Columbia University archives
[xiv] The Christian Cynosure June 6th, 1895
[xv] The Christian Nation, Vol 23 September 18th, 1895 page 10
[xvi] Proceedings of the first biennial conference of the World Federation of Educations Associations held in Edinburgh, July 20-27, 1925, Page 43.
[xvii] The Clarinda Herald, 7th April 1896 Page 1,
[xviii] The Christian Nation Volume 24, 13th May 1896 page 10
[xix] The Christian nation Volume 24, April 8th, 1896 page 10
[xx] Glasgow University archives correspondence
[xxi] Glasgow university archives enquiry service email 30th August 2017
[xxii] The Clarinda Herald, 16th June 1896, Page 1
[xxiii] Amity College catalogue for 1896-7
[xxiv] St Joseph weekly Gazette 2nd April 1897
[xxv] The Clarinda Herald, Page 1, March-09 1897
[xxvi] The Clarinda Herald, January 5th, 1897, Page 1,
[xxvii] Freeport Journal Standard, Wed, Sept 25th, 1907.
[xxviii] Medical directory for Great Britain 1896
[xxix] The Clarinda Herald, Page 1, 7th March 1896

[xxx] State Board of Health of Illinois certificate, Mid-western university, Downers Grove, Illinois, archives
[xxxi] Appendix to the twentieth annual report of the Illinois State Board of Health – Official Register of Physicians 1898 page 57
[xxxii] Polk's medical register and directory of North America 1898 page 447
[xxxiii] The Clarinda Herald, Page 1, 12th Jan 1897
[xxxiv] Christian nation Dec 9th, 1896, page 10
[xxxv] The Clarinda Herald, Page 4, 22nd oct 1895
[xxxvi] Kirksville Journal of osteopathy May 1900 page 539
[xxxvii] "early settlement and growth of western Iowa; or, reminiscences by Todd, john, 1818-1894 "chapter 12 amity or college springs
[xxxviii] Christian Nation June 7th, 1893 page 8
[xxxix] Clarinda herald 26th March 1895 page 1
[xl] The Christian nation Volume 25 2nd December 1896, page 10
[xli] The Christian Nation volume 26, February 24th, 1897 page 13
[xlii] The Christian Nation volume 28, June 8th, 1898 page 5
[xliii] Minutes of the Synod of the Reformed Presbyterian Church of USA May 22nd, 1897, page 14-15.
[xliv] Christian nation vol 10 Jan 1889, page 12
[xlv] The Clarinda Journal, 31st Dec 1897, Page 5
[xlvi] The Christian Nation Nov 13, 1895
[xlvii] The Clarinda Journal, April 12th, 1895, Page 3
[xlviii] Ibid
[xlix] The Clarinda Journal 22nd Feb 1895, page 4
[l] The Clarinda Journal, 13th March 1896, Page 4
[li] The Clarinda Journal, 8th March 1895, Page 3
[lii] The Clarinda Herald, 5th April 1895, Page 5
[liii] Audubon County journal 19 oct 1899
[liv] The Clarinda Herald, 27th May 1891, Page 6
[lv] Railroads and the American people page 171 by H R Grant 2012
[lvi] Iowa Railroads: The Essays of Frank P. Donovan, Jr. University of Iowa Press, 2000.
[lvii] Columbia University archives by email
[lviii] Preface of "Political theory of the Schoolmen and Grotius" J Martin Littlejohn, Submitted in partial fulfilment of the requirements for the Degree of Doctor of Philosophy in the Faculty of Political Science, Columbia University N.Y. 1896
[lix] ibid
[lx] Officers and graduates of Colombia College, general Catalogue 1754-1894, Page 70
[lxi] The Journal of Osteopathy, Kirksville, Vol. 4, No. 10, March 1898, page 489.

[lxii] Minutes of Testimony to House of lords select committee HMSO 1935, paragraph 3453, page 228
[lxiii] Journal of Osteopathy, Kirksville, Vol. 4, No. 12, May 1898
[lxiv] Christian Nation, Volume 22, February 27th, 1895, page 10
[lxv] List of degrees and honours, "Political theory of the Schoolmen and Grotius" J Martin Littlejohn, Submitted in partial fulfilment of the requirements for the Degree of Doctor of Philosophy in the Faculty of Political Science, Columbia University N.Y. 1896
[lxvi] "Political Theory of The Schoolmen and Grotius"; Submitted in partial fulfilment of the requirement for the Degree of Doctor of Philosophy, in the Faculty of Political Science, Columbia University, N.Y.: by J. Martin Littlejohn, Current Press, College Springs 1894. College Degrees and Honors
[lxvii] List of Degrees and diplomas in chronological order, attached to Letter from Hall and Canning to BSO graduates in 1935, Welcome Library holdings
[lxviii] Journal of Osteopathy (Kirksville), March 1898
[lxix] The Clarinda Herald, 12th January 1897, Page 1,
[lxx] The Christian Nation Vol 30, March 3 8th, 1899 page 12
[lxxi] The Clarinda Journal, 10th May 1895 Page 4
  Page County Democrat, 18th February 1897, Page 8
  The Clarinda Journal, 8th October 1897, Page 5; to give just a few examples
[lxxii] Philadelphia College of Osteopathic medicine: Pressly, Mason W., D.O. 1859 - 1942, Co-Founder
[lxxiii] The Daily Herald, Austin Minn. 13th January 1897
[lxxiv] The Christian Nation, Volume 10, Jan 16th, 1889.
[lxxv] The Chicago Clinic; Bulletin number 7; May 1898; Advert for the Chicago Clinical School, issued April 1897.
[lxxvi] P & S plexus college of physicians and surgeons and Chicago clinical school, Volume 3, Number 8, February 1898
[lxxvii] State Board of Health certificate held in the archives of Mid-western university, Downers Grove Illinois- previously The Chicago College of Osteopathic Medicine
[lxxviii] Chicago tribune Sept 22, 1895
[lxxix] The Daily Inter ocean, Saturday 23rd November 1895, Page 7.
[lxxx] Fort Worth daily gazette., June 08, 1890, PART TWO., Page 12
[lxxxi] ." Dunham Medical College Journal, Volume 1, Number 2, page 157; National Library of Medicine, Bethesda USA)
[lxxxii] Minutes of Testimony to House of lords select committee HMSO 1935, paragraph 3500, page 230
[lxxxiii] The History of Homeopathy; William Harvey King; The Lewis Publishing Company, 1905, Volume 3, page 121
[lxxxiv] John Martin Littlejohn An Enigma of Osteopathy; John O'Brien; 2019 Anshan ltd. ISBN 978 1 848291 386; page 41

[lxxxv] National Medical College (Chicago, I. Annual announcement. Chicago: Calumet Books & Eng. Co.
[lxxxvi] Dunham Medical College, 8th annual announcement, 1902/3; Centre for research libraries, Chicago
[lxxxvii] The History of Homeopathy; William Harvey King; The Lewis Publishing Company, 1905, Volume 2, page 431
[lxxxviii] The Christian Nation, volume 25, December 9th, 1896 page 10
[lxxxix] Columbia university archives, Minutes of Meeting of Council November 19, 1895
[xc] The Clarinda Herald, March 28th, 1895
[xci] The United Presbyterian, December 16th, 1896, quoted in The Christian Nation, Vol. 25, December 23rd, 1896, page 12
[xcii] The Christian Nation Vol. 27, December 29th, 1897
[xciii] The Christian Nation, Vol. 25, December 16, 1896
[xciv] City Directories for Chicago Illinois 1897. Page 1271
[xcv] The Christian Nation 17th March 1897
[xcvi] Journal of Osteopathy March 1898
[xcvii] The Clarinda Journal, 9th July 1897, Page 5

1897- 1899

1897 – Chicago prior to Kirksville

From one point of view it seems like a big jump for Littlejohn to go from Moral Philosophy to the study of medicine. However, if it is considered that the first divide in philosophy may be stated as being between "natural philosophy" which includes the biological sciences and medicine, and "moral philosophy"; it is not so much of a change in direction as a change in emphasis. Littlejohn, as mentioned above, came from a background that included many devoted anti-vivisectionists and would initially have been drawn towards the moral side of philosophy. Now, at this stage, he would have found himself in a dilemma. With his father's illness he would not have been able to minister to him as he would have been to any other individual-his father was himself a distinguished minister and therefore not needing Littlejohn's ministrations, but he could have had some benefit from James Buchan's medical experience. His own illness would also have given his enquiring mind a nudge in the direction of medicine. His direction towards a Homeopathic College rather than an orthodox one would be more in line with his wholistic view of philosophy, vital principles and arguing and deducing from a given set of principles

He notified the board of trustees of Amity of his intention to leave in December 1896 and in his own words "resigned my position in Amity in early 1897 and in 1897 and 1898 I was attending Dunham Medical College...I attended Dunham from March 1897 till 1898[i]

We have no reason to doubt his word, he was an ordained Minister in the Reformed Presbyterian Church and took oaths very seriously-he would not have perjured himself. (we can see this from a close examination of the whole of his testimony - see section on House of lords Select committee.)[1]

During 1897 he continued to maintain his close relationship with College Springs (Amity) up until he sold his house at the beginning of 1898[ii], lecturing at the Clarinda Chautauqua in June 1897[iii], regularly preaching[iv], preaching in the Reformed Presbyterian Churches locally and filling the pulpit in Page in November 1897,[v] (he was "an eloquent preacher"[vi]) and again in December 1897 and January 1898[vii] Lecturing[viii] and staying on as President until the position was filled in the summer of 1897. James B spent some time visiting with him at the time[2]

> ***J. W. Hewitt of Nodaway has purchased the Littlejohn property and will make this place his borne in the near future ...*** (The Clarinda Journal, Page 5, Jan 28th, 1898)
>
> *J. M. Littlejohn to J. W. Hewitt, blocks 3 and 4, College Springs. Consideration, $1,800.* (The Clarinda Journal, Page 3, Feb 4th, 1898)

---

[1] O'Brien in his book "John Martin Littlejohn an enigma of osteopathy" details his thoughts that Littlejohn attended the National medical college at this time. The Catalogues for the National medical College for 1896 and for 1897 do not mention Littlejohn as matriculant, Alumni or lecturer, so this assertion can be discounted. Unfortunately, the list of matriculants for Dunham for 1897/8 is not available.

[2] James B was in college springs paying his folks a visit (The Clarinda Journal, 21st May 1897 Page 3)

> "a called meeting of Kansas City Presbytery held Dec. 8, Rev. Wm. Littlejohn, D.D., of the R. P. fold, made formal application to be received into our fellowship. having satisfied the presbytery as to his standing in our sister church, and also as to his acceptance of our standards, he was duly received. Bro. Littlejohn has accepted an appointment as stated supply in our Second Topeka congregation. (The *United Presbyterian.* Dec. 16". Christian nation 23rd December 1896, page 12)

In summary then, Littlejohn announced his intention of leaving Amity and started his move to Chicago in December 1896. His brothers, David and James Buchan, registered as physicians in Illinois and moved to Chicago, living at 408 South California Avenue[ix], early in 1897 with James B taking a post in the Chicago Clinical School as an instructor in the ear nose and throat department[x]. During this time, December 1896, his other brother, William, left the Reformed Presbyterian Church to join the United Presbyterians.[xi] William's father in law, Mr. William Milligan Orr who passed away suddenly in July 1896, had been a United Presbyterian prior to joining the Covenanter Church[xii] and was for a long time associated with the Lind Grove congregation over which William had been minister prior to the North Cedar congregation[xiii]. This history may have influenced his change of Church.

It was during his last year as president of Amity College that Littlejohn started to have treatment from A T Still.

From his own testimony in 1935 to the House of Lords he said he started in Dunham in the March of 1897, - The Dunham college year ran from September to April, with the final exams and commencement exercises in the first half of April[xiv]. Mid-March to the middle of June would have been a busy time at Amity College. However, it should not be discounted that he had spent time at Dunham prior to the Fall, during the Amity college break in early March (between the Winter and Spring terms), investigating the possibility of studying at Dunham.[xv] Also it notes in the Dunham College 1896/7 announcement that *"The work of each year is complete in itself: final examinations and credits are given as fast as the work is accomplished. As far as possible. the work is assigned to meet the requirements of the individual student, and throughout the entire course of study every student practically stands alone. advancing as fast as his work is completed"*. Littlejohn being the industrious student that he was, would not have lagged behind in his studies in the absence of formal lectures.

From newspaper reports it appears he finally moved to Chicago in July, visiting his parents[3] who had moved there sometime earlier to live with his brother David[xvi]. At the same time James B visited College springs at Littlejohn's residence treating 'special cases'[xvii], possibly taking some leave from his position he had taken up as an instructor in the Chicago Clinical School prior to April 1897.[xviii] The Christian Nation carries a report that Littlejohn's residence had changed to 408 South California Avenue in February 1898, this is consistent with his move to Chicago in the summer of 1897. The explanation being, that he kept his house in Amity until the beginning of 1898, only confirming his move after the house sale, and only selling his house when he had obtained a position in the American School of Osteopathy.[4]

Littlejohn attended Dunham Medical college where he studied until about February/ March of 1898.

One of the unsaid reasons that Littlejohn might have chosen Dunham medical College may have been his attitude towards women. His history within the Reformed Presbyterian Church, and with Amity college and probably before that with Rosemount College in Glasgow, gives us a clear picture of a man who looked upon women as equals and that all professions should be open to them. He states this very clearly in his address to the graduating class on Thursday 13th June[xix] when he said: -

"Ladies, I am glad to congratulate you upon your admission to this noble profession. I hope the day is not far distant when our sisters and mothers will be admitted to every field and avenue of life it is their desire to enter"

---

[3] His Father probably moved to Chicago for better treatment and lived with David (who had just received his registration as a physician in Chicago), living at 408 South California ave.

[4] "With the opening of the February term of the American School of Osteopathy, Prof. J. Martin Littlejohn, recently President of Amity College, College Springs, Iowa, was chosen to the chair of Physiology, and to fill the vacancy caused by the resignation of Rev. M W Pressly". (Journal of Osteopathy vol 4 no 10 March 1898)

How Dunham was viewed at the time is again clearly stated by Theresa K Jennings, a graduate of Dunham in 1901 who was also the class valedictorian and, in her address, said

"Dunham stands as the first in its dealing to women of any co-educational institution in the world, where they really believe with our Doctor Hudson that 'Woman is man's equal! She would be only his equal! Nothing more! And less would sink her into nothingness'"[xx]

The article also tells of how hard it was for women who wanted to enter medical colleges, many of which did not admit women at all.

"She had an awful time getting into medical school...there weren't many women doctors back then. They tried to keep her out.... Once she opened her dresser drawer and there was a whole bunch of innards, intestines in there. She had a corpse in her bed one night and had to take it out before she went to sleep."[5]

Theresa K Jennings went on to teach at both Dunham and Herring College when Littlejohn was professor of Physiology

Littlejohn's father moved to Chicago during the first half of 1897, associated with the Covenanter Church in that city, was listed as assisting at communion on May 1st, 1898[xxi], and moved to Kirksville soon after, having been ill for some time[6] and not able to make the move earlier. According to his obituary[xxii] in the Journal of Osteopathy, Kirksville he moved to Kirksville in May 1898, his health having recovered sufficiently to make the Journey. During 1897 Littlejohn also travelled to Kirksville for treatment from Still.

---

[5] While the article gives the impression that these events happened at Dunham, it is much more likely that they happen when she was attending the Women's North-western Medical College, which she left after two years to attend Dunham

[6] Rev James Littlejohn, who had been ill for some time, has improved in health and moved to Kirksville (Christian nation 22nd June 1898, page 12 - quoting from Christian Instructor June 9th, 1898)

> *"we are gratified to learn that Rev. J Littlejohn has somewhat improved in health since his arrival at Kirksville, Mo., where he has three sons, two of whom are professors in the Medical College located there. Dr. J. B. Littlejohn is surgeon of the hospital, where they have some five hundred patients. The Fourth church, Chicago, were sorry to lose these good people. But they have the true savor and will impart it wherever they go, so that the loss of Chicago is Kirksville's gain.*
>
> Christian Instructor – Christian Nation
20th July 1898 page 12

It was Littlejohn's own treatment from Still that would have encouraged his father and mother to move there;

"he went to Kirksville, Mo, to receive treatments from Dr A T Still. He had been going there during his final year as president. The success which followed correction of his neck so impressed him that he determined to make the newly discovered Osteopathy his own life's work[xxiii]."

> *"There are Presbyterians who, on the creed question; Methodists on the question of rules on amusements; and United Presbyterians on the rule regarding secret societies; are like the fellow who was in favor of the Maine liquor law, but opposed to its enforcement"*(The Bellefontaine Republican., May 29, 1900, Page 3)

While osteopathy was not unknown in College Springs, it also worth noting that during 1897 Harry Still[7] was working in Chicago, and Littlejohn would almost certainly have been made aware of this during his visits to Kirksville.

Another point worth considering is that James Buchan was to be ordained as an elder in the 4th United Presbyterian Church in Chicago around the beginning of February 1898[xxiv] and became a member of the Candida Lodge of the Masons in February 1898. He had previously been a member of the Odd Fellows and other societies when in Munslow, so would not be a surprise that he would continue in that vein in Chicago.

> James Buchan Littlejohn was elected on the 6th February, initiated on the 20th February and passed on the 2nd March 1898 in the Candida lodge 927 Illinois.
>
> (Grand Lodge of A.F. & A.M. of Illinois archives)

Given the anti-secret society aspects of the Reformed Presbyterian Church and the less strictly implemented view of the United Presbyterians[8] it may be speculated that these events show an argument within the Littlejohn family with James Buchan going one way, John Martin and their father remaining loyal to their original

---

[7] Harry Still was in practice in Chicago with Hildreth and J H Sullivan, working from offices in the Masonic Temple office building. Journal of Osteopathy Kirksville, Vol 4, No 7, December 1897, Advertisements page xiv)

[8] "UP Synod June 1897 no action on removing ban on secret societies- newspaper report 1897" (The Bourbon news., June 04, 1897, Page 2,) "The greatest discussion in the assembly will be over the revision of the testimony on secret societies. Many members of oathbound organizations are now in the church and it is a causing trouble" (The Bellefontaine Republican., May 29, 1900, Page 2, in a report on the United Presbyterian Assembly in Chicago May 1900)

convictions. The fact that James Buchan was ordained as an elder in the 4th United Presbyterian Church[xxv] may be taken as an indication of a "peace offering" to his father- that his interest in the Masons was more for business and he was not moving from his fundamental Presbyterian beliefs.

The question still remains why did Littlejohn leave his studies in Chicago and take up Osteopathy in Kirksville? He had seen his and his father's health improve with treatment from Still. But I would suggest that the final piece of the puzzle was his interaction with the Rev. Mason Pressly. As mentioned above it is probable that he knew of Pressly, knew his story and probably had meet him prior to Kirksville. I would suggest that on one of his trips to see Still for treatment, he would have talked with Pressly, who at that time was not only taking up the teaching of physiology but was the Cumberland Church pastor in Kirksville so there would have been a commonality of thought between them. When Pressly was being forced into resigning his position at the American School of Osteopathy, it would not be too great a stretch to assume that he would suggest to Littlejohn, who had similar qualifications to Pressly, that he might apply for the position and thus take up the study of Osteopathy.[9]

---

[9] Pressly's resignation is noted at the January 4th, 1898 board meeting and J M Littlejohn's application and subsequent short talk on Physiology is noted at the 18th January board meeting (A T Still museum archives)

MOVE TO KIRKSVILLE

The two years 1898 – 1900 were fascinating and could make a wonderful soap opera containing as they do a burgeoning new career as the Prof. Of Physiology, tragedy in the loss of his father and the tornado that swept through Kirksville, intrigue, deceit, conspiracy over the appointment of Hildreth as dean, and in the background love and romance which flourished with David and his wife and which failed with Littlejohn and Blanche.

"Our Dr. Littlejohn is just what we want, wisdom minus wind. Smith has his literally equal, all like him." A.T. Still [xxvi]

"It was in 1897, while the old doctor was writing his autobiography[10] *that I first met him on the road near Kirksville. Dr. Still said to me, 'The cause of disease is to be found and exists in the limited or excited action of the nerves only which control the fluids of the parts or the whole of the body………. all diseases are mere facts, the cause being a partial or complete failure of the nerves to conduct properly the fluids of life."*[xxvii]
Thus, John Martin Littlejohn describes his first meeting with Dr. Still. This meeting would have presumably taken place when J.M. Littlejohn was on his way to Kirksville to have treatment and further explore the value of Osteopathy for his own and his father's health. [11]

He goes on to say *"being an enthusiast in the study of anatomy and physiology, and myself a sufferer, and exiled from my native land by the medical profession on the grounds of ill-health, I was fascinated by Still's ideas and then and there accepted the philosophy of his system, that based the foundation of this treatment of disease upon the medicine chest of the human body and laid the foundation for the prescription of remedies in the adjustment of the body structure, to normalise the production, distribution and application of these remedies in the cure of dis-ease."*[xxviii]

From this it is clear that he was taken almost immediately by this approach, it also fits in with his background and education in Theology and moral philosophy in the Reformed Presbyterian Church. Above all else Littlejohn was a reformist and an educator. His first educational foray was into law and divinity he then progressed to love of moral philosophy and from this it's a short step to the natural sciences and natural philosophy which would include physiology.

Also, given Professor Lorimar's influence on Littlejohn's early education and that his approach was to **"reason from cause to effect"** it's no wonder that he was immediately taken by Still's pragmatic, mechanistic approach to treatment and particularly with the emphasis of using the hands, not in the traditional lying on of hands as he would have been used to in the role as a Minister, but in a broader context more in

---

[10] Stills autobiography carries the date June 15th, 1897 in the preface by A T Still and was published in 1897.
[11] "Rev. James Littlejohn, of Chicago, whose illness was mentioned some time since in these columns, has so far recovered as to be removed to Kirksville, Mo., for a change of climate. He stood the journey without injury" Christian Instructor June 9, 1898, quoted in the Christian nation, Vol. 28, 22nd June 1898, page 12

conformity with the application of practical physiology than with a theological motive.

At the time he came to the school in Kirksville it was undergoing change and a period of some turmoil. The Board of Trustees on a motion had ordered the Dean to secure a Professor of Physiology at their meeting on July 1897[xxix]. This was partly due to the passage of the osteopathic bill on March 4th, 1897.[xxx] (the previous osteopathic bill being vetoed by the then Governor[xxxi]. Even though this had been overturned by the new Governor it was still a factor in the direction that the school was moving. and partly to improve the school's educational facilities. As Still himself had said: -

"It has been my design and desire to qualify the doctors of Osteopathy to a skilled use of the surgeon's knife, built upon a thorough knowledge of human anatomy in the field of battle or at home in this or any other government, or on the high sea. I am now prepared to teach anatomy, physiology, surgery, theory and practice, also midwifery, in that form that has proven itself to be an honor to the profession to date"[xxxii].

Having changed its syllabus and got recognition as a school of medicine from the governor it was starting to change its staff accordingly. The first effort to secure this was Dr. D.M. Desmond[xxxiii],[12] Although he didn't last very long and tentatively was to be replaced by the Rev. Mason Pressley[xxxiv] who was currently a student at the college.

---

[12] Dr. D. M. Desmond, M. D., A. M., D.O., who is in jail, charged with practicing osteopathy without having a filed certificate, has had the additional charge of murder brought against him. It is claimed he caused the death of Miss Minnie Nisle, upon whom, it is further claimed he performed a criminal abortion, in January last, which resulted in her death a few days later. His hearing will be Saturday. THE DAILY: IOWA CAPITAL FRIDAY, JULY 14* 1899.

Pressly was asked to take the classes in physiology for the last term and seemingly was in line for the position of Professor of Physiology. Unfortunately, he ran into difficult with students and was accused of inappropriate conduct. The charges were investigated by the board and found to have no substance. Unfortunately, this did not stop rumors spreading either amongst the students and within the town itself. Although he was subsequently cleared by the board rumors[13] and complaints persisted, and he had tendered his resignation which was accepted by the Board.[xxxv]

> *Mason W Pressly Ph.D. was recently elected to the chair of Physiology, by the trustees of the American School of Osteopathy. Dr. Pressly is a graduate of Princeton, having also taken a post graduate course in that institution, and attended Harvard university, winning a fellowship in the Divinity school of Harvard in 1889. At Princeton, he made a special study of metaphysics, philosophy, physiological psychology and biology. He has received the degrees of Bachelor of Arts, Master of Arts, and Doctor of Philosophy. Dr. Pressly is a gentleman of rare culture, a deep thinker, magnetic, and thoroughly alive to the Osteopathic idea, of which he is one of the ablest exponents. His course in physiology will be arranged to suit the needs of Osteopathy. The addition of Dr. Pressly to the faculty is a valuable one, both for the school and the science.*
>
> (Journal of Osteopathy, Kirksville, Vol. 4 No. 7, December 1897 page 347)

---

[13] "The evidence submitted is not sufficient to sustain the charges of gross immorality on the part of Rev Pressley as specified in the affidavits and the finding of the board is that Mr Pressly is not guilty of the said charges" (Minutes of meeting of the Board of Trustees of the ASO, Dec 22nd page 23; Museum of Osteopathic Medicine ref. 1987.1226.01)

A thorough description of the changes in the curriculum was published, before Littlejohn came to Kirksville, in the June 1896 Journal of Osteopathy as follows:

"Since the last issue of the Journal several important changes have been made in the curriculum of the school. The course has been lengthened from eighteen months to two years, and greatly improved. A more complete course in physiology has been added, together with a class in urine testing, use of the microscope, surgery in the treatment of accidents and injuries, an advanced course in obstetrics and diseases of women, symptomatology, and treatment of poisons. The general anatomical Class has also been made more thorough. A new dining room with a commodious amphitheater and every provision for the best practical demonstrations on the cadaver, was finished in May.

"The future graduates of the American School of Osteopathy will have the most complete knowledge of the human body that scientific research and up-to-date methods of teaching can impart. This knowledge will embrace all that is known of the human organism in health and in disease not according to Osteopathic principles alone, but also in accordance with the recognized authorities of the medical and surgical world, so that a student who goes out with a diploma from the American School of Osteopathy will be able to pass a rigid examination before any State Medical board upon all branches taught in medical colleges, except those branches in which treatment is concerned.

"Osteopathy is based upon absolute knowledge of every detail of anatomy and physiology, and neither pains nor expense will be spared to give the student the best the world affords in this line. In matter of treatment, of course, the entire Materia Medica is discarded, and Osteopathic principles and practice substituted." [xxxvi]

In any event Littlejohn let it be known to the then Dean, Hulett, that he was interested and was asked by the Board and Faculty to give a trial lecture so that they could access his ability.[14] This evidently was successful as he was then appointed to Chair of Physiology[xxxvii].

Apart from the controversy that we know about concerning Pressly, and ones we don't know about concerning Desmond, the school was facing other local problems.

The school also had opposition from the Columbian School of Osteopathy founded by Ward. The Columbian school opened in November 1897 and moved into their new building in 1898[xxxviii]. (the principle stockholder was R. M. Brashear who had previously (1894) offered to donate land to A T Still but that offer was not taken up by Still. Wards school opening in November 1897.[xxxix]

"Great animosity greeted the establishment of another osteopathic institution in the same town and in January 1899 the Weekly graphic stated that 'the town has seen enough bickering and he businessmen of Kirksville are getting tired of the fight between the American and Columbian schools'"[xl] Some people in the vicinity thought the school of osteopathy was a "gold mine" for the shareholders.[xli] (*"It is said to be a gold mine to its proprietors"*) and needless to say the local medical fraternity was not impressed.

Littlejohn set about his work with the same zeal, enthusiasm and dedication as he has with every other endeavor that he engaged in. Starting to write textbooks based on his lectures, publishing talks, participating in the academic world, serving on the athletic committee, engaging in the YMCA and Bible classes etc. Eventually moved his family[xlii] to Kirksville including his brother James who became Professor of Histology, Pathology and minor surgery and later major surgery[xliii]

---

[14] It's more than likely that Presley having come in contact with Littlejohn and knowing his background both as an educator and as an academic and his interest in physiology suggested to him that he might apply for the position of Professor of Physiology. They obviously remained in contact as they wrote the two closely connected articles on osteopathy and its development in the Encyclopedia Americana- digitized and available at Archive.org

and his brother David later who operated X ray equipment[xliv] and gave surgical clinics[xlv]

There's some controversy about his claim that he was the first Professor of Physiology and that this was the first time that the school had tried to teach physiology per say. However, on checking the records of the Board meetings and the Faculty meetings, it is found that while persons were appointed to the different chairs of anatomy, physiology etc., they were only finally approved by the Board in July 6th, 1898[xlvi]. The 1898 Catalogue states *"For the first time in the history of the school, practical work will be done in physiology and psychology"*[xlvii]. So even though others taught physiology before him, this was the first time that a full course was taught; and while Pressly had been appointed Professor of Physiology he had to resign before the appointment was confirmed.

During his first year in Kirksville it's reasonable to feel that Littlejohn felt that he had found his niche in life, his purpose, or preordained path if you like. He was enthralled by the natural philosophy of osteopathy and its application in the healing profession and this appealed to him not only as a philosopher but as a teacher in the educational field.

His health and that of his father was improved with treatment, his family was together with good positions and prospects, in particular James B was moved away from the influence of the Lodge in Chicago and back under the direct influence of his father. As ever he put himself to work with all the enthusiasm of a reformer, educator and philosopher.

The new science needed a good foundation and he preceded with trying to establish this in the field of education and research. To encourage students, he initiated a Gold medal for physiology[15] He started to write text books on subjects that hitherto had been missing or incomplete in the field of osteopathy – Physiology[xlviii], Psycho-

---

[15] H. H. McIntyre, M. D., of the Senior Class, won the medal offered by Dean Littlejohn in the competitive examination in physiology (Journal of osteopathy March 1899, page 402)

physiology and started experiments in philosophy with C. M. T. Hulett (the then Dean.) and a student H .V. Goetz[xlix].

"They carried out some experiments on dogs in an old barn in Osteopathy Street and their first work was concerned with the effects of stimulation and inhibition in relation to manipulation of the spinal area." (First School of Osteopathic Medicine by Georgia Warner, Walter page 79)

We also find evidence of this in the Osteopathic Physician when Goetz and Littlejohn were talking about how osteopathic research started.[l]

In this context we note that He was driven by his study of moral and natural philosophy and taken by the theory and philosophy of Still and terms of human health. Health being based on the principle of the perfection of the human body both physically, mechanically and physiologically. However, to quote a phrase often used by J. Wernham, *"if we let expediency override conscience then we lose"*. If Littlejohn did let expediency to overrule his conscience this would have, we can assume, hurt him to some extent.

There are a few occasions when we find that he may have crossed that line for reasons of expediency, and I feel that these costs him dearly. When you don't follow your conscience or go against your conscience it leaves a mark that is hard to erase.

We know that from his association with the Christian Nation as editor that he had close association with people who were adamant anti-vivisectionists. We have noted before the review of Salts book on animal rights and even though there is nothing directly in Littlejohn's writing about vivisection and his views on it, it would be hard to imagine that he would have been so closely associated with those of that belief without sharing at least some of their fundamental beliefs, implying that for him to use animal experiments there would have to have been overwhelming reasons.

The Reformed Presbyterian movement itself at that time had a considerable section of anti-vivisectionists who were in favour of the rights of animals that while man was given dominion over them, he was not to abuse them.

So even though it was expedient and practical and perhaps could be argued necessary to start experimenting on animals to give a firm foundation to the physiological aspects of osteopathy it would in my opinion have at least pricked if not wounded Littlejohn's conscience (I must admit to a strong bias here being particularly anti-vivisection myself, and perhaps I am simply reading my own views into this.)

Littlejohn, Still and Physiology

In the June – August 1935 edition of the Journal of Osteopathy, British School of Osteopathy, Littlejohn talks about his life at this time,

"He (Still) finally grasped the idea that the regulative control of the distributive machinery rested in the articulation fields of the body and the co-operation of all the articulating structures within the machinery of the body……..it was this thought that led to his final conclusion, the osteopathic lesion, which he defined as the abnormal fixation of any jointure in the machinery of the body inside the range of its own normal physiological movement. Time and again we sat beside him, walked with him along the road and listened to him repeating this wonderful, seemingly mythical idea. At last it dawned upon our mind, when his deft fingers rectified our own body mechanism, that while Dr. Still started out in his discovery in the realm of applied anatomy, the anatomical structures and relations of the many parts of the human body, he finally settled down in reaching his final conclusions in the realm of applied physiology, viz., the application of mobility to all parts of the machinery of the human body. It is for this reason that ever since Dr. Still revealed his principles to us we have spoken of applied anatomy and physiology as the great bedrock upon which osteopathy, its theory and technique, are built[li]

> *"What books and studies are necessary to a complete education in the science of Osteopathy? Is a question to which I have given much thought, and after a quarter of a century- in this work I have reached the conclusion that every successful operator should fully understand Anatomy, Physiology and Chemistry. Your knowledge of these three books and the principles which they teach must be thorough. When I say Anatomy, Physiology and Chemistry, I mean if you fully understand these branches you are a star of the greatest magnitude"* A T Still Aug 1897 Journal of osteopathy

In the same vain we find that Still himself wrote of the need for the student to understand chemistry and physiology for without this he would not be an efficient manager of the mechanism of the human body.

> "**An Osteopath...must master Anatomy and Physiology and have a fairly good knowledge of chemistry; then he can reason from the effect to the cause that gives rise to the abnormal effect or disease.**" A T Still on Adjuncts museum of Osteopathy Kirksville ref. 12/30/2016

Still and Littlejohn were in agreement on the issue of physiology[lii]. Some have said this was an area over which Still and Littlejohn had serious disagreements. This seems to be based upon the "no Physiology" story; which has been so perverted over the years that it has been related to me as Still bursting into a lecture being given by Littlejohn, pushing him aside, and writing 'no physiology' on the board!

Carol Trowbridge in her book on Andrew Taylor Still stated this quite clearly.

"The Littlejohn Smith influence irritated Still enough to write a terse note to Harry Bunting in 1899 concerning the improved status of the Journal of Osteopathy when he stated my school was chartered to teach osteopathy only, he eluded to series of disagreements within the A.S.O. One early osteopath recalled that on several occasions Still closed the school to argue with the staff over the compatibility of medical diagnosis and osteopathy. One student remembered the time Still stormed into a class and furiously wrote on the blackboard "no physiology".[liii]

It's an interesting quote, an interesting line of thought, unfortunately it is inaccurate.

Trowbridge seems to have quoted several people out of context. The one early osteopath recalling on several occasions that Still closed the school to argue with staff over the compatibility of medical diagnosis and osteopathy was H.S. Sullivan who was referring to his time in the school and he graduated in 1896[liv] and went to Chicago in 1897[lv]

In a talk in Oct 1926 (the Victoria incident) he says *"as I have said before, my close contact with Dr. Still for several years was a privilege of untold worth to me...His constant worry was over the introduction of medical textbooks into the school. On several occasions he closed the school for a day or two because of the conflict between medical diagnosis and osteopathy. I recall a controversy between those in control and the old Doctor, it was over the curriculum being enlarged. It was claimed the school would fall behind unless a more extensive curriculum was formulated."* [lvi]

As I mentioned above Sullivan graduated in 1896 and moved to Chicago to take over Harry Still and Hildreth's practice. He did maintain a close relationship with Still, but the likelihood is the School closure incidents he is talking about happened during his time at Kirksville and the other one refers to the extension of the curriculum after the Osteopathic Bill was vetoed 1895 and the subsequent changes in the teaching as published in Journal of osteopathy June 1896 .

> *"This Bill does not require any course of instruction in autotomy or physiology or knowledge of any science or knowledge of anything except osteopathy. Osteopathy consists of some description of manipulation of the human body or some part of it...   How all this can be done is a secret. This secret is called osteopathy."*
>
> W. J. Stone, Governor Missouri
>
> As published in Journal of Osteopathy March 1895

"When my building was completed, and I was ready to organize my college I employed such counsel and teachers, as I thought essential I to give instructions in the various branches necessary to make a qualified Osteopathic operator. I was careful to employ as secretary, one that would execute my plans-not his plans nor their plans, but my plans, both in construction of buildings and all conveniences. When the school was finally organized, **I called the professors together, in a body, and told them what I expected to have taught**[16]. I did not ask their opinion what was best to be taught, because they were not Osteopaths to begin with. I began and enforced special instructions in anatomy, because of its importance in Osteopathy; **Physiology of no less importance**[17] in health producing; Histology for its great importance as an auxiliary knowledge; and elementary chemistry for its comparative usefulness." (A T Still, Oct 1898 Journal of Osteopathy) [18]

The student who remembered a time Still storming into a classroom and furiously writing on the blackboard 'no physiology' was Edwin C. Pickler and his time in the school was much earlier graduating in 1895[lvii]. His actual quote, from the Journal of the American osteopathic association Jan 1921, is,

"One day he (Still) came in with fire in his eyes. Picking up a piece of chalk he walked to the blackboard and wrote two words: "No Physiology." We were amazed until he told us that physiology was a mass of contradictions and uncertainties, that we had better not believe any of it unless we could prove it up. He said: "Let the piffle and poppy-cock go." His attitude was afterwards modified to a certain extent, although he often told me that three-fourths of it was worse than useless."

---

[16] Bold emphasis by author

[17] Bold emphasis by author

[18] He was talking about the building of his school – probably in 1896; The new building is described in detail in the December 1896 issue of the Journal of Osteopathy and was completed in 1897 (First School of osteopathic Medicine page 22). The original building was dedicated on January 10th, 1895 (the Lengthening Shadow of Dr. A T Still, page 44)

He goes on in the next paragraph to refer to the tragic loss of Still's son, Fred, who died in June 1894[lviii] as being around this same time as the above incident.

So, neither incident has any connection with Littlejohn. In fact, Still goes further in his insistence on Physiology.

His attitude seems best summed up in the phrases **"we had better not believe any of it unless we could prove it"** and **""An Osteopath...must master Anatomy and Physiology and have a fairly good knowledge of chemistry; then he can reason from the effect to the cause that gives rise to the abnormal effect or disease."** But not let it lead into the application of drugs in the treatment of disease.

Also, it was in February 14th, 1899 that A.T. Still wrote the note to Bunting, the editor of the Journal of Osteopathy, saying that the journal was better now and suits him, but he had nearly considered cancelling it completely to stop the useless waste of money. He goes on to say that

"my school[19] was chartered to teach osteopathy only and now it must foot its own expenses or go to the waste basket I am willing to give it a reasonable time to do so. I think that it can easily be done if there is any brains in the running of it. Do the best you can."[lix]

This was at the same time as they were proposing a new journal. Still was considering dropping the old one and his reference to the school being to 'teach osteopathy only' can be taken in a number of ways. Others have taken it to mean that a reference to the teaching within the school.

However, if you read the note as it is written, it refers to the Journal of Osteopathy and that the school was to teach osteopathy not to produce journals and so on which would be a waste of money.

In other words, it had nothing to do with the teaching within the school itself.

The adage that the victorious write the history seems to be quite true. It's quite easy to take famous quotations and to place them in the context we want rather than where they belong.

---

[19] My School was underlined by Still in the original letter

Surgery and Osteopathy

The advent of the surgical sanatorium and the teaching of surgery in the School in September 1898 would have caused some controversy. It was announced as follows in the Sept 1898 Journal of Osteopathy:

"This is in line with the design of the school, one of the objects of which is, according to the charter 'improve our present system of surgery'. According to the statement published in the new catalogue of the American School of Osteopathy " the introduction of surgery into the realm of Osteopathy is the culminating point where these two accurate sister sciences are placed side by side."

"There are cases in which surgery is a necessity and recognizing such cases it is our intention to use the surgeon's instrument only where such a necessity exists, thus indicating the path along which regenerated surgery may be directed so as to set up the twin sciences, Surgery and Osteopathy, as correlative departments of the great science of medicine. Discarding the use of and denying the necessity of drugology we believe that we have a perfect science of medicine whose function is to preserve health and life, and when attacks are made upon the human system in any of its parts by disease, accident or malpractice so to employ the enlightened principles of Osteopathy and Surgery as to maintain the even balance of life and make life worth living".[ix]

The surgical sanatorium did cause some controversy as surgery by its very nature demands a high degree of resources of an institution and the introduction of the teaching of anaesthesia and drugs to some extent. However, at the same time it created an enhanced reputation for the Kirksville school, especially with the addition of the X-Ray equipment. This may have been the beginning of problems within the faculty and between the Littlejohns, Smith and Hildreth.

James B. Littlejohn, having arrived in Kirksville in the middle of the spring term, is listed as Professor of Histology, Bacteriology and Minor surgery[lxi]. He took over the Histology from Hazzard and freed him to concentrate on Principles of Osteopathy. By the August edition Major surgery was openly advertised "the A T Still Infirmary equipped for the most difficult cases."

Then for the term beginning in Sept 98 David Littlejohn[20] arrives in the School and it is announced that X-ray equipment is to be purchased.

In the august 1898 edition of the journal of osteopathy we find the first announcement that *"the A.T. Still Infirmary equipped for the most difficult cases…. Difficult cases will have the personal care of Professors (J B) Littlejohn and Smith with their able assistants…. Cases requiring careful and delicate surgery, the removal of fibroid tumors, and in fact any operation of whatever nature will receive the best and most scientific treatment and care in this institution…..Patients coming to the A.T. Still Infirmary may rely upon the fact that they will in no case be subjected to unnecessary surgical operations, as the knife is never used unless absolutely necessary."*

This was a major change with major surgery now on the curriculum and agenda for the first time. With this change the need for more technical education into the syllabus. J B Littlejohn also had part of the Infirmary building fitted with all the necessary improvements and equipment for a "complete surgical sanatorium" and would select cases for operation before the surgical classes.

Part of this was explained in the sept 1898 journal of osteopathy. *"in the classes in surgery however its (X-Ray) recognized usefulness will be fully explained and exemplified, and students will be carefully instructed in the technique of its operation as well as in the selection of cases for its application"* [lxii]

J.B. Littlejohn continued to improve and further the surgical wing of the college. This would have meant the introduction of the study of drugs, anesthetics and pain relief of necessity and this would have gone against the hardline views of Hildreth. Even though Hildreth himself would have felt the necessity of surgery at certain times but he would have tried to keep osteopathy separate from it.

---

[20] David Littlejohn PH. B., M.D., was still on the faculty of the Central medical college in March 1898 (The Saint Joseph Daily Herald, Wednesday March 2nd, 1898)

We can compare Littlejohn's ideas with those of Hildreth from the following quotes.

> ### Hildreth's ideas on surgery
>
> *"so far as our surgical sanatorium is concerned, it has been discontinued, and we never want it again in connection with the institution. There are plenty of good surgeons in the city, who have spent their lives to educate themselves for their work, and we want them to have it"* (Letter to Leslie D Smith May 1900, Museum of osteopathy, Kirksville)
>
> *"This hospital marks an epoch in the history of osteopathy."* Dedication speech for the new hospital and the introduction of teaching major surgery" (May 1906 Journal of Osteopathy page 190)
>
> *"our school at the present time (1903) was not even trying to qualify our graduates for the practice of surgery. We believe that when the need for osteopathic surgeons came, we would prepare them and make them better qualified than the majority of those medical men practicing surgery at that time.* (The Lengthening Shadow of Dr. A T Still, A G Hildreth, page 153)
>
> *Osteopathic surgeons who have been properly trained will know the value of preoperative and postoperative osteopathic care.* (Ibid, page 207)

Hildreth shows the expediency of a true politician. At one time saying that he doesn't ever want surgery in the American School of Osteopathy and is happy to leave it to Allopathic trained surgeons; later when the new hospital and surgical training were introduced he was perfectly happy to give the dedication speech, changing his attitude to say how much better osteopathically trained surgeons would be. His words were almost identical to those used in the September 1898

Journal of Osteopathy to describe the then introduction of surgery by Littlejohn and Wm Smith[21].

Littlejohn, in contrast, maintained the same view throughout his career, respecting and acting upon the foundation that Still had laid out in the charter for the American School of Osteopathy. In the charter it is stated, *'the object of this corporation is to establish a college of osteopathy the design of which is to improve our present system of surgery, obstetrics and treatment of diseases generally and place the same on a more rational and scientific basis"*[lxiii]

> *"If surgery is a necessity in certain cases, we ought to be able to deal with such cases: If we believe that modern surgery represents a mania for needless operations, the Osteopath can reform this only by applying Osteopathic surgery to cases that demand it. This is in line with the charter purpose of this Institution" which designs to improve our present system of surgery."*
>
> Littlejohn's address to the graduating class Oct 1898 Dec 1898 Journal of osteopathy

By March 1899 the surgical and X-ray departments had become so successful that it merited special mention-

---

[21] "so that the class of patients hitherto recommended to go elsewhere will be attended to in the future entirely under the supervision of the combined Osteopathic and Surgical operator. This has its advantage because Osteopathy can be of great service in preparing patients for surgical operation and also in toning up the system and regulating the circulation of the blood and the nervous system after the operation has been performed". (Journal of osteopathy, September 1898, page 202)

"It has become the custom for practitioners in surrounding states to bring their difficult cases to Kirksville for diagnosis in the X-Ray department. Dr. David Littlejohn's skiagraphs are as fine as are made anywhere in the world"[lxiv]

"The A. T. Still surgical sanatorium is now prepared to receive patients and to give them first-class professional attention in every respect. Within the last ten days several cases have been treated, notably an excision of the mammary gland and a resection of the rib. The latter being to overcome the results of an injury sustained several years ago by which the rib fractured and driven into the pleural cavity, keeping up a constant irritation of the lung.[lxv]

March 1899 edition also had a special article devoted to "unusual Osteopathic and Surgical opportunities offered patients at Kirksville. Again, putting the surgical side by side with the Osteopathic and giving full details of the qualifications (medical) of James B, David Littlejohn and Wm Smith. It finishes by saying "There is not another institution to be found where the same advantages for both Osteopathy and operative surgery are obtainable."[lxvi]

This progression would have brought to the fore the conflict found in most medical institutions between the demands for resources and recognition between physicians and surgeons. It would be a new experience for the osteopaths and for the ASO. Teaching Surgery also needed the teaching of anesthetics, pain relief and other "drugs" which would have been seen as amounting to heresy by some.

With Hildreth more or less in charge of the Infirmary during 1898 and his devotion to "unadulterated osteopathy" and lack of experience with surgery it would not be unexpected for him to react and to perhaps "provoke" reaction in the other infirmary osteopathic operators and students and for this to contribute further to the future problems between him Smith and the Littlejohns.

When we move into the next term and Littlejohn continues his work and Hulett decides to leave to form his own practice in Chicago, Hulett and the rest of the faculty nominate J.M. Littlejohn to succeed him as Dean. This was in December of 1898 with Hulett leaving in February 1899[lxvii].

Two other incidents, late in 1898, need to be examined. These are the unfortunate tragic deaths of two students.

Tragic deaths of two students

In the last quarter of 1898, a double tragedy struck the students at the Kirksville College. Just when the Littlejohns were settling in and John Martin impressing the faculty with his organizational and educational abilities, improving the syllabus of physiology and J. B. with his skill and passion for surgery. In the November '98 journal we find an announcement about the death of Edward Eckert, a young student in the school who was in the class of April '97 with I presume his two brothers George J. Eckert and W. H. Eckert. And then in the December '98 we note the sudden death of another student Miss Lelia Morehead, aged 26. She was in the September '97 class.

What I feel is important about these two deaths is the effect it would have had on their fellow students and on the debate, that was going on not only within the college but within osteopathy about osteopathy, the treatment of disease, and whether adjuncts or other modalities like medicine and drugs or even surgery should be used. In the In Memoriam about Miss Morehead we find no reference to osteopathic treatment, however we do find the following *"when the doctor was called in, he pronounced the case a low type of fever, between malaria and typhoid which ended in gastritis. ..... All was done for her that friends and doctors could do, but to no purpose."*[lxviii] It would be a natural assumption to make that these were medical doctors that were called and not doctors of osteopathy, particularly when 'not many of her classmates and other friends knew of her illness'.[lxix] However, we cannot be sure. However, the loss of someone so young and overtly healthy to a fever which osteopathy is said to be able to treat is bound to have raised questions and to some extent doubts.

The case of young Mr. Eckert is more problematic. The In Memoriam is written by William Smith who was a friend of Eckhart and he says *"Suffering cruel pain, the pain of peritonitis, he bore it like a man, fearing to give utterance to a groan lest it would distress his father and sister. Half an hour before his death Dr. J. B. Littlejohn and I called to see him. ..... And so, passes out of our school history one of the best, bravest, kindest hearted boys whom I have ever known, and I feel that there is a blank in my classroom which will take months to fill."*[lxx]

Smith was obviously deeply affected by the loss of this student and the fact that he brought J. B. Littlejohn to see him gives me the impression that he was seeking his opinion as to the case and as to whether surgery would be recommended.

> "I got to know Ed Eckert better out of school than I did in it; we spent two vacations together. His classmates know only one side of his character, the happy-go-lucky, jolly, laughing, dare-devil boy: the boy of whom they all said "No one can bluff out Ed Eckert", but there was a far other side to his character, the mind of a man of experience in the world, the gentleness of a woman; the tender solicitude and kindness of a nurse ; the unselfish devotion of a true friend. Poor boy, cut down on the threshold of manhood; dying just as life was beginning" "
>
> Journal of Osteopathy, Kirksville
> Nov. 1898, page 303; In Memoriam

Unfortunately, this consultation took place only half an hour before Mr. Eckert's demise. In this respect it's also worth noting that W. H. Eckert took over Hildreth's practice in St. Louis when Hildreth returned to Kirksville in September 1899. It would not be beyond imagination or unreasonable to assume that Hildreth had been involved in the treatment, even if in an advisory capacity, of young Mr. Eckert and if this was the case it would certainly be more than sufficient cause for Smith to have a serious problem with Hildreth

I know there is a lot of assumptions in this, and we may never get to the truth of the matter, but at the very least the loss of two students in the prime of their life in the home and heartland of osteopathy with the best of osteopathic physicians available to treat them would have brought into question whether something more than osteopathy could have been offered or perhaps should osteopathy not have been more involved in the treatment (of Miss Morehead). Given that W. H. Eckert went to work with Hildreth and took over his practice in St. Louis we can assume that the Eckerts including the unfortunate E. C. Eckert had great faith in Hildreth and continued to do so even after E. C. Eckert's demise. This would have meant that Smith would have been unable to express his concerns or his hurt or angst against Hildreth or the possible delay or refusal to consider surgery in his case. If this is true or even partially true it would certainly leave an undercurrent boiling up under the surface between Smith and Hildreth and would have almost certainly have affected J. M. Littlejohn and may answer the question as to how Hildreth had made himself so objectionable to Smith and the Littlejohns.

To understanding the possible relevance of these cases, in particular Eckert, it is necessary to look at the narrative at the time in the American School of osteopathy concerning appendicitis. Still wrote, in April 1898, *"successes in finding substances in the vermiform appendix, their removal, and successful recovery in some cases, have led to what may properly be termed a hasty system of diagnosis, and it has become very prevalent, and resorted to by physicians of many schools, under the impression that the vermiform appendix is of no known use and that the human being is just as well off without it.... as a general rule it is a useless and dangerous experiment. The percent of deaths caused by the knife and ether, and the permanently crippled, will justify the assertion that it would be far better for the human race if they lived and died in ignorance of appendicitis. A few general cases might die from that cause;* **but if the knife were the only known remedy, it were better that one should occasionally die than to continue this system,**[22] *at least until the world recognizes a relief which is absolutely safe, without the loss of a drop of blood, that has for its foundation and philosophy a fact*

---

[22] Bold emphasis by author; could this be referring indirectly to the death of Eckert and trying to end speculation regarding the lost opportunity of surgical intervention in that case.

based upon the longitudinal contractile ability of the appendix itself, which is able to eject by its natural forces any substances that may, by an unnatural move , be forced into the appendix. To a philosopher such questions as this must arise: ... Has God been so forgetful as to leave the appendix in such a condition as to receive foreign bodies without preparing it by contraction or otherwise to throw out such substances? If he has, He surely forgot part of His work. So, reason has concluded for me, and on that line, I have proceeded to operate without pain or misery to the patient and give permanent relief in seventy-five percent of all cases which have come to me. With the former diagnosis of doctors and surgeons that appendicitis was the malady and the choice of relief was the knife or death , or possibly both , many such cases have come for Osteopathic treatment , and examination has revealed that in every case there has been previous injury to some set of spinal nerves caused by jars, sprains, or falls . Every case of appendicitis, gall or renal stones can be traced to some such ca use."[lxxi]

In august 1899, the Journal carried a report of a case that two physicians had diagnosed as appendicitis and that an operation was the only recourse. It required only eight minutes of osteopathic treatment to cure the case.[lxxii]

With this narrative and Hildreth being, in his own words, so *'ultra-osteopathic and would tolerate none other than the strictest adherence to the teaching of osteopathy in the way that Dr. Still himself had taught"*[lxxiii], it is not hard to see how the situation with young Eckert could have played out.

The Agreement

"the protest we offered to you against the retention of Dr. Arthur Hildreth in violation of our contract with you that he was no to be connected with the school during the year 1899-1900".[lxxiv]

Hildreth had left the school in 1896 to go into practice in Chicago only to come back in 1897 and again leave to go into practice early in 1899. It could be argued that when Hulett resigned as Dean he may have felt slighted that the faculty recommended J M Littlejohn to the position and Still approved. He may even have felt that Littlejohn with just one year of osteopathy was poorly qualified compared to his 9 years – the reverse of what he said about his lack of higher education being part of the reason the Littlejohns did not want to work with him[lxxv]. Then when the infirmary's venture into serious surgery took off, he again may have felt his position as an "osteopathic surgeon" was under threat.

Hildreth announce his intention to leave the school and set up practice in St. Louis in the January 1899 Journal of osteopathy.[23] Thus his stay at Kirksville was relatively short, having only returned in May 1897 at the request of the trustees to again leave at the end of 1898. The coincidence of this with the expansion of the Infirmary to include major surgery and X-Ray diagnosis, the tragic death of the two students, the upcoming appointment of J M Littlejohn as Dean and the seeming approval of the faulty, students and his mentor A .T. Still of the changes is too much to ignore.

With Hildreth leaving to start his practice the conflict involving the Littlejohns, Smith and Hildreth could be avoided simply by entering into an agreement that Hildreth would "have nothing to do with the faculty" for the 1899/1900 term. This makes it seem likely that C E Still had made this agreement after Hildreth had left. His thinking might have been that this would solve the problem that had arisen because "Arthur Hildreth has made himself objectionable to us (Smith and the three Littlejohn brothers) in many ways"[24]. How Hildreth had made himself objectionable was probably related to all the factors noted above.

Later in the spring of 1899, Harry M Still joined Hildreth's practice in St Louis in response to the growth of the practice[lxxvi]. He was not due to stay long, returning to the school in May 1899.

"Harry Still Returns to Kirksville, Dr. Harry M. Still, second vice president of the American School of Osteopathy, has returned to Kirksville out of regard for the urgent demands for his services at the A. T. Still Infirmary. In the short time of his association with Dr. A. G. Hildreth at 708

---

[23] The announcement was carried in the Jan 1899 Journal of Osteopathy as follows:
"Dr. Hildreth Opens an Office in St. Louis, Dr. Arthur Grant Hildreth, one of the first disciples to whom Dr. A. T. Still imparted his system and who by his years of faithful friendship to his tutor won the title "Fidus Achates" (*A faithful friend or devoted follower*) among Osteopaths, has severed his connection with the A. T. Still Infirmary and will devote himself to office practice...The best wishes of all his former associates, and of students and patients-most of whom he had come to know personally in his years at Kirksville-go with him.

[24] Letter to Trustees Nov 23rd, 1899

Commercial Building, St. Louis. A large practice was built up and many new friends were won over to Osteopathy. Dr. Hildreth will remain in St. Louis to take care of this practice....Dr. Harry Still's extensive circle of friends and local patients are glad of his return".[lxxvii]

The Good Times

Even with all of this going on, 1898 went very well for Littlejohn and 1899 started out well and on a good note, with him being recommended by the faculty and made Dean. However, it was to turn out to be an altogether different year. The year started with his election as Fellow of the Royal Society of Literature in January. This nomination was by the usual method of two current members in nominating him.[lxxviii]

> "Kirksville is rejoicing with one of its prominent physicians over a new distinction that has come to him recently. Dr. Littlejohn, of the faculty of the School of Osteopathy, already a fellow of the Society of Science, Letters and Art, of London, has just been notified of his selection to membership in the Royal Society of Literature there."
>
> (Kansas City journal January 23rd, 1899)

Another event took place in January 1899 that would have brought joy to the Littlejohns and Smith.

"Dr. David Littlejohn, at the head of t h e X-Ray department, and Miss Mary Forbes, the sister of Mrs. Dr. William Smith, were united in marriage, January 26th, spending the honeymoon in Canada".[lxxix] John Martin Littlejohn and his father Rev. James Littlejohn officiated. It was reported that "The wedding was very quiet, only the families of the contracting parties, together with Dr. and Mrs. C. E. Still and little daughter Gladys, and Misses Blanche Still and Ethel Soles, being present...An elegant breakfast was served, and Dr. and Mrs. Littlejohn *left on the 10 o'clock train for a short trip to Chicago and other points in Illinois."*[lxxx]

As a counterpoint to this happy event, as stated in the introduction Littlejohn was associated with Blanche Still. She however had other designs and eventually married Laughlin, who became Dean in 1900/01.

At the end of the June 1898 he gave the Commencement address to the graduating class. In it he laid out his vision of Osteopathy as a drugless form of medicine[lxxxi]. The following phrases he used sum up his attitude;

"I have used the word medicine several times. It comes from medicus medicina and medeor to heal."

"The science of medicine deals with the preservation and. prolongation of human life and with the prevention and cure of those abnormal conditions, or diseases which threaten and destroy life. In the presence of the founder of Osteopathy I dare not attempt to define Osteopathy. It is sufficient to say it presumes that the body is a perfect mechanism and that when it becomes disordered, nature has within her own resourceful economy all of nature's remedies. All that is needed is the magic hand of a skillful operator to bring these remedies to the aid of a diseased part.

"The difference between allopathy and homeopathy on the one side and Osteopathy on the other, is that in the case of Osteopathy no medicine is used at all except nature's medicine.
Do not be content to go out and give general treatments.
Remember that here is the danger of Osteopathy as it has been the danger point of drugs.
"The operator who simply gives general treatments in the hope of hitting the right spot is in the same box. Hence, we need specialists who know just where and how to treat."
A theme he would continue in his address to the June 1998 graduates.)
"You are not sent out with a set of formulae to put down under the great R[25], *nor are you given a number of technical punches and movements like massage and fake Osteopaths; you are sent out with principles and a correct knowledge of anatomy and physiology to apply these in the correction of diseased and disordered conditions."*[lxxxii]

---

[25] The great R refers to the general shorthand for prescription R_x

After the commencement of the graduation exercises Littlejohn spent the summer in Britain and having got in touch with "literary and scientific friends in my native land, "he had been invited to give a paper on osteopathy to the Society of Science, Letters and Art in London in July 1898[lxxxiii]. There remains some confusion about the title of this talk. In the Journal of the British School of Osteopathy December 1929 and July/August 1935 it states that the topic he choose was "Osteopathy in the line of Apostolic Succession with Medicine"-. This would have been the one he gave to the graduating class in February 1899 However, in his notes on his European tour in the October 1903 edition of The Osteopathic World, he states that the talk was *"In 1898, the first paper on "osteopathy" was read in absentia, prepared from the substance of an address delivered to the graduating class at the A. S. O. June."*

It is true that if we read his addresses to the graduates in June and October 1898 and again in February 1899, we find a progression of thought. The article written in 1903 would seem to be more accurate. However, the February 1899 address, being more like a progression of thought and the 1929 article being written so much later and not by Littlejohn himself, secondhand errors do occur.

These papers show his thinking on osteopathy. That it was not a separate development from medicine but was an evolution of and a reformation of the medical system; That drugs had no place in it and that specificity in treatment based upon anatomy and physiology was the aim rather than quick single 'adjustment' or long 'general' treatments[26]. These ideas were in line with Still original thought that he wanted to re-form medicine and fits in with Littlejohn's approach as a reformer and educationalist.

The rest of his first year in Kirksville continued with more innovation and honours.

---

[26] There was during this time a debate about long vs short treatment **"the offending vertebra is treated (which it can be) in less than ten minutes. What is done during the other forty or fifty minutes"** (J H Sullivan; Journal of Osteopathy, October 1898, page 239). Others were quoted as saying **"don't allow anyone to give you three minutes shocks and call it osteopathy"** (Journal of Osteopathy June 1899, page 36).

> Kirksville is rejoicing with one of its prominent physicians over a new distinction that has come to him recently. Dr. LittleJohn, of the faculty of the American School of Osteopathy, already a fellow of the Society of Science Letters and art of London, has just been notified of his selection to membership of the Royal Society of Literature there.
>
> Kansas City journal January 23rd, 1899

He was instrumental in the establishment of the young men's Christian association in the college[lxxxiv], becoming the president[lxxxv] of the association and conduction regular bible classes[lxxxvi]. In December 1898, he was chosen to replace Hulett as the American School of Osteopathy's representative to the Associated Colleges of Osteopathy. In the same month, he was directly instrumental in the formation of the Student representative council in the school.[lxxxvii] This was to be a 'deliberative body only' but could petition the faculty or board on matters concerning student interest This was something he obviously felt strongly about having been involved in the student council in Glasgow university.

Then in mid-December, Hulett having announced his intention to resign, He was recommended by the faculty to the board of trustees for election to the office of Dean[lxxxviii], which was to become vacant on 1st February 1899. His regard within the faculty and board was also in evidence by his selection to give the address at the June and October graduating classes[lxxxix]

As the new year dawned his fortunes continued. In January 1899 his election as a member of the Royal Society of Literature was announced in the local papers.

Around this time Littlejohn received the Gold Medal of the Society of Science, Letters and Art, London for 1898 in recognition for his work contributing to science. "This work comprised, in the main, textbooks on 'Physiology, Exhaustive and Practical' and 'Physiological Psychology'[xc] which he prepared from the Osteopathic standpoint for use in the American School of Osteopathy" standpoint for use in the American School of Osteopathy"

The juxta position of the Royal Society of Literature and the Society of Science, Letters and Art of London in this notice was to cause some confusion later on. Some leaving out the 'L' in RSL and shortening it to 'Royal Society'[27], possibly thinking the 'L' stood for 'London'; others combining the two into 'Royal Science Society' and other variants adding confusion to an already confusing situation as we shall see later. Probably the most significant example of this is to be found in the December 1899 issue of the American Osteopath. Littlejohns paper in the Journal is titled;

"THE POSITION OF OSTEOPATHY IN THE FIELD OF THERAPEUTICS"
By J. Martin Littlejohn, Ph. D., L.L. D., F. R. S. L. & F. S. Sc. (London)

While' the 'Contents', on the front cover lists Littlejohn' as paper as

"The position of Osteopathy in the Field of Therapeutics"
By J. Martin Littlejohn, Ph. D., L.L. D., F. R. S. & F. S. Sc. (London)

The type setters taking the 'L' at the end of F. R. S. as meaning 'London' simply left it out and assumed that the two titles were from 'London'. So, even though Littlejohn, on the heading of the paper he submitted put the correct letters after his name, the effect from the type-setters error would be that the front cover implied something else. Remember what was happening with Littlejohn at this time in Kirksville. I don't think he would have noticed, given the confrontation he was having with the school management at that time. However, the journal was going out to many osteopaths and would be widely read.

He was also admitted to the Bar during April 1899[xci]

---

[27] A good example of this is found in The Philadelphia Times, November 19th, 1899, page 38. *"Osteopathy is young. Her literature is as yet scant, and save the Royal Society, of London, England, no recognized scientific body has thoroughly investigated her claims. The members of that society bestowed upon Dr. J. Martin Littlejohn, F.R.S., (London), the gold medal in appreciation of his most able article on 'Osteopathy' read before that august assembly last July."* Thus, confusing the Society of Science, Letters and Art (F.Sc.L.&A), The Royal Society of Literature, (F.R.S.L.) and The Royal Society (F.R.S.)

With David's wedding and him and James Buchan settling into their respective roles in the School, Littlejohn's life must have seemed content and full.

Graduating class commencement exercises February 1ST, 1899[xcii]

At the end of his first year Littlejohn wrote the lecture for the graduation ceremony for the February 1899 class. The topic he chose was 'Osteopathy in the line of Apostolic Succession with Medicine'. That Osteopathy was not a separate development from medicine but was an evolution of and a reformation of the medical system. This was in line with Still's original thought that he wanted to reform medicine and fits in with Littlejohn's approach as a reformer and educationalist. Putting this into context, it may have further influenced C.E. Still in his opinion of Littlejohn. It has been said that A.T. Still and Littlejohn got on well and that it was his son Charlie Still that was the problem. That Charlie saw that he may be not only losing influence with his father but perhaps losing control of the school to a better educated, more philosophical and perhaps better manager than himself.[28]

Littlejohn himself was too ill at the time to give the speech. It was given by Dr. Smith in his absence and at the end of it Still gave another clear endorsement of Littlejohn and the other teachers at the school at the time[xciii].

"It was the most auspicious commencement event that has yet dawned for the parent college of osteopathy. It was the largest class ever graduate into the profession of osteopathy. The average intelligence of

---

[28]Personal communication with Jerry Dickey D.O. also "They seemed to think Littlejohn had too much influence over their father, and when he began courting Blanche they had to act. The son's motives were anything but pure; they were waiting to inherit this money machine- ASO…. All this was told to me by Blanche's daughter Mary Jane Laughlin Denslow, who adopted me into the Still-Laughlin family in 1972." **This is of course just an opinion and conjecture and not stated as a fact.**

the class was high, and no previous graduates had enjoyed as great facilities for pursuing the several courses of the curriculum.

"The invocation was to be made by Dr. J. Martin Littlejohn but owing to a cold he was unable to deliver his address. Dr. Smith read it in his stead, giving every word of the able discourse utterance that might have reached even the deaf throughout the hall. The Glee Club interluded with two selections. Then this brief address was read for President Still by Dr. J. B. Littlejohn:

"As Dr. Still did not know in advance whether he would have strength enough to take a personal part in the program he committed this message to paper. With the enthusiasm of the hour, he felt a speech by proxy inadequate and just before the awarding of diplomas stepped to the speaker's rostrum and supplemented his first farewell with an eulogy of Dr. Littlejohn's address and a second God-speed to the graduates. He said, **'After listening to Dr. Littlejohn's masterly address I feel like saying to him and to you all what my old father said to his boys after he set us to plowing and doing other things which we came to do by degrees to his entire satisfaction: 'Boys, you are doing mighty well-I am not sure but you are beating me at it-yes, I think you are.'** "[29]

We find further evidence of Stills endorsement of what was happening at the school by two quotes, one in a letter concerning "all the old 'gods', have now left and all is smoother in the school"[xciv]

> "85 graduated Feb 2. had a good time School opened with 102. Over 100 more will be added says the clerk. **All the old gods are out of the school now**, and all is smothe(sic) now."

This was written at the beginning of 1899[30] (Hulett had his last faculty meeting as Dean on Jan 27th, 1899 and Littlejohn his first as Dean on the 7th Feb 1899)[xcv]. This gives the clear impression that Still held the view that with he was happy with LittleJohn as Dean.

---

[29] The Bold and italics are mine
[30] Letter dated 1899 Feb 7, A.T. Still to [the Orschel family] of Chicago

The second article was published in October 1898 Journal of Osteopathy were Still outlines how he set up the school, why he set it up and that when he did set it up everything that was taught in it was what he wanted to be taught.[31] While the incidents Still refers to in the article happened much earlier the timing of the article, October 1898, would seem to indicate that he was saying that what was taught in the school was as he himself wished it to be at the end of 1898.

Stills basic thesis in this article was that everything that was being taught in the school was being taught because he wanted it to be taught.

As already mentioned we can trace Littlejohn's thinking on this line right back to the beginning of his time at Kirksville., He gave addresses to the graduating classes in June 1898 and again in October 1898 when he clearly delineated his vision of osteopathy as Medicine—"an independent school of medicine"[xcvi] and that "the Doctorate in Medicine will be the appropriate title for the Osteopath as well as the allopath"[xcvii]

These ideas were also introduced in his article on Psychology and Osteopathy in the July 1898 journal of Osteopathy.

"In the definition of the science of medicine I have given, I think it is wide enough to cover osteopathy, because I believe Osteopathy is a part of the science of medicine and Osteopathy should claim the work medicine in its original sense, namely, that of healing."

The February 1899 graduation address was a pivotal moment in Littlejohn's career at the American School of Osteopathy in Kirksville. Having been elected Dean, he not only presented his vision for the School and Osteopathy but also, he received a glowing endorsement of his vision from A T Still himself.

---

[31] This contrasts with the interpretation of others i.e., that he called the faculty together, including Littlejohn to complain to them about what was being taught in the school, in particular physiology and medical subjects. As already mentioned, the incident he refers to actually took place in 1896, before littlejohn came to Kirksville.

Littlejohn's vision and work as Dean

> "Dr. J. Mart in Littlejohn, Ph.D., L L.D.; F S.Sc., and F.R.S.L. (Lond.), professor of physiology, was elected Dean of the American School of Osteopathy by the Trustees January 4th, and at once took up the duties of office".
>
> (Journal of osteopathy feb 1899 Page 454)

He Held his first faculty meeting as Dean on February 7th ,1899. In association with his appointment as Dean, Littlejohn did three things of interest, being associated with the formation of the Young Men's Christian Association[32]. Secondly being instrumental in the formation of the students' representative council[33], which we presume would have been formulated on the same basis as the one in Glasgow. During his time in Glasgow Littlejohn had not only being closely associated with the formation of the Student Representative Council but also had served as the law representative of it during his later years in Glasgow. He obviously saw the benefit of having the students involved at least on an advisory or an opinion basis in the running of the college.

The third thing of interest he did was to put the proposal to the Trustees that:

"Whereas it is provided in the charter of the American School of Osteopathy that this college 'shall grant and confer such honours and degrees as are usually granted and conferred by reputable medical colleges' and 'to issue diplomas and testimony of the same' and whereas the title of Diplomat or Doctor of Osteopathy has never being conferred by any medical college; it is hereby resolved that the faculty recommend to the trustees the execution of the charter powers of the school by hereafter conferring the degree of Doctor of Medicine, and in recognition of osteopathy as an independent school of medicine and system of healing as it is so declared by statute in

---

[32] Records of meetings of the Faculty of the ASO, December 14th, 1898: page 63; Museum of Osteopathic Medicine ref. B992

[33] Ibid, December 16th, 1898; Page 63

Missouri and other states that have recognized osteopathy, while carrying out the requirements of the charter that the designation and title shall be hereafter M.D. (Osteopathic)"[xcviii]

This was a reasoned step that LittleJohn took. Having developed and outlined his approach and ideas for the development of the School and Osteopathy in public with his addresses to the graduation classes, culminating with his address on February 1st, 1899, at which Still himself appeared to give his endorsement His methodology was to work through the proper channels. He would not have just sat in a room and come up with these ideas. He was a student of Still's[34] and as such would have entered into discussion with him and others who had more experience than him. Then formulated the ideas and published them in the speeches to the graduates before making a formal presentation to the faculty and through them to the board of Trustees. Others in his position may have used (or abused) their position of access to Still and tried to influence him and have it presented, as Hildreth tended to do, as coming from Still himself.

Littlejohn obviously saw the practical benefit of the M.D. degree as being that osteopathy would be recognized as medicine therefore not need separate legislation in any of the states and may also make it easier for practitioners to practice abroad. M.D.'s were already classified according to the school of medicine they practiced, e.g. Regular, Homeopathic, Eclectic Physio-medical,[xcix] To add osteopathy to this classification would have seemed the logical way to proceed However, even this would not have been without its problems. The Homeopathic colleges were under pressure to include 'regular Materia Medica' and other subjects that would take away from their own philosophy. One of the great supporters of Homeopathy, Wrigley, even went so far as to refuse to give any funding to homeopathic colleges in Chicago:

*"**William Wrigley** (1861–1932), of chewing gum and Chicago Cubs' Wrigley Field fame, was a major advocate for homeopathy. His*

---

[34] "Time and again we have sat beside him or walked with him along the road and listened to him repeating this wonderful, seemingly mythical idea" (Littlejohn talking about his time with A T Still, Journal of Osteopathy, BSO, June -August 1935

personal homeopath was **Julia Clark Strawn, MD**, *an 1897 graduate of Hahnemann Medical College in Chicago. She sought to obtain his financial support for various homeopathic causes, but he declined, not because he didn't appreciate homeopathy but because he felt that the homeopathic colleges were not teaching "real" homeopathy. Instead, the homeopathic colleges had been forced to teach so much conventional physiology and pathology in order for their graduates to pass the state medical exams that they were not teaching homeopathy in adequate depth or breadth (Kirschmann, 2004, 153)"* [c]

Purity of the system of medicine, whether it was homeopathy or osteopathy, occupied the minds of many and still does today. Littlejohn's idea was to be honest and develop Osteopathy as an independent 'drug free' system of 'Medicine', break the drug culture monopoly of the word 'medicine' that was taking hold in the legislature and in people's minds; and to keep Osteopathy out of the field of 'faith healing, massage, Turkish baths etc.[ci] .

This idea of keeping osteopathy 'pure', as put forward by Hildreth and others, would clash with Littlejohn's idea of being 'honest', i.e. admitting that diet, antiseptics, exercise etc. were all part of osteopathy. This clash of ideas would prove significant throughout Littlejohn's time in USA.

Following Littlejohn's approach may also have had the benefit of making it clear to prospective patients that Osteopathy and Osteopaths could treat diseases rather than being seen as some sort of 'bone-setter'[35]

Thus, we can see that he followed the same path as he did in any other occupation or position that he had. He put his full energy into not only understanding the position but also bringing forward and moving the college forward in its academic position and standing.

---

[35] As an example of how osteopathic treatment was associated with bone-setting This was in a relatively complimentary article on osteopathy "The good old reliable custom of neck-breaking-has been going. on for six thousand years, and it would be against tradition to have our faith broken in that sovereign cure for the blues". (The Clarinda Herald, 30th April 1897, Page 8)

In this line he supported, and probably was instrumental in originating, the proposed new Scientific journal, "The Arena". This was announced in January 1899 and Littlejohn was to be the editor. It's interesting to note also that **'an important notice'**[cii] was put up in the A.S.O. about a proposal to publish a true scientific journal 'devoted to the propagation and the elucidation of osteopathic ideas and kindred topics. No date is given for this notice it just says 1899 and it lists a committee including J. Martin Littlejohn Ph.D., LL.D, F.S.Sc. (London) together with his two brothers, C.E. Still, William Smith, Herman Goetz and Henry Stanhope-Bunting. If we note that Littlejohn does not have the F.R.S.L. after his name it is reasonable to assume that this would have been just before February 1899. It was included as an insert in the December 1898 issue of the Journal of Osteopathy[ciii], which would tally with this conclusion.

This was another plank that Littlejohn used in his educational process, creating a magazine for the purpose of spreading the word on the subject matter. From the educationalist point of view this fitted in with his approach of the leadership role of the Dean, the involvement of the students by way of representative council and then the educational cohesive force of the magazine.

However, by June 1899 it was abandoned due to failure of subscribers to "pay up" and it was announced that "The Journal of Osteopathy will cover the field of scientific work in future as well as printing plenty of popular literature upon the science and practitioners may expect from eight to ten pages of good, solid, carefully edited clinic reports each month hereafter"[civ]. Given its failure Littlejohn would proceed to fund a new journal in Jan 1900 "the journal of the Science of Osteopathy"[36]

We continue to see Littlejohn's popularity and work to improve the curriculum, when he Introduced an optional class in dietetics the attendance was so large there was standing room only.[cv]

---

[36] In the March 1900 edition of the Journal of Osteopathy the editorial notes the publication of the 'Journal of the Science of Osteopathy' but also that the American School intends to publish a similar journal entitled the Osteopathic Arena and that this would appear about June 1900. In any event the Osteopathic Arena was never published

The M.D. Osteopathic Idea

Given that he had put these views clearly before he was appointed Dean, that the faculty clearly endorsed them when they approved the motion to recommend to the Trustees that the correct diploma was M.D.O. (osteopathic) and that A. T. Still apparently gave his endorsement of them at the Feb 1899 graduation, how did things go so wrong for him in the later part of 1899.

One factor was Littlejohn's persistence in his line of thought that the correct and best/easiest way forward was to recognise that osteopathy was medicine in the true sense of the word and the diploma should recognise this as M.D. (osteopathic) or M.D.O. Given his growing popularity and the success of his brothers this fermented some opposition, even though Still himself give it his endorsement at the February 1899 graduation.

> "Chicago, Dec 21st. The grand Jury voted yesterday to indict Professor William Smith, of Kirksville. Mo., for the robbery of the Dunning morgue on Oct. 24 last. With him it was voted to hold Henry Ullrich, watchman, and John Ludea, teamster. The charge upon which indictments were voted was burglary, and not body stealing. Under the laws of Illinois, a human body has no value unless It is in the grave."
>
> (Rock Island Argus., December 22, 1897, Page 3)

A.T. Still was said to have been against the use of the M.D. title even though he used it himself and was a registered medical practitioner himself.[37]

---

[37] His title was given as 'Andrew Taylor Still, M.D.' on an article he wrote published in the May 1899 Journal of Osteopathy, Kirksville, Vol. 5, No. 12, page 568. Also, the front cover of the Journal of Osteopathy, up to the first issue of volume 6 in June 1899, had on its front cover, a picture of Still under the banner heading "A. T. Still M.D."

Dr William Smith

Before Littlejohn's arrival Smith had already been in trouble with Still. Harry still is said to have been aware of the problems "his father had working with Dr. Smith, because, except for their shared interest in medicine, they had very little in common" Smith had a wanderlust and looked continually for new challenges and adventure, so was not to settle in one place for long [cvi]. These differences were to keep surfacing despite Stills admiration for Smiths ability to teach anatomy. His raid on the morgue at Dunning in Chicago is often told as an act of heroism but Still seemed to think otherwise as evidenced in the short note he wrote on Jan 16th, 1898, just three months after the raid.

"now Dr. Smith wrote a four-column saucy, idiotic letter and it came out last Sunday. He would be in Illinois State Prison dead today but for the brains of Ellison, Shelton, Gov. Stephens dishonouring the requisition for him. Smith is tame enough now and we will keep him straight or give him the bounce. We have had all the fooling we want out of him and he knows it. Otherwise all is good. We will likely have G.O. Nason[38] to teach physiology but he must not preach and teach. We have had all the hell we want. I have five trustees and God on my side and not a politician or preacher to bother and never will be paid a day unless our teachers teach and nothing else even though they be angels."[cvii]

---

[38] G. O. Nason was associated with the founding of the Southern School of Osteopathy. It was established in March 1898. He is not to be confused with Mason Presley who had already resigned from the A.S.O.; This was just before Littlejohn was asked to give a talk on physiology to see if he was suitable for the position.

As we have already mentioned the surgical and X-ray departments had become so successful that it merited special mention in the Journal of Osteopathy.

During this time Smith's own medical qualifications had come under attack with him suing the Medical Age journal for $25000 for damages. It is of interest to note that the editor of the Journal of Osteopathy states that,

"Osteopathy has nothing to do with this matter…Dr Smith merely happens to be a teacher in this school It is his fight for his character…Osteopathy is not on trial…Dr, Smith asks neither "sympathy" nor "support" in defending his professional ability" (Nov 1898)[cviii]

While this distancing itself from the proceedings may seem appropriate and to have the support of Smith, I cannot help feeling it would have at the very least upset Smith and probably left him vulnerable to any negative inferences about his ability or education. on the same page in the Journal we find Smiths in memoriam for his friend Ed. Eckert. I don't think there can be any doubt that these too events played into each other in Smiths mind and affected his relationship with the School.

After he was dismissed in November 1899, Smith instigated legal proceedings for unfair dismissal[cix]. During 1900 he left for Edinburgh[cx], returning in 1902[cxi] after a "long and severe illness"[cxii] The cause of his illness, Smith put it down to *"worry, and that he recovered by leaving his worry in America and going to Europe. In this case there was no adjustment by skilled fingers to remove an anatomical lesion""*[cxiii]

The Turning Tide

On 25th February 1899, Littlejohn's father, the Rev. James Littlejohn passed away. His father's passing was a landmark in Littlejohn's life as we see from the letter, he wrote to the Christian Nation;

"Writing from Kirksville, Mo., Rev. J.M. Littlejohn says:

"Just a line. We are prostrated with grief. Our beloved father passed away from our midst at noon yesterday. Our family has lost a noble head and the church has lost one of her bravest veterans. It came so sudden we did not anticipate it. He had been confined to the house and in bed for about a week, but for the last few years he had always had a prolonged sickness every Winter and Spring. Saturday night at midnight he had an attack of syncope out of which he revived. We watched around his bedside till 12 noon on Sabbath when he passed away. Peaceful, happy, blessed death. O, not death, for Jesus has said he that liveth and believeth on Me shall never die. And he did not die, only passed away from a little weeping circle here, to the glorious company of the Master whom he loved and served. He had a message of love for us all and a blessed counsel to the Church he loved to be 'faithful unto death. Among the last things he said was that he had displeased many because he had remained the same; but he said, I am the same, the same, the same, and so is Jesus. He passed away glorying in those blessed Psalms he had loved and leaned upon all his life. The life here is closed—we have lost him—but God wanted him, and we submit. He has left us his life. It was Christ like, humble and faithful, and his passing away was the same. I may ask you to give a more extended notice in the Christian Nation, that he loved to read, but now I am so filled with sorrow I cannot do it.

Your sorrowing brother,
Martin[39] Littlejohn."[cxiv]

One particular quote from it is that his father said that he had annoyed many people during his life because he had remained the same throughout his life thus implying that he had stuck rigidly to his principles. This was something that Littlejohn took to heart and tried to follow throughout his own life by sticking to his own principles.

---

[39] This is how he signed his name after his letter.

Shortly after this, his brother James Buchan, re-joined the Masons. He joined the Adair lodge of the Masons in June 1889[40]. It's noteworthy that he didn't do this prior to his father passing, as joining an oath bound "secret" society was more than frowned on by the Reformed Presbyterian Church and indeed may have been subject to censor if he had remained a member of it.

This is in contrast to his brother J.M. Littlejohn who always maintained his accreditation and association with the Reformed Church. Thus, remaining a 'Practical Covenanter', trying to live according to their principles throughout his life. It's quite possible that J.B. being pragmatic, and businessman joined this organisation to further his career. It was Warren Hamilton and Ben. F. Henry that recommended his application. Hamilton, at that time was the secretary of the Board of Trustees of the American School of Osteopathy.[cxv] Ben F Henry was a prominent business man in Kirksville and ran a pharmacy, advertising in the Journal of Osteopathy as "the Druggist" specialising in 'fine perfumes and toilet articles'[cxvi] His son Clifford Henry went on to be an Osteopath, famous for 'Henry's lines and triangles' well known to classical osteopaths. These two persons alone would have given J. B. a position of influence in the community and within the school. In this light, this could have been seen as a threat by Charlie Still and lead to him joining the Masons himself early in 1900, when he saw the Littlejohns as possible rivals, not only from the point of view of the educational influence of J.M. Littlejohn but also from the business point of view now that his brother was in the same fraternity as the Schools business manager, Warren Hamilton, who not only had been a member of the Adair Lodge since 1891 but also had put J B forward for initiation.

This, I believe led C E Still to join the Kirksville Lodge in March 1900. A Mason would be expected not to do something that would dishonor a fellow Mason.

---

[40] James B. Littlejohn, Adair Lodge No. 366, Kirksville, Adair County, MO; Initiated as an Entered Apprentice 19th May 1899; Passed to the Degree of Fellow Craft 2nd June 1899; Raised to the Sublime Degree of Master Mason 16th June 1899
Charles E Still was initiated into the Kirksville Lodge on 21st March 1900 (Grand Lodge of Missouri records)

J M Littlejohn would have probably felt some conflict as he held family relationships to be important as well as his faith in his religious believes. However, if we note that his method was always from the positive, that is to show by example and educate, not by dwelling upon the negative aspects of Lodge life but extolling the virtues of truth and morality.[cxvii]

Littlejohn shows in his attitude, while strict, he is not intolerant when he says "should be large enough of heart and mind to hold to the old and receive the new.... avoid one-sidedness and faddism".[cxviii]

We can get a good idea of what Littlejohn and his father's reaction to J B joining the masons might have been, from the following from the minutes reformed Presbyterian synod 1896:

"Secret societies are peculiarly dangerous because of their secrecy. Secrecy is an essential feature of all such societies. This it is that makes them so attractive. But this it is also that condemns them. Secrecy robs of true manhood. To swear or promise to conceal what is as yet unrevealed degrades the conscience. Secrecy becomes one of the strongest temptations to engage in evil practices. It gives unlimited power to work mischief; power that has often been used to defeat justice and been made to serve every evil purpose. To attack secret orders is to fight a foe hidden in ambush.[41] Secret orders often claim to afford superior social advantages, but they provide social amusement generally at the expense of good morals and the best interests of the home. Lodge life and club life have to an alarming extent taken the place of the quieter, safer enjoyments and comforts of home life.
That our Church, her ministers, officers, and people be encouraged to stand firm in bearing an unpopular testimony against all secret oathbound societies of whatever name."[cxix]

This view has not changed since Littlejohn's time as we can see from the following taken from the website of the of Newtownards Reformed Presbyterian Church Northern Ireland:

---

[41] This sentiment resonates with Littlejohn's conflict with Hildreth, Hamilton and Charles Still over the move of the school form Kirksville.

There are several secret societies in existence. Some are older than others and some are more prominent than others. The Church's attitude to such organisations must be determined by a study of Scripture. From such a study we find that the teaching and practice of secret societies are in conflict with the Word of God in the following ways: -

1. Unscriptural Secrecy

The practice of secrecy is contrary to the teaching of the Word of God, and to the example of the Lord Jesus Christ. He said "I have spoken openly to the world, ... I said nothing in secret." Secrecy is also damaging to society and is contrary to its well-being....

2. Unlawful Oaths

Membership in secret societies involves taking an oath before being aware of the obligation. No man is at liberty to bind his conscience by oath without a knowledge of the nature and extent of his undertaking.....''It is a trap for man to dedicate something rashly and only later to con-sider his vows':

3. Unsocial Benevolence

The benevolence of secret societies is confined to a "brotherhood" which is not warranted by the Word of God. Scripture gives clear direction for our good works. "Therefore, as we have opportunity, let us do good to all people, especially to those who belong to the family of believers".[cxx]

The Tornado

In between these events tragedy was again to strike Kirksville. This time in the form of a tornado. It was on the evening of 27th April 1899.

Headlines of "thirty or more killed and scores injured" filled many local and even British papers. While one student and the wife of another were among the many dead the school of osteopathy was largely spared- the tornado striking the opposite side of the town.

The students and staff of the school, including Smith and the Littlejohns, along with the local medics spend most of the night searching for and attending the many injured in near total darkness with only the light from burning buildings to help.

> **50 DEAD IN A STORM**
>
> *The storm first struck the eastern portion of the town, near the part occupied by the boarding houses of the students of the American School of Osteopathy, State Normal School and McWard's seminary. These three institutions escaped the wind*
>
> *The storm then went northeast and wiped out Patterson's nursery, pulling the trees out of the ground and hurling them through the town.*
>
> *A second of edition of the tornado followed the first, twenty minutes later. It came as an inky black cloud, widely distributed and covered the whole town.*
>
> The Bulletin, Linneus, mo. May 3rd Page 3

This was not without controversy. One newspaper reported

"*about the neatest piece of surgery ever done in Kirksville was the removal by the Saturday mail of the hide of the local correspondent of the metropolitan papers who basely perverted facts in his cyclone write up in order to boon the Still school at the expense of every other institution and of the local physicians*"[cxxi] [42]

Almost immediately after this several more important events took place. The Kirksville journal of 28th April, the day after the tornado, reports that Littlejohn has been called to the bar and that "Prof. J. Martin Littlejohn has been invited to deliver a scientific address before the **Royal Science Society**[43] of London,

---

[42] That this report was in not only in the same edition but also the same column of that newspaper as the item about Littlejohn repudiating his statement about the American School Moving from Kirksville shows just how linked and tangled all these events were.

[43] Bold emphasis by author

England, which body will convene July 15th Next[cxxii]" This is the beginning of the controversy concerning his talk.[44]

(His paper was subsequently published in the February 1900 journal of osteopathy and credited as read before "royal Society of Literature" and reprinted with permission from the American Osteopath; and later in the American osteopath of Sept 1st as being to the "London Society of sciences" on august 19th 1899, which is more correct.[45] More confusion was to follow on this subject which we will see later.)

---

[44] See chapter on The Dispute
[45] Professor Littlejohn had been invited to deliver the address before the Society of Science, Letters and Art, August 19, 1899, and went abroad for that purpose, his subject being: " The Prophylactic and Curative Value of the Science of Osteopathy " (The American Osteopath, Monthly, Sept. 1900, page 3)

The A S O to Move from Kirksville

It was also during this time that there was considerable debate and even open strife amongst the Trustees of the College, in particular within the Still family, about the school moving to a larger city. For example, Harry Still, in a letter dated 27th April 1900 says,

"our school, as you know, has 700 students and we will have to seek a larger place for more clinical material however, Chicago or St Louis will be the city. I am rather in favour of Chicago myself. But Dr. Chas and Dr. Hildreth think more favourably of St Louis as it is a Missouri city."[cxxiii]

On the same date he wrote to another osteopath

"There is only one thing that will keep me out of New York and that is our school. Chas. is quite anxious for me to locate in St. Louis so as to pull our school there this coming February"[cxxiv]

While the story is told a that A T Still requested Harry to return Kirksville because of the increase in patients in the infirmary and students in the school, another explanation comes to mind given his admission in that letter. A T Still new of his sons scheming to move the school and that building a large practice in St Louis was to be part of that plan, then it is reasonable to assume that recalling Harry to Kirksville was a way of putting pay to their scheming and the increase in patients in the infirmary was just a good excuse.

It might be instructive to say a few words about Harry M Still at this point. On the 13th of April 1900 he wrote.

"I have started something like fifteen offices and all of them have been successful. I went to Chicago in 1895 where Osteopathy was known very little. The first month my receipts run over $2000, at the same time I was persecuted and arrested daily. With all of this staring me in the face I made a success. My second year cleared me close to $30,000, and I believe if I had not left Chicago to come to Kirksville to be associated with the school, I could have had a practice to-day worth $75,000 per annum. We have now something like 700 students in school, but I have become sick of the school business and intend to get out immediately."[cxxv]

This was about a new venture he was thinking of starting in New York and looking for a partner. Trowbridge says *"a Doctors life did not suit Harry. In fact, he did not like even to be around sick people"*. Despite this he built several successful practices and was more of a businessman than osteopathic practitioner. He returned to Kirksville in 1907 with 'his health broken' and served as president of the Citizens national bank and invested in diverse businesses"[cxxvi].

This being said, given the problems mentioned above about salaries within the school, and his Fathers lament that the school must 'foot its own expenses or go to the basket'[cxxvii] putting proposals such as that contained within the quoted letter was sure to contribute to the conflict.

On top of this he was clearly involved in the idea of moving the school out of Kirksville even after his father had definitively stated that it was staying. In the board of trustee's minutes, we find further evidence of conflict over money when the trustees voted themselves large salaries, although these were not to be paid until all the schools' expenses were taken care of.[cxxviii]

I don't want to give the impression that there was open conspiracy within the still family, simply to point out that at the time the Littlejohns were at Kirksville there was more going on than teaching osteopathy.

For J M Littlejohn in particular, with his simple, straight foreword attitude of stating his vision, this would have been the next thing to an alien environment.

To return to the first week of May 1899, Littlejohn is quoted as saying that the school would definitely be moved within eighteen months to a larger city Des Moines, Chicago or St. Louis.

And then one week later, May 12th, he is reported as retracting that statement.

> *"Dean Littlejohn now repudiates his interview in which he said the Still school of osteopathy would be moved from Kirksville, but that institution has received just as much free advertising as if the interview had been genuine"*
>
> The Macon Citizen Macon MO 12th May 1899

This is quite unusual for Littlejohn to make such a definite statement unless he had been given that information as a definite fact and then when he found out it was false; he would have taken the necessary steps to correct it.

This begs the question as to who would have fed him that information and why. It's not unusual for politicians or others who want to judge public reaction to get someone else to leak the information to see how it will be received. The ones in this case that would benefit from that would be C.E. Still, Harry M. Still or A.G. Hildreth. It is possible that one or other could have done this. Charley and Harry Still from the point of view of getting it out, without risking their father's ire; A.G. Hildreth on the other hand may have been getting it out into the public domain as he was later said to be in favour of the school moving to St. Louis.

> *"Dean Littlejohn authoritatively announces that the American School of Osteopathy will be moved from Kirksville within eighteen months, either to Des Moines, Chicago or St. Louis. This will be a worse blow to the town financially than the death-dealing cyclone which ravaged it last week"*
>
> The Macon Citizen Macon MO 5th May 1899

Then on May 13th a delegation from the school including C.E. Still, Warner Hamilton, J.B. and J.M. Littlejohn, Judge Ellison and William Smith went to Des Moines to investigate if it would be a suitable city to move to. C.E. Stills remarks here would have certainly irked his father if not angered him. When he said,

"we have outgrown the village we are located in."

That and other remarks would not have found favour with his father and we see his father's reaction by his clear statement put into the newspapers on June 7th that the school would not be moving anywhere, and that Kirksville was his home and he was staying there. He also put in the Rider that he would do his job if the residents of Kirksville would do theirs.

> "A special party of Kirksville men who are connected with the Still school of Osteopathy, arrived in De Moines this morning and will spend some time being driven over the city and hearing what sort of a proposition Des Moines has to make for the location of the Kirksville school. The party is made up of C.E.Still, who is in charge of the Kirksville institution and is a son of Dr A T Still the originator of osteopathy,, W Hamilton, business manager of the institution and (J.B.) Littlejohn, Chief Surgeon, J. M. Littlejohn, Scientist, Judge Andrew Ellision, lecturer on medical jurisprudence and W Smith, in Des Moines to investigate if it would be a suitable city to move the school to; C. E. Still "we have outgrown the village we are located in. Kirksville cannot be called more than a village and it does not afford the accommodations which our patients and students require" …
>
> (the daily Iowa Capital May 13th, 1899)"

In this quote it is also of interest to note that C E Still is listed as being in charge of the school and Littlejohn as being *"a scientist"* and not as Dean-perhaps showing C E Stills worry or insecurity about his position in face of Littlejohns success and popularity, especially with his Father.

We have to consider the fact that Littlejohn stated quite clearly in his letter of November 23rd, 1899 to the Board of Trustees that Hildreth had made himself objectionable in many ways. He was referring to his association with the school in the 1888 –'89 term. So, it is quite possible that one of the ways he did this was by feeding Littlejohn false information about the potential movement of the school.

Another point worth noting is that the local papers also stated that the school had got much free publicity from the talk about moving the school out of Kirksville.

Still himself put pay to these discussions about moving the School out of Kirksville in a very strongly worded document published in the local newspapers as well as the Journal of Osteopathy June 1899.

> "Rumors have been rife for several weeks to the effect that the American School of Osteopathy was shortly to be moved to one of the prominent western cities. Dr. A.T. Still president of the institution wishes this impression to be corrected. It is not true that any agreement has been made looking to the removal of the school or infirmary. Several cities have made overtures to Dr. Still offering considerable bonuses to secure the American School of Osteopathy but they were not accepted. The school is making every arrangement to increase its occupations and equipment for the fall term; a large incoming class is regarded as a certainty; and patrons may rest assured that osteopathy in the future as in the past will be taught best at its birthplace – Kirksville.
>
> **"Dr Still gave out this statement June 7th through the Kirksville papers;**
>
> **'To the citizens of Kirksville and all others concerned: Kirksville is my home. I have no intention of leaving the place. My interests are here for life as far as I know now. Let this answer all questions or rumors. Do your part and I will do mine. A.T. Still"**
>
> *Journal of osteopathy Kirksville June 1899, page 38*

When we skip forward to 1903, we find a clear statement associated with C E Still and Warren Hamilton among others in an article in a local St Louis paper:

> "The American School of Osteopathy, which has been conducted at Kirksville Mo., for thirteen years is soon to be moved to St, Louis"[cxxix] [46]

Further in a letter, written on 27th April 1900, about the possibility of moving the school form Kirksville Harry M Still says

> "I am rather in favor of Chicago myself, but Dr. Chas and Dr. Hildreth think more favorably of St. Louis as it is a Missouri city."[cxxx]

So, we see that even after this definitive statement from the head of the institution A T Still, his sons, Hildreth and Warren Hamilton were still going about the business of trying to move the school against Stills wishes.

At the same time there was a degree of angst regarding the publicity that surrounded what the osteopaths had done in the aftermath of the cyclone compared to the ordinary M.D.s.[cxxxi]

> "About the neatest piece of surgery ever done in Kirksville was the removal by the Saturday mail of the hide of the local correspondent of the metropolitan papers who basely perverted facts in his cyclone write up in order to boom the Still school at the expense of every other institution and of the local physicians."

There had always been game play from the Still family regarding staying in Kirksville. Even at the beginning of the idea of building an infirmary Still had more than hinted that he wanted the support of the townspeople of Kirksville.

---

[46] It did print a correction saying that the ASO was not going to leave Kirksville and said *"It is anticipated, however, as a result of the success attained by the St. Louis summer school, that a complete three-year course may be instituted here*(St Louis) *within a year. If that is accomplished the school will still be an auxiliary establishment and the parent school will continue its two-year course at Kirksville"* (The Osteopathic Physician; October 1903, page 1)

In 1894 the citizens of Kirksville showed their loyalty to Still by offering land and money to help build an infirmary. R. M. Brashear offered ten acres in the eastern section of the town. Still was impressed with their support, declared his intention to stay in Kirksville but declined the offers of land in favour of staying on the north side and to build his infirmary with his own money. Brashear was later to support Ward in setting up the Columbian school, in 1897, in opposition to Stills school[cxxxii]

Attempts were made to say that they were responding to approaches from larger cities to attract the school to move to their location. No doubt it was relatively common for a town to try and attract a large organisation, hospital, university etc to move to their location. However, when we read the letters and newspaper interviews the impression is clearly given that Charles and Harry Still and Hildreth not only supported the idea but at the very least made it known that proposal would be favourably received.

The M. D. O. question comes to a head

Even in the midst of all this intrigue Littlejohn was trying to put the school first. Having been invited to give a talk on Osteopathy in London in July, he felt it would be advantageous to the mission of putting osteopathy on the map in Europe if he were not only the Dean of the American School of Osteopathy but also a graduate, and hence a Doctor of Osteopathy. He made his case in a letter to the board of Trustees on June 6th.

"I am going to London and will have an opportunity of presenting from a scientific standpoint the science and art of osteopathy and would like to do so not only as an official of the American School but also as one of its graduates. I think that I can do something for the science of osteopathy that may bear fruit in the future recognition of our standing and reputation, respectfully submitted, J. Martin Littlejohn"[cxxxiii]

This was seemingly rejected as he had not been in the school long enough to graduate, (under its bylaws which required attendance of four terms of five months each, two terms being held in each year; September to January and February to June), as he wrote a second letter on the 7th June in which he outlined his previous studies which he felt could be taken into account as he had only been in school since February 1898 and at most attended 3 terms. He also asked for *"the degree of M.D. (osteopathic school) because I (Littlejohn) believe that is the right one by the intent and expression of our charter and as a matter of policy for the recognition of Osteopathy as an independent school of Healing".*[cxxxiv]

    This appears to have been turned down as he did not graduate until January 1900. It would not have come as a surprise to him, as he was Dean and well aware of the bylaws, but he would probably have seen it as a lost opportunity for the School and osteopathy. Others may have had a different opinion, particularly regarding the M.D.O. degree as we shall see later. Remember that the 7th June was the same day that Still expressed his firm conviction that he would never leave Kirksville – what must have seemed as a strong rebuke to his son Charles. As such Charles would not have be in a mood to give any concession to Littlejohn; having seen the failure of the attempt to get Littlejohn to front the idea of the School moving from Kirksville and his Fathers apparent approval of the idea of the M.D.O. degree at the February graduation, he would have seen Littlejohn as a rival for his father's confidence.

In any event, Littlejohn chaired his last faculty meeting 24th June for the routine business of approving the students to graduate on June 29th.

Summary

Littlejohn was also called to the bar and elected a fellow of the Royal Society of Literature during this time. He was also invited to give a lecture again in London to the Society of Science, Letters and Art. Now I would speculate that the invitation for this talk was in two parts, one that he was elected fellow of the Royal Society of Literature and then invited to give a lecture to the society. It was then and is still today the practice for new members of a society to give a talk or present a paper as part of their introduction to the society. This would have given Littlejohn certainly the impression that the talk was to be to the Royal Society of Literature, and this is confirmed by the title opening remarks and the title of the talk as it is given in the Journal of Osteopathy. We get an idea of how excited he was about the prospect of this by the two letters he wrote on June 6th and June 7th to the Board of Trustees asking that he should be graduated in June 1899 and requesting that the degree should be M.D. Osteopathic. The tone of these letters gives an idea of how delighted he was about the prospect, and how he felt about the honour of being a fellow of the Royal Society of Literature and the opportunity it would give for him to present the scientific basis of osteopathy in England.

The secretary of the Society of Science, Letters and Art, Dr. Sturman[cxxxv] was a long time Fellow of the Royal Society of literature, and it was probable that he was one of the members who proposed Littlejohn. Also, the enthusiasm and eagerness to promote osteopathy back home and that he could do this better and with more authority if he attended not only as Dean but as a graduate of the college. I've no idea if there was any reply whatsoever to this but given the timing of it, the timing of A.T. Still's declaration in the local papers about Kirksville being his home and the effect of this declaration on his son C.E. Still who had openly and enthusiastically promoted the idea of moving the college it wouldn't surprise me if C.E. Still on receipt of these letters from Littlejohn did not put them forward to his father at that time.

Littlejohn duly sailed for England on 1st July having sent telegrams of congratulations to the graduating class for the graduation ceremony on 29th June[cxxxvi]. The purpose was twofold. They had lost their father on the 25th February and he and his brother

James Buchan were escorting their mother to England to see their sister Elizabeth Margaret. She had married in 1894 and their mother had left to join the rest of her family in America in 1896. It was important to see her daughter and grandchildren, one born in 1896 and 1897, and to offer Elizabeth comfort and condolences for the loss of her father.

Secondly, Littlejohn intended to make a tour of Europe. Rev Tucker in his article in the American Osteopath in September 1900 puts the purpose of Littlejohn's tour as having the *"especial object being to investigate the latest physiological and psychological work at the leading universities. One result of his visit was a great interest on the part of the leading physicians in England and Germany in Osteopathy, and a promise on the part of the professors of Physiology at the Universities of Edinburg, London, Cambridge and Oxford, (Schaffer of Edinburg, McKendrick of Glasgow, Michael Foster at Cambridge, Burdon Sanderson of Oxford) to pursue their investigations during the year on the lines of Dr. Still's discoveries "*[cxxxvii]

Unfortunately, on his way to England he received notification that his friend, the secretary of the Society of Science, Letters and Art, Dr. Sturman had passed away on 20th June. This meant that the lecture would be postponed and that he had to deliver the lecture to be read in absence. In his own words, written in October 1903.

"In 1898 we were especially invited to deliver an address for the society at its annual meeting and preparations were in process of completion when the secretary, our personal friend, and a warm friend of science suddenly died. Following his death, which took place while we were on the ocean crossing to England, the address that we prepared in the library of the Campania, on route, was presented to the society, read in abstinence at a later meeting and published as an "in memoriam" to the deceased secretary"[cxxxviii].

---

[i] Minutes of Testimony to House of lords select committee HMSO 1935, paragraph 3497 and 3501 page 230
[ii] The Clarinda Journal, Page 5, Jan 28th, 1898
[iii] Page County Democrat, 17th June 1897, Page 8
[iv] The Clarinda Herald, 24th December 1897, Page 7

[v] The Clarinda Journal, 19th November 1897, Page 5
[vi] The Clarinda Journal, 9th July 1897, Page 5
[vii] The Clarinda Journal, 31st December 1897 Page 51
[viii] The Clarinda Herald, 19th February 1897, Page 8
[ix] Fold3 1897, page 1271, City Directories for Chicago, Illinois
[x] The Chicago Clinic, bulletin number vii, page vi: Also, Cap and Gown 1897 Page 208
[xi] The United Presbyterian. Dec. 16". Quoted in The Christian nation 23rd December 1896, page 12
[xii] The Christian Nation October 14th, 1896 page 12
[xiii] The Christian Nation October 14th, 1896 page 12
[xiv] Dunham Medical College circular of information 1895/6 and Announcement 1896/7
[xv] Amity College catalogue 1896/7
[xvi] The Clarinda Herald, 9th July 1897, Page 8
[xvii] Ibid
[xviii] Cap and Gown 1898 and The Chicago Clinic Bulletin no 7
[xix] Journal of Osteopathy August 1898, page 115
[xx] The Times -Press, Streator, Illinois, Monday September 20th, 1982, page 3
[xxi] – Christian nation May 25th, 1898, page 12
[xxii] Journal of osteopathy March 1899, page 402
[xxiii] The Clarinda Herald Journal, 11th February 1954, page 5
[xxiv] Christian Nation 9th February 1898, Page 11
[xxv] The Christian nation 9th Feb 1898, page 11
[xxvi] museum of osteopathic medicine, Kirksville, Catalogue number 2010.02.722: no date but details in letter place it in February 1898.
[xxvii] The Journal of Osteopathy, British School of Osteopathy, October 1932
[xxviii] Ibid
[xxix] Minutes of Board of American School of Osteopathy, July 1897; A T Still Museum archives
[xxx] The Lengthening shadow of Dr. A T Still, Arthur Grant Hildreth, page 97; also pages 77-80; Andrew Taylor Still; Carol Trowbridge, the Thomas Jefferson University Press, 1991 Page 171
[xxxi] Ibid
[xxxii] Still in Journal of Osteopathy, Kirksville, Dec 1896
[xxxiii] Journal of Osteopathy, Kirksville, October 1897, page 218
[xxxiv] Journal of Osteopathy, Kirksville, December 1897, page
[xxxv] Minutes of Board of American School of Osteopathy, January 4th, 1898; A T Still Museum archives
[xxxvi] Journal of osteopathy, Kirksville, June 1896 page 4
[xxxvii] Journal of osteopathy, Kirksville, March 1898 page 449
[xxxviii] The First School of Osteopathic Medicine, Georgia Warner Walter; The Thomas Jefferson University Press, 1992 Page 45-46

[xxxix] Ibid page 18
[xl] Ibid page 47
[xli] Kirksville Journal 28th April 1899
[xlii] The Christian Nation Volume 29, July 20th, 1898, page 12
[xliii] Journal of Osteopathy, Kirksville, August 1898 page 141; October 1898, page 209
[xliv] Journal of Osteopathy, Kirksville, March 1899, page 489
[xlv] American School of Osteopathy Catalogue 1899/1900 page 6; A T Still Museum
[xlvi] Minutes at July 6th on page 43 of the board of trustee's minutes, A T Still Museum ref. 1/3/2017
[xlvii] American School of Osteopathy Catalogue 1898/89 page 19; A T Still Museum ref. B1801
[xlviii] History of Osteopath and twentieth-century medical practice, E. R. Booth Ph. D., D.O. 1905, Page 284; and Psycho-Physiology by J Martin Littlejohn, Preface dated Kirksville November 1899.
[xlix] The First School of Osteopathic Medicine, Georgia Warner Walter; The Thomas Jefferson University Press, 1992 Page 79
[l] The Osteopathic Physician November 1908 page 8; December 1908 page 11
[li] The Journal of osteopathy, British School of Osteopathy, Vol 6 June-August 1935, BSO.

[lii] Video: Still Littlejohn and Physiology, a presentation to the ICO by C. Campbell 2020
[liii] Andrew Taylor Still; Carol Trowbridge, the Thomas Jefferson University Press, 1991 Page 176
[liv] AMERICAN SCHOOL OF OSTEOPATHY ALUMNI, 1894-1924; Museum of Osteopathic Medicine, 800 West Jefferson St., Kirksville, MO 63501
[lv] Journal of Osteopathy, Kirksville, advertisement page viii
[lvi] Museum of Osteopathy, Kirksville ref. 1980.373.08 _Victoria episode
[lvii] AMERICAN SCHOOL OF OSTEOPATHY ALUMNI, 1894-1924; Museum of Osteopathic Medicine, 800 West Jefferson St., Kirksville, MO 63501
[lviii] Journal of Osteopathy, Kirksville, June 1894
[lix] A T Still museum of osteopathic medicine, Kirksville, Letter(1899 Feb 14) to Henry Stanhope Bunting, Ref 1899-02-14
[lx] Journal of Osteopathy, Kirksville, September 1898, page 202
[lxi] Journal of Osteopathy, Kirksville, May 1898
[lxii] Journal of Osteopathy, Kirksville, Sept 1898, page 201
[lxiii] Journal of Osteopathy, Kirksville, November 1894, page 1
[lxiv] Journal of Osteopathy, Kirksville, March 1899, page 492,
[lxv] Journal of Osteopathy, Kirksville, Oct 1898 page 212/3

[lxvi] Journal of Osteopathy, Kirksville, March 1899, page 489
[lxvii] Faculty Meetings minutes, December 16th, 1898 page 65; Museum of Osteopathy, Kirksville, ref B992
[lxviii] Journal of Osteopathy, Kirksville, December 1898, page 355
[lxix] Ibid
[lxx] Journal of Osteopathy, Kirksville, November 1898, page 303
[lxxi] Journal of Osteopathy, Kirksville, April 1898, page 516-7
[lxxii] Journal of Osteopathy, Kirksville, August 1899, page 98/9
[lxxiii] The Lengthening shadow of Dr. Andrew Taylor Still, page 120
[lxxiv] Letter from the Littlejohn Brothers to the Board of Trustees of the ASO, November 30th, 1899; Museum of Osteopathic Medicine ref. 1980.375.02.01
[lxxv] Ibid page 121
[lxxvi] Journal of Osteopathy, Kirksville, march page 403
[lxxvii] Journal of Osteopathy, Kirksville, May 1899, page 594
[lxxviii] Minutes of Testimony to House of lords select committee HMSO 1935, paragraph 3510 page 230; also, Correspondence with the Royal Society of Literature archives that this was indeed the norm.
[lxxix] Journal of osteopathy, Kirksville, February 1899, Page 454
[lxxx] To Teach, to Heal, to Serve; page 17, Theodore A. Berchtold.
[lxxxi] Journal of Osteopathy, Kirksville, August 1898, Page 115-121.
[lxxxii] Journal of Osteopathy, Kirksville, December 1898, page 329
[lxxxiii] Journal of Osteopathy, British School of Osteopathy, July-August 1935
[lxxxiv] American School of Osteopathy, Record of Proceedings of the faculty, Dec. 14, 1898, pages 63; Museum of Osteopathic Medicine Kirksville
[lxxxv] Journal of Osteopathy, Vol. 5, No. 10, March 1899, page 402
[lxxxvi] Journal of Osteopathy, Vol. 6, No. 8, page 346 January 1900
[lxxxvii] American School of Osteopathy, Record of Proceedings of the faculty, pages 65; Museum of Osteopathic Medicine Kirksville
[lxxxviii] American School of Osteopathy, Record of Proceedings of the faculty, pages 63-4; Museum of Osteopathic Medicine Kirksville
[lxxxix] Journal of Osteopathy, Kirksville, Vol. 5, No. 7, December 1898 Page 325; and Vol. 5, No. 3, August 1898 page 115
[xc] Journal of Osteopathy, Kirksville, Vol. 5, No. 12, May 1899, Inside Front cover and page 537
[xci] The Kirksville Journal, 28th April 1899
[xcii] Journal of Osteopathy, Kirksville, August 1898, Page 115-121.
[xciii] Journal of Osteopathy, Kirksville, February 1899, page 431-434
[xciv] **Letter [1899 Feb 7] from A.T. Still to [the Orschel family] of Chicago.** (Missouri Digital heritage; (Orschel Family)-letter from Andrew Taylor Still Accession number 2009.10.650; original date 1899-02-07)
[xcv] American School of Osteopathy, Record of Proceedings of the faculty, pages 69-71; Museum of Osteopathic Medicine Kirksville
[xcvi] Journal of Osteopathy, Kirksville, December 1898 Page 329

[xcvii] Journal of Osteopathy Kirksville, February 1899 page 429
[xcviii] Minutes of the faculty meetings of the A.S.O. March 22nd, 1899, page 72/73.
[xcix] Polks medical and surgical register of the united states of America and Canada, Various edition.
[c] The Homeopathic Revolution; Dana Ullman MPH; North Atlantic Books, Berkeley California .2007, page 263
[ci] Journal of Osteopathy Vol5 No3 August 1898
[cii] Museum of osteopathic Medicine, Kirksville ref 1997.04.147
[ciii] Journal of Osteopathy, Kirksville, December 1898, insert after front cover, New York Academy of Medicine library holdings
[civ] journal of osteopathy, Kirksville, June 1899
[cv] Journal of osteopathy, Kirksville, February 1899, March 1899, page 402.
[cvi] Frontier doctor- medical pioneer, C. E. Still Jr., The Thomas Jefferson University press 1991, university press' page 168 C E Still jnr
[cvii] A T Still museum, Kirksville' ref. 1990.10 Dear Awl January 16th, 1898
[cviii] Journal of Osteopathy, Kirksville, November 1898, page 302
[cix] The Republican Friday December 15th, 1899 (newspaper archive)
[cx] Journal of the History of Medicine, April 1967, Peripatetic Pioneer, William Smith, M.D., D.O., by E. R. N. Grigg
[cxi] The Osteopathic physician, August 1902, page 2
[cxii] Ibid
[cxiii] The Osteopathic World July 1904, page 176, 'Death of the Lesion Controversy by C. W. Young, Ph.B., D. D.
[cxiv] The Christian Nation, Vol. 30, March 8th, 1899, page 12
[cxv] Catalogue of the American School of Osteopathy 1898-9; Museum of Osteopathic medicine, Kirksville
[cxvi] Journal of Osteopathy, Kirksville, January 1898, page 402 and v
[cxvii] The Christian Nation vol 23 Nov 13, 1895, page 309
[cxviii] Ibid
[cxix] minutes reformed Presbyterian synod of North America, 1896 page 36.
[cxx] http://newtownards.rpc.org/ April 2020: Presbyterian Church Northern Ireland
[cxxi] The Macon Citizen Macon Mo. 12th May 1899
[cxxii] Kirksville Journal 1899, courtesy of Truman State University archives
[cxxiii] A T Still Museum of osteopathy ref .2006.76.01 – ASO Business Letters Ledger 1900, page 718
[cxxiv cxxiv] A T Still Museum of osteopathy ref. 2006.76.01 – ASO Business Letters Ledger 1900, page 720
[cxxv] A T Still Museum of osteopathy ref. 2006.76.01 – ASO Business Letters Ledger 1900, page 628
[cxxvi] Andrew Taylor Still, Carol Trowbridge, The Thomas Jefferson University Press, 1991, page 207/8

[cxxvii] A T Still Museum of Osteopathy; A. T. Still Letter, 1899, Feb 14, to Henry Stanhope Bunting.
[cxxviii] A. T. Still Museum of Osteopathy; 1898 Board of Trustees minutes, July 14th, page 42
[cxxix] The St. Louis Republic., August 23, 1903, PART I, Page 8
[cxxx] A T Still Museum of osteopathy ref. 2006.76.01 – ASO Business Letters Ledger 1900, page 720
[cxxxi] The Macon Citizen 12th May 1899
[cxxxii] First School of Osteopathic Medicine by Georgia Warner Walter, The Thomas Jefferson University Press, 1992, page 18 and 45
[cxxxiii] ASO letters museum of osteopathy Kirksville, ref. 1980.375.02.04.
[cxxxiv] ASO letters museum of osteopathy Kirksville, ref. 1980.375.02.03
[cxxxv] transactions of Royal Society of Literature 1878
[cxxxvi] Journal of Osteopathy Vol 6 No 2 July 1899, page 84
[cxxxvii] The American Osteopathy, sept 1900; vol 2 number 1 "Osteopathy, Its History and Treatment. Rev. Ernest EL Tucker, Mobile, Ala;
[cxxxviii] The Osteopathic World, October 1903

LITTLEJOHN'S RETURN FROM SUMMER IN ENGLAND 1899

On the 26th august 1899[i] Littlejohn, his brother James Buchan and their mother set sail from Liverpool to return to Kirksville onboard the Campania arriving back in Kirksville shortly before the first day of term, the 4th September.

During his absence a number of things occurred which were to have a bearing on future events.

Hildreth the A.A.A.O, and Harry

First amongst these was the commencement exercises on 29th June 1899[ii]. Littlejohn was on his way to England, so missed the ceremony. However, both Hildreth and Harry Still were present. As mention above Harry had no great love for the work involved in the school and it may be postulated that he started a process of "encouraging" Hildreth to return to the school. In his book "the Lengthening Shadow of Dr. A. T. Still" Hildreth says that "late in August (1899) he (Harry Still) told me his father and Dr Charlie wanted me to return once more to Kirksville". And he replied, "if your farther thinks he needs me I will go back"

Harry had written to Hildreth on August 7th, 1899 saying:

"I am very glad you have found a little time to take a vacation. I only wish I could be with you. I tell you they run me a merry chase now. There are only two of us here to do the work and one hundred fifty patients to take care of.

You spoke to me of whether I was thinking of keeping house this Winter. It is my intention to do so unless you throw me out for lack of rent.

Every indication is now that we will have the largest class in the history of the school, and I would not be surprised to see it run up to 200. The other schools are straining every point to get students. The two northern schools are represented here now.

There is no use talking, you are missed in the Infirmary and school every day and I only wish you could be with us this Fall and Winter. Up until two o'clock today I have treated fifty patients."[iii]

Hildreth was made president of the A.A.A.O. at the meeting on the 5th and 6 the of July[iv]. This appointment meant that he could not hold a position[1] in a school of Osteopath[v]. The general rationale for his being recalled to the school was the growth of the student population, the intake in September 1899 was to be over 200 and the total student numbers over 700;[vi] making the need for experienced operators in the infirmary essential.

C M T Hulett and the M.D.O.

In the summer of 1899, an incident occurred which probably influenced Still's attitude towards the journal of osteopathy and how he would react when Hulett broached the issue of the definition of Osteopathy on the inside cover of the magazine and the MDO question. This involved Bunting, the then editor of the Journal of Osteopathy and a student at the American School of Osteopathy, and Dr. S. R. Landes, who graduated from the American School of Osteopathy in 1895. They had entered into a partnership to work a practice at Petoskey and Mackinac Island, Michigan during the summer of 1899. They ordered 1000 copies of each of the May and June issues of the Journal of Osteopathy to use in promoting the practice, with their professional cards printed on the inside front cover. Someone informed A T Still of this and he intercepted the order, confiscated the copies and had the cards torn out. Landes and Bunting then had to buy up the bulk of their own confiscated papers

---

[1] "the Faculty, Officers and stockholders of schools shall be ineligible for election to official positions and duties" Constitution of the AAAO quoted in The Popular Osteopath October 1899, page 232

through others in smaller orders, after their cards had been torn out, and to have their cards reprinted and pasted in again after receiving the magazines.[vii]

Bunting said of the incident *"While I learned little by little on returning to school next fall (1899) that many of my old classmates had both heard and believed these accusations I could never ascertain who was responsible for starting them; nor find anyone who admitted believing them. I therefore maintained difficult silence."*[viii]

While this[2] is not related specifically to Littlejohn or the MDO issue it would have created an angst in Still's mind concerning the Journal of Osteopathy and that would probably have influenced how he reacted to Hulett's concerns as they also related to the inside front cover.

The question of the definition of Osteopathy and the MDO degree was raised in an article by C M T Hulett in the September 1899 edition of the Journal of Osteopathy. In this article he criticizes the use of M.D.O. and Still gives his approval of his criticism.

"One undergraduate said to the writer sometime since; " D. O. does not mean anything. Our title ought to be M. D. O. " In the minds of some of us D. O. stands for Dr. Still's work and means just what that means. Where did that student get the suggestion for any other idea?
Why is there such an apparently eager desire to ring the changes on "medicine?"
Why is the last item in the standing definition of Osteopathy in the JOURNAL eliminated?
These things must mean something, and we who are but learners and separated far from the fountain head, and hence can only occasionally catch a spray from its life-giving streams, can but stand and wait and wonder, and hope that in some way and in due time, we may be permitted a deeper and more satisfying draught
(I approve the above article. The D. O. in the definition of Osteopathy was left out without my knowledge or consent and was added as soon

---

[2] A full description of this incident and its resolution in 1903 is given in the December 1903 issue of the Osteopathic Physician

as I noticed the omission. We want no M. D. O. in our school-for the American School is strictly Osteopathic-and D. O. means just what it stands for, Diplomate in Osteopathy.) [ix]

This Would seem to be a condemnation of Littlejohn's idea of the M.D. (osteopathic) degree. It has been suggested by Gevitz that perhaps Still did not understand what Littlejohn had said at the February 1899 graduation:

"Had Still understood Littlejohn's meaning? Had he just endorsed all that Littlejohn said? Did Still believe that "ultimately...the Doctorate in Medicine will be the appropriate title of the Osteopath as well as the Allopath"? [x]

It seems unlikely that Still had misheard or indeed misunderstood Littlejohn as Littlejohn had made no secret of his ideas regarding the meaning of the word "medicine" and that osteopathy should reclaim it in its true sense and not in the drug or pharmaceutical sense. Also remember that Littlejohn had written to the board of trustees requesting to graduate with the June 1899 class with the degree M.D. Osteopathic (M.D.O.). While it is possible that these letters/requests were not passed on to A T Still, it is doubtful that Still himself would have remained unaware of these ideas over such a lengthy period. But, as Gevitz said the minutes of the board of Trustees meetings are not available for the relevant period, so we may never know for sure.[xi]

The main text of the article by Hulett concentrated on the legislation in Illinois with the above comments appended to it- giving the impression of a quote from a conversation with Still rather than an appended note. It is difficult to fully understand Hulett's position. He criticizes a previous article on the relationship of osteopathy to surgery, (*April 1899 Journal of osteopathy*) firstly on the grounds that it is unsigned and then that it is inaccurate but gives no details or references.

The article being unsigned would seem to be in line with the direction of A T Still to the editor, S Bunting, in a letter dated 8th Feb 1899[3] and may indicate that the article was written by the editor, S Bunting himself. (Bunting would put his name as editor on the last issue he was in charge of. Probably so he could have quick proof of his tenure for his C.V.)

On reading the article the only "complaint" that I can find that fits with his own article is that the writer is suggesting that under the original meaning and origin of the word "surgery" Osteopathy can include surgery. The article appears to build upon Littlejohn's article "Osteopathy in Line of Apostolic Succession with Medicine," in which he reclaims the word "Medicine" and progresses to reclaim "surgery"[4] in its original meaning. The article finishes with the statement:

" It is deserving of record that within recent years, nearly all the British universities have commenced to give Surgical as well as Medical Degrees."

Indicating the separate nature of surgery and medicine as such.

Hulett's argument on the one hand that the *legislation "In effect it places the Osteopathist on the same plane as the midwife, the nurse, the masseur and the chiropodist, good people all of them, and highly necessary, but from a professional standpoint, regarded as*

---

[3] 8th February 1899; "Your letter received, there will be no change in the journal at present. I object to my name or any other individuals name being used as Editor or associate Editor. Let it be edited and published by the American school of Osteopathy only"(A T Still papers, museum of osteopathic medicine; D 299; ATSP 1.1.27, Missouri digital heritage on line)

[4] "Dr. J. Martin Littlejohn 's masterly discourse on "Osteopathy in Line of Apostolic Succession with Medicine," has sounded the signal note to the osteopathic profession to claim legitimate succession with medicine. The new school doubtless will follow out his advice and make a stand for rescuing the term medicine from its later degenerate and more limited meaning of *drug* medicine to the older, more general and wider meaning which includes *all* schools of the healing art. Osteopathy therefore *is* a " school of medicine," statutes to the contrary notwithstanding, although the laws are plain that it may not be construed as under the control of those statutes regulating drug medicine and major surgery."(journal of Osteopathy April 1899)

simply " valets" and "maids de chamber" by the medical profession,......" lamenting that osteopathy is not included in the definition of medicine under the act and on the other hand complaining is *" Osteopathy indeed entitled to be considered as a distinct system, or is it simply an adjuvant to the practice of medicine"?*. Then going on to complain about the title M.D.O.".

Sullivan, in the Nov 1899 journal[xii] gives a reply to Hulett's article and says, *"the title is a misnomer as Dr. Hulett 's queries rather consist of a gratuitous expounding of ponderous ideas and adverse opinions of our new law in Illinois."*. He does not mention the M.D.O. degree at all. This is rather curious as he was as ardent a follower of Still as you could find. He concludes by saying that he only wants to be known as an "Osteopath" and if Hulett wants to be called a "doctor" he will need to pass an exam in Materia Medica in Illinois.

So, where does this leave Still's comments about the title M.D.O. He does not mention it anywhere else that I have found, Sullivan didn't comment on it, given the time lapse from Littlejohn's proposal in February to the comments in the Sept journal, it would appear to me that someone "pushed Still's buttons" and produced an immediate visceral response that was out of context and not well formulated. The angst against the use of the word medicine and the title M.D. always seemed to be partisan rather than real. As A T Still used the title Dr. and was referred to as Doctor Still.

This was deemed acceptable, but the word "medicine" was said to be associated in "people's minds with drugs" and therefore taboo. The inconsistency in this argument seemed lost on some osteopaths as the title Doctor in most people's minds, even today, would mean someone who would prescribe a medicine (drugs).

Also, in the May 1899 edition of the Journal of Osteopathy, printed an article by
"ANDREW TAYLOR STILL, M. D."[xiii]

The Southern School of Osteopathy's magazine, The Southern Journal of Osteopathy, published an article entitled 'Osteopathy Described' by
"A T Still M.D., founder of Osteopathy"[xiv]

It is also noteworthy that the front cover of the Journal of Osteopathy, up to the first issue of volume 6 in June 1899, had on its front cover, a picture of Still under the banner heading "A. T. Still M.D."

The change of cover in volume 6 had a picture of Still from a medal and opposite page 1 of the June issue, the medal is shown and the inscription
"A T Still, M.D.
He who first acted on
Shakespeare's adage:
'Throw physic to the dogs'"

The last line was one Still used in the April 1895 issue of the Journal of Osteopathy. While the cover continued to show only Still's head the inscription does not seem to have been included in other issues, only the July issue having the inscription 'A. T. Still, M.D.' under the picture of the medal on page 78.

Further, if we look forward to May 1909, in the Osteopathic Physician, we find Still referred to as "Andrew Taylor Still M.D." in one large advisement he apparently endorsed, exactly opposite a large advert for American School of Osteopathy. If this was a single advert in a single edition of the magazine it could have been overlooked. However, as it appeared in the Osteopathic physician through 1907, 1908, 1909 and 1910, it is hard to believe that it was not seen by those who were ardently against the use of the title M.D. Other references to Still having the title M.D. can also be found.[5] As we can find no complaints about the use of the title Doctor or Still's use of the designation M.D. what are we to make of Hulett's article?

It would seem that Still was not immune to responding viscerally to arguments that appealed to his ego; *"In the minds of some of us D. O. stands for Dr. Still's work"*. On the other hand, he would respond positively to well put arguments like that of Littlejohn in his February 1899 address to graduates. Something annoyed Hulett, but we cannot be sure what, given that his article assailed many different aspects of legislation and opinion and came many months after Littlejohn made his views about his opinion on the proposed title M.D. (osteopathic). Given the personal remarks by Still, it would seem likely that Hulett had communicated personally with him rather than sending the article to the editor and the editor then bringing it to Still for comment. It would also seem probable that it was a deliberate act on Hulett's part and that he and others had discussed it in advance.

Another incident recorded in Booths History of Osteopathy gives an insight into how Charlie Still, Hildreth and others tried to influence Still when they thought he was 'endangering' the College. This concerned the building of the college buildings in 1895/6. The story is told by M. F. Hulett. When it appeared that Still was overspending *"His staff of co-laborers were taken by surprise, and the forces would be gathered to protest. Patterson said, `This must stop'. Charlie, ditto, Harry declared, `We can't raise the money'. Hildreth added, `We must not allow it'. The latter, being perhaps suave and*

---

[5] Dr. Wilfred E. Harris, president of the Massachusetts College of Osteopathy, spoke on "Some. Thoughts on the Research Institute." Among other things he said: "He would like to see the Massachusetts College grant an M. D. degree after four years' work; that our beloved founder, Dr. Still, usually signed his name A. T. Still, M. D. and D. O. Carl P. McConnell, of Chicago, had the appendages M. D., D.O., and other osteopaths, too, that I need not mention at this time." (osteopathic Physician June 1912 page 13)

more diplomatic, was appointed to deliver the ultimatum"[xv]. In this case Hildreth was chosen as the mostly to be heard by Still, However, Still held his ground and Hildreth" *returned from the encounter with temper and feathers much bedraggled and with little to say"*[xvi] In this case, appealing to Still on the basis of finance did not work. While there is no evidence that C. M. T. Hulett was sent in as the result of discussions involving Hildreth and Charlie Still, the sequence of events makes it seem likely. Particularly if McConnell's later comment, in 1902, is taken into consideration; He also reminded osteopaths *"I wonder if these few know how perilously near a great many osteopaths came to having, the M. D. degree conferred upon them, instead of the degree of D.O., a few short years ago?*[xvii]*"* It could be argued that Still was actively considering the use of the M.D.O. degree as suggested by Littlejohn, but was turned against it by the use of the appeal to his 'emotional side' by Hulett with the backing of Charlie Still and Hildreth.

We see another clear example of the political maneuvering of Hulett and Hildreth at the annual meeting of the American Osteopathic Association in Minneapolis in 1909. At the eighth session, after the Associated Colleges had adjourned to another room and the demonstration by Hildreth and Laughlin had finished *"Dr. C. M. Turner Hulett took the floor and said : I move that this Association deplores the radical and dangerous departure from the ideals of the profession on the part of some of our institutions in their published purpose to grant the M. D. degree…. So strongly are we impressed with the dangers involved that we recommend to the Committee on Education and Board of Trustees that no college which grants the degree of Doctor of Medicine shall be elected or continued as a co-operating organization with this association".*

Before the resolution could be passed Dr. Louisa Burns spoke up *"There is not now present any member representing the colleges which are concerned in this motion. There was certain college business which needed to be attended to…. I appeal to every one of you on the score of fairness not to take such action as this without giving these people an opportunity to be heard"*[xviii].

Hulett agreed to wait but the damage, which I suspect was deliberate, was done. As Dr. Peck said in a letter about this *"First, an appeal to the emotions always produces a stronger reaction in the human mind than an appeal to reason. Consequently, a speaker who* clothes some pleasing generality in poetical language is apt to receive more enthusiastic support than is one who deals with some specific fact which has arisen in his practice of the healing art"[xix][6].

    I don't think there was any chance neither Hildreth nor Hulett did not know the members of the Associated Colleges, including Littlejohn, were out of the room. It is a very good example of the clash of cultures that Littlejohn faced.

    Littlejohn had no problem with discussing with Still, even when they disagreed.[7] His method would not involve emotion or ego. Rather he would rely on argument and logic. We see good example of this in his discussion on the 'Alabama decision'[8]

Changes to the Journal of Osteopathy

    The inside of the front cover of the Journal had been more or less consistent with the 'definition of osteopathy' being the main or only content. This included the definition of 'Diplomate' and D.O. the designation of graduates as 'diplomate or Doctor in Osteopathy'. The announcement for the ASO was consistently on the inside back cover and ended with a call for those wanting more information to write for the catalogue for more information. The person whose name was associated with it varied from 'A T Still, president, 'Hulett, Dean'

---

[6] While Takser, a leading osteopath, thought the meeting in Cleveland in 1903 was an overall success, he had some criticism. These included Tasker had made the comment *"The is still too much emotion about our conventions. We are not held together by our emotions. It is unity of experience which holds us and so long as we profess to be a scientific body we must not befog the points at issue by redundant phraseology, adjective piled on adjective, fulsome praises or any other of the so-called arts of oratory."* In august 1903 in an article on 'The things which contributed to the success of the A.O.A. Cleveland meeting'. (The Osteopathic World, August 1903, page 366)

[7] An example of this is found in the Osteopathic Physician, October 1902, page 1, when Littlejohn was settling into his time in Kirksville **"I know that Dr. A. T. Still opposed the A. C. O. from its inception, as I personally discussed the matter with him at the time of the origin of the A. C. O. I told Dr. Still then I believed he was mistaken, and I still believe so."**

[8] The Osteopathic Physician of September 1902 pages 6-8.

'Hulett, Secretary' with no apparent rhyme or reason to the changes. During 1898, with Hulett as Dean the designation changed almost randomly.

In June 1899, with the change to the new volume, volume 6, the front cover was changed, the definition of osteopathy had the last paragraph, the definition of 'Diplomate in Osteopathy and D.O., left out and Littlejohn's name as Dean was given at the end of the Announcement on the inside back cover. At the same time, Bunting was to leave as editor and was replaced by Minnie Dawson in July 1899. Miss Dawson was in Littlejohn's graduation class in January 1900.

If this seems a little complicated, it is because it relates to the re-inclusion of the definition of D.O. by Still in the September 1899 edition. In his reply to Hulett Still said that the definition was The D. O. in the definition of Osteopathy was left out without his knowledge or consent and was added as soon as he noticed the omission. This means that he only noticed it in time for the September edition, and probably only when Hulett mentioned.

The coincidence in timing is too much to think otherwise. This edition also reverted to the school announcement that did not include the name of the Dean. This could be taken as a deliberate act by Still, thus reinforcing the argument that he 'sacked' Littlejohn as Dean. On the other hand, it may simply be an artifact of the printing process, or just like during 1898, when this detailed varied, it is of no significance. Remember, the editor had just changed to Miss Dawson in July.

The rationale for this would have been the time frame. It is unlikely that Hulett's article came direct to the printer and was then brought it to Still, who then wrote his endorsement and gave instructions to change the definition of osteopathy back to its original. The most likely scenario would have been for Hulett to communicate directly with Still. Remember he was a nephew of Still's wife. This would then have put time pressure on the printers to include not only the article but also to change the inside of the cover.

Bunting gives some idea of the exchanges he had with Still during his term as editor.

"When he had anything to say to me, he used to go by the school, pick me up, and we would go down to LaPlata, or down to the farm where he did much of his work... This place was about seven miles out of town, where we would have a good farm dinner, and the

'Old Doctor' would rake me over the coals and give me enough instruction to last two or three months[xx]

So, Minnie Dawson, having just taken over as editor now faced Still's ire about the exclusion of the last paragraph in the Definition of Osteopathy. Still having earlier in the summer dealt with the incident of Bunting and Landes ordering copies of the Journal with their cards printed on the inside cover.

Now both inside and outside covers would have had to be changed. My view is that Still, fueled by Hulett's comments gave the order in a fit of angst. This does not mean he sacked Littlejohn, just, in my opinion, that he was upset or angry, not necessarily with Littlejohn, but more likely as a reaction to Hulett's promptings and the previous incident with Bunting.

"SOMETHING NEW OR NOTHING AT ALL"

Another piece published in the July 1899 journal adds to the confusion:

"SOMETHING NEW OR NOTHING AT ALL. stale habit and imitation and quotations from the honest though ignorant dead will not be tolerated in this school any longer than I can ascertain the osteopathic instructor who will come before the class with lists of quotations from medical authors who hate osteopathy in their bigoted way. I wish no books with such productions presented to the honest seeker for osteopathic knowledge, and I advise the student who reads any book abounding in quotations to take it to some competent osteopath who will probably tell you how badly the author has missed the object and how unwisely you have spent your money. A. T. Still"[xxi]

It is given over Stills name and comes after a section from his new book "The Philosophy of Osteopathy" which was due to be published. It has been quoted to me as further evidence of the putative argument between Still and Littlejohn. However, if we read it as it is written and in the context of his new book it is fairly clear it has nothing to do with Littlejohn. Remember, Littlejohn was not even in the country at the time. In the May issue of the Journal the publication of McConnell's book 'The Practice of Osteopathy" was announced.

Others have suggested that *"In this book, McConnell attempts to merge the ideals of Still and Osler. At the time of its writing, osteopaths were divided as to where medical philosophy fit in with osteopathic philosophy. McConnell serves to bridge that gap through this work."* [xxii]

Indeed, in the preface McConnell says:

"I am specially indebted to Osler, Anders, Tyson, Loomis, Raue, Goss, Stephens, and Hughes practices of medicine and to the writers in Allbutt's System of Medicine and the American Text Book on the Practice of Medicine. Also, to American Text Books, Landois and Sterling's, Schaeffer's, Foster's, Flint's, and Yeo's Physiologies and to Ziegler's, Greene's and Stengel's Pathologies for many valuable ideas". [xxiii]

We know Still did not rate McConnell's book as he writes in January 1900: -

"I think Barnes helped McConnell[9] write his book. [It] is about all taken from old medical authors. It is a total failure to an Osteopath Barnes[10] did not write nor say a word that is in it" [xxiv]

Still's preface to his book makes his position clear:

"When I saw others, who had not more than skimmed the surface of the science, taking up the pen to write books on Osteopathy, and after having carefully examined their productions, found they were drinking from the fountains of old schools of drugs, dragging back the science to the very systems from which I divorced myself so many years ago, and realized that hungry students were ready to swallow such mental poison, dangerous as it was, I became fully awakened to the necessity of some sort of Osteopathic literature for those wishing to be informed". [xxv]

---

[9] Underlined words are by Still himself; Bold emphasis is by the author, McConnell is spelt 'McConnel' in original

[10] "I am under special obligations to Mr. Samuel D. Barnes, a senior student in the college, who has been a most able and untiring assistant in the correcting of the manuscript. CARL PHILIP MCCONNELL." (The Practice of Osteopathy, 1899 C. P. McConnell, page 9)

The truth is more likely to be that it was just a statement about his own book and not directed at anyone in particular. Another quote from the Philosophy of Osteopathy puts the above in context.

"Several books have been compiled, called "Principles of Osteopathy." They may sell but will fail to give the knowledge the student desires"[xxvi]

Barbers 'Osteopathy Complete' was published in 1898 and his school, National School of Osteopathy, had caused some trouble for Still's college.

"The recent novel and extraordinary decision of the Kansas City Court of Appeals in the case of the State vs Barber's so called School of Osteopathy, at Kansas City, seems to leave the doors wide open for all kinds of "fake" institutions and " diploma mills" to follow their business without legal interference."[xxvii]

Smith had gone to the school under an assumed name and obtained a diploma without attending any classes, as a result of which a case was taken by the State.

"Dr. Smith secured a diploma from the school, upon payment of $150 as a graduation fee, without attendance, which diploma certified that its holder had "completed the full course of study prescribed by the National School of Osteopathy"[xxviii]

However, I do feel that Still himself did not have a good grasp of how his 'plain speaking' manner would or could be interpreted by people. His statement had a purpose, to publish his book and to make people think about who had written what - was it just a series of quotes without understanding or did it serve a purpose in osteopathic education

An example of the effect of his 'plain speaking' quotes is to be found in the reminiscences of his students. Most often these are centered on Still performing some deft maneuver and the patient was then cured. Two examples will serve to illustrate. The first concerns a student, Charles F. Bandel[11], who had been treating a patient for several weeks with no real improvement. On this day the patient had

---

[11] Littlejohn's last recorded act as Dean was at the faculty meeting of September 7th, 1899, was to add Bandel's name to the list to be graduated in June 1899

talked to Still who then came into the treatment room and, after examining the patient, asked him to treat the patient.

"I gave the patient before me about twenty minutes of all the energy my body could supply. You can imagine how anxious I was to make a decided hit; I relaxed every muscle in the patient's back; stretched the spine for good measure; treated his neck, and rotated his legs thoroughly so as to be sure I was omitting no 'movement' within my knowledge. "I really worked hard (perhaps never perspired so much before or since), and all this time the 'Old Doctor' was pacing up and down the room with his keen eyes fixed upon me."

Still's reply was

"'All done, Bandel?" Yes, doctor,' I replied, and complacently awaited his compliments upon my untiring efforts in behalf of our poor patient. Imagine my dismay when he stepped in front of the patient and said, 'Oh, Bandel—how long will it be necessary for you to remain in this college? You have heard me speak dozens of times, and I have talked with you privately; how long, in God's name, shall I have to be around you before you will comprehend our simple principle? Why, my son, the treatment you have given this man is nothing short of that done by an ignoramus; you are simply an "engine-wiper;" you rubbed, you pulled, you did everything under the sun, except the right thing; an "engine-wiper" rubs up the whole machine when the trouble lies in one mal-adjusted part. You can imagine how my castles in the air were tumbling during this reprimand before a patient. The 'Old Doctor' then stepped behind the patient, used his left arm as a lever, placed his thumb and his forefinger upon the second lumbar, gave a peculiar rotary movement and the result was a pop, so loud that it seemed incredible. He then said, "Now, Bandel, come round and pat your patient on his back and tell him he will be walking in three days."[xxix]

A second example concerns Dr W A Potter and Dr Joe Sullivan, both students at the time, who had been treating a case for several months with little or no improvement. Sullivan said: -

"they had just finished giving her a general treatment[12]*, adding all the turns and twists they knew, when Dr. Sullivan, wiping the*

---

[12] It is interesting to speculate as to who taught the 'General Treatment' at this stage in the ASO. This was well before Littlejohns time. Sullivan graduated

perspiration from his brow, said, 'The "Old Doctor" is always talking about setting these hips in one treatment; I'd give a farm to see him set this one...' He (Still) came and walking up to the girl, said in his kindly voice, 'Hello, sister, what's the matter here?' He did not stop to ask her age, get her family history, take her blood pressure, or make an X-ray examination. He simply placed a chair against the wall, asked the little girl to .be seated. To Dr. Sullivan he said, 'Hold the pelvis firm, —now, Potter, take hold of the good leg and keep her firm on the chair.' He then placed one hand on the great trochanter, took hold of the foot with the other, gave two or three turns of the limb, the whole operation lasting less than one minute. 'Now stand up,' he said. When she arose, the leg was in normal position, just as long as the other one."[xxx]

In general, what I have found over the years is that people only remember the 'quick and effortless' cure and do not remember the words of others who tell of how long it takes in most cases. For example: -

"An Osteopathic adjustment is and must be one of precision." "As you advance in your understanding, you will find it is always the deeper structures that are responsible in keeping the parts in lesion when they have once formed, and no amount of massaging of the superficial tissues will adjust a bony lesion." "And when there exists an excessive irritability of the nerves that innervate the structures that govern the joints, you must first normalize it; otherwise, the adjustment will not stay put." **I have known him to take weeks and even months to do this**[13], *especially, when the joints having the larger range of motion were involved and his adjustment stayed put when he made them."*[xxxi]

---

in 1896 and Potter in 1897 and Hildreth and H. M. Still as the main lecturers listed for the Practice of Osteopathy, with McConnell and W. J. Conner as lectures in the Clinics (ASO Catalogue for 1897). Bandel graduated in 1899 with Hildreth, H.T. Still, W. J. Conner and McConnell listed as demonstrating in Clinic or teaching the theory and practice of Osteopathy in the 1898/1899 catalogue.

[13] Bold emphasis by the author.

Wernham, my teacher and mentor at the Maidstone College of osteopathy, used to put this problem succinctly. To paraphrase him;

People only want to be shown how and are not interested in the why. Those who have a natural aptitude for manipulation and do not get a deep grasp of the Principles of Osteopathy together with a solid foundation in anatomy, physiology and mechanics tend to become **'crack merchants'** as Littlejohn would call them. Those who have less natural aptitude tend to become **'engine wipers'** as Still would say.

Wernham himself used to call them ' **the all you need merchants'** These would take simple phrases from Still's works, like the 'no physiology' story, mentioned earlier, and use it to defend their attitude of ' just show me and never mind all the theory', without any thought for how often Still said how essential Physiology was. As mentioned above Still also said "An Osteopath...must master Anatomy and Physiology."

> "He (Still) said it would take six months before I saw any pronounced change and maybe a year before the parts would gain sufficient strength to keep them in place"
>
> The Gravett Papers Journal of the American Academy of Osteopathy 1954, pages 38

All of this is just to illustrate my opinion that Still, when he made his 'proclamations' did not have a good grasp of how the words might be misinterpreted or taken out of context or to extremes. It does not mean that the early osteopaths in general, did only quick cures. In fact, we find more stories in the literature giving details of it taking months of preparation to be able to affect an adjustment. It is sad that the stories that are remembered are those that appeal to the emotions and these in general involve 'miraculous cures' at the hands of Still or other leading osteopaths when other methods, especially regular medicine, had failed.

So, if the statement *'something new or nothing at all'*, was taken as a definitive statement or directive, then it would almost certainly have been one that Littlejohn would disagree with. Littlejohn always insisted upon crediting those who went before and whose labors you built upon- especially in anatomy and physiology. However, we find that Still did use quotes when it suited his teaching purposes. E. G. In his 1902 Philosophy and Mechanical Principles of Osteopathy' and his 1910 "research and Practice" he quotes from Dunglison's and Dorland's works[xxxii]. So, my opinion is that it was simply about his new book. He did have a problem with the continuous use of medical texts in his school[xxxiii], but this was something that had to be put up with until similar texts were written by Osteopaths. Littlejohn had set in motion this with his texts on Physiology, and Smith with his notes on Anatomy.

As an aside to this, it would be my opinion that Still's book, Research and Practice' was prepared from his earlier works but someone else and put into a 'more modern' style. The writing style does not, in my opinion, read like Still's. I would say the same about the piece 'Our Platform' published in the October 1902 Journal of Osteopathy and reprinted, slightly modified, in 'Research and Practice'.

Still had intended to write a larger book on the treatment of disease. From his description it would appear the he was at least considering including 'comparative therapeutics' to some degree. This would have been in line with Littlejohn's ideas of showing how superior Osteopathy was to other forms of medicine. This book never came to fruition and may have ended up as 'Research and Practice', which would appear to be a watered-down version of what Still had envisioned. I often wonder what would have happened if Still and Littlejohn had been left alone to work together, what wonders of Osteopathy might have emerged.

Another aspect should be mentioned here. That is Still's inherent honesty. George H. Fulton, D. O. put it this way,

> Kirksville Mo. Dec. 14. 1899
>
> *I have begun to write a <u>book</u> that will be as large as Gray's Anatomy. It's title is Treatment by <u>A.T. Still</u>.* All parts that I write will be shown by colored plates. Say when I write on lungs or bowels or any part I will give colored plates of chest or abdomen. On [xx: left] right hand or pages Book will have two colums:
>
> | New Stile | Old stile |
> |---|---|
> | Osteopathy | Alopathy |
> | | Homeopathy |
> | | Eclecticism |
>
> It will be a textbook on disease and treatment for the osteopathy only.
>
> Museum of Osteopathic Medicine. Kirksville, A T Still, Letter to Thekla Orschel. [1899 Dec 14]. [2009.10.654] Andrew Taylor Still Papers.
> (spelling is as in Still's writing)

"I have never known anyone who put greater emphasis upon honesty than did Dr. Still. Honesty was the basis on which his life was builded and the crucial standard by which he judged others. For the deceitful and dishonest he held a lasting contempt. He stood honestly and squarely on all issues, and he demanded honesty on the part of his associates. And with this irrefutable integrity of character went another notable characteristic of the really great, and that was his simplicity of manner".[xxxiv]

So, you might imagine how he would react when rumors were spread questioning Littlejohn's honesty in connection with his Lecture to the Society of Science[14] in London in the summer of 1899. Charles Still, in his letters to Dr. E Roberts says

"We have in our employ one J. Martin Littlejohn who has been filling the chair of Physiology, and last year he made the announcement that he had been invited by the Royal Society of Science to deliver an address before that body which convened in Crystal Palace, July 19th. His subject was to be Osteopathy. It was heralded by our Journal as being quite an honor for a young man. Sometime last summer in the city of Buffalo, N. Y., a gentle man spoke to our secretary stating that it was quite a joke that was published in our Journal. It was again brought to our notice this fall that such a thing did not happen."[xxxv]

Littlejohn's attitude to honesty would have been similar to Still's. He made many pleas to the profession for honesty, particularly in regard to the word 'Medicine' and the use of antiseptics anesthetics etc.[15]. This would have set up an interesting dynamic between the honesty or lack of it, of Charles Still and Hildreth on one side and Smith and the Littlejohns, particularly James Buchan, on the other. A clash between 'political honesty' (with its inevitable appeal to emotions rather than reason), mid-western culture and the honest nature of Reformed Presbyterian Culture.

---

[14] The official short title that was to be used by members of the Society of Science, Letters and Art. *"Fellows are requested to describe themselves as Fellows of the Society of Science : the Society of Science being the short name of the Society of Science, Letters and Art, of London"* (journal of the Society of Science, Letters and Art of London, January 15th, 1895, page 23)

[15] "One of the chief factors that militated against us in Illinois during our last campaign was the fact that while many of the osteopaths were preaching "no drug, no knife doctrine" —the catalogues of the A. S. O. were in the hands of the legislators announcing pages of surgical operations. The A. S.O. is quite right in adding surgery to the curriculum, and a course in the fallacies of medicine, that is, comparative therapeutics; but let us be honest" (Trying to Solve M. D. Degree Proposition, JAOA May 1910, page 407)

Hildreth's Recall to the A. S. O.

Another event was the recall of Hildreth to work in the infirmary. As mentioned above, the school and infirmary had been growing fast both in numbers of students and patients. Even Warren Hamilton, the school business manager saying they had tried to control it without any prospect of success;

"We have been trying to shut down, but they still come and will break in. we now have 190, and I believe I can surely say by the end of the month, we will have at least 200"[xxxvi]

> Owing to circumstances which I am unable to control, it has become necessary for me to leave St. Louis and again join the American School of Osteopathy, at Kirksville, Mo. And in order to leave my friends in good hands, and the profession with an able exponent in my office, I have transferred the same to Dr. W. H. Eckert, graduate of our home school and a man in whom I have the utmost confidence. both as an Osteopath and a gentleman. It gives me pleasure to recommend him to my friends and to the public. Thanking you for past favors and with the hope for a continuance of the same for my successor, I am, Very respectfully yours,
> ARTHUR G. HILDRETH, D. O. (Journal of Osteopathy Oct 1899)

This is an even more difficult event to find the "truth" about. He was elected president of the A.A.A.O.[16] in July, a meeting that Charlie Still attended. This appointment meant he could not hold a position in an Osteopathic School.

We can assume that Charlie had nothing directly to do with his recall as it seems he had given Smith and the Littlejohns an agreement that Hildreth would have nothing to do with the school in the 1899/90 session[xxxvii].

---

[16] American Association for the Advancement of Osteopathy, this was to evolve into the American Osteopathic Association.

It is more than likely that is was Harry Still actively encouraging his father, A T Still, that the infirmary needed more experience staff, especially given the large expected intake of students in Sept 1899. His motive, as mention above, would have included his desire to get out of "schoolwork". It seems just as unlikely that A T Still had any knowledge of the agreement that *"Hildreth would have nothing to do with the school"*; nor that he would have acted in such an underhanded way against Littlejohn to appoint Hildreth as Dean while Littlejohn was in Europe.

Hildreth's Version of Events

At this stage it is appropriate to look in detail at Hildreth's account of what happened when Littlejohn returned from Europe, to continue in his position as dean. Hildreth's return was announced in an Important announcement as follows;

"*On account of the growth and magnitude of both the School and Infirmary, they have deemed it wise to have more assistance, and with the interests of both students and patients foremost in their minds, have succeeded in securing Dr. A. G. Hildreth, who for so many years has been associated with Dr. A. T. Still and his sons, but has been, for the past year, located in St. Louis, Mo., where he has established an excellent practice.*
Dr. Hildreth has accepted an offer from Dr. Still and his sons to again associate himself with them—not as a salaried man—but to have an interest in the entire work of both School and Infirmary. Dr. Hildreth has been too long associated with the parent institution, and with the growth and development of the science of Osteopathy, to need any comment from us. His experience in the operating-rooms has been almost limitless, and combining his ability with that of Drs. Charles and Harry Still will give the A. T. Still Infirmary the strongest corps of able and experienced Osteopathic practitioners to be found in the land."[xxxviii]

That Hildreth was dedicated to A T Still and Osteopathy no one can doubt. Born on 13th June 1863 near Kirksville he was more or less continuously associated with the college for 10 years following his graduation in 1894. He and his family settled in St Louis in 1903 and practiced there until the spring of 1914 when he took charge of the Still- Hildreth Sanatorium at Macon MO. His mother was a practitioner of Water Cure (*not the hydrotherapy of Kneipp*) and consulted with Still for a patient of hers that had goiter and the young Hildreth witnessed this – his association with Still had started at that young age and would continue up to Stills death in 1917.[xxxix]

He is recorded as leaving Kirksville in November 1896 to Join Harry Still in Chicago. " *He said he did not want it understood he had completely severed his connection with the school and that at present while duty called him to the front, at any time when he could do more for the advancement of the science of Osteopathy here (Kirksville) than elsewhere he would gladly return"*[xl]

On the 23rd of May, 1897, he again took up work in school at a salary that *"at that time was considered large"* This was in response to a invitation from *"the founder of osteopath and his sons"* to return from their practice in Chicago to help in the school due to the increasing number of students and patients. They sold their practice to J H Sullivan. It is interesting to note that the invitation was given via Harry Still and he passed it on to or perhaps seemed to extend[17] it to Hildreth.[xli]

In his book "the Lengthening shadow of Dr. A T Still" he relates his version of events in the fall of 1899 as follows;

"During that fall -1899- quite a dissension arose over the fact that a man who was not a graduate of a recognized higher educational institution had been made dean and been placed in a position which gave him great power. There were four men on the faculty at that time who were graduates of the allopathic school of medicine. Their opinion was that I was ultra-osteopathic and would tolerate none other than the strictest adherence to the teaching of osteopathy in the way Dr. Still himself had taught it for a number of years. A written protest was sent to Dr. Still, his sons and family, and to myself, all of whom were members of the board of trustees. It was signed by the four graduates in allopathic medicine and said that they refused to serve as members of the teaching staff of the American School of Osteopathy if I were to be retained as dean. I was opposed then, as I have always been, to any and all tendencies toward mixing the teaching of drugs and osteopathy...

"through experience I had learned that the greatest opportunity for service for those who wished to study osteopathy as well as for

---

[17] They way Hildreth wrote about this is a little ambiguous. First saying the letter to Harry asked for 'both 'of them to return, then Harry asking him if he would be willing to return, then the invitation was said to come from 'the founder and his sons'

those who wished to be aided by osteopathy, must come from an absolutely independent system. Perhaps I might have been a little radical, at least that was the feeling of the four graduates of medicine. Among them was Dr. William Smith, the man who had done so much in the beginning, in his teaching of anatomy and kindred subjects, in laying the foundation of the osteopathic profession. I have complimented his work highly in an earlier chapter. He and his associates seemed to think that because my education was not equal to theirs it was beneath their dignity to serve with me. I was so opposed to having anything taught but osteopathy that they resented it. It was very clear that the objectors felt that a combination of "old school" medicine and osteopathy would mean most. They had a perfect right to their opinions, just as I had to mine, just as Dr. Still had the right to think and fight for the truth as he saw it.

"The students took up the matter and a very large majority of them were loyal to Dr. Still and osteopathy. Such men as Drs. McConnell, Proctor, Hazzard, W. M. Clark, Will Laughlin-in fact nearly the entire faculty of the college- went to Dr. Still and his sons and demanded that the medical influence be eliminated. In other words, they stood by me in my position, and plainly stated that unless the medical influence was eliminated, they would resign from the positions they occupied. With the majority of the students taking the same attitude, or a least throwing their influence with the osteopathic teachers in the college, the only thing these four men could do was to retire. Dr. Smith resigned at once, the other doctors completed the year and then resigned."[xlii]

Hildreth's recollection of events in around the years 1899-1900 have been taken as fact by most authors so much so that this "fight" against the medical influence has become part of osteopathic folklore within the putative argument being between Littlejohn and Still.

If we examine it closely it is found to have many errors which are listed below:

Only 3 were graduates of allopathic medicine – J M Littlejohn was not. True he had studied in Dunham, but this was a homeopathic school and he had not yet graduated. The other M.D. was McConnell, the publication of whose book was announced in the May issue of the Journal of Osteopathy and about which Still was not impressed. McConnell became an 'outstanding ACOM&S faculty member' joining Littlejohn in his school, The **A**merican **C**ollege of **O**steopathic **M**edicine and **S**urgery in Chicago in 1900.[xliii] So it is very unlikely that he supported Hildreth in the way Hildreth mentioned above.

Hazzard had left the school in June 1899 and therefore was not a member of the faculty.

"Dr. Charles Hazzard of the faculty of the American School of Osteopathy, and member of the staff of operators in the A. T. Still Infirmary, will sever his connection with these institutions July 1st, and about July 15th will open an office for the practice of Osteopathy in Detroit, Michigan."[xliv]

In fact, it took a lot of pleading and several letters from Charlie Still to get him to come back to teach in the 1900-1901 term, after McConnell had left. Part of the reason was that he felt McConnell was being paid much more than him. If he 'supported' Hildreth it is likely that money had as much to do with it as principles.[xlv]

The written protest was sent to the Board of Trustees and not to any individual. It did not say they refused to "serve as members of the teaching staff". It said **"He (Hildreth) is in the school in violation of a contract made with us last term, and in spite of the distinct statement made at the beginning of the term that he was to have nothing at all to do with the faculty….we decline to associate with him as teacher because we believe it detrimental to the school, to our reputation and the good name of Dr. A.T. Still our president"**[xlvi]. The Littlejohns made this clear in further letters and by continuing to work in their given roles in the college.

It had nothing to do with the teaching of drugs or medicine. If we look at Littlejohn's writings no one could be clearer on their opposition to Drugs" Two quotes from that time period serve as examples

"The difference between allopathy and homeopathy on the one side and Osteopathy on the other, is that in the case of Osteopathy no medicine is used at all except nature's medicine."[xlvii]

"Osteopathy goes beyond this skeptical stage, for it claims that the use of drugs is a disadvantage to the system and represents an unscientific method of attempting to cure diseases." [xlviii]

It would be my opinion that Hildreth himself caused much of the angst by impugning the methods and lectures of the Littlejohns and Smith, in particularly, the movement towards more complex surgery at the infirmary.

At the 1899 AAAO meeting in Indianapolis, quite a discussion took place regarding the inclusion of Surgery in Osteopathic schools. Hildreth stated that *"I am opposed to osteopathic schools teaching surgery. What has brought us here to-day? …was it surgery that brought us here? No sir; it was the mistakes of surgery that brought us here. I am not here to condemn surgery, I am not here to fight any other school, but I am here to preach with all my might Osteopathy in its purity and simplicity, believing that in so doing we can do the greatest possible good for suffering humanity."* [xlix]

It is interesting to note that at the same meeting he also said **"That Osteopathy is the practice of medicine in its broadest sense no reasonable-minded man can deny, for he who heals the sick by manipulation, with a tub of hot eater, or in any manner whatever, is a practitioner of medicine in the sense of healing disease"** [l]

He went on to say *"that we as osteopaths must court the strongest feeling of good fellowship and eliminate forever from our schools the petty jealousies, the personal prejudices and envy, which I am sorry to have to admit exist so largely to-day in the older schools of medicine"* [li] – not quite the sentiments he engendered on his return to the American School of Osteopathy in September 1899.

Even within the medical profession we find the tug of war between physician and surgeon to be an ongoing battle. Surgery demands so much resources in terms of facilities, education and drugs and anesthetics, staffing and recovery compared to the physician's side of medicine that it does create potential for disharmony. And this would be particularly so in the young osteopathic college that here to fore had no experience of this type of conflict.

It would also give fertile ground for those who wished to move against this by latching on to the increased curriculum in the area of drugs and Materia Medica as this would have been necessary for surgery but would have been potentially totally out of favour with those committed to 'ten fingered osteopathy'. Also, many students were from poor educational backgrounds and found themselves taking to the practical side of osteopathy very quickly.

"My class had a number who had little or no preliminary education, but when the time came for them to enter the clinic, they gave a wonderful account of themselves and they have also done so in the field. True, they lacked much in some of the things which go to make a fully rounded doctor, and I hold no brief for that; yet they were taught that structural abnormalities were responsible for bodily ills; and also taught to recognize and remove them. With what astonishing success many of them meet." Dr. Harry M. Vastine who graduated in the 1900, with Littlejohn [lii]

I would speculate that the same students, and graduates including some teachers, may not have relished the prospect of more detailed study and thus 'opposed' the expansion of the syllabus.

As has been detailed earlier, Littlejohn had always been in favour of persons of poor educational standards being given opportunities and never put anyone down in this regard. Any objections he would raise would always have been with the ability to do the job. Nowhere in Littlejohn's writing do we find anything other than support for those who have come from lesser educational backgrounds to better themselves. Nowhere in the faculty meeting minutes for that period do we find anything other than wanting to expand the college curriculum as supported by Still in the aftermath of the osteopathy's recognition in Missouri.

Littlejohn was the class representative for the Jan 1900 graduation class[liii] - this would seem to indicate that he had the support of that class at least.

The class poem for the poem for the February 1901 graduating class has one full stanza devoted to the teaching of Littlejohn. No other teacher is mentioned by name. This again would tend to indicate he had made a good impression on them.

"There is one rugged road o'er which we came

J. Martin's Physiology by name"[liv]

It seems Smith did not resign but was dismissed – see letter of Nov 30th to the Board of Trustees from the Littlejohns.

*"We beg respectfully to state to the Board of Trustees of the American School of Osteopathy the **dismissal of Dr. Smith**[18] is not Satisfactory to us as a settlement of the protest we offered to you against the retention of Dr. Arthur Hildreth in violation of our contract with the school during the year 1899-1890"*[lv]

Not only did he not resign, he instigated proceedings to sue the school for "**illegal dismissal**"[19]

See the section "tragic Death of two students" for a viewpoint on how Hildreth may have made himself objectionable during the spring/summer term of 1899 and how the Littlejohns and Smith may have got a contract that Hildreth would have nothing to do with the teaching faculty.

While there is some controversy about when Hildreth was appointed Dean, we can be sure he was not recalled to be Dean. Why? The important announcement makes it clear. It states that it was due to the 'growth and magnitude of both the School and infirmary'

It does not mention him being Dean, nor imply it in any way. The announcement comes later. Littlejohn was clearly Dean during the first part, if not all of September 1899. He signed the Faculty meeting minutes for the meeting on 29th June 1899 as "J. Martin Littlejohn Dean"[lvi]. This would have been done at the subsequent Faculty meeting on 7th September 1899. It was, and is still, the convention to read, agree and sign the minutes of the previous meeting at the current meeting.

---

[18] Bold emphasis by the author
[19] "Dr. William Smith has sued the trustees of the American School of Osteopathy of Kirksville for illegal dismissal" The Republican Friday December 15th, 1899 (newspaper archive)

One other incident that Hildreth mentions in his book, is of importance. That is the 'class rush' as it was called. He says directly that this took place in the first few weeks of term at the beginning of September 1899 tells it as an interesting anecdote about Stills love for the American flag while promoting his own heavy workload[lvii]. However, newspaper reports of the time place it in the week of the 20th November 1899.[20]

> "the trouble culminated in a fight on the roof of the American School and the bone setters were just pushed to the railing and it was about to give when Dr. Still appeared and quelled the riot. The school is four stories high and if Dr. Still had not arrived when he did there would have been plenty of work for the rival school"
>
> Macon citizen November 24, 1899

This is important as it may have been associated with Smiths dismissal. Even though he is not mentioned in the reports, it was the kind of event he would probably have been involved in. it also would have been the type of event that involved alcohol consumption. This and the timing of the event just prior to the first letter from the Littlejohns and Smith complaining about Hildreth dated 23rd November, and the second letter (this time from the Littlejohns, mentioning Smiths dismissal) on the 30th November, would tend to indicate a connection rather than coincidence.

---

[20] Also noted in the Brookfield gazette November 25, 1899 as occurring during the past week; putting it as during the week of the 20th November

A T Still in a letter to Mrs. Orschel dated Dec 14th, 1899 says:

"all is in good shape in school and infirmary- Dr. Smith is dropped out of the school. You will learn why when you come, we had to much boss and drug to suit"[21]

The word "boss" is clearly written as he has done in other letters but does seem out of place. But Still was not renowned for his use of grammar. The date does imply that he was happy with the settlement between the Littlejohns and his son Charlie and that Smith was been given the "blame" so to speak.

As a last word on this episode we have to ask what Still was saying about having surgery in the School. An often-quoted demand from Still is that

"Our duty is to fence strongly against the poisonous effects of old theoretical medical trash; **purge our school of such**, and all dim lights that are not blaring with the oil of up-to-date reason and progressive osteopathic skill and the thunders of effective execution against disease" …

This would appear to in line with Hildreth's version of events except for one thing. It was written in the January 1902 edition of the Journal of Osteopathy under the title of Dr. A T Still's Department, eighteen months after the Littlejohns had left the School. So, it is clear it had nothing to do with LittleJohn. Further, in the same article Still seems to be bemoaning the lack of surgery and surgical training for osteopaths.

"What osteopathy needs in Kirksville is a large surgical sanitarium of its own, to which the diplomates could send all cases needing surgical treatment When we get that, then we will be complete as a scientific brotherhood. A person educated in a school of osteopathy should have protection by having such a sanitarium to which he could send or to which he could recommend his patients. It would be a protection for him….

---

[21] Bold emphasis by the author.

"Thus, the demand for some reliable place to which our doctors of osteopathy can recommend patients requiring surgical attention such as the busy osteopath cannot accommodate, is urgent."[lviii]

Again, this was less than two years after the Surgical Unit in the American School of Osteopathy was closed down because the surgeons had left, or in the case of Dr. Smith, been sacked. So, I would say that it was on account of the experience of having the Surgical Sanatorium run successfully by Smith and James B. Littlejohn during 1899 that generated such a statement by Still and gave him the impetus to have designed and built the hospital and surgical unit, that opened in 1906, which Hildreth endorsed, giving the dedication speech.

JOURNAL OF OSTEOPATHY APRIL 1901 GRADUATING CLASS FEB 1901 CLASS POEM

LAST TWO STANZAS

There is one rugged road o'er which we came
J. Martin's Physiology by name:
'Twas on this march we fought our hardest fight;
We labored all the day and half the night
To learn the action of Depressor Nerve,
Which from its path of duty does not swerve
But keeps the fountains of the heart at play
In smooth and even tenor day by day.
We tracked the Vagus Nerve and saw it run
Into the golden Plexus of the sun.
Sensation, motion and nutrition, all
Lie motionless and useless 'till a call
From some nerve center brings them into play,
Nerve impulse keeps them active night and day,
'Til something interferes with Nature's breath,
Then nervous action stops, we call this death.
Let's not forget that death is sure to come,
We know not when we shall be summoned home
To render an account of what we've done
These past two years. Those days were full of sun,
While scarce a shadow fell across our way.
Since now we've seen the dawning of our day
Of usefulness, let's crown it with success;
Do your full duty – stop with nothing less,
For when at last our race of life is run
We shall remembered be, by what we've done.

The Seeds of Discontent

So, what were the seeds of discontent? Mostly the rise of and success of the surgical sanitorium, followed closely by the suggestion of the M.D.O. Degree. Undercurrents were always there and must include the blossoming new schools of osteopathy. Charlie Still, instead of seeing this as an advantage tended to see them as competition. Still himself was opposed to the Associated Colleges if Osteopathy, and Littlejohn had discussed this with him and explained why he thought he (Still) was wrong. There was also another undercurrent. The southern school, the Philadelphia school and the northern school all had close connections through the Cumberland Presbyterian ministers involved in their inception. Nason- a well-known Cumberland minister, whom Still had thought would teach physiology at the ASO, started the Southern School and entered into it as a student. Pressly, who had left the ASO under a cloud and moved first to the Northern school before setting up the Philadelphia college was also a well-known Cumberland Presbyterian. Littlejohn's church, the Reformed Presbyterian, was a closely related church to the Cumberland Church. These 'new' schools all were locating in large cities and this may have added fuel to the effort, by Charlie and Harry Still, Hildreth, Hamilton and others, to move the ASO to a larger city. It is possible, given the events about this mentioned earlier, that Littlejohn was set up as a fall guy for this failed effort, and as time has shown unnecessary venture.

With this background of under currents, change and too fast progress a backlash of some sort was inevitable. I feel Littlejohn made the same mistake in Kirksville he had with his first ministry in Creevagh. He moved too fast and without due consideration for the reaction of the congregation. In Creevagh this was the financial hardships they had been through. In Kirksville, it would be the hardships the early osteopaths had faced from 'medicine', so much so that the word was almost anathema to them.

Hildreth, as one of the earliest and most devoted followers of Still would have the strongest reaction.

Hildreth left the school in 1896 to go into practice in Chicago only to come back in 1897 and again leave to go into practice in January 1899. Thus, his stays at Kirksville were relatively short, having only returned in May 1897 at the request of the trustees to again leave at the end of 1898. He was followed by H M Still[lix] who joined his practice in St Louis in response to the growth of the practice

The coincidence of this with the expansion of the Infirmary to include major surgery and X-Ray diagnosis, the appointment of J M Littlejohn as Dean and the seeming approval of the faulty, student body and Hildreth's mentor, A. T. Still, of the changes together with Hildreth's probable involvement in the tragic death of at least one of the two students that died in 1898 is too much to ignore.

It could also be argued that when Hulett resigned as Dean Hildreth may have felt slighted that the faculty recommended J M Littlejohn to the position and Still approved. He may even have felt that Littlejohn with just one year of osteopathy was poorly qualified compared to his 9 years – the reverse of what he, himself, said about his lack of higher education. Then when the infirmary's venture into serious surgery took off, he again may have felt his position as an "osteopathic surgeon" was under treat. When Still backed Littlejohn so dramatically at the Feb 1899 graduation exercises it may just have been too much for him, especially as it included, not only the rehabilitation of the word Medicine, but also a totally different approach to legislation compared to the one, he had been following. (Hildreth, although now practicing in St Louis, attended the commencement exercises on 1st February 1899)[lx] It is worth recalling Littlejohn's words from that eventful first day of February 1899: -

"In medicine there are different schools and as the constitution does not allow discrimination in behalf of certain persons, the statute law does not permit any discriminations in behalf of one school against another ….

"…The statute law of Missouri, Indiana and other states provides that nothing in the medical laws shall authorize the board of health to make any discrimination against the holders of genuine diplomas under any school or system of medicine, the same statute law declares that Osteopathy is a system or science of healing….

"....If it is not a school of medicine then it can only claim statutory privilege where such statutes exist . Medicine will ultimately be interpreted in the wider sense to include the whole art of healing and the laws up on which this practice is based, so that the Doctorate in Medicine will be the appropriate title of the Osteopath as well as the allopath. The Encyclopedia Britannica defines the Science of medicine as 'the theory of diseases and of remedies.'....

"....We must claim that we are a school of medicine and demonstrate this fact....

"...This means we must raise for ourselves a standard of professional skill and educational qualifications that will challenge the admiration of the world and show t hem that we are not charlatans or impostors or believers in the miracle working power claimed by some who impose on the credulity of the people. Here and here only lies the secret of success to osteopath.

"This seems to me is the idea that instinctively and almost unconsciously guided the movements of the distinguished founder of this science and his early co-workers. This is the idea that lies buried in all his work, plainly stated in the charter of this parent school of Osteopathy under which since 1894 this science has been taught. In the charter it is stated, 'the object of this corporation is to establish a college of osteopathy the design of which is to improve our present system of surgery, obstetrics and treatment of diseases generally and place the same on a more rational and scientific basis, and to impart information to the medical profession, and confer such honors and degrees as are usually granted and conferred by reputable medical colleges; to issue diplomas in testimony of the same to all students graduating from said school' here is the policy of the school, and the purpose for which as a faculty we are engaged in the task of preparing physicians competent to deal , with all the problems of the curative science and art, is 'to teach such sciences and arts as are usually taught in medical colleges and in addition thereto the science of Osteopathy'....

"Dr Still just before awarding the diplomas stepped to the speaker's rostrum and supplemented his first farewell with an eulogy of Dr. Littlejohn's address and a second God-speed to the graduates. He said:

"after listening to Dr. Littlejohn's masterly address, I feel like saying to him and to you all what my old father said to his boys after he set us to plowing and doing other things which we came to do by degrees to his entire satisfaction. 'Boys, you are doing mighty well – I am not sure, but you are beating me at it-yes, I think you are'" [lxi]

The School was to lose another lecturer Prof. Hazzard in June 1899. A letter from C. E. Still to Hazzard on May 7th, 1990 [lxii] when he was trying to get him to come back to the school gives another indication of what was happening during the year 1898/99. C. E. Still had previously spoken of Hazzard as giving him (C E Still) the "Marble heart" (an expression for a cold unresponsive person) and this seems to have something to do with Hazzard being under the impression that another lecturer, Mc Connell, was on a much higher salary than he was. This gives the impression that salary could have been a sore point in general for the staff and not as Hildreth in his book implies related to the Littlejohns and Smith.

So, at the end of 1898 as Hildreth intended to devote his time towards practice in St Louis; he wasn't going to be on the staff for the next year, 1899, and the agreement that the Littlejohns and Smith had with the Trustees, through C. E Still, may have been more diplomatic than real. C.E. Still trying to calm things down at this time. Other events that had had an unsettling effect on the school included the effect of the hurricane[22], the battle over the move of the school, Littlejohn's request for graduation and the M.D.O. qualification. It would seem that Charlie thought he could placate things by giving the Littlejohns and Smith the impression that Hildreth wouldn't be coming back to the school on account of their protest while he knew that Hildreth wasn't coming back to the school because he was going to practice in St. Louis, thus avoid the possibility of further conflict with his father, who had probably scolded him over the attempts to move

---

[22] that the local papers also stated that the school had got much free publicity from the talk about moving the school out of Kirksville and also there was a degree of angst regarding the publicity that surrounded what the osteopaths had done in the aftermath of the cyclone compared to the ordinary M.D.'s.

the school from Kirksville[23], and who was a longtime friend of Hildreth.

On July 6th, 1899 Hildreth was elected President of the A.A.A.O.. C.E. Still also attended the same meeting. This meant that he wouldn't be able to hold a position within the school or any school as this would conflict with the position. It is likely that Charlie knew of, and possibly had an influence upon, this upcoming appointment, so again would have had no problem giving a pledge to the Littlejohns and Smith that Hildreth would not be in the school during the 1899/1900 school year.

Another aspect that needs to be mentioned is the surgical aspect. It has been said that one of the first things Hildreth did was to close the surgical sanatorium which was commissioned and constructed "without A T Stills knowledge but clearly sanctioned by members of that still family"[24] However, if we look at Charlie Stills letters we find that it may have been due to the lack of surgeons and not out of a political statement that it was closed. When you lose your three surgeons, J. B. and D. Littlejohn and W. Smith, you cannot have a surgical sanatorium.[25] The only direct comment we have from A T Still I have found is in a letter he wrote on 14th December 1899; -
"all is in good shape in school and infirmary- Dr. Smith is dropped out of the school. You will learn why when you come, we had to much boss and drug to suit" [lxiii]

In the Journal of Osteopathy, June 1899, it is stated

"Infirmary and Surgical Sanitarium Staffs Were Never Stronger. Patrons of the A. T. Still Infirmary at a distance often hear that they will not be able to be examined or take treatment from "one of the Stills " if they come to Kirksville. **Dr. A. T. Still, president of the**

---

[23] "Dr Still gave out this statement June 7th through the Kirksville papers; '**To the citizens of Kirksville and all others concerned: Kirksville is my home. I have no intention of leaving the place**" (June 1899 journal of Osteopathy)
[24] John Martin Littlejohn an enigma of osteopathic, page 34 John O'Brien; but unreferenced in his book
[25] "*About the operation—I do not believe we are in shape at the present time to undertake anything of that order. I do not care to assume the responsibility of major surgery, and to be successful in such cases one must be in practice every day. I am sorry that that we are not able to do something for you, but these are the facts.*" C E Still to W A McKeehan D.O. April 1900; ASO business letters page 653

Infirmary[26], takes this occasion to make the announcement that such reports are an injustice to the institution. The Infirmary is now under the personal conduct of Dr. Harry M. Still and Dr. Charles E. Still with President A. T. Still in consultation. Dr. C. L. Rider, one of the old and experience operators, has been recalled from Herman, Texas, and is again on the operative staff. Dr. C. P. McConnell, senior professor of Osteopathic practice, and Dr. Marion L. Clark, with Drs. J. B. and David Littlejohn and Dr. William Smith, surgeons, who conduct the surgical sanitarium, make up a complement of the most skilled Osteopathic physicians and surgeons to be found on earth. And these are the physicians whom patients at the A. T. Still Infirmary meet and take treatment under on coming to Kirksville".[lxiv]

Both of these, together with the advertisements for the surgical facilities, in the Journal of Osteopathy, that started in August 1898 and continued through to December 1899, would indicate that not only was Still aware of the changes in the Infirmary but clearly approved of them.

When Hildreth returned to the ASO in September 1899 he wrote a number of articles for the Journal of Osteopathy. The first was called "osteopathy unadulterated" in the October 1899 edition. This concentrated on the relationship of Osteopathy to medicine and surgery and the tendency for osteopaths to want to expand their knowledge by studying other systems.

"I mean by this that as we increase in numbers there is a tendency on the part of some to want to study medicine, surgery, magnetic healing, mesmerism, etc., and I know that it is a mistake to do so." Specifically, on surgery he says: -

"Yes, and in many cases, death occurs, which, if rightly called is nothing short of legal murder. Legal because the law protects them in their butchery."

This brings to mind the tragic case of young Mister Eckert and the reaction of Dr William Smith to the loss of his friend. It seems

---

[26] Bold emphasis by the author

not only possible, but probable that Hildreth was, in this article, setting the scene for his 'rehabilitation' around this affair, in the way that politicians often do.

Another aspect of Littlejohn's relationship to Hildreth that might have contributed to the seeds of discontent, maybe found in their approach to treatment.

Hildreth, while a good and conscientious osteopath was inclined to give short and 'specific' treatments. Littlejohn would not only include osteopathic treatment, both specific and general, but also lifestyle, including diet, hygiene and work. The so-called general treatment advocated by Littlejohn was highly specific in nature.

In his collected papers called 'Principles of Osteopathy' Littlejohn gives great detail on what he means by 'general treatment'. The tendency for students and so called 'specific treatment' advocates to lack the understanding of the highly specific and detailed nature of the 'general treatment' lead John Wernham, who trained under Littlejohn in the British school of osteopathy during the early-part of the twentieth century to change the name to 'Body Adjustment'

> "The osteopathic system brings out certain landmarks of the human body as a basis for its diagnosis and treatment. The masseur simply gives a general treatment with respect to the fact that there are particular muscles, bones, etc. in the body. The osteopathic physician must be thoroughly trained in anatomy, physiology and kindred sciences, and must know every nerve in the body and the direction of every soft tissue and ligament, as well as the path of the fluid streams….
>
> Among the general treatments called for we note the following.
> THE GENERAL CIRCULATION TREATMENT...
> THE GENERAL RESPIRATION TREATMENT...
> THE TREATMENT FOR GENERAL NUTRITION….
> (a) General treatment from the mechanical anatomical standpoint;
> (b) Specific treatment from the physiological standpoint of relation; and
> (c) General physiological treatment is also of value in stimulating or inhibiting the fluids and forces of the body so as to develop a more or less active condition.
>
> Principles of Osteopathy; J Martin Littlejohn; published by L. S. Meyran, 1903; Mid-western University Archives, Chicago, Illinois

Littlejohn's attitude, on the other hand, tended towards the inclusion of the 'general treatment', not as 'engine wiping' but as a specific treatment applied to the whole body.

> "you are not sent out with a set formula to put down under the great R*, nor are you given a number of technical punches and movements like massage and fake osteopaths;
>
> You are sent out with principles and a correct knowledge of anatomy and physiology to apply these in correction of diseased and disordered conditions".
>
> *"R$_x$ "= prescription
>
> Journal of Osteopathy Vol 5 No 7 1898 December; Littlejohn's address to the Graduating class oct 27th 1898

> *"Do not be content to go out and give general treatments…The operator who simply gives general treatments in the hope of hitting the right spot is in the same box. Hence, we need specialists who know just where and how to treat."*
>
> Journal of Osteopathy Vol 5 No 3 1898 August; Littlejohn's address to the Graduating class

In this context Littlejohn would have had no time for the sort of 'races' or games that Hildreth, Charles and Harry Still engaged in. We find this exemplified in the following reminiscence quoted in the Osteopathic Physician in 1904: (this particular 'race' may not have been when Littlejohn was in Kirksville, but I would assume the 'legend' of these activities would have been.)

"(The) Kirksville infirmary, where he, (Harry M. Still), and Sam Landes and Arthur Hildreth and Charley and others used to run races to see

how many patients an average, healthy, hard-working Osteopath could treat in a. day, anyhow....I think these are the comparative statistics as furnished me by Dr. Harry when the records were still fresh in his memory:

Harry M. Still. 95 patients in eight-hour day.

Charley Still. 72 patients in ten-hour day

A. G. Hildreth. 68 patients in ten-hour day.

S. M. Landis. 49 patients. in ten-hour day.

Herman Still. 13* patients in two-hour day"[lxv]

When we see the advice he gives students about how to approach a person on the treatment table we can imagine how he would have reacted when he came across one of the races mentioned, or someone who practiced that way.

"When your hands are laid on the sick, lay them on reverently as if you were dealing with the master mechanism of earth and heaven, the body of man than which no more perfect embodiment of Divine wisdom ever appeared. But you are to remember that even from the standpoint, of science your profession is noble. The pure love of science for sciences sake is a noble Ideal...Do not let the auri sacra fames[27] eat out the vitals of your life." [lxvi]

---

[27] *auri sacra fames* = The accursed greed for gold. An expression that voices St. Paul's dictum that the desire of money is the root of all evil (I Timothy 6:10)

THE DISPUTE

When Littlejohn returned from England in September, he found that Hildreth may be coming back to the school. As mentioned above, there was an important announcement that was put up around this time for which we don't have an exact date, but it is reasonable to assume it was put up at the beginning of term. It says that Hildreth is coming back to assist in the school and infirmary, due to the large number of students coming in. This was in direct violation of the contract they had made in the previous term, presumably with Charlie Still.

In their letter of the 23rd November 1899[lxvii] the Littlejohns and Smith indicated that they had been given a "distinct statement" at the beginning of term that Hildreth would not have anything to do with the faculty. This implies that on his return, Littlejohn on finding out that Hildreth was to return to Kirksville, had talked to Charlie Still and was reassured that Hildreth was to have nothing to do with the School, only the Infirmary. We also note that the '99 /90 catalogue does not list Hildreth as part of the faculty.

Prior to this, we find two faculty meetings, one on the 7th September 1899 and one on the 9th September 1899. The one on the 7th has C.E. and H.M. Still, J.M. and J.B. Littlejohn, McConnell, Proctor, Laughlin, Smith and Clarke present. It's not signed, and the handwriting looks to be that of C.E. Still. The one on the 9th follows as a result of the one on the 7th to consider a special case of a student. Again, those present C.E. and H.M. Still, J.M. and J.B. Littlejohn, McConnell, Proctor, Laughlin and Judge Ellison. Again, there is no signature and again it seems to be in the handwriting of C.E. Still. As was noted earlier, Littlejohn had added a note to the June 1899 minutes to add the name Charles Bendel to the list of graduates for June 1899 as per "resolution of the faculty a 7th September 1899 JML". No such resolution is recorded in that meeting. However, in the minutes of the meeting on 7th Sept 1899, we find that the minutes of the last meeting were read and approved, and that Littlejohn signed the minutes of the last meeting (24th June) as "J. Martin Littlejohn Dean",[lxviii] thus indicating that he was Dean for the meeting on the 7th Sept. but not taking the minutes as would have been one of his duties as Dean.

The next meeting is on September 20th and here again it looks as if it is in the handwriting of C.E. Still. This time there is no list of those present and it simply states "all faculty present except A.T. Still, D. Littlejohn, C.E. Still in chair". This one has the signature of A.G. Hildreth as Dean which would have been added at the next meeting.(It was the usual practice to sign the minutes of the previous meeting when they were read and agreed at the next meeting- that is Hildreth signed it as Dean on October 4th, 1899)

September 27th[28], 1899 the A.A.A.O. accepts A.G. Hildreth's resignation[lxix] so that he can take up position in the American School of Osteopathy. One may speculate that at least the first two meetings, and more probably the first three meetings, not having anyone sign as Dean, with Littlejohn present, indicates that he may have been protesting at those meetings at the prospect of Hildreth coming back into the faculty and therefore not acting as Dean, a means of protest commonly used in Political Dissent. So rather than having been demoted it seems that he may have been protesting by not taking the minutes of the first three meetings of the faculty in Sept 1899. In his mind he would probably say his tenure ended in June when he left for England. (In his depositions for 'The National School of Osteopathy VS (No 838) The American School of Osteopathy'[lxx], he states that he was 'Dean for five months, bringing him up to the end of June 1899, when he left for England)

Hildreth then being appointed Dean at the end of September to fill the "vacant position"[29]. None of this is recorded which indicates to me a rather heated debate in the background.

We then move on to November. It is in the Littlejohn's letters of the November 30th[lxxi] that we clearly see that Smith has been dismissed rather than resigned. Again, we might see

---

[28] This is the date of a Letter from the Board of Trustees of the AAAO passing a resolution, having received Hildreth's resignation, acknowledging his work and congratulating him on being 'in his selection by our Alma Mater as a representative member of her corps of Professors'. It does not mention him being 'Dean'.

[29] Dr. Arthur G. Hildreth, who for many years, was associated with Dr. A. T. Still and his sons, but who has been for the past year located in St. Louis, Mo., has returned to the parent institution, where he serves the school in capacity of Dean, and the Infirmary as a member of its operating staff. Journal of osteopathy Oct 1899 page 198

the hand of C.E. Still in the background here trying to smooth things over, perhaps, as suggested above, using the problems arising from the class rush, as an excuse.

Some further letters then exchange between the Littlejohns and C E Still, as trustee. Hildreth insinuated that some of these letters were written to the family rather than to the Board of Trustees. But this is absolutely not true. Littlejohn would always go through the formal method of doing things and he wrote to Charles Still as a Trustee and a Vice-President of the institution and not on a personal basis to the members of the Still family. It is noteworthy that J B Littlejohn insisted that C E Still talk to all "four" together in his letters of 2nd Dec[lxxii], thus including William Smith who at this stage had been dismissed. This reinforces the impression that the initial argument was between Smith (and J B Littlejohn) and Hildreth. Further evidence of this is to be found in Charlie Stills letters[30] during early 1900.

In a letter of December 9th[lxxiii], the Littlejohns demand a final settlement and we see in this Littlejohn's hand trying to make or find a resolution to things. C.E. Still apparently prior to this had announced to the students that he felt that the Littlejohns had lied and were dishonorable and this had pushed things even further in the rift between them[lxxiv].

After this, it seems Charlie Still and the Littlejohns settled their differences. In a letter signed by the three Littlejohns and C.E. Still stating that they had talked over their differences and had come to an agreement. This would appear to be in the middle of December even though the letter itself has no apparent date on it. Their letter of the 9th December asked for *"a settlement of the*

---

[30]*"You remember young Wilcox that you assisted in getting here from Peoria. I understand that he has taken a strong stand for Hon. Wm. Smith. Since he has been out of our school, he has been trying to get up a class from some of our students much to the annoyance of students and Faculty*(letter to Dr Hazzard, 9th Feb 1900; ASO business letters page 82); *"It has come to the ears of Osteopaths here time and again that Dr. Smith [wrote] a letter to the President of the Medical Board denouncing Dr. Hildreth."* (letter to W Ammerman; Feb 17th, 1900, ASO business letters page 174)

matters presented to you in our previous communications before 6 p.m. today Sat. Dec. 9th."[lxxv]

It may be reasonable to assume the settlement letter was also on December 9th. The only thing that might indicate otherwise is that in the settlement letter we find the phrase; -
"The undersigned Drs. Littlejohn"

This would, if taken literally imply that J. Martin Littlejohn was a 'Doctor'. While he was a Ph.D. and intitled to use the title Doctor; to put in this context was to imply the same use of the title Doctor as his brothers had., which he wasn't, since he did not graduate until January 1900. Even then, it is likely he obtained a diploma 'diplomate in osteopathy'. This is evidenced by his title, 'Diplomate in Osteopathy', as editor of the Journal of the Science of Osteopathy February 1900 to December 1900.[lxxvi] However, the signatures at the bottom indicate that David signed on behalf of Littlejohn and it is more likely just a minor error in syntax, or a matter of convenience in writing.

One point of specific note in this letter is the line "Dr. J. B. Littlejohn recognizes his mistake in hypothetically imputing to the Trustees any possible breach of faith with the students". This presumably refers to the action of C.E. Still telling the students that the Littlejohns had lied, and also breaking faith with the students in terms of bringing Hildreth back against the wishes of the faculty and presumably the students. This also tends to lend support to the argument that J martin Littlejohn was trying to act as a peace maker with him defending his brother J.B. in the argument with the Board of Trustees and C.E. Still. This does not conflict with his principles that if an agreement was entered into it should be stood by, but rather is in line with his education as a minister; if there was a conflict over an agreement or contract then his role as a minister would be to try and resolve it without a breach of the contract.

This settlement is followed in time sequence by Stills letter to Mrs. Orschel dated Dec 14th, 1899 where he says, *"all is in good shape in school and infirmary- Dr. Smith is dropped out of the school."*

Taking these letters in sequence it would appear that Smith got the blame and A T Still was happy that the Littlejohns were staying.

The last mention of Hildreth as Dean is in the Dec 1899 journal of Osteopathy in connection with the Freshman social (page 300). Charlie Still is seen signing letters as Dean from 9th February 1900 (ASO Business letters page 85) onward and is listed as Dean in the

June Journal of Osteopathy[31]. Faculty meeting minutes stopped on January 10th, 1900 with the last one in Hildreth's handwriting being on November 1st, 1899. No minutes were recorded between these two dates. Hildreth did not occupy the position of Dean for long. Doctor George Laughlin was to be Dean from the start of the 1900/01 term (ASO Business letters page 914). So Hildreth's influence was short lived. It would appear that part of the settlement might have been that Hildreth would no longer be Dean or on the faculty and possibly it was expected that Littlejohn would again become Dean. Charlie Still only started signing his name as Dean from the 9th of February 1900, the day after the Littlejohns dated their letters of resignation (J M Littlejohn's letter of resignation is dated 10th February, but he states that he had already told C E Still of his decision prior to this) (ATS museum records)

The question must be asked, why did Littlejohn resign if a settlement he was happy with what had been agreed? The best answer seems to be that his brothers were not happy to continue to work with someone who had acted in such a dishonorable way towards them and their colleague W. Smith; also the damage that had been done to the surgical work in the infirmary with the sudden dismissal of Smith and the probable continued interference by Hildreth made it difficult for them to continue to provide a professional service[32]. Another factor may have been that while

---

[31] "Pettit, Dobson, Eastman and Geo. Cleary, accompanied by Earl D. Jones, manager of the track team, Harvey Maver and Dr. Chas. Still, dean of the faculty, composed the party from Kirksville" (Journal of Osteopathy, Kirksville, June 1900, page 25)

[32] *"Surgery, no man can question but what it is scientific when scientifically applied, but Dr. Still's life work and the experience of those of us who for years, have been associated with him and engaged in this practice, prove that hundreds, yes, thousands of people are operated upon- when there is no necessity for an operation, and when he who operates does not even know what is the matter with his patient, thus proving that surgery as practiced to-day by thousands of incompetent men who profess to be surgeons is only one more avenue to drain the purse of the Ignorant, and leave in many instances hopeless cripples or maimed bodies for life....*

... I am aware that this is strong language, but I am also aware that it is truth". (Osteopathy unadulterated; A. G. Hildreth; (Journal of Osteopathy, October 1899, Page 189).

Littlejohn and David graduated in January 1900, James Buchan was told he could not. In a letter dated 31ˢᵗ January 1900, he said; -

"My request for Graduation with the present class being considered incompatible with the requirements, I beg to ask, should my connection with the American School continue, upon what terms that graduation is possible?"[lxxvii]

At the time, the Littlejohns were told they would have to pay for their Diplomas or tuition.

"Mr. Hamilton, as secretary and treasurer of the American School of Osteopathy came to me (J. Martin Littlejohn) on the afternoon of the Graduation in January 1900[33] and stated that the Trustees expected us to pay for the tuition. He said at the same time that they intended to withhold the diploma until it was paid for. I (J. Martin Littlejohn), said it was all right".[lxxviii]

There seems to be a correlation between these two events. However, James Buchan's testimony is rather vague on the issue of his diploma or Doctor's Certificate. Littlejohn implied that he thought a Diploma had been prepared for James B. but withheld for payment of a fee.[lxxix]

Littlejohn himself seemed to be alright with paying a fee to graduate, but his brothers, especially James B. apparently were not. This would indicate another source of angst given that the resignations followed quickly after this.

Also, from Littlejohn's point of view, with the upcoming wedding of Blanche Still, A T Stills only daughter, to George Laughlin[34], he probably could not see much of a future for his position as Dean. Another aspect is that given Hulett's intervention around the idea of

---

[33] Graduation took place 30ᵗʰ January 1900

[34] "George M. Laughlin and Miss Blanche Still, both of Kirksville, were united in marriage on Wednesday evening, April 11ᵗʰ" (Macon Times April 13ᵗʰ, 1900 page 2)

the M.D. Osteopathic degree, Littlejohn could see no prospect of that being achieved in the American School of osteopathy.[35]

John Martin and David graduated in January 1900 with John Martin being the class representative, the commencement exercises taking place from 28-31st January[lxxx]. (Journal of osteopathy February 1900 page 339). We unfortunately have no minutes of board meetings for this time. The faculty meetings that exist show that the Littlejohns worked as they would honorably and consistently with the other faculty members doing their jobs to the best of their abilities.

Littlejohn moved forward with the Journal of the Science of Osteopathy but as he did so more opposition from the School came forward and they tried again to resurrect the 'Osteopathic Arena' in opposition to it.

"The Journal of the Science of Osteopathy is the title of a bi-monthly publication edited by J. Martin Littlejohn. It is a Journal for the profession, and it is the intention of the publisher to include nothing but what is scientific. The field has long been open for such a publication and it no doubt will be appreciated by the profession. It is the intention of the American School to publish a similar Journal entitled " The Osteopathic Arena. " This publication will appeal' about June 1, 1900. A complete announcement will appear' in the April number of the Journal of Osteopathy"[lxxxi]

The Osteopathic Arena was again given a large write up in the May 1900 issue, but it never materialised. The Journal of the Science of Osteopathy appeared in February 1900 and continued for three years when it merged with the 'Osteopathic World' with Littlejohn remaining as editor.[lxxxii]

This was not the only thing that C E Still did in opposition to Littlejohn. Smith had an upcoming court case for "illegal dismissal" and Charlie Still tried to stir up angst towards him in respect of a letter

---

[35] The school changed its charter to replace the words "reputable medical colleges" to usually conferred by Osteopathic schools and colleges" in august 1903 (A T Still Museum of Osteopathic Medicine;ASO record book 1903-1924, Page 3) Thus, making it almost impossible to award the M.D. osteopathic degree..

he had allegedly written to the President of the Kentucky Medical Board denouncing Dr. Hildreth

"I want you as President of the Kentucky Association of Osteopaths also get a number of Osteopaths in the State to make an affidavit stating just what Dr. Smith has done. If you will do this, I will consider it a great favor." [lxxxiii]

At the same time, he was to write to John Hopkins, Yale, Harvard and other universities to try and find a replacement Professor of physiology for Littlejohn.[lxxxiv] (ASO business letters pages 121, 135, 136 etc.) Even though he had no connection with these universities, Charlie Still must have thought Littlejohn was a hard act to follow. In this context we find an undated fragment from the writings of A T Still were he says *"the greatest struggle of O.P.is to get men to teach opy from Harvard, Yale or (hog? Illegible) who know nothing about the philosophy nor anything belonging to (the) our system. The school would be far better off without them."*[lxxxv]. It would not be surprising if Still wrote this as a comment on his son's efforts to recruit a physiology professor from Harvard, Yale or John Hopkins, but this is just speculation.

The most negative aspect of Charlie Still and his brother Harry's activities regarding Littlejohn at this time was his attempts to find some sort of dirt on J.M. Littlejohn. He wrote to many people connected to Littlejohn's past including Reformed Presbyterian Minsters in the Amity, College Springs region, New York and to others trying to find something on J.M. Littlejohn[lxxxvi]. The general tone of these letters can be judged by the following quotes;

"If it is not asking too much, I wish you would give me some information in regard to J. M. Littlejohn. I understand that you were associated together in the same College, and it has been reported to us that he did not give satisfaction and caused a great deal of annoyance while there, on the other hand this has been contradicted, and I am quite anxious to know the facts in the matter. He is Professor of Physiology in the American School of Osteopathy and as a teacher has been giving satisfaction, but he seems to be interested in making trouble in the Faculty. Yours truly H M Still" Mr. J. W. McKinley, Ex-Treas. Amity College, College Springs, Ia. Feb 19th, 1900 [lxxxvii]

"Rev. J. M. Wylie,
"I have been referred to you as to the Standing of J. M. Littlejohn. I hear that you are acquainted with his past history. He has been a teacher in our institution during the last sixteen months, and in that time has caused a great deal of disturbance in the Faculty. I wish you would enlighten me upon this subject as it is of great importance to us. "
Yours truly, [C. E. Still signature] Vice President A. S. O. March 16th, 1900[xxxviii]

    The impression these letters give is of someone who is afraid of possibly losing control of the school and wants to "nullify" the influence that his possible "enemies" may have. In this regard Smith is gone but is agitating amongst osteopaths and students, probably trading upon his past history with A T Still; J B Littlejohn was a skilled surgeon with impeccable qualifications, but he was a member of the local Masonic Lodge, Adair No 366 in Kirksville, were he had been sponsored by Warren Hamilton. Charlie proceed to join another local lodge[36] in March 1900, thus putting himself into a different relationship with J B Littlejohn. David, while a skilled surgeon with good qualification, would not have been seen as having a "seat of power" outside of his control of the X-Ray department in the School. So, when he resigned, he would be no threat. John Martin Littlejohn was a different proposition. He was well qualified, held in respect by students, staff and other osteopaths and more importantly, seemed to have a good relationship with A T Still. This would explain the lengths to which Charlie Still went to find dirt on him.

    As a politician, Charlie would not be able to understand that Littlejohn was a man of honour, possessing of no guile and did things in a straightforward, honest and deliberate manner. This was contrary to how Hildreth as a politician and C.E. Still himself as another politician would have expected other people to act. There is quite a contrast in culture between these two sets of individuals. On the one

---

[36] Charles E. Still; Kirksville Lodge No. 105; Kirksville, Adair County, MO
3/21/1900 Initiated as an Entered Apprentice
9/24/1901 Passed to the Degree of Fellow Craft
3/29/1904 Raised to the Sublime Degree of Master Mason
7/6/1955 Dies in Good Standing (email from Grand Lodge of Missouri researcher Lloyd G. Lyon, 21st June 2017)

hand the Covenanter, Reformed Presbyterian who had no guile, straight forward, honest and deliberate with a deep reverence for contracts and the binding nature of one's word on one hand and the 'classic' politician to whom guile, subterfuge and not taking people at their word was not just second nature but their bread and butter.

So, find C.E. Still doing his best to find some sort of dirt on J.M. Littlejohn and to undermine the publication of the Journal of the Science of Osteopathy. Having written to many people with past association to Littlejohn, what did he find?

From the letters that have survived it seems that the only negative thing he found was concerned with Littlejohn being called to the Bar. In normal practice this would have involved the taking of an Oath contrary to the Reformed Presbyterian code. We know that the Kansas presbytery to which Littlejohn was affiliated at the time, was informed of this and that they raised objections to their Presbytery about him, including

"*Paper No. 19 is a reference from Kansas Presbytery for advice.*
At its last regular meeting, Presbytery instructed the clerk to notify Rev. J. M. Littlejohn, one of its members, **to show cause why his name should not be stricken from the rolls**, *as he had not attended the meetings for about five years, nor performed any work under its direction for three years. Presbytery forwards his reply dated May 14, 1900, with its request for advice. With the present information, the Committee recommends that the matter be left with the Presbytery*"[lxxxix]. *(May 30th, 1900)*

We also know that Littlejohn answered this objection by showing that he had not taken an oath or in any other way contravened the Reformed Presbyterian codes. This was investigated by synod and they found that he was in good standing, that he hadn't taken an oath but had taken a "declaration of intent" to become a lawyer.

> Rev. J. M. Littlejohn presented a certificate transferring him from the Kansas to the Iowa Presbytery. While action on this certificate was pending, Rev. Littlejohn was asked if it were true that he was enrolled as a lawyer. He admitted that it was true. When asked if he had taken the oath of allegiance before his enrollment, he replied that he had not, but had "declared his intention" and was enrolled on his declaration. He was received into Presbytery and his name added to our roll.
>
> Reformed Presbyterian Standard, Volume iv, No. 11, June 2nd, 1902, Page 7, meeting of Iowa presbytery

This was in conformity with the Reformed Presbyterian Creed at the time.

> "Granted to J. M. Littlejohn a letter of standing requested by himself with a view to connecting with another presbytery."
> (Page 124 1901 synod, Kansas presbytery report)
>
> "We have certified the Rev. J. M. Littlejohn to Iowa"
> (Presbytery, 1902 synod, Kansas reports page 47)

One could speculate that this action by the Kansas presbytery was, if not instigated at least pushed in the right direction by others in Kirksville who would have been or had friends in the local Reformed Presbyterian Church. Given Charlie Stills letter dated 4th April 1900 in which he asks; -

"D. H. Colter[37], Winchester, Kans.
Dear Sir:
"I have been referred to you by J. M. Wylie of Evans, Colo. and would like for you give me the information as to the standing of J. M. Littlejohn in the Kansas Presbyter." [xc]

It seems reasonable to assume that the origin of these inquiries can be traced back to Charlie Still himself.
What were the results of the Kansas Presbytery inquiries?
They found him to be in good standing and granted him a

> "A Bible class, conduct ed by Dr. J. M. Littlejohn meets every Friday at 4 p. m. This is a rare opportunity and all young women are urged to attend the meetings"
>
> Journal of osteopathy January 1900, page 346),

certified this to the Iowa presbytery. This is not surprising as the Presbytery knew and recognised that he was laboring in the Medical College of Osteopathy at Kirksville, Mo.[xci] and that while there he continued to be engaged in ministerial duties, holding regular bible study classes.

He regularly contributed to the YMCA, of which he was involved in the formation and was Honorary President[xcii]. [38]

Charlie did seem to have some 'success' in his endeavors when he wrote to Dr. Ernest Roberts in England regarding the meeting of the Society of Science, Letters and Art in July 1899. I have been

---

[37] D H Coulter was "for many years was called "The Father of Kansas Presbytery." (Sketches of ministers of Reformed Presbyterian church of north America 188-1930 by THE REV. OWEN F. THOMPSON)

[38] The College branch of the Young Men's Christian Association is doing good work. All men are invited to the 2 o'clock Sunday afternoon meetings…. Officers are: Honorary President, Dean Littlejohn; President, S. D. Barnes; (journal of osteopathy March 1899 page 402)

unable to trace a Dr Ernest Roberts at the address on Charlie Stills letter but have found Arthur Roberts who registered as a physician in 1869 who resided at the same address, viz. 2, princes square, Harrogate. He had visited Still in Kirksville in 1896[xciii], and read Still autobiography.[xciv]

> Kingswood House PRINCE'S SQUARE, HARROGATE, LONDON, ENGLAND May 24th, 1897
> My DEAR DR. Still. I was heartily glad to receive the papers on Osteopathy, showing that you have secured State recognition. Your science deserves it, and you will triumph. I am delighted as I study it more and more carefully. Many thanks to you for your kindness to me when at Kirksville. kindest remembrances to all my friends.
> Yours, very sincerely, Arthur Roberts.
> (journal of osteopathy June 1897 page 106)

It could be the same person or a relative, perhaps a son. There was a Doctor Ernest Roberts, born in 1878 who lived in Peckham Rye London in 1890[xcv]

In any event the letter gives the impression that Littlejohn had, at the very least, misrepresented himself.

However, if we remember, as stated above, that the two events, his election as Fellow of the Royal Society of Literature and the invitation to give the lecture to the Society of Science, Letters and Art came at about the same time the origin of the confusion is fairly clear. Newspaper reports added to the confusion by 'dropping the superfluous' 'L' from the letters F.R.S.L. London, thus making it F.R.S. London. Others followed suit homing in on the advantageous use of the adjective 'Royal'

Dr. C. L. Goban D.O., who graduated in the same class as Littlejohn[xcvi], wrote a newspaper article in March 1900, which is a good example of this when he quotes Littlejohn in his article.

March 28, 1900
Dr. Ernest Roberts, Kingswood House, 2 Princes Square, Harrogate, England.
Dear Doctor:
Yours just at hand, and I thank you for the same. We have in our employ one J. Martin Littlejohn who has been filling the chair of Physiology, and last year he made the announcement that he had been invited by the Royal Society of Science to deliver an address before that body which convened in Crystal Palace, July 19th. His subject was to be Osteopathy. It was heralded by our Journal as being quite an honor for a young man. Sometime last summer in the city of Buffalo, N. Y., a gentle man spoke to our secretary stating that it was quite a joke that was published in our Journal. It was again brought to our notice this fall that such a thing did not happen. This was my reason for writing to you some few weeks ago as I did. I was not surprised at the answer. It seems to me that one has to have an unlimited amount of nerve to pose as this gentleman did when he knew the facts would come out. He received a great deal of free advertising for his supposed lecture or address. Some have suggested that maybe he did write this address, and then presented it in the way that some political speeches or addresses are mailed out over the country. I would like to know if this address was presented to this body to be pigeonholed and read by any one that might be interested. I am thoroughly disgusted with the whole affair and am almost ready to believe anything.

This man further states that Prof. Shafer one of the recognized physicians of the country had congratulated him upon the address and told him that he was interested and would not criticise until he had seen Osteopathy tried.

I hope I have not asked too much of you, but it seems to me when such a thing had been done that it should receive its just deserts.

My father joins me in wishing you success.
Yours truly, [C. E. Still signature]

"Dr. J Martin Littlejohn (a member of the faculty of the American school of osteopathy at Kirksville, Mo.) in a paper on osteopathy, read before the Royal Society, in London says..." [xcvii]

The Journal of osteopathy February 1900 gives Littlejohn his correct letters after his name with a minor mistyping (F.S.S.C. instead of F.S.Sc.), and correctly, states that the paper was **presented** to the Royal Society of Literature.

The Journal of the Science of Osteopathy for the same month (its first issue Feb. 1900) does not mention were the paper was presented. In the text of the paper it says, in the first paragraph, **"your charter rights as a Royal Society..."**, giving the impression that it was presented to a Royal Society.

Littlejohn himself, I believe was of the opinion that the lecture was to be to the Royal Society of Literature. It was and still is a common occurrence in societies for new members to deliver a talk or lecture so as to introduce themselves.[39] The text, as mentioned earlier, was written while he was on board the Campania to London, during which journey he learnt of the death of his friend, Dr. Sturman of the Society of Science, Letters and Art. Also, we noted earlier that Tucker, in an article in the American Osteopath, Monthly September 1900, clearly said the it was to "London Society of Sciences" and not to a 'the Royal Society' of any sort, that Littlejohn was to have delivered his talk.

Littlejohn, Himself, in the August issue of the Journal of the Science of Osteopathy, makes it clear what happened.

"The Editor (Littlejohn) was privileged to present in printed form his previous address to the same Society as an 'in memoriam' of Dr. E. A. Sturman, the secretary of the Society and the beloved friend of the editor who died last summer (1899) after a life devoted to science and literature. Dr. Sturman was the first to take an active interest in Osteopathy in Europe."[xcviii]

---

[39] One can postulate an invitation from Dr. Sturman including a line saying something like ' I have sent a special invitation to all members and fellows of the Society of Science who are member of the Royal Society of Literature', thus while being accurate would be sufficiently ambiguous to give the impression the talk was to a section of the Royal Society of Literature.

Later, things were compounded when the lecture was republished and widely distributed. For Example, as a booklet by H J. Omstead D.O., under the title of "osteopathy explained" and listed as "delivered in London before the Royal Society".

in the Kirksville journal of the 28th April 1899 it was announced that Littlejohn was admitted to the Bar and in the same issue, noted his invitation to "deliver a scientific address before the Royal Science Society of London" The 28th of April 1899 was the day after the Tornado struck Kirksville, so the error in the announcement could easily have gone unnoticed. This came just three months after it was announced that he was made a fellow of the Royal society of Literature.[40] Thus the prefix of "Royal" was in added to the Society of Science.

However, from the wording of Charlie Stills letter were he says "It (the lecture) was again brought to our notice this fall (1899) that such a thing did not happen.", it would appear that the only source of this information would have been one or the Littlejohns themselves. At that stage, on their return for England, they would have been the only ones who knew. Also, given that Charlie goes on to outline, nearly exactly, what Littlejohn himself said happened, it would suggest that Littlejohn did not make a secret of the whole story of sudden loss of his friend and colleague Dr. Sturman's death, the postponement of the lecture etc.

Could Littlejohn have done more to clarify the situation? He could have put out a simple statement and asked people not to confuse things by giving the wrong title or using the adjective 'Royal' inappropriately. However, this was not in his character. A simple statement of what had happened, with no explanation was all he did. This was in line with his general approach to rumours. He stated this quite clearly in letters he wrote to Thomas Edward Hall in the 1920/30's. Hall was one of Littlejohn's star pupils and became his

---

[40] *"Kirksville is rejoicing with one of its prominent physicians over a new distinction that has come to him recently. Dr. Littlejohn, of the faculty of the School of Osteopathy, already a fellow of the Society of Science, Letters and Art of London, has just been notified of his selection to membership in the Royal Society of Literature there."* (Kansas City journal January 23^{rd,} 1899)

deputy in the British School of Osteopathy. At the time of the letters, Hall had been taken to court by his ex-fiancée for breach of contract. During the court case many of Hall's personal letters had been read out in public and published in the newspapers. Littlejohn said words to the effect that He paid no attention to gossip, especially of those who have no interest in osteopathy beyond gossip; when he hears any such gossip, he puts it under his feet and tramples it out of existence[xcix]. The following quote gives a flavor of his attitude to gossip.

"I pay no attention to the chatter and gossip of those who have no interest in Osteopathy bar gossip. I could tell you of things reported to me regarding yourself and others but when any such gossip comes to me I put it under my feet and trample it out of existence...It is a great pity some give themselves to these things".[c] September 17th, 1932.

Littlejohn had no time for rumors or gossip. Even if he had put out a clearer explanation it would probably not stopped the spread of the rumor, but perhaps it might have made things a little clearer for history.

It is understandable given that when he did return to the college instead of finding things as he had left them (starting to settle down and move forward despite the problems of the arguments about moving the school out of Kirksville and the angst following the publicity of the schools and osteopath's involvement in the aftermath of the cyclone) he found himself involved in turmoil around the return of Hildreth to the teaching faculty in violation of the contract they had with the "trustees" and the publication of his journal of the science of osteopathy and the proposed 'rival' magazine Osteopathic Arena, he didn't really get a chance to correct any mistakes in the publicity about the Lecture.

We have given some examples of the Political maneuverings of Hildreth and others earlier. This example is directly related to the American School of Osteopathy and relates to future events regarding the Associated Colleges of Osteopathy.
Dr. S. S. Still, a nephew of A T Still, left the ASO in July 1898 under a cloud, after a 'testimonial' he had apparently given a student was

used by that student in a misleading way to insinuate that he had graduated from the ASO when he had not and was just a student "[ci] and founded his own school, The S. S. Still College of Osteopathy. The February Class presented him with an elegant solid silver table set, a demonstration one could take as showing upset at his leaving.

Later, in the journal of Osteopathy he was reduced from being "one of the best teachers of Anatomy in the west" (November 1896), *"Prof. S.S. Still cannot be excelled by any such teacher in America"* (March 1897) to being *"simply junior professor of Anatomy"* (October 1898). It seems that using the Journal politically against possible competition was not beneath the management of the American School of Osteopathy when it suited them.

> *"There are other teachers and practitioners. and good ones, too; but the best are undeniably at the American School of Osteopathy at Kirksville. The impression has been created in certain quarters that this or that man was the real head of the Kirksville institution. This has been said of Dr. S. S., Still, a nephew of Dr. A T. Still. The fact is that at Kirksville, Dr. S. S. Still was simply junior professor of Anatomy"*
> (Journal of Osteopathy Vol 5 No 5 October 1898; IMPRESSIONS AND OBSERVATIONS OF A REPRESENTATIVE OF THE DAILY NEWS, OF DES MOINES, IOWA.)
>
> ---
>
> In the grades this month, of the students of Osteopathy, under Dr. S. S. Still an average of 97 was attained Dr. Still is one of the best teachers of Anatomy in the west and is much pleased with the work accomplished by his 165 students. He insists that students must take every examination, as it comes, and be in prompt attendance, -
> (Saturday Mail, Kirksville Journal of Osteopathy Vol 3 No 5 November 1896)

All in all, it seems that any augment Littlejohn had with A.T. Still, if there was one of any significance, had more to do with the M.D.O. classification, and that this was possibly used as a means of diverting Stills attention (by C.E. Still, and others possibly Hildreth) from their involvement in the move to get the school to relocate to a larger city. This would probably been relatively easily dealt with if it had not been for the affair over their contract regarding Hildreth's involvement with the school overtaking other events.

SOME LEGAL MATTERS, DEPOSITIONS AND COURT CASES

When Littlejohn and his brothers left Kirksville for Chicago, they also exchange a series of heated letters concerning the refusal of the ASO to pay their salaries[cii]. In essence this, was on the instructions of the "Trustees", in leu of the demand from the Trustees that they pay for their diplomas[ciii]. The case was eventually dismissed by agreement[civ]. The exchange of letters between James B. littlejohn and Warren Hamilton finally reached an agreement and the case was listed as discontinued in May 1903[cv]. All in all, during the nearly three years that this court case dragged on no papers were ever lodged apart from the change of venue and postponements[cvi]. James B. seems to have used his influence with Warren Hamilton and their past relationship in the Adair Lodge to bring the case to its conclusion.

"I will take it as a personal favor if you will attend to this matter right away. Time is running along and the matter ought to be fully settled".[cvii] (J. B. Littlejohn to W. Hamilton Nov 5th, 1902)

In the settlement the ASO was to pay $400 to the Littlejohns for their salary for June 1900[cviii], which was accepted as final settlement of the case.

Littlejohn's letter on the subject to Warren Hamilton, Secretary of the ASO shows not only his legal mind but also his attitude to contracts that has been mentioned before.

"Having refused to pay me my salary due on June 1st, I beg to notify you that I shall hold you responsible for failure to fulfil contract from this day with the legal consequences involved therein. Respectfully J. Martin Littlejohn June 15th 1900[cix]

The court case of "The National School of Osteopathy VS (No 838) The American School of Osteopathy" has been mentioned above. Essentially this was about Smith obtaining a diploma from the National School, under an assumed name and without attending any classes, simply paying a fee. Thus, it was labelled a "diploma mill". The deposition[cx] of Littlejohn gives some useful information but has often been misquoted.

A common quote that has been used to try and discredit Littlejohn comes from a deposition taken from him in 1900 for the case of "The National School of Osteopathy VS (No 838) The American School of Osteopathy" (Still National Osteopathic Museum, Kirksville, Mo.) It usually takes the form of "Littlejohn said under oath that he was never a student at the American School of Osteopathy", so how could he have earned a diploma or learnt Osteopathy?

A simple examination of the deposition clears this up immediately.

He stated that he had never attended any classes or received any instruction "as a student". He did attend classes. However, not as a registered student, but as a Professor in the School to further his own learning of Osteopathy.

In his letter of 6th June 1899[cxi], (in which he makes application to graduate in June 1899), he states he has *"been 17 months in the American School of Osteopathy during which I have taken up all the Osteopathic work of Dr. Hazzard and Dr. McConnell"*[cxii]. He also made it clear in the deposition that he took instruction from and discussed Osteopathy with Still.

Quotes from the Deposition
What has been your place of residence during the past two or three years prior to corning to Chicago?

Question 10. Did you ever attend any classes or receive any instruction in that institution?
Littlejohn's Answer 10. *I was matriculated as a student by special permission of the faculty.*
Question 11. Did you ever attend any classes or receive any instruction in the institution?
Littlejohn's Answer 11. *You mean as a student?*
Question 12. As a student.
Littlejohn's Answer 12. *No...*
.....

Cross examination Littlejohn's Answer 29. *When the diplomas were first issued, Mr. Hamilton as Secretary and Treasurer of The American School of Osteopathy came to me on the afternoon of the graduation in January 1900 and stated that the trustees expected us to pay for the tuition. He said at the same time that they intended to withhold the diploma until it was paid for. I told him that was all right...*

Question 10. Doctor, how did you acquire your knowledge of Osteopathy?
Littlejohn's Answer 10. *I acquired my knowledge of Osteopathy by personal investigation.*
Question 11. Did you ever take any lessons or instructions from any professor in the American School of Osteopathy?
Littlejohn's Answer 11. *No, Sir.*
....

Cross examination; Littlejohn's Answer 1. *Doctor Still may have ---did tell me several points in regard to Osteopathy, but these points were entirely in reference to new points that he was investigating on the subject.*
Question. and he has as often asked your opinion as you his?
Littlejohn's Answer. *Yes, Sir.*

---

[i] Find my past passenger lists
[ii] Journal of Osteopathy, Kirksville, Vol 6 No 2 July 1899
[iii] A T Still museum of osteopathic medicine ref Transcripts of letters from [1979.290.18]

[iv] Journal of Osteopathy, Kirksville, Vol 6 No 3 August 1899
[v] The Popular Osteopath October 1899 page 232
[vi] Journal of Osteopathy, Kirksville, Vol 6 no. 5, October 1899, page 198
[vii] The Osteopathic Physician, December 1903, page 23
[viii] Ibid page 22
[ix] . Journal of Osteopathy, Kirksville, Sept 1899 some queries. C. M. Turner Hulett, D. O.
[x] The "Diplomate in Osteopathy": From "School of Bones" to "School of Medicine" J Am Osteopath Assoc. 2014;114(2):114-124 Norman Gevitz, PhD
[xi] IBID
[xii] Journal of Osteopathy, Kirksville, Vol 6, No 6, November 1899, Page 251
[xiii] Journal of Osteopathy, Kirksville, Vol 5, No 12, May 1899, Page 568
[xiv] The Southern Journal of Osteopathy, February 1898, Page 15; National Library of Medicine, Bethesda, Washington, Reference NLM Unique ID: 20920550R, call number W1 SO954D
[xv] OsteoLib® (Vol. XIII): History of Osteopathy and Twentieth-Century Medical Practice, E. R. Booth; Cincinnati press, 1924, page 445; HISTORY OF OSTEOPATHY.
[xvi] Ibid
[xvii] The Osteopathic Physician, October 1902, page 5
[xviii] Journal of the American Osteopathic Association, Volume 9 September 1909, page 36
[xix] Journal of the American Osteopathic Association, Volume 9 October 1909, page 81
[xx] History of Osteopathy and twentieth -century Medical Practice; E. R. Booth; Cincinnati press of Jennings and Graham; 1924, page 452
[xxi] Journal of Osteopathy, Kirksville, Vol 6 No 2 July 1899, page 67
[xxii] Osteolib® Vol. VIII The Practice of Osteopathy (1899) C. P. McConnell About the book…Editor of the online-publishing and reprint: JOLANDOS eK, 2006
[xxiii] The Practice of Osteopathy, McConnell 1899, Page 8
[xxiv] Museum of Osteopathic Medicine, Kirksville, Reference 2009.10.656, A T Still letter to Thekla Orschel January 2nd, 1900,
[xxv] The Philosophy of Osteopathy; by A T Still September 1st, 1899 Preface
[xxvi] The Philosophy of Osteopathy; by A T Still September 1st, 1899 Page 12
[xxvii] Journal of Osteopathy, Kirksville, Vol 5 No 7 December 1898, page 352
[xxviii] History of Osteopathy and twentieth -century Medical Practice; E. R. Booth; Cincinnati press of Jennings and Graham; 1905, page 167
[xxix] OsteoLib® (Vol. XIII): History of Osteopathy and Twentieth-Century Medical Practice, E. R. Booth; Cincinnati press, 1924, page 511- 512 HISTORY OF OSTEOPATHY.
[xxx] Ibid page 515

[xxxi] ECHOES FROM DR. STILL'S LECTURES TO THE CLASS OF NINETY-SIX; H. H. Gravett D.O.; Journal of the American Academy of Osteopathy, 1948, page 50

[xxxii] Osteopathy' Research and Practice, Kirksville, A T Still 1910 Preface page vi, page xxi of the Eastland Press, Seattle 1992 edition

[xxxiii] The Victoria Episode, J. H. Sullivan D.O.; Museum of Osteopathic Medicine, Kirksville, MO., reference 1980.373.08

[xxxiv] OsteoLib® (Vol. XIII): History of Osteopathy and Twentieth-Century Medical Practice, E. R. Booth; Cincinnati press, 1924, page 517 HISTORY OF OSTEOPATHY.

[xxxv] A T Still museum of Osteopathic Medicine, Business letters ledger, reference 2006.76.01 – ASO Business Letters Ledger 1900, page 516

[xxxvi] A T Still museum of osteopathic medicine ref Transcripts of letters from [1979.290.18] page 2, Letter from Hamilton to Hildreth, 13th September 1899

[xxxvii] Museum of osteopathic medicine Littlejohn letters - November 30th, 1899, reference 1980.375.02.07 Letter to the American School of Osteopathy... also letter of Dec 9th, 1899, ref. 1980.375.02.12

[xxxviii] A T Still Museum of osteopathic medicine, ref. 2009.49.198

[xxxix] The lengthening shadow of Dr. Andrew Taylor Still, A G Hildreth, D.O.

[xl] Journal of Osteopathy, Kirksville, Vol 3 No 5 November 1897, page 7

[xli] The lengthening shadow of Dr. Andrew Taylor Still, A G Hildreth, D.O. page 105/ Journal of Osteopathy, Kirksville, Vol 3 No 8 March 1897, page 4

[xlii] The Lengthening Shadow of Doctor Andrew Taylor Still ;1942, A G Hildreth, page 121

[xliii] To Teach, To Heal, To Serve; Theodore A. Berchtold; Chicago college of Osteopathic medicine, 1975, Page 20 and 24

[xliv] Journal of Osteopathy, Kirksville, Vol 6 No 1, June 1899, Page 42

[xlv] A T Still museum of osteopathic medicine, Kirksville, Ref. 2006.76.01, American School of osteopathy, Business letters ledger 1900, pages 804, 764,259

[xlvi] Letter from J. Martin, James b., David Littlejohn and William Smith to The Board of Trustees of the American School of Osteopathy, dated Nov. 23rd, 1899, A T Still museum of Osteopathic medicine ref. 1980.375.02.06

[xlvii] Journal of Osteopathy, Kirksville, Vol 5 No 3 August 1898 Page 118, Littlejohn's address to the June 1898 grad class

[xlviii] Journal of Osteopathy, Kirksville, Vol 5 No 9, February 1899 page 425 Littlejohn's speech "Osteopathy in Line of Apostolic Succession with Medicine

[xlix] The American Osteopath, Vol Sept 1899, Minutes of the AAAO meeting, page 66; National Library of Medicine Bethesda holdings

[l] IBID page 52

[li] IBID page 54-55

[lii] The Lengthening Shadow of Doctor Andrew Taylor Still ;1942, A G Hildreth, page 436
[liii] Journal of Osteopathy, Kirksville, Vol 6 No 9 February 1900, Page 399
[liv] Journal of Osteopathy, Kirksville, April 1901, Page 128

[lv] A T Still Museum of osteopathic medicine, Kirksville, ref 1980.375.02.07
[lvi] A T Still Museum of Osteopathic Medicine reference B992; American School of Osteopathy, record of meetings of the Faculty, page 80 (Missouri Digital heritage; Collection Name; American School of Osteopathy Collection, Title; American School of Osteopathy Record Book, 1897 – 1900; Accession Number 1981.519.03)
[lvii] The Lengthening Shadow of Doctor Andrew Taylor Still ;1942, A G Hildreth, page 123-4
[lviii] Journal of osteopathy, Kirksville, Dr. A T Stills' department January 1902
[lix] Journal of Osteopathy, Kirksville, March 1899, Page 403
[lx] Journal of Osteopathy, Kirksville, Feb 1899, page 454
[lxi] Journal of Osteopathy, Kirksville, Feb 1899,
[lxii] A T Still museum of osteopathic medicine, Kirksville, Ref. 2006.76.01, American School of osteopathy, Business letters ledger 1900, Page 804,
[lxiii] A T Still to Mrs. Orschel Dec 14th, 1899.

[lxiv] Journal of osteopathy, Kirksville, June 1899, page 38

[lxv] Museum of Osteopathic Medicine, The Osteopathic Physician, 1904, Page 2
[lxvi] Journal of Osteopathy, Kirksville, Volume 5, No. 7, December 1898, page 326
[lxvii] A T Still museum of osteopathic medicine, Kirksville, Ref 1980.375.02.06
[lxviii] Museum of Osteopathic Medicine, Minutes of the faculty meetings of the A.S.O. reference B992, March 22nd, 1899, page 729-84.
[lxix] Journal of Osteopathy Vol 6 No 5 October 1899 Hildreth page 197
[lxx] A T Still museum of osteopathic medicine, Deposition of J Martin Littlejohn, David Littlejohn, and James B. Littlejohn; The National School of Osteopathy VS (No 838) The American School of Osteopathy Question Q 9- A 9
[lxxi] A T Still museum of osteopathic medicine, Kirksville, Ref 1980.375.02.07
[lxxii] A T Still museum of osteopathic medicine, Kirksville, Ref 1980.375.02.10
[lxxiii] A T Still museum of osteopathic medicine, Kirksville, Ref 1980.375.02.12
[lxxiv] Ibid
[lxxv] ibid
[lxxvi] Front cover of the Journal of the Science of Osteopathy February 1900 to December 1900, British Museum Library
[lxxvii] A T Still museum of osteopathic medicine, Kirksville, Ref. 1980.375.02.14

[lxxviii] A T Still museum of osteopathic medicine, Deposition of J Martin Littlejohn, David Littlejohn, and James B. Littlejohn; The National School of Osteopathy VS (No 838) The American School of Osteopathy Question X Q 29 and answer.

[lxxix] A T Still museum of osteopathic medicine, Deposition of J Martin Littlejohn, David Littlejohn, and James B. Littlejohn; The National School of Osteopathy VS (No 838) The American School of Osteopathy Question Q 37- A 40

[lxxx] Journal of osteopathy, Kirksville, Volume 6, No. 9, February 1900, page 339).

[lxxxi] Journal of osteopathy, Kirksville, Volume 6, No. 10, March 1900, page 442

[lxxxii] OsteoLib® (Vol. XIII): History of Osteopathy and Twentieth-Century Medical Practice, E. R. Booth; Cincinnati press, 1924, page 290 HISTORY OF OSTEOPATHY.

[lxxxiii] A T Still museum of osteopathic medicine, Kirksville, Ref. 2006.76.01, American School of osteopathy, Business letters ledger 1900, page 174, C E Still to W. W. Ammerman, D. O., Harrisville, Ky. 17th Feb 1900

[lxxxiv] Ibid pages 121, 135, 136 etc.

[lxxxv] A T Still Museum of Osteopathic Medicine, reference 2009.10.165; Missouri digital Heritage)

[lxxxvi] A T Still museum of osteopathic medicine, Kirksville, Ref. 2006.76.01, American School of osteopathy, Business letters ledger 1900, page 198 etc

[lxxxvii] ibid

[lxxxviii] Ibid page 442

[lxxxix] Minutes of the Synod of reformed Presbyterian Church, USA May 30th, 1900, Page 89.

[xc] A T Still museum of osteopathic medicine, Kirksville, Ref. 2006.76.01, American School of osteopathy, Business letters ledger 1900, page 552

[xci] Minutes of the Synod of reformed Presbyterian Church, USA June 1899Kansas presbytery reports page 52

[xcii] Museum of Osteopathic Medicine, Minutes of the faculty meetings of the A.S.O. reference B992 page 63, minutes Dec 14th, 1898: journal of osteopathy Kirksville, March 1899 page 402)

[xciii] Journal of Osteopathy, Kirksville, Volume 3, No. 5, November 1896, Page 7

[xciv] Journal of Osteopathy, Kirksville, Volume 4, No. 11, April 1898, Page 555

[xcv] Epsom college register 1890, page 189

[xcvi] Journal of Osteopathy, Kirksville, Volume 6, No. 9, February 1900, Page 399

[xcvii] Bryan morning eagle, Bryan, Texas, Saturday, March 17th, 1900, page 2

[xcviii] The Journal of the Science of Osteopathy, Volume 1, No. 4, August 1900 page 149

[xcix] AS told to the Author by John Wernham. Copies of the original letters are in the Wellcome Library Littlejohn collection and the A T Still Museum of Osteopathic Medicine archives and verify the story, even though I suspect Wernham has tied together two different episodes, one of which is definitely related to Hall's court case with this ex-fiancée, the other comes approximately two years later.

[c] Letter to T. E. Hall from J. Martin Littlejohn, September 17th, 1932; Copies of the original letters are in the Wellcome Library Littlejohn collection and the A T Still Museum of Osteopathic Medicine archives. Quoted with permission of the European School of Osteopathy, Maidstone, Kent.

[ci] Journal of Osteopathy, Kirksville, Vol 5 No 2 July 1898, pages, 89, 93-95

[cii] A T Still Museum of Osteopathic Medicine reference 1980.375.02.32; 1980.375.02.31; 1980.375.02.30; 1980.375.02.29; 1980.375.02.28_; 1980.375.02.27; 1980.375.02.26_; 1980.375.02.22; 1980.375.02.21; 1980.375.02.20; 1980.375.02.19

[ciii] The National School of Osteopathy vs The American School of Osteopathy; Depositions for the Plaintiff 27th August 1900; Depositions from J. Martin Littlejohn, David Littlejohn and James B. Littlejohn; Courtesy of The Still National Osteopathic Museum, Kirksville Mo.

[civ] Chariton courier., November 29, 1901; Chariton courier., May 08, 1903.

[cv] Ibid

[cvi] Telephone conversation with Circuit court clerk re court papers relating to the case- in essence there were none.

[cvii] A T Still museum of osteopathic medicine, Kirksville, Reference 1980.375.02.32; Letter to Warren Hamilton, Secretary and Treasurer of the American School of Osteopathy, from James B. Littlejohn

[cviii] A T Still museum of osteopathic medicine, Kirksville, Reference 1989.375.02.28; Letter from Warren Hamilton, Secretary and Treasurer of the American School of Osteopathy, to James B. Littlejohn October 2nd, 1902

[cix] A T Still museum of osteopathic medicine, Kirksville, Reference 1989.375.02.20; Letter to Warren Hamilton, Secretary and Treasurer of the American School of Osteopathy, from J. Martin Littlejohn

[cx] A T Still museum of osteopathic medicine, Deposition of J Martin Littlejohn, David Littlejohn, and James B. Littlejohn; The National School of Osteopathy VS (No 838) The American School of Osteopathy

[cxi] A T Still museum of osteopathic medicine, Kirksville, Reference 1980.375.02.04 June 6th letter from Littlejohn to the Trustees of the ASO, re graduation

[cxii] A T Still museum of osteopathic medicine, Kirksville, Reference 1980.375.02.04

1900-1913

MOVE TO CHICAGO
FAMILY UPDATE

The move to Chicago was in many ways a complete change in Littlejohn's life. He no longer had the headship of his father to rely on and before settling into his work in Chicago he spent the summer of 1900 in England and Europe, got married to Mabel Alice Thompson and gave his third and final lecture to the Society of Science, Letters and Art. The wedding took place on the 11th August 1900 in Ipswich. Mabel Alice was deprived of her father at an early age[1] and she lived with her grandparents, grocers in the Ipswich area and was known to the family of Littlejohn's sister who lived in the same area and was married to Thompson J. Anthony.

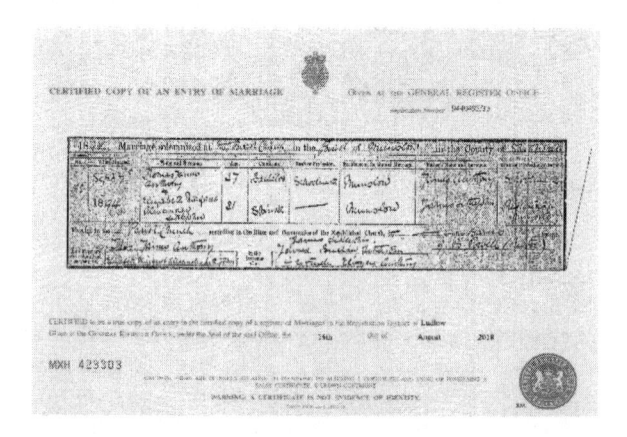

---

[1] Her father passed away in 1893 aged 39 (http://www.findmypast.com: 2012); citing Death, Ipswich, Suffolk,
England, General Register Office, Southport, England.)

"The bride...wore a white silk dress, and carried a handsome shower bouquet, the gift of the bridegroom."

"On Tuesday afternoon, a choral wedding was solemnised in St. John's Church, Ipswich, the contracting parties being Dr. J.M. Littlejohn, of Chicago, and Miss Mabel Alice Thompson, daughter of Mrs. Thompson, Saddington Villa, Woodbridge Road, Ipswich. The bride, who was given away by her mother, wore a white silk dress, and carried a handsome shower bouquet, the gift of the bridegroom. The bridesmaids were: - Miss Martha Mills, Miss Nellie Thompson, and Miss Maggie Anthony, who wore white dresses, and carried baskets of white flowers. Master James L. Anthony acted as page, and was dressed in a suit of green velvet, with old gold collar and front. The bridegroom was accompanied by Mr. T.J. Anthony, who acted as best man. Before the service and during the signing of the registers, Miss Crossley (organist of St. John's), played appropriate music, and the "Wedding March" as the bridal party left the church. The Rev. W. S. King, M.A., Vicar of St. John's officiated. The bride has been for several years connected with St. John's parish schools, and large numbers were present to witness the ceremony. The bridegroom is President of the American College of Osteopathic Medicine and Surgery at Chicago, Illinois. He was born in Scotland and is a triple graduate with honours of the university of Glasgow. The bride and bridegroom sail to-day from Liverpool in the Lucania for America. The presents were numerous."[i]

Birth Certificate for Mable Alice Thompson[2]

---

[2] Some have suggested to me that his wife was under the age of twenty-one when they got married, even going as far as saying she was only 16 years old. Her birth certificate puts pay to these suggestions as do the records of the 1881, and 1891 censuses. This is just another example of the attempts to discredit Littlejohn after the 1935 House of Lords select committee report

When the happy couple returned to Chicago the settled in to 928[3] West Adam Street where they lived until they moved to Lake Bluff in spring of 1911.

Lake Bluff had strong association with the Chautauqua movement and deep connection with Scottish Presbyterians who sought refuge from the hotbed of vice and sin that was nineteenth century Chicago, found a quieter home in the country up north. As such it would have had a special attraction for Littlejohn.[ii]

LITTLEJOHN AND HIS WIFE HAD SEVEN CHILDREN [iii]

Mary Elizabeth born 8th June 1901

Mabel Emma born 19th September 1903

James born 15th March 1905)

Edgar Martin Born 29th January 1907

John Martin born 14th November 1908

Elizabeth Alice born 14th September 1910

Stuart William born 8th March 1915.
Died 27th June 1915[4]

I think it is fair to say that Littlejohn followed in his father's footsteps. His father being a minister in a remote area of Scotland spent many days, weeks away from home tending to other congregations in far parts of the Highlands of Scotland and it would seem that Littlejohn did the same when he was living in Chicago. This time not attending to the spiritual needs of his flock but to the osteopathic education. Spending many weeks travelling, attending conferences and lecturing. This is not to say that he neglected his

---

[3] Later renumbered to 2331 West Adams
[4] After a short life Stuart William died from a congenital debility and heart failure in his Fathers presence. (Essex County council archives; Death Certificate REF.1301933)

family per say but as one of his sons, James, commented the **"only thing he did to excess was work"**[iv]

Another comment that is worth mentioning is that Wernham in his book on Littlejohn states "it was said that the father had a cruel mouth over which he wore a moustache in later life" [v]. In this section of his book He was giving a description of Littlejohn's family. My feeling is that this comment was partly to show his personal relationship with the Littlejohn family and also to show that he is not afraid to make a somewhat negative comment about his mentor J.M. Littlejohn. The Scots and Glasgow/Belfast tendency to laconic phraseology, together with their sharp accent can be misinterpreted as perhaps being "cruel". This may also have been accentuated by age. In this context it is noteworthy that Littlejohn either had a moustache or a beard for all of his adult life. (Wernham knew Littlejohn only after his return to England.)

His writing, speeches and lectures that have come down to us do not give impression of having a "Cruel mouth". They contain too much kindness and understanding for that. We see examples of his kindness and understanding in some of his writings for the Christian Nation.

"Do parents realise the responsibility that rests upon them, and do they use their influence always in the right way?"

*".... The life of the child is **like a force that stands unengaged** looking for some groove along which to move; it stands **waiting for direction** and if the childhood influences that are brought to bear on its young life are such as make for God the issues rest with him for the best."*

"Bring up a child in the way he should go, and when he is old, he'll not deviate from it."

"Such is the design of parentage and of the influence of the home upon the young and rising generation."

"Yonder is a child that plods on from day to day performing the small tasks of its childish life; it searches into the parent's eye, aye into the parent's heart, for a smile of approval. Does it meet with such a glance as would cheer its heart? The

parent is engrossed with business, perplexed by the harassing troubles of life; and instead of a smile and an encouraging word, the child receives a cold glance, and its tender heart is chilled. Coldness leads to carelessness, carelessness to indifference, indifference to open dislike, and open dislike to separation. Does the blame rest with the child? We think not. The child may have done some trivial wrong. For this it has suffered chastisement, the chastisement of alienation, not of love. Parental influence that reigns supreme in a Christian home in which Jesus preside, tempers discipline with kindness and confidence, in leading, not driving from paths that are dangerous to better and holier ways. Parents should not repress their children, unless they can take them into their confidence, lead them by the hand into their bosom and point them in their own heart and life the way on which to walk. Such an influence is for God and heaven."[vi][5]

These quotes set the scene for how Littlejohn approached the task of parenthood. This does not mean he achieved this, but he aimed for this high goal, in the same way as he aimed to show a better way of doing things, in health care through osteopathy, in education through the college organization and in life in general through his Reformed Presbyterian code. This was his way, rather than pointing out and dwelling upon the deficiencies in others or their mistakes, he would concentrate on the better outcomes that could be achieved by choosing a more rationale path.

Wernham's comments may be an attempt to show intimacy with the family rather than being a factual description of Littlejohn's character, since, apart from his youth, Littlejohn either had a beard or a moustache throughout his life.

While his brother, James B.[6]., had moved away from the strict principles of the Reformed Church, Littlejohn tried to stand by them

---

[5] Bold emphasis by author

[6] He was ordained elder in the 4th UP church in Chicago (The Christian nation 9th Feb 1898, page 11) and continued his association with the Masons (Grand Lodge of Missouri records)

all his life. When he moved to Chicago he again asked and got for his credentials from the church to be associated with another presbytery in Chicago. The complaint made against him for having become a lawyer, was successfully defended by demonstrating that, he had not taken an oath but had taken the 'Declaration of Intent' instead. This was allowed as it was not seen as "forswearing" or swearing allegiance to an oath bound society.

His brother James. B, on the other hand, joined the Masons before the summer of 1889 and this may have caused quite a stir within the family and particularly with their mother. Their mother was a strict Reformed Presbyterian and had stood by her husband not only when he seceded from the main church as a probationer but all through her life. It's certain that she would have seen James. B's actions in joining the Masons as being at the very least an embarrassment but also a possibly an insult to their father.

One aspect of the Covenanters was that despite their strong personal convictions they would associate, in daily life, with others of different, sometimes quite opposing beliefs, with tolerance provided it did not mean compromising on their own convictions. Thus, while Still[7] himself professed to be a Mason[vii], Littlejohn had no problem in not only associating with him but in following his Medical Philosophy because it did not conflict with his own Reformed Presbyterian beliefs. In essence, he did not have to take an oath of allegiance to Osteopathy or to Still. The same was true of his association with his brother, James Buchan. He may not have approved of his membership of the Masons but was prepared to work with him for the betterment of Osteopathy so long as it did not impinge on his own fundamental beliefs. However, the rather insidious and pervasive influence of 'secret societies' in American life in general and in the College scene in particular did seem to cause Littlejohn problems as the College grew.

---

[7] Still's funeral service was conducted by the local Masonic Lodges. "The services at the grave were conducted by the Masonic lodges of Kirksville, in charge of Judge Edward Higbee, Past Grand Master of Missouri Masons". (Journal of Osteopathy, Kirksville, Vol 25, January 1918, page 13)

Another example of his principles in action, is found in his report on his European tour in 1903 when *"we decline to be tempted by the Rhine wines but ultimately exchange the courtesies of Germany and America over some coffee and lemonade"*[viii]. He was a strict teetotaller and temperance advocate and he has a lot to say about the harmful effect of coffee on health[ix]. Which makes us assume that when he says over some coffee and lemonade, he himself took the lemonade and not the coffee.

His departure from Kirksville to Chicago was not without some difficulty. When he moved from College Springs to Kirksville, he received a letter of standing and was received by the Kansas presbytery. But when he asked for a letter from the Kansas presbytery with a view to uniting with some other presbytery there was a disciplinary action taken against him on the grounds that he had become a lawyer and as such may have taken an oath and also that he hadn't being active in the presbytery during the past few years.

This was investigated by synod and they found that he was in good standing, that he hadn't taken an oath but had taken a 'declaration of intent' to become a lawyer. The following year 1901 he was received by certificate by the Ohio presbytery.

In Chicago, as we have come to expect of him, Littlejohn continued in the same vein as he had elsewhere, putting his whole energy into the new venture as president of the American College of Osteopathic Medicine and Surgery, at the same time continuing in the political field and educational field associated with osteopathy. During his first two years in Chicago he continued his studies at Dunham medical college, matriculating in 1901[x] and obtaining his M.D. (homeopathic) in 1902[xi]. He also taught physiology in Dunham and other colleges in Chicago.

The American College of Osteopathy and Surgery of 405 Washington Boulevard, Chicago, was founded under the laws of the state of Illinois in the early part of 1900.

"the American College of Osteopathic Medicine and Surgery, Chicago; Educational: incorporators, J. Martin Littlejohn, James B. Littlejohn, and Edith M, Williams."[xii]

Edith M Williams was in the Sept 1899 class in the ASO[xiii], and while listed as graduating in 1902[xiv] she was listed as registering in Official Register of Legally qualified other practitioners (drugless Healers) Licensed in Illinois prior to July 1st, 1917"[8] as being first certified as an osteopath on October 30th 1901 which is consistent with her graduating with her class in June 1901. She also graduated in January 1902 as Doctor of Osteopathy from the American College of Osteopathic medicine and Surgery[xv]

Her name was not included in the list of the graduating class with her classmates in June 1901[xvi]. This may simply have been because she did not attend.

She married James B. Littlejohn in Shelby county, Tennessee, on the 3rd July 1900. The ceremony was performed by her father the Rev. Hugh Spencer. Williams[xvii]

Her father was, once a pastor in Wales and who had preached in Kirksville on occasion and was associated with the Cumberland Presbyterians.[xviii]

Regarding the American College of Osteopathic Medicine and Surgery, as reported in the Christian Nation that Prof J.M. Littlejohn was president, David Littlejohn secretary and James B. Littlejohn M.D., treasurer and manager and that President Littlejohn would be spending the summer in Europe. And further noted that he sailed in the early part of July for Ireland[xix]

Before looking at the college in detail, on a human front, it is worth noting some of the tragedies that beset students in the college. One of the student's wives committed suicide, leaving a note thinking that her husband and his friend who were studying for their exams at the time had more interest in each other than in her.

"well, Willie: it seems that you and I cannot get along well together. You act as if you do not love me any longer, you see, you go out every night, and if you loved me you would not do so. I love you and can not get along with you. Dr. Hill has done it all, for you

---

[8] PUBLISHED BY THE ILLINOIS STATE BOARD OF HEALTH SPRINGFIELD, ILLINOIS, 1917

and I never had any trouble until he and you started to go together. Well, Willie, I will say good-by. Your loving wife, SUSIE"[xx]

Willie Hartford and his friend Frank E Hill explained – the annual state board of health examinations were coming up and both had been cramming to pass with much of their time spent at the American College of Osteopathic Medicine and Surgery where they were students.

It is a rather extreme story, but it does serve to show the stress that students were under, in particular around the Board of Health exams. The pressure on students would have been an important factor in Littlejohn's attitude towards the Board of Health legislation in Illinois.

Another student was charged with wife abandonment and had to be rescued by the other students in the college coming to his aid. This was in 1909/10 and is a rather more complicated human story. On the one hand it shows the close bond of students in Littlejohn's college. On the other hand, it shows some of the deep-seated student problems Littlejohn may have had to deal with as Dean.

"Rah, Rah, Rah, Maxwell" was part of a vocal demonstration at the police station were a fellow student, Guy Maxwell (21 yrs old) was being held. The entire complement of his classmates of the junior class at the Littlejohn College rallied to contribute $375 as bond for his release. Maxwell was charged with "wife abandonment", a charge he and his classmates considered was caused by the father in law, Rev. Ira Durfee. It was said that the Rev. Durfee agreed to the marriage as long as there were no children. In Maxell's own words:

"I don't know why they have made this charge against me, as the only reason I am not living with my wife is because her father won't let us live together. I was just a kid- about 16 years old when I first met Anna. She was an awful sweet girl and I was head over heels in love with her. At that time Mr. Durfee and his family lived at Akron. Anna attended Buchell college and I was finishing up at high school. My mother, who resides in Cleveland, was opposed to my marrying the girl on account of our age and financial condition. I explained these matters to Mr. Durfee and his daughter. Mr. Durfee overcame the objection by saying he would give us a start and I was so happy I

cried. About this time Mr. Durfee got hold of a pamphlet advertising the Littlejohn Osteopathic College. He became deeply interested and the first thing I knew the Durfee family pulled up stakes and moved to Chicago. Anna and I were married September 23rd, 1908 soon after our arrival here. Anna, her father and myself all became students at the Littlejohn school and for a short time everything was fine. When it became known that Anna was to be a mother in a few months, Mr. Durfee made life unbearable for me. One of the stipulations of our marriage – a stipulation imposed by Mr. Durfee – was that Anna and I were not to have any children. From the day it became known that Anna was to be a mother until I went to my mother's home in Cleveland, I was continually nagged by my wife's father. Morning, noon and night the burden of his talk was 'baby'. I sent her to pay her railroad fare to Cleveland. She did not come, and I came to Chicago July 4th to see her. I found she had left the city on the advice of her father. For months, until I returned in the fall to resume my studies at college, I did not see or hear from her. I wrote more than fifty letters in an effort to find her but was unsuccessful. Finally, when I returned in September, I saw her at school. She asked me to treat her as a stranger. It was hard for me to see her every day and not speak to her. My heart was breaking.

Just before Christmas the baby was born. She was at school the day before. The child lived but a few hours. I went to the undertaker's establishment and kissed its cold lips. A few days later I met Anna and we spoke a few words. She is such a sweet, good little girl, but her father won't let her live with me. I have not abandoned her and would be only too glad to live under the same roof with her. When a fellow loves a girl the way I do, he'll go through fire and water for her" [xxi] (Chicago tribune March 31st, 1910)

The story did not end there. Anna sued for divorce on the grounds of cruelty, claiming that on several occasions Maxwell beat her with a yard stick.

"in April 1909, we quarrelled one Sunday after coming home from church about the sermon my father had preached. When father left the house, Guy told me that he would punch me for sticking to my opinion of the sermon. He dragged me across the room, but my mother interfered. I would have left him sooner, but we were

attending school and he was not earning any money. The baby came, and I was unable to combat the circumstances".[xxii]

So, while they attended the same classes from September 1908 to 1910, they did not speak to each other during most of this time. This story and the one above about the suicide of the student are very sad and difficult cases. While they are extreme and not typical, the point in retelling them is to illustrate the type of problems that Littlejohn would have to attend to and deal with as Dean, to give a broader context other than the Osteopathic, to his work. At the same time, while using these extreme stories to illustrate at point, that Littlejohn's College produced some of the finest osteopaths in America, including Fryette and Comstock who are household names to osteopaths to this day.

On the personal front an interesting incident happened in 1908, when his mother witnesses a fatal shooting and had to testify at the coroner's court in December. In short, a picture dealer had been delivering a framed picture to one of two sisters living at 778 West Adams street. The cost of the framing was far in excess of that expected and Mrs. Chambers, one of the sisters, and the framer had an argument and the other sisters, Estelle Stout, shot him as she feared for her own and her sister's life Littlejohn's mother, who lived at 928 West Adams street, gave testimony that was crucial in the coroner's verdict that "Estelle Stout not responsible when she shot the agent"[xxiii]

During this time Littlejohn's writing and editing skills continued to attract attention even outside of Osteopathy; -

In 1906 *"Dr. J. Martin Littlejohn has been appointed a member of the editorial staff of the United Editor's Association. He has been commissioned to write an article of two thousand words on osteopathy for the encyclopedia which the Association will publish"*[xxiv].

And again in 1907

"Dr. J. Martin Littlejohn has recently been elected to membership in the National Historical Society. This is an unsolicited honor which he greatly appreciates."[xxv]

Another important incident happened during this time and that was the death of his brother David's wife. It is noted in the November 19th, 1902 edition of the Christian Nation.

"Mary Forbes, wife of Dr. David Littlejohn, died at her residence 55 Laffan Street, Chicago October 10th at 4.00 p.m. She was twenty-seven years and seven days old. Mrs Littlejohn was born in Scotland in October 1875 and came to this country in September 1898 and was married to Dr. Littlejohn in January 1899. She had a sister living in Kirksville, Mo., where she lived herself after her marriage till June 1900 when the family moved to Chicago. For the past six months she had been ailing, frequent attacks of heart failure weakening her until the end came in one of these attacks, from which she never rallied. She passed away in the midst of a promising womanhood brightened by kindness and a cheerful disposition that made her a genial companion. She followed into the presence of her Master two little babes[9], beside whom her body was laid to rest in the family burial ground at Highland Park, Missouri.[xxvi]"

The loss of his wife[10] and the seeming failure of osteopathy to restore his wife's health may have contributed to David moving away from working in the school to other interests, In 1907 he moved from osteopathy taking up more interest in surgery and then public health issues and administration.

"Feeling the necessity of a change and finding also that in after years he was tending more and more to specialization in surgery, he has associated himself with Dr. White, of Freeport, Ill., In the Dr. White sanatorium. Relieved from the strain of teaching he now is giving

---

[9] At least one of these would appear to have been buried in Kirksville. (Jane Stark correspondence, copy of certificate of purchase of burial plot by J. M., J. B., and David Littlejohn in Kirksville

[10] (David remarried in 1904, but was divorced in 1913, only to remarry again later that year; (To, teach, to heal, to Serve page 17) David also attracted criticism from medics over his qualifications, as mention earlier; and also at one point was arrested as a forger- charged with forging the name of a friend on a check. The case was, I believe, quickly cleared up. (Chicago Sunday Examiner May 16, 1909)

almost his undivided attention to his specialty, surgery of the head, eye, ear, nose and throat. He finds himself quite at home in this fine institution, for previous to his becoming associated with Dr. White he was visiting surgeon in that institution for the five years last past.[xxvii]"

Apart from the osteopathic side of things, these incidents give a flavour of the trials and tribulations that Littlejohn had to face in his time in Chicago. During this time he also had to content with being severely ill with Typhoid during 1907[xxviii], the change of name of the college to the 'Littlejohn College' and started a long association with the Reverent Minifie; all of which would play an important part in his life's path.

I don't know when he first met Rev. Minifie. This newspaper report[xxix], from 1909, is the first I have found. I do suspect he may have met earlier, perhaps during one of his trips to England. During the 1899 trip he apparently spent time at the international YMCA convention in London[xxx]. Minifie, when just 16yrs old, founded the youth section of the YMCA London[xxxi]. So, it is possible that they met at that convention. Minifie and Littlejohn continued to have a close association in England.

> *Dr. J. Martin Littlejohn, who has been president of the Littlejohn College and Hospital of Chicago since it was founded in 1900, has resigned from active connection with the institution, and has been succeeded by Dr.Jas. B. Littlejohn.*
>
> Journal of the American Osteopathic Association Vol 11, No. 3 November 1911 page 795

Perhaps the hardest and the one that ultimately lead to him leaving America and moving to England was the death of his mother in November 1911. She fell ill in the latter half of the summer of 1911, passing away on 22nd November. It is hard to imagine the effect this had on John Martin, especially as his brother James Buchan, had, only two days before, on the 20th November, re-established his connect with the Candida Lodge of the Masons in Chicago. At least when they were in Kirksville he had waited until after their father's death before joining the Adair Lodge. Littlejohn, with his wife having to look after six young children, the youngest having been born in September 1910, resigned his positions with the Littlejohn College, in October 1911[xxxii]

We know his mother was ill for four or more months prior to her death, and we find that he missed the American Osteopathic Association's meeting in Chicago in July 1911 on account of this.

"Dr. littlejohn was unavoidably detained at home due on account of illness in his family and his paper was read by Dr. Elfink[11] of Chicago"[xxxiii]

His mother's health, the burden on his wife in taking care of the family, his own health, and his brother's actions, were probably all factors. After his mother passed away, he obviously considered his position carefully and started to act on his decision to move his family from America to England. His mother would not have considered moving from America when her husband was buried in Kirksville. It would have been her wish to be buried with her husband as would have been the tradition. evidence of this is to be found in the will Littlejohn made in 1912. He obviously had been quite ill and was considering his own passing. In this he says that his mother and father were to be exhumed and reinterred in the family plot of his mother in Glasgow[xxxiv]

The first concrete evidence of his planning to move to England is that in and around August 1912 he asked for a letter of standing from the Iowa Presbytery with the intention of attaching to the R P Church in Scotland. This was granted at the presbytery meeting on September 10th, 1912.[xxxv]

---

[11] Dr. Elfink was a lecturer at the LittleJohn College, but also the editor of the Vegetarian Magazine and an advocate for Vegetarianism

> "A letter was read from J. M Littlejohn asking for a letter of standing to present to the R.P. Church of Scotland and the request was granted"
>
> The Christian Nation vol 57, September 18th, 1912, Page 10

Like all things he did, he took his time and would have personally informed everyone involved before taking any formal action.

Some idea of his mother's standing in the community can be had from the obituary notice that was printed in the Christian Nation.

"ELIZABETH SCOT WALKER LITTLEJOHN
Elizabeth Scot Walker Littlejohn was born in Lesmahagow, Lanarkshire, Scotland, March 5th, 1835. She was married to the Rev. James Littlejohn, a minister of the Reformed Presbyterian Church of Scotland in 1858. For many years she lived in Glasgow while her husband travelled in all parts of Scotland, preaching the gospel to the scattered covenanter congregations. These were the trying times of the disruption in the church of Scotland, 1863, when but few remained faithful to the Church of their Fathers. Mr. Littlejohn was one of five or six ministers that stuck to the Covenanter Church. From 1870 to 1875 she resided at Easdale, in the west highlands of Scotland, where her husband ministered to the scattered Covenanters in the western Highlands. In 1876 she went to reside in Ireland, where her husband ministered to the congregations at Garvagh. From here she moved in 1893, to live with her son, James B. At Munslow in England, on account of the breakdown of her husband's health. In 1896 she came to the United States with her two sons J. B. and David, her husband having preceded with her son J. Martin. Her and her husband resided with J. M. at College Springs Ia., until 1897, when she came to Chicago, where she remained until the summer of 1898, when the family moved to Kirksville Mo. While there, Feb 19th, 1899, her husband died after being in the ministry of the Covenanter Church for 40yrs. Since 1900, she has resided with the family of J. Martin

Littlejohn[12]. *On Wednesday morning, Nov. 22nd, after an illness of four months, she passed away in the presence of her son J. Martin Littlejohn and his wife, Mabel, and Mrs. J. B. littlejohn. A true mother in Israel, she represents probably the last of the worthy mothers of the Covenant, who in Scotland in 1863, "loved not their lives", that they may be true to the Covenanter Church."*[xxxvi]

---

[i] The Evening Star and Daily Herald, Saturday, August 11th, 1900, page 4
[ii] Conversations with David Forlow, member of the Illinois' St. Andrew Society, Lake Bluff, Post Card History Series Lyndon Jensen and Kathleen O'Hara, Arcadia Publishing, Chicago; Lake Forest-Lake Bluff Historical Society
[iii] Mable Emma and Mary Elizabeth as published in the Littlejohn family trees on Ancestry; James, Edgar Martin, John martin and Elizabeth Alice birth dates as recorded on Littlejohn's Certificate of naturalisation Home office No. 370,747; cert no 620 January 1925; Stuart William from his Birth and Death Certificates from Essex County Council
[iv] J Wernham. J M Littlejohn biography Page 12
[v] Ibid page 14
[vi] The Christian Nation Vol 19, July 19th, 1893 (Littlejohn was a co-editor.)
[vii] Journal of Osteopathy, Kirksville, 1901 October,
[viii] The Osteopathic World, October 1903, the editors own, Page 473
[ix] Journal of the American Osteopathic Association, November 1912, page 188
[x] Annual announcement of Dunham Medical College, 1902-3; Courtesy of the Centre for Research Libraries, 6050 South Kenwood Ave., Chicago
[xi] History of homeopathy vol 3, page 122; William Harvey king, m. D., LL. D.; the Lewis publishing company 1905
[xii] Chicago Tribune (Chicago, Illinois) · Wed, May 23, 1900 · Page 13
[xiii] Journal of Osteopathy vol 6, no. 6, Nov 1899, Page 254, Edith Williams
[xiv] ASO alumni directory by name, 1894-1924, A T Still Museum of Osteopathic Medicine
[xv] Diploma held in the Archives of the Chicago College of Osteopathy

---

[12] O'Brien, in his book John Martin Littlejohn, an enigma of osteopathy, on page 57 says ' there is ample evidence the Elizabeth, after their father's death, had lived with various family members around Chicago until her own death'; he gives as reference 'littlejohn family and sundries'. While she may have visited other family members from time to time it is clear she lived with J. Martin and his family for the whole of this period.(See for example, 1910 census, Chicago Examiner, Dec. 4th 1908; Christian nation mothers memorial April 17 1912 vol 56 page 10

[xvi] Journal of osteopathy July 1901 graduating class, page 229
[xvii] "Tennessee, County Marriages, 1790-1950," database with images, *FamilySearch* (https://familysearch.org/ark:/61903/1:1:QKH9-SR2C : 22 December 2016), J B Littlejohn and Edith Mary Williams, 03 Jul 1900; citing Shelby, Tennessee, United States, Marriage, p. , Tennessee State Library and Archives, Nashville and county clerk offices from various counties; FHL microfilm 1,148,814.
[xviii] Hopkinsville Kentuckian, Sept 11th, 1903: The Weekly Graphic, Kirksville Sept 18th, 1880
[xix] The Christian Nation, Volume 33, August 1st, 1900, page 12
[xx] Decatur review March 31st, 1904
[xxi] Chicago daily tribune Thursday March 31st, 1910, page 1
[xxii] Chicago Daily Tribune 25th May 1910, [page 9
[xxiii] Chicago examiner December 4th, 1908, page 1
[xxiv] The Journal of the American Osteopathic Association vol 6 1906 page 454
[xxv] The Journal of the American Osteopathic Association vol 6 1906 Page 236 Feb 1907
[xxvi] The Christian Nation November 19th, 1902, page 15
[xxvii] The Freepost Daily Journal. Sept 26th, 1907, page 5
[xxviii] Journal of the American osteopathic association, Vol 7 no 2 oct 1907 page 69
[xxix] Boston Post June 9, 1909 page 4
[xxx] Journal of Osteopathy, Kirksville, Volume 6, Number 6, November 1899 page 252
[xxxi] The Arbroath Herald, Friday 27th 1914, page 6
[xxxii] Announced in the November 1911 Journal of the American Osteopathic Association, page 795
[xxxiii] Journal of the American Osteopathic Association, august 1911 page 613 - minutes of the fifteenth annual session of the American Osteopathic Association, in Chicago 25-28 July 1911
[xxxiv] 1912 Will and testimony of John Martin Littlejohn, NOA now held in the Wellcome Library
[xxxv] The Christian Nation vol 57, September 18th, 1912, Page 10
[xxxvi] The Christian Nation, Vol 56; April 17, 1912 page 10

The American College of Osteopathic Medicine and Surgery

The move to Chicago allowed Littlejohn to pursue his ambition of developing a truly Osteopathic College of Medicine in its fullest meaning. At his heart, He was an educator and a minister. These two aspects of his character would be fulfilled as an Osteopathic Physician and as Professor of Osteopathic therapeutics and Dean of the College. From the beginning of his association with Osteopathy he maintained that Osteopathy was 'Medicine' in its original meaning, and that the best way forward was to claim it as such. While osteopaths in many states and court battles rejoiced when a court case for practising medicine without a license was dismissed, they seemed to ignore that this placed osteopathy in the same category as masseurs, nurses, Turkish baths and others ancillary to the physician. Others felt that their education in osteopathic colleges, including the ASO, did not fit them for general practice and that their education, to quote LittleJohn, was "*not rounded out until they are able to dabble in drugs with the license of the law*"[i]. In the same article he lamented that "*we have several schools in Chicago that graduate Osteopaths without seeing them, professing to give by mail or otherwise in a few weeks or even days the principles and practice of this great system*".

It was in this atmosphere that he set the standard for his school, in conjunction with his surgeon osteopath brother, James B.; a standard they aimed to be in line with the best schools of medicine in the country. They aimed for the college to have "*a complete course, including everything that is embraced in the new Osteopathic system. Yet it was a system with rigid qualifications, for 'none but a perfectly trained and thoroughly skilled hand shall deal with the body'*"[ii]. To do this they started with the standard two-year course in osteopathy and a further two years, as part of a four-year course "*in which every branch and department of medicine and surgery required by all the states in the Union and in foreign countries will be taught*"[iii]

"*a College of Osteopathic Medicine, Surgery and Obstetrics, the object of which shall be to discover, formulate and teach the improved methods of surgery, obstetrics and the treatment of diseases in general so as to systematise and place on a scientific basis the osteopathic methods of healing and treating diseases and conditions of the body; to impart this scientific system of healing to the medical profession, and others attending this College"*[iv] [1]

Osteopathic Principles, techniques, diagnosis, and practice being substituted for pharmacy and Materia Medica and the therapeutics of the other schools of healing.

His view on this was unequivocal, and always very clearly stated-**"One thing that is tending to destroy the scientific nature of Osteopathy is the tendency to mix Osteopathy with something else. They do not mix, however, because the Osteopathic system is independent. We cannot hope to make much advance by trying to consider disease or its treatment from a dual standpoint"** [v]

Unfortunately, the inclusion of the word 'medicine in the school's title and the need to teach anaesthetic and associated drugs/pharmacology for the practice of surgery gave some in the osteopathic profession and the State Board of health of Illinois, cause to complain.

This argument would persist within the osteopathic profession and while it took many forms the essential argument would seem to have been

'is osteopathy a specialism in which disease is "considered from one standpoint, viz : Disease is the result of anatomical abnormalities followed by physiological discord"[2]

Or

is **"Osteopathy is a complete system of therapeutics and as such is both medicinal and surgical in its own peculiar way."**[3]

---

[1] This is very similar to the original charter of the ASO
[2] Taken from 'our Platform' Published in The Journal of Osteopathy, Kirksville October 1902

An excellent account of the College and its development is given by Theodore A. Berchtold, *in his book*

'To Teach, To Heal, To Serve'

"This College shall maintain a standard of requirements for entrance equivalent to that laid down by the American Association of Medical Colleges, shall teach such sciences and arts as are usually taught in reputable medical colleges and in addition the science of osteopathy in all its branches; and members of the medical profession graduated from reputable colleges shall be allowed to complete the courses, both practical and theoretical, in osteopathy and on the completion of such courses, shall be entitled to receive the diploma in osteopathy; (b) This College shall be and represent an independent medical school or system or method of healing or treating diseases and conditions of the body, said College using, applying and teaching the osteopathic theories of diagnosis and therapeutics, surgery and obstetrics so as to maintain the same as an independent system or science of healing; and finally (C) This Corporation shall not be conducted for profit but shall be solely conducted as an educational institution, with annexed infirmary, as the Board shall determine, in accordance with the laws and constitution of the state of Illinois. The College was empowered to confer degrees and diplomas upon all those who shall have attended the prescribed course and passed examinations satisfactory to the faculty in each and every branch required to be taught and studied in the course."

To Teach, To Heal, To Serve; Page 19-20

---

[3] Minutes of convention, The American Association for the Advancement of Osteopathy; at Indianapolis July 1899; F. W. Hannah D.O., The American Osteopath, Quarterly, Vol 1 sept 1899, page 46

OSTEOPATHY AN INDEPENDENT SYSTEM CO-EXTENSIVE WITH THE SCIENCE AND ART OF HEALING.

Paper read before the A. O. A. Convention at Kirksville, Mo., by Dr. J. Martin Littlejohn, President of the American College of Osteopathic Medicine and Surgery, Chicago, Ill.

I thank you for the privilege and honor of addressing this body. A few weeks ago, the chairman of your committee asked me to give a paper and selected for me the above title. I am glad that it is my privilege to speak on this topic. **In some mysterious way my personal attitude to Osteopathy has been misunderstood. I find that some of my fellow Osteopaths here have the idea that the College over which I have the honor to preside teaches medicine in the sense of drugs.** I am an Osteopath and delight to be connected with a College which regards Osteopathy as an independent system. The charter of our College, the only recognition that Osteopathy has in the commonwealth of Illinois, contains this provision, "this college shall be and represent an independent medical school or system or method of healing or treating diseases and conditions of the body, said college using, applying and teaching the osteopathic theories of diagnosis and therapeutics, surgery and obstetrics, so as to maintain the same as an independent system or science of healing." Every member of our faculty is pledged to this principle and I hope to demonstrate to you why we are pledged to this fundamental conception of Osteopathy. osteopathy and medicine.

We do not say that medicine is a generic term with Osteopathy as one of its subdivisions or branches. We do not place Osteopathy, medicine and surgery as co-ordinate branches. Osteopathy is not a branch of medicine or surgery. Dr. F. W. Hannah, at the Indianapolis convention, said: "Osteopathy is a complete system of therapeutics and as such is both medicinal and surgical in its own peculiar way." Minutes of convention, American Osteopath, Vol. I. page 46.)

The Journal of the American Osteopathic Association vol 1-2
Sept 1901-page 22
(Bold emphasis by the author)

Part of this argument centred around the sixth point found in 'Our Platform'

Bunting, who had studied with Littlejohn in the American School of Osteopathy, edited the Journal of Osteopathy and as editor of the 'Osteopathic Physician', was quick to challenge this view, writing in January 1903;

"Under the heading "Our Platform" the sixth plank contains this sentence: 'The fundamental principles of Osteopathy, however, are different from those of any other system and the cause, of disease is considered from one standpoint, VIZ.: disease is the result of anatomical abnormalities followed by physiological discord'. This may be the sum total of some people's Osteopathy, but it is not mine. I would like really to know how many men of five years' active practice are willing to balance themselves on this two-inch strip of a plank. Those who desire to confine themselves to this narrow doctrine are at perfect liberty to do so. I doubt whether a man who is satisfied with it could be convinced by any line of reasoning whatsoever, that life in its-manifold phenomena has any other side than the mechanical. Those who make this doctrine, that structural defect is the sole cause of physiological perversion, the mainspring of their therapeutic methods claim that the Maker of All Things has placed in our bodies all the materials necessary for health and repair. This is granted by all Osteopaths, but we also have appetites, desires, passions, etc., which subject us to excesses. People have to work for a living in damp, cold, poisonous places; have little to eat and little to wear. Others live in luxury, have too much to eat and to wear, are cursed with nothing to do. There are the occupation diseases, those resulting from fatigue and excesses either in the line of too much work or too much gratification of appetite. When these have had their resistance lowered, they are subjected to overwhelming amounts of parasites, bacteria, etc."[vi]

Others took the same view

"A so-called platform is published, and this statement is taken from one of the planks: 'The cause of disease is considered from one standpoint, viz: Disease is the result of anatomical abnormalities followed by physiological discord.' This I cannot believe, and utterly fail to understand how anyone who has studied the subject can set

forth such a doctrine. Notice it says one standpoint. According to this the boy who eats green apples must have an anatomical abnormality when his stomach aches, or the office man who takes little or no exercise and eats three hearty meals a day and overworks every organ in his body must have an anatomical abnormality when the digestive system refuses to do its work" (Warren B. Davis. Milwaukee. Before Wisconsin Osteopathic Association Meeting at Madison, February 24th, 1903)[vii]

Littlejohn, himself, would put even more forcefully:

"To state the principle of Osteopathy as it has been stated, namely that disease is the result of anatomical abnormalities followed by physiological discord, is as absurd as the statement of the older medical schools. On this supposed principle osteopathic therapeutics is limited to the cure of diseases in which the abnormal parts must be adjusted to the normal. This principle of therapeutics is equally absurd, because anatomical abnormalities represent only one field in the aetiology of disease. The trouble here is that the osteopaths do not understand the principle of Osteopathy. The principle of Osteopathy is not bone adjustment, but body adjustment. Hence, any maladjustment affecting the body, or any of its parts- structural, environmental or toxic - falls under the osteopathic aetiology, and any means of correction - manipulative, dietetic or surgical - that tend to correct the adjustment and thus elaborate the forces and fluids of the body so as to normalise the body, belong to the osteopathic system.

"Drugs are entirely eliminated because these represent elements foreign to the proximate principles of the body and not in line with the therapeutics of increased resistance. The only exception to this to be noted in the case of germicides, antidotes and antiseptics, because these substances are instrumental in removing the toxic and septic conditions that prevent the organism from maintaining, or returning to, its normal condition.

"This is not a new principle in Osteopathy, although it has been contended that Osteopathy is an absolutely drugless condition. Dr. A. T. Still recognises this himself. He recommends the inhalation of cantharidin for a smallpox patient and the vaccination by the use of cantharadin as a preventative for smallpox. He recommends the

use of glycerine and water in cases of diphtheria. These are substances that belong to the field of medicine, and to be just to ourselves, as well as to the practitioners of other systems, if we use these as antitoxins or antiseptics, it is simply honesty to admit that we do use them"[viii]

Of course, we have to remember that many things attributed to Still were 'rewrites' of his words. The text, Our Platform, was included in the book 'Research and Practice', but this may not have been written directly by Still. Littlejohn, writing in response to the quote in 'our Platform' quotes Still from the August 1902 Journal of Osteopathy:

"Disease is the result of physiological discord in the functioning of the organs or parts of the physiological laboratory of life. The cause of disease can be traced to boney variations from the base of the skull to the bottom of the foot; in the joints of the cervical, dorsal and lumbar vertebrae, the articulations with the sacrum; also the arms and lower limbs." [ix]

This he quotes before attacking the phrase used in 'Our Platform'

Still, in his book 'Philosophy of Osteopathy, which was written by himself – **"I have written all that is in it from end [to] end"**[4] says;

"The Osteopath seeks first physiological perfection of form, by normally adjusting the osseous frame work, so that all arteries may deliver blood to nourish and construct all parts" [x]

Late in 1902, in his book 'Philosophy and Mechanical principles of Osteopathy' he says;

"The blood vessels carrying the fluids for the construction and sustenance of the infinitely fine fibres, vessels, glands, fascia, and cellular conducting channels to nerves and lymphatics, must be absolutely normal in location before a normal physiological action can

---

[4] From a letter written to Thekla Orschel on January 2nd, 1900 about his book 'Philosophy of Osteopathy' which had just been published (A T Museum of Osteopathic Medicine, Kirksville, ref. No. 2009.10.656)

be executed in perfect harmony with the health sustaining machinery of the body. (Page 34)

"If health is perfect, it only proves perfect harmony in the physiological action of the body in all its parts and functions. Any variation from perfect health marks a degree of functional derangement in the physiological department of man "(Page 86.)

No matter what the origin of the phrase in 'Our Platform'[5], it crystallised the division within osteopathy into two factions, the 'specialists' and those who wanted osteopathy to be a complete system of medicine. Unfortunately, this division meant that those who wanted to mix Osteopathy with drugs etc found a home on one side; and the 'all you need merchants' who used only specific manipulation and nothing else, found a home on the other side.[6] This had the inevitable consequence of blurring the debate and those that appealed to base emotional response had the upper hand compared to those whose had a rational approach. The Mid western Politician's method verses the Practical Covenanter.

We see some of the strength of feeling amongst osteopaths, about the word Medicine and Drugs, especially in Illinois, from a report in the JAOA sept 1904 titled 'the M.D., D.O. in osteopathic societies'. In this it says that

" *the Illinois osteopathic association has caused the resignation of Dr. W. A. Hinckle M. D., D. O. of Peoria Illinois, as a member of the association, on the ground that he has not been convinced that drug medication may not be beneficially employed in some cases where osteopathic adjustment fails to accomplish all that is to be desired. It is a rule of the association to exclude from membership any M.D., D. O. that prescribes drugs.*"

In pursuance of its aims of the American College of osteopathic medicine and surgery, made application to the State Board of Health to be recognised as a Medical College (osteopathic) in good standing

---

[5] In my opinion, even if Still did not originate this phrase, he certainly led people along that route, possibly without being aware of the effect his 'plain speaking' had on his followers.

[6] It is rather unfortunate as the two genuine factions could have lived in peaceful co-existence as they were not mutually exclusive.

so that its graduates would have full rights to practice Medicine in all its branches **except** Drugs,. on completion of the full four-year course. This idea, as mentioned above, was put forward by Littlejohn in 1899 in Kirksville.[7] This led to a prolonged battle with the Board of Health, and conflict with the American Osteopathic Association.

The College was incorporated by J Martin Littlejohn, his brother James B. and Edith W. Williams (who married James B. Littlejohn in 1900), with the original directors being J. Martin Littlejohn, James B. Littlejohn, David Littlejohn and their mother, Elizabeth W Littlejohn.[8]

" The American College of Osteopathy and Surgery, 405 Washington Boulevard, Chicago, has been founded under the laws of the State of Illinois, Prof. J. M Littlejohn is President, David Littlejohn is Secretary, and James B, Littlejohn, M , D., is Treasurer and Manager. We are in receipt of the Catalogue for 1900-01; President Littlejohn is spending the summer in Europe".[xi]

---

[7] The ASO removed the term "reputable medical colleges" and replaced it with " osteopathic colleges" in 1903. This meant that Littlejohn's claim that the ASO could legitimately award the degree M.D. (Osteopathic). would no longer be valid. (ASO record book 1903-1924 page 3)

[8] "Elizabeth W. Littlejohn, who is listed as one of the four directors, was the mother of the Littlejohn brothers. Five officers were listed for the Board of Directors in the 1900 Announcement Catalogue: J. Martin Littlejohn, President; T. J. Anthony, Vice President; David Littlejohn, Secretary; James B. Littlejohn, Treasurer and Manager; and Judge J. M. Longenecker, Attorney". (To Teach, to Heal, To Serve Page 41); Officers of the Board are not to be confused with Board Members.

Thomas J Anthony, who had married Littlejohn's sister in Munslow England in 1894 was listed as 'vice president[xii]' for several years. His year of emigration to USA is given as 1902 in the 1930 Census of the USA:[xiii].

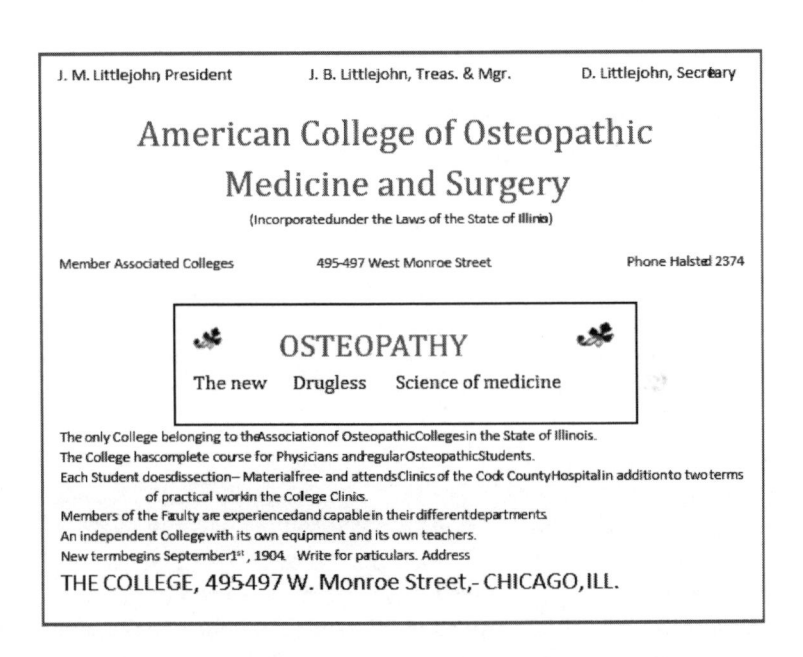

J. M. Littlejohn, President   J. B. Littlejohn, Treas. & Mgr.   D. Littlejohn, Secretary

American College of Osteopathic Medicine and Surgery

(Incorporated under the Laws of the State of Illinois)

Member Associated Colleges   495-497 West Monroe Street   Phone Halsted 2374

OSTEOPATHY
The new   Drugless   Science of medicine

The only College belonging to the Association of Osteopathic Colleges in the State of Illinois.
The College has complete course for Physicians and regular Osteopathic Students.
Each Student does dissection – Material free- and attends Clinics of the Cook County Hospital in addition to two terms of practical work in the College Clinics.
Members of the Faculty are experienced and capable in their different departments
An independent College with its own equipment and its own teachers.
New term begins September 1st, 1904. Write for particulars. Address

THE COLLEGE, 495-497 W. Monroe Street,- CHICAGO, ILL.

David was not to stay long as a director, although he maintained an interest in the School and hospital[9], for which he organised fund raising and helped develop the associated school of nursing[xiv]. He tragically lost his wife in 1902 and began a move towards surgery[xv].

"Dr. David Littlejohn, a resident of Oak Park, is one of the promoters of the plan to ... establish an osteopath hospital in Chicago. Walter Wellman, who seeks to reach the North Pole by airship, will donate the proceeds of his lecture in Orchestra hall Monday evening" [xvi]

---

[9] The listing of new incorporations in the Illinois Medical Journal for January 1908, page 120 includes the "American Hospital of Medicine, Surgery and Osteopathy, Chicago; incorporators, A. F. Heimlich, D. Littlejohn, J. B. Littlejohn."

> "Last month the Littlejohn Osteopathic Hospital pulled off a lecture at Orchestra Hall, which was a great credit to the profession. Walter Wellman, the Arctic explorer, gave an illustrated stereopticon lecture, showing his dash for the Pole in an airship. It was great."[xvii]

After David left as director and to accommodate the introduction of their attorney as director, the Littlejohns, in 1906, filed a request with the Illinois Secretary of State to increase the board of directors to six from four[xviii] Rolla Rudolph Longenecker their attorney, who was to play a crucial role in the fight with the State Board of Health, was a long-time member of Candida Lodge 927[xix], to which James B. originally joined in 1898. This change in the Board of Directors would give James B., his wife Edith Williams and his fellow Mason R. R. Longenecker as a group virtual control. The sixth member was John H. Lucas. This would become important when the issue of the change of name came up in 1908/9.

Another factor that comes into play was the increase in staff. Some of this was to help with the case for recognition by the State Board of Health, but mostly it was to improve the quality of teaching. When the ACOM&S took over "the Chicago School of Osteopathy". in 1903, some of the lecturers of that school were retained by the ACOM&S, others came from other institutions like the Illinois Institute of Osteopathy. Some prove worthwhile, for example Dr. William McClelland, from the Chicago School, who became assistant manager.[xx]

> "The American College of Osteopathic Medicine and Surgery Chicago has consolidated the Chicago College of Osteopathy with its 29 students. This gives the former college the whole field in Illinois which will be of advantage both to it and to osteopathy. The American College is one of the associated colleges and as such will work harmoniously with the others of that organisation for the promotion of the osteopathic interests. The American College will graduate 30 students next June."
> (The Osteopathic World May 1904; page 157)

Others helped fuel the accusation that the ACOM&S was tending to mix Osteopathy with orthodox medicine.

Dr. Hamlin is a good example of this.

"In 1904 he was elected president of the Illinois College of Osteopathy, situated at No. 167 Dearborn street, which was later discontinued. He is now professor of clinical diagnosis in Littlejohn College and is a member of the Chicago Osteopathic Association.... Dr. Hamlin made the following statement: "I do not believe in the physician practicing anyone teaching or system of medicine. Each and every school has its good qualities, but no physician, no matter what school he may have graduated from, is capable of meeting all conditions and carrying them through to a successful termination with one line of practice — for that matter he could not do so if he had all the knowledge embodied in all the schools, but his failures would be less numerous if he were broad enough to inform himself of what some other school would do under like circumstances and then decide which to employ... No patient cares what you give him so long as he gets well. He is not paying the physician for living up to the ethical laws of some medical society. Medical ethics tend to make physicians narrow. They try to fit the patient to their one system of treatment instead of trying to fit the treatment to the patient" [xxi]

So while Littlejohn and his brother James B. held strongly to the concepts of osteopathy, promoting the necessity for sound education and standards through talks before professional groups, their commitment to the Associated Colleges of Osteopathy (ACO), or through papers published in professional journals they would continue to face opposition from within the profession; At the same time, others within their faculty would tend to undermine their efforts and give credence to the charge that they mixed osteopathy with drugs. This was in addition to the continued clamour for 'pure osteopathy and no drugs' from some quarters like the American School of Osteopathy in Kirksville, Hildreth and others. This clamour being accompanied by literature which tended to give the opposite impression.

> *"One of the chief factors that militated against us in Illinois during our last campaign was the fact that while many of the osteopaths were preaching "no drug, no knife doctrine" —the catalogues of the A. S. O. were in the hands of the legislators announcing pages of surgical operations.*
>
> *"The A.S.O. is quite right in adding surgery to the curriculum, and a course in the fallacies of medicine, that is, comparative therapeutics; but let us be honest"*
> (J Martin Littlejohn, Trying to Solve M. D. Degree Proposition, JAOA May 1910, page 407)

This would come to a head with the inspection of the school by Dr. Charles C. Teall on behalf of the American Osteopathic Association (AAO). To put this into context we first need to look at the Associated Colleges of Osteopathy (ACO) and its relationship with the AAO.

The Drs. Littlejohn Sanatorium, Windsor Park, near the shore of Lake Michigan.

THE ASSOCIATED COLLEGES

The idea for the associated colleges of osteopathy was, at least in part, the brainchild of Littlejohn. During 1898, the ASO recognised that many other schools of osteopathy had opened up and, in an effort, to help maintain standards invited representatives of all the schools to meeting in Kirksville on the 28th June. The ASO together with the Northern, Pacific, S. S. Still, Bolles and the Milwaukee schools met and formed the Associated Colleges of Osteopathy[xxii]. At the faculty meeting of the ASO on December 14th, 1898 a motion was passed that *"Dr. J. Martin. Littlejohn be elected as the representative of this school in the Associated colleges of Osteopathy to succeed C. M. T. Hulett"*[xxiii]

Hulett wrote an interesting article in the American Osteopath, September 1899, which not only gives an indication of the rationale for the Associated Colleges but also illustrates that even then it was recognised that Still's plain speaking could lead to problems.

"But the reason which explains all other reasons, and which underlies the whole subject, is the fact that the early graduates of the American School of Osteopathy were not qualified to plan and carry out a system of education such as is necessary to fully furnish students for its practice. They did not know because they had not been taught. The old doctor's conception of the errors of the medical profession was so vivid that to the students' minds it was all-inclusive, **and some of them went quite convinced that the entire store of supposed knowledge of the medical profession was a mass of error and should be wholly disregarded, and osteopathy built up of a little anatomy and some clinic work-** *Physiology, pathology, symptomatology, chemistry, everything, was totally tabooed, and students were strictly forbidden to "waste their time on any such foolishness." In fact, the idea was cultivated that "a good physiologist made a poor operator*[10] [11]*," and that, therefore, scholastic attainments or*

---

[10] Bold emphasis by the author.

ambitions were not to be considered as of special advantage in the lifework of an osteopathist. Those who did not see the fallacy of this position, (and there were many who did), were therefore, not wholly to blame if they considered that they were doing a legitimate act in founding a school on such lines. This, of course, was very unfortunate. **Everyone now sees its error, but that does not change history, nor does it undo the harm (and in a sense the injustice) to many students, who, through hard experience, are getting in their practice what ought to have been given them in their course;** or if they have not the realization of their needs which leads them to such results, they simply settle down to being, what the old doctor calls, "engine wipers."[xxiv]

In 1900 the ACO had to deal with problems concerning the business methods of the S.S. Still school. They recognised that if these methods continued and the S. S. Still school remained in the ACO it would "lessen the benefits and destroy its efficiency". Hence it was decided to suspend the S. S. School from the associations.[xxv]

By 1902, this situation had been resolved and the S. S. Still school was welcomed back. At the same meeting, Littlejohn's college, the ACOM&S joined the association, having completed the minimum of one complete cycle of education, graduating its first full class that year. Unfortunately, at the same meeting the ASO resigned from the Associated. This defection resulted in almost universal condemnation from all the other schools. The main rationale for their withdrawal from the Association would appear to be two-fold. Firstly, the reinstatement of the S. S. Still College with the admittance of Littlejohn's College. Secondly, the fact that the ASO would not be in control of the association.

Hildreth and Charlie Still seemed content to use A T Still's opposition to the ACO as the basis of their withdrawal, but when the other schools and many osteopaths came out against their move Hildreth published a 'fuller explanation' in an effort to deflect from criticism of

---

[11] It is interesting to note how the phrase '**"a good physiologist made a poor operator'** has been taken out of context and become associated with Littlejohn during the second half of the twentieth century. The implication being that it was directed at LittleJohn

him and the ASO that arose and was printed in the August Osteopathic Physician: Hildreth explained:

"Dr. Hildreth Makes a Statement

Editor Osteopathic Physician/ Chicago, -

"Dear Sir; In your report of the action of the A. S. O. at the meeting of the Associated Colleges of Osteopathy held at Milwaukee August 8th, "The O. P." says; "Dr. Hildreth addressed the meeting on behalf of the American School of Osteopathy, and said, it is reported that the life and usefulness of the Associated Colleges of Osteopathy were now evidently about concluded; that the American Osteopathic Association was now big and strong to do the work hitherto falling to the province of the 'Associated Colleges'; and that the time was ripe, therefore, to disband the Association;" that the Old Doctor said to me, just as I left Kirksville: "Arthur, go up to Milwaukee and tell the boys that I said I wish they would disband the Association of Osteopathic Colleges."

"Now, Mr. Editor, I did address the meeting, and did say that we came there with -our minds fully made up to withdraw the A. S. O. from the Association, and that now, since everything had been concluded in a business way between all the colleges, agreeable to all, we felt it would be the best time to withdraw; that we did so without any feeling whatever toward any of the other colleges, and purely because we felt in so doing we were doing the most for Osteopathy as a profession;....that there were schools as members of the Association which were not doing the work they should do to place Osteopathy where it belongs; and we did not believe we could afford to help maintain a reputation for these schools that tended to weaken the profession by putting incompetent practitioners in the field. Further, that no matter what might be said as regarding the Association as a scientific organization and for the benefit of the profession as a whole, yet the fact remains that the schools, as conducted at present, could not help but have more or less rivalry, because they were actuated more from a financial standpoint than a scientific standpoint. In other words, the competition of certain schools was due largely to the desire of financial gain, when it should not be the case.

"Again, we believe the American Osteopathic Association should be the power behind the throne which should help to guide the schools of

Osteopathy into a channel which would mean the greatest good to the profession. In other words, an organization that was disinterested from a financial standpoint and only interested in the best good of the profession could do more to guide the management of the school aright than the Associated College could do; and for those reasons alone, as well as some others, we took the position we did, believing it would mean most to the profession as a whole in the end. I did not say in the "words reported that the Old Doctor said to me just as I left Kirksville: "Arthur, go up to Milwaukee and tell the boys that I said I wish they would disband the Association of Osteopathic Colleges;" but I did say the Old Doctor said to me he wanted me to go there and see that Dr. Charles Still and our people did withdraw from the Associated Colleges; and further, I said, personally I would be glad to see the Associated Colleges disband. That was my own personal view and expressed independently by myself.....I will say further that our action was done with best feelings toward all members of Associated Colleges and done purely because we believed that action meant most to the. profession in the end. Yours very truly,
"A. G. Hildreth, D. O[xxvi]."

Littlejohn and others thought the withdrawal was the wrong thing to do and was done, in essence for the wrong reasons. Charles Still was of the opinion that if the ASO stayed in the association it would only give the other schools an advantage they did not deserve, setting a standard that made "weaker" schools seem as good as the ASO. Perhaps Mason w. Pressly, of the Philadelphia School (who incidentally came up with the definition of osteopathy that A. T. Still used on the inside cover of the Journal of Osteopathy), said what others only thought:

"The withdrawal of the American School of Osteopathy from the Associated Colleges of Osteopathy is susceptible of several interpretations:

1.   Because of personal differences between the American School and the S. S. Still College. These are generally known to exist, and to be of such oppugnant character as to make the cordial affiliation of the two enterprises impossible. The A. S. O. seemed satisfied to remain in the Associated Colleges after the failure to elect Dr. S. S. Still as

President of the Associated Colleges, but when Dr. S. S. Still was re-elected President of the Associated Colleges, the A. S. O. withdrew[xxvii]."

He went on to say that he felt this was the main reason.

Littlejohn's opinion was more diplomatic but just as to the point. It is worth quoting him at length as it gives a clear impression of how Littlejohn thought.

"The Associated Colleges a Part of the A. O. A.

"You ask me to express my views upon the withdrawal of the A. S. O. from the Associated Colleges of Osteopathy. I regret the action very much. I know that Dr. A. T. Still opposed the A. C. O. from its inception, as I personally discussed the matter with him at the time of the origin of the ACO. I told Dr. Still then I believed he was mistaken, and I still believe so. The A. S. O. claims to stand for an independent system of healing and for the best interests of the science. This action, however, in my opinion, does not mean that. We all recognize the A. S. O. as the parent school and A. T. Still as the first discoverer of the system. That does not mean, however, that the old doctor, however much we respect him, is the only exponent of the science or that the A. S. O. is the only school of Osteopathy. The reasons given are not in our estimation sufficient to justify the action.

"(1) Associations are formed for mutual benefit. That is true. The A. S. O. has not proved the failure of this in the A. C. O. It seems to claim that money making, not osteopathic teaching, is the policy of all the other schools. That has not been proved. It has yet to be demonstrated that anything taught by any other school is non-osteopathic. The purpose of a college is the advancement of liberal education. The charter of the A. S. O. 'declares that Its policy is to teach every science, and art taught in the reputable medical schools'. The A. O. A. has definitely declared (see Indianapolis resolutions) that its ideal is to teach every therapeutic equipment taught in any medical school, except Materia Medica. Yet the A.S.O. endorses the A.O.A. and repudiates the A. C. O. We know of no college of Osteopathy in the A. C. O. that is teaching Materia Medica. Everything else taught is part of a liberal education designed to fit the Osteopath for his, general and special practice.

There may be business and educational methods in vogue among some schools which are not perfect. This, however, is not to be wondered at, because Osteopathic colleges are in their infancy. The bettering of this condition is not to come from isolating the strong from the weak or dividing forces. The question of what is purely osteopathic and unosteopathic is yet an open one. We are in favor of thoroughly osteopathic procedures and none else, but we do not believe if an osteopath uses water, heat, proper food, as nature's means of recuperation, he is entitled to be branded as an heretic. Osteopathy gave birth to the principle that nothing foreign to the nature of the body may be used as a curative remedy, but every proximate principle of the body means body life. Deep breathing is osteopathic, although taught by Hanish, because It is a means of furnishing the 65 percent of O[12] necessary to life; physical exercises by, the patient are osteopathic, because they bring out the principle of mobility, which is the primary property of all living matter, water internal, external, for cleansing as well as drink is osteopathic, because the body substance consists of solids suspended in fluids, the fluid and fluid motivity being the foundation of every body function.

"(2) The A. S. O. does not indorse the business methods of certain schools. This does not, we think, furnish good reason for secession. If certain schools employ questionable methods be manly to name these certain schools and do not attempt to slap at all the schools for the sake of some. I can only speak for the college of which I am president. I trust the other schools will do likewise. If the A. S. O. will point to anything in our business methods un- ethical, our college will frankly admit it so if it exists, and at once reform the same. Our college corporation exists by charter in such a way that profit is impossible. Every cent made belongs to the college and is bound to be held in trust under the charter. If the corporation does not follow straight business methods, it is liable to impeachment. And the trustees are ready to invite closest investigation along these lines. Every other college of osteopathy should be in the same position:

"(3) The A. C. O. is unnecessary, because the A. O. A. can do all that is necessary. The A. S. O. surely knows that according to the

---

[12] Oxygen

constitution of the A. O. A. the A. C. O. is really a part of the A. O. A. Article VI section 5 gives to the committee on education of the A. O. A. general oversight of all educational institutions. The mode of execution is clearly and carefully outlined. The education committee of the A. O. A., with the executive committee of the A. C. O., is to form a joint committee of inspection, oversight and report regarding colleges. This report is then submitted to the board of trustees of the A. O. A. and the A. C. O. If these agree, then the decision is final as to acceptance or rejection; if they do not agree a final appeal goes to the A. O. A. This, we think, is a well-considered and carefully guarded system of jurisdiction, control and cooperation. The A. O. A. recognized that certain academic questions could best be looked after by the A. C. O. at the same time making the A. C. O. an affiliated position of its own committee on education and its Board of Trustees. How can the A.S.O. heartily "commend the A. O. A. when it secedes from a part of the A. O. A. organization? To withdraw from the one certainly endangers association with the other. If the A. S. O. knew of existing methods of business or education deserving condemnation, it had a constitutional right to bring the matters in question before the final court of appeal, the A. O. A. In failing to do so, the action of withdrawal seems to be against the A. O. A. constitution. This, in our opinion, is a cause for regret. We are sincerely sorry that the A. S. O. did withdraw. We trust they will withdraw this withdrawal. The science needs a united front. When vital questions are at issue, we cannot afford to divide our forces. Many a cause has been lost, not because of enemies, but from internal division. In union of osteopathic colleges and practitioners lies the hope of final victory for our beloved science. (J. MARTIN LITTLEJOHN, M. D., D.O., LL. D." [xxviii]

Littlejohn was at heart an educationalist. He believed that a profession, if it was to grow, needed three things:

1. A strong professional association that would look after professional ethics and all maters dealing with the practice, in this case, of Osteopaths in the field. The A.O.A.

2. Strong schools, with a solid educational standard, governed by an association of the schools. In this case the Associated Colleges of Osteopathy.

3. Co-operation of the two strands on an equal basis. The Professional Association giving feedback from the field on how the education may need to be adjusted, upgraded or otherwise improved to meet the needs met in practice. But this should be done without compromising on the basic principles of Osteopathy.

At the same time, within colleges, there would be a need for faculty meetings and a student body. The same co-operation within the colleges or schools as on the macro scale, was taking place between the professional organisation and the college/school association.

He would put these views strongly and without compromise. Unlike Hildreth, he was not a politician. Hildreth, as seen above, saw the need to roll back on what he had said at the conference, so as to appear less controversial, in the face of almost universal criticism. The quote that is often used is *"The old Doctor said to me just as I left Kirksville, 'Arthur, go up to Milwaukee and tell the boys that I said I wish they would disband the Association of Osteopathic Colleges'"* (Osteopathic Physician August 1902, page 2). Which is rather different from the revised version he claims in his letter in the October edition quoted above.

Charles Still seemed to think differently, he seemed to fear the development of other schools and perhaps, given that the ACOM&S seemed to be succeeding and was accepted into the ACO at the same meeting as the S. S. Still school was readmitted, he had not overcome his apparent fear of Littlejohn.

As an aside, the ACOM&S was referred to as **'The Littlejohn School now recognised'** on page one of the August Osteopathic Physician. It certainly flows easier off the tongue that the full title – The American College of Osteopathic Medicine and Surgery. The ASO was often referred to as Kirksville; it could not be referred to as the 'Still College' as Still's nephew, S. S. Still had usurped that privilege. Littlejohn, when asked, plainly stated his opinion on the naming of schools;

"Personally, we are against the use of individual names to designate colleges, schools, infirmaries etc because it savours of egotism. Any school is above a mere individual, however great that individual may be, and an incorporated college is a public trust,

when a specific name is chosen that name should be scrupulously adhered to, to avoid any possible misrepresentation".[xxix],[13]

This conflict about the ACO and the AOA would resurface again during Littlejohn's time in Chicago.

> One writer put the conflict very succinctly when he said;
> *"Dr. Still is fond of calling himself "Pap', and his children needn't get nervous because he is a 'Grandpap'. He and they ought to be proud of all the Associated Colleges, and not fret because some of them are big enough to go it alone".*
>
> (The Osteopathic Physician October 1902 Vol. 2, No. 5, page 8)

---

[13] This was in an article, in the Osteopathic World, in May 1903, in connection with about the S.S. Still College calling itself the "Still College".

THE ALABAMA DECISION AND MATERIA MEDICA

The legislative battle for osteopathy in Alabama provided a pivotal point in the history of osteopathy. In short, the supreme court decided that osteopathy was 'medicine' in the meaning of the then current law and that if an osteopath did not have a licence form the Medical board they were in violation of the law. The osteopath, Dr. E. E. Bragg against whom the case was taken, had not applied for a license and was told that if it was refused and he felt discriminated against, the remedy was to take a civil action

"The board of medical examiners is only an agent to execute the medical law and are under the superintendence of the court and cannot act otherwise than within the spirit of the law they are constituted to help administer. The courts are perfectly able to prevent them from abusing their trust. "[xxx]

"Thus it is made entirely clear both by definitions and history that the word medicine has a technical meaning, is a technical art or science, and as a science the practitioners of it are not simply those who prescribe drugs or other medical substances as remedial agents, but that it is broad enough to include, and does include all persons who diagnose diseases and prescribe or apply any therapeutic agent for its cure. "[xxxi]

This was the first time that 'Osteopathy' was formally recognized as 'medicine'. Prior to this osteopath rejoiced in court decisions that let the defendant osteopath 'off' under the charge of 'practicing medicine without a license', as osteopathy was not covered by the legal definition of 'medicine'; medicine meaning 'drugs'. They rejoiced even though it placed osteopathy in the same category as massage etc.

This brought into focus the two factions within osteopathy, those who wanted it as a 'specialism' and those who saw it as an independent system of medicine in its broadest meaning. At the same time this argument within osteopathy was side-tracking into a debate questioning **'are you a lesion osteopath?'** This seemed to start in the Milwaukee meeting of the AOA after a demonstration by Dr. Forbes on the treatment of spinal curves. Forbes was on the staff of the S S Still college, which alone made him suspect in the eyes of Charlie Still and Hildreth. On top of this he had studied under Ward, in the Columbian College in Kirksville and not under Still in the ASO[xxxii]. This made it almost unacceptable to Charlie and Hildreth that his ideas were being lauded as 'something new' at the convention. Hildreth took the political route in challenging him saying " *You understand," said Dr. Hildreth, "I do not say this is the way to treat these cases I say merely that it is my way, and I believe it to be the best; and I make these comparisons here-not to challenge the methods of Dr. Forbes, but to give a chance for free discussion that we may learn more about everybody's way and all be benefited. "*[xxxiii]

Charlie took the more direct personal approach;

""What do you know about the subject Dr. Charley Still shot up at the platform in the acrimonious sarcasm of which he is a past master. "How long have you been in this business-what's your experience?"[xxxiv]

Hildreth's approach, and by implication of his reputation this would be seen as A T Still's approach, was to go directly to the 'lesion'. Forbes approach was that *"the best work on such lesions is not to work first and foremost upon the spot most involved, but to approach it from above and below, and build up the nutrition of the spine somewhat gradually by this means";*

The editor of the Osteopathic Physician headed the report up as;

"Are You A "Lesion" Osteopath?"

He then asked for the debate to be carried on in the pages of the Osteopathic Physician over the next year. The result was an intrenchment of the divide, with the ASO holding itself up as the standard by which osteopathic schools should be judged, while at the same time restricting its syllabus to exclude anything which might be seen as 'adjunctive' including diet, environment(except for sanitation required for control of contagious disease necessary for passing state health board exams), occupation etc. The debate over adjuncts, lesion osteopaths, drugs etc. were all part of the same division within osteopathy; i.e. the so-called advocates of 'osteopathy pure and simple- correct the anatomical lesion and nature with do the rest; and those who saw osteopathy as a 'complete system of medicine which had no use for drugs, but did recognize the need to correct diet, exercise, habit etc. Unfortunately, of these two factions one would

attract the 'all you need merchants' while the other would attract the 'eclectics' – taking from and mixing all different schools of medicine.
While LittleJohn did not seem to engage directly in the debate about lesion osteopaths, except in so far as he commented on the proposition 'that disease is the result of anatomical abnormalities followed by physiological discord', he did put his views very clearly regarding the Alabama decision.

Regarding the debate as to whether you were a 'lesion osteopath' or something else, Littlejohn's opinion was simply that there's no such thing as anything other than a lesion osteopath and osteopaths must believe in the lesion.

"Some spoke of the 'lesion osteopath', others of adjuncts necessary to complete osteopathy. In a seeming difference of opinion there exists no divergence. Every osteopath believes in lesions. However, osteopathic lesions are not, solely. 'bone lesions', but include muscular, osseous, osseo-ligamentous, organ and vital or psychic lesions, as well as dietetic lesions."[xxxv]

But his lesion concept was more than just a structural lesion and included the environmental and mental aspects as well.

We see particularly if we look at the Alabama decision, the Lesion osteopath and medicine debates, how Littlejohn came into conflict with others in the profession and particularly with Hildreth, who approach these aspects by appealing to the emotional side of their audience. We quote Dr Littlejohn on the Alabama decision from the September 1902 edition of the Osteopathic Physician.

"I am glad of the opportunity to express my opinion to the O.P. regarding the decision of the Alabama Supreme Court that osteopathy is medicine and in this same conclusion to place myself on record as to the policy of the osteopath taking the M.D. degree for the purpose of being able to explain the inefficiency of drugs – or for whatever reason. Both topics can be conveniently discussed together. As a student in two of the old schools of medicine regular and homeopathic as well as an osteopath I can speak somewhat impartially. I hold that the word medicine, in the larger sense as Dr. E.R. Booth puts it: "MEANS LITERALLY THE WORK OF HEALING THROUGH THE AGENCY OF A PHYSICIAN." In this sense I have always contended that

osteopathy is in the line of apostolic succession in medicine. To use the word medicine in the narrow and limited sense of drugs is not warranted, either by the etymology or the most common use of the word, nor by the history of medicine." (E.R. Booth D.O.)

"We as osteopaths are medical practitioners in the widest sense of the term and are entitled to equality in rank, privilege and obligation with the practitioners of other systems. Our methods are more in harmony with not only nature, but also the principles of primitive medicine or healing.

"In the recent decision of the Supreme Court of Alabama, Judge J.R. Tyson says the difference between practitioner of osteopathy and other practitioners of medicine IS "IN THE MATTER OF THERAPEUTICS" the word medicine being a "technical word denoting the science or art of curing disease."

"Thus, he claims that the word is "broad enough to include and does include all persons who diagnose disease and prescribe or apply any therapeutic agent for its cure". We do not follow this eminent jurist in all his laboured opinion. But as practitioners we are not to be regarded as up-starts without any ancestry. We are not like the Melchisedec[14] priesthood. We are entering a profession which has a history, certain rights and privileges under the law, both constitutional and statute. Hence if discrimination takes place against us there is, as Judge Tyson states, a civil procedure remedy in the case of refusal to recognise the granting of licenses. This means equality in law.

"Now granted equality in right privilege and obligation the question is one of qualification and educational status to back up the qualification. Who shall judge the qualifications, the old school of practice? Certainly not. Because the therapeutics of "osteopathy is new. This means the judging of osteopaths from osteopathic therapeutic standpoint.

---

[14] Also spelt 'Melchizedek' He is described in the Scriptures as having no known genealogy, with apparently no account of his descent, or of the beginning and end of his life. He is "without father, without mother, without descent, having neither beginning of days nor end of life" (Hebrews 7:3)

"Now the question revolves itself into this what knowledge is necessary to enable the practitioner to become a thorough DIAGNOSTICIAN and a thorough THERAPEUTICIAN from the osteopathic standpoint? Our system is independent, has its own independent ANATOMICAL PHYSIOLOGICAL and CHEMICAL basis hence

"1.   It will be no advantage to the osteopath to go to another school because he will not learn anything of advantage in his diagnosis and treatment of disease. We can gain nothing either by mixing osteopathy with some other methods or by "trying to consider disease from a dual standpoint. To do the latter is to perplex and probably to pervert. Some are claiming that it is an advantage to study the drug system so that we may see disease from an all-round point of view and even give the remedies of other systems if necessary[15]*.*

"2.   We do not sacrifice the brotherhood of the healing profession when we stand upon our own independent ground claiming that we have a system co-extensive with the healing arts. It seems to me instead of needing a medical education we need greater research from the strictly osteopathic point of view rather than attempting to spend efforts in studying regular medical courses.

"3.   This does not prevent us in our own colleges from doing all that is necessary to supply the demand for information of those who want an all-round view of disease. Some at least are real seekers acknowledge, the only way to study the other systems is from a COMPARATIVE standpoint, taking the osteopathic system as the independent basis and comparing other methods in theory and practice with our own. This cannot be done except within our own college walls. And here we want to say an osteopathic college must exist in fact, not in the office of a medical college. The extensive pharmacology and Materia Medica of the symptoms of other schools by themselves would throw light upon osteopathic methods ... I for

---

[15] The Journal of Osteopathy, Kirksville, commented on this saying "We are also glad to see Dr. J. M. Littlejohn of Chicago, make his position plain on this subject (Osteopathy Unmixed.) and come out uncompromisingly for osteopathy as an independent system healing. (Journal of Osteopathy October 1902, page 341)

one will never be satisfied with special legislation as any legislator that gives one system advantage or precedence over another. Such I consider arbitrary and discriminating and therefore unconstitutional. Meantime, the principle thing is to stand together, to pull together, to cultivate loyalty to our system and to give it the best chance that we can by developing the best that is in it and wait with patience for that victory which crowns all truth and truth seekers with the laurels of recognition in the good done for humanity." J. Martin Littlejohn M.D., D.O., L.L.D., Chicago.[16][xxxvi]

It's a long quote but it states his philosophy quite clearly and distinctly and why he pushed for the M.D.O. degree. Not that he wanted to mix medicine with osteopathy but if we were to look at the medical approach it would be on a comparative basis and in light of osteopathy. Osteopathic therapeutics replacing the Materia Medica of the standard medical colleges.

The American College of Osteopathic Medicine and Surgery

Our Therapeutics is based upon principle and requires no pharmacy - no Materia Medica - but instead a thorough knowledge of Anatomy, Physiology and neurology in physical application to the human system. In addition, Comparative Therapeutics, embracing the entire field of medicine, physiological and Surgical Medicine, are taught as a basis for Complete Surgery.

Catalogue 1907-8 page 20

---

[16] Capitalization by Littlejohn in original article

Littlejohn as ever presented his case logically, philosophically and in a straightforward manner. His belief that osteopathy was the natural progression in medicine and that it should stand as medicine in the truest sense of the word.

It is a peculiar thing in osteopathic history that after meetings like the one in Milwaukee in 1902, reports would be printed saying *"One of the most gratifying manifestations at the convention was the almost universal sentiment in favor of osteopathy pure and simple, osteopathy without adjuncts- osteopathy without drugs, without electricity, without hydrotherapy, etc."*[xxxvii]
The truth being quite the opposite as evidenced in this case by the 'Lesion osteopath' debate and the Associated Colleges correspondence.
Then researchers and historians would take these reports as evidence that Littlejohn was isolated in his views. The fact was that Littlejohn was always trying for unity and not division and his views were held by a large number of osteopaths, osteopaths who had to go to medical colleges to complete their education or fill in the subjects they were not taught in their alma mater. His views are aptly summed up by his letter, although written in 1931, when he was in England, its sentiments equally apply to his time in America

"I have been hoping against hope for unity among us but I have given up the hope and now for the future I go ahead on my own— my slogan is Osteopathy and I don't care who says yea or nay— it is the osteopathy of A. T. Still and like him, we will win. The keynote is adjustment and whatever falls under adjustment correction, diet, antisepsis, sunlight, and other natural ways are mine to use and hope for results."[xxxviii]

Littlejohn was an educationalist and minister at heart, not a preacher. Preachers often use 'sound bites' that appeal to the emotions, rousing their audience sometimes into a frenzy, and not unusually this is in a negative, i.e. against something rather than in favour of a principle. Phrases like 'osteopathy pure and simple' were coupled with 'no drugs- no knife' and a general reaction to the antagonism of the 'regular' medical fraternity. This would appeal to the 'all you need merchants' in particular and antagonize loyal Osteopaths who aimed to provide a full service to their patients.

He would always demand honesty, which in turn demanded the admission that the spinal lesion on its own was a very limited view of osteopathy; He took the view that osteopathy was **'a system of medicine'** and this did not mean abandoning its principles nor using so-called 'drugs'. Bunting put this quite well;

"To be a science at all, any system of knowledge most be capable of growth and improvement. If there could not arise one day more learned and more skilled Osteopaths than Dr. A. T. Still, then, indeed, our system would fall short as a science, and our work be in vain. Osteopathy would be-not a science but a craft, a cult, a matter of imitating merely one man's cleverness; and if there is anything on earth the Old Doctor despises it is the imitator-of himself or any other person. This is the sort of teaching we heard from the lips of A. T. Still. Let us not forget it. Says he again and again to his group of eager disciples: "Boys and girls, I have made a beginning merely. You have all I have and can give you. Yon begin where I leave off. Now, go ahead. Build the Osteopathic structure higher and higher upon naked truth, until it shall be a perfect house!" Let us not in a spirit of hero worship forget the science for the man. It is not just to the man to thus dwarf his work. It is human history that each generation carries truth some stage further than its forefathers. Let Osteopathy be no exception to this rule "[xxxix] (HENRY STANHOPE BUNTING A. B. D.O., Editor.)

It is a shame, in my opinion, that the efforts of Charlie Still, Hildreth and others to keep osteopathy 'pure and simple' after the style of the founder, A T Still, forced it into being a 'specialism'; a specialism needs a home and the only home it could possibly find, when they rejected 'Osteopathic Medicine,' was within 'regular medicine'. In this respect their efforts were self-defeating.

This dilemma is aptly summed up by McConnell[17]

---

[17] He also reminded osteopaths "I wonder if these few know how perilously near a great many osteopaths came to having, the M. D. degree conferred upon them, instead of the degree of D.O., a few short years ago?" in the context of pointing out that "Endeavoring to make it appear that Materia Medica and the degree M. D. are synonymous terms will not do" – a reference to Littlejohn's proposal for the M.D. (Osteopathic) degree (The Osteopathic Physician, October 1902, page 5)

"We can never, legally, reach the position of a "school of medicine" until our college course represents it, and osteopathy unadulterated cannot survive unless it is represented as a school. Somewhat paradoxically our apparent troubles have started from within the fold. Our friends are demanding us for family physicians and surgeons. They are expecting us to take care of them during confinement and in the major operations as well as in the acute and chronic diseases. They are not content to allow us to practice our osteopathy as a specialty and choose the cases; but we are obliged to administer the antidote, give an anesthetic, adjust the fractured bone, and the thousand and one things that make up the practice of an all-around practitioner. Is it any wonder the practicing osteopath is calling for a larger college course? Veritably osteopathic practice has largely been restricted to a specialty while its basis has covered the entire field of etiology and therapeutics. We simply are obliged to enlarge (not our horizon) our practice. Osteopathy pure and simple is what the public wants; but it wants the practice under all conditions and circumstances. Osteopathy has more than proven its worth. It has been rendered indispensable. … "Dr. J. Martin Littlejohn has long been an advocate of the ultimate necessity of legislating osteopathy as a distinct school, of osteopathic medicine and surgery, in contradistinction to special and separate legislation. Upon this point he states: … 'So far as status is concerned, if we stand together and fit ourselves for the full profession of the osteopathic physician and surgeon, we will in the end maintain equality of status with other practitioners"[xl].

McConnell was almost dismissive of the attitude of some osteopaths to the inclusion of Materia Medica osteopathic colleges

"Just a word more about this 'bugaboo' Materia Medica…. How could we mix the therapeutics? They are incompatible. It would be. antagonistic to one of the basic principles of osteopathy, viz., the body is an entirety, and consequently contains within its tissues all forces and agencies necessary for growth and repair. Therefore, when anatomical freedom is combined with pure air, pure water and the right food~ disorder cannot exist.[xli] Thus while teaching antidotes, antiseptics, exercise, diet etc. it did not mean mixing drug medicine with osteopathy nor abandoning nor diluting Osteopathic Principles.

Unfortunately, this would have meant Hildreth, the ASO (Charlie Still included) and others to stop claiming that the only thing needed was

'Osteopathy Pure and Simple', Meaning the Spinal lesion only, and to stop treating those that might disagree with them as somehow diluting Osteopathic Principles.

In this same vein, Hildreth found his accusation *that "THE GREATEST OBSTACLE IN THE WAY OF OUR SUCCESS was an article published in Osteopathic Physician over the signature of Secretary A. B. Shaw, of the Des Moines college, claiming that the existing law in Alabama was good enough and that Osteopaths should pass the examination"*[xlii] did not go unchallenged. H. S. Bunting, the editor of the Osteopathic Physician took Hildreth to task on this issue, devoting much of the December 1903 issue to setting out the facts and showing Hildreth's accusation to be just an attempt to deflect from his own failings.

"A. G. Hildreth, was open to criticism and earned it, in mild degree, for the poor way in which he represented his office; … the exact facts regarding defeat were known to the Osteopaths of Alabama when they went into the last fight-or that they had, at least, every opportunity to know them"[xliii]

As if the politics within osteopathy were not confusing enough another aspect was not far from the surface. That was the State regulation and the make up of Medical registration boards.

Independent Boards

The regulation of the practice of medicine in the USA was and still is, governed by local State law and State Boards which grant practitioners a license to practice. In some of the States, Osteopaths were prosecuted under the Local Acts for 'practicing medicine without a license' and when it was declared that osteopathy was 'not medicine' in term of the act, the Osteopaths tended to celebrate. The Alabama decision, that osteopathy was medicine, brought into focus the debate within osteopathy as to what it was- medicine, healing trade, a specialism or something else.

Flexner, in his 1910 report on medical education said;

"The state boards are the instruments through which the reconstruction of medical education will be largely effected. To them the graduate in medicine applies for the license to practise. Their power can be both indirectly and directly exerted. They may after examination reject an applicant, —— an indirect method of discrediting the school which has vouched for him by conferring its M.D. degree".[xliv]

Further, he makes the point of the different 'schools' of medicine that were 'recognized', emphasizing that no matter which school it was, there should be a minimum standard in the fundamental sciences:

"In making this study the schools of all medical sects have been included. It is clear that so long as a man is to practise medicine, the public is equally concerned in his right preparation for that profession, whatever he call himself, —allopath, homeopath, eclectic, osteopath, or whatnot. It is equally clear that he should be grounded in the fundamental sciences upon which medicine rests, whether he practises under one name or under another".[xlv]

Within Osteopathy, part of the argument was whether Osteopathy should have a Board entirely separate from the established State Board, or if it should have representation on the State Board so that the Osteopathic practitioner would be examined in their own subjects by an Osteopath.

The term 'Independent Board' was often used in this context to mean a 'Separate Board'. In other contexts, it was taken to mean a Board independent of any school – teachers and professors working in medical school were not eligible to be members of the State Boards. Thus, Sate regulation, the composition of State Boards and their independence with regard to practice osteopathy in any given State of the USA became a vexed one. Littlejohn gave his opinion very clearly outlining the options available:

"It is a manifest injustice that we should try to secure a position of equality if we are not willing to make our profession of equal scientific and professional standing by equality of equipment. Special legislation has placed us in many states in complete subordination to the medical profession. In some states, like Ohio we are not fit socially and professionally to sit with the examining body for the other professional systems, but we sit under the table in a committee. There are only two possible positions we can occupy in justice to ourselves and our system as science and truth. We must have

1. *As in Wisconsin, a member sitting side by side with the representatives of other systems. This we can have if we stand by our guns where all systems are represented on one board.*

2. *We should have an independent board with no affiliation, and not serve as a subcommittee on a medical board. Where the different systems are thus separately looked after it is just and proper, we should have this.*

"In the state of Illinois, we are in the nondescript class. Neither education or qualification or status are at all necessary. The man who can crowd through an examination in certain branches in two or three weeks and get his certificate to "TREAT HUMAN AILMENTS," while the law says he is practicing medicine is just as good as the one who has spent years in trying to master the principles and practice of osteopathy. In the proposed new medical bill the position of inferiority is made still more plain, and all this is done by the medical profession in the attempt to deny us equality, while we sit idly by and never lift a finger, when the regular, homeopathic, eclectic and physio-medical are licensed to practice medicine and surgery in all their branches although not one of them know an iota of the osteopathic branch, while the osteopath is to be licensed to practice restricted medicine – whether under the sun that may mean. In the name of science, we ask what incarnation of devils formulated the plan of this proposed legislation?"[xlvi]

LittleJohn has often been accused of wanting to mix medicine with osteopathy and it may seem that his belief that osteopathy was 'medicine', albeit in the true sense of the word, was in contradiction to his statement, made in the 1930's, about Independent Boards

"I have always stood here as in the U.S. For seventeen[18] years I have fought for independent boards in the U.S. and I mean to continue so here.[19]"[xlvii].

What did LittleJohn mean by 'Independent Boards'? He put it simply as follows:

"A non -partisan, independent board representing all the therapeutic systems could foster and build up the Colleges to equality of equipment and educational facility and at the same time do no injustice to any system"[xlviii]

His ideal was not separate boards but a board independent of Political maneuvering of the different 'schools' of medicine (Regular, homeopathic, Eclectic, Osteopathic etc.), the aim and objective of which was to succor the development of the Colleges so as to maintain a uniform minimum standard within each independent school or system of medicine. In this he also saw the necessity for practitioners only to be licensed to practice the therapeutic system they were qualified in and not 'medicine in all its branches' He wasn't so naive as to think that State Boards or politicians were not open to corruption. However, he did feel that if the starting point was the *"the granting of freedom of practice, freedom of choice to patients as to their method of treatment"* [xlix] and then, with the upbuilding of the Colleges, the negative effect of Boards which may be *"composed of political doctors who are by no means representative of the highest and most scientific attainments in science"*(April 1903, page 167) could be nullified. He developed this line of thought to the extent of saying

---

[18] This counts his time from the beginning of his treatment by Still in 1897 through to 1913 inclusive.
[19] Bold emphasis by the author

"The Time has come when there is too much attempted regulation, too many boards" [l]

and that *"If regulation is required, as we have stated before, the proper field of that regulation is the College"*[li]

This ties in with his view on the Associated Colleges and its role in partnership with the professional association the A.O.A. as the way forward in developing Osteopathy as a practice of medicine.

He found many within the profession agreed with him, even referring back to his time at the ASO and the defining of Osteopathy as Medicine: As Bunting, the editor of the Journal of Osteopathy, Kirksville, in 1898-9 and editor of the Osteopathic Physician in 1903 said

"There is no personal opinion about this. It is fact. It is statutory law. Dr. J. M. Littlejohn and the editor, with a few others, accepted this view four years ago, Judge Ellison dissenting. It required an Alabama decision to make it universally accepted. (editor page 1 the osteopathic physician; April 1903.)

In response to the Alabama decision that Osteopathy was medicine he reiterates his view

"Our principal failure is a failure to appreciate the true position of osteopathy in the field of science, healing or medicine and in the field of law. Osteopathy is in the line of succession, apostolically to all that is good and true and scientific in medicine. It is a system of medicine. By special legislation, we have tried to legislate ourselves out of the field of medicine, while the law, both common and statutory, places medicine in the field of healing, recognizing different systems, complete, independent and all sufficient in themselves to deal with disease, ill health, accident etc."[lii]

Adding that the opponents of Osteopaths were trying everything to stop them getting recognition, including saying that Osteopaths were afraid of taking the medical board examinations.[liii] He encouraged the profession to *"come out boldly as an independent system, claiming* equality, fraternity and liberty, that trinity of true democracy"[liv], reminding Osteopaths that the greater part of their work was actually surgical in nature, quoting Still: *"Dr A.T. Still, in his latest work (1903) on the Philosophy and Mechanical Principles of Osteopathy says; "Osteopathy is surgery from a physiological standpoint. The osteopathic surgeon uses the knife of blood to keep out the knife of steel. He must use freely a skilful knowledge of physiology, remembering all the time that cures come only as a result of physiological action after the most skilled surgeons of this and past ages have done their best work"*[lv]

As always, Littlejohn would start from a point of principle. In the case of medical legislation, he applied the fundamental principle Osteopathic practice – find the cause and then delineate a definite etiology of the condition:

"Will you tell us how the passing of a theoretical examination for license, makes men literary products or trains them to think. Existing laws are a slam at colleges. Colleges are presumably chartered to teach and qualify men and women for a profession. If the college is non compos mentis[20], by all means strike at the root of the evil. Medical legislation is a good example of allopathic medication in general? It deals with an alleged condition without attempting to deal with the supposed cause. Osteopathic philosophy in the legislative field calls for the definite etiology of condition. If the colleges are corrupt, full of commercialism, incompetent to teach, why strike at the root of the evil[21], face the unworthy colleges. We should remember however that state boards are not incorruptible, their judgement is not infallible, and they are often composed of political doctors, who are by no means representative of the highest and most scientific attainments in science....A regularly chartered college is a state

---

[20] In English law when a person is declared by a judge to be 'non compos mentis', they can't legally speak for themselves. And here Littlejohn is using the term 'root of the evil' to refer to the State Board examinations

[21] Meaning the State Board examinations

institute, as much a part of the state economy as an artificially created state board. The fact that a college is small, not credited with the wealth of Croesus, is no proof of its incompetency. The state board examinations have often demonstrated the fact that the small colleges turn out the best men."[lvi]

He went on in a later editorial to put his views on legislation and freedom of choice for the Patient, who is often forgotten in these discussions, in clear and simple terms;

Practical stand we ought to take for our profession – equality with members of other schools, recognition of our own as an independent system of practice, justly entitled to be called the practice of medicine and claiming legislative recognition and protection as such. The extent of this should be simply the granting of freedom of practice, freedom of choice to patients as to their method of treatment" [lvii]

A word about Hildreth the Politician

During the fight for recognition in Alabama there arose an altercation between Hildreth and the editor of the official magazine of the AOA, H. S. Bunting. Hildreth made the statement *"that the greatest obstacle in the 'way of our success was an article published in osteopathic physician"*[lviii] He stated that the article claimed *"that the existing law in Alabama was good enough and that osteopaths should pass the examination.*[lix]*"* Bunting was clearly upset by this and in the December edition of the Osteopathic physician he published a rebuttal under the heading "DR. HILDRETH IS UNMASKED" The article that Hildreth was talking about simply stated that the law that had been passed in Alabama exempted osteopaths from examination in Materia Medica and if they did not wish to practice major surgery they would be also exempted from that examination; if they then passed all other examinations set by the State Board they would be *"entitling him to treat "in any manner that he may deem best"*. While it did not mention osteopathy in particular, the argument was that it could serve the "well educated Osteopathy fully" provided that it was implemented fairly. As it was written by the Secretary of the Still College it is possible that the old angst against the Still College had something to do with Hildreth's stance. Or was it, as Bunting put it *"that A. G. Hildreth grasped at a straw-out of his long training in the work of misrepresentation-and was able to use it for a time successfully as a flimsy lance with which to assail and belabor innocent friends and allies and laying responsibility for treachery to the cause upon their hapless shoulders!"*[lx]

Possibly both were a factor. Hildreth needed an excuse for his failure and the article from the old enemy, the Still College in Des Moines, provided the opportunity.

In any event, Bunting was not to take it lying down. Note only did he reply but he showed that the senators who voted against the Osteopaths bill were mostly unaware of the article and that those who were found it did not influence them at all. Their main concern was that they had already passed a bill that should satisfy all the different schools of the practice of medicine and had no patience left to give time to anything else. One of the Senators going further and saying:

"Dr. Hildreth was tactless-even insinuated that Alabama and Alabamians were behind the times and other such impolitic things and argued along lines more calculated to antagonize us than to enlist the sympathy and cooperation of the senators whose votes he sought to win. I could not but notice also that the New York gentleman with Dr. Hildreth [Dr. Charles Hazzard, no doubt. -Ed.] was visibly embarrassed by his leader's want of diplomacy and delicacy, as well as his bearing of condescension toward us Alabamians. I felt a little sorry for this gentleman. he could not but show his discomfiture."[lxi]

This incident gives a different view of Hildreth that is usually given in the history books. It is not meant to take away from his contribution to Osteopathy nor to the fight for legal recognition. Indeed, Bunting himself saying in his editorial comments, February 1903, "Dr. Hildreth wins new laurels as the chief Osteopathic legislator every time a new skirmish develops".[lxii]

However, the whole article gives a clear idea of how Hildreth operated on the political field.

Another interesting rumor was put to rest by Bunting in the same December 1903 issue of the Osteopathic Physician. This one relates back to an incident which happened during the summer of 1899. In essence, during that summer, *"the story was industriously circulated that I had been guilty of a breach of trust; guilty of defalcation; guilty of stealing 2,000 copies of the Journal of Osteopathy for the use of Dr. Landes and myself* (Bunting) *at Petoskey, Mich.; guilty of surreptitiously trying to get these magazines out of Kirksville; and lastly, that I had been forbidden to return to complete my course at the American School of Osteopathy".*[lxiii]

It could be a coincidence that this rumor re-emerged at the same time as Bunting was having the altercation with Hildreth. However, the timing seems suspect. Bunting again gave a vigorous defense, not only explaining himself but also quoting A T Still himself who said:

"President of the American School of Osteopathy."I was told, Bunting," said Dr. till, "that you were going to use the Journal's second-class mail privilege to mail out that special edition, with your own card in it, and that was the only reason why I intercepted the order, I did not want to have the Journal cut off from second-class mail privileges, and I knew such a thing would do it. "I am very sorry, Bunting, that It caused you such trouble-very sorry. It was misrepresented to me entirely. Your work was good and loyal to me *and you and I always got along well together when they let us alone-- didn't we?"*[lxiv]

As mentioned earlier, not long after this incident in 1899, there followed the incident with Hulett and the MDO degree.

THE 1906 AOA INSPECTION

The education committee of the AOA, at the Milwaukee meeting in August 1902, presented a report on the problems of osteopathic education after consulting with the Associated Colleges of Osteopathy. Littlejohn was very much involved, not only as president of his college but also in his role within the Associated Colleges.[lxv] In the report they stated the problems clearly:

"The problem of securing the highest results in osteopathic education comprises three factors. The first is the establishment of a written standard outlining the requirements for a college of osteopathy. The second is the character and attainments of the men by whom the standard is administered and the third is the kind of students who receive its benefits...These three factors of the problem need each to receive due attention. The suggestions of the committee as to the second and third factors are in consonance with the spirit of osteopathy, in that they seek to correct the cause, to establish normal conditions at the beginning, instead of dealing with effects after the damage is done.."[lxvi]

It went on to outline the proposed organisation of colleges, matriculation requirements, educational methods, standard of education and syllabus. These included surgery and the teaching of *"pure and unmixed"* osteopathy while noting that *"this does not exclude such accessory procedures in prophylaxis and therapeutics as are in consonance with tis principles and therefore apart of the science of osteopathy, nor does it prevent any college from teaching surgery as a cognate professions."*[lxvii]

All of this was completely in line with Littlejohn's ideas and the organisation of his college, the ACOM&S and met with his *"unqualified commendation"*[lxviii] This report then lead to an inspection of the colleges by the AOA in 1903 with E. R Booth being appointed as the inspector. In general, the report was encouraging while pointing out general weakness that needed attention while not singling out specific colleges.

One point in the report of the 1903 inspection of colleges has a bearing upon the following inspection in 1906.: *"In one school I found that the osteopathic students attend, as a part of their work, clinics in a county hospital. The question naturally arises whether or not such influences would be beneficial to the osteopath. If he is as thoroughly grounded in the underlying principles of osteopathy and the sciences pertaining to an osteopathic education as he should be before reaching the senior class,* **I believe his knowledge would tend to confirm his good opinion of osteopathy when compared with other systems and enable him to more fully realize their shortcomings.**[22] *If not, he surely would be laboring under a disadvantage by having his attention so often directed to principles at variance with our system"*.[lxix]

This point does not mention the ACOM&S however as that college made a point in its announcements and advertisements that students attend the clinics of Cook County Hospital in addition to the college clinics[lxx] it seems likely that it was aimed at it. Littlejohn. Then in 1906, the A.O.A. carried out another inspection of Osteopathic Schools. The report from this inspection, by Charles Teall, was very critical of Littlejohn's college, the ACOM&S. In his response to the 1906 inspection Littlejohn give a detailed explanation for the rationale and benefits of the Clinics held in the Cook County Hospital as well as answering the other criticisms. - this is dealt with below.

Berchtold[lxxi] goes into detail about the inspection carried out by Dr. Charles C. Teall on behalf of the AOA in 1906. Teall's report was published in the October 1906 journal of the AOA and severely criticised the ACOM&S. In particular, he honed in on the fact that the building was shared with the College of Medicine and Surgery, the use of M.D.'s as instructors, and that while the laboratories were well equipped, the clinics well supplied, *"things seemed to run rather loosely, as if no one was at the head"* and *"under such conditions the emphasizing of osteopathic principles could not be expected to be very strong"* [lxxii].

James Buchan LittleJohn gave a strong reply, saying the there was no relationship between the ACOM&S and the College of Medicine and surgery; they *simply "rented the use of the building and has no other relation to our college (the ACOM&S) whatever. The college represents*

---

[22] Bold emphasis by author

a system of medicine which has been very friendly towards our college and ourselves, and we did this to help them out of a difficulty"[lxxiii].

However, it was Littlejohn himself that wrote the most vigorous rebuttal of Dr. Teall's charges. It is worth quoting it in full, as it not only rebuts Teall's charges but also gives a good description of how Littlejohn engaged in teaching. He first paragraph also gives a clear indication of the difficulties he faced in setting up his college, not only from the regular medical fraternity but also from within the osteopathic community.

"Editor of The Journal of the A. O. A.

"*I am very sorry that it is my duty to enter my protest against some statements in the report of the inspector of colleges, Dr. C. C. Teall, published in the Appendix to the Journal of the A. O. A. for October. For six years past we have been loyally trying to uphold the banner of osteopathy in this college.* **We have had "to meet medical tyranny in many forms and above all to contend against a registration law that places osteopathy with the mongrel breed of know nothings…... We have been taunted again and again with teaching medicine by men who know not of what they were speaking because they have never visited our college**"

He then goes on to defend the qualification and experience and loyalty to osteopathy of the faculty in his college, the American College of Osteopathy Medicine and Surgery. As already said, Littlejohn's background and character gave him a tendency to take people at their word. This may have led him to overestimate the loyalty of some of his faculty to osteopathy or even to overlook or not see the attitude of some lesser members of the faculty towards eclecticism'. So, while defending his faculty it may be said that he displayed a certain naivety in this regard. The example of Dr. Hamlin mentioned earlier comes to mind. This does not, however take away from his defence of his College, in which, while he accepts there are problems; "**As a college we realize that we have failures and we are trying to improve on these. The college, like the system, is young. We are not incompetent, dishonest or disloyal to osteopathy. Any reasonable counsel is welcomed**". However, he would rather the criticisms were made in the spirit of "*helping us to make this college a center to represent osteopathy*" rather than condemnation.

"Instead of the inspector coming to us and giving us a word of encouragement to help us in bearing aloft the banner of osteopathy, he comes with cold water on his shoulder and insinuates that we are disloyal to osteopathy and incompetent to teach"

Littlejohn then gives a point by point defence and rebuttal of Dr. Teall's criticisms.

Firstly *"The building is shared in common with the college of medicine and surgery."* The secretary of the college replied to Dr. Teall's query and yet doubting this statement Dr. Teall says *"just how far this union extends I have not found."* Dr. Teall was told there was no union. There was no mixing of students. In chemistry and histology some of the students of the College of Medicine and Surgery received special permission to attend our classes under our own professors. And yet when Dr. Teall knew this he gets a fling at the college when he says, *"the medical end was "still at work."* There was no medical end. He was not sent to inspect the College of Medicine and Surgery and to our college there is no medical end.

Secondly: *"Dr. Teall says there was no roll call. In some classes there is, in others there is not probably a roll call. But each one keeps a roll, marks his roll, hands it to the assistant secretary each day and signs the roll of the faculty after each lecture. If Dr. Teall wanted to know what was done, he could have inspected the roll of every class and the record of every lecture, clinic, demonstrations from the first day of the session. When he was told about these, he did not want to examine them.*

Thirdly: Dr. Teall says *"instructors seemed to be changed frequently in the midst of work."* I do not know what he means. If he means that our instructors were changed during the course of the term or year work that is absolutely false. We have kept in the main our instructors from the very opening of the college, adding year by year new members from the ranks of our graduates.

Fourthly: Dr. Teall states that we employ students as instructors, three of the instructors he says were undergraduates. One of these our teacher in biology, is a certificated teacher in Great Britain, certified in science under the South Kensington, London, governmental board, and a teacher for over fifteen years. Another, our teacher in chemistry, was *a high school teacher of chemistry for years and acknowledged by everyone as an excellent teacher. Dr. Teall spent five minutes in this class of chemistry.*

Fifthly: *Dr. Teall says "the instructors, outside of Drs. Littlejohn, were not of a class to insure the best results. With two exceptions the instructors were M. D.'s, etc." I wish to call Dr. Teall's attention to positive misrepresentations. Excluding myself and my brother there were nine M. D.'s on our faculty; of these six were supplying the material for our class in post-graduate work on comparative therapeutics. The other three are our own graduates who completed a medical course after graduation for the sake of surgery.... Instead of two osteopathic graduates as instructors, excluding my brother and myself, there were seventeen D. O.'s, pure and simple, actually engaged in the teaching work of the college as regular instructors when Dr. Teall was here.*

Apart from his clear defence of the teaching in his college, he gives us a good description of his own teaching methods. In examining patients in front of a class littlejohn would talk for an hour *"on the lesions, their significance, the line of treatment and the possible benefit, demonstrating the mechanical basis or the lesions found and their treatment"*

In the public clinics in the Cook County Hospital during the first three years of the college existence, when he was acting as assistant to Dr. Duncan, he personally took *"the students and examined with them all the cases"*. In this work in surgery, eye, skin, heart and diagnostic clinics at the County Hospital the students *"could see a variety of operations and acute cases not seen anywhere to better advantage in this (USA) country"*

In addition to this he conducted a two-hour class on osteopathic therapeutics in which he *"compared the osteopathic theory and practice with that of the other systems and told why ours was better"* and held a class in osteopathic technique, diagnosis and manipulation which met twice a week.

Unfortunately from the fourth year of the college on he had not been able to *"spend the forenoon of each day on account of other work"* We could be forgiven for coming to the conclusion that he felt he had 'allowed things to slip' when he, due to other work, stopped personally taking the students through the exam of the patients in the hospital Clinics, although his clinics in the College itself were kept up on a thorough and completely osteopathic basis.

Teall said, regarding the clinics at the Cook County Hospital, in 1906 *"The benefits derived are problematical, outside of what might be seen of strictly medical procedure. This, with the combining of the medical school under one roof, as well as mixed classes, would seem like a contaminating influence."*[lxxiv]

One major difference between the clinics in the Cook County hospital in 1903 those in 1906 was that Littlejohn was conducting these clinics in 1903 and he had stopped personally being present by 1906. One is left wondering if this change affected the observance of the clinics and Teall's report.

Littlejohn goes onto say that "**During the last year I gave to my students thirteen hours a week on the principles, practice and "technique of osteopathy and comparative osteopathy. And it is not medicine either as my students can testify. Dr. Teall says there was a class scheduled in the fourth-year practice of medicine. Yes, the Supreme Court of the State of Illinois has decided that the practice of osteopathy is the practice of medicine (see catalogue of school 1905-6, p. 10-12.)"**

He makes it clear that not only does he believe osteopathy is an independent system of medicine but also, he practices and teaches in the same way; so as to keep Osteopathy as an independent and distinctive System or science of healing. Osteopathy, as his definition makes clear," **includes all that is commonly included in the field of the practice of medicine, namely, diagnosis, therapeutics and surgery, from its own distinctive standpoint. It is not the practice of medicine by drugs"**

In conclusion he says:

"I am sorry that Dr. Teall was not generous enough to give one word of commendation. I protest against the wholesale denunciation of my

colleagues, some of whom have been years in osteopathic practice. We did not parade anything for display. Dr. Teall came at the close of a long and tedious year of work. We were near the close of the ninth month of work. It may be some of us were fagged, but I know that we are as loyal to osteopathy as our critic. I feel satisfied that our condemnation will bring us more friends than other wise, because those who know us best, know that we have not hesitated to spend our time and money in the defense of osteopathy and even in research work that the world has not yet even heard of..[lxxv] J. MARTIN LITTLEJOHN, President, Chicago, Illinois., Nov. 28, 1906

Dr. Teall says '"under such conditions the emphasizing of osteopathic principles could not be expected to be very strong."

Littlejohn again emphasises that he and his college were purely osteopathic, did not use drugs and were loyal to the principles of osteopathy as laid down by Still himself. In the highlighted parts of his defence we get a glimpse of how he felt about the internal workings of his college., including how "**The clinics conducted by us free of cost as a labor of love give us cases that amply repay the time expended in developing and extending the osteopathic field here.**"

It would appear that the result of the deal, apparently made by his brother, James Buchan, to allow the College of Medicine and Surgeon to rent part of their building, seems to have fuelled the negative inspection by Teall and given credence to the charge that the college was 'mixing, medicine with osteopathy'. Having to continue to defend himself against the charge of 'teaching or mixing osteopathy' with medicine was a difficulty that Littlejohn did not shirk from. At the same time, he had to almost demand that others, especially those who claimed to be in favour of "osteopathy unadulterated" to be honest. We can get a flavour of this from the following exchanges;

As he and James Buchan put it in the JAOA 1909/10;

"If you would be a physician worthy of the name you must be educated in the broadest way, taking in the field requisite to comprehend the defects of the organism and the methods of restoration available. Some of our practitioners are averse to the study of anything but anatomy, physiology and osteopathy as they comprehend it. They go so far as to say that we have good

practitioners who acquired it all in six months. Have we? Did your respected and honored A. T. Still acquire it all in six months? I am sure he would be the last one to breathe such a thought. He had a medical education first, and a long course of experience; He was a medical practitioner first. and became an osteopath afterwards. It took Him years to work it out-to acquire it He got it at nature's fountain. and I doubt much if many of his followers could really honestly say that one year could teach or convey that principle to another. "[lxxvi]
(J B Littlejohn)

"*Do you wonder that a wider and larger course is demanded? The public demand osteopathy not under limited conditions but under all conditions. Practitioners....* **The greatest damage we have suffered has been at the hands of those who have gone into medical colleges to complete their course. They have admitted the incompleteness; -- they have acknowledged the subserviency of their qualification.**
"Do we blame them? No. we cannot because our colleges have not risen to the situation and provided what is demanded. Most of our legislation is in negatives, not the practice of medicine, not use medicines, not use operative surgery-while our system is a school of medicine if it is a true system of healing.
"*Do we teach surgery as a part of the osteopathic system? Do we teach and use antidotes, anesthetics and antiseptics? Do we practice obstetrics without the aid and counsel of another obstetrical master?* If so **let us come out flatfooted and say we have an osteopathic system which includes thus and so, that our colleges teach all the arts and sciences usually taught in reputable medical colleges, but that these are taught. even the physiological action of drugs used in the fields of antidotal, surgical and preventive medicine. from the purely osteopathic standpoint of adjustment and that this constitutes osteopathic medicine, surgery and obstetrics our school of practice.**
"Do not let us say we do not use drugs when, we do use them in the field of surgery, anesthetics and antidotal medicine." JML; Osteopathy and its Colleges, JAOA Jan 1910, page 225[lxxvii]
The subject of 'Materia Medica' for the field of surgery would prove to be a difficult area for many reasons, the most salient of which was

well put by Teall in his report on the Massachusetts College of Osteopathy

"The teaching of surgical Materia Medica leaves but a step to internal medication and the circular on this course shows it to be a possibility."[lxxviii]

> **Hildreth is getting heretical for he has publicly announced he recommends both the hot water bag and the enema.**
> Journal of the American osteopathic association September 1909 page 21

By this stage they would appear to be getting fed up with the dishonest claims of the so-called old guard of "10 fingered, pure osteopaths". Even the grandfather of this group, Hildreth, eventually **admitted he used enemas etc**

The continued acrimony towards the word 'Medicine' and the inclusion of 'Materia Medica' albeit for surgery, antidotes anaesthetics, contributed in no small measure to the change of name of the college to The Littlejohn College.

This division within Osteopathy was difficult, acrimonious and sometimes personal. As we mentioned above, Charles E. Still certainly had a personal grievance against Littlejohn, and Hildreth showed the depth of his 'distain' for the Littlejohns in his book, The Lengthening Shadow of A. T. Still' when he would not even mention them by name in his erroneous piece on their time in Kirksville.

Change of Name to
THE LITTLEJOHN COLLEGE

As a result of the criticisms by osteopaths and the fight against the State board of health, the Littlejohns decided it would possibly of benefit to change the name, leaving out the word 'medicine'

> "Dr. Littlejohn announces that the name of the American College of Osteopathic Medicine and Surgery has been changed to the Littlejohn College and Hospital. This eliminates the word medicine".
> (JAOA, December 1908, page 183)

This was in contradiction to Littlejohn's stated belief that " *use of individual names to designate colleges, schools, infirmaries etc because it savours of egotism*".[lxxix]

So how did this happen? Firstly, the board of directors of the ACOM&S was increased from four to six by an amendment to its charter on July 10th, 1906. The Directors being Dr. J. Martin Littlejohn, Dr. Edith Williams Littlejohn, Dr. James B. Littlejohn, Elizabeth W. Littlejohn (mother of the Littlejohn brothers), Judge J. M. Longenecker (the college's attorney), and John H. Lucas.[lxxx]

Another factor was the continuing quest for recognition by the State Board of Health as a 'Medical College in Good Standing'

> *The question of recognition of the College by the State Board of Health was being considered and in order to obviate some difficulties as to the name it was changed in 1909 to The Littlejohn College and Hospital.*
>
> James Buchan Littlejohn,
> on the early history of the college.
> (1929 CCO Reflex, pp. 62-63.)

A third factor was the continuing accusation, from within the Osteopathic fraternity, that the college was teaching or mixing medicine with Osteopathy

All of this meant that to drop the word 'Medicine" from the title may remove the obvious criticisms from within the profession and to drop the word 'Osteopathy' may help their case with the Board of Health. Littlejohn's position of not wanting to use individual names to *"designate colleges, schools, infirmaries etc because it savours of egotism"*, had to take second place to the other consideration of the board of Trustees. These considerations included the formation of the 'Littlejohn Hospital and Training School for Nurses'.[lxxxi]

His view would have been that if it was a matter of a 'tenet of Conscience' then you should resign; however, if it was a deeply held personal belief rather than a matter of conscience then, if the majority of the committee, in this case the board of directors, passed the motion, then it should be adopted as if it was unanimous. This is how it would have worked in presbyteries in the Reformed Presbyterian Church. This said, I have no doubt that this would have caused him some pain, in like manor to the experimenting on animals mentioned before. It would have been in this light that he, as President, signed the documents to change the name.

"Documents in Cook County and Illinois State offices indicate that the name change was agreed upon by the school's Board of Directors at a meeting held on October 4, 1908. A report of this meeting, typed on the College's official stationery and on file in the Cook County and the Illinois Secretary of State offices, reads: At a special meeting of the Board of Directors of the American College of Osteopathic Medicine and Surgery held on the 4th day of October 1908 after due notice the following resolution was adopted—
Resolved that the articles of incorporation be amended so that the name of the College be changed to "The Littlejohn College and Hospital"; and that section 2, paragraph (C) be amended by inserting the words "Hospital and Training School for Nurses" after the words "annexed infirmary" so that the section would read. . . . "with annexed Infirmary, Hospital and Training School for Nurses. . . .'[lxxxii]

> "The report was signed by J. Martin littlejohn, President, and James B. Littlejohn, Secretary, and officially filed with the Illinois Secretary of State on January 9. 1909".
> (To Teach, To Heal, To Serve, page 32)

It was around this time that time his association with the Rev. Minifie[23] was developing and that he had been engaging in his research into cancer[24] and the use of antidotes in osteopathic

---

[23] Boston Post, June 9, 1909
[24] First published in the March 1907 Journal of the American Osteopathic Association

practice, a subject he had developed a serious interest in during his tour of Europe in the summer of 1903[25]. He said of that tour,

"Our trip abroad was one of pleasure combined with investigation and exploration of the fields in the great central cities of Europe. We started out to carry on a line of investigation, begun four years ago, into (1) the tendencies toward osteopathic ideas in the writings' and teachings 'of die 'medical' profession; (2) the methods of instruction, hospital facilities and methods used in the mechanical forms of treatment; (3) the tendencies toward the newer methods of surgical work; (4) the position and practice of the different systems of treatment, especially in cases of nervous and mental diseases and abnormal growths of a tumorous and cancerous nature. ... In London we visited especially the cancer hospitals. The superintendents kindly extended to us the courtesies of the wards[lxxxiii]*"*

His work in the field of cancer and tumors involved the use of animals in the experiments. An expediency that may have also caused his conscience discomfort.

On this tour of Europe in 1903, we also find his continuing adherence to his covenantor principles. While he wanted particularly to visit the pathological museum of the Allgemeine Kraukenhaus but found it only open on Sundays. He said:

"There is a large collection of bones and especially skeletons, that will repay study representing scoliosis and kyphosis of the spine. This is open only on Sundays, but by the kindness of the curator we had the privilege of a private admission[lxxxiv]*"*

---

[25] On this tour we also find his continuing adherence to his covenantor principles. While he wanted particularly to visit the pathological museum of the Allgemeine Kraukenhaus but found it only open on Sundays.

EXPERIMENTING ON ANIMALS

During his early education in physiology in Ireland Littlejohn had been introduced to experimenting on animals as a means of gaining knowledge that could be used for the betterment of humanity.

At the same time the Presbyterian church, including the Reformed Presbyterians, had groups who were entirely opposed to vivisection.

"The whole spirit of the Bible, the whole teaching of Christ, the whole life and practice of Christ was one of eloquent living protest against the horrible barbarities of Vivisectors. Kindness, mercy, love and charity, these were the things that Christ and the Bible placed before us as those which we should aim at possessing and practising, and these things were wholly and entirely irreconcilable with Vivisection" [lxxxv]

During his time as editor of the Christian Nation, he would have associated with many with this view. The following report of a resolution at the Women's Christian temperance union is a good example;

'*Experimenting on live animals and birds in public schools in teaching physiology should be put away with, for it dulls the finer sensibilities of a child, aside from the cruelty practiced on the creatures themselves. We should have laws against vivisection. A resolution was passed by the Convention that we give up the use of bodies, wings, and feathers of birds for ornamentation, with the exception of the feathers of the ostrich, who feel no pain in losing theirs. This was carried by a rising vote*"[lxxxvi];

In fact, a book review, which might even have been written by Littlejohn himself, appeared in the December 19th 1894 edition of the Christian Nation gives a strong endorsement of the Anti vivisection movement while acknowledging that no substitute has been offered for vivisection.

"When we contemplate the horrors of vivisection which the best of physicians declare has after all been of no true worth in the medical field, we cannot help but stand amazed that something has not been done towards putting a stop to such wholesale cruelty, and that laws are not made and enforced for its prohibition. A remedy has been presented for the wearing of birds in the substitution of artificial ones and of bead ornaments and flowers, but still the rage for feathers continues. What substitute has been offered for vivisection and hunting of animals we know not, but certainly the Saviour of mankind reminds us forcibly that not a sparrow falls to the ground unnoticed by our Heavenly Father, and that even the wild beasts were made by Him, and certainly as all life emanated first from God, it is a fearful thing to rob any creature of a gift that unites them still to God and is certainly a part of Him."[lxxxvii]

So, what justification could he have used to convince himself of the benefits of the animal experimentation he started to undertake when he took up the teaching of physiology in Kirksville. The use of animals for the 'noble' cause of reducing humanities suffering would seem to be the only justification for Littlejohn's engagement in serious physiological research. In this regard, Osteopathy was at that time, lacking a firm physiological basis. To overcome this and thus help spread the 'gospel' of osteopathy I would suggest was his rationale.

He would continue using animals for experimentation to forward the physiological and 'scientific basis of Osteopathy and develop his thesis on the Osteopathic approach to toxicosis. This was published in the Journal of Osteopathy and even commented on in the book Chicago its history and builders.[26]

"His latest contribution is the result of laboratory experiments conducted for some years in relation to toxicosis and mechanical obstruction as the causes of the so-called malignant diseases,

---

[26] The same article on Littlejohn says *"He has not sought to confine his knowledge to those branches taught by a single institution, and the result is that he is able to choose from the various schools and methods of practice that which he deems most essential and valuable for specific cases".* I doubt that he would have been in agreement with this statement given his views on Osteopathy and how osteopathy and regular medicine are incompatible. This would indicate that he did not write this biographical piece himself.

published in the Journal of the Osteopathic Association and in the annual bulletin of the research institute for 1910."[lxxxviii]

There is always a price to pay 'if we let expediency overrule conscience'. In Littlejohn's case I would suggest this affected his health. This is in line with the approach of Littlejohn, his approach about the physic or mental influence on our health as well as the mechanical and physiological aspects and the driving force behind our body of the vital force.

"we introduce into our curriculum the study of the mind, mental conditions and operations and mental phenomena because these have an important bearing upon health and the comfort of life". [lxxxix]

Osteopathy is based on a principle. According to religious beliefs our life should be based on principle. if we step outside of our principles then we may cause damage to our health.

We find an interesting aspect of his view on this in his lectures on Psycho-physiology;

> "Recognizing the osteopathic principle that drugs are unnatural and that all of nature's remedies are stored up in the human system, we have this psychic law of the mind's ascendancy and to carry it out in the removal of these diseased conditions, **the beginning must be made within.** The adjustment must be made by the mind and the mental condition must first be adjusted to the body conditions of perfect health"
> (J. Martin Littlejohn, Lectures on psycho physiology page 7)

It wasn't only in the Religious field that Littlejohn associated with those that held strong beliefs about vivisection.

For example, Professor Mills Fowler in Dunham medical College had strong feelings in this regard including;

Dr. Fowler, Professor of the Practice of Medicine in Dunham Medical College, was listed in the Annual report of American anti-vivisection society 1900[xc], as a prominent member and quoted as saying *"The brutality manifest in the employment of vivisection is a disgrace to our civilisation".*[xci]

Walter Elfink, who taught in Littlejohn's college was editor of the vegetarian magazine and against vivisection as we can see from the following comment about Dr. Samuel R. Landes D.O[27]., another anti-vivisectionist osteopath;

"There is one thing about "Sam" that always makes me laugh. He is an anti-vivisectionist of the most sincere type and he will raise his hands in horror as high as Dr. Walter Elfrink of Chicago, at the mention of vivisection experiments for the
investigation of physiology. He thinks it is a cruel practice-but, mind you, Sam will go a-fishing and hook the finny prizes and he'll catch a boat-load of 'em if he can, and anti-vivisection principles have no relation whatsoever to a good day of sport
when Sam goes a-fishing[xcii].

We find yet another comment on vivisection in the March 1906 issue of the Osteopathic Physician, this time with a counter by the editor;

"I am very sorry to notice a tendency among Osteopaths to follow in the steps of the medical profession in a matter which constitutes one of the darkest blots on their record, the
experimenting on helpless animals for the sake of increasing the knowledge of physiology".[xciii]   By DR. E. D. BURLEIGH, of PHILADELPHIA, PA;

By way of reply the editor, Bunting;

" It is not understandable to us how the "antis" can doubt what vivisection has done and is doing for physiology, and directly, therefore, for Osteopathy. But it is with vivisection just as with meat-eating. Some will, and some won't and argument on both sides seldom changes anybody's position; some people are just born for that philosophy, and anti-vivisectionists are very frequently, if not usually, vegetarians, to boot. It is but a short step further into Nirvana and chanting the hymns of the Vedas".[xciv]

Vivisection was a controversial subject in Littlejohn's time as it is today, with many shades of opinion, as the above shows. Littlejohn, himself, did not discuss it as far as I can tell. In general, he tried to keep Religious views and 'moralising' out of his discussion on

---

[27] Dr. Landes graduated from Kirksville in 1895

Osteopathy and Health, except in so far as general principles were concerned. His aim was to make Osteopathy available for all humanity and not just for those who follow a particular creed or sect. In his paper on The Theory of the Treatment of the Spine, he clearly states leaving aside his personal views, that it does not matter what you believe in so long as you believe in some sort of higher power:

"I do not care whether a man is a believer in the superhuman or whether he is not, it does not make a bit of difference, the one who believes in the superhuman cannot object to this point and the other who disbelieves cannot object. Man has a higher being; I do not care whether it is called a soul or a spirit or a life power or a sun power, or whatever else it may be called; the higher being comes into relation with the body. The body of itself is absolutely lifeless but when that life power, or soul
or sun power is brought into contact with the body, the body represents the earth substance. A connection established between these two, the life power and the body, gives us what we call objective mind".[xcv]

Regarding vivisection it was even suggested that osteopathy would render the 'need' for it unnecessary, although the editor of the Journal of Osteopathy did not agree;

"In Vogue, the fashion journal issue of March 25th, it is stated 'The structural treatment known as Osteopathy' is eliminating the vivisection of animals for experimental purposes. As an ever increasing number of persons are coming to realize that nourishment and proper elimination and sanitary environment are the only roads to permanent health. There is apparently some misunderstanding on the part of the contributor of the work done in laboratories on animals as well as the purpose for which undertaken".[xcvi]

However, someone who was described as having **" the kindest eyes"**[28], someone with the attitude towards children and life in general, that we have discussed earlier can hardly have been immune to the suffering caused by animal experiments no matter how important the rationale. In this context, I would suggest that it caused

---

[28] From description of treatment of Elsie Goddard, who was treated by Littlejohn in England during world war 1, by her daughter Audrey Harry

his conscience at least some discomfort; and would mean, given his statement that " ***the beginning must be made within. The adjustment must be made by the mind and the mental condition must first be adjusted to the body conditions of perfect health***" that he would need to spend some time dealing with his own 'mental condition'. The conflict would have been between the inevitable suffering of animals used in experiments and the perceived need to put Osteopathy on a sound 'scientific' basis.[29]

> "The past years have been very active in research, tending more and more to take medicine out of the realm of hypothesis and dogmatism, and establish it on a firm foundation of facts."
> J. M. Littlejohn
> JOA DEC 1898 volume 5 number 7 page 326
>
> "In the days of the reformation when Humanism began its positive work of upbuilding, it was almost a necessity that the Reformers should declare war against the method and the principles of the Scholastics, in order to break the galling chains of dogmatism and pave the way for the intellectual renascence". J. M. Littlejohn
> (THE POLITICAL THEORY OF THE SCHOOLMEN AND GROTIUS page 3)

---

[29] This whole discussion on his attitude to vivisection is of course, very speculative on my part

DEFINITION OF OSTEOPATHY

Many authors have given a definition of Osteopathy, including Littlejohn. Littlejohn came after Pressly in the American School of Osteopathy. It was Pressly who formulated the definition of Osteopathy that graced the inside front cover of the journal of Osteopathy for many of the early years.[xcvii]

In 1899 Littlejohn put forward his own definition and reiterated it in a Paper read before the A. O. A. Convention at Kirksville, in July 1901.

"We have seen no reason to alter our definition of Osteopathy, formulated nearly two years ago, with the approval of Dr. A. T. Still, Dr. A. G. Hildreth, Dr. C. P. McConnell, Dr. D. L. Tasker and others.
"Osteopathy is that science or system of healing which emphasizes, (a) the diagnosis of diseases by physical methods with a view to discovering, not the symptoms but the causes of disease, in connection with misplacements of tissue, obstruction of the fluids and interference with the forces of the organism; (b) the treatment of diseases by scientific manipulations in connection with which the operating physician mechanically uses and. applies the inherent resources of the organism to overcome disease and establish health, either by removing or correcting mechanical disorders and thus permitting nature to recuperate the diseased part, or by producing and establishing anti-toxic and anti-septic conditions to counteract toxic and septic conditions of the organism or its parts; (c) the application of mechanical and operative surgery in setting fractured or dislocated bones, repairing lacerations and removing abnormal tissue growths or tissue elements when these become dangerous to organic life. The legal description of Osteopathy is, 'a system, method or science of treating human diseases'.".[xcviii]

It is informative to see that his definition was formulated during his second year in Kirksville with the approval of not only A. T. Still but also of Hildreth. In the same talk he again states his position and that of his college, the ACOM&S.

"In some mysterious was my personal attitude to Osteopathy has been misunderstood. I find that some of my fellow osteopaths here have the idea that the College over which I have the honor to preside teaches *medicine* in the sense of *drugs*. I am an Osteopath and delight to be connected with a College which regards Osteopathy as an independent system…. Every member of our faculty is pledged to this fundamental conception of Osteopathy…. Osteopathy starts out with a new principle in therapeutics, namely; 'the self-sufficiency of the organism' the grandest triumph of this old time principle is found in the Osteopathic System, mechanical, physiological, anatomical, all combined in one, the fruitful discovery of Dr. A.T. Still…the system as I understand it recognizes the basic medicine in the field of toxicology, surgical anaesthesia and the physiological medicine of the organic constituents[30] of the body organism"

---

[30] A complicated way of saying a good balanced diet, while putting the word medicine into context rather than allowing it to be used in the narrow sense of 'drugs'

The **Masonic Temple Building, built in 1892,** was a skyscraper became the tallest in Chicago. It stood on the northeast corner of Randolph and State Streets rising 21 stories. The building featured a central court ringed by nine floors of shops with offices above and meeting rooms for the Masons at the very top. Many osteopaths had offices in the building, which was described as a city within a building. Dr. J. H. Sullivan D.O., had his offices on the 5th floor, Littlejohn had his on the 13th floor. Having offices in the building did not mean having any association with the Masons. It was demolished in 1939.

"Its grand height alone has made it world-famous, the grand promenade being twenty-eight feet higher than any other point of observation in the city. The observatory alone draws to the building hundreds of people daily, while the walls of Italian marble, the mosaic floors and bronze grills and balustrades tend to make it attractive, bright and grand in every detail. We have a Postal Sub-Station; telegraph companies maintain offices here. Tenants receive their mail earlier in the morning and later at night than in any other building in the city".[xcix]

ISSUE OF TOXICOSIS

Another point worth making at this time is his defence of his articles on toxicosis. In this series of articles, Littlejohn described his research into the treatment of cancer and gave case notes on some seventy cases. In his research, he had used animal experimentation with the sole aim of finding a way of treating Cancer a *"comparatively modern disease, said by some to be a disease of civilization"*.[c] He goes on to say;

> *"I have not been able to demonstrate that manipulative treatment without an antidote for the poison can effect & cure. Why? I believe we must dearly distinguish between two classes of cases (I) those in which drug or poison substances have never been introduced into the system.... (2) those cases in which drug or poison substance have been introduced into the body..."*

"In regard to the technique of the antidotal treatment only a mere outline can be offered. Where the poison in the system is active and on the surface of the circulation, regular toxicological measures are adopted to antidote the active poison. Where the poison is passively cumulative in the system, assimilated into the tissues, representing the accumulated effects of crude drugs, adulterated food[31], auto-intoxications and disease toxins, a deeper effect must be produced to liberate from the tissues.... The high potency antidotes and throws down for elimination, as well as destroys the effect of crude remedies or substances.... These points have been demonstrated by us by the application to animals and to the human subjects".[ci]

---

[31] His researches in this area led him to the conclusion that a simple life and a vegetarian diet was better for health and indeed almost essential in the case of constitutional diseases like cancer -"Among the inhabitants of China, Burma and India who live on a vegetable diet, it (cancer) is very rare" (JAOA April 1907, J M Littlejohn, Etiology of Cancer, page 287). In his latter days, when very ill, he used a vegetarian diet (letter to T. E. Hall, April 2nd, 1936.)

Some accused him of reinventing homeopathy and again Littlejohn clearly point out that the principles were not the same as the homeopathic principle. The principle of auto intoxication and anti-doting the toxicosis on the bioplasmic plane was a very different principle from that at the foundation of Homeopathy and was or should be in his opinion part of osteopathy.

> *My principle is to convert the antibody(sic) into a force and attenuates through an inert medium like distilled water or alcohol, then use it as a force antitoxin instead of a serum antitoxin. In this I am using the method of homeopathic attenuation, although not the principle of homeopathic medication. Mine is not the principle of similia similibus curantur but it is that of the same substance in attenuation force form meeting and anti-doting the action and effects of the same substance used in the crude. This is physical and physiological toxicology".* J. M. Littlejohn
>
> Journal of the American Osteopathic Association, volume 8, number 16, February 1909, page 261-2
>
> "We have been criticised for presumably discovering homeopathy. Not by any means. This is not the homeopathic principle. The homeopathic principle is sinidimum based on symptoms. Our principle is that of the same substance in its dynamic or vibratile force equivalent". J. M. Littlejohn
>
> Journal of the American Osteopathic Association, volume 7, number 10, June 1st ,1908. Page 441.

In fact, he went further and stated that any osteopath who didn't antidote toxicosis within their patient was professionally negligent.

> *If a surgeon in the operative field permitted toxic degenerative substances to accumulate in a wound without the use of antiseptic treatment or anti-dotal treatment, if necessary, he would be CRIMINALLY NEGLIGENT of the life of his patient...If an osteopath treats the gross anatomy of his patient and forgets to provide for antiseptic and anti-dotal treatment to dispose of insidious poisons that are sapping the very life centers of his patient WE CONSIDER HIM EQUALLY NEGLIGENT.*
>
> J. Martin Littlejohn, in his article on Cancer, Journal of the American Osteopathic Association, 1906/7 volume 6, number 9, May, page 320

To many at the time this was seen as the mixing of other forms of medicine with osteopathy whereas Littlejohn saw it as the proper place of osteopathy to take the whole lesion into view rather than narrowing it down to just one aspect of the patient's life. To the "pure and unadulterated" osteopath the assertion that manipulation alone could not tackle deep seated toxicity, and that antidotal treatment was necessary must have seemed like heresy. They did not seem to, nor want to understand the difference Littlejohn was making about ordinary toxicity and auto-intoxication where the toxic accumulation was such that it was the body itself is producing the toxic substance. They could understand simple poisoning and its treatment, but not auto-intoxication, which by definition is an extension of poisoning onto the vital or bioplasmic plane.

This was a hard battle for Littlejohn. He continually came up against those who would not have the same vision as him and who thought that his vision stepped outside the bounds of osteopathy and moved into the realms of medicine. It is important to remember that he was not alone nor isolated in his views, nor even the most outspoken. What made him different was his insistence on being loyal to Osteopathy and not mixing it with regular medicine nor allowing it to become a specialism. His view was that if we try and legislate osteopathy on a very narrow basis and exclude the wider vision of the osteopathic lesion then osteopathy will by force die. In this he was to be proved right. Osteopathic medicine in the United States is now basically ordinary medicine and drug medicine, with 'osteopathic manipulation therapy' as a 'speciality'. It is sad to see that his vision was not accepted and that his prophesy for want of a better word came true.

Replenishing his Conscience

During the summer of 1909 Littlejohn spent some time with the evangelist Dr. Minifie[32], traveling with him for part, at least of his tour.[33]

> " **Dr. Minifie leaves for Europe June 25th**
> The Rev. William C. Minifie, D. D., the English evangelist, who is at present conducting the tent services at WInthrop, will leave Boston on June 25 for an extended trip abroad. Dr. Minifie will be accompanied by Mrs. Minifie, the Rev. Dr. Fairbanks and daughter of Avon, Mr. and Mrs. Green, Mrs. Irwin and Mr. McGill of WInthrop; Miss Ashton of Benedict College of Columbia, S.C., and Dr. J. Martin Littlejohn, professor at Chicago University and one of the leading physicians of Chicago"
> (Boston Post, June 9, 1909)

It could be argued that after the trials of his endeavours in the research field, including the effect of experimenting on animals, the controversies around the colleges' fight for recognition and the name change, he needed to refresh his spirit. We know he continued to preach at least occasionally while in Chicago and remained in good standing as a minister.

He was very much connected with the Chicago congregation, (which was organized in April 1897[cii], around the time the Littlejohns

---

[32] Rev Minifie and Littlejohn had a long friendship that continued in England.
[33] Another example of misinformation in the newspapers, referring to Littlejohn as 'professor at Chicago university', a minor story for the reporter who would not put in a great effort, but at the same time would try to make everything sound more impressive - a general tendency for which Littlejohn cannot be held responsible.

moved to Chicago) especially during 1902. During this year he not only had his child baptised but also preached at this church

"Commission of Iowa Presbytery met according to appointment June 17th and 18th at Church Hall, 6532 Cottage Grove ave., Chicago, for the purpose of ordaining and installing Licentiate Robert Clarke as pastor of the First Reformed Presbyterian congregation, Chicago...Rev. J. M. Littlejohn and Rev. W . J. Sanderson being present, were invited to sit as consultative members.... At same time the infant child of Rev. and Mrs. J. M. Littlejohn was baptised....Rev. Mr. Littlejohn delivered the charge to Mr. Clarke and Mr. Brodie and the congregation came forward and extended a hearty greeting to the newly ordained and installed minister and elder.".[ciii]

"Rev. J. M. Littlejohn is expected to preach for us the four last Sabbaths of August, and we expect to have Rev. Dr. McFarland Sept. first Sabbath".[civ]

"on Nov. 2nd (1902) we were privileged to enjoy a pleasant and profitable observance of the Lord's Supper. Our pastor was ably assisted by Rev J. M. Littlejohn, and attendance at both morning and evening service was good".[cv]

As his duties within his college and the osteopathic profession at large increase he would have been unable to continue to devote as much time as he would have liked to his religious duties. Also, His preaching services would have been less in demand with the Ordination of Robert Clarke in 1902. Clarke stayed with the Chicago congregation until September 1909[cvi]

Littlejohn's relationship with the charismatic Minifie would play an important role in Littlejohn's life, and death as one of Littlejohn's last requests was his funeral service should be conducted by the Rev. Minifie "as he knows me better than anyone else".[cvii]

THE STATE BOARD OF HEALTH

The main areas that have come down to us as controversial are the fight for recognition from the State Board of Health, the relationship with the Associated Colleges of Osteopathy and the American Osteopathic Association, and the change of name to 'The Littlejohn College' and finally the dissolution of the Littlejohn College with the formation of the Chicago College of Osteopathy.[34]

From the start the idea was to get the school recognised as a bone fide school, in good standing, of medicine. Using the word medicine in the broadest term possible, Littlejohn and his brother, James Buchan, fought a long battle with the Board of Health over this and always came back with the stumbling block that their charter stated that the school was a school of osteopathy and taught osteopathy therefore the Board of Health couldn't grade it as a school of medicine.

Another part of the problem with the Board of Health came from their inspection of the college on February 1908. One of the criticisms by the State Board of Health was *"there are no Physiological and Pathological Laboratories, and it is impossible to give their students proper training in the department of Pathology, Histology, Physiology, Chemistry and Bacteriology with their present equipment. The Department of Surgery, Obstetrics and Osteopathic Medicine is conducted by Dr. James B. Littlejohn, and we are unable to find indications that surgical clinics were conducted, either in the College Building or in any Hospital"*.[cviii]

On receipt of this report, and the said "poor state of the physiological laboratories" within the college the Littlejohns installed further equipment in the laboratories and the college, spent "about $18,000 and bought new and additional equipment at a cost of about $3000, and in addition thereto imported equipment to the value of about $1000".[cix] They even changed the name from 'the American college of

---

[34] An accurate account the development of the American College of Osteopathic Medicine and Surgery (ACOMS) can be found in 'To Teach, To Heal, To Serve' by Theodore A. Berchtold.

osteopathic medicine and surgery' to 'The Littlejohn College'.[35] This was for two very different reasons. Firstly, it took the word 'osteopathic' out of the title, thus removing the criticism from the State Board that it was an osteopathic college and therefore removing, or so they hoped, one reason why the State Board could not list it as a medical college. Secondly, it took the word 'medicine' out of the title in an effort to overcome the criticism from fellow osteopaths that it was mixing osteopathy with medicine.

The State board refused to carry out another inspection and the Littlejohn College then tried to force the issue in court. In the end the state board relied upon the charter and announcements for the Littlejohn College to refuse it recognition and won in the state supreme court on that basis.

> " the jury decided the subject of therapeutics is shown by the announcement of the college to have been taught only as required in osteopathic practice"
>
> Chicago daily tribune April 24th, 1912 page 3

While John Martin Littlejohn had retired[36] from the College at this time, his brother James Buchan, portrayed it as a victory

---

[35] In their submission to the court they claimed that the State Board of Health had stipulated that they would never be granted the status of 'Medical College in good standing' while the name 'American College of Osteopathic Medicine and Surgery' remained, in particular the word 'Osteopathic' was the main objection.(The people of the state of Illinois, ex rel Littlejohn College and hospital vs Illinois State board of health; gen No. 303742, term 8881)

[36] His announcement was carried in the November 1911 issue of the Journal of the American Osteopathic Association

> "We think this a great victory for our Osteopathic College to be declared eligible to recognition as a college of medicine in every respect save in therapeutics and in that to be recognized by them as teaching such therapeutics as should be known by osteopaths. This decision does not affect the standing of our college or our graduates in any particular whatsoever. We are stronger in our osteopathic faith and principles than ever.
> Yours fraternally,
> James B. Littlejohn, President."
>
> JAOA June 1912, page 1196

During this time the State Board of Health was itself embroiled in controversy.

The Chicago daily tribune, April 24th 1912, carried an article reminding readers that it *"is not long since that the state board of health of Illinois was severely criticised for recognising medical schools whose curriculum and physical laboratory work were deemed inadequate"*.

Another aspect of the State Board of health's attitude is to be found in the accusations that it faced, especially from the National Medical University, that some members took bribes to register some colleges as being in good standing. This was widely reported, including in the Journal of Osteopathy, Kirksville;

> **Smejkal's Claim on the Doctors**
>
> *Legislator Smejkal's especial claims on the medical profession are cited as his opposition to the osteopathic and optometry bills at Springfield. He recently came into the limelight of the medical school's scandal, It being indicated that he received $700, in a move to secure from the state board of Health the reinstatement of National Medical university. Dr. L. D. Rogers of the University Dr. and Egan, secretary of the state board of health, said that Mr. Smejkal, who was formerly attorney of the State Board, did nothing in return for the $700.*
>
> **Journal of Osteopathy, Kirksville**
> Volume 17, No. 10 October 1910

In a rather sarcastic article a note on the same subject, quoting from the 'Chicago American', was carried in the 'Chicago Clinic and Pure Water journal in October 1905. Despite the sarcastic nature of this article does give some indication of how long this scandal involving bribes, hush money etc. had been going on.

"Under the heading 'Healers Say State Board Accepted Hush Money' sub-heading 'Christian Scientists, Osteopaths and others declared they paid cash to be allowed to carry on their business in Illinois ... it's also charged by those who belong to the irregular medical profession that the State Board of Health officials have taken from them thousands of dollars in the past few years. It is said that unless they pay (hush) money they are not permitted to do business. It is claimed that magnetic healers, Christian scientists, osteopaths etc from all parts of the state are ready to confirm these charges under oath." [cx]

This is another aspect of the political battle in Illinois. We have the two strands, the determined opposition of the secretary of the State Board of Health to irregular practitioners and osteopathy in particular and the taking of hush money by members of the Board of Health to ignore the practice of certain practitioners. It paints a pretty poor impression of the state board and one which if you try to battle on legal grounds, you're likely to lose. The payment of bribes would have been something that neither Littlejohn brother would have countenanced given their upbringing under their parent's watchful eyes.

This was the case with the Littlejohns and their college looking for recognition as a medical college in good standing. One has the impression that if they had taken a less robust challenge and had been more politically astute and used what is regarded as "hush money" or greased the wheels of power they may have been more successfully. This of course is just an opinion but is based on what I have read about the times.

John Martin Littlejohn, in particular, would not go down this route. His background as a Reformed Presbyterian Minister and his beliefs stemming from that meant that he would not hold political office but would try to campaign for political rights from the side-lines and push for the rights on a legal and formal basis. He would not engage in bribery or corruption[37].

So, we find the State Board, which had been under-fire for bribery and again from the Flexner report, found various technicalities to avoid recognising the Littlejohn College as being a medical college in good standing. First criticising the equipment or lack of it, then the Lecturers and when these were attended to they turned to the 'failsafe' of saying it was an Osteopathic College and therefore not under their remit to classify it as a medical college, never mind a medical college in good standing and that it was therefore "useless to make an investigation of the Littlejohn College and Hospital at the present time".[cxi] Dr. Egan wrote formally to James Buchan Littlejohn,

---

[37] Littlejohn had already engaged in research into the Fee system of payment (Journal of Osteopathy, British School of Osteopathy, June- August 1935, page 8.) and would have been very aware of the possibility corruption

Secretary of the Littlejohn College and Hospital to inform him of the State Board of Health's rejection of their application to be granted the status of 'Medical College in Good Standing' on January 18th 1911. This rejection led to the court case, which as detailed above, they lost.[38]

The points made in Dr. Egan's letter seem to acknowledge the Littlejohn college's claim to be teaching an unmixed pure system of osteopathy. In detail the letter, says:

"A complete system of healing in the Osteopathic System is taught"

" the curriculum of the Littlejohn College and Hospital is devoted principally to Osteopathy.

"That Materia Medica and Pharmacology are not properly taught in the Littlejohn College and Hospital

"Therapeutics is ignored in the Littlejohn College and Hospital except in so much 'as should be known in Osteopathic Practice'

"that the degree conferred by the Littlejohn College and Hospital is M. D. Osteopathic

"in view of these findings the State Board of Health decided that the Littlejohn College and Hospital is an Osteopathic rather than a Medical College, and for this reason recognition as a Medical College, according to the purposes of the act to regulate the practice of Medicine in the State of Illinois, approved April 24th 1899, can not be accorded".[cxii]

Illinois was regarded as one of the most difficult states in which to practice Osteopathy legally. Some idea of the difficulty that

---

[38] Littlejohn wrote the first letter to James A Egan, Secretary of the State Board of health, Illinois, concerning their application for recognition as a medical college in good standing on September 27th, 1900 which was replied to on Oct 1st, 1900. Unfortunately, i have not been able to find copies of these. All later correspondence seems to have been handled by J. B. Littlejohn and their attorney, R. R. Longenecker.

the Littlejohns faced can be gleaned from the following article in the April 1905 Chicago Clinic and Pure Water Journal:

"Illinois stands practically alone in a unique position. The efforts of osteopaths in the state have been stubbornly resisted although the battle has been vigorously fought in legislative halls. The veto powers of Governor Tanner and of Governor Yates are required to stem the tide after the osteopathic ship has successfully weathered the seas in both houses and senate. In Illinois today the osteopaths are not recognized as osteopaths. They have no Board of Examiners of their own. They've no representation on state examining bodies. They are permitted to practice as those who are permitted to treat without the internal or external use of drugs or the use of operative surgery, just as magnetic healers and other peculiar cults are permitted to ply their trades ... The osteopathic lobbyists are making an energetic fight, but their efforts are met with as vigorous opposition on part of the secretary of the State Board of Health." [cxiii]

This describes very well how complex the legislative fight for the right to practice as full general practitioners and physicians was in Chicago at this time, and in particular, how determined a foe Dr. Egan, Secretary of the State Board of Health, was to Osteopathy.

After the Flexner report was published, the State board of Health went as far as writing to neighbouring states to ask what their attitude was to the 'inferior' medical schools in Chicago. The results may surprise some, particularly with regard to the standing of the Littlejohn College.

Letters were sent to the executive officers of Indiana, Ohio, Pennsylvania, New York, Kentucky, Missouri, Iowa: Minnesota, Wisconsin, and Colorado:

Up to the time of going to press, October 1911, they had received replies from six of these states.

State of New York education department: Dear sir..."**The Littlejohn College and Hospital (Osteopathic) is accredited with three years"**.

Minnesota State Board of Medical examiners: *"Minnesota has its own Board of Osteopathic Examiners"*

Iowa State Board of Medical Registration and Examination: did not mention The Littlejohn College and Hospital or Osteopathy

Wisconsin Board of Medical Examiners " *Gentlemen :—In reply to your favor of the 19th inst. we wish to state that we recognize none of the graduates of the medical colleges mentioned in your letter, nor do we have anything to do with any graduates of the schools mentioned in the second paragraph of your letter, except* **the Littlejohn School of Osteopathy, whose graduates are accepted for examination the same as other reputable medical colleges".** "Yours sincerely, "John M. Beffel, Secretary

The State of Ohio *"A list of medical colleges acceptable to the Ohio Board will probably be acted upon at the meeting on October 3. We have been registering applicants from the Hering Medical College and have also recognized credentials from the Chicago School of Medicine and Surgery, likewise the Jenner Medical College. We have never had occasion to pass upon the credentials from the Reliance Medical College nor the National Medical University.* **The Littlejohn College and Hospital (Osteopathic), has also been recognized in the past.** No *applications from either of the other schools mentioned in your communication have come before us for consideration".* "Very Respectfully, "George M. Matson, Secretary

Indiana State Board of Medical Registration and Examination

" Dear Sir :—*Replying to your inquiry of some days ago, beg to say that it is the policy of this board not to pass upon the standing and credibility of a medical school until an applicant comes up for examination from said school, then the matter is brought to the board's attention and passed upon. Graduates from the National Medical University, the Jenner and Reliance Medical Colleges are not admitted to the Indiana examination for license to practice medicine.* **"Graduates from the Littlejohn College and Hospital (Osteopathic), who have, by documentary evidence, satisfied this board that they have attended four courses of instruction in said institution, of not**

less than eight months each in separate calendar years, are admitted to the osteopathic examination. W. T. Gott, M.D., Secretary. ([cxiv]) (Illinois medical journal October 1911)

The replies[39] may surprise some, as the Littlejohn College seemed to fare well in many areas.

However, the final result of the attempt for recognition was that the supreme court of Illinois refused the appeal by the Littlejohn college and upheld the State Board of Health's decision not to recognise it as a 'medical college in good standing'.

James Buchan's initial reaction was to say they would continue the fight right up to the Supreme Court of the USA. However, this never happened. J. Martin Littlejohn's resignation from the college, the possibility of losing at the highest level and the need to re-organise the college all probably being factors in this decision.

As an interesting aside to James Buchan's standing, the following quote, talking about The Littlejohn College, in 1917, from a studious opponent of osteopathy is worth reading.

> "Littlejohn (James Buchan) is a doctor; many who are teaching are doctors. He gives a pretty fair course in medicine, and it is apparent to me from his talks, that Littlejohn's idea is this: He is going to make osteopathic doctors, he is going to run a medical school, and he wants them to be known as osteopathic doctors, the same as they were formerly known as homeopathic doctors. He thinks he can establish another cult of doctors and put the name 'osteopath' in front and make them popular with the people."
>
> Illinois Medical Journal July 1917, page 53;

---

[39] Bold emphasis by author

THE FLEXNER REPORT

The Flexner Report or the Carnegie Foundation Report into medical education in the United States 1907 – 1910 has been held up by many as an example of how an examination of a profession should be carried out and the results of it are held in high esteem by many people. Before we look at it in particular it is important to put it into context of the time.

"In 1907 in an effort to raise educational standards and put pressure on poor quality schools to improve or close the American Medical Association Council on medical education carried out inspections of American medical schools and created a classification system (i.e. rankings) for these schools. Following this, the Council decided in 1908 that it would be advantageous to solicit the Carnegie Foundation for the advancement of teaching to work on this issue (medicine pays tribute to Dr. Flexner. American Medical Association News October 5th, 1959). This was because many physicians in medical schools were bitter that their institutions were under pressure or had already closed as a result of the Council efforts." [cxv]

The A.M.A. may have being carrying out its own investigation into medical schools and putting pressure on those which they thought were of a lower standard to close. To further this they enlisted the Carnegie Foundation to carry out the work as an 'independent educational foundation'.

"The Council and Carnegie Foundation believe that the observations and recommendations in the report would be more widely accepted if they came from the neutral educational foundation of high standing." [cxvi]

The result was that the Carnegie Foundation appointed their own investigator Abraham Flexner to lead the investigations of medical schools. Flexner had a wide knowledge of general education and was believed to be "genius for this sort of work".

An excerpt for the minutes of the December 1908 meeting of the council states (at one of clock an informal conference was held with

President Pritchett and Mr Abraham Flexner of the Carnegie Foundation.

"Mr Pritchett had already expressed by correspondence the willingness of the Foundation to co-operate with the Council investigating medical schools ... He agreed with the opinion previously expressed by members of the council that while the Foundation would be guided very largely by the Council's investigation, to avoid the usual claims of partiality no more mention should be made in the report of the Council than any other source of information. The report would therefore be and have the weight of an independent report of a disinterested body, which would then be published far and wide. It would do much to develop public opinion." [cxvii]

Thus, the initial motive behind it was clearly from the American Medical Association with the Carnegie Foundation acting as a front for their views so as a pretence could be maintained of neutrality. The study was begun in January 1909 by Mr Flexner of the Carnegie Foundation and Dr. N.P. Colwell of the Council. The results were published in 1910 in what is referred to as the Flexner Report.

Jafet Arrieta[cxviii] comments in a report on the Flexner Report that the impact was amongst other things an elimination of alternative medicine courses from the curriculum, domination of American medicine by well-off white males and the report tended to de-legitimise existing women doctors and doctors of colour. Implementation of the university medical based model meant that medical education became more expensive and the number of graduates was cut from four and a half thousands to two thousand and the number of schools American Medical Schools were reduced to thirty-one in total.

Another aspect of this is that Chicago was particularly set out for investigation and 'cleaning up'. In his report, Flexner states that:

"The city of Chicago is in respect to medical education the plague spot of the country. The state law is fairly adequate for it empowers the Board of Health to establish a standard of preliminary education, laboratory equipment and clinical facilities thus fixing the conditions which shall entitle a school to be considered reputable. In pursuance of these powers the board has made the four-year High School or its

equivalent the basis and has enumerated the essentials of the medical course including amongst other things clinical instruction through two annual terms. With the indubitable connivance of the State Board these provisions are and have long been fragrantly violated. Of the fourteen under-graduate medical schools above described the majority exist and prepare candidates for the Illinois State Board examinations in unmistakeable contravention of the law and the state board rules."[cxix]

When we read deeper behind this, we find that the American Medical Association itself regarded Chicago in particular as a black spot of medical education and that it needed to be cleaned up. Flexner in his report talks about the difference between the scientific method and medical sectarians. That the scientific method should be applied throughout the education not just in one part and therefore he classified the homeopaths, the eclectics, the physio medicals and the osteopaths as sectarians.

In not so many words he sets out a bias against these institutions without a firm understanding of their underlying principles. He goes on to say, in terms of homeopathy, that the number of schools have been decreasing and that the graduating classes are falling from 1900 – 1909 stating that logically there can be no other outcome:

"The ebbing vitality of homeopathic schools is a striking demonstration of the incompatibility of science and dogma."

He then launches an attack[cxx] on osteopathy which says that the eight osteopathic schools fairly reek with commercialism, their catalogues a mass of hysterical exaggeration alike of the earning and the curative power of osteopathy. It is impossible to say upon which score the "science" most confidently appeals to the crude boys or disappointed men and women whom it successfully exploits.

"In no case has a competent osteopath made a failure in his attempt to build up a paying practice ..." taken from the catalogue of the Los Angeles College of Osteopathy. He quotes from other colleges' prospectus in the same manner to substantiate his argument that the schools are commercial.

The catalogues quoted are from the Pacific College, the Los Angeles College, the Central College of Osteopathy, the Philadelphia College and the Massachusetts College. He attacks the assertion that dissection should come after book learning of anatomy despite that fact that Still and others in the osteopathic profession said that anatomy should be learned first in the living before the dead so that you don't get stuck in thinking of the body as being dead.

He makes a point about the Littlejohn College in Chicago whose catalogue says that:

"The physician should be imbued with a knowledge of the healing arts in its widest fields and here is its opportunity."

He states that it has lately in rebuilding wrecked all of its laboratories but that of the chemistry without in the least interfering with its usual pedagogic routine. He also makes a sub note that this school teaches medicine as well as osteopathy. It offers instruction in Materia Medica,[40] therapeutics and practice in medicine, yet it is a three-year school.

Again, he doesn't pay much attention to the meaning of the word Materia Medica or medicine in terms of osteopathy, thinking only of medicine as being drug use. At no point does he display an understanding of osteopathic philosophy or indeed of homeopathic or any other alternative but tries to maintain his impartiality by saying that all schools must adhere to a scientific approach thus applying the American Medical School model and philosophy to those who are in strict opposition to them.

This is in line with the approach that he was instructed on by the American Medical Association and indeed the conclusion that was reached by some investigators that the effect of his report was to allow the American Medical Association to close down all schools, not just those of a so called lower standard, which didn't fit the white male middle class or upper middle class model. In other words,

---

[40] Even though as we have already shown, it only teaches Materia Medica as part of comparative therapeutics and in relation to Surgery.

schools specifically for women, for African Americans, for alternatives were all to suffer at the hands of this report.

Flexner was criticized by many colleges and organizations after his report was published, some, like Littlejohn[cxxi], questioning if he ever even visited their college. Given Flexner's own admissions this is hardly surprising. One researcher describing his methods as 'roughshod'

"In terms of research methods, Flexner's data gathering was roughshod at best, even by his own description... Hastily written notes summed up his observations...To a great extent, Flexner's study was an exercise in foregone conclusions".[cxxii]

In his own words Flexner's gives a description of his methodology:

"In half an hour or less I could sample the credentials of students filed in the dean's office, ascertain the matriculation requirements (two years of high-school work, high-school graduation, two years of college work, or finally a college degree) and determine whether or not the standards, low or high set forth in the school catalogue were being evaded or enforced. A few inquiries made it clear whether faculty was composed of local doctors, not already 'professors' in some other local medical school, or the extent to which efforts had been made to obtain teachers properly trained elsewhere. A single question elicited the income of a medical school.[cxxiii]"

If this describes the time he spent in the Littlejohn College it would; hardly be enough time to walk around the college never mind interview the professors, students or other staff that may have been there. Flexner also made the point when he visited the school, they were in the process of rebuilding their laboratory, so he saw it at a particularly dysfunctional time though it still managed to function. Littlejohn in his defence of it says that he has no recollection of Flexner actually visiting the school itself;

"I was surprised to find in your columns this morning the so-called Carnegie Foundation Report. So far as our college is concerned it is a malicious libel. Neither Flexner nor any of his confreres ever entered our college and therefore incapably of judging. For ten years

this college has supported and carried out a standard of High School entrance and four-year college course in spite of the fact that there is no law governing our system as laying down any standards in this state. We have a charter requiring us to maintain a standard of requirements for entrance equivalent to that laid down by the American Association of Medical Colleges ... shall teach such sciences and arts as are usually taught in medical colleges, in addition the science of osteopathy in all its branches..."[cxxiv] J. Littlejohn, President of College and Hospital.

He put his opinion even stronger in the Osteopathic Physician

"This is part of the policy of extermination evidenced by the report of the Carnegie Foundation formulated by Abraham Flexner. I can only speak for our college in Chicago. That college he condemned without ever being within its doors to the knowledge of the officers of the college. The manifest untruth of such a report evidences its malice with determination to destroy by fair means or foul."[cxxv]

Further evidence of the lack of time Flexner had to carry out his inspections is found in his itinerary:

"By way of illustrating the speed and energy with which I worked, the following itinerary, found among my papers, is enlightening

November	4th	Des Moines, Iowa
	5th	Sioux City Iowa
	6th	Omaha Nebraska
	7th	Kansas City
	8th	Lawrence, Kansas
	9th	St. Louis, Missouri
	11th	Oklahoma City
	12th	Norman, Oklahoma
	14th	Dallas, Texas
	15th	Little Rock, Arkansas
	16th	Memphis, Tennessee
	17th	Vicksburg Missouri
	19th	Nashville, Tennessee
	20th	Louisville, Kentucky"[cxxvi]

This itinerary hardly gives enough time to visit let alone inspect any of the Colleges.

Flexner's attitude towards osteopathy in general is well summed up in his own words, *"From Kirksville, Missouri, fountain spring of osteopathy, I wrote, I have seen much gullibility in the last ten months but commend me to the father of osteopathy and his sons as past masters therein"*.[cxxvii]

Not much need be said about the report itself, it has been shown to be what it evidently was, a political stunt masquerading as a well-designed investigation. However, in case it is thought that Littlejohn's claim that no one of the staff of the Littlejohn College knew anything about a visit by Flexner or his associates, is hard to believe, let's look at the response of another college.

"W. Henry Wilson, register, Hahnemann Medical college- Abraham Flexner, who got up the report, is not a medically trained man. We do not feel that we were fairly treated. No officer of the college knew that anybody was there, and we were not asked for information at the time. The information was obtained from the janitor and the students, as far as we have been able to determine."[cxxviii]

Not only alternative colleges had the opinion that Flexner's report was all about medical politics, but also many of the Allopathic Colleges. "J. Newton Rowe, secretary of the Chicago College of Medicine and Surgery-"This is medical politics."[cxxix]

Even Dr. Egan, Secretary of the State Board of Health condemned the report:

"Dr. James A. Egan, secretary of the Illinois State Board of Health, roundly denounced the report as 'asinine and betraying but little knowledge of the real conditions in Illinois'... Dr. Egan asserted that the report in parts is false. The report of the Carnegie Foundation calls for but little attention from the people of Illinois. It evidenced a lack of knowledge on the part of those by whom it was prepared, of the legal requirements in Illinois and the rules of the state board of health. It a deplorable ignorance as to what is a medical college....

"The inspections of the medical colleges were made for the Carnegie Foundation by a gentleman who is not a physician and who, so far as I have been able to learn, does not possess the knowledge enabling him to intelligently determine whether a college Is adequately equipped to each medicine".[cxxx]

The one thing we do see is Littlejohn's unwavering defence of his College and of Osteopathy. The Flexner report and the case against the State Board of Health confirm that his college taught "osteopathic therapeutic"[41] as the osteopathic equivalent to orthodox Materia Medica, anti-dotes on the basis of dynamization on the bioplasmic plane, and antiseptic and analgesic medicine as needed for surgery, but all in the context of pure unadulterated Osteopathic principles.

---

[41] Littlejohn published his lecture notes, given in his College, "Osteopathic Therapeutics" in 1908

FURTHER DETAIL ON
THE A.O.A., A.C.O., THE M.D. DEGREE
AND DRUGS

Perhaps nowhere more so than at the A.O.A.'s annual meeting in Minneapolis in 1909 do we see the debate on medicine, drugs and the M.D. degree come more clearly into perspective.[42] The meeting was proceeding in usual manner when the subject of the request to the state legislature, by the Massachusetts college of osteopathy to give the M.D. degree came up for debate. Hildreth in his usual manner invoked not only the name of Still but also of God in his speech;

"But, brothers mine, tell me, in the name of osteopathy, which I know you love; tell me, in the name of our beloved founder, Dr. Andrew Taylor Still ; nay ! in the name of God who created us and made all this great work possible — tell me why you do a thing that you apologize for doing, even in the announcement of your future policy?" [cxxxi]

Dr. M. W. Peck of the Massachusetts College gave his rationale in a straightforward manner that is worth reproducing in full;

"The trustees of the Massachusetts College wish to confer the degree 'M. D.' for four reasons:

"The first reason is that there are many student graduates in osteopathy who desire the M. D. degree. At present it is necessary for

---

[42] Dr. Bunting reports his opinion that "the dominant note of the meeting at Minneapolis was the practical unanimity expressed by the resolution forbidding the extension of our college curricula to include Materia Medica" even though it was more of a political stunt than a unanimous expression. He did make some attempt to put this into context by adding "in their honest zeal the convention almost violated the proprieties and forgot to give the advocates of this new policy a fair hearing"(Dr. Henry Stanhope Bunting JAOA sept 1909. Page 13/14). It was an unfortunate tendency of many, including Hildreth, to report things as 'almost unanimous' thus closing the possibility of debate.

him to take a four-year course in a medical college where the atmosphere is decidedly unfriendly to osteopathy. In order for our school to give the M. D. degree we will have to increase the course in order to give more complete instruction; but unless he prefers the M. D. degree it would be a hard matter to keep him in school that long.

'The second reason is that in our school we have students from England and Canada, and in those countries, it is impossible for an osteopathic graduate to have any legal standing without the degree, M. D.

"Third, if the osteopathic physicians had the degree M. D. it would clear up to a large measure all the legal difficulties that we are now experiencing all over the country.

"Fourth, there is in the association in the minds of all people of the physician and doctor with M. D.; and this association is fixed and immovable, and if we could also confer the degree M. D. it would not weaken but strengthen the osteopathic schools". [cxxxii]

In many ways his argument echoes Littlejohn's thoughts on the M.D. Osteopathic degree, that he first put forward in 1899. The subject was further discussed the next day, without any action and then the convention moved on to other subjects. However, on the Friday morning, four days later, after a paper by Dr. George McLaughlin on the treatment of quiescent hip disease, Dr. C. M. T. Hulett took to the floor and recommended *"to the Committee on Education and Board of Trustees that no college which grants the degree of Doctor of Medicine shall be elected or continued as a co-operating organization with this association. I move the adoption of the resolution"*.[cxxxiii] The motion was seconded and carried. It was pointed out that the representatives of the Colleges were not present, they were at a meeting of the A.C.O. and therefore could not offer their viewpoint. Hulett relented, saying it was not his intention that the motion should be carried in the way it was and then asked for it to be reconsidered when those opposed to it have had an opportunity to express their views. This seems to be a good example of politics in action. His motion could have been put forward at any time, especially when the subject of the Massachusetts College was being discussed. However, he 'chose' to do it when the A.C.O. meeting was on, and therefore the college representatives would not be present.

Littlejohn, who was chairing the A.C.O. meeting, in his reports put it as follows;

"On receiving intimation that a resolution was presented to the A. O. A., instructing the Board of Trustees and the Educational Committee to debar from membership in the A. O. A. any College giving and conferring the M. D. degree, the A. C. O. resolved, not to express any opinion on the subject at the present time, as neither the A. O. A. nor the A.C.O. has ever adopted any official degrees the matter having been left entirely to the Colleges. With the broadening of the education of the osteopathic physician, especially to include surgery, surgical medicine, antidotes, anaesthetics and antiseptics, some definite degree or degrees or legal definitions must be adopted to make plain the position we take as Colleges and practitioners. Hence it was decided to appoint the President of the A. C. O. to present a resolution to the A. O. A. referring the matter of degrees and the laws in the different states relative to the same to the committee on education and the A.C.O. for investigation and report at the next meeting. The A. C. O. desires a thorough investigation of the subject of degrees from its constitutional and legal standpoints, as well as from the point of view of the demand of so many osteopaths to receive the M. D degree".[cxxxiv]

The session then heard for representatives of the Colleges with Littlejohn and others putting amendments, which were defeated, and the original resolution adopted.

This would seem to put Littlejohn's college and others in a position of jeopardy. To understand this, we must look at Littlejohn's response.

"Dr. Littlejohn on the Proposed Degree
"*I am prompted to write the Journal, because I do not think that the Associated Colleges have been quite fairly represented. You give in full the resolution offered by Dr. Hulett, but do not give the amendment offered by me on behalf of the A. C. O.*
His proposed amendment on behalf of the ACO was that there should be a full and proper debate on the subject of degrees after a complete report had been presented by the education committee of the AOA and the ACO. This would take the emotional 'knee jerk' response out of the matter. He goes on to say:

> "Drs. Bunting, Bernard, Achorn and others, misunderstood entirely the matter in discussion. It is not a question of Medicine, versus osteopathy, or Medicine mixed with osteopathy. That was settled years ago at Indianapolis, when it was agreed that every therapeutic equipment except Materia Medica should be included in our college curriculum" [cxxxv]

Again, we see Littlejohn being diplomatic, thinking only of the position of Osteopathy and how it's college would be best suited to teach. Materia Medica to him was not drugs but Osteopathic therapeutic, and if pharmacology was taught it was from a comparative point of view, showing the superiority of Osteopathy. He made a plea for honesty;

> "No Medicine was raised at all, except what Dr. Hildreth and others admitted as I stated that there are Medicines, the common property, of all Schools, antidotes, anesthetics, antiseptics. But it is a question of calling these Medicine. An antidote of carbolic acid is not any the less Medicine, because given by an osteopath, than by an M. D. Why not call it so and be consistent?" [cxxxvi]

The question is, could he have expected honesty?
He again made this plea for honesty in 1910;

> "One of the chief factors that militated against us in Illinois during our last campaign was the fact that while many of the osteopaths were preaching "no drug, no knife doctrine" —the catalogues of the A. S. O. were in the hands of the legislators announcing pages of surgical operations.
> The A. S.O. is quite right in adding surgery to the curriculum, and a course in the fallacies of medicine, that is, comparative therapeutics; but let us be honest". [cxxxvii]

To put it into perspective, the argument was about the degree M.D. and how many osteopaths found the use of this title offensive. This goes back to earlier days, as we saw when Hulett got Still to come out against the M.D.O.(Osteopathic) in 1899. However, in the May 1909 edition of the Osteopathic Physician, on page 12, we find a large advertisement for the American School of Osteopathy in Kirksville with the founder and president listed as "Dr. A. T. Still"; no D.O. or accolade of 'Osteopath' attached to him. On the same page we find a large advertisement for the 'Edinburgh University Stereoscopic Anatomy' with the following endorsement:

"this new method is a good one, very helpful to students and practitioners in their anatomical studies. I cordially recommend it to the osteopathic profession. Andrew Taylor Still, M.D."

The use of the title M.D. could be excused if this was a one-off advertisement. However, we find the same advertisement, with Still using the title M.D. in the Osteopathic Physician during the years 1907 through to 1910, long enough for Hildreth, Hulett and Still himself to see them and put a stop to the use of the designation M.D.[43] If they did not, how did they expect the osteopathic profession as a whole to take them seriously.

Another aside to this is in Hildreth's drive for 'pure and unadulterated' osteopathy. In the same journal we find a note that **"Hildreth is getting heretical for he has publicly announced he recommends both the hot water bag and the enema"**. [cxxxviii] which if true would put much of what he is saying into the realm of politics rather than the practice of osteopathy.

Another aspect of Hildreth is to be found in his response to an article entitled "A Plea for Honesty" by a friend on his, Frederick W. Sherburne, D. O., in the April 1908 journal of the American Osteopathic Association. This article was along the lines that many, including Littlejohn, had made. In it he says:

"These writers contend that osteopathy is "a complete system," "good for everything," and yet would limit practitioners so that of necessity they must turn quite a percentage of their cases over to M. D's". [cxxxix]

Here he was referring to those *"prominent osteopaths entreating the profession to keep away from all adjuncts and adhere strictly to lesion osteopathy"*

Hildreth, in his response, he refers to Dr. Sherburne as *"a good personal friend of mine and a man whose opinion I value highly"*, and goes on to say:

---

[43] We have noted before other places where Still's name is followed by the designation 'M. D.', including his own Journal of Osteopathy.

"As to adjuncts, I feel that Dr. Sherburne and many others do take the writings of some of our osteopaths too literally. Dietetics, hygiene, the enema, and many other simple things constantly used everywhere as means of relief, belong to no school and are common to all people all the time, everywhere. They are not allopathic, homeopathic, electic nor osteopathic. As to the anesthetic, anticeptic, antidote or the opening of a boil, neither one is internal medication, unless it be the antidote, and every individual, whether physician or layman, has a right to give antidotes whenever and wherever required. No law that grants the osteopath the right to handle sick people can prevent their use".[cxl]

This seems very much in tune with Littlejohn's opinion. It would seem that, when referring to an opinion of a 'close friend' Hildreth's attitude was a lot softer and less evangelical than when he had to deal with Littlejohn, against whom he seems to continue to hold a grudge or angst.

The arguments between the two factions, those who wanted it as a specialism, and those who want to be osteopathic physicians, within Osteopathy is well put by Dr. Peck in the September 1909 Journal:

"All the discussion about adjuncts is really a consideration of this more general question in one of its aspects. Likewise, behind most of the argument for and against granting the M.D. degree and in all matters of dispute, was hidden the real question, is osteopathy a specialty or is it not.
By no means (can) a.,(sic) the profession ignore or evade this question. Dr. Charlie Still, stated from the platform, that he considered osteopathy a sort of specialty and that he wished to be considered himself as an osteopathic specialist....
It was stated by several in their impressions of the meeting, that the question of the M. D. degree had been settled once and for all. I do not agree with them. I venture to say that the great majority of members present had never given consideration to the matter before and that many had never even heard of it. It must be clear to any impartial mind, that no question of such great importance can be settled by a few hours thought and a few minutes discussion in an atmosphere

where feeling was running too high to even permit listening to argument.
I consider that the question of the M. D. degree was just begun at the Minneapolis meeting rather than that it was definitely settled".[cxli]

If we look at the A.O.A. at the time of this convention in 1909, we see them lamenting that only thirty-five per cent of osteopaths were members,[cxlii] so again to claim to be representative of the profession as a whole was stretching things just a little. In true fashion, Littlejohn does not use any of this as 'political ammunition.' Instead, he concentrates on the heart of the argument, use the term medicine in its true meaning and teach osteopathy in its fullest extent to include anti dotes, antiseptics, analgesics for use in surgery. In the November JAOA the editor puts Littlejohn College perspective clearly;

"With the Littlejohn College It is largely a matter of meeting the peculiar legal conditions in the state. They teach surgery and of course surgical medicine, anesthetics, antiseptics and antidotes, etc. Dr. Littlejohn argues that these are drugs, as much drug when used by the osteopath as when administered by the allopath, hence it is not right for us to say we do not use drugs, and using them it is proper that we should have the degree that indicates their use, tho' limited to osteopathy (M. D. osteopathic, or osteopathic medicine.).... Dr. Littlejohn says he does not care what the degree is, he wants to do justice to his students and keep within the law".[cxliii]

He goes on to say that the resolution adopted was *"possibly not parliamentary; perhaps it has no standing under the constitution, as not coming through the proper channels...that, (the convention) was not the place for discussion...Feeling ran too high and there was too much temptation to appear ultra-orthodox as a play to the galleries"*

This, I feel gives an honest assessment of the situation. Littlejohn's brother, James B. was a little less diplomatic in his choice of words;

"The law in most of the states requires a four years curriculum to prepare for the practice of medicine. We do practice medicine, ladies and gentlemen, fool yourselves as you may by thinking or trying to think otherwise. Osteopathic practice is the practice of medicine —that is, healing. Encyclopedias say the practice of medicine is the practice of the healing art. Is that what you want to

be? Would you rather Be a masseur, licensed to rub, to knead, to collect a fee, but not heal the sick as a physician?... The word practice of medicine seems to convey the idea of degrees only to some. Just as the letters M. D. do to some. That is their conception of it only. I am proud that I am an M. D., I Am proud that I am an osteopath, and I Want to fight for the principle for you."[cxliv]

In all his writings, Littlejohn was clear that he had *"no use for drugs because they belong to the class of alien principles and elements which can find no place in the normal economy of the body. A poison can at its best but poison the organism; a cathartic can at best but deplete; a serum can only enter the organism as a foreign substance and a virus remains a virus when it enters the commonwealth of body cells."*[cxlv]

He made the point that as osteopaths "we ought to know why these things are so". Thus, defining why comparative Materia Medica might be of benefit. His main point, put very succinctly in this article Osteopathy and its Colleges, was that *"if the practitioner is to be the family physician and surgeon, to practice surgery, to differentiate between osteopathic and surgical cases, to give an antidote, to administer an anesthetic, to determine the extent of the evil effects upon the system of the use or overdose of certain drugs and to devise means of overcoming these effects and getting rid of the drug action in the system.... he should be thoroughly qualified for such practice."* It is evident that many agreed with him, and that the "M.D. Osteopathic" degree had the potential to overcome many difficulties. The degree, itself, he felt was "a minor consideration". The all-important matter is the course of study, the college equipment and above all loyalty[44] to the osteopathic principle".[cxlvi]

---

[44] Having laid the foundation as an independent school of practice, I do not believe we mean to back down, or permit ourselves to be assimilated. As colleges we need to stand shoulder to shoulder. Do not let dissensions weaken our ranks. Do not let jealousy open the entering wedge of dismemberment. My individual viewpoint of the osteopathic principle and its application may be and must be different from yours. This however does not alter the unalterable principle, nor does it diminish my loyalty or yours to the principle of osteopathy. (Littlejohn; Osteopathy and its Colleges; JAOA February 1910, page 226).

However, osteopathic politics got in the way. Here we see the clash between the principled Reformed Presbyterian culture and the American Politician. Hildreth and Charles Still seemed to play to the galleries, not recognise the fundamental problem that their education system did not provide those graduating with the tools to become fully fledged family physicians. Sticking to their restricted ideas, an Osteopath was a specialist, someone who would step in were others failed. Littlejohn, on the other hand, saw the problem, and what was a greater sin, saw a solution and tried to put it into action.

When the leadership, the A.O.A., did not grasp the problem then those who felt their education was lacking, not necessarily lacking 'drugs', had nowhere to go except medical colleges.

Politically, Littlejohn was no match for the politician. Simply put he would not engage in political manoeuvring. As we have said before, Hildreth had a personal against Littlejohn and Charles Still showed how far he was prepared to go to get dirt on Him. Both of these seemed determined to undermine an idea if it came from Littlejohn, using the invocation of "our founder" as a rallying call to generate "temptation to appear ultra-orthodox as a play to the galleries". Littlejohn would have been seen as a dangerous foe as he had a compelling argument that did not lead to subservience to orthodox medicine, at the same time he was putting his ideas into practice while recognising that many osteopathic graduates were going to medical colleges to fill in the gaps in their education. He wanted to get away from negative legislation.[45] This was something that Hildreth and Charles Still amongst others seemed content to rant about but not offer anything positive.

---

[45] "Most of our legislation is in negatives, not the practice of medicine, not use medicines, not use operative surgery-while our system is a school of medicine if it is a true system of healing. The parent school was chartered to teach such sciences and arts as are usually taught in medical colleges and in addition thereto the science of osteopathy." and was authorized to grant and confer such honors and degrees as are usually granted and conferred by reputable medical colleges."(Osteopathy and its Colleges; JAOA February 1910, page 225).

(Charles Still, in 1914,[46] even went as far as opening a school for granting the M.D. degree in Kirksville, even though it was opposed by the osteopathic student body in Kirksville and the British Osteopathic Association[cxlvii] and was short lived).[cxlviii]

The debate continued in the JAOA, and again came to a head in 1911 when Comstock wrote an article, published in the Bulletin of Health and the Journal of the American Osteopathic Association, titled 'The Littlejohn College Idea.' In the September edition of the JAOA, the editorial made a critical analysis of the article and accusing Comstock of getting 'entirely away from the Osteopathic idea' and the Littlejohn College of being 'apologetic of drugs'. In conclusion it says that 'If the letter printed in this issue and the article from which these excerpts are made from the official bulletin of the college represent the position of the college accurately, it is safe to say that either the Littlejohn College is wrong or almost the entire profession, which believes differently, is wrong."[cxlix]

Comstock's idea was straight forward. He found *"In conversing with a number of the visiting osteopaths at the A. O. A. Convention in July, I found that there is a misunderstanding among many of them regarding the principles of osteopathy as taught in the Littlejohn College and Hospital",[cl]* and he wanted to correct this impression. He explained that all lesions need attention, including Structural, environment, mental, diet and occupational fields. The other articles the editor quotes are from the 'Bulletin of Health', published by the Littlejohn College and whose editor at the time was Dr. W. E. Elfrink. In the December 1910 edition he had laid down what could be seen as a challenge to the A.O.A. and the upcoming convention in Chicago, saying that the A.O.A. must take "*a more

---

[46] The announcement is made in Kirksville that Drs. Charles E. Still, George A. Still, S. S. Still and Mr. E. C. Brott will open the Missouri Valley Medical College in the old Ward School property in that city, in which full credit will be given to graduates of osteopathic colleges for the work done in securing their D. O. degree. That is to say, those who studied two or three years and received their osteopathic degree may enter it and study two or one year more, respectively, and receive an M. D. degree. There is nothing new in this except the location of the proposed school and the names mentioned as responsible for it.(Journal of American Osteopathic Association, March 1914, page 379; see also May 1914, page 535)

enlightened attitude towards the field of therapy generally or there will be a new organisation to give this sentiment expression" [cli]

He also made the point how the Littlejohn College, as the only osteopathic college in Chicago, had been largely ignored by the organisers of the A.O.A. Convention to be held in July in Chicago. Obviously, relations between the A.O.A. and the Littlejohn College were not great at the time. This and the events at the convention, gives some background to the editorial in the September 1911 issue of the J.A.O.A.

The Editor attributes the quotes which he says are 'apologetic to drugs' as being indicative of the policy of the college. They come from an article by Dr. Elfrink titled 'Why not tell the truth' in the August 15th, 1911 issue of the 'Bulletin of Health'. He had not printed Comstock's article saying, *"we declined to print until it had been submitted to Dr. J. Martin Littlejohn and at his request given publicity"*, thus implying that it carried Littlejohn's imprimatur. Littlejohn's comments are worth reading in full as they not only deal with the criticism but also give us an indication not only that he had left the College but also some of the reasons why he did so. Littlejohn's comments were a published in the October issue of the J.A.O.A., were he says:

"As you make me personally responsible, in your editorial on the Littlejohn College Idea, for the publication of the letter of Dr. Comstock, I ask you to publish a brief statement. I had no idea when it was submitted to me that such approval meant publication on my say-so. It deserved publication on its merits

In the first place it meant to call attention to certain unjust criticisms which demanded attention. In the second place, a careful reading of the entire article will show that it fulfilled that purpose in a clear cut and concise manner. Dr. Comstock was one of the best students in an exceptionally bright class and understands what osteopathy is and its claims. Osteopathy will be painstakingly advanced by his work. Third, I believe you have somewhat misinterpreted his meaning.

He goes on to explain that if something is missing in the diet it should be provided and if the cause is lack of assimilation, then the lesions should be corrected. It was not to be taken that food elements should be used as 'medicine/drugs'.

"Nowhere does he (Comstock) recommend the use of medicines except as emergency remedies, antiseptics, anaesthetics, and antidotes for poisons. He says in the paragraph quoted "which might be termed medicinal" —to cover the well-known fact that olive oil, cod-liver oil, bone-marrow, etc., have been classified as medicinal. I do not think myself that you are correct in saying this is beyond osteopathic thought and procedure. These supplied, as he stated, on a food basis, are a part of the adjusted constituents of the body.... Remember, however, it is not a question of medicinal action, but one of body assimilation —dietetic"

. **In the other quotation you give you quote from a signed article representing the personal opinions of a single writer**. You might have quoted other statements from the Bulletin. Dr. Inwood, in the July number, writes, "Our chief and distinctive method is manipulation. Success is based on the fact that our physical treatment is converted into its physiological equivalent. We believe in and use antiseptics, antidotes, anaesthetics, scientific dieting, psychology, etc." Here, as in other quotations that might be made, the extent to which drugs are used is stated specifically and this is in line with our osteopathic ideas.

In this he gives a very robust answer to the accusations dismissing the comments about Elfrink's article as "*a signed article representing the personal opinions of a single writer*". This would seem to be a clear indication that he did not agree with the content of Elfrink's article " Why not tell the *truth*?"

In particular, Elfink's question " *if we ask, 'do drugs cure disease?' The answer must be no. But if we ask whether or not drugs are useful in the treatment of certain diseases, we must answer 'yes', if we would tell the truth. Is there a drug which will cure pneumonia? Emphatically, no. Are any drugs useful in the treatment of pneumonia? Yes, but they are not indispensable. An osteopath can do more in this disease than any drug or combination of drugs. But in the absence of an osteopath a skilful physician can often give remedies which will to a certain extent alleviate the symptoms and possibly shorten the course of the disease. If he is called early, he may even be able to abort the disease altogether. Shall we in view of these facts, which cannot be disproven, go before the world and say that drugs are useless in pneumonia? We have a right to say that osteopathic treatment is better than drug treatment, but we have no right to say that drugs are entirely useless.*

This kind of misinformation spread abroad will be certain to do harm especially if it has the sanction of the profession as a body".[clii]

Elfrink goes on to describe the case of a friend of his who died from Tuberculosis. His friend, in Elfrink's opinion, had died because he had *"blundered in his diet"* and had believed that *"nothing mattered except fresh air and diet"* and this because he had absorbed a lot of misinformation he had read in popular journals. In an article he wrote called 'The Differentiation between food and drugs' he makes clear his viewpoint that while to some it is easy to make the distinction between food and drugs, it is in fact quite difficult when looked at from an unprejudiced viewpoint. This gives some background to Elfrink's reasoning.

From the political osteopath's point of view, it did not matter what Elfrink's reasons were, just that he seemed to be 'apologetic for drugs." This article by Elfrink was part of a trend in the Bulletin of Health, under Elfrink's editorship[47], going further than Littlejohn in his reasoning about drug therapy and putting the case that " *if there is any virtue in drugs at all Osteopaths ought to avail themselves of it*"[cliii] This was part of the argument of whether osteopaths should or would be 'office specialists'- and thus limited in their practice to being specialists in mechanical adjustments; or family physicians. Another aspect of the so-called drug/medicine argument within osteopathy was again summed up by Elfrink

"But even though drugs were absolutely useless, it would be a serious mistake to continue the plan of prohibiting osteopaths from using them. The very fact that we are not allowed to use them places us in an inferior position. It is one thing not to use drugs because we

---

[47] He became editor in 1910 after Littlejohn who had been editor from 1905: *"Unfortunately, some factional feeling is shown n criticisms of graduates of other colleges for their attitude towards the Littlejohn institution. However, notwithstanding the expression of this feeling, a willingness is expressed to co-operate with the Illinois Osteopathic Association and the American Osteopathic Association to make the national convention in Chicago a big success". The Osteopathic Physician, January 1911, page 13*

do not believe in them, and quite another thing to be deprived of the right to use them by law"[cliv]

This has to be seen, not as wanting to be able to use drugs, but as part of the wider discussion about restricted or 'second class' practice. Even Hildreth tended in this direction while avoiding the use of the taboo word 'Drugs':

"I want to go farther and say to you that I as an individual am strictly opposed to any legislation whatever looking to the control of the practice of medicine. I believe in the broadest possible freedom. —a freedom which will guarantee the greatest possible liberty to scientific investigation and research. discovery and progress...I believe to-day the people of this country would be better off if there was not a medica practice act on the statutes except one directing handling the of contagious diseases, and all schools should be obliged to use the same care to prevent the spreading of those diseases, but should be allowed to treat the cases as they please."[clv]

Littlejohn, in response to the editorial on Comstock's article, clearly and unequivocally put his opinion on 'drugs':

"The Littlejohn College has never believed in or taught the use of drugs as medicinal agents, nor has it ever represented that "the physician schooled in drugs is the only learned and adequately equipped practitioner." In fact, it has taught just the opposite, that the osteopathic system is an independent system of therapy, that the osteopathic practitioner is a physician just as truly as any other physician of any school and as such is entitled to equalled rights and privileges. The only recognition it has ever given to medicines has been as stated above, the antiseptics, anaesthetics and antidotes of surgery and toxicology, and these only when used in compliance with the principles of adjustment"...

"Many times, I have stated, in the A. O. A. Journal, on its platforms and elsewhere, that I have no use for drugs, beyond knowing the uses other doctors have made or them, first, to avoid them, and, second, to compare our methods with theirs and the results..... This College has applied these principles to the treatment of diseases generally, to the surgical field, to the field of diet, to the field of emergency, because the osteopath should be competent to deal with all conditions that arise in connection with disease"...

"I do not believe that we need to take on drug therapy or take our manipulation into drug therapy. We must realize, however, that manipulation is not osteopathy, but is a means used by the osteopath when such adjustment is called for. There are cases in which other means, such as diet, climate, Nature herself represent osteopathy.

Then to put into a clinical setting he cites the case of tuberculosis that had been mistreated by so-called specific osteopathic treatment:

"A schoolteacher who had tuberculosis was treated osteopathically and so great was the damage done that the patient claimed the ribs were broken, which they were not. Patient was out of school work for two years. Now she is back in school work perfectly well, cured in Chicago climate, and during three years received about twenty manipulative treatments, absolutely no medicine of any kind".

Then to again show how this approach was put into practice in the Littlejohn College, he gives detail of the hours devoted to teaching each subject, showing that its approach is distinctly osteopathic in diagnosis and therapy, with the inclusion of other subjects to "complete the general education of the practitioner, not to make him a drug therapist."

"It is but justice to state, that no College has taught more forcibly the self-sufficiency of the organism than Littlejohn College. Granted normal structural adjustment with the adjusted conditions of diet and environment the body will be in a state of health. During the last year, 1910-11, In the four-year course 864 hours were devoted to the osteopathic principles and practice, outside of the time spent in clinical treatments and the specialties, such as osteopathic obstetrics and gynecology over 300 hours; whereas only 108 hours were devoted to the physiological action and uses of anaesthetics, antiseptics, anodynes and antidotes and comparative therapeutics; in the latter class most of the time being given to the comparison of drug and osteopathic methods of action to show the excellence of the osteopathic."

In finishing this defence of his College, he reaffirms his conviction and belief in the principles of Osteopathy:

"*Personally, I have ever been loyal to osteopathy. Its principle is an abiding truth, the comprehensiveness of which we have not yet begun to realize in its application to the human organism.* It remains for the researches of patient laborers to demonstrate that when this principle is applied to the fields of pathology, diagnosis and treatment to the full extent of its application, there will be built up a system that will survive every other system, because that system is based upon the eternal truth of the self-sufficiency of the organism.".[clvi]

The article is then signed:

J. Martin Littlejohn, D. O.; Lake Bluff, Ill.

As we mentioned earlier, there were persons within his own college that did not help his argument that the Littlejohn College, or as it was known earlier, The American College of Osteopathic Medicine and Surgery, was purely osteopathic and did not mix osteopathy with regular medicine or drugs. We mentioned Dr. Hamlin previously as an example of this.

Dr. Elfrink could also be put into this category, even though, in truth, he was ever loyal to the osteopathic principle. His tendency to push for truthful recognition of the position of the regular Physician's work was often taken as him being in favour of mixing treatments, as evidenced by the editorial the September 1911 JAOA., mentioned above.

Littlejohn's opinion on 'medicine and drugs' can be put into the wider context of the arguments within osteopathy.

Dr. E. M. Downing's' classification of osteopaths was quoted by Elfrink in the June 15th, 1911 issue of the Bulletin of Health. In this article Downing, who was an associate editor of the JAOA and on the Board of Trustees of the American Osteopathic Association and the A. T. Still Research Institute[clvii], gave the following classification:

"*There are those who insistently proclaim themselves as 'bony-lesion osteopaths.' They cry aloud their allegiance to the Old Doctor. Since the revered founder of the osteopathic system, Dr. A. T. Still, is a bony-lesionist, it seems to them disloyal to acknowledge the possibility of any other cause of disease than a displacement. or abnormal relation of tissues. They are willing to be called narrow; yea, they glory in it. For is not Dr. Still narrow? Since their concept of disease causation is limited to tissue displacement. Their treatment is limited to replacement, or correction of lesions; and they rarely undertake any cases that call them away from their offices. They deserve and receive our respect, for almost without exception, they are among the most successful practitioners.*

"There are others, also bony-lesion osteopaths, who through observation and experience, have become convinced that there exist other causes for disease than displacement of structures. They find hereditary factors that often compel consideration and they discover habits, as well as lesions of the spine that need correction. They study the environment and methods of thought of their patients, and their treatment is often directed more to other conditions than to palpable structural faults. We must respect these osteopathists, for they sire sincere. earnest students, and successful practitioners.

"Still others there are, who maintain that they, too, are bony-lesion osteopaths, who find cases and conditions which according to their best judgment require something besides manipulative treatment. These are not content to do only an office practice. It is their ambition to be general practitioners, to minister to suffering humanity, whatever aliment is presented. They do not wish to have to refuse a ease of smallpox or syphilis, a compound fracture, or a tubercular joint with abscesses pointing in several directions, hemorrhoidal tumors complicated with fissures and fistulae, acute indigestion, and extensive burn involving the deep structures, or any acute infectious diseases. They are earnest, studious workers and thinkers, whose sincerity cannot be called into question, and they, too, command our respect.

"Then we have a small class who are indifferent who are content to just " go along," as politicians say; who do not fraternize or affiliate with their fellow practitioners. Not all of them are indifferent in the sense that they are indifferent operators; some are very successful practitioners. But they are not advancing osteopathy. They are building up a following around their own personality, which in no wise counts for the advancement of osteopathic principles. This class, though by no means negligible, is quite small.

"Now it happens that I have had unusual opportunities for confidential talks with a large number of osteopathists in all of the classes mentioned. I know whereof I speak when I say that (leaving out the indifferent ones), the profession as a whole is loyal in the superlative degree to the basic osteopathic principle. To a man they believe in it, work for it, and will, if need be, fight for it. This is equally true of' the liberal minded practitioner and the osteopathist of one idea, and it is one of the most telling facts in osteopathic annals.

"I have observed that, generally speaking, the men who have taken medical courses and obtained medical degrees, remain firm and steadfast in their adherence to the fundamentals of osteopathy. I have observed also that those who limit their practice to office work are frequently the ones who are most vehement in proclaiming that " simon-pure" osteopathy (the ten-finger kind, limited to manipulative methods Alone) constitute a complete system, adequate to cope with any and all emergencies – that the osteopathist is not a specialist, but an all-around physician.[48]

"I present these observations as having a distinct bearing on the status of the profession. and have no doubt that others will verify them."[clviii]

Elfrink comments on this saying: "Dr. Downing's attitude toward the unification of the profession to the extent of doing away with all sectarianism in medicine seems to be well taken.
..... Those osteopaths who specialize in office work and treat only the chronic conditions which can be treated entirely without medical measures, should learn to appreciate the position of their brother osteopaths who are in smaller cities or are trying to conduct general practices including every kind of' acute illness met with in the life of a visiting practitioner."[clix]

This classification puts the division within osteopathy into perspective. It was widespread and Littlejohn himself occupied a clear middle ground within it.

It would be a simple opinion to come to that the middle ground of those like Littlejohn, Downing etc would be overshadowed by the extremes that appealed to the strong emotional responses. However, it is also plausible that the personal angst of Hildreth and Charlie Still in particular was an influential strong undercurrent.

---

[48] He studiously avoids the drug question except for one sentence; "This, it should be understood, does not mean the inclusion of discredited drug therapy"

This tendency of some of those associated with his College to move towards the extreme end of wanting to be 'Osteopathic Physicians, by wanting to be allowed to use 'drugs etc.' if they felt it necessary would have been one factor in his resigning from the College. Another, within the college itself, may have been the growth of 'Fraternities'. However, to get a clearer picture the important thing is to put the timing of this debate and events into the context of what was happening in his life in general, not just within his college. It is quite easy to forget that Littlejohn was a family and religious person and not only an osteopath.

In 1907/08 he had completed his research into cancer[49] and published the results in the JAOA. The use of anti-dotes, using potentization or dynamization on the bioplasmic plane brought some criticism-again on the grounds of using 'medicine' or re-inventing homeopathic medicine; further we have to remember the possible effect of using animals in experiments may have had on him. This was quickly followed by the 1909 A.O.A. convention discussed above, the Flexner Report in 1910, the arguments about the M.D. degree and the meaning of 'Drugs', the continued failure in the fight with the State Board of Health, the strain on his wife and family and the hardest blow on a personal level, the Loss of his Mother in 1911.

Littlejohn had six children at this time, the youngest, Elizabeth Alice, was born on 14th September 1910, in the middle of the worst of the controversy. The last part of this, the so-called 'Littlejohn College Idea' came at a time when his mother was on her last illness and just before his resignation was published in the November 1911 issue of the J.A.O.A.

The next notable thing about his response was his signature. It simply said, ' **J. Martin Littlejohn, D. O.; Lake Bluff, Ill'**. It did use his normal title of 'President of the Littlejohn College' or mention any connection with it. This would tend to imply that he had already

---

[49] Dr. J. M. Littlejohn has reached the tentative conclusion that the neoplasmic diseases, like tuberculosis, cancer, etc., are all based on toxicosis, the toxic conditions involving primarily the blood and nervous system; localization taking place through injury, hyper-irritation, sub irritability, and non-use of organs and structures. He is fully equipped for experimental work and will continue along the lines of his previous work. (A. T. Still research institute report, JAOA Sept 1909 Page 12)

resigned and that he withheld publicity until the November issue of the J.A.O.A., that is until after he had informed family and colleagues. The announcement was as follows:

> *"Dr. J. Martin Littlejohn, who has been President of the Littlejohn College and Hospital of Chicago since it was founded in 1900, has resigned from active connection with the institution, and has been succeeded by Dr. Jas. B. littlejohn".*[clx]

This would, in all probability, date his resignation to, at the latest, somewhere in October 1911. However, if we consider his signature to his letter in the October issue, which would have to have been written in September, it is more likely that his resignation came around the beginning of the College term on September 18th. The annual announcement for 1911/12 was published in June 1911 and listed Littlejohn as President[clxi]. He had to forgo presenting his paper at the A.O.A. Convention in Chicago in July 1911, in all probability due to his mothers' illness. In December 1911, Charles Still wrote to James Buchan Littlejohn, while offering condolences for his mother's death, asked if it was correct that "JM has severed his connection with the school",[clxii] which confirms the timing.

All of these things influenced his move to Lake Bluff, his resignation from the Littlejohn College and Hospital and finally to his move to England.

LAKE BLUFF

Early in 1911 Littlejohn purchased a property in Lake Bluff. This purchase was completed on April 12th, 1911 for a price of $1715.[clxiii] He then sold his property in Adams street on May 17th, 1911[clxiv] and moved his family from Chicago. Lake Bluff was about a 60-minute train journey from Chicago, so not a difficult commute.

One of the attractions of Lake Bluff would have been its strong Scottish community and its association with the Chautauqua Movement. It was in the summer of 1881 that the national Prohibition Party was form at a meeting in Lake Bluff; and this resulted in the passage of the 18th amendment to the United States

> *"The Lake Bluff camp meeting was greatly influenced by the Chautauqua movement that began in Upstate New York at Lake Chautauqua. The concept was to provide cultural, social, religious educational, and recreational experiences for families in a beautiful natural environment. This new summer resort, enhanced by direct train transportation from Chicago, was modeled. After Oak Bluffs Martha's Vineyard….*
>
> *Thousands flocked here during the summer months to enjoy the lake's cool breezes, the white sandy beaches, and the leafy shade of the ravines while participating in the. many lectures assemblies, and events offered by the Lake Bluff Camp Meeting- Association. Classes were held in such. things as foreign language, music, photography, and elocution. Kindergarten was offered for young children, allowing the adults to enjoy the varied activities offered by the Chautauqua summer programs".*
>
> Post Card History series
> Lake Bluff Lyndon Jensen and Kathleen O'Hara;
> Arcadia publishing

Constitution By 1911 Lake Bluff was evolving from summer resort into a North Shore suburb of Chicago.[clxv]

Why, at this stage would he move his family? Many factors would probably have played a part. We know from the number of trips he made back to Scotland and Europe that he longed for his homeland. A report in the Clarinda Herald April 7, 1896, gives a clue of how he felt about his homeland and his family.

"Dr. Littlejohn's mother and two brothers arrived from Scotland. Of course, the Dr. never gets homesick, but he does look real cheerful since the completion of the family circle. One of his brothers will assist him in conducting his classes."

His mother was getting on in years and it would be reasonable to assume she longed for real Scottish company. She would not have considered moving back to Scotland as her husband was buried in Kirksville and it would be inconceivable for her, given her background, both Presbyterian and Scots, to be buried anywhere other than with her husband. She did express this wish before her passing to Littlejohn.[50] He would not return to Scotland and leave his mother. Lake Bluff would seem like a good compromise.

Another aspect would have been the young children, a move to a more country type environment, away from the difficulties and temptations offered by the city again might have been a factor.

---

[50] In a will written in 1912, Littlejohn attests to his mothers' wish to be buried with her husband in the 'family plot in the Necropolis, Glasgow'. (NOA archive, Wellcome Library). Her two children that had passed away in childhood were buried in that plot. The Index to the burial registers shows that only 4 burials took place in lair no 89 in compartment Petra and the information from the burial registers is below. Elizabeth and James Littlejohn were certainly not buried in this grave post 1899.
Littlejohn, Buchan   Buried 16/11/1863; Age 6y 6m; 27, Taylor St,
Littlejohn, David   Buried 27/11/1869; Age 41y; Royal Infirmary,
Littlejohn, Janet A Buried 4/11/1863; Age 4y 6m; 27, Taylor St,
Scott, Mary   Buried 11/10/1865; Age 23y; 93, Rottenrow, Glasgow
(Historical and Genealogical Researcher, Friends of Glasgow Necropolis)

The move was not to go well, however. His mother fell ill during the summer of 1911 and Littlejohn had to miss the A.O.A. convention in Chicago[clxvi] to look after her and his young family, his wife having recently given birth to their sixth child, Elizabeth in September 1910.

This event was to change the course of his life. It would undoubtedly become clear to Littlejohn, the physician, that his mother was very ill. Given his devotion to his family and mother, he would want to spend as much time with her as possible, also his wife would need help with the children with the recent arrival of their sixth child. In this light and given the 'support' of some of the College lecturers for the use of 'drugs', albeit in certain circumstances only, the drift in the life of the college to Fraternities, and the strain of the previous years with the fight with the State board of Health, the Flexner report and prior to that the Teall report, it would seem to have been the logical thing to retire from the college.

It was duly announced in the November edition of the Journal of the American Osteopathic Association. As detailed above, this would, in all probability, date his resignation letter to somewhere in September/October 1911.

Littlejohn always followed proper procedure and would have personally told those closely associated with him in the college of his decision prior to making a public announcement. This would tend to imply that the decision may have been made as early as September or even August, prior to the start of the 1911/12 term.

If we take into account that he stopped editing the college magazine at the end of 1910 and that Walter E. Elfrink M.D., D.O., was editor in December1910[clxvii], we could say he started his move from the college work when he was starting his move to Lake Bluff.

We can see that he had made the decision to move his family from America back to Great Britain by august 1912, as he had he ask for a letter of standing from the Iowa Presbytery, which was granted at the presbytery meeting on September 10th 1912, so he could attach to the R P Church in Scotland[clxviii].

His personality was such that he would have told those who would be personally affected by this decision prior to taking any public action. this would seem to indicate that he had discussed this matter with his brother, which led him to take the action he did. The fact that Littlejohn was going to leave the country and therefore not going to rejoin the College seems to have been the force behind James B. moving to reorganize, or close, the college.

The next steps for Littlejohn was to clear up his affairs in America and make arrangements for a life across the water.

The Will he wrote in 1912, undated apart from the year, paints a picture of a man who thought that he was in the last throes of life and was intent on putting his affairs in order. In this document he sets out detailed instructions on his assets and outlines his desires and wishes for his children. He wanted them to have a *'suitable education' and that 'some or all of them qualify themselves in Osteopathic Science so as to take up and continue the work to which my own was dedicated. It was my purpose to establish a sanatorium in England for the maintenance of this method of Treatment and if my wife and Children can see their way to devote the home that I have made provision for to the purpose it would be a fitting memorial of my life work'*[clxix] Why England and not Scotland? The best answer I have come across was when I asked J. Wernham why did Littlejohn leave America? He said he had asked Littlejohn the same question and Littlejohn's reply was **"Mabel wanted to come home"**. In the Will mentioned above Littlejohn gives a clear expression of his feelings for his wife, saying that he had *'devoted his life to her love and service. Often misunderstood there was but one ambition, to remain loyal to the first and only love of my wife and children, I cannot give them more than the remembrance of that love and its perpetuation in the land of love in the presence of Jesus Christ My Lord'*[clxx] It seems likely Littlejohn himself would have preferred to move to Scotland, Glasgow in particular as he considered this his true home. However, he deferred to his wife. She had had a hard life before her marriage, losing her father at a young age.[51] Then she moved to America at 21yrs old, possibly under the impression that her

---

[51] Her Father died of 'Acute Rheumatism Pericarditis in 1893 (Death Certificate from Ipswich archives

new husband would be returning to England/Scotland and not making America their permanent home. It would be easy, given Littlejohn's numerous trips home from America and his referring to himself as an "exile from my native land by the Medical profession on the ground of ill health",[clxxi] to see him giving his wife to be the impression, if not the promise, that they would make England/Scotland their permanent home in good time.

The best times for crossing the Atlantic was during the summer months. This would point to summer 1913 as the proposed time to move. Finding a suitable property in England was the main stumbling block. The best way would be to employ an agent in England to search/advertise and to liaise until such a property was found

He booked to sail on the S. S. Corinthian from Montreal and Quebec to London, departing Sunday June 29th, 1913[clxxii], arriving in London in or around 11th July 1913. From there the family travelled to their new home at Badger Hall Thundersley, Essex. In respect of this journey, consisting of his family and wagons laden with his goods, furniture etc, his student John Wernham said, "it must have been quite a sight travelling through the English countryside".

THE PATH TO ENGLAND

It is important to understand not only what led to his return to England but also the sequence of events. One source of information is the following quote from an article by J. O'Brien on the Littlejohn brothers:

"Rumblings of discontent among faculty and Illinois colleagues came to a head when JML was told by a delegation of the LCO faculty, he must reapply for the position of LCO president. There were only two applicants for job, JML and James, who had been propositioned by the staff to apply. The result was a foregone conclusion, James was appointed, in his place JML resigned from the faculty to make plans to return to Britain. James's action was perceived by JML as an act of treachery, both brothers sold their controlling interests in the LCO to a consortium of Illinois colleagues, headed by osteopathic heavy weight, Carl McConnell. From this sale emerged the Chicago College of Osteopathy (CCO) under McConnell as head and James, his deputy".[clxxiii]

It is well known that events are often mis-remembered even by those involved. Therefore, the best way of unravelling history is to look at the timeline of events, whose dates have been recorded.

- **October 1911** (announced in November JAOA) - Latest date of Littlejohn's resignation from the Littlejohn College given his announcement in the November 1911 JAOA
- **Sept/October 1911**. Article in JAOA in response to criticism of Comstock's article ('The Littlejohn College Idea in Sept 1911) he signed it 'J. Martin Littlejohn, D. O.; Lake Bluff, Ill.' (JAOA, October 1911 Page 727-8) – no mention of being 'president of the littlejohn College'
- **November 1911** - Mother passes away; James B. "Raised to Master Mason" two days prior to mothers death.
- **December 8th, 1911-** Charles Still writes to James B. Littlejohn asking for confirmation that Littlejohn has severed his connection with the Littlejohn College.[clxxiv]
- **May 21, 1912** - Charles Still writes to James B. Littlejohn about "fight lost by osteopaths" (concerning the case against the State Board of Health)[clxxv]

- **July 26, 1912** - Unsigned letter, from the C. E. Still. Collection, concerning "finishing up the Littlejohn College and what to do with the buildings and students".[clxxvi]
- ***1912** - James B. and his wife Edith Williams were the only members of the Littlejohn College left with the college, this led to consideration of widening its scope and broadening the board of trustees.[clxxvii]
- **July 24, 1912**-J. B. Littlejohn writes by telegram to Charles Still "for good of Osteopathy have endeavoured harmonise all interests in Chicago. Name made Chicago College of Osteopathy Strictly Osteopathic"[clxxviii](ATSU museum 1980.375.02.45) (given the date of this telegram, July 24, and the date of the 'unsigned letter, July 26 and the source of the letter, in the C. E. Still collection at the ASTU, it seems reasonable to assume the letter was from Charlie or Harry Still.)
- a letter of standing from the Iowa Presbytery, which was granted at the presbytery meeting **on September 10th, 1912**, so he could attach to the R P Church in Scotland
- **September 1912** - Osteopathic Physician notes that the Littlejohn College would be known as the Chicago Osteopathic College sometime in the future.[clxxix] (Osteopathic Physician Sept. 1912, page 5)
- **September 7th, 1912;** The littlejohn College Alumni meeting heard remarks on "Efforts to unite the Illinois Osteopaths" by Dr. J. B. Littlejohn
- **October 1912-** group of representative osteopathic physicians of Chicago met in offices of Dr. Carl P. McConnell to consider the future of the College. This led to an agreement that a new organisation, representative of all groups of osteopaths in Chicago should be formed to continue an Osteopathic college and that the Littlejohn College should cease to exist[clxxx].
- "During the **Autumn of 1912** some of the alumni of the Littlejohn College and Hospital began a series of conferences with Dr. J. B. Littlejohn to see if means could be devised to convert the College into a professionally institution instead of one privately owned. After several such conferences a meeting of several Chicago osteopaths was called at the

offices of Dr. Carl P. McConnell in October for the purposes of taking steps to accomplish this change. (Edgar S. Comstock, The Reflex 1923)

- *February 1913 - mass meeting of Chicago Osteopaths, in Mrs. Ellis's Tea Room, to consider the matter.[clxxxi]
- *March 4th, 1913 - a permanent organisation was made, and board of trustees elected.[clxxxii]
- *July 1st, 1913 - the new organisation took control[clxxxiii] (*History of Chicago College of Osteopathy; J. B. Littlejohn, The Reflex 1929.
- **June 26th, 1913** Littlejohn transferred the title of the College Building to James B. Littlejohn for $10 (ten dollars) said to be valued at $15,000. At the same time, 1420 west Monroe (the next door building as far as I can tell) was transferred to J. B. Littlejohn by B. A. Eckhart for a nominal fee, the building said to be valued at $10,000.[clxxxiv]
- **Sunday June 29th, 1913**[clxxxv], Littlejohn sailed on the S. S. Corinthian to London, departing arriving in London in or around 11th July 1913.

From this it becomes immediately clear that Littlejohn resigned before the efforts to re-organise the College which eventually led to the formation of the Chicago College of Osteopathy; the loss of the fight with the State Board of Health was the next major event after Littlejohn's resignation, followed closely by the 'unsigned' letter offering to help wind up the college and James Buchan's telegram saying that "for good of Osteopathy have endeavoured harmonise all interests in Chicago. Name made Chicago College of Osteopathy Strictly Osteopathic".

This gives a different picture from the account by O'Brien quoted above which implied that Littlejohn was sacked and had a serious falling out with his Brother James B. If he did have any cause to 'fall out' with his brother it was more likely to have to do with his mother's death and the fact that James B. re-joined the Masons only two days prior to their mothers passing.

In any event he transferred the ownership of the college buildings to James Buchan for $10 fulling his claim "*I am glad to see the consummation of unity and harmony in the establishment you announce (Formation of the new Chicago College of Osteopathy). For this I hoped earnestly during the passing years. If I am not there it is because, like one greater than myself, I "laid down my life" in trying to establish a foundation upon which such a college might be built; and I helped to hold the fort until the greater developments you announce were rendered possible."*

The building was purchased by J. Martin Littlejohn in June 1908 for $10,000[clxxxvi]. This was described as Monroe St., 75 feet west of Loomis and was transferred to James B. Littlejohn by his brother on June 26th 1913, improved with two story dwelling for $10 (ten dollars) said to be valued at $15,000[52]. At the same time, 1420 west Monroe (the next door building as far as I can tell) was transferred to J. B. Littlejohn by B. A. Eckhart for a nominal fee, the building said to be valued at $10,000.[clxxxvii]; James Buchan apparently consolidating the College and Hospital buildings in his name.

---

[52] It is likely the building had mortgage or debt on it and this was transferred together with the building

A REVIEW

1910 was a mixed year for the college. It moved into a new building, fraternities[53] and 'secret society' membership,[54] became more established within the college and the fallout from the Flexner report all having an effect.

> *"Membership in secret societies involves taking an oath before being aware of the obligation. No man is at liberty to bind his conscience by oath without a knowledge of the nature and extent of his undertaking. In doing so he is being bound to a law other than, and, in the light of further knowledge, possibly in conflict with, the revealed law of god".*
> (the website of the of Newtownards Reformed Presbyterian Church Northern Ireland)

It is important to understand what it was about 'secret societies', fraternities etc that Littlejohn would have objected. It would not necessarily have been their objectives. In many cased he would have supported the objectives, for example building a sense of

---

[53] The Bulletin of Health announcement number for 1911/12 lists the following fraternities; Phi Alpha Beta; Iota tau Sigma; Phi Delta Sigma sorority.

[54] For example ; **Dr. Fryette is professor of osteopathic technic in the Littlejohn College.** Dr. Fryette is an independent republican in his political connection, usually supporting the principles of the party, and yet not hesitating to support his honest convictions, whether at variance with the opinions of political leaders or not. He is **prominent in Masonry**, holding membership in Lake View Lodge, No. 774, A.F. & A. M., in Oriental Consistory and in Medinah Temple of the Mystic Shrine. (CHICAGO: ITS HISTORY AND ITS BUILDERS vol 4 Page 448 Chicago: its history and its builders, a century of marvelous growth, by J. Seymour Currey. (Josiah Seymour), 1844-1928. Chicago, The S. J. Clark publishing company, 1912.)

loyalty to the profession, giving support to each other in their studies, charitable objects, helping those less well-off etc. The effect of 'keeping secrets' would have been seen as a negative, which could create division. The main objection was that of taking an oath to swearing allegiance to an organisation without knowing how that organisation may evolve in the future. Even today this is frowned upon in the Reformed Presbyterian Community.

He had no problem working alongside others of different beliefs, so long as they all worked for the same end, in this case Osteopathy. Renting offices in a building called "the Masonic Temple" was not a problem as it did not involve any obligation other than paying rent. As we saw earlier in Ireland, the Reformed Presbyterian synod saw no problem with the congregation in Liverpool renting their building to the Good Templars. The main problem was the oaths and swearing allegiance, even if it was to his school, together with the idea of 'secrecy'..

One incident that illustrates the problem from a point of view that would have been similar to Littlejohn's was reported in the Christian nation on October 23rd, 1895.

"A struggle in one of the denominational colleges, which recently culminated in the brutal treatment of two anti-fraternity students, may serve to call the attention of Christian people to the character of these college secret orders. The inhuman and indecent treatment found its only excuse in the fact that these students had used their influence against the secret orders. Many of the students insisted that the Faculty should take severe measures to break up the fraternities, but they found, as many have found before them, that secretism which, like its first representative, coils and strikes in the dark, has many advocates in the high places of the earth. In both Faculty and Board were found members of the orders and they did not fail the guilty brethren in the time of need. When it was seen that no redress was to be had from the college authorities, a large body of the best students in the institution, some at considerable sacrifice, went to other schools where there is a quality of fraternity which does not find expression in midnight assaults."[clxxxviii]

This illustrates how the members of so-called secret societies and fraternities may use their influence to assist their own members at the cost of others, irrespective of the rights or wrongs of the situation. A situation that Littlejohn would not have approved off.

While he had no power and probably no inclination to ban such activities of themselves, the growth of them and the idea of secrecy and brotherhood within the fraternity overruling the brotherhood of 'Man' in general, would have worried his conscience. His method was not oppressive nor censorial. We see this in his attitude to osteopathy and osteopathic education. Banning or prohibiting something generally has a negative effect. The method he always favoured was to show a better way and were possible illuminate the defects of such activities.

It is interesting to note Still's attitude to the Masons, as he stated in the Journal of Osteopathy in 1901:

"MASONIC secrecy seems to be a fat, fearful bugaboo or spook. I have been a mason for forty years; I took no obligation that I would be ashamed to take before God or man. I took no obligation of disloyalty to God or government, none to be found in a saloon drunk. I took no obligation to hate everything but masons because they did not see as I did. I took no obligation to meddle with people's religious views, but I did take or promise to be a good citizen with all that means. We have a few signs and words of recognition. In free America that is our privilege under the personal privilege granted! to us in the constitution of the United States".[clxxxix]

In this he speaks of all the aspects that Littlejohn would have been in agreement with but shows no understanding of the problems of 'forswearing'. This is another good example of the difficulties in 'culture' that Littlejohn had to face when he moved to America and thence into the political field of health care in America. The secrecy aspect, while important, would have been a less important objection than forswearing. The taking of an oath and thus making a covenant would have been the main objection. In his life he always took the road of "a declaration of intent" instead of taking an oath of allegiance to 'man made' organisations, whether it was for citizenship[55], to become a lawyer or anything else. College life in America seemed to be moving more in the direction of belonging to some 'secret society' or fraternity/sorority, with some colleges even boasting in their catalogues of how many 'secret societies' they had.[56]

We can get an indication of how he worked with his conscience from part of the text of his talk on 'Osteopathy and its Colleges' published in the February 1910 JAOA. In this talk he advances the role of 'thought' in the "reconstructing process of adjustment" and reconciles Stills dalliance with spiritualism and clairvoyance with his own beliefs.

"Mental force is not outside of the osteopathic field. It was recognized as one of the original factors in the therapeutics of nature by the founder of osteopathy. What a powerful force we have here in our adjustment work. Suggestion pure and simple in all its comprehensive significance as applied to every expressive activity of the body. **Clairvoyance in the sense in which it is understood by the old doctor himself as the power of intercommunion among the spirit forces of the world for the betterment of humanity.** *Thought, what a power! The thought of ugliness, bad temper, suspicion often acts as a disturber of the peace in family and in social circles. Thought, what a factor in the erotic dreams of the neurotic, in the criminal appetites of a Eugene Aram, in the depraved tastes and impulses cultivated and created by the dime novel, in the brutal instinct brought out by formal companionship with the brute element in fellow beings! Osteopathically we must dignify thought, for we are our thought-selves when the guise of hypocrisy wears away."*[57]

The same idea, of his beliefs and background culture in the Reformed Presbyterians, is seen in the 1928 catalogue of the British School of Osteopathy, when he says *"Divine healing is not the healing by miracles....it means the use of all the gifts of healing, the methods of making life pleasurable, which the divine has imparted to the human for the benefit of the body...the spirit has been active in the minds of*

---

[55] The one apparent exception to this was when he re-affirmed his British citizenship in 1924-see chapter on England
[56] Under the heading "Secret Societies at The University of Chicago", the university magazine, 'Cap and Gown', 1898, lists 19 societies and clubs.
[57] Bold emphasis by the author

men... to devise ways and means of preserving the integrity and healthfulness of the human body...we have hands and minds and these can be used as healing agents"

I don't know how he came to the conclusion of the sense in which Still used the word 'clairvoyance'. However, given his predilection to discuss points of theory and philosophy and that the was 'no ordinary student' of Stills, I feel it is safe to assume it was from discussion with Still himself.

One thing he could not reconcile would have been the tendency towards fraternities/sororities in the Littlejohn College, especially if this meant taking an oath or swearing allegiance to the School itself, and thus making a covenant without knowing the extent of the commitment – no one would know how the school would develop it the future and therefore not know if they would or could remain loyal. This would have been especially so given the tendency of some in the Faculty to move towards the 'extreme' end of the 'osteopathic physician' scale, wanting amongst other things full access to all drugs and to use whatever means available in treating patients no matter what school of medicine it came from.

" *Littlejohn College Notes;*

"The completion of the new building is creating considerable interest among the students and outside friends. As evidence of student anticipation and preparation for larger things, two new and healthy fraternities have recently been organized. We are informed that they are not organizations of Hilarity and revelry," but are rather united efforts to further and uphold the principles of osteopathy and maintain a high and worthy loyalty to our college. The friendly enemies are the Pi Alpha Betas and the Sigma Apsilons. The class entering next fall promises to be the largest on record, so far. Many practitioners will enter for post-graduate work. There has also been a demand for night school work. The Seniors report some very good obstetrical cases at the hospital recently.... Publisher Meryren has recently announced Dr. Ford's new book on Surgical Anatomy....

"Dr. Ford, after visiting dissecting rooms of some of our largest medical colleges, informed his students of the Junior class that they were doing as good dissection as he ever saw anywhere".[cxc]

The completion of the new building was, as we can see, accompanied by an expansion, or rather a consolidation of the Fraternity as part of college life. These, of themselves, seem to have been orgainised to 'uphold the principles of osteopathy and maintain a high and worthy loyalty to our college'. However, the inclusion of 'initiation rites and oaths of loyalty would have caused littlejohn some concern, given his deeply held views on 'oath bound societies'. So long as it was not a requirement of being accepted as a student, while he wouldn't be in favour, he would not interfere, but rather put energy into alternatives like the YMCA and YWCA as he did when in Kirksville.

Add to this the extra burden of having a young family, the youngest being born towards the end of 1910, especially on his wife, the stress involved in moving to Lake Bluff, his mother's illness and death in 1911 and his brother's re-involvement in the Masonic order and we get a picture of the complex reasons for Littlejohn's resignation and his move to England.

From this timeline we see that Littlejohn had left the college, voluntarily resigning for personal reasons, the Health of his mother and his own health, stress and strain on his family etc., prior to any meeting about the re-organisation of the college. In fact, the 'unsigned' letter in July 1912 shows that James B. Littlejohn seemed to be at a loss as to what to do with the school now that his brother had left.

There is some confusion as to whether James Buchan started the process or if it was started by a group of alumni including Comstock[58]. From the historical point of view the important point is that J. Martin Littlejohn was not driven out by a revolt or any other activity of alumni or other Chicago osteopaths. It is also important to note

---

[58] James B. Littlejohn gave a talk, on the "Efforts to unify the Illinois Osteopaths" to the Alumni association of the Littlejohn College in September 1912. At the same meeting Comstock gave a talk "The Probable Future of the Profession in this State," (The Osteopathic Physician September 12 page 13)

that in his own words, he moved to England because "Mabel (his wife) wanted to come home"[59]

In his will he also mentions that Dr. George W. Short was to take over practice. Rev. Short is listed in the Chicago Blue Book 1904, as a congregational minister at a church in Roberts Avenue, Chicago and his history is given as

George Washington Denver Short born in Ohio abt 1868, parents also born in Ohio.

1900 Clergyman Sycamore Street, Pleasant, Putnam County, Ohio
1910 Dr Geo Short lived at 3110 Logan Blvd, Chicago
1920 Physician 3110 Logan Blvd
1940 Doctor 3110 Logan Blvd[cxci]

He was also listed in the "Official Register of Legally qualified other practitioners (drugless Healers) Licensed in Illinois prior to July 1st, 1917"[60] as being first certified as an osteopath on June 1st, 1912.

A final point that needs to be addressed is why Littlejohn never fulfilled his mother's "desire that he should place her body and the body of his father in said burial ground (at the Necropolis Glasgow) "wish to be buried with her husband in the family plot in the Necropolis, Glasgow".[cxcii]

The burials that took place in the Littlejohn family plot in the Necropolis are listed in the Index to the burial registers. This shows that only 4 burials took place in lair no 89 in compartment Petra and the information from the burial registers is below.

Littlejohn, Buchan Buried 16/11/1863; Age 6y 6m; 27, Taylor St,
Littlejohn, David Buried 27/11/1869; Age 41y; Royal Infirmary,
Littlejohn, Janet A Buried 4/11/1863; Age 4y 6m; 27, Taylor St,
Scott, Mary Buried 11/10/1865; Age 23y; 93, Rottenrow, Glasgow .
Their records also show that Elizabeth and James Littlejohn were certainly not buried in this grave post 1899.[cxciii]

---

[59] Wernham would give slightly different answers to this question on different occasions. The essential point was always the same, "Mabel wanted to return, and I wanted to retire" was another version

[60] PUBLISHED BY THE ILLINOIS STATE BOARD OF HEALTH SPRINGFIELD, ILLINOIS, 1917

The obvious explanation would be that he was the only member of his family in the Great Britain, all his remaining brothers and sisters had moved to and lived in the United States. Another possibility would be that the plot would not have been deep enough to hold 2or 3 more bodies. However, the researcher at the Necropolis while not sure, did not think this was the case. A third possibility was that, as in his will of 1912, the arrangements were left to his cousin William Brown
"my cousin William Brown will see to the final execution of this desire".[cxciv] It is hard to say but it is likely that the final reason would contain elements of all of the above.

THE CASE OF THE MYSTERIOUS GROCERY BILL

The final grocery bill that the Littlejohn had with the Lake Bluff grocery store has been publish and with it a story that he may have left it unpaid, with the implication that he left Lake Bluff in a hurry. O'Brien, in his book, Littlejohn an enigma of osteopathy, says *"it is postulated that he never settled a substantial debt to the local store in Lake luff before embarking on the SS Corinthina, 29th June 1913"*. [he gives as his reference a local historian who communicated via emails on the 22/8/2012'. (copies held in NOA. J. Martin Littlejohn Archive)]

However, when checked into, it appears that it was a simple misinterpretation of remarks that lead to the postulated accusation that the bill was unpaid. When I talked with members of the Lake Bluff historical society, they had never heard of any indication that it was unpaid. Further, the bill is made up to a final amount, indicating that it was presented for payment. The local historian O'Brien gives as a reference said " *Dr. Littlejohn had a high credit balance owed to Rosenthal & Helmings in Lake Bluff but* **I've never heard that he didn't pay. I've seen an image of the amount owed and new purchases being made on credit..... The grocery store ownership has changed multiple times in the last 100 years....** *I'm pretty sure I was given a copy of that grocery bill by one of the osteopathic centers and not a local Lake Bluff area source.* **The people at the Lake Bluff Museum as well as the people at the Lake Forest – Lake Bluff Historical Society had never heard of Littlejohn.... I have no evidence that he ever skipped out on the bill without paying and don't recall ever suggesting so. My original comment was intended simply to point out that, adjusted to today's dollars, it was a fair sum. It could be that such bills were commonplace. It could also be that he was held is such high regard that he was asked to settle his bill only periodically. I hope the good Dr. is not rolling in his grave....**[cxcv] "

Littlejohn did not sell his Lake Bluff property until 1916/7, if any money was owed in the community, I am sure a lien would have been made against his property. After all it was a small community. In his will written in 1912, he puts a 'first charge' on his assets.

"My funeral expenses and debts shall be paid as a first charge"[cxcvi]

Paying his debts was a duty for Littlejohn and not something he would neglect. In this will he also says that some debts owed to him are "in the hands of Charles Daniel, Collector", showing the other side of the duty to collect what is owed - the two sides of a contract- paying what you owe and collecting what is owed to you.

That his wife kept the bill along with other mementos of her last days in America, the ticket back to England etc, is more in line with sentimentality.

THE CHICAGO COLLEGE OF OSTEOPATHY

When the Chicago College of Osteopathy was formally announced in the April 1913 edition of the Osteopathic Physician, the article made a big issue of it being NON-PROFIT, almost to the point of being accusatory without actually saying it, about other Colleges, particularly The Littlejohn College.

"A NEW osteopathic college of prime national importance and undoubted power -The Chicago College of Osteopathy has just been launched in Chicago on the **nonprofit** making basis. For some months past the movement for this new **non-profit making** school has been quietly organized by the leading osteopaths of Chicago, assisted and encouraged by numerous progressive members of the profession in many widely separated places in the country. ...

"**None of the funds** will accrue as profits to any individual or individuals whatsoever. All funds coming into the school, whether in the form of fees from students in the under-graduate or post-graduate courses, or in the advanced and special courses projected, or in the form of endowments, will be converted at once into actual concrete development, so that **the benefits of the money** shall go to the students who have paid it in, and who are to be the osteopaths of the future, or to the post-graduate workers who shall take advantage of the attractive and practical post-graduate courses to be offered. The Chicago College of Osteopathy has been chartered by the State of Illinois as a corporation "**not for profit**," thus making the "**not for profit**" principle the Cornerstone of the new institution. The basic principle of the school will be to spread **every dollar of its funds on osteopathic education**[61]". [cxcvii]

This article obviously upset Littlejohn as he felt compelled to reply and to set the record straight as he was about to leave the country, sailing for England on the 29th June from Montreal.

In this letter, published in the May 1913 edition of the Osteopathic Physician, he also clearly states that it was for health reasons that the resigned from the College, (in the summer of 1911).

---

[61] Bold emphasis by author.

Littlejohn College Was a Non-Profit Institution

"Editor Osteopathic Physician: Permit me to say a few words about your statement in last issue regarding the new college of osteopathy. You do not say, but what you say creates the impression that this new college represents a new principle, as this is your cue, namely "not for profit." The college that this new college succeeds, or rather continues, the Littlejohn College, formerly the American College of Osteopathic Medicine and Surgery, was founded in May 1900, **on a non-profit principle and was conducted on that principle during its entire existence. No profits ever accrued to anyone.** *I worked for eleven years as head of the institution and gave two hours a day or more to teaching and never drew a cent out of it. One-half of the equipment of the college and the hospital represents time, money and labors I spent in building up for osteopathy an institution representing absolutely the non-commercial in osteopathic education.* **My physical strength could not any longer stand the strain.** *I am glad to see the consummation of unity and harmony in the establishment you announce. For this I hoped earnestly during the passing years. If I am not there it is because, like one greater than myself, I "laid down my life" in trying to establish a foundation upon which such a college might be built; and I helped to hold the fort until the greater developments you announce were rendered possible. From the field of my rest in the far-away I shall look on with eagerness to see the prosperity of this movement for the perpetual upbuilding of osteopathy, that we all love".* **J. Martin Littlejohn, D.O.** [cxcviii]

A brief summary of his time in Chicago is given on Page 557 of Chicago its History and its Builders, Volume 4, as follows:

"During the period of his residence in Chicago he has occupied the Professorship of Physiology at the Hahnemann Medical College and also in Herring Medical College. Becoming the founder of the Littlejohn College and Hospital in 1900 he has since being its president and his Professor of Theory and Practice of Osteopathic Therapeutics ... He is a member of the Chicago Osteopathic Association, Illinois Osteopathic Society, the American Osteopathic Association and the Regular Homeopathic Society ... He was editor of the Journal of the Science of Osteopathy 1900-1903, of the Osteopathic World 1903-1905, and is now editor of the Bulletin and Journal of Health, Chicago. Dr. Littlejohn is also a member of the United Editors Association of the United States. His scientific and literary articles have covered a wide range and on various subjects he has being heard on the lecture platform. He's author of Christian Sabbateanism (1892) a political theory of the school men and Grotius (1894) the Evolution of the State (1895) Lecture Notes of Physiology (1898), Textbook on Physiology (1898), Lectures of Psycho-physiology (1899) Lectures of Psycho-pathology (1900) Journal of Science of Osteopath (1900 – 1903) Science of Osteopathy (1899), A Treatise on Osteopathy (1902), Principles of Osteopathy and Theory and Practice of Osteopathic Therapeutics (1907) and Psychiatry (1908). His latest contribution is the result of laboratory experiments conducted for some years in relation to toxicosis and mechanical obstruction as the causes of so-called malignant disease, published in the Journal of the Osteopathic Association and in the annual bulletin of the Research Institute for 1910. He's a contributor on osteopathy in the Encyclopaedia Americana and the International Congress of Arts and Sciences".

It goes on to say: "Such in brief is the history of Dr. John M. Littlejohn, who is continuously carrying his research far and wide into the realms of science and who day by day learns from actual practice and experience lessons that have not only been used for the benefit of his pupils but have also formed the basis of writings that, widely read in this and foreign lands, have made his service of unmeasured value to humanity. He is ever actuated by high ideals — to know something higher, to do something better, than he has known and done the day before, and thus he is constantly reaching out along far reaching lines of usefulness for his fellow man". [cxcix]

Comment

As has been mentioned earlier, it is apparent that Littlejohn himself did not write the biography in the book 'Chicago its history and builders'. It is also probable that he did not see it, or he would have objected to the following lines;

> "He has not sought to confine his knowledge to those branches taught by a single institution, and the result is that he is able to choose from the various schools and methods of practice that which he deems most essential and valuable for specific cases". Pages 554-5

The sentiment expressed in this paragraph go against everything Littlejohn has written about Osteopathy, the Osteopathic principle and that only those practices that not only do not contradict the basic tenets of Osteopathy but actively fit into them are acceptable. It is true he had a broad view of the Osteopathic lesion, to include not just structural but also diet, environment, occupation and mental or emotional states; but that is as far as it went. He was adamant that Osteopathy and regular (drug) medicine practices were incompatible. The paragraph quoted would, on face value, seem like a good summary of Littlejohn's approach given the material supplied. So, it would be reasonable to put it down to an attempt at good, but unfortunately incorrect, editorial.

In works like this, material would be supplied and correlated before being put together by the editors. Only three osteopaths seem to have been included. Littlejohn, Fryette and Hamlin. Only in the case of Hamlin is a direct quote given.

> " Dr. Hamlin made the following statement: 'I do not believe in the physician practicing anyone teaching or system of medicine. Each and every school has its good qualities, but no physician, no matter what school he may have graduated from, is capable of meeting all conditions and carrying them through to a successful

termination with one line of practice —for that matter he could not do so if he had all the knowledge embodied in all the schools, but his failures would be less numerous if he were broad enough to inform himself of what some other school would do under like circumstances and then decide which to employ. No one would undertake to build one of our modern sky-scrapers with only a hammer, saw and square, but the average physician undertakes to do that which is much more impossible with a few tools—the teaching of one school only. Each of the various schools or systems of medicine have a reason for being or they would soon pass out of existence and that reason is some small light which it may shed on one of the most difficult of problems — keeping the human body healthy. There should be but one school of medicine and that should be universal and embody all the valuable technique of all schools. The physician should be taught from the day of matriculation to be broad-minded, to gather knowledge from any source and to make use of that which has proven itself of value. No patient cares what you give him so long as he gets well. He is not paying the physician for living up to the ethical laws of some medical society. Medical ethics tend to make physicians narrow. They try to fit the patient to their one system of treatment instead of trying to fit the treatment to the patient'." 'Chicago its history and builders pages 607-8 vol. 4

In this case we can accept the views expressed as those of Hamlin himself. Of course, it is possible that the quote is made up, but that would be incompatible with the quality of the editors.

[i] JML Osteopathy an Independent system Co-extensive with the Science and Art of healing; Journal of the American Osteopathic Association, September 1901, page 28
[ii] To Teach, to Heal, to Serve; page 21, Theodore A. Berchtold.
[iii] Ibid page 20
[iv] Ibid
[v] JML Osteopathy an Independent system Co-extensive with the Science and Art of healing; Journal of the American Osteopathic Association, September 1901, page 28
[vi] The osteopathic physician Jan 1903 editorial page 3
[vii] The Journal of the American Osteopathic Association, Vol. 2, No. 9 May 1903, Page 253
[viii] The Principles of Osteopathy, J M Littlejohn, Page 13, Published by L Meyran 1903
[ix] The Principles of Osteopathy, J M Littlejohn, Page 13, Published by L Meyran 1903 page 12
[x] The Philosophy of Osteopathy, A T Still, Kirksville 1899, page 27
[xi] The Christian Nation, Vol. 33, August 1st, 1900, page 12
[xii] first annual announcement of ACOOM&S1901-2
[xiii] 1930 Census of the USA; enumeration district 51-43, supervisors district 10, sheet 1b, Pueblo city Colorado, precinct 40
[xiv] The exact reference for this could not be rechecked prior to publication due to the Covid 19 lockdown. However, I am confident of the accuracy of the statement.
[xv] Freeport Daily Journal, Thu. Sept. 26, 1907, page 5
[xvi] Oak Leaves, Illinois, Page 29, 1908-03-14
[xvii] The Osteopathic Physician, April 1908, page 8
[xviii] To Teach, to Heal, to Serve; page 30, Theodore A. Berchtold.
[xix] Email from Grand Lodge of AM & AF of Illinois; historical records
[xx] To Teach, to Heal, to Serve; page 23, Theodore A. Berchtold.
[xxi] Chicago: its history and its builders, a century of marvellous growth, Volumn 4, by J. Seymour Currey; page 607
[xxii] The American Osteopath, Quarterly, December 1899, page 150
[xxiii] A T Still museum of osteopathic medicine ref B992; Record of the proceedings of the Faculty of the American School of Osteopathy, Page 63
[xxiv] PSEUDO-OSTEOPATHIC SCHOOLS—CAUSE AND REMEDY. C. M. T. Hulett. The American Osteopath, quarterly September 1899, page 108
[xxv] (Journal of the American Osteopathic Association, Sept 1901 page 27
[xxvi] The Osteopathic Physician October 1902 Vol. 2, No. 5, page 7/8
[xxvii] The Osteopathic Physician October 1902 Vol. 2, No. 5, page 1
[xxviii] The Osteopathic Physician October 1902, page 1

[xxix] Page 211 Editor's Own by J. Martin Littlejohn: Osteopathic world May 1903
[xxx] Journal of Osteopathy, Kirksville, August 1902, page 277-8
[xxxi] IBID
[xxxii] The Osteopathic Physician, August 1902, page 3
[xxxiii] The Osteopathic Physician, August 1902, page 3 and 7
[xxxiv] The Osteopathic Physician, August 1902, page 7
[xxxv] The Osteopathic World, May 1903, page 210, quoting from an Editorial of The Journal of the Science of Osteopathy
[xxxvi] The Osteopathic Physician, September 1902, page 7&8
[xxxvii] Journal of Osteopathy, Kirksville, September 1902, page 309
[xxxviii] The Osteopath, No. 192. November 1931, page 8
[xxxix] The Osteopathic Physician, September 1902, page 5, signed the Editor.
[xl] Journal of Osteopathy, Kirksville, Dec 1902 page 389- 395 ORGANIZATION AND LEGAL STATUS. DR. CARL P. MCCONNELL, 57 WASHINGTON ST., CHICAGO
[xli] The Osteopathic Physician, October 1902, page 5
[xlii] The Osteopathic Physician, December 1903, page 3
[xliii] The Osteopathic Physician, December 1903, page 2
[xliv] Medical education in the United States and Canada a report to the Carnegie foundation for the advancement of teaching by Abraham Flexner with an introduction by Henry S. Pritchett president of the foundation, bulletin number four (1910); page 167
[xlv] Ibid page viii
[xlvi] The Osteopathic World May 1903. page 213
[xlvii] The Osteopathic Technique and Philosophy of John Wernham; DVD section 9 'a brief biography of J. M. Littlejohn'; 1996 C Campbell and The Institute of Classical Osteopathy; Original from a letter by Dr. Streeter in the Pacific Journal (possible of Osteopathy) in unknown year – Taped interview with Dr. Stoddard 1993, at 9 minutes 37 seconds
[xlviii] The Osteopathic World July 1904 page 183-4
[xlix] The Osteopathic World May 1903 page 214
[l] The Osteopathic World April 1903, page 166
[li] The Osteopathic World sept 1904 page 43
[lii] The Osteopathic World, April 1903 – Editors own page 164
[liii] The Osteopathic World, April 1903 – Editors own *page 163*
[liv] The Osteopathic World, April 1903 – Editors own *page 167*
[lv] The Osteopathic World, April 1903 – Editors own *page 165*
[lvi] The Osteopathic World, April 1903 – Editors own *page 167*
[lvii] The Osteopathic World May 1903 page 214
[lviii] 1903 October Journal of Osteopathy. Kirksville, page 329
[lix] Ibid

[lx] The Osteopathic Physician, May 1903, republished in the October 1903 edition page 2
[lxi] Ibid page 7
[lxii] The Osteopathic Physician, February 1903, page 6
[lxiii] The Osteopathic Physician, December 1903, page 22
[lxiv] Ibid page 22
[lxv] Journal of the Science of Osteopathy, Vol. 3, No. 6, December -January 1902-3, page 244; report of the committee on education of the AOA
[lxvi] Ibid
[lxvii] Ibid
[lxviii] Journal of the Science of Osteopathy, Vol. 3, No. 6, December -January 1902-3, page 278
[lxix] Journal of the American Osteopathic Association, Vol 3; Sept 1903, Supplement on reports of committee of Education Page 15.
[lxx] See advertisements in the Journal of the Science of Osteopathy from vol. 1 no. 6 onward
[lxxi] To Teach, to Heal, to Serve; The Story of the Chicago College of Osteopathic Medicine, the First 75 years., Theodore A. Berchtold
[lxxii] To Teach, to Heal, to Serve; page 26, Theodore A. Berchtold.
[lxxiii] SUPPLEMENT to The Journal of the American Osteopathic Association for October I, 1906 Vol. 6 No. 2, page 21
[lxxiv] Journal of the American Osteopathic Association, Vol 3; Sept 1903, Supplement on reports of committee of Education Page 21
[lxxv] . The Journal of the American Osteopathic Association Nov. 1906, page 167; J. MARTIN LITTLEJOHN, President, Chicago, Illinois.,
[lxxvi] Journal of the American Osteopathic Association, Dec 1909J B Littlejohn; Should Osteopathic Colleges maintain a Standard of Education equal to or Higher than Medical Colleges,
[lxxvii] Journal of the American Osteopathic Association, January 1910, page 220-228; J. Martin Littlejohn; Osteopathy and its Colleges,
[lxxviii] SUPPLEMENT to The Journal of the American Osteopathic Association for October I, 1906 Vol. 6 No. 2, page 18
[lxxix] Page 211 Editor's Own by J. Martin Littlejohn: Osteopathic world May 1903
[lxxx] To Teach, To Heal, To Serve Page 30; Theodore A. Berchtold
[lxxxi] To Teach, To Heal, To Serve Page 34; Theodore A. Berchtold
[lxxxii] To Teach, To Heal, To Serve Page 32; Theodore A. Berchtold
[lxxxiii] The Osteopathic World, October 1903, The Editors own page 472&475
[lxxxiv] The Osteopathic World, February 1904, page 75
[lxxxv] The Anti-Vivisection Movement; Presbyterian witness vol 13 1889, page 284

[lxxxvi] The Christian nation Volume 16/17 January 1892, page 9, Last Days of the N. W. C. T. U. Convention. Monday, November 15 1891
[lxxxvii] Christian Nation Vol 21 Dec 19 1894 page 8 Review of Animal rights by H S Salt
[lxxxviii] Chicago: its history and its builders, a century of marvelous growth, by J. Seymour Currey. Volume 4 page 558
[lxxxix] Lectures on Psycho-physiology, J. Martin Littlejohn; American School of osteopathy, Kirksville, 1899; page 1 Introduction.
[xc] Annual report of American anti-vivisection society 1900, Page 29
[xci] The Baltimore Sun, November 6th, 1902, page 6
[xcii] The osteopathic physician, June 1908 page 12
[xciii] The Osteopathic Physician, volume 9 number 3, March 1906 DR. E. D. BURLEIGH, of PHILADELPHIA, PA; page 14,
[xciv] Ibid page 10
[xcv] The Journal of the Science of Osteopathy, Volume 3, Number 6, December-January, 1902-1903; pp. 258-277
[xcvi] Journal of Osteopathy, Kirksville, April 1909, page 299
[xcvii] Philadelphia Journal of Osteopathy July 1902, page 2
[xcviii] Journal of the American Osteopathic Association, volume 1 sept 1901, page 25; OSTEOPATHY AN INDEPENDENT SYSTEM CO -EXTENSIVE WITH THE SCIENCE AND ART OF HEALING; a Paper read before the A. O. A. Convention at Kirksville, Mo., by Dr. J. Martin Littlejohn, President of the American College of Osteopathic Medicine and Surgery, Chicago, Ill
[xcix] Chicago, Illinois, City Directory, 1907
[c] Journal of the American Osteopathic Association; volume 6, number 9, May 1907 *page 252*
[ci] Journal of the American Osteopathic Association; volume 6, number 9, May 1907 *page 321-323*
[cii] Glasgow's Record of the Elders of the RPCNA; available from the Reformed Presbyterian archives website rparchives.org.
[ciii] The Christian Nation Vol. 36, June 25th, 1902, page 14
[civ] The Christian Nation Vol. 37, August 6th, 1902, page 11: also noted in the Reformed Presbyterian standard, Vol. iv, No. 18, September 15th, 1902, Page 9
[cv] Christian nation November 12th, 1902, page 12
[cvi] Sketches of the Ministers of the Reformed Presbyterian Church of North America, 1888 to 1930, By The Rev. Owen F. Thompson. Page 61
[cvii] Letter by Littlejohn to his son James re his will and funeral arrangements; National Osteopathic archive, now held in the Wellcome archives (courtesy of conversations with John Wernham)
[cviii] The people of the state of Illinois, ex rel Littlejohn College and hospital vs Illinois State board of health; gen No. 303742, term 8881; report of inspection of the American College of Osteopathic Medicine and Surgery (1908)

[cix] Ibid
[cx] The Chicago Clinic and Pure Water Journal, Volume 18, 1905, page 54
[cxi] The people of the state of Illinois, ex rel Littlejohn College and hospital vs Illinois State board of health; gen No. 303742, term 8881; report of inspection of the American College of Osteopathic Medicine and Surgery (1908) exhibit C.
[cxii] Ibid
[cxiii] Chicago Clinic and Pure Water Journal, April 1905, page 112
[cxiv] Illinois medical journal October 1911 page 477
[cxv] The A.M.A., N.M.A and the Flexner Report of 1910 prepared by Ololade Olakanmi for the writing group of the history of the African Americans and the medical profession.
[cxvi] A History of the Council of Medical Education and Hospitals have the American and Medical Association, 1904 – 1959, page 10.
[cxvii] Reprinted in A History of the Council of Medical Education Hospitals the American Medical Association 1904 – 1959, page 10
[cxviii] Arrieta, J. (2009). Flexner Report Overview. Monterrey, MX
[cxix] Medical Education in The United States and Canada; a report to the Carnegie Foundation for the Advancement of Teaching by Abraham Flexner: bulletin No. 4; 1910, page 216
[cxx] Ibid page163-4
[cxxi] The Chicago Tribune, June 8th, 1910, Page 6
[cxxii] Another Flexner Report? Pondering Flexner's Role in Reforming Education; by Rose Asera;, American Association of Colleges for Teacher Education, Washington,
[cxxiii] I Remember: The Autobiography of Abraham Flexner Simon and Schuster, 1940, page 121
[cxxiv] The Chicago Tribune, June 8th, 1910, Page 6
[cxxv] The Osteopathic Physician, July 1910, page 2
[cxxvi] I Remember: The Autobiography of Abraham Flexner, page 129
[cxxvii] I Remember: The Autobiography of Abraham Flexner, page 129
[cxxviii] The Osteopathic Physician, June 1910, Page 8
[cxxix] The Osteopathic Physician, June 1910, Page 8
[cxxx] The Chicago Tribune, June 6th, 1910
[cxxxi] Journal of the American Osteopathic Association, September 1909, Page 27
[cxxxii] Journal of the American Osteopathic Association, September 1909, Page 28
[cxxxiii] Journal of the American Osteopathic Association, September 1909, Page 36
[cxxxiv] Journal of the American Osteopathic Association, September 1909, Page 11, J. Martin Littlejohn President A.C.O.

[cxxxv] Journal of the American Osteopathic Association, October 1909 Page 79-81, Dr. Littlejohn on the Proposed Degree
[cxxxvi] Ibid
[cxxxvii] Journal of the American Osteopathic Association, May 1910, page 407; Trying to Solve M. D. Degree Proposition.
[cxxxviii] Journal of the American Osteopathic Association, September 1909, page 21
[cxxxix] Journal of the American Osteopathic Association, February 1908, A Plea for Honesty, Frederick W. Sherburne, D. O., Boston, Mass., page 261
[cxl] Journal of the American Osteopathic Association, April 1908, A Plea for Honesty, from another point of view, A. G. Hildreth, page 358
[cxli] Journal of the American Osteopathic Association, September 1909, Martin W. Peck. D.O., How Dr. Peck viewed the Meeting, page 82)
[cxlii] Journal of the American Osteopathic Association, September 1909, page 6
[cxliii] Journal of the American Osteopathic Association, November 1909, page 115/6
[cxliv] Journal of the American Osteopathic Association December 1909, Page 140, Dr J. B. Littlejohn, Should Osteopathic Colleges Maintain a Standard Equal to or Higher Than Medical Colleges.
[cxlv] Journal of the American Osteopathic Association February 1910, page 226, Osteopathy and its Colleges.
[cxlvi] Journal of the American Osteopathic Association February 1910, page 228, J M Littlejohn, Osteopathy and its Colleges.
[cxlvii] Journal of the American Osteopathic Association, May 1914, page 535.
[cxlviii] Journal of the American Osteopathic Association, March 1914; also, The Chanute Daily Tribune, March 11th, 1914, Page 2; The Erie Record, March 13th, 1914, Page 5
[cxlix] Journal of the American Osteopathic Association, September 1911, page 673
[cl] Journal of the American Osteopathic Association, September 1911, Page 675-6
[cli] Bulletin of Health, December 15th, 1910, page 3
[clii] Bulletin of Health, August 15th, 1911, Page 16
[cliii] Bulletin of Health, Volume 4, number 8, January 15th, 1911, Page 3
[cliv] Bulletin of Health, Volume 4, number 8, January 15th, 1911, Page 4
[clv] The American Osteopath, September 1899; Discussion of the work of the AAAO, page 53
[clvi] Journal of the American Osteopathic Association, October 1911, Page 727
[clvii] Journal of the American Osteopathic Association Volume 10, September 1910 – August 1911; pages 617/8,633
[clviii] Journal of the American Osteopathic Association, October 1910, page 70-71

[clix] The Bulletin of Health December 15th, 1910 page 16-17
[clx] Journal American Osteopathic Association, November 1911, page 795
[clxi] Bulletin of Health volume 4 number 4, June 15th, 1911
[clxii] Museum of Osteopathic Medicine, Kirksville, Letter from C. E. Still to Dr. James B. Littlejohn, December 3(or possibly 8), 1911; Reference 1980.375.02.42
[clxiii] Lake county, Illinois, record of deeds, Number 134979, 12th April 1911
[clxiv] Chicago examiner May 23rd, 1911
[clxv] Post Card History series; Page 20; Lake Bluff Lyndon Jensen and Kathleen O'Hara; Arcadia publishing
[clxvi] Journal of the American Osteopathic Association, August 1911, minutes of the fifteenth annual session of the American Osteopathic Association, held at Chicago July 25th -28th 1911; page 613
[clxvii] Book of Chicagoans 1911, Albert Nelson Marquis Chicago A. N. Marquis & Company, 1911, page 422: bulletin and Journal of Health, Vol. 3, No. 12, Dec. 1910
[clxviii] The Christian Nation, vol 57, September 18th, Page 10
[clxix] NOA archive, Wellcome Library, NOA/JML/BSO Owned/File box 2 Deepstore B000002313598
[clxx] Ibid
[clxxi] Journal of Osteopathy, BSO, October 1932, page
[clxxii] National Osteopathic archive, BSO: and passenger lists
[clxxiii] "J Martin Littlejohn (1865e1947) and James Buchan Littlejohn (1868e1947): Two distinct directions in Osteopathy and the birth of osteopathic medicine John C. O'Brien; National Osteopathic Archive, 275, Borough High Street, London, UK; international journal of osteopathic medicine 2017, 23 pages 4-10; page 8.
[clxxiv] Museum of Osteopathic Medicine, Kirksville; ref. 1980.375.02.42
[clxxv] Museum of Osteopathic Medicine, Kirksville; ref. 1980.375.02.43
[clxxvi] Museum of Osteopathic Medicine, Kirksville; ref. 1980.375.02.46
[clxxvii] The Reflex, 1939, History of the Chicago College of Osteopathic Medicine, Richard O. Gifford, Literary Editor: Also "Historical Sketch of the Chicago College Osteopathic College 1923 reflex.
[clxxviii] Museum of Osteopathic Medicine, Kirksville; ref. 1980.375.02.45
[clxxix] Osteopathic Physician Sept. 1912, page 5
[clxxx] The Reflex 1929, Page62-63; History of Chicago College of Osteopathy, Dr. J. B. Littlejohn D.O., M.D.,
[clxxxi] the Chicago College Osteopathic College, Its History 1923 reflex, Page 99, Edgar S. Comstock D.O.
[clxxxii] Ibid
[clxxxiii] The Reflex 1929, Page62-63; History of Chicago College of Osteopathy, Dr. J. B. Littlejohn D.O., M.D.,

[clxxxiv] Chicago Tribune, July 1st, 1913, page 21; Chicago tribune Sunday 26th June and 25th July
[clxxxv] National Osteopathic archive, BSO: and passenger lists
[clxxxvi] Chicago Examiner June 10, 1908
[clxxxvii] Chicago Tribune, July 1st, 1913, page 21; also, Chicago tribune Sunday 26th June and 25th July
[clxxxviii] The Christian Nation Vol. 23, October 23rd, 1895, Page 4
[clxxxix] Journal of Osteopathy, Kirksville, October 1901
[cxc] The Osteopathic Physician, June 10, 1910, page 14
[cxci] Personal communication by email from D. Forlow.
[cxcii] Littlejohn's last will and testimony written in 1912: NOA archive, Wellcome Library, NOA/JML/BSO Owned/File box 2 Deepstore B000002313598
[cxciii] Email correspondence from Historical and Genealogical Researcher, Friends of Glasgow Necropolis.
[cxciv] Littlejohn's last will and testimony written in 1912: NOA archive, Wellcome Library, NOA/JML/BSO Owned/File box 2 Deepstore B000002313598
[cxcv] Personal emails and communication
[cxcvi] Littlejohn's last will and testimony written in 1912: NOA archive, Wellcome Library, NOA/JML/BSO Owned/File box 2 Deepstore B000002313598
[cxcvii] The Osteopathic Physician, April 1913, Vol 23, No. 4, page 1
[cxcviii] The Osteopathic Physician May 1913, Vol 23. No 5, Page 4
[cxcix] Chicago its History and its Builders, Volume 4, Page 557; The S. J. Clarke Publishing Company Chicago, 1912.

JML'S CAREER IN ENGLAND

Having been through the trials of the past decade in Chicago, in the long battle from the beginning of 1900 with the Board of Health, the arguments with the AOA, the change of name of the School and his own poor health, and finally the loss his mother[1] which allowed him the freedom to think about moving from America his feelings are aptly summed up in the quote from John Wernham " **Mabel wanted to return (to England) and I wanted to retire**"

His mother's passing was the final tether which held John Martin Littlejohn to the U.S.A. Thus, after breaking from the school he set about organising himself for his return to the U.K. Some say it was in haste, however if we look at the timeline it took well over a year to organise. The latest date for the definite start of this process was when he asked for his letter of standing from the Iowa Presbytery in order that he could attach to a Reformed Presbyterian Church in Scotland. This was granted at the presbytery meeting on September 10th 1912[i]. Thus, he was planning from August 1912 or earlier. That certainly isn't in haste. It takes time to organise the purchase of a property from a distance through friends. It takes time to organise the removal and transport of himself and his family to England and then to have arrangements made for the goods household effects etc to be picked up at the port in England and moved to their new home.

Thus, we see that he came to England, settled down, opened a practice to maintain a living and set about looking after his family. His own words describe it well.

"After settling down in England to rest, in 1913, my friends demanded osteopathic treatment, and the first month that I opened my office at 69 Piccadilly Square, London, I found that I had as many patients as I could treat. During the past ten years (1913-1923) I have been kept more than busy, and now I have four centers for

---

[1] As stated earlier His mother would not have envisaged returning to England and thus not having the opportunity to be buried with her husband in Kirksville

OSTEOPATHY: at 48 Dover St., Piccadilly; at Enfield, Middlesex: at my home in Thundersley; and in Thorpe Bay, Essex, these centers I am keeping open for my four children, who are well on their way in osteopathic education.

"In regard to the practice of osteopathy in England there is no law for registration or regulation of the practice. It is different here than what it is in the United States. The practice of medicine regulated by registration through licensing bodies, but this does not forbid the practice by anyone unregistered the only disadvantage being that as such we have no privileges".

"During the war we were kept busy giving treatments to officers and private soldiers. While there was no official recognition of our work, each individual case could have the treatment, if so desired, by the individual himself. For the past seven years I have conducted clinics at my home and in Enfield, treating twenty to thirty patients at these centers weekly

"Several attempts have been made to secure recognition for our science. The last attempt before the Board of Trade brought forward this question from the officials: you tell us   "what you have done in research in American —but what have you done here? This stimulated Dr. Horn and myself to apply for a charter for a school of Osteopathy, which was granted to us March 7, 1917. The British School of OSTEOPATHY thus founded by us has been enlarged and is now in close affiliation with the British Osteopathic Association. As dean of the British School of Osteopathy I send greetings to the Chicago College of Osteopathy. From a small beginning, like your own school, we hope to develop this first school founded in the British Empire to a large institution in the future. It is dedicated to OSTEOPATHY as a science and is pledged to maintain unadulterated manipulative science as the foundation of therapeutics. From the first we have maintained the practice of OSTEOPATHY as a science in its purity, a system unmixed by any others." [ii]

It would seem that it had always been his intention or desire to return to the British Isles as is evident by the number of trips that he made back to the British Isles, his writings and his interest in obtaining a position in Glasgow University, or the interest in the preaching position in Penfold in Scotland and even in his own testimony to the House of Lords, Select Committee meeting when he states:

"I think Dr. Horne, another osteopath who is now dead, was associated with you in the establishment of the school? – yes, in 1903 I visited this country and we discussed the subject of establishing a school of osteopathy in this country but I was called back to America to continue my teaching there and I returned in 1913".[iii]

The remark *'I was called back to America'* indicates that at some part of him at least would have preferred to stay.

Wernham was wont to say when he asked Littlejohn why he came back to England his answer was in two parts, one he wanted to retire and two Mabel (his wife) wanted to return to the U.K. *"Mabel wanted to return, and I wanted to retire".*

Littlejohn's wife ran his home in the true fashion of a Reformed Presbyterian Ministers wife and may have felt isolated from the rest of Littlejohn's associates who were "high academics" if you like and driven by their profession. This included James Buchan and his wife Edith Williams Littlejohn, who worked and supported J.B. in the clinic and College.

Badger Hall

Wernham, in lectures and conversation would always give a good description of the conditions that Littlejohn found upon his return to England; He eventually published his childhood recollections; -

" *Badger Hall was an early 19th century farm house, centered in 45 acres of not very productive arable land and a pleasantly wooded valley hard by. In 1895 the Victorian style manor house was erected in juxtaposition with the older structure and, although a handsome facade, the house was innocent of central heating and somewhat chilly. The water supply required daily pumping from a well in the valley which boasted a most peculiar taste but apparently possessed no poisonous qualities. Lighting was limited to oil-lamps and candles at bedtime. Life was simple in those days and modern aids to living, water, light, heat and the telephone were only added much later in the history of the family home*

"... the six American children made themselves heard in the good old American style and the old house was a chatter of activity. It was wartime and this alien family was not permitted to travel a distance greater than three miles and it was only by special permission that John Martin was allowed to travel the 40 miles to London[iv]*."*

Regarding Littlejohn's work and practice in London Wernham said that the reasons why Littlejohn travelled to London were not really talked about[2] and only *"vague references were made to 'hospital work' and 'teaching".*[v]

Wernham often said that, in his childhood recollection of Badger Hall during the first world war, that Littlejohn *'remained a*

---

[2] Littlejohn in the Reflex of 1923 gives an accurate description of what work he was doing at this time.

silent, remote figure[3], and that "Life must have been difficult: here was a man at the top of his profession, at the head of one of the leading colleges and with a scholastic history second to none, now thrust into a country at war, with a large family, a large house and practically no income"

While the above gives a good description based upon personal experience, of life at Badger Hall, it is also a good example of easy to create a myth, good or bad, without reference to the facts. Wernham would have known the children and been a visitor to the house and would have been recalling events from his own childhood. He was only 7 in 1914.

Apart from starting his practice at 69 Piccadilly, London, Littlejohn and his friend Rev. Minifie involved themselves in charitable work raising funds for the relief of American and other allied prisoners of war with the International bible Institutes war relief fund. In an article written in 1923 Littlejohn says;

""During the war we were kept busy giving treatments to officers and private soldiers. While there was no 'official' recognition of our work, each individual case could have the treatment, if so desired, by the individual himself"[vi]

---

[3] While Wernham's words, based upon his childhood memory, may have been true of Littlejohn in his later days, it was not his true nature; *"Widely read, thoroughly cultivated, he has such margin that men of widely differing education and antagonistic opinions admire him and cherish his acquaintance and friendship. Yet, enjoying as he does, these evidence of appreciation, he is the modest J. Martin Littlejohn, who has turned his back on promotion that he might pursue the truth as first discovered and formulated by Andrew T. Still. Honoured by learned societies, tempted by the luring parks of literature, he prefers to be and to be known as an osteopathic physician."* (Wm Dobbyn, The Osteopathic world oct 1903).

Life in England

When Littlejohn came to England, he had sold properties and almost certainly had other savings. Then in 1916 he sold his home in Lake Bluff for around $4000, having purchased it for $1715 in 1911[vii]. $4000 in 1916 would equate to approximately £1000, which by today's prices and inflation would be worth over £80000. So, while he could not be termed Rich, he would have been relatively comfortable while he built up his practice. He bought Badger Hall for £4000 and in 1925 had an annual income of about £4-500.[viii]

One aspect of his early life in England that is not often mentioned is the loss of his son Stuart William at just three months old. He died, at his home in Badger Hall, of heart failure brought on from 'congenital debility' and LittleJohn is listed as being present at his death. It is heart breaking to lose a child and it is difficult to imagine the grief that Littlejohn and his wife went through during the three months from March to June 1915, nursing their sick child only to watch as he died in their arms.[ix]

Wernham described Littlejohn's first ten years in England in the following words;

"How John Martin survived this period of his life during the first world war and the time immediately following is unknown. The first sign of recorded activity is an osteopathic clinic in Enfield followed by a private osteopathic practice in Dover Street, Piccadilly; the third hint came to the surface in Victoria, where we find John Martin teaching a small group of students in Vincent Square, alone and unaided. The time is around 1925 and John Martin was beginning to lay the foundations of the final chapters in his career, the practice and school showed a measure of growth and prosperity that was remarkable, if we remember that it was the work of one man, frail in health and without fortune except an indomitable will and (as Fryette once remarked) a head full of brains. In 1923 he became the president of the British Osteopathic Association, the membership of which was restricted to graduates of the American osteopathic colleges. In 1924, he resigned his office. The reason for this brief tenure is unknown and only conjecture can make a shrewd guess that the shades of Kirksville and Chicago had not yet faded. Many years later, a prominent

member of the B. O. A. stated publicly that he "never knew what went wrong".[x]

This account would now be considered inaccurate as it is known how Littlejohn worked during the war, his connection with the International Bible Institute, his practice in Piccadilly and Enfield. However it does serve as an introduction to his work at the British School of Osteopathy.

Regarding his reason for resigning from the British osteopathic Association, Littlejohn states it quite clearly in a letter. This letter was written on August 23rd, 1926 to an osteopath prominent in the political field in England. He says:

*"During the year of my presidency of the British Osteopathic Association I gave you a place on our legislative committee. Now all the time I tried to keep to the front the ideas you advocate. An independent system and independent recognition nothing else will help us. I need not go into the troubles of these days, the **B.O.A. has been gradually drifting into the position of subservience to medicine against that I have always stood here as in the U.S. For seventeen**[4] **years I have fought for independent boards in the U.S. and I mean to continue so here.**[5] I advocate the B.O.A. inclusion in attempted legislation to get a standard entirely independent of medicine. I'm sending you a copy of a draft bill I prepared in 1925 for the B.O.A. and submitted again during my presidency in 1926 It was of course turned down. Now I have severed my connection with the B.O.A. because no good can be accomplished by propaganda work that is alien to our ideals and only antagonise popular feeling against an independent osteopathy".*[xi]

Being an educationalist at heart he became involved in osteopathic education again and having gained the support of other

---

[4] His involvement with osteopathy stated in 1897 and he left the USA in 1913 which gives 17yrs inclusive.
[5] Bold emphasis by the author

osteopaths, opened the British School of Osteopathy in 1917[6]. In conversation with those who had the privilege of studying under him at the British School of Osteopathy in the 1920's and 1930's it was gratifying to hear that he continued to teach in the same manner as he had in Chicago. In clinic, with a team of tutors, he would diagnose and then explain, in pure osteopathic terms, his findings, how this led to treatment and then demonstrate the treatment. All agreed that he would not give a 'medical diagnosis' but was only interested in the Osteopathic aetiology of the patient's condition. Some thought this was a fault, as they wanted the 'medical diagnosis'; others thought it was ' pure osteopathy- in line with that of A. T. Still[xii]. However, when he came back to England, he did not seem to produce any original from that time until his death.

What he published, what he taught was all from work he had published and produced while in the States. He used his books, Osteopathic therapeutics and practice, current literature from the Journal of the American Osteopathic Association, from new books that were published like 'The Theory of Osteopathy'[7] by 'Tuckers and Wilson'[8] etc. but he wrote no more original work of his own. In essence, he had in essence retired.

Wernham describes Littlejohns daily routine as catching the 7.15 a.m. train to London, working all day and returning on the 8.30 p.m. train. Once home he would remain fully occupied until bedtime at around 2.00 a.m. On Saturdays the return train was a little earlier at 6.30 p.m. *"Sunday was a day of rest, with the exception of those occasions when*

---

[6] " In March 1915, An attempt was made to incorporate the British school of Osteopathy. But the Treasury refused to sanction the organisation of any Body involving capital in any field not actually associated with the war service.... The British School of Osteopathy was incorporated in March 7th 1917 on condition than not more than two shares of stock be issued during the continuance of the war" Journal of osteopathy, British School of Osteopathy, December 1929

[7] The Theory of Osteopathy; 1936. By Ernest E. Tucker and Perrin T. Wilson, published by the authors, printed in Kirksville, Missouri.

[8] As an interesting anecdote, he seemed to dictate this book to his students who then as a collective typed it up to share, The author found a typed version of what appeared to be the students typed version in John Wernham's kitchen in the mid-1980s.

he was called upon to preach at the local (Congregational) church. In addition, he often presided at the local Sunday afternoon Men's Brotherhood and served on the Parish Council".[xiii]

Retirement wasn't to mean sitting around doing nothing.

In letter, to a colleague in America published in the Osteopath, he says:

"I have been trying to find time to write to you, but you know how busy I was in 1898, at it morning, noon and night and now in 1931, I am still the same. In all these years, I have kept real well and like yourself I have done a great deal. We are thousands of miles apart but as I pen this, I am looking up at your picture on the wall in the old group taken at Kirksville.

"I want to thank you for your kind reference to myself and my little journal. It is small but ten thousand of them go out all over the world. Some to the U.S., Canada, Australia, India, Africa and the Isles of the Southern Seas. So, you see we have friends everywhere".[xiv]

His continued devotion to the pure science of osteopathy is unquestioned. He continued to practice osteopathy, continued to be devoted to osteopathic principles and the teaching of osteopathy and the practice of osteopathy, but didn't write any new material and didn't do any new experimentation. That is until towards the end of his life. it was suggested that, towards the end of his life he started to do further research into children damaged by vaccination and birth.[xv] This seems to have been a return of his interest in toxicosis research but, this time, not using animals; instead using his previous results and the principle of osteopathy.[9]

He continued in the same vein his whole life dedicated to the osteopathy and that is the osteopathy of A.T. Still. Two major events were to mar his 'career' in England and have perhaps done more

---

[9] This contains speculation on the author's part, but it fits with the character of Littlejohn and his emphasis on Toxicology in his teaching at the British School of Osteopathy as evidenced by the detail in the typed and handwritten student notes on the subject in Wernham's collection and the National Osteopathic Archive.

damage than anything else to detract from his legacy. The first was the investigation into the 'International Bible War Relief Fund'; and the second, more well-known one, was the House of Lords Select Committee on the Registration and Regulation of Osteopaths Bill 1935.

Before we look at the 'International Bible War Relief Fund' it is necessary to give some background on Littlejohn's friend the Reverent Doctor William C. Minifie.

Reverent Doctor William C. Minifie

Since Littlejohn's connection with Rev. Minifie goes back to at least 1909, it seems apt to give some more detail. Especially as this relationship illustrates, in some measure, how Littlejohn's belief system and cultural background influenced his life.

"Minifie, William Charles was born on March 8, 1869 in London, England. Son of John Holloway) Minifie and Isabella (Curtis) Minifie.

"Educated Sherburne Grammar School, and Metropolitan Pastors College, London, 1886-1889. (Doctor of Divinity, Washington and Tusculum College, Tennessee, 1901. Doctor of Civil Law, Potomac U., 1905, Doctor of Philosophy., 1908. Doctor of Letters, Alfred University, New York, 1914".[xvi]

Rev. Minifie was a charismatic evangelical preacher as evidenced by the many newspaper accounts; for example;

"Dr. Minifie is known on both sides of the Atlantic Ocean as a lecturer of high repute. The Boston Herald says of him: 'He is an orator and lecturer of remarkable ability, from whose lips epigrams and metaphors fall with as little effort as pearls and diamonds from those of the fabled princes. His pictures and scenes at the front and in camp are remarkably vivid and life-like'".[xvii] *(1918 Texas)*

"Dr. Minifie, as a speaker, chiefly remarkable for the coining well-sounding and often very apt and telling phrases, generally embellished with touches the rosy colours which | distinguish the flowers of the poetic mind, and given a manner which seldom failed elicit the round applause which lie evidently accustomed, and by which his speech was plentifully punctuated".[xviii] (England 1903)

He started his ministerial career by studying at Spurgeon's[10] College, (Metropolitan College) for Baptist ministers in London, becoming at one time assistant private secretary to D. Spurgeon[11] himself, he quickly established himself as a Charismatic Preacher as illustrated by the following newspaper account, from 1892 (just six months after the passing of his mentor Rev. Surgeon), of him as a young minister:

"......The presence of a young London Minister whose good fame as a preacher and a worker among the poor has spread far beyond the scene of his labour at the Arthur Street Baptist Chapel in Camberwell Gate. The young minister is the Reverend W. J Minifie whose marriage about two months ago with Miss Rossitor of Weston- Super-mare is still fresh in the memory of many. Mr Minifie was one of C.H. Spurgeon's college students, but his vocation of preacher began when at the age of fourteen he was known at the Grand Theatre, Islington, as the boy evangelist. An interesting sketch of the young ministers short but busy life appeared with a portrait in a recent number of the Christian Globe. In all the work he did whether labouring for the Young Men's Christian Association or as secretary of the Students Missionary Association and the pastor's college or since July 1890 as in his present pastorate, Mr Minifie threw his whole body and soul. He it was who organised single handed the government undenominational missionary convention of young men in the Metropolitan Tabernacle in October 1889 gaining for himself a warm and characteristic eulogium from the great head of the Tabernacle. Towards the end of his college, as the Globe informs us, Mr Minifie went to assist the

---

[10] Charles Haddon Spurgeon, also known as the "Prince of Preachers," was a Calvinistic, Baptist minister. Born in 1834, he was pastor at the New Park Street Chapel and the Metropolitan Tabernacle and founded a college for prospective ministers, The Metropolitan Pastors College, named 'Spurgeon's College' after his death.

[11] In the London news 30 May 1907, we find a letter claiming that Dr. William C. Minifie being described as "at one time Charles Haddon Spurgeon's private secretary" as being a false claim. He actually said he was an 'assistant private secretary', this being misquoted. I found no other objections but many quoting him, accurately, as being Sturgeons assistant private secretary for a time. In Spurgeon's magazine, 'Sword and the Trowel' 1889 we find him "Mr. Minifie (secretary of the students Missionary Association)". page 43

Reverend J. W. Harold at Thornton Heath, and also helped in secretarial work at 'Westwood', and undertook those responsible duties whilst Mr Spurgeon was at Mentone during the winter of 1889".[xix]

This gives a brief history of his association with Spurgeon and his secretarial duties as "assistant private secretary" to Spurgeon while he worked at Westwood which was Spurgeon's home.

Spurgeon's attitude towards education, (although somewhat limited to the education of ministers), which surely had an effect on the young Minifie, had a close affinity to that of Littlejohn.

"From the beginning Spurgeon recognised the plight of young men who were desperately keen for ministerial training but who had not received the formal academic education required for entry to the existing colleges".[xx]

Minifie served as a Baptist minister in Lansdowne road, Bournemouth from 1893-97[xxi] ,for some time in the early 1900's as minister in the Sion Baptist church in Bradford[xxii] and in America was minister in the Clarendon Street Baptist church, Boston, a position he took up in 1907[xxiii]. On his departure from England, in 1907, he was presented with a "purse of Gold" as tokens of the esteem he was held in by the congregation at Newport, were he had been for three and a halve years. During that time, he was said to have taken a prominent part in "Free Church Life in the town and county".[xxiv], He was initiated in the Albert Edward Prince of Wales Lodge Newport of the Masonic Order in 1907.[xxv]

He resigned his ministry at Clarendon Street in 1909 to take up a more evangelical missionary role with the Chapman-Alexander band of evangelists,[12] conducting revival services at Winthrop, in the greater Boston area. (It was at these meetings that we find him associated with Littlejohn. How this association came about I do not know. But it was to last the rest of Littlejohn's life- Littlejohn asking that Minifie conduct his own funeral service as he knew him better than anyone else.[xxvi])

However, his style of preaching was not to everyone's taste and he faced some criticism, even though the numbers attending the Clarendon Street Baptist church had increased by 400% since he started that type of worship, which included pictures, slide shows and music.[xxvii] This criticism may have led him to his decision to resign. He did however retain the support of many parishioners and ministers who attended a farewell reception for him to offer him there best wishes and a financial purse to help him on his new venture.[xxviii]

> "it is reported that on Sunday last Dr. Minifie illuminated the outside of his church in New York with electric arc lights, while inside he had provided an orchestra, magic lantern slides, white gowned pew openers and picture postcards for the congregation"
>
> Yorkshire Evening Post, April 30th, 1908

---

[12] In 1905, John H. Converse, a wealthy Presbyterian philanthropist, offered to underwrite Chapman's expenses if he would re-enter the evangelistic field full-time... Chapman accepted the offer and in 1907, joined forces with popular gospel singer Charles McCallon Alexander to launch the "Chapman-Alexander Simultaneous Campaign.... Chapman's biography reports, "The first Chapman-Alexander worldwide campaign left Vancouver, British Columbia on March 26, 1909, and returned on November 26, 1909. (John Wilbur Chapman-Wikipedia). He was also associated with the Moody Bible Institute in Chicago "Moody's confidence in him was further shown in that he served as the vice-president of the Chicago Bible Institute (later Moody Bible Institute)" (Believers Web biography).

By 1912 he had again settled in England and was 'a Freeman of the City of London' in February 1912.[xxix]

Although still listed as a minister in the Boston Presbytery, his address was given as London, England and was listed as absent 'without excuse' from the Synod in 1912.[xxx]

One of the ventures he was involved in was the "Cuba Christian Mission",[xxxi] of which he was listed as a Director. This was an idea to bring bible and bible studies to those in Cuba and to help the poor farmers of that region.

In this regard, he was also involved in a company which sold shares in fruit groves in Cuba on an 'instalment plan'. His son was living in Cuba at this time and listed as 'manager of cattle ranch'.[xxxii] And was said to be 'employed as assistant manager in connection with the cultivation of some of these groves'.[xxxiii] During a lecture on Cuba, after which a collection was taken on behalf of the 'Cuba Mission' Minifie gave details of this scheme.[xxxiv] He was giving lectures regularly during 1914-5 titled 'Through Cuba with a Camera' with funds being collected on behalf of the 'Cuba evangelical Mission'.[xxxv] This led to an article in Truth magazine commenting on the ethics of this type of scheme. So, he was no stranger to controversy. Some may argue that the change of name was in part due to this negative publicity. In the March 10th edition, the editor says:

> "I fear that all is not going well with hose wonderful investments in orange groves in Cuba upon which the Rev. Dr. W. C. Minifie has discoursed so persuasively. Personally, I am not surprised. For one thing, I instinctively dislike any business proposition emanating from a minister or ex-minister of the Gospel…. There was too much conjecture and too much philanthropy about the business for my taste, and the fact that Dr. Minifie had the effrontery to represent these "orange groves" as a better investment than an annuity or a life assurance policy convinced me that he was, to say the least, a very reckless and unsafe counsellor of the investors whom he addressed".[xxxvi]

The reference to this in the Police report makes it sound like a fraudulent investment. However, the editor seems is indicting his own bias against 'Philanthropy' and 'ministers of the Gospel' being financial advisors and using this once apparently successful and now failing investment as an example.

After the start of the first world war the objects of this charity were expanded, and the name changed to the 'International Bible Institute' with the added aim of providing a Bible study correspondence course.[xxxvii]

"This Institution (the International Bible Institute) was originally founded by Dr. Minifie to promote the study of bible and Christian evidences, to carry on missionary work in Cuba and to conduct pictorial and other services in halls theatres and prisons, Recently it added a special relief campaign on behalf of war suffers in Europe".[xxxviii]

According to a brochure advertising his lecture series in 1916 called "With the British Fighting, Forces in Camp and Field".·· "A portion of the proceeds of this CINEMATOGRAPH WAR LECTURE will be devoted to the work of " The International Bible Institute." I, Charing Cross, London"[xxxix]

The Colman Institute, Redhill.

CINEMATOGRAPH
WAR LECTURE

Dr. WM. C. MINIFIE,

AUXILIARY CHAPLAIN.

With the British Fighting Forces in Camp and Field.

THURSDAY. MAY 18th, at 7.30 p.m.

Realistic Cinematograph and Steriopticon Pictures

Minifie's Canadian and USA fundraising trip 1916

Minifie had been earning his living from his preaching and evangelical lecture tours when the first world war broke out. He then volunteered with the Chaplain's office of the City of London National Guard as an 'auxiliary chaplain'.[xl]

During 1916, he then went on a fund-raising trip to Canada and the USA on behalf of the International Bible Institute, a trip that was to lead to personal tragedy and some controversy. Littlejohn gave the following description of the purpose and financial organization of the trip

"Dr. Minifie is not attached to any Church and depends solely upon the results of his lectures for his living. Dr. Minifie went to America specifically to obtain funds for the Bible Institute. The arrangement was that he should cover his expenses. I understand the term "expenses" does not include, for instance the rent of his house at Finchley and household expenses there".[xli]

"The Rev. Dr. William C. Minifie, formerly of Bournemouth, is journeying to Canada and the United States on a lecturing tour. Since the war began, Dr. Minifie has been engaged among the troops in England and France, as auxiliary chaplain: and his repertory includes a lecture, with cinematograph pictures, entitled " With the British Fighting Forces in Camp and Field." He is accompanied by Mrs. Minifie and does not expect to return before spring"

The Bournemouth Graphic:
oct 13 1916, page 8

During this trip, on April 24th, 1917, his wife tragically drowned in an accident in which he also nearly died while trying to rescue her.[xlii] This took place on the shores of Lake Huron. During the next couple of months, he continued in the Canada/ New York area, giving talks in Buffalo and surrounding areas.[xliii] During these talks he was sometimes accompanied by Colonel Williams, senior chaplain of the Canadian Army.[xliv]

During this time, he probable meet Ellen Brown, a nurse who was attached to the Harvard Unite of the American Ambulance Corp and who had been under fire several times in Europe.[xlv] He subsequently married her on 22nd October 1917 in All Saints church Highgate Middlesex.[xlvi] The speed of this romance, just months after the tragic drowning of his first wife was probably a source of conflict with those who had supported him in his fund raising endeavors up to this time. He was to return to Canada and The United States later in 1917 and listed his residence as Newburyport Massachusetts, the home of his new wife, with his office in Tremont Temple, Boston[xlvii].

Prior to his visit to Canada in 1916, Minifie followed correct procedure in trying to get letters of introduction so that he would have the best chance of raising funds for the International Bible Institute's war relief fund. In this case he wrote to and called upon Lieutenant Colonel John W Carson[13]. Carson then wrote to Sir Sam Hughes requesting information about Minifie, who had apparently intimated that Sir Sam Hughes would give him a letter of introduction.

Minifie tended to do things by the book so that when he intended to go to Canada in 1916, he asked for a letter of introduction and suggested that this would be forthcoming from Sir Sam Hughes the then General Minister of Militia and Defence. While we have no idea of the response to the letter requesting a letter of introduction, we do know that two letters were written to Sir Sam, by Lieutenant Colonel John W Carson requesting some direction, both dated September 1916[xlviii]. We also know at that time that Sir Sam Hughes was deeply engaged in his own controversies and was soon to be forced to tender his resignation in November 1916. He was a

---

[13] John Wallace Carson was appointed in August 1914 by Sir Sam Hughes, the minister of militia and defence, his "special representative" or agent in Britain. Sir Samuel Hughes, KCB PC (January 8, 1853 – August 23, 1921) was the Canadian Minister of Militia and Defence during World War I

controversial figure and had managed to earn himself the reputation of a bigot amongst the French Canadians.[14]

"**Sir Sam Hughes**, *Canada's minister of militia at the start of the First World War, was a bombastic **bigot** who despised Roman Catholics, French Canadians and professional military officers. He was a man of great passions and unshakable beliefs, traits which initially endeared him to many. But the boasting and bravado that came with those traits would eventually bring him down. Some thought he was eccentric. Others simply called him mad".*[xlix]

It would be hardly surprising if he himself did not reply but handed it to a junior who on looking for the Reverend Minifie as a member of either the Canadian or British Armed Forces found that he was neither.[15]

It is true that he was a Chaplin or more correctly an assistant Chaplin in the City of London National Guard. This position became redundant when the National Guard was re-organised under army control in and around 1916 and "officers were no longer appointed by the Colonel in Command, but by the war office, and the number of commissions were greatly reduced. As a result, the Chaplin's Department was reduced to one namely 'Dr Rosedale'".[l] Minifie is recorded as given four days and ten hours at the Euston Station Section of the National Guard during 1916.[li] This work involved meeting soldiers on transit, helping them with accommodation, food, information and anything else that they might need. The National Guard was formed in and around December 1914 and was principally a creation of the City of London and from the very beginning the question of uniform was a matter of some controversy. "Originally it had been intended to provide dark blue jacket and trousers or

---

[14] Hughes was an Orangeman prone to anti-Catholic sentiments, who was not well liked among French Canadians. (Wikipedia) His Anti-Catholic views resonate with those expressed by Spurgeon and Minifie

[15] Another factor was that "the Militia Department in Ottawa was corresponding with the War Office and three separate individuals in England. MacDougall and Steele had separate commands of the two Canadian contingents in England. Completely divorced from these two officers was an honorary colonel, J. W. Carson, whom Hughes appointed as his special representative in England". (Recommended: Canada's Controversial Sir Sam Hughes (1853–1921) By Carol Whitfield at the Parks of Canada Website)

breeches – not so much a uniform as uniformity of clothing. After the affiliation it was agreed to adopt the recognised grey green of the existing volunteer training core."[lii] In fact in the early days the men had to pay most of their own expenses including their own uniform. With this background it is not surprising that Minifie, who probably had to supply his own uniform, pushed his claim to wear the Khaki to the limit. (He was several times photographed in uniform in England during the war- the Bournemouth Graphic May 12th, 1916 with the caption "Chaplain the Rev DR. William C. Minifie"; Unfortunately, the caption was changed to "Captain Minifie" in some American papers. Note that his name was also mis spelt[liii].)

Given all this 'confusion' it is not surprising that the 'information' that Minifie was not an 'Officer and Gentleman' would make its way back to Canada and into the hands of two people in particular, W. H. Griffith Thomas of Toronto and Joseph W. Ward of New York. Griffith Thomas was of Wycliff College in Toronto and Kemp was of the Metropolitan Tabernacle in New York. These men took it upon themselves to write a warning about Minifie stating that:

"we think it right to mention on the highest official British authority that Dr. Minifie is not and never has been a Chaplin either in the British or in the Canadian Army and therefore has no right to be called Captain as he is sometimes referred to or to wear the khaki as he frequently does. It need hardly be said there is no such post as Honorary Chaplin". [liv]

They went to great pains to state that they had on the *"highest British authority that Dr. Minifie was not and never had been a Chaplain in the British or Canadian army"* and had no right to be called 'Captain'[lv] They go on to say *"Rev. Dinsdale T. Young, disowns all association with Dr. Minifie, who, it seems, is using (but without consent) Mr. Young's name as a President of this International Bible Association or Institute"*[lvi]

All this published under the large heading:

"Caution Concerning Dr. Minifie"

Like many evangelists, Minifie could upset those who had a more orthodox approach. The mission of a charismatic evangelist may be said to 'stir up the faithful and revive the faith in those who may have strayed'. In doing so it is to be expected that they will also stir up controversy, jealousy and other emotions, especially if they are seen to be 'too successful'. Those listening will not only hear what is said but will play it up on retelling. This is especially true in newspapers and applies to both the good and the bad. There is no doubt from the reports that Minifie was not only Charismatic but also very successful and attracted large crowds who would, in all probability been associated with other ministries in the area that he preached.

Collecting monies, for worthy causes, during war time meant that people gave what they could and therefore would not be in a position to give to other more familiar causes, like their local churches. Some ministers may have taken exception to this, even to the extent of being jealous. (Littlejohn maintained that Minifie was 'not a fraud but the victim of professional jealousy'.[lvii])

This activity led to such conflict while he was in America, even to the extent of the funds he had raised for the war relief effort being held up while he was investigated[16]. This prompted him to write a letter in response; -

FROM DR. MINIFIE
Riverside. Cal- - March 23.
Editor El Paso Herald:

My attention has been called to a "warning" which appears in a certain Presbyterian weekly stating that I am not a British chaplain and have no right to wear the khaki, and that the International Bible Institute which I represent is only another name for the International

---

[16] "Funds for W. C. Minifie are held up temporarily. Funds collected by a local church for the International bible association's war work, now represented in Arizona by Re. W. C. Minifie, formerly pastor of a Boston Baptist church, have been held up by the church trustees. They have received work from the head of the British recruiting service in New York that any claims that Dr. Minifie is a chaplain of the British or Canadian forces are unwarranted."
El Paso Herald (El Paso, Tex.), Monday, March 25, 1918,

Bible Students' association and that I am an advocate of "Russellism[17]," etc.

As these falsehoods are doing the Bible Institute and myself serious harm, will you kindly allow me to state that I have in my possession military, Masonic and official papers which prove beyond a doubt that I am what I claim to be, and especially my "commission," which I received on my appointment as a chaplain to the city of London regiment, whose uniform I am fully entitled to wear?

As for the International Bible Institute, it has no connection whatever with the International Bible Students' association but is an evangelical organization with offices in London and Boston, doing a good, genuine and growing work.

As proof positive of the genuineness of the same, it may be stated that I have just received from London an official Intimation that the international Bible Institute has been registered under the "war charities act of 1916, " which means that our relief work has the sanction and endorsement of the British government and that our accounts are audited by the appointed auditor. Nothing more need be said, as this is conclusive, except that I have been empowered by our British board to receive funds for our work and to handle all matters as I may deem expedient. For confirmation of these statements any doubters are referred to our treasurer. Dr. J. Martin Littlejohn, 69 Piccadilly. London.
Yours still in the fighting line.
Wm. C. Minifie.[lviii]

---

[17] "Russellism" teaches that Christ was not Divine before he came to earth, but only a created spirit of an order higher than the angels, and that He was not God in any sense. It teaches that, when Christ came to earth, He dropped that spirit nature and became simply a human being, nothing more nor less— not a man and God, but only man in body, soul and spirit; while He was on earth, He was in no sense Divine. On the cross a man died, and whatever atonement was made for sin was made by the sacrifice of a mere man. Charles Taze Russell, by name Pastor Russell, (born Feb. 16, 1852, Pittsburgh, Pa., U.S.—died Oct. 31, 1916, Pampa, Texas), founder of the International Bible Students Association, forerunner of the Jehovah's Witnesses. (The Editors of Encyclopaedia Britannica)

In this they make several mistakes. Firstly, Minifie was an 'honorary chaplain'. Having presented himself for service to the Chaplain general in England at the beginning of the war *"He explained, however, that he did not desire an ordinary commission, since it would be inconvenient for him to be assigned definitely and for a length of time to any one place. As a result, he was made a special honorary chaplain with power to conduct services from camp to camp as he saw fit".*[lix] The usual mistake- you only get the answer to the question you ask i.e. he was not a 'Chaplain' but he was an 'honorary Chaplain' and as such could be entitled to wear the uniform. He was an auxiliary Chaplain in the national guard but did not continue with this commission when the army took over this unit in 1916[lx]

Secondly, they seem to have mixed up **'The International Bible Institute'** with **'The International Bible Student Association'** which was very active in England and associated with 'Russellism' during the same period as Minifie's organisation and had no association with Minifie.

Kemp, in particular disowns all knowledge of the Bible Institute even though minutes of 'the Cuba Mission' (which changed its name to the International Bible Institute in 1916), clearly names him at meetings as having consented to be Director of the Bible Correspondence College,, and also mentions looking for a replacement for Rev. Dinsdale T. Young as President[lxi]. This begs the question as to why these gentlemen 'turned on' Minifie.

This seems to be traceable to the year 1917. During that year Minifie's wife was drowned in a tragic accident in which he himself almost died. After this, he was interviewed by the Canadian police, returning to England in to marry his second wife in October 1917. Hence to again return to America, arriving I early November 1917[lxii]

These are the type of trials that a charismatic and successful person like Minifie is put through. In all his work, philanthropic and preaching, he had to use the work to fund himself as he had no other source of income. His style of preaching was going out of style.

> "No organized, aggressive evangelistic campaign has been conducted by the church, in this Synod, within the past two years. Spectacular methods, with the big tabernacle and the big band play, have fallen into desuetude (discontinuance from use); quieter methods of a kingdom which cometh not with observation are being resumed. The most effective work in the churches of this Synod seems to have been done by the method of pastoral evangelism."
>
> Minutes of the synod of new England of the Presbyterian church of the united states of America meeting October 28-29, 1919; page 254

It was also the case with the 'Cuba mission' and the 'International Bible institute', that he had to use his lectures/talks to earn his own living and expenses. This left him open to criticism that he was using these organisations for his own benefit. The fact that he does not help himself by the use of hyperbole in his talks and generally, if not encouraging at least not dis-encouraging newspaper reports to 'exaggerate' his stories also leads to inevitable conflict. One interesting anecdote is that at his meetings, when he was a minister in Boston, no charge were made, and new members of the congregation were made to feel welcome and the 'plate for offerings would pass their pew without a hint'-avoiding putting pressure on 'newcomers to give donations but 'offerings or pledges would be accepted'. [lxiii]

This led into the International Bible Institute Affair and his association with Littlejohn being called into question.

The work undertaken by the International bible Institute war relief fund was said, in newspaper articles, to include;

- *"to put a bible in the kit of every soldier who goes to the battle front of France".*[lxiv].
- *"the maintenance of a great military hospital in Loudon, where wounded and gassed soldiers of the allies are being nursed tenderly back to life. This hospital now has its American ward, decorated with the Stars and Stripes. Another department of service, perhaps its greatest, is that of relieving the civilian population in the re-captured portions of northern France, where the British and American armies are now operating. Last year Dr. Minifie collected thousands of dollars for this work; and much more is required this year, to provide tents and tarpaulins, boots, beds and blankets, a field dispensary. traveling soup kitchens, condensed milk for the children, warm clothing, stoves and huts and such other essentials as will be needed for the suffering peoples relieved of the hated Hun rule".*[lxv]. In effect the Institute had taken responsibility for the expense of the ward in a hospital in Enfield, London, devoted to the care of soldiers
- Goods parcels sent to prisoners of war. These were said to contain 1lb . biscuits, 1lb. Gorda cheese, 1 Lb. herring, 1lb. beef and vegetables, 1lb. canned milk, 1/2lb. margarine, 1/4lb. sugar, and 2lbs soup square".[lxvi] [18]
- "Providing active assistance to American soldiers as they pass through London, including lunches and other temporary assistance".[lxvii]

---

[18] This article notably spelt Minifie's name incorrectly and titled him as 'Captain'

Littlejohn and Minifie

At first glance it seems like an odd mixture, Littlejohn a devoted Reformed Presbyterian Minister and Minifie a charismatic Evangelical Baptist Minister. However, they both shared a deep love for the bible and had an interest in healing. Minifie as mentioned above had wanted to study medicine to become a medical missionary but had to forego that because of health reasons and Littlejohn had come to osteopathy from the missionary and from education because of health concerns. In Littlejohn's case, as he saw his own church, the Reformed Presbyterian Church in North America, shrinking would have seen the charismatic and evangelical Minifie commanding large audiences particularly directed at those who had falling away in their beliefs. Littlejohn had even seen his two brothers William and James leave the Reformed Church and move to the United Presbyterian Church though with William eventually becoming a Baptist – the same as Minifie origins. Another factor that may come to mind is that Minifie was initiated into the Masonic Order in 1907[lxviii]. This may seem confusing to some that Littlejohn would associate with him. However, you must remember that the Reformed Presbyterians thought that for the most part orders like the Masons and the Templars did good work, but they objected to the need for them to have an oath or secrecy built into their initiation. So, in fact they may admire the good work that they may do but not the method of membership. Littlejohn's own brother James was a Mason as were many of the lecturers in the Chicago College including Fryette and R. R. Longenecker their solicitor or legal representative.

Littlejohn seems to have met Minifie in 1907 when Minifie was conducting Evangelical Missions in the Boston region and spent some time accompanying him. This was a time in Littlejohn's life when he had undergone many trials including possibly impinging on his own conscience by the use of experimentation on animals even though this may be justified in terms of the benefit to mankind, and thus may have been in need of refreshing his soul so to speak. While himself and Minifie were almost opposites in terms of their character Littlejohn, when he had a message to give, either in preaching or in the educational field, was an inspiring lecturer in his day. His style may have been different from the Rev Minifie's but the effect on the audiences would have been similar. (This may not have been true in Littlejohn's latter days in England in the British School of Osteopathy. but then we have to remember at that stage he was an old man, chronically in pain and still overworking).

Littlejohn's personality led him to be loyal to those that he trusted. Taking them on their word and being open to forgive their errors and mistakes provided they demonstrated a contrite heart and that this was reflected in their actions. We see this demonstrated quite clearly in his relationship with Thomas Edward Hall the same can be said of Minifie. He supported Minifie when Minifie started the Cuba mission. This was an idea to bring bible and bible studies to those in Cuba and to help the poor farmers of that region. Littlejohn lent his support to this noble cause as he saw it. When Minifie was attacked by The Truth Magazine[lxix] on account of this Littlejohn stood by him because he knew the facts.

The Truth Magazine was prone to sensationalism, as this sold copies. When the editor of Truth investigated the London Society of Science Letters and Arts, The chairperson of that society voluntarily went to the editor to give an interview so as to distance his organisation from his similarly named one in France which had run into difficulties regarding possible fraud. During the interview the editor of Truth Magazine plied the chairperson of the society with hard liquor, getting him intoxicated[lxx] and then took comments made by him under the influence of alcohol and published those as fact. Not exactly the actions of a reputable magazine editor.

The same editor apparently accused Minifie of a 'get rich quick scheme' in Cuba. This would be where he would take the local farmers and try to 'presale' their crops in shares to those in England. There are many similar schemes used in England even today to help indigenous farmers so that they can be guaranteed a wage. The downside of it is that it can be used in a fraudulent manner as a possible scheme. Minifie didn't seem to become rich by these activities so I think we can discount it as a pyramid scheme and Littlejohn remained loyal to his friend.

When war broke out, they changed the name of the Cuba Mission to the International Bible Association and aimed at expanding activities to include a bible corresponding course. This would have fulfilled one of Littlejohn's deep interest and love in his life. The study of the bible. It would also have meant that he could have pursued this while at the same time pursuing his other love the practice of osteopathy and the development of the educational system in England, The British School of Osteopathy, without being overly involved in the bible institute. As Minifie then began to raise funds it became clear that the Bible Institute would have to register under the War Charities Act in order to be able to distribute these funds, so they set about that activity. This has been described above. After the fall of the International Bible Institute Minifie went back to his first 'vocation' i.e. as a healer. This may have been the result of Littlejohn's influence. His attitude to healing and its origins is well expressed in the British School of Osteopathy's brochure from 1926:

"From time immemorial there have been " Workers who have devoted themselves to the healing of the sick. Among the ancient this was chiefly confined to the Ministers of Religion. This was countenanced by the fast that Divine healing was the order established by Jesus of Nazareth, the Model Healer"[lxxi]

From this it is easy to see how he might have influenced Minifie, another minister, to find in Osteopathy a path similar to his calling, especially as his first interest was to be a 'medical missionary'.[lxxii]

He started to study under Littlejohn in the fledging British School of Osteopathy[19] but during his studies emigrated to America, possibly under the influence of his second wife. He seems to have settled in Reno, Nevada for a couple of years, practicing as

Dr. Minifie, D.C., PH.D.,

(former London Practitioner)

New Drugless Methods."[lxxiii]

On returning again to England he completed his studies in osteopathy and then helped Littlejohn in the British School of Osteopathy and

---

[19] 'in 1918, he entered the BSO and in 1926 he was awarded the 9th diploma, having returned to the USA during 1920-24' Osteopathy in Great Britain, the first hundred years, Dr. martin Collins, page 21.

practiced osteopathy in his own right. Littlejohn described Minifie as someone "who knows me better than anyone else[lxxiv]". This is a good description because he would have been one of the few people if not the only person who would have been involved not only in his osteopathic life but also directly involved in his spiritual life. So that Littlejohn's two loves, osteopathy and the bible would have been shared with him.

The one thing that we see for definite in this relationship is Littlejohn's almost naive acceptance of somebody who overtly demonstrates love of osteopathy and the love of the bible, accepting their failings provided they show a contrite heart and an effort to change. His attitude, as mentioned earlier, was not to dwell upon the weakness of others, but to point out and demonstrate a better way or path. We see that Minifie after his trials with the Bible Institute and the Cuba Mission left the evangelical world and moved into private practice in osteopathy. He moved from the world of evangelicalism and public speaking into what seemed to have been one of his first inclinations, that was healing, and into osteopathy, to which he gave good service right up until his ninety second year This change of direction in itself was not a straightforward conversion.

After the war, Minifie entered the British School of Osteopathy to study under Littlejohn. He had previously studied anatomy, physiology and first aid at London teaching hospitals and the Royal College of Surgeons with the aim of becoming a medical missionary, an aim which had been thwarted by the missionary society deciding that his health was not up to work in the tropics. He graduated for the British School of Osteopathy in 1926 having spent the years 1920-24 in America[lxxv]

.

> **DR. MINIFIE, D. C.**
> Ph. C., Ph. D., F. R. S. L. (England)
> **New Drugless Healing**
> Consultations Free
> 129 N. Virginia St., Reno
>
> Nevada State Journal.
> Oct 05, 1920, page 6

On returning to England again in 1926 he helped Littlejohn establish the first osteopathic clinic in the UK, lectured at the British School of Osteopathy, served as a member of its council and practiced as an osteopath both in London and in the French Riviera, even at the grand age of 91.[lxxvi] He died in Newton Abbot, Devon, in 1961 aged 92.

The change from evangelist to osteopath may seem a big step, but his history was that the wanted to be a medical missionary, 'laying on of hands' is a part of the ministry so a hands-on approach to healing would inevitably seem attractive.

"Sometimes religion seems overmuch concerned with souls. The Devine mission and commission to preach the gospel included, not only saving men's souls but healing the sick."[lxxvii]

After giving himself so completely to the ministry, and as an evangelist missionary and then to raising money to help with and personally tending to war victims I don't find it surprising that he would change to working on a one to one basis with a system of medicine using only his hands as tools – laying on of hands – especially after the criticisms that he had faced.

Swapping as it were preaching to the fallen masses to helping individuals develop their health. The health, as we know from Littlejohn's writings, involve not only the physical health but their mental health and their ethics.

It is hard to say what to make of the good Dr. Minifie. He certainly was charismatic, energetic and passionate about anything he did. Was he a fraud? After all I have read about him, I have to say, in my opinion, he wasn't. He did sail close to the wind and with his turn of phrase and 'journalistic license' it is easy to see how 'honorary chaplain' becomes 'captain', 'international bible institute' becomes 'international bible association', the money raised reaches '$500,000'[20] and so on. This seems to be a misquote from an article he wrote saying *"Minifie was able to collect last year thousands of dollars but the need is so great that $500,000 will soon be required ..."*[lxxviii]

It is always hard to say why two people become close friends especially when they come from very different aspects in their lives. It may be a case of opposites attracting. Or simply that their shared love for the bible and healing in all aspects of people's lives would override any differences in their overall approach to the subject.

---

[20] If he had indeed raised $500,000, I think the relief work he was involved in would have become much better known, or, if he was a fraud, he would have been a rich man'. The most I have found reported to have been raised at a meeting was in the order of $500, most of which was pledged, so may not have materialised. Full audited accounts for the International Bible Institute were rendered to the Charity Commission when it was wound up in 1920 (Letter dated 14th April 1920, War Charities case file 545 ; Title War Charities act 1916 - Register of applications - Cases 1-550; Reference Code LCC/PC/CHA/03/001; From Collection LONDON COUNTY COUNCIL)

Reverend Minifie, Littlejohn and the International Bible Institute War Relief Fund

Minifie was a boy wonder, in modern parlance, charismatic, eloquent and an engaging preacher almost to the point of that you could call him an entertainer. While it is evident from the newspaper cuttings and his writings that he never engaged in untruths he did present the truth in a manner to maximise its importance and effect. This would leave it open to misinterpretation usually in a manner which would be of benefit to him in attracting audiences. For example, we find that he always said of himself that he was at 'one-time Assistant Private Secretary to Spurgeon'. In a number of newspaper reports we find this being transposed to being 'Private Secretary'. The only complaint noted about this was from the Reverend J.W. Harold for whom Minifie acted as assistant in Thornton Heath for some time[lxxix].

In the same vein he presented himself as an 'auxiliary Chaplin' and wore the Khaki of the British army. He was in fact, a Chaplin or more correctly an assistant Chaplin in the City of London National Guard. A position which became redundant when the National Guard was re-organised under regular army control in 1916. At the beginning of the war the men had to pay for their own uniform. So, it is not surprising that Minifie pushed his claim to wear the Khaki, even to the extent of a 'Captains uniform[21]' His tendency to "stretch the truth to its limits of credibility" would rebound and eventually lead him to move from the ministry and evangelical work and into osteopathy.

Another aspect of Minifie's methods that needs to be mentioned is his use of the so-called 'silver collection'[lxxx].

---

[21] At meetings held in England, he openly wore the Uniform and was addressed as honorary Chaplain (Bournemouth Graphic, may 12th 1916). I found no complaints in England about this except in the police report into the International Bible Institute war relief fund

This is where only silver coins would be given in collection thus, aiming to maximise the return or from a more charitable viewpoint, to put a minimum entrance fee of three old pence on the event. The more modern equivalent of this would be the so-called 'silent collection' or the 'sea of green' as they were called. These practices were looked on with distain by many evangelists whereas others used them quite openly and freely with the viewpoint to maximising the collection on the day. Usually the Minister, in this case Minifie himself, would make the determination how much of the collection would go to a particular cause and how much would go to his own living. This left it open to considerable possible abuse on the one hand and to accusations of abuse on the other hand. There is evidence that when he was in Boston his practice moved away from this in that at least one report mentions that when the collection came around those who had not been regular attenders at his meetings were avoided so that they were not put into a position of having to give a donation[lxxxi]. This would tend to indicate that while he used these controversial practices his underlying motivation may have been towards the nobler aspect of putting a minimum fee on the event while encouraging those of more means to subsidise those of lesser means.

The International Bible Institute Affair

The 'International bible Institute war relief fund' was registered under the war Charities Act, 1916 and was removed from the register in September 1918. Why it was removed from the register is dealt with below, but would seem to be the result of the letter of warning written by Joseph W. Kemp of the Metropolitan Tabernacle New York in February 1918, which reverberated across America and to England whence it led to an investigation by the Charity commissioners. Why Kemp, who had been an associate of Minifie, 'turned on' him seems to relate to incidents in 1917 including the tragic death of Minifies first wife in April 1917 and his subsequent remarriage in October 1917 in England.

In his meetings held in England, during the first world war, Minifie openly wore the Uniform and was addressed as honorary Chaplain. I found no complaints in England about this except in the police report into the International Bible Institute war relief fund. In this document it is stated that *"Dr. Minifie was formerly an assistant chaplain of the national Guard, but was not reappointed when that body was taken over by the Army Council, and a question has been raised as to this user of the military uniform subsequent to that event"*.[lxxxii] However, no further information or enquiry seems to have been made. It is unbelievable that during the war years, if he was not entitled to the rank of Chaplain and to wear the uniform that no complaints would have been made in England or in the army camps that he attended and gave sermons in. Even after the Institute was removed for the register of the Charity Commissioners, Minifie was recorded as still giving lectures in October 1918[lxxxiii] as 'Dr. W. C. Minifie, Director of the Bible Institute of London'[lxxxiv].

Kemp and Griffith Thomas go on to disown Minifie and to discredit the 'International Bible Association', which they mix up with Minifie's association 'The International Bible Institute'[lxxxv]. And even go as far as saying that the Reverend Dinsdale T Young disowns all association with Dr Minifie even though Dr Young was or had given his name to be used in connection with the International Bible Institute.

This turn of events seems very much to be related to Minifie's request for a letter of introduction from Lieutenant Colonel John W Carson[22] so that he would have the best chance of raising funds for the International Bible Institute's war relief fund while in Canada and the USA.. This then , apparently, led to circulation of information that Minifie was not a Chaplin in either the British or Canadian forces; However, the fact that he had been a Chaplin within the National Guard and therefore entitled to wear the uniform was omitted.

---

[22] John Wallace Carson was appointed in August 1914 by Sir Sam Hughes, the minister of militia and defence, his "special representative" or agent in Britain. Sir Samuel Hughes, KCB PC (January 8, 1853 – August 23, 1921) was the Canadian Minister of Militia and Defence during World War I

This lead Kemp who was also associated with Minifie in the International Bible Institute to not only distance himself from him but to orchestrate a campaign to discredit Minifie during his time in America. The net effect of this was an investigation by the United Presbyterian Synod and Minifie to be put on the suspension role of the United Presbyterian Synod. He was summoned to account for himself at the synod in 1918 however this synod did not take place because of the 1918 flu epidemic[lxxxvi] and as far is known Minifie never did attend nor was asked to attend a synod after that date to offer any explanation.

This misinformation that Minifie was never a Chaplin in the army and not entitled to wear the 'khaki' and the investigation in America into his activities came back again to England and lead to the investigation by the CID into the International Bible Institute War Relief Fund and its subsequent deregulation by the Charity Commissioners.

At the end of its investigation the Charity Commissioners did get audited accounts of the Charity and acknowledged that the funds were distributed correctly; no charges were ever made against the Directors of it.[lxxxvii] The Charity Commissioners seemed to take the "easy way out" for when an appeal against their decision to deregister the International Bible Institute War Relief Fund was made and it was found to be outside the rather short required time for an appeal to be lodged "the commissioners saw no reason to extend the time".[lxxxviii]

Regarding the CID investigation on behalf of the Charity Commissioners, it is open to criticism on a number of points:

It seemed to ignored all previous investigations which were made at the onset of the registration process, including all the references of good character for Minifie, Littlejohn and the others involved.

It seemed to ignore the contradictory evidence of people like Kemp and others taking only one version of events and not looking at the contradictory statements they had made.

It seemed to take the route that if there might be a scandal then it is best to avoid it and with such a small organisation who is going to notice.

(The following account is based upon statements in the file *War Charities Act 1916- Register of applications - Cases 1-550 Reference Code* LCC/PC/CHA/03/001 held in the London Metropolitan Archives unless otherwise stated)

The International Bible Institute was a continuation of a charitable organisation known as the Cuba Mission which was started in America in and around 1909 by Dr. Minifie. Littlejohn, by his own admission had been associated with Dr. Minifie and his work since "practically the inauguration of the societies" but he only took over as treasurer at the International Bible Institute at the beginning of world war 1. At that stage there was practically no money standing to the credit of the Cuba Mission and Dr. Minifie was the only person who had drawn power on the accounts Towards the beginning of world war 1 it was decided that the Cuba Mission should be renamed as the International Bible Institute and it was the intention to establish correspondence colleges for bible studies within America and England. However, on account of the outbreak of the war it was not possible to carry out any of these projects. Joseph W. Kemp apparently had agreed to become Director of the Bible Correspondence Colleges. At a meeting in 1914 at the Stand Palace Hotel in was decided by the executive committee which comprised Mr. Ward, Littlejohn and Minifie to devote their energies towards the relief of war sufferers in Europe and not to continue with the Cuba Mission as such.

Dr Minifie was not associated with any particular church or organisation at this time and earned his living from evangelical work, missionary meetings and lectures that he gave on the subject of the bible. He also at this time he presented himself to the chaplain general and offered his services. At the time he did not desire an ordinary commission since it would be inconvenient for him to be assigned definitely and for a length of time to any particular place. As a result, he was made a "special honorary chaplain" with the power to conduct services from camp to camp as he saw fit[lxxxix]. During 1915 and 1916 he lectured and covered expenses for the institute. These lectures were not only in England and Europe but also in America. Unfortunately, during his time in Canada in 1917 his wife died in a drowning accident in which he almost died from hyperthermia. From the reports of the Scotland Yard investigation into the charity it appears that Dr Minifie was interviewed approximately one month after his wife's death and the CID or Scotland Yard reported this as him being "interrogated"[23]. The people in the region seemed content with the results of the investigation while others, like, H. Griffith Thomas of Toronto and Joseph W. Ward of New York., were not.

"Charity is a great virtue, but it can be overdone. Investigation of some of the unfavorable rumors about Rev. (Caps) Minifie coupled with a feeling of sympathy for him in the loss of his wife appears to have convinced the good people of Kincardine that he was 'straight'"[xc24]

. However, from minutes of the meeting of the Advisory Board to the

---

Aug. 17th, 1917

It was arranged that letters from the British Advisory Board should be sent to Kincardine, St. Catherines, Ont., and Buffalo, refuting the charges and insinuations made against him in those places and thanking contributors for their offerings.

Minutes of the Advisory Board
to the
International Bible Institute

---

[23] Police report 29th May 1918; He (Minifie) Is a widower his wife having been drowned on the 24th April,1917, at Kincardine, Lake Huron, Canada. On the 30th May 1917, Mr. Minifie was interrogated by the police of St. Catherine's, Ontario, Canada, with regard to his movements in Canada. He was then touring the Country dressed in the uniform of the Captain of the National Guard of the City of Landon, preaching, giving lectures and collecting money on behalf of the Institute. (page 2 of metropolitan police report 29th May 1918 in the War Charities Case file 545). Note, at this time Minifie had remarried and therefore not technically a widower.

[24] The author of this article while accepting that the people of Kincardine were happy with the explanations he was not.

Bible Institute taken by Littlejohn it would appear that the CID interviews ranged into other areas including Minifies wearing of the uniform and his collection of money on behalf of the Institute. It would also appear that Minifie was upfront with Littlejohn and the 'Advisory Board' about these problems.

In this we see Littlejohn's tendency to accept the word of those he worked with, especially if they appealed to his love of the bible (or osteopathy). In this instance he had volunteered not only his osteopathic skills to help treat injured solders but also his skill in Bible studies to take on the Direction of the Bible Correspondence Department in Great Britain.

Another example of this tendency is to be found in his dealings with T. E. Hall. In one letter to Hall, on 16th August 1928. In this he says *"I have trusted you to keep your promise. I was very much surprised; I confess when I found your name attached to a paper which if it meant anything meant I was not capable of conducting the school*[xci]..." From subsequent letters it would appear that Hall apologized and Littlejohn accepted and forgave him even to the extent of commiserating with him when he had his own troubles in November 1930 *"Please do not let any of these things mar our friendship...I admire the way in which you stated specifically the grounds based upon financial circumstances*[25xcii]..." Thus, showing that their friendship had continued despite the earlier 'breach of faith'. This was consistent with Littlejohn's values and how he tried to live his life. This could be seen as a weakness or a strength depending upon your viewpoint..

Another aspect of Littlejohn's character is illustrated in his friendship with Minifie. Minifie's usual method of preaching and lecturing was to appeal to the emotions of his audience in a direct and often 'inflammatory' manner. For example:

"Romanism, once flung out of England's back-door, now, arrayed in the guise of Ritualism, is boldly walking up John Bull's front step and entering into his drawing-room, there wiping its dirty boots on our

---

[25] This episode was concerning Halls court case for breach of promise and the surrounding publicity. This is dealt with latter on.

best Axminister, and it is about time we showed it the back door again, and gave it a little assistance in getting there"; The Education Act is designed to hang Protestantism upon the gallows of Popery, and not merely so, but to make it pay for the rope". He concluded a sermon by making an appeal to his hearers not to surrender their consciences to "a power which blows out the lamp of knowledge and dams back the stream of liberty"(loud applause)[xciii]*

This type of retoric is reminiscent of the type of appeal some early Osteopaths including Hildreth[26] would use. In their case read Drugs, Medicine and M.D. instead of Pope, Romanism and Priest/Jesuits.

Littlejohn on the other hand would use reasoned argument as in this extract from an article of Cardinal Satolli's views upon schools;

"He comes with all the prejudices of Papal Europe to destroy the free thought and enlightened sentiments of the Western Christian civilization. He may possess sufficient tact to compromise the petty priestly squabbles of his own faction and to secure peace on the surface, but he show s an amount of ignorance in dealing with institutional and constitutional questions purely American, excusable only on the ground that he is a foreign prelate. If he fancies that the American people will accept...

---

[26] For example: "My God ; why is it men and women will continually keep trying to pollute our calling; why is it that they constantly seek to sap the life of our great science, born in the same manner and of the same principles as the divine law that guides and guards every single atom of this wonderful universe. Every heart-beat of the great osteopathic body which now exists should revolt against any movement that does other than to carry us closer to, and give us more knowledge of, the laws which have made our existence possible".; "But rather, my part in the action taken there regarding the granting of M. D. degrees by some of our osteopathic colleges came from the same pure, holy, divine source that hurls the frantic mother bird or the giant tigress, between seeming impending danger and her cherished offspring — the same desire that would impel a mother to twine her arms around her child and guard with her life, if need be, her loved ones." Hildreth; The Journal of the American Osteopathic Association Vol 9 sept 09, Aug 1910. page 196/7

"He will learn, we hope, ere long that no sectarian school system can represent or safeguard the Constitution of this country…. He places high eulogium upon the Romish schools, as model specimens of education.

"American citizens have learned to value, not the sectarian school,— this they abhor, because of its tendency to instill the embittered prejudices of Romanism into the minds of the rising generation—but the public school, because in it there is found one of the main defences against an aggressive denominationalism and one of the best influences in producing enlightened citizens. The Christians of America do no desire to hinder the growth of denominations within their proper sphere, but all truth loving Christians desire to see a system of education free from the over-mastering influences of any one sect."

With Minifie, Littlejohn developed a strong and lasting relationship. With Hildreth no such relationship was possible. Hildreth seemed to hold an angst against Littlejohn up to the point of not even mentioning his name in his book "The Lengthening Shadow of Dr. Andrew Taylor Still". As mentioned earlier, Hildreth dealt very differently with a friend who expressed ideas similar to Littlejohn's in regard to being honest about the use of antiseptics, antidotes surgery etc.[27] So it would seem that personal matters rather than style of presentation was the problem.

Littlejohn's friendship with Minifie extended into his influence over him, supporting him when his rhetoric ended in catastrophe and guiding him into the profession of Osteopathy while keeping his underlying Christian values and missionary spirit. This was very much Littlejohn's way, to look after the wayward and 'damaged' and try to help them find their way. We see this again in his friendship with Thomas Edward Hall.

To return to Minifie, he presented to the advisory board of the institute a report and statement of the amounts collected and his expenditures, and also letters from the First National Bank stating what monies had been deposited to the credit of the institute[xciv]. This

---

[27] "A Plea for Honesty" by a friend on Hildreth, Frederick W. Sherburne, D. O., in the April 1908 journal of the American Osteopathic Association.

meeting was held at Littlejohn's office in Piccadilly, probably because it was the most convenient place to do so and not because that office was associated in any way with the institute. In fact, Littlejohn rented a room at that address from another osteopath during that time. During this time, it was found that before they should be collecting money on behalf of the war victims or distributing money for that cause the charity should be registered with the War Charities Board under the War Charities Act 1916. They then proceeded to apply for registration. Littlejohn as treasurer was advised by the board not to distribute any money until the registration was secured.

Dr Minifie stated in a letter that he wrote to Littlejohn in May of 1917 that there seemed to be some misunderstanding as to the auspices under which his meetings in Canada were organised and he thought it was wise to hand all the monies over to a bank in Canada and to get them to forward the same to John Lowden treasurer of the Christian Men's Federation of Canada to be thereafter forwarded to Mr. W. Ward of the "Brotherhood National Counsel" as this organisation was authorised to raise funds for relief work. And he suggested that until they receive their own registration that the institute should raise money on their behalf. It is interesting to note that Mr. Ward in his statement to the police denied all knowledge of the institute even to the extent of saying *"the (national Brotherhood) Counsel has not the remotest connection with the International Bible Institute, nor has it received any monies from that institute"*

He goes on in the statement to contradict himself then by saying that Minifie had given his services and which did result in financial benefit to his fund.

"He may have given, and I believe he did give his services in Canada which did result in financial benefit to the Fund. The meetings at which he gave his services were raised by the National Brotherhood Council".

He also denied that he had ever met or heard of Littlejohn even though back in 1914 he seems to have been at one of the advisory committee meetings for the Cuba Mission; Littlejohn, in his statement says the *'Executive Committee which comprised Mr. Ward besides myself and Dr. Minifie, to devote our energies to the relief of war sufferers in Europe. This meeting was held at the Strand Palace Hotel in 1914'*

It may have been that he simply didn't register that the International Bible Institute was an outgrowth of the Cuba Mission or that more likely, he tried to distant himself as far as possible from any police investigation.

It is also worth noting at this stage that at a meeting of the institute on the 17th August 1917 they were looking for a successor to D.T. Young as President. This contradicts some of the statements in the police statements where they have *"on good authority"* that Dr Young was never associated with the institute. This again may have been as a result of the confusion between the International Bible Institute and another organisation called 'The International Bible Student Association', which was an organisation devoted to 'Russellism' and therefore an organisation which Dr Young would not want to be associated with.

The phrase "we have it on good authority" has been used more than once in the report of the Charity Commissioners. However, the 'authority' is never stated nor is any evidence given. This together with the lack of challenging the statements of Ward, Broughton and other inconsistencies puts the whole investigation into a poor light, appearing to be agenda driven as opposed to one which is looking for the truth.

The Institute came about from a name change of the Cuba Mission in 1916 and applied for registration under the War Charities 1916 Act and on 28th February 1918 was duly registered after a full enquiry into the Bona fides of all involved including Littlejohn and Minifie.

> Subject of enquiry a Baptist Minister, Dr of Divinity, and Fellow of the Royal Society of Literature, has been in residence in East End Rd, East Finchley, for several years, where he maintains a fair home. He bears an excellent reputation, has travelled extensively in Canada, and the United States, and is also well known in Yorkshire where he was most successful in his ministry. We are given to understand he is not at all likely to enter into an engagement he could not see his way clear to meet.
>
> Perry and Stubs report on Dr. Wm. C. Minifie
For War Charities Act, 1916. Case No, 697.
>
> ------------------------
>
> Subject of inquiry is a Doctor of Philosophy and reputed to be a man of considerable educational attainments. As far as we can gather, he has a comfortable income and is regarded locally as of undoubted respectability and paying his way satisfactorily
>
> Perry and Stubs report on Dr. J. Martin Littlejohn
For War Charities Act, 1916. Case No, 697.

Around the same time in America their colleague Joseph W. Kemp, who had been named as wanting to be the director of the Bible Correspondence Colleges wrote a letter of warning concerning Dr Minifie. This resulted in a cable from the British Counsel in Boston looking for the bona fides of the Institute and of Dr Minifie and the opening of the CID Scotland Yard investigation. This investigation would eventually lead to the charity being removed from the register in August 1918.

In between time with what little money had been transferred to the charity Littlejohn was able to start distributing funds. However, this ran into some difficulty in the beginning as the accounts had not been changed to allow him to write cheques under his signature and the cheques were returned. He corrected this immediately and increased the amount of the donation to the particular charities.

At the same time more money could not be transferred from the funds collected in America because they had been frozen by the bank while, as a result of Kemp's 'warning' Dr Minifie and his cause were investigated by the United Presbyterian Synod of New England, with which Rev. Minifie was registered as a minister. Dr Minifie had been a former pastor of the Clarendon Street Baptist Church in Boston and that some members of the clergy in that area did not like the way that he preached or the methods that he used. This investigation was on the foot of the warning published by Kemp and a colleague of his W.H. Griffith Thomas of the Wycliff College in Toronto[xcv].

It is also interesting to note that the whole matter came up for public attention and discussion at a Baptist Ministers Conference in Tremont Temple and that the president of that David M. Lockrow appointed a committee to investigate the matter. This is the same man who is mentioned as a member of the committee of the International Bible Institute.[xcvi]. Minifie had previously transferred the funds collected legitimately to the 'National Brotherhood' organization via John Lowden, Treasurer of the Christian Men's Federation of Canada to the Mr. W. Ward of the National Brotherhood Council.

The police investigation itself and the reports makes interesting reading. One of the points that they make is regarding the Secretary of the Bible Institute in Britain, Violet G Minifie, a daughter of Dr. Minifie. Miss Dorothy Minifie Hall, her sister, was Dr Minifie's secretary, but she left London in 1917 and her sister Violet Gwendolyn Minifie took over as secretary but didn't change the name on the office or on the literature for the institute. The police investigator made a big thing about this, charging that the secretary of the institute named as Miss Dorothy Hall turns out to be the daughter and that this was done to hide the family connection. Dorothy had married Graham Hall in 1914[xcvii]

But they didn't seem to acknowledge that both sisters had lost their mother not a year previously in a drowning accident in Canada and that her father had remarried at the end of 1917 and during that time they were both trying to hold their lives together in their various ways and were probably still in shock. Nor did they mention that Dorothy Hall was the secretary for 3 years and her name was already on the literature, and therefore changing the name would involve additional expense. In the same report the investigating officers refer to Minifie as 'a widower' even though he had remarried some five months before they did their report.

There were many failings in their report. The report complains that they didn't disperse any money and produce letters from some of the charities to that effect. However, they didn't follow that up by showing that Littlejohn had dispersed money to charities but was stopped from further dispersals due to the investigation in America and the Police investigation in England. Another point they raised was that the auditor Mr. Broughton in his statement says that *'he has never been connected in any way with Institute and has not even seen the books of the society. He was certainly asked to act as auditor for the Institute but has never been called upon to carry out such duties'*. The date of establishment of the Charity is given as 30th August 1916, meaning that, in normal circumstances, a full year's accounts would not have been available for audit until, at earliest September 1917. The extract from the minutes sent to the Charity Commissioners on the 13th September 1917 adds the note *"This branch of the work is new, therefore there are no accounts to present"*. Also, during that time and until registration under the War Charitie Act had been approved, they should not make appeals to the public for funds. This restriction caused Minifie some difficulty. Until the registration had taken place, 28th February 1918, as state above, moneys collected in America had been transferred to National Brotherhood Council.

In Mr. Broughton's statement that, while he had agreed to be Auditor, he had not undertaken the duties of an auditor starts to make sense. Until registration had taken place there was little for him to do. The absence of audited accounts was noted on the Institutes application but did not prevent or impinge on its registration. Its rather surprising that in the subsequent investigation nobody seemed to acknowledge or understand that there were no books or other things to be investigated because the Institute had been told not to collect or distribute any funds until registration had taken place.

One last word on the International Bible Institute is that in the file of the Charity commission a letter dated 14th April 1920, states:

"I am to refer you to the letters which were addressed to you from this office on 16th and 29th

August 1918. The committee appealed against the removal of the Charity from the Register, but the appeal was not presented within the prescribed time and the Commissioners saw no reason to extend the time.

Audited accounts of the Charity were obtained and with the approval of the Commissioners[28] a sum of £9-9-0 was paid to the treasurer of the Charity and the residue of the funds amounting to £103-5-4 was paid to the Enfield Voluntary Aid Detachment Hospital. **A final audited account showing the application of the funds was rendered to the Commissioners".**

So, after all the investigations it is to be seen that the Charity accounted for its actions in a satisfactory manner despite not having its appeal heard on purely technical grounds, probably, in no small measure, due to Minifie not being in the country at the right time. Apart from t Dorothy Hall's name being continued to be used as secretary even though her sister, Violet Gwendoline Minifie had taken over that role, the Charity was not only handled properly but concluded properly despite all the negative charges thrown at them. Much of this can be put down to Littlejohn as he seemed to be the main person who stuck by the Institute and dealt with the flak that arose from the investigation.

Another charge that was made against Dr Minifie during this episode, was that he was not entitled to wear the kaki of the British army. This was particularly made in Canada and followed up in America. In his defense he stated that he was auxiliary Chaplin of the City of London volunteers. However, it would seem to be more appropriate that he was *"formerly an assistant Chaplin of the National Guard but was not reappointed when the body was taken over by the army counsel and a question has been raised as to his use of military*

---

[28] Author's emphasis

uniform subsequent to that event"[29]. It seems to be a debatable point and perhaps he would have been better off not continuing to wear the uniform and particularly as the uniform he seems to have worn did not have the cap emblem for the Chaplaincy but for the Regiment. (as mentioned earlier he may have had to purchase the uniform himself, and he had worn it in England at numerous events without any complaint).

It is worth noting that in his application for renewal of his British Citizenship in 1924, and the associated police investigation concluded that *"there is no suspicion attaching to the applicant (Littlejohn) personally over the Minifie incident and he apparently acted in good faith"*[xcviii]

This entire episode illustrates a number of points. Firstly, when you work outside of the establishment you attract a certain type of person to you and the methods that you use become questionable to the establishment merely because you are outside of it. This is illustrated in the police reports where they use phrases like *"Littlejohn has absolutely no qualifications in this country"* and where they take selective extracts from certain statements and use them in a negative manner, e.g. taking statement from a Major Leggatt of the Enfield Auxiliary Hospital in which he states that "Dr Minifie promised financial assistance which has never been received nor has any help been offered or received from the International Bible Institute". Even though quite clearly the hospital later does acknowledge the receipt of monies from Littlejohn towards the expenses of the hospital. They also take Mr. Wards statement that he only heard by accident of the existence of the International Bible Institute even though it is shown in the minutes of the Cuba Mission that he was at a meeting in 1914 and does not seemed to have re-examined Ward on this point.

When the establishment is asked to make an investigation into something that is outside of the establishment it cannot help but being biased to some extent.

---

[29] Quote taken from the police report in 'War Charities case file 545; Title War Charities act 1916 - Register of applications - Cases 1-550; Reference Code LCC/PC/CHA/03/001; From Collection LONDON COUNTY COUNCIL

The police report for Littlejohn's renewal of his British citizenship application in 1924, makes a similar point when talking about the medical opinion of Osteopaths in general and Littlejohn in particular. They came across and reported the very antagonistic attitude of the British medical association and the medical practitioner's union in the course of their standard enquiries. The report say *"this somewhat antagonistic attitude may be due to a certain extent, to professional jealousy, as it is understood that the number of men taking up Osteopathy as a profession, and obtaining substantial fees, is on the increase"* and the opinion was that *"the statement by the Secretary of the Medical Practitioners Union that osteopathy is quackery in its crudest form is far too sweeping to be taken as a considered view"*[xcix]

All of Minifie's associates seemed to have either come out with statements seemingly corroborating the negative allegations against him, without any evidence as such or distanced themselves as far as they could from him. The sole exception to this was Littlejohn who seemed to stick by Minifie. Later on, when Minifie was qualified as an osteopath he accepted his assistance in teaching in the British School of Osteopathy and even as a member of the board of governors. This is an element of Littlejohn's character that is sometimes overlooked. He was loyal, he also tended to take people at their word and to help the wayward if possible. Some may see this as naivety, which it may be, but it is also reflective of his upbringing and that a person's word was their bond. And he expected others to fulfill that as much as he would.

> An interesting anecdote about his views was given in the El Paso Herald, March 9th, 1918, page 12, when in answer to a question he said
>
> **"Just what is the nature of the House of Lords. The House of Lords is a back number and is due for the junk heap. We have no more use for lords, or for kings for that matter, except as ornaments".**
>
> Given Littlejohn's background I can't help but feel these sentiments echo his feelings at least to some extent.

---

[i] The Christian Nation Volume 57, September 1912, page 10
[ii] The Reflex 1923 page 96; Osteopathy in Great Britain, J Martin Littlejohn
[iii] Select Committee on the Regulation and Registration of Osteopaths Bill 1935; minutes of Evidence; paragraph 3073
[iv] John Martin LittleJohn biography by John Wernham, page 54-55; Private publication by The Maidstone Osteopathic Clinic.; and private conversations and recollections given in lectures
[v] John Martin LittleJohn biography by John Wernham, page 54-55; Private publication by The Maidstone Osteopathic Clinic.
[vi] The Reflex 1923, Osteopathy in Great Britain, J Martin Littlejohn
[vii] Lake County Recorder of Deeds online access point; Document #134979 in Deed Book #177 Pg. 527; Document #175069 in Deed Book #208 Pg. 632
[viii] NATIONALITY AND NATURALISATION: Littlejohn, John Martin, from the United States of America; Catalogue reference: HO 144/4540
[ix] Essex County council archives; Certificates of birth and death
[x] John Martin LittleJohn biography by John Wernham, page 54-56; Private publication by The Maidstone Osteopathic Clinic

[xi] The Osteopathic Technique and Philosophy of John Wernham; DVD section 9 'a brief biography of J. M. Littlejohn'; 1996 C Campbell and The Institute of Classical Osteopathy; Original from a letter by Dr. Streeter in the Pacific Journal (possibly of Osteopathy) in unknown year – Taped interview with Dr. Stoddard 1993, at 9 minutes 37 seconds

[xii] Personal interviews with John Wernham, Douglas Mann, Dr. Stoddard, Ralph Hardy; Tape recordings of T. E. Hall, J Canning and others. Some of these are now in the National Osteopathic Archive

[xiii] John Martin LittleJohn biography by John Wernham, page 56; Private publication by The Maidstone Osteopathic Clinic

[xiv] November 1931 issue of The Osteopath, No. 192

[xv] Personal interview with Anne Kennard

[xvi] Who's Who in America, a biographical dictionary of notable living men and women of the united states, Vol X, 1918-19 Page 1716; edited by Albert Nelson Marquis; Chicago: A. N. Marquis & Company

[xvii] Temple daily telegram, feb 28 1918, page 10

[xviii] Cheltenham chronicle, sept 19th, 1903

[xix] The Western Times, Thursday May 26th, 1892

[xx] http://www.spurgeons.ac.uk/about/history

[xxi] https://www.lansdownechurch.uk

[xxii] Bradford daily telegraph, March 23rd, 1900

[xxiii] Who's Who in America, a biographical dictionary of notable living men and women of the united states, Vol X, 1918-19, page 1716; edited by Albert Nelson Marquis; Chicago: A. N. Marquis & Company

[xxiv] London Daily News, May 28th, 1907

[xxv] Library and museum of Freemasonry, England, Membership register; country Q 1391-1482 to country R 1486-1575; reel number 480

[xxvi] Letter from Littlejohn to his son concerning his funeral arrangements National Osteopathic Archive, British School of Osteopathy, material

[xxvii] Boston Post, May 7th, 1908, page 4

[xxviii] Boston Post, March 8th, 1909, page 4

[xxix] London Metropolitan Archives

[xxx] Minutes of the Synod of New England 1912

[xxxi] Who's Who in America, a biographical dictionary of notable living men and women of the united states, Vol X, 1918-19, page 1716; edited by Albert Nelson Marquis; Chicago: A. N. Marquis & Company

[xxxii] New York Passenger Arrival Lists (Ellis Island), 1892-1924", FamilySearch (https://familysearch.org/ark:/61903/)

[xxxiii] West Sussex county times and standard May 9th, 1914, page 5

[xxxiv] Ibid

[xxxv] South of England Advertiser May 7[th, 1914], page 11: The Newcastle Daily journal, January 7th 914:
[xxxvi] Truth, March 10th, 1915, page 371; British Library Holdings
[xxxvii] Minutes of Advisory Board meeting held at 69 Piccadilly, London, August 30th, 1916. On file at London Metropolitan Archives; War Charities Act 1916, Reference Code LCC/PC/CHA/03/003, Case 545
[xxxviii] London Metropolitan Archives; War Charities Act 1916, Reference Code LCC/PC/CHA/03/003, Case 545; Charity organisation society, inquiry department; report number 3/5555; September 10th, 1918
[xxxix] Library and archives of Canada; File block 6 - First series of CEF personnel files from the Overseas Military Forces of Canada Headquarters [textual record] (R611-438-8-E)
[xl] The Bournemouth Graphic, October 13[th, 1913], page 8:
[xli] London Metropolitan Archives; War Charities Act 1916, Reference Code LCC/PC/CHA/03/003, Case 545: Statement of John Martin Littlejohn, 20th March 1918, re the International Bible Institute to Sergeant Eveleigh of Scotland Yard.
[xlii] The Northern Daily Mail, July 6th, 1917; The Leeds mercury, July 30th, 1917, page 3: Archives of Ontario, Ontario Deaths, 1869-1937...
"Ontario Deaths, 1869-1937 and Overseas Deaths, 1939-1947," database with images, FamilySearch (https://familysearch.org/ark:/61903/1:1:JXQ7-6QY: 27 April 2019), Ivy Helen Lindsay Minifie, 24 Apr 1917; citing Kincardine, Toronto, Ontario, yr 1917 cn 8745, Registrar General. Archives of Ontario, Toronto; FHL microfilm 1,862,471.
[xliii] Christian Advocate, New York, of June 14th, 1917/ The Christian Advocate, New York May 17th, 1917
[xliv] Christian Advocate, New York, of June 14th, 1917/ The Christian Advocate, New York May 17th, 1917
[xlv] Miami-daily-Arizona-silver-belt-mar-12-1918-p-4
[xlvi] Marriage record and record of Bans of Marriage from the All Saints Church; Copies on file.
[xlvii] Who's Who in America: a biographical dictionary of notable living men and women of the united states: Vol. X' 1918-1919; edited by albert nelson marquis; Chicago: a. N. Marquis & company
[xlviii] Library and Archives of Canada; Item 135420'
http://collectionscanada.gc.ca/pam_archives/index.php?fuseaction=genitem.displayItem&lang=eng&rec_nbr=4228122
[xlix] http://ww1.canada.com/faces-of-war/sam-hughes-canadas-minister-of-militia-in-1914-bombastic-eccentric
[l] The National Guard in the Great War; 1914 – 1918; a. E. Manning Foster, 1920, Cope & Fenwick, London; page 121
[li] Ibid page 263

[lii] Ibid page 17
[liii] Arizona Republican March 18th, 1918
[liv] The Herald of Gospel Liberty, March 14th, 1918, Page 23
[lv] The Christian workers magazine. Vol. 18, No. 7-12, 1918 Mar-Aug, Page 638.
[lvi] Ibid
[lvii] NATIONALITY AND NATURALISATION: Littlejohn, John Martin, from the United States of America; Catalogue reference: HO 144/4540
[lviii] El Paso herald, Tuesday April 2, 1918; (texashistory.unt.edu/ark:/67531/metapth143597, University of North Texas Libraries, The Portal to Texas History, texashistory.unt.edu.)
[lix] Boston-Sunday-globe; oct. 17, 1915, p-55
[lx] London Metropolitan Archives; Charity commission case 545 page 6 of metropolitan police report
[lxi] London Metropolitan Archive; Charity commission case 545; Minutes of the Advisory Board held at 69 Piccadilly, August 17th, 1916
[lxii] "New York Passenger Arrival Lists (Ellis Island), 1892-1924", database with images, FamilySearch (https://familysearch.org/ark:/61903/1:1:JJCR-8NY)
[lxiii] Boston Sunday Post March 7th, 1909
[lxiv] Texas history, San Antonio express, March 1, 1918, page 7
[lxv] Riverside daily press 13 March 1918, page 3: California Digital newspaper Collection
[lxvi] Arizona republican, March 18, 1918, page 10
[lxvii] Boston Sunday Post, Nov 18, 1917, page 7
[lxviii] Library and museum of Freemasonry, England, Membership register; country Q 1391-1482 to country R 1486-1575; reel number 480
[lxix] Truth, March 10th, 1915, page 371; British Library Holdings
[lxx] Truth; April 21st, 1893, page 817; Courtesy of the British Library
[lxxi] British School of Osteopathy announcement brochure 1926
[lxxii] Osteopathy in Great Britain, The First hundred year; Dr. Martin Collins; ISBN: 1-4196-0784-7; page 18-20
[lxxiii] Reno-evening-gazette- Nov 27th. 1920, page 9; May 21st, 1921, page 10; Dec-15-1921-p-8
[lxxiv] Littlejohn's Letter to his son James re his will and funeral arrangements; NOA archive, now in the Wellcome library archives.
[lxxv] Osteopathy in Great Britain, The First hundred year; Dr. Martin Collins; ISBN: 1-4196-0784-7; page 18-20
[lxxvi] Ibid
[lxxvii] British School of Osteopathy announcement 1927
[lxxviii] Modern Missionary Movement; War Charities case file 545; Title War Charities act 1916 - Register of applications - Cases 1-550; Reference Code LCC/PC/CHA/03/001; From Collection LONDON COUNTY COUNCIL
[lxxix] The Western Times, Thursday May 26th, 1892

[lxxx] E.G> The Motherwell Times and General Advertiser; November 12th, 1909; both the @silver collection and the minimum fee of 3d (3 old pence) are advertised.
[lxxxi] Boston Sunday Post March 7, 1909
[lxxxii] Charity organisation society report Sept 10 1918; case file 545; Title War Charities act 1916 - Register of applications - Cases 1-550; Reference Code LCC/PC/CHA/03/001; From Collection LONDON COUNTY COUNCIL
[lxxxiii] The Horsfield and Bishopston record oct 4 1918
[lxxxiv] Shipley times and express 18 oct 1918
[lxxxv] The Christian workers magazine. v. 18 no. 7-12 1918 Mar-Aug -April.
[lxxxvi] Minutes of Synod of New England of the Presbyterian Church of the United States of America, 1919, Page 256
[lxxxvii] War Charities case file 545; Title War Charities act 1916 - Register of applications - Cases 1-550; Reference Code LCC/PC/CHA/03/001; From Collection LONDON COUNTY COUNCIL
[lxxxviii] Letter dated 14th April 1920; War Charities case file 545; Title War Charities act 1916 - Register of applications - Cases 1-550; Reference Code LCC/PC/CHA/03/001; From Collection LONDON COUNTY COUNCIL
[lxxxix] Boston-Sunday-globe; oct. 17, 1915, p-55
[xc] Lucknow Sentinel, 17 May 1917; courtesy of Bruce County Museum, Southampton, Ontario, Canada.
[xci] Littlejohn letter to Hall, on 16th August 1928, courtesy of the European School of Osteopathy; copies held in the A T Still Museum of Osteopathy, Kirksville.
[xcii] Littlejohn letter to Hall, in November 1930, courtesy of the European School of Osteopathy; copies held in the A T Still Museum of Osteopathy, Kirksville.
[xciii] Cheltenham Chronicle 19 sept 1903, page 6
[xciv] Minutes of the British Advisory Board, August 17th, 1917, Held at 69 Piccadilly, Presided over by J. Martin Littlejohn; War Charities case file 545; Title War Charities act 1916 - Register of applications - Cases 1-550; Reference Code LCC/PC/CHA/03/001; From Collection LONDON COUNTY COUNCIL
[xcv] The Continent, March 14th, 1918, page 278; The Christian workers magazine. v.18 no.7-12 1918 Mar-Aug April, page 638
[xcvi] Letter and minutes of the British Advisory Board 13th September 1917, War Charities case file 545 ; Title War Charities act 1916 - Register of applications - Cases 1-550; Reference Code LCC/PC/CHA/03/001; **From Collection** LONDON COUNTY COUNCIL
[xcvii] "England and Wales Marriage Registration Index, 1837-2005," database, FamilySearch (https://familysearch.org/ark:/61903/1:1:26D7-PSJ : 13 December 2014), Graham R Hall and null, 1914; from "England & Wales

Marriages, 1837-2005," database, findmypast (http://www.findmypast.com : 2012); citing 1914, quarter 4, vol. 3A, p. 793, Barnet, Middlesex, England, General Register Office, Southport, England.

[xcviii] NATIONALITY AND NATURALISATION: Littlejohn, John Martin, from the United States of America; Catalogue reference: HO 144/4540

[xcix] ibid

1935 HOUSE OF LORDS SELECT COMMITTEE HEARING

Much has been written about this episode in his life. With phrases like "then came the Littlejohn Debacle (This thy body, Mrs Cecil Chesterton) it is difficult to get an unbiased view. It is important to hold in mind the different backgrounds or cultures of Littlejohn, on the one hand and, the House of Lords on the other. Minifie's opinion of the House of Lords, *"Just what is the nature of the House of Lords. The House of Lords is a back number and is due for the junk heap. We have no more use for lords, or for kings for that matter, except as ornaments"*[j], may echo Littlejohn's feelings in this regard. He did, however, regard the committee hearings as following 'Court Procedure' this meant that, in his view, he could not present the material he had put together himself, but it had to be introduced by counsel by direct questioning[ii]

The Reformed Presbyterian Church has been described as a state within a state. They had their own view of life, they were involved in political dissent, not recognizing the state or government agencies as being above the headship of Christ, while at the same time obeying all the legitimate laws of the state that didn't conflict with their religious beliefs. This difference in culture can be seen in many aspects around education, degrees and especially 'honours.'

So that, while they may have attended university and took degrees, they did not take the graduation if it meant taking an oath that conflicted with their beliefs[1]. This did not stop them from recognizing their

---

[1] It seems that Littlejohn had softened his stance on the format of Oaths by this time as he took the standard Oath of Allegiance when renewing his British citizenship in 1924. This did not mean he took oaths less seriously. The reason for the Oath was that he had to apply for the reinstatement of his British Citizenship. As he said in his application in 1924, he was without citizenship after returning to England in 1913 and in 1916 the United States refuse to honour his citizenship after being out of the US for 3years. The application took more than 7 months to process and he needed a passport for a holiday. This time pressure may also have been a factor. In the application itself he made a 'Solemn declaration'. However, when his application was approved after more than 7 months and many delays, he had to submit the oath within one month. It is possible that on going to the Justice of the Peace that the proper form for the 'Solemn Declaration' was not

educational attainments and using the letters B.A., M.A., and Ph.D., etc after their names, even though they were not properly entitled to do so in the view of the universities or others in the educational field. Littlejohn, in particular, had great affinity for those who could not afford education either financially or due to life circumstances. This led him to associate with Christian Universities and those offering education via distant learning and taking life experience into consideration.

To Littlejohn, education in the 'Garvagh Science Academy', Glasgow university or anywhere else was looked upon as of the same value, having achieve the same standards, irrespective of how 'prestigious' the institution. In the House of Lords community, it would be more likely that the prestige of the institution would take precedence.

Another aspect of this 'cultural clash' is to be seen in the different views on so called 'honours'. On the one hand we have Sir William Jowitt, Counsel for the BMA, saying, in connection with the Society of Science, Letters and Art, "who gave that degree, because in England we do not do these things, do we"?[iii] and in relation to his degree LL.D. referring to the Add-Ran university in Texas in the following words "LL.D., 1895-that is the one you had from that Christian College at Texas"[iv]; and in general, being derogatory about Littlejohn's degrees, in particular his Honorary degrees.

From Littlejohn's background the recognition of his own peers would have been viewed in the same light as the recognition of the peers of someone like Jowitt, who had got the 'honour' of a knight hood from his society, and the sitting Lords whose 'honour' was for the most part hereditary, for which they recognised the authority of the King or Queen and their government. Littlejohn, on the other hand did not acknowledge the authority of the state as such, as it was considered to have broken its covenant with God and therefore was ungodly and he would not have put it above his religious beliefs. He did try to make some reference to this when he referred to the system in England and the meaning of giving a title by 'courtesy', in relation to the title LL.D.,

---

immediately available. The fact was that all that was needed was for him to sign the standard oath. Waiting for alternative form meant not only more delay but also the possibility of his application being rejected because the Oath was not made within the one month allowed. This would have put him under pressure to allow expediency to overrule his conscience. As Rev. Allen said, *"This perhaps reflects the gradual change in his stance on a matter he came to see as peripheral rather than foundational"* (John Martin Littlejohn-A Practical Covenanter; Rev Geoffrey Allen))

"The same as might make many of our Universities here make the Prince of Wales or anybody else, Doctor of Laws"[v] and the use of the title 'Doctor' referring to medical Doctors, *"by courtesy, the same as medical doctors here"*[vi].

We gain some insight into the 'cultural' attitude in England at the time from a letter to the editor of The Spectator, in 1925;

"The quality of teaching is as important as its duration. I suppose we may take the osteopathic college in Kirksville (Missouri), founded by Andrew Still, as the flower and pattern of the rest. Mr. Streeter is proud to write, " D.O., Kirksville," after his name. Kirksville is stated by Longman's Gazetteer for 1920 to have 4,000 inhabitants (probably less in Mr. Streeter's day). How miserably equipped for the recognition and the treatment of disease in general must the freshly qualified "graduate" be whose experience has been gained solely in this primitive hamlet. In British schools the teachers are great scientists, great physicians, great surgeons, great specialists in every branch of instruction; what sort of clinical material exists —and who are the teachers in Kirksville, Missouri? I challenge all the osteopathic colleges put together to produce a single teacher in " anatomy, physiology, chemistry, pathology, bacteriology, diagnosis, practice of medicine, surgery, physiotherapy, and leading clinical subjects" (I take Mr. Cooper's list of subjects "taught") whose name is known outside his own classroom. Kirksville is smaller than Keswick (in the English Lake District); what measure of confidence would the " M.D., Keswick" (if such existed), command? I call the bluff of the osteopathic colleges in the little matters of the duration and the quality of their medical teaching as compared with the medical teaching in this country."[vii]

So that without any knowledge of the school or hospital or anything else it was to be judge simply on its remoteness from a 'great centre of learning' like London, Oxford or even Glasgow and Edinburgh.

These are cultural differences we don't always recognise unless we are in a position like Littlejohn, who would have known he had absolutely no chance of getting his point across in that arena.

During my research I had the privilege of interviewing four osteopaths who had been at the British School of Osteopathy (BSO) during this time and who had direct contact with Littlejohn. It was somewhat of a surprise to find the consensus view given by them. That is Littlejohn did not answer or refused to answer questions about his degrees and that the report of the select committee concluded that the BSO was in thoroughly dishonest hands-meaning Littlejohn was 'thoroughly dishonest'. Even Wernham's wife, who was present in the gallery when Littlejohn gave his evidence, said much the same *"a little man with white hair who just stood there saying and doing- nothing"* [viii] Wernham goes on to say The counsel for medicine *threw much scorn on Littlejohn's possession of three doctorates; 'no mean achievement' quoth he, but the Dean stood mute with proof of his doctorates rolled up in his hand"*[ix].

This shows how myth becomes history. The testimony itself shows he actually did answer the questions and answered them well when given a chance. For example, on the question of his Ph.D.

Sir William Jowitt questioning

3425;. My word ! That is a great deal. Just tell me 'some 'more about Dunham because that· is what' interests me particularly, about · this Medical Degree. Have you more to tell us about' that?—*I have the diploma* ' (handing ·same . to learned Counsel) .

3426;. ." Dunhamense Medicinal ' Collegium,Chicagoniense ' Illinoisense."There is a lovely seal. 'What date did you get this?—*1902.*

3427;. .This describes (**The diploma from Dunham Medical College)** you as J. Martin Littlejohn, Doctor of · philosophy. "Is that right?—*No; that is a matter of courtesy. That. should be erased.*

3428; It · seems a very odd ·courtesy. Do you, as a matter of courtesy, call people "Doctor of. philosophy," who are not? No.· 3429. What is the courtesy then? —*They might make a mistake, my Lords...* **(Interrupted by)**:. Lord Dawson of Penn.] "Who Might

3430; (Sir William Jowitt continues) They might make a mistake in making out the Diploma? *In Making out the Diploma*

There follows a discussion between Jowitt and Viscount Elibank on the signatures on the Diploma after which Jowitt continues

3435; Before we go on to something else, I want to know about that little mistake on this thing. How do you suggest they came to make that mistake, calling you on this thing a " Doctor of Philosophy "?—

I do not know. I did not know it was on it until I hunted it out yesterday.

3436. You saw it yesterday for the first time ?—*Yes.*

3437; You never noticed ii before ?—*No.,*

3438; Do you really mean that, when you say to their Lordships that you never noticed until yesterday that they describe you as a " Doctor' of Philosophy " ?— That is an entire mistake about that " Doctor of Philosophy,"-is it? —Yes, I do.

Lord Dawson interrupts with questions about the location of Dunham College

The Jowitt continues

3344; That is an entire mistake about that "Doctor of Philosophy" is it? - Yes

3445. You would never willingly describe yourself as " Doctor of Philosophy "? —*No, I should not...*

· 3446. It would be dishonest, would it not? If you had seen that before, you would at once have corrected it?—*Yes, I would..*

3447. Have you ever described yourself as, "Doctor of Philosophy "?—*I should erase it*

3448. Have you ever described your-self as " Doctor of Philosophy," Sir? — *Not that I know of.*

In this he was being questioned about his medical degree and not his Ph.D. The questioning confused the two subjects by taking the description on his certificate of him as being 'Doctor of Philosophy' and Littlejohn, correctly say that should not be there and not being allowed to give a full answer to explain that the certificate was 'Doctor of medicine" and not for 'Doctor of Philosophy.'

Jowitt then then abruptly changed the questioning to the British School of Osteopathy and read a piece from a British School of Osteopathy document – presumably the school's announcement, giving Littlejohn's qualifications.

3450 Let me read to you this Passage ". The School Organisation. J. Martin Littlejohn, Dean of the School and Superintendent of Education, MA., B.D., LL.B., Foundation Scholar (Glasgow), University Medallist in Forensic Medicine and Henderson University Scholar, 1892. Fellow of Columbia University, New York, 1892. President of Amity College, Iowa, 1894-97, Ph.D., 1894 "·? —*That is a mistake.* (The mistake was that the Ph.D. was granted in 1895 and not 1894. While the degree was conferred by the Chicago National university in 1895; his thesis mentioned was submitted to Columbia in 1894).

3451. Look at it. This is your own book. (Book is handed to the Witness.) How did you come to make that mistake? —*It was put in, I presume, on the basis of the thesis—that book I handed round.*

Interruption by the Chairperson

3452,. The Thesis on political theory? —*Yes.*

Interruption by Lord Dawson of Penn,

3453. Was that an accepted and completed Thesis? —*That was accepted*:

3454, Is there any record of your having been granted a Ph.D. degree on that?

Jowitt continues before Littlejohn can answer

Sir William Jowitt.

3455. Were you granted a Ph.D.:?—*Not by Columbia.*

3456. Why, when you were not granted a Ph.D. do you describe yourself as a Ph.D.?—*That is a mistake.*

3457. Why did you make that mistake? —*It was put down by somebody else.*

3458. Did you never notice that before? —*I could not say that.* 3459. I want you to tell my Lords as to that: Did you notice that before? —*Yes, I did.*

Interruption by Lord Carnock

3460. Did you not correct the Proofs? —*No.*

Jowitt then changes the subject again and continues the cross examination with questions on Littlejohn's LL.D and the Society of Science, Letters and Art and his time at Dunham Medical College with continued interruptions by the Chairperson, Viscount Elibank and Lord Dawson of Penn.

The whole episode, and this is only a short part of his testimony, is very confusing with all the interruptions and changes in direction of the questioning, just to read. One can only imagine how it must have felt to be interrogated in that manner, especially at 70 years of age and not in the best of health, and knowing that he could never bridge the gap in culture between the House of Lords and his education ideals and experience in America from 1892 to 1913.

As it was 'court procedure'[x], to quote Littlejohn, he would await the response from his counsel – which never came. Even during the interruptions, the Counsel for the supporters of the Bill said nothing. It became 'history' to put the blame on Littlejohn. In essence he became the scapegoat for the whole affair despite Hall's efforts. One of the osteopaths, Ralph Hardy[xi], specifically gave Hall credit for calling a meeting in Manchester at which he settled the issue of Littlejohn's degrees and rallied the graduates of the BSO to continue to back Littlejohn.

"You have doubtless read some of the very biased and incomplete Press reports of Dr. Littlejohn's evidence and cross examination before the House of Lords Committee which appears to indicate that Dr. Littlejohn is falsely claiming to possess a Ph.D. Diploma and that he has dishonestly issued Diplomas of the B.S.O."

"The undersigned, in company with Dr. Harvey R. Foote, have personally examined and verified all Dr. Littlejohn's Diplomas and Degrees and the appended chronological list should make it evident that his qualifications as Dean of the B.S.O. are beyond adverse criticism.

"The origin of this false impression has a very simple explanation and will, we hope, even be turned to advantage in the final summing-up by our Counsel.

"The misunderstanding arose over the method of cross-examination by the opposing Counsel who asked, Have you a Ph.D. of Columbia University?" On the Dean attempting to explain that the Ph.D. was conferred by Chicago National University and not Columbia, he was demanded to give a straight "yes" or "no". The apparently unreasonable

demand by Counsel provoked in the Dean that characteristic trait of which we are all aware – that of retiring within himself and refusing further explanation. While admitting that this was a decidedly mistaken attitude, in the vital interest of the profession we can only assume that the Dean failed to realise fully the dangerous false impression this might create in the minds of the public and how prejudicial the issue might be to the value and status of the B.S.O. Diploma

"<u>Re Looker Graduates.</u> You, as a graduate of the B.S.O. are aware of the reason for, and the condition under which the members of this Association were absorbed. This letter is an appeal for you wholehearted loyalty and support, for your School and its Dean at a time when Osteopathy in this country is passing through a critical period in its history.

Signed by J Canning (Faculty Rep. Of Students Union) and T. E. Hall (Hon. Secretary to the faculty)[xii]

List of Degrees and Diplomas in Chronological Order[xiii]

M.A.   Glasgow University 1899
B.D.   Glasgow University 1890
LL.B. Glasgow University 1892
Graduated from Garvagh Academy, 1878. Honours and Prize.
   Intermediate Education Board, Ireland, 1879-80.
University Foundation Scholar, Glasgow University, In
   Mathematics and Philosophy, 1884
Honours and First Class in Mental Philosophy, 1884.
Tutor at Glasgow University, 1883-85.
Honours and First Class in Divinity, with special prize in Oriental languages. 1885.
Lecturer in Theology, Ballybay Union Hall, 1886-1887.
Henderson Fellowship in Theology, 1890. (Thesis – The Sabbatism of Hebrew, Vol. iv, 9. 1892), With honours.
First Class in all branches of Law, University Medal in Jurisprudence and special prize in Federal Law.
Law Member of Students' Representative Council, 1891-2.
Member of Glasgow University Council for life. 1889.
Principal of Rosemount College, 1890-92.
University Fellow in Political Philosophy, Columbia College 1892-3.
Student in Cathedral, and University Librarian of England, France, Germany, Switzerland and Italy during summer 1893.
President of Amity College, Iowa, 1894-7.
Joint editor of Glasgow University Magazine, 1891-2.
Joint and departmental review editor of Christian Nation, U.S.A., 1892-4

Ph.D. of Chicago National University, 1895.
Diploma, American School of Osteopathy.
Dean of American School of Osteopathy.
Founder and Dean of the Chicago School of Osteopathy.
M.D. of Dunham Medical College, 1902.
M.D. of Herring Medical college, 1904.
Professor of Applied Physiology in: -
   Dunham Medical College.
   Herring Medical College.
   Chicago National Medical University.
   Hahnemann Medical College.

If Littlejohn had made a statement giving a summary of his qualifications and the cultural background to them one wonders if he would have fared any better. I doubt it as the Committee seemed to have too many hidden agendas. The following is a summary of his qualifications and the cultural background.

When he was a minister in Ireland in 1886-8, he used the post-nominal letters M.A. This was with the approval of his Church and Colleagues as he had completed the required course for the degree M.A. at Glasgow university but had not taken the final graduation. This was in line with the philosophy, custom and beliefs of the Covenanter Church to which he belonged. Later, in 1889, when customs within Glasgow University had changed somewhat, he returned and graduated with the degrees M.A., B.D., LL.B. On moving to America, he completed the course for the degree of Ph.D. at Columbia University (1892-4), including handing and having the thesis accepted, but not taking the final graduation. In this case the reason was not a conflict of beliefs or philosophy but rather due to serious illness that required two operations on his throat, thus meaning he could not complete the process of graduation on time due to the college regulations. He then took the degree of Ph.D. from the National University (Chicago) in 1895 and LL.D. from the Ad-Ranx[2] University of Texas. Hall, in his letter to the Graduates did not mention Littlejohn's LL.D. for the Ad-Ranx university in Texas. This was presumably due to the unfair negative association of it being a 'Christian University'[3], particularly in light of Jowitt's remarks – E.g. LL.D., 1895 "—that is the one you had from that Christian College at Texas, is it not?[xiv] *The implication being that it was not a 'proper' university.*

---

[2] Many different versions of the spelling are to be found the most correct seems to be Add-Ran, used today by the Texas Christian University as AddRan from the names of the founders -**Add**ison and **Ran**dolph Clark.; Ad-Ranx is the one used in the Select committee report.

[3] "Texas Christian University's mission is to educate individuals to think and act as ethical leaders and responsible citizens in the global community. This ideal is the continuation of a quest that began in 1869, when brothers Addison and Randolph Clark dreamed of creating a college where men and women could acquire a classical education and develop character. The 1873 charter stated that AddRan Christian University would fulfil its mission to "promote literary and scientific education." The relationship with the Disciples would continue to be one of heritage and values. It still flourishes today. (website of https://addran.tcu.edu)

In publications his qualifications have been quoted as 'In 1892 he became University Fellow in Columbia University, N.Y., completing the Doctorate course (Ph.D.) in one year by special permission of the University council. In the summer and fall of 1893 he visited Europe for the purpose of investigating the field of Medieval Literature with the result that early in 1894 he presented to Columbia a Doctoral Thesis entitled " The Political Theory of the Schoolmen and Grotius .'

This is misleading to some as it implies that the post-nominal letters, Ph.D. after his name are from Columbia University. He would not have seen the need to correct this as he had completed the course, including having his thesis accepted but he simply had not taken the final step. Although the rationale was different this would have been culturally similar to his first use of M.A. in Ireland, giving due recognition for the work done. In this case the reason was ill health and he also had a genuine Ph.D. from the National University in 1895. Upon his return to England, he tended to sign his name as 'J. Martin Littlejohn M.D. (Dunham), LL.D., D.O' on all B.S.O. letters and as editor of the official journal of the BSO. He did not continue to use the letters Ph.D. as this college no longer existed and had fallen into some disrepute. Some confusion still remained due to one mistake in the biographical information on him in the School announcements, in the which stated his Ph.D. was in 1894 and did not list the college it was from. He did not see any reason to correct this minor error.

On looking at his own use of letters, in private correspondence etc., it is found that on all the letters he wrote to Hall on British School of Osteopathy headed paper he was listed as

"J. Martin Littlejohn, M.D. (Dunham US), D.O., LL.D."

The British Medical Associations approach

Having read through the briefing documents prepared by the British Medical Association for their counsel Sir W Jowitt[xv] and the minutes of evidence from the inquiry, I have come to the conclusion that they had a three-pronged strategy, with Dr. W. k. MacDonald as their unwitting fall-back champion. *(The following is taken from those briefing notes and the minutes of evidence of the Committee published by His Majesty's Stationary Office and Lord Dawsons personal notebook held in the Wellcome Library archive)*

1. Attack the concept of osteopathy. To this end they corresponded with their medical colleagues in America, gathering material on the fight for recognition of osteopathy and the weaknesses of the colleges there, including reports of inspections of the osteopathic colleges. This coupled with many "quotes" from osteopathic literature, especially the writing of A T Still in his autobiography, to show that it was a "cult" and not based upon 'science'. In one letter from a leading Doctor in America to the medical secretary of the BMA he says 'we shall be greatly interested in seeing how the fight against these cults develop in England'[xvi]

2. Exploit the division within the Osteopathic profession in England. They were aware that the British Osteopathic Association (BOA) and the BSO had serious disagreements and that the four agencies, BOA, BSO, Osteopathic defence league and Incorporated association of osteopaths, had only put aside their differences to support the Bill. They suggested that one of the chief witness for the osteopaths was a qualified Doctor[4] and If he gives evidence well it was suggested that it might be useful to attribute this to his medical qualifications and imply that if he could make a good osteopath then it would be right and fitting to make all would be osteopaths take a medical degree first and thus have a full medical education. ("*Dr MacDonald suffers none of the disabilities of which unqualified persons such as Mr. Streeter complains*") .This would be especially useful as this qualified doctor was elevated to the position of '**professor of osteopathic principles**' in the founding school of osteopathy while still a student[xvii]. Thus, he was placed above other qualified osteopaths of long standing, implying that his medical degree was of considerable merit. This division was well exploited during the evidence of Dr. MacDonald. When he was asked about the BSO by Sir Wm Jowitt "*so far as you and your Association (the BOA) are concerned, you do not regard the diploma obtained by the study at that school (the BSO) as a satisfactory standard?*" he said "*We do not*".[xviii]. Prior to this he said "*it has not yet been enabled to bring its educational standard up to the level at which we would like it*"[xix]. Part of the background to the division between Littlejohn and the BOA had been Littlejohn's opinion

---

[4] This was Dr. William Kelman MacDonald who graduated, Bachelor of Medicine and Surgery in 1907 from the University of Edinburgh and went to Kirksville in 1910 graduating D.O. in 1912

that *"the B.O.A. has been gradually drifting into the position of subservience to medicine against that I have always stood here as in the U.S."[xx]*

3. They claimed the British School of Osteopathy was a *"fraudulent establishment ... the standards of which are Despised by the British Osteopathic Association"*. It was also suggested that a fruitful line of questioning would be to find out why the Dean of the BSO, who was a past president of the BOA, was no longer a member, thus implying that Littlejohn himself may not have been of a satisfactory standard for the B.O.A. A follow up of this was to examine the relationship of the BSO with the Looker College and Dr. William Looker. Dr. Looker had apparently left America in a hurry, a fact that was in the public arena and not contested the Osteopathic community. The had assembled a lot of 'information' on the Looker School and that diplomas were granted to the school's graduates by Littlejohn after what they thought was only one year on top of a six-month course. It may even be that Littlejohn's M.D. was 'Master Diagnostician' and not a real medical degree.

Collins, in his book 'Osteopathy in Britain – the First Hundred years' gives a sound account of the Looker School and the path that Littlejohn set out for the graduates of that school to receive a diploma from the BSO.

"William Looker had spent many years in America, practicing in Pennsylvania, before returning to England. He established an osteopathic practice in Manchester in 1920 and founded 'The Looker School of Bloodless Surgery, registered in 1921. In 1923 the name changed to the Looker College of Osteopathy and Chiropractic," but the majority of its graduates elected to practise only Osteopathy. It then transferred to London as the Looker College. It 'taught the science in an admirable manner and... did most excellent work and turned out many able and efficient practitioners.' The Prospectus apparently outlined a three-year course. Hill and Clegg claim it was of only three to six months' duration, but their book contains many inaccuracies.

Littlejohn claimed it was a three year course[5].........

".... In 1925 a few graduates of the Looker College formed the 'Incorporated Association of Osteopaths Ltd' (IAO), as they were unable to join the BOA. As Littlejohn explained in 1935, 'The object of that Association was first of all, to support, advance, maintain and carry out investigation into the principles, theory and practice of Osteopathy; to train, teach and graduate students therein. They set themselves to work in 1925, to teach themselves and to be taught by others, who went and lectured to them from time to time'.

"'It met with much adverse criticism in a certain section of the press (details unknown)," but made progress, conducting study circles, periodic meetings, lectures and clinics to assist in the development of the profession." Members were granted the privilege of the title of 'osteopathic physician', 'osteopathic surgeon' or both.'

"After Looker's death, the Looker College closed and in 1926 some of its graduates, all members of the Incorporated Association and in practice for several years, applied to the BSO to qualify for the BSO Diploma. Negotiations between the IAO and BSO commenced in 1927. The son of John Leary recollected his father speaking of 12 such students and consequently Littlejohn referred to them as 'the Disciples'. From details of the background of students recorded in Littlejohn's ledger of graduates, it would seem that 19 joined the BSO accredited with work at the Looker School. 15 were mentioned at the Select Committee of the House of Lords (1935) ·

"Accreditation of IAO members with work at the Looker School was consistent with the regulations regarding credited work of the Associated Colleges of Osteopathy in the US, of which Littlejohn had been President for

---

[5] In his testimony to the House of Lords Select Committee, Littlejohn was very specific and clear on this point: He did not claim that the Looker School was a three-year course. He stated that "...We are allowed to accredit graduates of an unrecognized School to come in on three years' credit and to require one year's work....Credit him with three years' work on the certificates that he furnished to us from the unrecognized college... first of all that they should produce their credits from the Looker School ... and secondly that they fulfil a certain amount of work in our School ". The main condition he said was that they must not only supply the information, but it must be proved. Paragraphs 3326 – 3371, pages 222-224. The Looker graduates had, after their school closed "set themselves to work in 1925, to teach themselves and to be taught by others, who went and lectured to them from time to time. They carried that on from 1925 to 1927 when we took them in and gave them credit, as I said already for work done irregularly for three years."
(Paragraph 3629, page 238)

three years. There was a record of some 20 'irregular' schools in the US in which the same plan and principles were carried out,'

"IAO members were obliged to attend monthly study circles in Manchester, conducted by BSO graduates. From time to time even Littlejohn taught there. On 14 July 1928 he conducted a formal practical examination in the Milton Hall, Manchester. After 12-18 months, during which eight test papers were set which students worked through at home, they sat a final examination in accordance with the requirements governing all the other students of the School." Those who passed were granted a Diploma. The same requirements applied to graduates of the British College of Chiropractic (see below). All became successful practitioners and some, such as Willis Haycock and Arthur Millwood, made significant contributions to the profession. Not all members of the IAO agreed to this arrangement with the BSO and some who considered that they already held 'reputable' qualifications were not willing to spend further time and money and either resigned from the IAO or allowed their membership to lapse. In due course, they ceased to be any longer eligible for membership, as it was later only open to graduates from the BSO.

"At the Select Committee of the House of Lords held in 1935 to discuss the possible statutory recognition of Osteopathy Littlejohn was one of the witnesses called to defend Osteopathy but the lawyers representing those opposing legislation were intent on demonstrating that the Dean of the only school in existence was dishonest. Sir William Jowitt accused Littlejohn of issuing diplomas to Looker graduates who had not completed 'a full and rigorous' four years at the School.

"Jowitt read out the certificate of George Spencer, a Looker graduate, who was taught at the BSO for one year:[6]

" 'To whom this may come, Greeting. Be it known that George Spencer having completed the required study and attended the full course of Lectures, Clinics and Demonstrations during the regular 4 years' course, and having passed satisfactory examinations in all branches of training taught in this school including Clinics and other practical demonstrations, is hereby admitted to the Diplomate in Osteopathy D.O., given at London 22 December 1928.' Littlejohn explained that in accordance with the conditions of the Associated Colleges of Osteopathy students were credited

---

[6] Littlejohn gave a very robust response to this in paragraph 3629. *Is it an honest document? —Yes. We are conforming to the conditions, as I explained before, that have been followed out all the time by the. Associated Colleges of Osteopaths"*. See below

with three years' work, but were required to undertake one further year's work, pass an examination and undertake clinic work in Manchester. They also had undertaken three years' work as graduate members of the IAO.' (incorporated Association of Osteopaths – formed by a few graduates of the Looker College in 1925)
"It is ironic that it is now quite commonplace for students to join institutions with credit for work undertaken elsewhere.,[xxi]

Since he wrote the above some letters from a now deceased South-west of England osteopath who was influential in the spread of osteopathy in that region, have come into the National Osteopathic archive. These letters have been said to show evidence that the osteopath had been given a DO certificate claiming he had attended and graduated from the BSO course, when he had not, and that Littlejohn had sworn him to secrecy.[xxii] This osteopath had graduated from the British College of Chiropractic[7] in 1928 but did not get his diploma from the associated Western School of Osteopathy due to the impending amalgamation with the B.S.O. He says "Had I been given a diploma of the W.S.O. (Western School of Osteopathy) it would have born an identical date with that of my B.C.C.(British College of Chiropractic) Diploma, namely 8th September 1928"[xxiii]. Having not followed with the other graduates of the Western School of Osteopathy and taken further study with the British School of osteopathy, test papers and a final exam in 1928/9, it would appear that with the upcoming Osteopathic Bills he was anxious that his Osteopathic qualification would be recognized. To this end he then made contact with Littlejohn in about 1932. Littlejohn wrote to him in July 1932, saying "I am glad to hear form you. I remember your name is still on my books at the School" and recommended a patient to him, giving advice on the condition and treatment approach.[xxiv]

In his letters to the Osteopath concerned Littlejohn was quite explicit in asking for all the details of his previous studies, examinations and the attendance records. In fact, on reading these letters it is quite clear that LitteJohn was very strict about the evidence of previous studies before granting diplomas or credit for previous study. In this particular case, the Dean of the Western College of Chiropractic and Osteopathy advised the student to reply to Littlejohn's question and he, the Dean of the Western

---

[7] At this time Minifie was president of the British College of Chiropractic (Diploma of T. D. Michell held in the National Osteopathic Archive.)

college, would supply the necessary records[xxv]. The only thing 'wrong' Littlejohn did was to backdate the diploma from 1934 to 1931. This seems to have been in response to the Osteopaths 'complaint' that he was practicing as an osteopath all these years and had not received his diploma from the western college as they were at the time arranging for the students to transfer to the British School of Osteopathy with credit for work done. He had only received his Diploma in Chiropractic. Littlejohn acknowledge that he had the students name on his records and seemingly, out of regard for his situation and his kind and helpful nature, backdated the Diploma, as the student was concerned about the upcoming osteopathic Bill. One item in the Students newspaper cuttings from that time contained an article about people granting themselves diplomas in Osteopathy.

Littlejohn wrote to him saying: **"I told your mother you had passed. No one need know you did not take the exam in 1929".** This one line, taken out of context, has been used to 'show' the LittleJohn was lax about giving diplomas, up to the point of being dishonest. In fact, if it is taken in the context that it was written, it shows the opposite; that Littlejohn, even with someone he knew well, had worked and corresponded with, still insisted that he provide proof of the prior study, examinations and work before crediting him with advanced standing.

Then and only then was the further one years work done under Littlejohn's auspices (which, while not necessarily done in the buildings of the BSO, was in essence done in the BSO.), the test papers sent out and check before the final exam undertaken. Littlejohn, in his note to him regarding his matriculation certificate says;

'I do not want to get you into any trouble but what I do want is a short statement of the length of time you were at work and work. Would you send me a history of yourself, school you attended, dates of and any examinations taken. What I need is to have our record book filled in. I have looked out the test papers and will send them on if you will give me the information and if you wish I will ask Mitchell Fox for the statement. He gave me one for all the rest"[xxvi].

In June 1933 he wrote to the Dean of the Western College saying he would send on the information Littlejohn had requested further evidence of his studies with Littlejohn is found in another letter from Littlejohn in which he examined a patient for the student and gave a detailed description of what he found. This one was written in December 1934.

This same line, **"no one need know you did not take the exam in 1929"** is taken from a scrap of a letter, so the whole content is not available, nor is the full context. As Collins says, *"The truth regarding what tuition these* *students received and what examinations were set by Littlejohn is difficult to determine[xxvii]."*

Given Littlejohns character, principles and history it would seem that his assertion that diplomas were only issued if the student fulfilled the requirements set out in the standards of the BSO is closer to the truth. The only issue being the distance learning criteria and assessments, which Littlejohn detailed in his evidence to the Select Committee.

Further to this Littlejohn was very familiar with, if not an expert in distance learning, having been part of the Chautauqua movement and then in Amity College both of which have organised and taught by this method, methods which today have become common place – a study program, a self-administered quiz or 'exam' to review your study progress and a final exam. The same procedure that Littlejohn followed with the Looker graduates and those from the British College of Chiropractic and Western School of Osteopathy. *"The former, founded in London in 1925, transferred to Plymouth in 1927 with T. Mitchell- Fox as Dean. There he formed the latter in 1928. The two colleges floundered, and some students were taken on by the BSO"*[xxviii]

A final word needs to be said about 'Littlejohn had made him swear not to tell a soul. (keeping it under wraps was a polite understatement) The poor man, a catholic, spent his life riddled with guilt'[xxix] It is impossible to imagine Littlejohn making anyone 'swear not to tell a soul' given his Covenanter background. This comment appears to originate[8] from the fragment of a letter written by Littlejohn saying, *"I told your mother you had passed. No one need know you did not take the exam in 1929."* This fragment coupled with a comment made by that Osteopaths son in a letter' to whom it may concern' (in the BSO) *"He (his father) always felt badly about his academic and therapeutic background I have not found him (his father) very communicative on this subject.(His background)*[xxx]*".*

---

[8] Ongoing through the correspondence in the National osteopathic Archive I have found no other evidence of this

Littlejohn's approach

Littlejohn's approach seems to have been the same as he had followed in America. That is to present the school in terms of its objects and how it was moving towards improvements despite lack of facilities and support and to put this into its best light even if it was open to criticism. He never claimed that the BSO had no problems or that it was perfect, but that it had done a good job under these circumstances and if the Bill was passed doors that had hitherto been closed, like the anatomy labs in medical schools, would be opened. The medical schools having a monopoly in these areas presented an impediment to the development of the BSO. Rather naively, perhaps, he thought that when Streeter had got the groups of Osteopaths to present a united front for the Bill, it would work out well for Osteopathy.

He went further and stated in the school's prospectus

"In the Bill at present before Parliament, the British School of Osteopathy is the only school referred to and it is given full recognition by having its representative on the Board to be appointed to carry out the provisions and regulations of the act when passed"[xxxi]

While this was true it proved to be counterproductive, given that it was used by the BMA in its briefing to their counsel to focus attention on the BSO.

Unfortunately, when any group is formed the first thing that tends to happen is the 'election' of a scapegoat, not usually consciously or overtly. In this case it would seem that the BSO, and by inference, Littlejohn were 'elected' to this position. The BOA did not recognise the BSO as being of good enough a standard and had ambitions of its own to set up a school and hospital in conjunction with the medical profession[9].

"The College Committee of the British 'Osteopathic Association have had as their policy for a good number of years now the establishment

---

[9] This is in line with a statement by a leading member of the BOA *"we have reason to believe we can establish a college in London which will be a credit to existing Medical standards and also teach the principles of osteopathy."* E T Pheils Clinical special consultant BOA quoted in the BMA proof of evidence document.

of a college in London where students can be trained from beginning to end, and where medical students and medical practitioners who are anxious to learn osteopathy can get training".[xxxii]

The division between the BOA and LittleJohn has been described as follows:

"The British Osteopathic Association was not prepared to take a leading part in operating a school until legal recognition of osteopathy would permit the highest possible standards and an ambitious programme, whereas Dr. Littlejohn believed that the best school then possible was better than none. With this chasm of thought separating them the osteopaths of the British Osteopathic Association continued their own line of development and Dr. Littlejohn followed his"[xxxiii]

So, it was no surprise that their main witness, Dr. Kelman MacDonald, stated very early on that'

"There is no college in this country that has been recognised, whose educational standards come up to the level required by the British Osteopathic Association".[xxxiv]

"The British School of Osteopathy has been conducted by Dr. Littlejohn and we all admire his effort. It is an individual effort and it has not yet been enabled to bring its educational standard up to the level at which we would like it".[xxxv]

Mr. Thorpe, counsel for the supporters of the Bill pressed Dr. Kelman MacDonald on whether Littlejohn was a member of the BOA saying;

 ``Is Dr. Littlejohn a member of the British Osteopathic Association? – Yes, I think so. Of course, he is. He was President of the British Osteopathic Association in 1925".

Mr. Thorpe then stated "he is not now. He can speak for himself, but he tells me he is not now"?[xxxvi]

It seems rather extraordinary that the counsel for the supporters of the Bill should introduce so strongly a conflict between the BOA and the BSO, so much so that Dr. MacDonald felt compelled to come to the defense of the BSO.

"Dr. Littlejohn and the Incorporated Society of Osteopaths have worked along this line. The thought: 'well, the Rt. Hon. Neville Chamberlain said on a previous occasion that you must start colleges. They have done so, and they have made to my mind a most commendable effort. The wonder is not that the college is in such a state that critics can find fault with it, but the wonder is that it exists at all. I want to make that point strongly. The British Osteopathic Association has, rightly or wrongly, gone on the idea that they suddenly want a full-blown college to come into existence, all of a sudden with hospitals, five years training, and everything. Those two lines they have not made yet, but they will under this Bill meet and make in the first instance the British School of Osteopathy an institution worthy of our practice."[xxxvii]

It would seem that there was more going on in the background than what came into light during the Select committee hearings. It is clear that the BOA did not want the BSO as it stood, it being said that the "The standards of the school are despised by the British Osteopathic Association".[xxxviii] And Littlejohn thought "the B.O.A. has been gradually drifting into the position of subservience to medicine against that I have always stood here as in the U.S."[xxxix]

But for their own counsel to bring this into prominence seems like a foolhardy exercise unless he was directed to do so. The only body to gain, of the supporters of the Bill, would be the BOA. If the Bill passed, then they could either take over the BSO to bring it up to standard or start up their own college so as to be able to set the proper standard.

It would appear that the BOA had close or were trying to develop close relations with the BMA. Pheils, as chairperson of their College Committee had had meeting with Mr. Mennell[10] and invited him to attend meetings of their committee meetings[xl], even if these meetings were informal and Mennell was not officially representing the BMA.

Another aspect that has been suggested is that Littlejohn was reluctant to take part. This was not on the basis of being afraid of being

---

[10] Mr. James Beaver Mennell was a medical consultant who practice manipulative surgery as a specialty and was Medical Officer of the Physico-therapeutic department of St. Thomas's Hospital. He had also been accused of practicing Osteopathy in essence.

exposed or having his degrees subject to scrutiny but because he did not think the proposed bill was the right one

Wernham was wont to say that *"Littlejohn did not want to be involved in this, he thought it was a bad piece of legislation and felt forced to be involved by those around him"*[xli]

"the truth is that the Bill was prepared by one man, Dr. W. A. Streeter, without any consultation with the B. S. O."[xlii]

> *"I remember walking down Buckingham Gate and catching a glimpse of the Dean in a passing taxicab, a diminutive figure sitting alongside the burly physique of Streeter. The Dean waved to me and I was left with the strong impression that here was a lamb being led to the slaughter;"*
>
> Osteopathy
> a historical and auto biographical account John Wernham page 56

Further, in private conversation, Wernham would say that Littlejohn had been briefed by Streeter and their Counsel and from reading the testimony and Littlejohn's assertion that the Committee Hearings followed 'Court Procedure[11]' it seems that he had been prepared to give testimony about the BSO and that his degrees and his teaching in America was only for background material. It seems purely by chance that Sir Wm Jowitt stumbled upon this avenue of enquiry. It appears he was trying to go down the same line with Littlejohn as had been suggested with Dr. MacDonald. That is to show that the medical degree was not only an advantage but

---

[11] "We have to go over all the ground and I myself have to supply the information. I have handed over 94 typed foolscap pages of material to Counsel. He says it is a pity I can't present it myself. But this committee is court procedure." Letter to Dr Mitchell February 26th, 1935; National Osteopathic Archives.

could be a prerequisite to the study of osteopathy. His cross examination started with the loaded question "You have, of course, the advantage of having a full medical degree?" followed by "Where did you get it?" Littlejohn had already given this information in full at the beginning of his testimony *"You hold the Degree of Medicine of, the Dunham and Hering Medical college in Chicago? —Yes, and State licenses in several of the States. And you are a Doctor of Osteopathy"*[xliii] So, when asked again he simply said *"In Chicago"*[xliv]. Jowitt then led him into a discussion about the University of Chicago and how Dunham was not a part of the University of Chicago. LittleJohn answered saying:

"Not in Chicago University. At the time when I got my degree Chicago University was simply in formation, and development. There were a number of medical schools in Chicago which were all separate. The majority of those have all been incorporated now under a University".[xlv]

He then went on the explain that it was from Dunham Medical College.

We find in the Chicago University magazine 1898, "The Cap and Gown"[xlvi], evidence of just how young and in formation the University of Chicago was in 1898, just four years before LittleJohn got his M. D. degree.

"Already members of the Class of '96, the first regularly graduated class, are returning to regale the students of the present with tales of "the old days " and wonder if the fun now can compare with the larks of '94 or the wild freedom of '93 before the Midway was cleared away."

This side-track seemed to fluster and irritate LittleJohn to some degree so that when he was asked about his LL.D. it led into a trap to get him to say 'yes' in answer to the question "you are an honorary member of the Texas University"[xlvii]. Littlejohn had never said he got his LL. D. from 'Texas University' but that he had got it "in Texas" This led into a discussion about the meaning of a 'Fellowship' with Jowitt impugning that his fellowship at Columbia as bogus as compared to the meaning of a Fellowship as usually understood by leading English universities like Oxford.[xlviii]. This illustrates a difference in culture and language, between the educational system in America and England, that may have been lost on Jowitt[12] and served to

---

[12] Another explanation is the Jowitt was well aware of this difference and was using it as a ploy.

further irritate and fluster Littlejohn. This whole episode about his degrees came about almost by accident and was made worse by Jowitt continually referring to Littlejohn's LL.D. being from 'Texas University' and Littlejohn not correcting him. Neither did Littlejohn's counsel come to his aid as would have been expected. This was made worse again when the cross examination was continued the next Monday. Littlejohn produced his degrees showing that the LL.D. was from 'The Ad-Ranx University of Texas' and said that

"I beg your pardon; I made a mistake on. Friday[13]: The Ad- Ranx University was in existence 10 years before the University of Texas"[xlix]

The time that Littlejohn was talking about was during the formative years of the university. The 'culture' in England, and perhaps particularly those in the House of Lords, would not have readily appreciated this, being more used to 'old universities' like Oxford, Cambridge and even Glasgow. Given that the atmosphere was hostile to Littlejohn what chance did he have of getting his point across.

The distinct impression was given by comparing Littlejohn's career in America with what would be expected from so called high level institutions in England like Cambridge and Oxford was that he fell short of the mark. As indeed did the institutions in America. This was like comparing chalk with cheese. Universities in England were seen as being of long standing, hundreds of years in existence, to be made a 'Fellow' was one of the highest honours and an 'honorary degree' was a 'lifetime achievement'. This was confounded by Littlejohn's association with 'Christian universities' like the Ad-Ranx university of Texas. Speaking of which, Littlejohn tried to explain saying;

"That refers to the fact that it was founded by what they call in America The Disciples, a body of Christians called the Disciples, that is what I was going to explain. At that time there was a great controversy between the Universities proper and what were called the Christian Universities. ... For example, according to our custom here in the Universities they had Chapel exercises. The Universities which were supposed to be non-Sectarian abolished those Chapel exercises, This University, among others, adhered strictly to the idea of opening the day in the University work by a short

---

[13] Even though LittleJohn himself had not made the mistake, except in so far as he did not correct Jowitt's repeated use of the phrase 'Texas university'

Chapel exercise of 10 minutes. When I was President of Amity College in the State of Iowa, we followed the same rule. I was a member of the Executive Committee in connection with what is called Chateauqua, lecture work, and I lectured in practically all the centres in the Middle West from Cleveland, Ohio, to Denver, Colorado, and from the University of Minneapolis to Selma, Alabama, It was in connection with that work that I received this honorary degree"[i]. -

At this stage it would have been reasonable to expect the Counsel for the supporters of the Bill to intervene and explain that in fact Littlejohn had only said he got the degree 'in Texas' and it was Jowitt who continually said the 'University of Texas' and that the system in the USA was only just forming at that time and for Jowitt to infer anything else was unreasonable. But of course, they did not. Why? It has been suggested by Wernham[ii] that the BOA in particular, did not want the BSO to come out of the inquiry in good standing; in fact their own counsel and their witness, Dr. MacDonald, had already opened up this avenue of examination by stating that the BOA did not recognize the diploma of the BSO to be of good quality. Jowitt was following the BMA's advice of exploiting that difference between the BOA and the BSO. It was Mr. Thorpe, counsel for the supporters of the Bill, who emphasized the divergence between the BOA and Littlejohn.

This again points to possible background of liaison between the BOA and the BMA. It would seem reasonable to speculate that some in the BOA had fed information to the BMA and maybe even gone as far as suggesting that if the BSO was discredited and the Bill amended to exclude it, then the BOA and BMA together could develop a college to the benefit of both. Perhaps the BOA was naive enough to believe that the BMA would go along with such an arrangement and the BMA being political enough to let them believe it. However, everything in the correspondence between the BMA and their American associates, the AMA, indicates that they had no intention of ever letting the Bill pass.

The briefing from the BMA to Jowitt also emphasized the connection to the Looker school and the degree of 'Master Diagnostician' that some of the graduates had been awarded.

Another suggested line of questioning that was suggested to Jowitt in his briefing by the BMA was:

"have you throughout the years, say 1919-1934, insisted upon a full four years courses of study?

"if yes – then ask; Did you ever know a Dr. William Looker, or at any rate an American called William Looker, now diseased?

"if no, then ask; were you ever in touch with an osteopathic school in Manchester?

"if yes then ask; who ran that school? The reply must be Looker"

So, it was hardly surprising that Jowitt seemed intent on showing that Littlejohn's medical degree 'M.D.' was in fact the same as '**M**aster **D**iagnostician' awarded by Looker and not '**M**edicinae **D**octor' and that Dunham College did not really exist[lii]. After asking Littlejohn to bring in his LL.D. and M.D. degrees for inspecting he then introduced the concept of the M.D. meaning 'Master Diagnostician'.

When questioned about Dunham college Littlejohn said he could not recall the names of the Professors and according to Hall's account[14], when he tried to explain Jowitt would cut him short and demand simple yes or no type answers.

This led to a rather confused situation, discussed above, with Jowitt changing the subject of his questions with the probable aim of confusing the witness as to the reason it said 'Doctor of Philosophy' on Littlejohn's Medical Degree.

The result was that he was on record as saying he would not describe himself as having a Ph.D., while it seems fairly evident that what he meant was that the did not have a Ph.D. from Columbia, but as Hall said in his letter of support, he was never given the chance. Halls hope that "the origin of this false impression has a very simple explanation, and, will we hope, even be even turned to advantage in the final summing-up by our counsel" never materialised.

The questioning wandered all over the place with the probable aim of finding ways to 'discredit' Littlejohn and the British School of Osteopathy. In this light even Sir William Jowitt K.C., counsel for The British Medical Association, got caught in his own web; pouring scorn on the 'Royal Society for literature' -asking 'Is it a London thing? …. what right has it to call itself Royal Society…'; The Chairman having to remind him 'it is a well-

---

[14] In the Letters of support of Littlejohn written by Hall and other senior figures at the BSO, after the failure of the Bill.

known body'[liii] Again, the question must be asked as to why Littlejohn's own counsel did not intervene or refer to this in his re-examination. His counsel, Mr. Harold Murphy, did, however, at the end of Jowitt's questioning, Mr. Radcliffe and Mr. Harold Beverage's cross-examining, take LittleJohn through a re-examination that went over his qualifications[15] but without covering his Ph. D. It seemed a rather perfunctory re-examination that left the question of Littlejohn's Doctor of Philosophy hanging in the air.

He also made no reference to the Looker school or students. Nor did he try to elaborate on the differences between the state of the BSO at its inception, its development to its state at the time of the inquiry and its proposed development if the Bill was passed as other avenues of co-operation in the educational field were opened up as a result.

The only rebuke Jowitt received during his examination of Littlejohn was that mentioned above, i.e., when he attacked the existence of the Royal Society of Literature. Given his repeated misrepresentation of Littlejohn's answers this seems extraordinary, and it seemed to suit everyone other than the BSO.

Another extraordinary exchange happened in the middle of Dr. MacDonald's testimony:

Radcliffe[16] asked :
2468. You agree that the practical side is very important?—Yes, it is most important. Dr. Elmer Theodore Pheils an osteopath in Birmingham, could answer all your questions with regard to the plans we have in the Association for our College.
Mr. Thorpe.] My learned friend will tell me something on which he wants information, and if I have no evidence available, I will procure it. I am not sure what he wants at the moment.

---

[15] A misprint in the minutes of evidence: 4083. *You got the honorary degree of LL.D. from a University in Texas?* — Yes.
"4084. *Having already got your **LL. D**. degree from Glasgow University?* — Yes.
It should read; "4084. *Having already got your **LL. B**. degree from Glasgow University?* — Yes.

[16] Mr. Cyril K Radcliffe, K.C., Counsel for the Royal College of Physicians; Mr. Thorpe K.C., O.B.E., was counsel for the supporters of the Bill; and the witness was Dr. MacDonald

Mr. Radcliffe.] Dr. Macdonald agrees with me that the practical side of what is going to be done is of the first importance.

Mr. Thorpe.] The future policy which will follow on this Bill becoming an Act?

Mr. Radcliffe.] I do not want to help you too far.

Mr. Thorpe.] Helping me? I am standing up and offering to find you what you are asking for.

Mr. Radcliffe.] If you do not propose to call the evidence, I am not going to assist you.

Mr. Thorpe.] 'If you want evidence to that effect, I will call it. I have none at the moment and I was not proposing to call it. It. is complete 'hypothesis.

Witness.] If you want evidence on the question of the college educational procedure, I suggest Dr. Elmer Theodore Pheils of Birmingham; he has the thing absolutely at his finger-ends.

Mr. Radcliffe.] If it is regarded of complete hypothesis, I ani quite willing to leave it so". [liv]

Pheils was never called as a witness and the plans of the BOA for a college never explored further in the inquiry. Again, this points to behind the scenes politics by the BOA and probably by Pheils, leaving the BSO to be 'exposed' as not up to standard and to be discredited. Pheils was Clinical special consultant on the 'College Committee' of the BOA and had held meetings with prominent Medical men like Mr. James Beaver Mennell[lv], and has been quoted as saying "we have reason to believe we can establish a college in London which will be a credit to existing Medical standards and also teach the principles of osteopathy"

These extraordinary interventions by Mr. Thorpe, Counsel for the BOA and other supporters of the Bill, taken together and in conjunction with the liaison between Pheils on behalf of the BOA and Mennell on behalf of the BMA lead to to probable conclusion that Thorpe was briefed to make sure the BOA's opinion of the BSO was not only exposed but opened up for full examination and the BSO discredited.

Littlejohn was not averse to criticism if it was of a positive nature. This was in line with his general approach to life and teaching/education. However, if it was of a purely negative nature designed to 'destroy' then he would not only not accept it but would almost aggressively defend his school and position. For example, twice before, when his college in Chicago was under attack, in 1905 with the AOA inspection and latter from the Flexner report he published a full defence of his College and staff in

Chicago. In this case we find in the British School of Osteopathy's journal the following response:

> "In the evidence given on behalf of the B.S.O. the cross-examination consisted of insinuations and personal attacks on the qualifications, integrity and honesty of the Dean of the School and the sincerity of those working with him in the School. **The leading Counsel for the supporters of the Bill never gave a helping hand although all the information was available. Everything could have been completely adjusted on re-examination following cross-examination**[17]. When the cross-examining Counsel suggested " I have been told " he introduced an element into examination contrary to legal procedure. Here is the account of what happened in a recent case. In the Revelstoke case reported in the " Daily Mail," May 15th, page 4, Mr. Justice Swift is reported as laying down the court law, " Let us observe the bounds of propriety. We do not know and do not care, and we ought not to be told what you have been told." This covered, for example, the statement of counsel that the Looker School had a six-months course, no proof being either offered or suggested."[lvi]

It seems clear that, although he was in favour of legislation, he didn't want to be at the meeting, for a variety of reasons, not least was the attitude of the BOA to his school and the disregard shown to his graduates. Wernham's wife described the same feeling. She was present as a spectator during the interrogation of Littlejohn at the select committee meetings. This was before she had met Wernham or knew anything about Littlejohn. She recalled that she had the distinct impression that he didn't want to be there, that he was reticent, he held in his hands diplomas which he had but no made effort to show them or to answer the questions that were being put.

> "He looked as if he did not want to be there, he had a bundle in his hands, I take it was his degrees, but did not show them"[lvii]

---

[17] Author's emphasis.

Littlejohn was a man of principle. He tried to state that the Doctorates were honorary and given for work done in the educational field[18], and as such were earned and not bought and then to elaborate on the state of the educational system in the United States during 1890-1910; In particular his affiliation with those institutions which made education available to women, minority groups and those who could not afford or did not have the opportunity to avail of higher level education; and that this affiliation was founded on both his religious and educational beliefs and principles. His views were clearly elucidated in a talk he gave to the Mediapolis, Iowa, Lecture Association, at the opening of season 1892-3.

"The lecturer (Littlejohn) pled for an enlargement of the field of popular education commensurate with the advancement of knowledge in every department; in the maxim of Pestalozzi, "Education is the generator of power." This advance, he shewed, could be made by receiving an inspirate of nature, identifying oneself with the brotherhood of man, opening up the treasures of antiquity, and especially by an exhaustive study of individual personality and placing oneself under the influence of the Christian ideal in private and public life".[lviii]

However, his explanations landed on deaf ears, a clear class of cultures, with the added factor of 'not wanting to hear' as it did not suit their agenda. Wernham and Hall give a splendid summary of the events;

"The failure of the Parliamentary Bill to regulate the practice of Osteopathy in Great Britain in 1935, is a matter of history. There can be little doubt, and it is generally agreed, that the Bill was premature. The real cause, however, was to be found in the discord and disunity among the members of the osteopathic profession and the lack of accord between the four separate organisations that represented Osteopathy at that time. Graduates of the British School of Osteopathy formed the nucleus of the Incorporated Association of Osteopaths; membership of the British

---

[18] Dr. Littlejohn has Just received, from the Chancellor of his Alma-mater, the following letter:
"I take pleasure in Informing you that the honorary degree of LL. D., will be conferred upon you by this university at the November graduation by a unanimous vote of its council, as an evidence of their appreciation of your success both pedagogical and literary, and a token of the high esteem In which you are held as a man and scholar." This is the second university which has conferred this honor upon Dr Littlejohn within the past year. (The Clarinda Herald, Page 4, 1895-10-22)

Osteopathic Association was drawn exclusively from American trained osteopathic practitioners; The Osteopathic Defence League was sponsored by an American practitioner who was not a member of either of these associations.

"... As a matter of fact, the British School of Osteopathy was never considered beyond the fact that the possibility of its support and help was projected.... When the Select Committee was appointed by the House of Lords the spokesman for the British Osteopathic Association (Dr. MacDonald) announced that the association did not recognise the British School of Osteopathy. Dr. Streeter said that "He did not know, and the British School of Osteopathy could speak for itself." ......

"Hence when The British School of Osteopathy was blackballed it was ULTRA VIRES and it was done on the principle of bullying and blustering to defeat the Bill by side-ventures[lix]*"*

Littlejohn, true to character tried to put the insults, innuendoes and lies behind him and to continue to put his energies into the continuance of the BSO and the 'Osteopathy of A T Still' But unfortunately the 1939-45 war and the tragic loss of his son Edgar, as a victim of the war, intervened. In a letter to a colleague in August 1935, he said

"Thanks so much for your kind letter. Such things as these – insinuations and lies – do not move me. For 38 years I have been used to such apelets and worse than these. Long years ago, Dr Still and I and his disciples were possessed with the devil – wretched, miserable, unfit to associate with holy hearts – so that all these things pass over me like a dewy rain."

"The reflection will come someday as it did in Pasteur's and Listers days. I won my Hunter Gold Medal in medicine and still have the William Hunter Spirit..........I am trying to rest, still weak and easily tired but undaunted – see our Journal in press for the answer – all good wishes."[lx]

The Destruction of Littlejohn's Reputation

An oft quoted book is 'This thy Body' by Mrs. Cecil Chesterton. In this she gives a very critical account of Littlejohn. Even Viscount Elibank, who introduced the Bill to regulate Osteopathy in 1934 and sat on the House of Lords committee, without naming Littlejohn added to the misapprehension of what had happened in the Committee hearings. In his introduction he commended Dr. Streeter as the main, if not only osteopath without whom 'Osteopathy would probably be little known in Great Britain today'

"The reader, as he proceeds, will gather that the Osteopaths were ill-served during the proceedings of the Select Committee by one of their own number"[lxi]

This shows how much Littlejohn had become the scapegoat for a very sad and politically driven agenda to discredit the BSO (and from the BMA's perspective, Osteopathy) while, hopefully in the eyes of the BOA, leaving the field open enough for them to start their own college.

In respect to Littlejohn the comment by Chesterton *"Memory failed to precipitate the essential thing at the imperative moment, and the spectators of the scene were left with the impression of a startling discrepancy between Dr. Littlejohn's recollection and the actual facts"*[lxii] does not tally with the testimony. The only thing he claimed not to recall was the names of professors in Dunham College from over 30 years previous.

She goes on to say *"Then there was the matter of the degree of LL.D. Doctor of Law. Dr. Littlejohn stated that it was the University of Texas which had conferred the degree, but on closer investigation it became apparent that it was not Texas University from which he had received the honour, but the Ad-Ran, a Christian University in Texas. It was only under extreme pressure that the witness seemed to realize the difference.*[lxiii]*"*

We get a similar example of 'bias' in the official report by the British Medical Association, which states on page 65 *"Dr. Littlejohn admitted that it was a mistake when he had stated at the previous hearing that he held a degree of the university of Texas; the degree was that of the Add-ran Christian University in Texas"*[lxiv]

The actual testimony was; -

"3264. Which University conferred that degree (LL.D.) upon you? - 'in Texas'

"3265. You are an honorary member of Texas University? - Yes

"When did they confer that degree upon you? – I could not tell you exactly the date. I could show you my diploma if it is necessary[19]."

So, he did not say from the university of Texas, not even "from Texas"; in answer to the question 'were did the degree come from?' It was the BMA's counsel, Sir W Jowitt, who kept referring to the University of Texas. This would appear to be a common trick to get the witness to inadvertently say something inaccurate.

Again, we find in Chesterton's book more misquoting of the testimony, giving a totally false impression

"The next point of examination was the degree of Doctor of Philosophy, which the witness said had been granted by the University of Columbia. Alas, interrogation elicited the amazing admission that: 'I am not a Doctor of Philosophy of Columbia—I would describe myself as a Fellow of Columbia."[lxv]

She goes on to say, **"the witness on his own admission, is not a Doctor of Philosophy; the origin of his degree in Law is dubious, and he is not an M. D. of Chicago University".**[lxvi]

Even a cursory examination of this statement by her shows that none of it is true. He never claimed to be a M.D. of 'Chicago University' and is clearly an M. D. of Dunham Medical College and was licenced to practice in several states. His Law degree from Glasgow is unquestioned, even by Jowitt, His LL. D. while from a Christian University and is 'honorary' is real and valid.

---

[19] He continually offered to show his diplomas throughout his testimony, not trying to hide anything.

However, in all of the testimony he did not get to mention his Ph.D. from the 'National University Chicago'.

One explanation, put forward by Hall, probably after discussion with Littlejohn himself, was that:

"The misunderstanding arose over the method of cross-examination by opposing counsel who asked ' Have you a Ph. D. of Columbia University? On the Dean attempting to explain that the Ph.D. was conferred by Chicago National University and not Columbia he was demanded to give a straight 'Yes' or 'No'. The apparently unreasonable demand by counsel provoked in the Dean that characteristic trait of which we are all aware that of retiring within himself and refusing further explanation".[lxvii]

While this is not quite what happened in the cross examination it does capture the essence. It is doubtful if Hall or Littlejohn, at that time had the transcript of the testimony[20].

Jowitt went on to poor scorn on not only Littlejohn's positions at Dunham and Herring Colleges as Professor of Physiology, but also on their very existence, saying *"What puzzles some of us who have made exhaustive reference to text-books and directories, both of that time and of the present time, is that (I speak for myself), I cannot find Dunham, and I cannot find Hering anywhere".*[lxviii]

Again, we find the Chairman correcting him and pointing out were Herring College was located: *"Chairman.] Hering. Medical College and Hospital, 823 Rhodes Avenue".*[lxix]

Again no one made the point that apart from the rather mild comment by the Chairman, no one else, especially not the Counsel for the proponents of the Bill, came back on this point and made it clear that these Colleges not only existed, but were recognised by the State Board of Health in Illinois. Thus, leaving Littlejohn looking like a 'fraud'.

Regarding the Ph.D., it is possible that another aspect played on Littlejohn's mind at the time. He did not get to say that his Doctorate was from the Chicago National University due to the line of questioning. However, it is also quite possibly, the fact that this particular university

---

[20] This has been dealt with above.

had a history in England and the Houses of Parliament, albeit in 1897, played on his mind.

"Harkins defence of the National University; AMERICAN DEGREES. Sib, — Great public interest having been excited by the discussion raised by a question in the House of Commons, "Whether there was any such institution in the United States as the National University of Chicago, and whether the Government would consider whether any steps could be taken to stop this alien interference with the duties and prerogatives of our authorised Universities," [lxx21]

It is interesting to note that in Littlejohn's correspondence with Hall and others, on British School of Osteopathy headed paper, he is listed as 'Dean: J. Martin Littlejohn, M.D. (Dunham, U.S.), D.O., LL.D.'. No mention of Ph.D.[lxxi]

It is hard to imagine how Littlejohn felt at this juncture in his testimony. His trait of character of 'retiring within himself', his probable promise to Streeter[22], his oath on being sworn in at the Inquiry, to answer questions honestly and truthfully, together with his view that the inquiry was 'Court procedure' and that it was up to the Counsel to present the evidence through him all adding up to a very confusing time. In particular the fact that Thorpe, the "leading Counsel for the supporters of the Bill never gave a helping hand although all the information was available". Littlejohn must have felt dumbfounded at this stage, awaiting as he would have, for the re-examination to clear up all the insinuations and false impressions. But this did happen with Mr. Harold Murphy only taking LittleJohn through a rather perfunctory re-examination.

On top of all this there was the scheming between some in the BOA and the BMA on the issue of an Osteopathic College, which continued after the Select Committee hearings

---

[21] See appendix on Colleges Littlejohn was associated with for full details

[22] I say probable as it is inconceivable that he did not as Streeter was the architect of the Bill and Littlejohn agreed *"The BSO recognises that Streeter has worked unselfishly for Osteopathy for many years, and has done his best to try and get legislation to recognise the Osteopathic profession and Osteopathy as a system of healing. Recognizing this, the B.S.O. told Dr. Streeter that it was willing to follow his leadership in litigation, as the B.S.O, was devoted to the educational side of Osteopathy, provided the Osteopathic profession as a whole and its educational aspects were safeguarded by a united front".*(Journal of Osteopathy, BSO, June-August 1935, page 3)

"The animosity to and criticism of the BSO did not end with the Select Committee. On 5 April 1935 Kelman MacDonald asked the BOA Council for absolute secrecy in regard to a long talk he had had with Viscount Elibank. Assuming that the Bill in its present form would not pass: they would like to put a very strong recommendation 'for the creation of a voluntary register with high standards; The establishment of' a first class, trustworthy School of Osteopathy (i.e. a BOA School); graduates of certain osteopathic colleges with a 4 year course, to undertake postgraduate work at the BOA college in order to satisfy a Board in all respects. This would not apply to those who have already started and an agreed plan of education to include a number of years at ordinary medical schools, pending the establishment of a full course at the Osteopathic School.' "[lxxii]

In these circumstances, at the age of 70 years and not being in good health, it is no wonder that his efforts to present his evidence, which was supposed to be on the evolution and place of the BSO in the context of the proposed Bill ended in a personal attack on his reputation. His past experience in America was that he would support any legislation to make Osteopathy legal but would not do so if it put his students in a position that they would have to practice in violation of the law. This had led him into conflict with others in Illinois. Here he tried to avoid such conflict as much as possible, the result was his reputation was assaulted.

In the editorial of the journal of osteopathy June-august 1935 a response to the criticisms of Littlejohn was given. In particular it was stated that "The leading Counsel for the supporters of the Bill never gave a helping hand although all the information was available. Everything could have been completely adjusted on re-examination following cross-examination".

One is left with to wonder why? If it is remembered that The BOA started life in 1911 as "the formal wing of the American osteopathic association (AOA), for American trained osteopaths"[lxxiii] and its ambition was to have a school of osteopathy under its control modelled upon medical schools, and that it "despised the BSO" it is not surprising that Littlejohn was made into a scapegoat. If the BSO was discredited that would leave the way open for them to start a college in conjunction with the BMA. Their apparent scheming in this with the BMA would never have achieved anything other than played into the hands of the BMA who were totally opposed to Osteopathy. In one letter to his American counterpart the Medical Secretary of the BMA said, *"we are, of course, preparing our case and hope to destroy the Bill at this early stage."*[lxxiv] This would seem to sum up their attitude towards the Bill and Osteopathy in general.

They would not have seen that their own approach, of putting Dr. MacDonald forward as the champion of osteopathy played entirely into the hands of the BMA and opponents of the Bill. After all, if he was a qualified doctor and he could legitimately practice osteopathy, after postgraduate training, under the exist law, what was the point or necessity of further legislation. Nor would they have agreed with the BMA's assessment of Streeter's evidence; *The first witness called for those who are sponsoring the Bill, namely Mr. Wilfrid a. Streeter, the author of "The New Healing" made, in my judgment' a lamentable show. when our Counsel gets to work on him, he should 'tear him to bits '. Unfortunately, it is only too evident that the majority of the Select Committee are in favour of the Bill, and therefore we must lose no opportunity to convert them to our way of thinking".*[lxxv]

Lord Dawson of Penn who sat on the committee, thought *"the importance of this enquiry is that it concerns other 'quack' systems besides osteopathy"…"If witness throws over osteopathic principles and accepts as he does in the Bill the same training – he removes ground for separate training and discards fundamental principles of osteopathy. The memo to the Bill – calls osteopathy 'treatment of disease by manipulation methods' that sure nails them… the only good of the enquiry it to discredit this last assertion and purpose"*[lxxvi]

Some Additional Context

A final point on the House of Lords Select committee report that needs to be mentioned is the oft quoted remark in the report that the British School of Osteopathy is **"above all in thoroughly dishonest hands"**[lxxvii]. This has often been quoted as 'proof' that Littlejohn was dishonest. However, let us examine the facts. The draft report said, ***"the only existing establishment in this country for the education and examination of osteopaths was exposed, in the course of evidence before us, as being of negligible importance and inefficient for its purpose."*** The line ***"above all in thoroughly dishonest hands"*** was proposed as an amendment by Lord Redesdale[23]. In the absence of the chairperson, Lord Amulree, (due to ill health), who had drafted the report, Lord Redesdale was made chairperson. Who was Lord Redesdale? His more famous daughters were known as the 'Mitford sisters' It was said that they *"grew up in an aristocratic country house with emotionally distant parents and a large household with numerous servants; this family dynamic was not unusual for upper-class families of the time. There was also a disregard for formal education of women of the family, and they were expected to marry at a young age to a financially well-off husband."* [lxxviii]

"*Redesdale wealth was seriously depleted in the late 1920s by a series of poor investments. During this period, he developed extreme right-wing opinions and became a member of several anti-Semitic organizations including the Anglo-German Fellowship and The Link. His daughter, Diana Mitford, married Oswald Mosley, leader of the British Union of Fascists, in 1936. Another daughter, Unity Mitford, went to Nazi Germany and met Adolf Hitler, Heinrich Himmler, Herman Goering, Joseph Goebbels and other leaders of the Nazi Party. Hitler told newspapers in Germany that Unity was "a perfect specimen of Aryan womanhood.*[lxxix]

So, we have one Lord, who ostensibly did not believe in educating[24] women and was described as **'one of nature's natural fascists'**[25] making sure a disparaging remark about Littlejohn is published, with parliamentary privilege, without any real justification for the accusations. How bizarre is it that this remark has been used so frequently to discredit Littlejohn?

---

[23] AS to why Lord Redesdale added this sentence we can only speculate. One reason may simply be that he took a personal dislike to Littlejohn; another possibility, following the line of thought-'who benefits'- is that the BOA colluded with him to make sure the BSO and Littlejohn were totally discredited in the report.

[24] "As a child he was prone to sudden fits of rage. He was totally uninterested in reading or education, wishing only to spend his time riding. (He later liked to boast that he had read only one book in his life" Talking about Lord Redesdale. (http://enacademic.com/dic.nsf/enwiki/9069115)

[25] "British fascist leader Sir Oswald Mosley, described him as "one of nature's fascists", but it seems he never joined any fascist party" wikipedia.org/wiki/David_Freeman-Mitford,_2nd_Baron_Redesdale

Jowitt's speech and the Looker Students

When the committee met on Friday 23rd of March, Jowitt made a speech before calling his next witness. It seems astonishing that the detail in this speech went unchallenged.

"I do not want to say very much about the British School of Osteopathy, or about Dr. Littlejohn. The divergence between Dr. Kelman MacDonald, on the one hand, and Dr. Littlejohn, on the other, is about as great as the divergence between the North Pole and the South Pole: I cannot imagine two men more wholly and utterly different than those two people. I will content myself with saying to your Lordships, that one thing at least is plain in regard to this matter, that the British School of osteopathy cannot be regarded as in any way a satisfactory, or, I regret to say, a reputable school. Of the 96 old boys, some 15 are Looker students; the particular Looker student I took was one Spencer. So far as Dr. Littlejohn knew, the Looker course was six months. Spencer comes to the British School of Osteopathy and gets a certificate from the British School of Osteopathy, saying that he had attended the four years' course, because that is the effect of it. That, in my submission, and I had better be quite plain about it (I have tried to be quite polite), is not an Honest, certificate, and Dr. Littlejohn, I will say quite plainly, is not an honest, man. I am quite certain that your Lordships and anybody who has the interests of the osteopaths at heart would regret very greatly to see, or to think for a moment that a man of the quality and calibre of Dr: Kelman MacDonald is in any sense mixed up with a man of the quality and caliber of Dr. Littlejohn. I should ask your Lordships to make, and I am sure your Lordships would make this quite plain, that, whatever else is plain, if you are going to have a satisfactory education hereafter in osteopathy (I will say quite frankly what I mean) the less Dr. Littlejohn has to do with it the better. If there were only more people like Dr. Kelman MacDonald (unfortunately one swallow does not make a summer), if only you could get some of them, who could give their time and attention to the development of the School and give their time and attention to the development of a hospital attached to the School, then I conceive that your Lordships would approach this Bill from a very different point of view." [lxxx]

The basis of the charge that Littlejohn was 'dishonest' was built upon his evidence regarding the Looker students, in particular one student, Spencer and on the format of the Diploma issued by the British School of Osteopathy. The testimony went as follows:

3623. Tell me this: Would it be honest, do you think, if a man had attended, let us say, for two years, at some school or other (take a reputable medical school; let us take Edinburgh); supposing he had attended for two years at Edinburgh and then had come to your school for two years, and two years only, would it be honest for you to give him a Certificate to say that he had attended lectures at your school and been at your school for four years? — **We do not give a Certificate to say that he attended lectures.**

3624. That is not the question. It is a simple one: If he had been two years at Edinburgh and two years only at your School, would it be honest to give him a Certificate to say that he had been four years at your school? — **We do not give such a Certificate.**

*3625. It would be dishonest, would it not? —***I do not answer that question. It would be dishonest. My point, as I stated before, is that we require a four-year course, and if we require them to attend somewhere else for two years of that course, we take them as third year students. We have had students from Cambridge University Medical School who have attended their first two years there, and we have taken them in as third year students.**

*3626. Do you remember a man called George Spencer; he was one of the Looker Students, was he not? —***Yes.**

*3627. George Spencer, who had been a Looker Student of the school of Osteopathy and Chiropractic, came to you for one year, did he not? —***Yes.**

3628. George Spencer, having been with you for one year and one year only, receives this Certificate. - I will read this out to you: " Be it known that George Spencer "—it is from the British School of Osteopathy, Limited, London—" To whom this may come, Greeting " it is a Royal kind of' thing[26]*; let us read on: " Be it known that , George Spencer having completed the required study and attended the full course of Lectures, Clinics and Demonstrations during the regular four years' course, and having passed satisfactory examinations in all branches of training taught in this school*

---

[26] Jowitt could not resist diverting attention by pouring scorn on the wording of the Diploma and imputing a different meaning to the greeting.

including Clinics and other practical demonstrations, is hereby admitted to the Diplomate in Osteopathy D.O., given at London "— not " given at our Court of St. James[27] *' ". That is dated the 22nnd" day of December 1928, signed' ". J. Martin Littlejohn, Dean of the School and Superintendent of Education." Look at that. Tell my Lords if that is an honest document. Here it is?* —**I know.**

3629. *Is it an honest document?* —**Yes. We are conforming to the conditions, as I explained before, that have been followed out all the time by the. Associated Colleges of Osteopathy.** *Here we are taking in a student who give us the evidence that he has completed three years of work in an irregular school, and we have required him to take one year's work; pass the examinations and attend clinic work. There was a special clinic for these people held in the City of Manchester in order that ·they might· complete that work, and it is on that basis that we give, and gave him and the others the Diploma. I want to explain that we had no definite relation whatever to the Looker School of Osteopathy and Chiropractic. In 1926 a certain number of the graduates of that School who had formed an Association called the Incorporated Association of Osteopaths Limited made application to us for admission to our School, and to get credit for the work they had done in the irregular school. That Association was formed in 1925. The object of that Association was, first of all, to support, advance, maintain and carry out investigation into the principles, theory and practice of osteopathy; to train, teach and graduate students therein. They set themselves to work in 1925, to ·teach themselves and to be taught by others who went and lectured to them from time to time.* **The carried that on form 1925 to 1927 when we took them in and gave them credit, as I have said, for work done irregularly for three years, and we required them, on that basis , to complete one years work, pass examinations, and take a final exam**[28]. *It was on that basis that they got their diploma."* ...

---

[27] Again, imply that the wording was arrogant rather than just formal.

[28] In the Chautauqua and other distant learning courses it was common for study circles to meet and learn together with the help of a local tutor were available and a final exam supervised by a local nominee. A final exam did not mean coming together in a central location with 'external supervisors' etc as we might expect in modern colleges. *"The Chautauqua Literary and Scientific Circle (CLSC) was started in 1878 to provide those who could not afford the time or money to attend college the opportunity of acquiring the skills and essential knowledge of a College education. The four-year, correspondence course was one of the first attempts at distance learning"* (https://chq.org/about-us/history)

3392. My question to you is simple and clear: Is it honest to give a certificate to say that a man has attended four years at your school when in fact he has not? – **He has completed a four-year course according to our requirements.**

3633. Do you suggest as plainly as can be there that he has done a four years course at your school? – **No.**
        Lord Dawson of Penn] It says so.
        Lord Redesdale.] Yes, it says so."[lxxxi]

The diploma did not say he attended the BSO for four years - simply that he had *"completed the required study and attended the full course of Lectures, Clinics and Demonstrations during the regular four years' course"* The counsels for the opposition to the bill uniting to make it sound different, while the counsels for the proponents of the Bill remained silent.

Littlejohn answered all the questions simply, in a straightforward and honest manner and yet because of the wording of the diploma and Jowitt's persistence with the help of Lord Dawson's and Lord Redesdale's interventions the accusation of Littlejohn being dishonest was allowed to stick. No help or rebuttal coming from the counsel for the supporters of the Bill. The matter of the 'four years' being simply a matter of interpretation and if was to be a problem could easily be changed in the future as was made plain in earlier testimony – One of the purposes of the Bill was to set a standard and iron out any anomalies that existed, either by lack of support from the 'established' educational and medical authorities or the lack of the financial ability of the existing school to bring itself up to the ideal it set for itself. In essence the BSO was run by one person, others helping were and when they could. One past student said that he spent many an afternoon playing bridge waiting for a lecturer to arrive, but not in the case of Littlejohn who unless ill was extremely reliable[lxxxii]. In these circumstances it could hardly be expected that every possible detail could be dealt with. Did they really expect the diploma to be changed to say 'having attended some lectures at the college and other lectures elsewhere' or 'having attended one year at the BSO and been given credit for 3 years elsewhere' or some other wording. No reasonable person would expect this.

As to the BSO being of *'negligible importance and inefficient for purpose'*, it was the only school at the time, working under difficult conditions with opposition from the BOA, who wanted to have control. Littlejohn would not let this happen as he felt it was *'not in the province of the BOA, any more that it would of the BMA or AOA to own schools.'*[lxxxiii] Educationally, he always felt the profession needed a professional body and an educational body, independent of each other but working in co-operation. Alongside of this, within the schools he would have a board of governors, a teacher's body and a student body as the necessary functioning units for a healthy system. It could hardly be said to be of negligible importance as it was the only one. The only justification for this remark could be the stated intention of the BOA to have a school with a five-year course modelled upon the then current medical educational system. An aim that apparently was deliberately not presented for examination during the enquiry. Littlejohn never claimed perfection for his school; Under examination by Mr. Harold Murphy he said *"We do not claim perfection because we have had many obstacles to fight against and many difficulties to try to overcome, and we have done our best under the circumstances; .*

For instance, -'your ' course is at present 4 years. Have you any objection to a course of 5 years being-substituted? —No, we Should welcome it. As a matter of fact, we ourselves have considered that, independently of this investigation" [lxxxiv]

Afterwards, he did receive support from some of his colleges, especially T E Hall and J Canning, who wrote to graduates and others giving details of Littlejohn's degrees and the Looker graduate situation. It is sad that Littlejohn became the scapegoat to such an extent that no one cared to see the contribution of the BOA, MacDonald and Streeter. It suited the BOA as they were let off the hook so to speak and could continue to venture down the medical route. It suited the BMA, who seemed to be happy that the bill was defeated, and they always had their fall-back – Dr. MacDonald who 'showed' that a medical degree could indeed be the prime requirement for doing postgraduate work to become an Osteopath.

The viewpoint of MacDonald and Littlejohn, at first sight, may not seem far apart. Both were in favour of a 5-year course[29] the first part being the same as for medical doctors, in anatomy, physiology, chemistry etc.

---

[29] LittleJohn intimated as much even earlier in a letter to T E Hall in October 8th, 1926

However, while MacDonald seems to have held a medicalised view, with drugs being a last resort-especially when a disease was full blown[30]. Littlejohn, on the other hand, held firmly to Classical Osteopathy as taught by A T Still, drugs being poisons and therefore of no use medicinally - the two systems being incompatible and it being a matter of the free choice of the patient which system to choose and then follow that line of treatment. On meeting the then minister of health, Neville Chamberlain, in 1925. *"Dr. Littlejohn, President of the British Osteopathic Association[31], said that the deputation had not come with any antagonistic feelings to the medical profession, they felt that their spheres of activity were quite different"*[lxxxv]. This was typical of his approach, no antagonism, ill feeling or negative comments, just a positive approach extolling the benefits of the osteopathic system, with no desire for recognition from or association with the medical profession as such, just mutual respect, and the freedom of the individual to choose their system of medicine. This idea would be in a similar vein to that espoused by Br. Benjamin Rush.

"Dr. Benjamin Rush (1746-1813), "the Hippocrates of America," "the American Galen," "the American Sydenham," "the father of medicine in America," signer of the Declaration of Independence, true patriot that he was, read the signs of the times….it is not surprising that he should say: …"The Constitution of this Republic should make specific provision for medical freedom as well "as for religious freedom. To restrict the practice of the art of healing to one class of physicians and deny to others equal privileges constitutes the Bastilles of our science. All such laws are un-American and despotic. They are vestiges of monarchy and have no place in a republic."[lxxxvi] [32]

---

[30] Dr. William ' Kelman Macdonald. - *"Whenever I can I avoid using drugs, whenever necessary I push them on to other people "* (Minutes of Evidence Taken Before The Select Committee On Registration And Regulation. Of Osteopaths Bill 2889)

[31] Littlejohn was not only a member of the BOA at that time but also President. He later left the BOA because of its drift towards medicine, as mentioned earlier.

[32] This particular quote has been said not to be a true quote from Dr Rush but rather to be a later misquote of this quote "Conferring exclusive privileges upon bodies of physicians, and forbidding men of equal talents and knowledge, under severe penalties from practicing medicine within certain districts of cities and countries. Such institutions, however sanctioned by ancient charters and names, are the bastilles of our science."

Thomas Jefferson, writer of the Declaration of Independence, *"I hope and believe that it is from this side of the Atlantic that Europe, which has taught us so many useful things, will be led into sound principles in this branch of science, the most important of all, to which we commit the care of health and life."* [lxxxvii]

As for the pre-osteopathic work at the BSO, Wernham gives a personal account of his time;

"having only physics and chemistry, it meant going back to school to struggle with biology, anatomy and the rest. In those days Chelsea Polytechnic College was open to osteopathic students and the Kings road became my familiar path to knowledge – there we dealt with dead frogs, rats and bits of fish. I remember being instructed to rush up and down the main stairway to increase my blood pressure for experimental purposes, but there was no change in pressure and the experiment failed. I must have been very fit in those days. Much of the work carried out was a matter of private study." [lxxxviii]

The Bill was withdrawn upon the request of the Supporters of the Bill giving the *reason "That they could not properly ask for a measure which required for its full operation the granting of powers to the British School of Osteopathy, the present constitution of which the "principal supporters did not approve".* [lxxxix]

It is evident that this did not include the BSO or Littlejohn. Throughout the inquiry it was made clear that part of the purpose of the Bill was to set and help the BSO implement an improved standard of education, opening doors to educational material that were closed to them and helping provide the necessary financial backing. Up to this point Littlejohn was the main if not sole provider of finances to run the school. As Streeter said *"The British School of Osteopathy has been conducted by Dr. Littlejohn and we all admire his effort. It has been an individual effort and it has not yet been enabled to bring its educational standard up to the level at which we would like it."* [xc] It does seem a strange rationale given that that was one of the points of the Bill, unless of course, we see the putative background scheming of the BOA having backfired on them, in that they were not going to get the support of the BMA for amending the Bill to exclude the BSO.

Littlejohn and Hall

Hall left us a treasure trove in the letters that Littlejohn wrote to himself. We are indebted to the European School of Osteopathy in Maidstone, Kent, for preserving and allowing full access to these letters. In these we find great insights into Littlejohn's mind and character. Of hall he wrote:

"you and I are old friends and I want it to last. You are one of the few among my students who has followed myself and kept in this line of osteopathy with no adjuvants". August 29th, 1934.

It was in this vein that Hall, together with Wernham and others founded the 'Osteopathic Institute of applied technique, later called the "Institute of Applied Osteopathy' and now the 'Institute of Classical osteopathy"

He found in Hall not only a friend but someone who like himself had a great love of osteopathy and supported him not only financially but also in the face of criticisms. When Hall was a student, he supported him financially not charging him for his treatments and allowing him to pay his fees how and when he could.

"I will not charge you for your treatment. But if you feel you can give at any time give towards your fees in the school." -August 18th, 1928

Even when he found Hall to be or tending to be 'disloyal' Littlejohn still found it in his heart to forgive him to support him provided he was contrite and working in the right direction for osteopathy.

"I was very much surprised I confess when I found your name attached to a paper which if it meant anything meant that I was not capable of conducting the school and when I was told that I lectured sometimes about what I did not know or understand I was more than surprised." – August 16th, 1928.

He went on to openly tell Hall that he expected to find him loyal and expected and felt that Hall would make good and be a credit to the school otherwise he would not have trusted him.

Later on, when Hall found his name sullied and dragged through the mud in the newspapers due to a case for breach of promise by his fiancée, Littlejohn again expressed his feelings of brotherhood and clearly stated,

"do not think that anything that has happened or been reported in the papers in any way prejudices or alters my opinion of yourself. Please don't let any of these things mar our friendship or interfere with your work with and among us either in the school or association." November 26th, 1930.

The incident must have caused Hall a great deal of embarrassment and even shame. His private letters to his fiancée were published in the newspapers not just in a small column, but sometimes up to even half a page. He had described himself in these letters as being unfit to be married:

"I wanted to do this for the last few weeks only being such a contemptible cur I dared not. Things have been going far worse than I let you suspect, and I am simply surrounded with debts and no future prospects and cannot see any marriage ahead until six or seven years. First let me tell you there has been no other woman…. Although I have been such a selfish beast as to take other women out, and therefore have lost all my self-respect, and may be my failure in my practice is Fate's own reward"… I shall never marry, and my dreams of a home must go- I am not fit to black your shoes. It may sound queer on top of all this when I say you are the finest woman I have ever known. It is for that reason I write because I can only wreck your life when you are worthy of a man".[xci]

This would have given Hall's critics within the British School of Osteopathy ammunition. O'Brien[xcii] felt Hall *"was starting to suffer from hereditary mental problems, especially those of mild paranoia and were exasperated by regular bouts of drinking and his increased dependence on alcohol"*.[xciii] The old saying that just because you are paranoid does not mean that people are out to get you seems to apply in this case. Before this incidence Littlejohn had to deal with the outcome of what he calls *"chatter and gossip of those who have no interest in osteopathy beyond gossip"* – (September 17th, 1932) with regard to Hall.

He made it quite clear in that letter to Hall, that he never spoke to anyone about his case and that he had appreciated everything that Hall had done and if others would give help and assistance instead of bantering criticism and misrepresentation the school would get on better.

This was particularly true in the case coming up to the osteopathic bill. The legislation that was presented in 1931 had to be withdrawn because of disagreements between the B.O.A and other osteopathic institutions only to be brought forward again in 1935. He reminded Hall on occasion of what he himself had been through. In a letter dated May 16th, 1935 he told Hall of a dream he had about the incident in Louisville in Kentucky when Dr Smith and himself appeared for the A.S.O. and were called everything from a liar to a knave and to a fool and that they were crucified for osteopathy but the A.S.O. came through this.

"Last night I dreamed of Louisville Kentucky when before Judge Toney and the supreme court Dr. Wm. Smith and I appeared from the A.S.O. and were called everything from a liar to a knave and a fool. Isn't it funny how all these old memories come back? And yet, after we were Crucified Osteopathy and the A.S.O. made its biggest victories." – May 16th, 1935.

This an interesting incident that he is recalling in this letter. It became the main topic of his address as Class Representative at his Graduation at the American School of Osteopathy, Kirksville, in January 1900.

"Next followed the address of the afternoon by Dr. Littlejohn, which was a most able effort[33]. He began by attacking Judge Toler (Sic.) of Kentucky, who stated in a decision in the Nelson case from Louisville, that the American School of Osteopathy had incompetent professors and the whole institution was a farce. Judge Toler's (Sic.[34]) decision and an accompanying article in the American Medical Journal, is a slanderous lie. He, and as Dr. Littlejohn said, the author is worse than the father of liars. He then went into the discussion of Osteopathy, comparing to other systems of

---

[33] This quote "a most able effort" has sometimes been made use of in a derogatory manner to imply that Littlejohns' speech was not very good. However, the whole quote puts it in a very complimentary context. A simple example of how careful one has to be when interpreting remarks using small quotes. See bold emphasis

[34] The misspelling of Judge Toney's name is interesting, but probably nothing more than a typographical error.

*Therapeutics, some of a kindred nature and others of the very opposite, such as drug Therapy. His talk lasted on hour and a quarter and was **listened to with rapt attention**. His advice to the class was fine and we trust will be heeded. The address was **most eloquent in thought and delivery** and while not honoring him here, for he is and has been well honored, the class feels the honor to have so able a representative.....*

*During the exercises Dr. Hildreth received a telegram from Buckmaster & Nelson announcing the shooting of William Goebel, the contesting candidate for the governorship of Kentucky. Dr. Littlejohn read it and then **said it was a pity it wasn't the Judge who rendered such a nonsensical decision** and whose decision it is said are nearly all reversed by the court of appeals" (Kirksville Journal February 1st 1900, courtesy of The State Historical Society of Missouri)*

His remark that "it was a pity it wasn't the Judge (Toney)" was rather out of step with his ethics and principles. It would seem that having given a talk that was heavily critical of Toney and being on the stage with Hildreth he let the mood of the occasion get the better of his principles. It is easy to forget that while he had lofty ideals and principles does not mean that he had lost the frailties of being human.

The purpose of quoting these letters to Thomas Edward Hall from Littlejohn is to show the same spirit that he showed in his relationship with the Rev. Minifie and that these attributes could be found throughout his career. That is, he would approach matters from the point of view of demonstrating and elaborating the positive effects of his cause whether it was in the bible or in osteopathy or in his attitude towards life. He would not engage in destructive or negative thinking regarding anything if this was avoidable. He was loyal to his friends and those that supported the cause that he was involved in. His attitude towards rumours, innuendoes and gossip is best summarised by his statement to Hall on September 17th, 1932

"I pay no attention to the chatter and gossip of those who have no interest in osteopathy beyond gossip. I could tell you of things reported to me regarding yourself and others but when any such gossip comes to me, I put it under my feet and trample it out of existence. I hope you will do likewise. I haven't the time or the energy to attend these petty things. It's

a great pity some give themselves to these things." - September 17th, 1932.[35]

This was his attitude throughout his life and even in his last decade. Many of these letters written by him to Hall were written when he was going through illness or recovering from illness and being in great pain. At times he may come across as being a little bitter or forceful. But this was not in his nature. It can be difficult at times to see the line between holding on to a principle and overt stubbornness. Principle can descend into an appearance of awkward stubbornness especially as we get older. Littlejohn had spent his life in defence of the non-established, the Covenanters and the Osteopaths (non-established medicine); not in fighting against the establishment rather wanting and looking for recognition and the freedom to practice both in the religious sense and the medical[36] sense. This has always been a difficult 'fight' especially when one is trying not to 'fight' but simple demand one's 'rights'. He put this ably in the British School of Osteopathy's announcement for the year 1927:

"In modern times, Colleges of Physicians and Surgeons have been set apart for Medicine and Surgery after the pattern of the Apostolic College, and these Colleges have been incorporated for the purpose of educating those who should be considered " qualified " to engage in the profession, and thus certifying the " qualified." These Colleges have in recent years debarred all others not possessing their qualification as "unqualified" just as the Conformist in religion branded the unbeliever as a heretic and non-conformist... Hence there has sprung up in the healing profession a body of dissenters or non-conformists just in the same way as there arose in the history of religion dissenters from the predominant established religion."[xciv]

---

[35] Still expressed similar sentiments "There has been too much tattling and trouble-making and I have always been pained to see it," said Dr. Still. "I rebuke it severely whenever I see it going on, too". Osteopathic Physician, December 1903, Page 22.
[36] Medicine is used in its full meaning i.e. the science or practice of the diagnosis, treatment, and prevention of disease and not as the use of drugs

The Last Decade

Littlejohn passed away on the 8th December 1947[xcv].

"A pioneer of osteopathy In Britain, well-known Thundersley resident and former councilor. Dr. John Martin Littlejohn, M.A., B.D., M.D., died at his home. Badger Hall, Thundersley, on Monday at the age of 82... shortly before the 1939-1945 war he retired. but he afterwards returned to public life until 1946." Obituary from unknown local paper

in 1940 Littlejohn himself ceased to have active involvement in the school, not attending meetings and not teaching because of suffering from deteriorating health for which he had spent two weeks in hospital and was having x-rays and other diagnostic procedures to find out the cause of the trouble. [xcvi]

His last decade was one of failing health and reputation due in no small measure to the report of the Select Committee the net result of which was the slating of Littlejohn's reputation despite the fact that he tried to set the record straight in the publications of the British School of Osteopathy. This coupled with outbreak of the war interfered with any further progress at the British School and Littlejohn's health, which had been poor during the late 1930's, deteriorated, especially after the death of his son, Edgar, who died after an acute attack of nephritis, while in India on active service in 1944[xcvii].

Wernham, from his own personal experience, gives an excellent description of this period: *"John Martin could hardly be called a 'good mixer' but he was a generous host who was never heard to complain and was content to relax privately until the last guest had departed. This happy state of affairs continued until about 1935, a time that was to prove a kind of watershed in the life of Badger Hall and in the professional status of the B. S. O.; the heavy blow that the medical opposition dealt the school and its Dean finding reflection in the social and private life of the family home. The ever-flowing stream of guests was gradually filtered off and it is doubtful if the school ever recovered its former buoyancy in the four years prior to the outbreak of war"* [xcviii]

> *Littlejohn's illnesses as mentioned in letters to Hall*
> **Dec 29th, 1928** – *I have been fighting severe abdominal pains for some weeks.*
> **May 16th, 1935** – *I am sitting comfortably at present in my Morris chair. I am feeling better today. I have had no sickness and feel more like moving around. It is so biting cold and I can't go out and enjoy the fresh air.*
> **May 22nd, 1935** - *I am better and gaining strength and hope to be back soon to help*
> **April 2nd, 1936** – *I had a throat of my own – tonight it is a little better- my first meal since Monday night. Milk and Bovril has been my diet – vegetarian … … anyway I am feeling more free and easy tonight.*
> **May 26th, 1937** - *I haven't felt too good myself but have to keep on.*
> **Aug 15, 1938** – *I haven't been very much up- have felt limp and weakly. I hope my little holiday will build me up.*
> **October 5th, 1938** – *I feel I can't go to the diner on October 14th as I feel when it comes to 6 o'clock in the evening I can only sit in my lounge chair and rest. I must keep up the schoolwork although it is a hard task to keep going. I must for the present avoid all other work*

He would often Imply[xcix] that not only was Littlejohn's reputation affected but also his social standing. Despite his own attitude *that "Such things as these – insinuations and lies – do not move me*^c*"*[37] it would appear that this had a negative effect on his wellbeing, as it would on any normal human

---

[37] In this letter He went on to say ". For 38 years I have been used to such apelets and worse than these. Long years ago, Dr Still and I and his disciples were possessed with the devil – wretched, miserable, unfit to associate with holy hearts – so that all these things pass over me like a dewy rain."

being. Added to this it has been said that he *"never got over Edgar's death and rather lost the will to continue himself"*[ci]

What happen was in contrast to his view of what his final years would be. In a letter written in March 1937, Littlejohn set out his attitude to what would be his final decade:

"Regarding myself I can't see where this rumour came from. I have never spoken of retiring and you may take it from me I shall never retire until called to a higher sphere of life and service. I have worked for 40 years in osteopathy and mean, like the old doctor, to finish my course still fighting. I haven't the endurance of earlier years, but I still keep going – after which others lag behind"[cii].

His own attitude was to continue and to continue to give his life to Osteopathy but *"although the indomitable will remained, the frail body was now burdened with these many years and recent events must have taken their toll. He continued to teach and practice, the school and clinic never ceased to operate, but the bitter attack from medicine and the unhappy report from the Select Committee had left their marks and the brief period between the dismal affair, commonly known as 'the Bill' and the outbreak of the war were but twilight years, ending in closure with the exception of the clinic, which still gave a limited service"*[ciii]. He had Thomas Edward Hall at his side as vice principle of the college for most of the time up until the time Hall resigned in the early 1940's. Of Halls resignation, Littlejohn wrote:

"I, personal, am fully appreciative of your long service to the school, and of your great assistance in affecting the many improvements which have marked its progress. It is for me a great disappointment not to have your continued support. I trust, however, that the school will have your continued support in its efforts" [civ](2nd April !940)

In spite of Hall's resignation his contribution to the school was invaluable during this period; Wernham was adamant, in all conversations on the subject that *"It is well, perhaps to place on record that it is doubtful if the British School of osteopathy would have survived the second Great War or survived at all if T.E.H. had not exercised considerable authority and control in 1940"* [cv]

In January of that year Hall wrote to the Dean criticising the school and resigned from the Board and other offices[cvi]. The main tenor of his criticism according to Wernham [cvii] was the lack of teaching of osteopathic principles particularly the physiological movements of the spine, Littlejohn's treatment of diseases and the general osteopathic treatment. According to Collins[cviii], Hall explained his resignation was the accumulative result of a series of small incidents over a long period. His resignation was accepted by the Board and Littlejohn, with regret[cix]. However, later on as the school faced problems with a declining number of students and patients during the war together with a lack of teachers again due to the war "a letter was sent requesting him, 'to give the directors the benefit of his knowledge to the school and his special organisation ability at this difficult period".[cx] When Hall's resignation was accepted Joselyn Proby was appointed Deputy Dean of the B.S.O. and he seemed to be instrumental in getting Hall to return. Proby himself moving to Ireland in 1943 to open a clinic in Kilmuckridge[38]. Hall was again appointed Vice-Dean and re-elected as a governing director. However, there was strong objection to his appointment with Webster Jones and Clem Middleton resigning.

In the midst of all of this Littlejohn who was in poor health wrote to Webster Jones asking him to withdraw his resignation and asking him to ask Clem Middleton to do the same. The row between Hall and other faculty members rumbled on through the years even after Littlejohn's death. According to Wernham the main bone of contention that Hall[39] wanted osteopathy taught as Littlejohn taught it and as Still taught it, that the student must be bathed in osteopathic theory first, last and always and practice. Or as Collins put it in his book "Edward Hall contended that the osteopathic student must soak himself in his osteopathic environment, he must be taught to think osteopathy and osteopathic theory first, last and always." Collins says of Hall that he was "very influential at the B.S.O. from 1943 'til his resignation in 1964". He passed away on the 24th March 1979.

This all could be summed up as the natural 'power struggle' for succession, that took place when Littlejohn had to take a step backward in the 40's due to ill health and then after his death in 1947. When a strong

---

[38] In County Wexford, Ireland. and was the clinic where Wernham came to do locum work in 1947 after he was demobbed from the army and where he met his wife who was a patient in Kilmuckridge at that time.

[39] Hall and Wernham became fast friends in the cause of osteopathy and founded the 'Osteopathic Institute of Applied Technique' which later was renamed the 'Institute of Classical Osteopathy'.

personage like Littlejohn has to relinquish power there inevitably follows a power struggle.

Regarding the British School of Osteopathy, it has been said that *"in 1940, over a celebratory lunch, Littlejohn complete the contracts* (to transfer his shares to an independent board of trustees) *and by doing so relinquished not only control but his presence at the school too"* and this for settlement of £240.[cxi] In March 1949 his solicitor wrote:

"All J. M Littlejohns shares went into a Trust Deed to ensure that the school is governed and conducted in the best interest of the profession of osteopathy. This was Dr Littlejohns arrangements and all his shares went into the arrangement."[cxii]

If indeed he received a settlement, surely, he would have been entitled to it. From all sources consulted, past students, Letter to Hall, archive material etc., it would appear that Littlejohn himself not only subsidised the School but also many students at considerable cost to himself and his family. His rationale was simply stated by him:

"instead of spending all my time doing practice for myself I try to teach others so that the work may expand and be carried on"[cxiii].

From what he said at the end of his time in Chicago it would appear his intentions were the same at the 'end' of his time at the British School of Osteopathy. *"If I am not there it is because, like one greater than myself, I "laid down my life" in trying to establish a foundation upon which such a college might be built; and I helped to hold the fort until*[40]*"* that is until his health failed.

His last decade saw not only failing health, but also the struggle for the heart and soul of the British School of Osteopathy, which ended with the epitaph from the Select Committee's report **"being of negligible importance, inefficient for its purpose, and above all in thoroughly "dishonest hands"**[cxiv] becoming his legacy, leaving it to others to save the School from extinction by rewriting the syllabus, leaving out much of Littlejohn's or Still's direct writings or teachings. It has been said that he stopped going to church "In his later years, even though JML stopped attending church, his Christian message in limited osteopathic articles and

---

[40] Taken from the letter he wrote to The *Osteopathic Physician May 1913 page 4*, when he talked about the development of the Chicago College of Osteopathy.

letters was as strong as ever"[cxv] This gives a rather mixed message as it does not give any reason for him stopping attending church. The source quoted was interviews with his family. However, in my own interview with those that knew him and his family the reasons for non-attendance was given as 'due to his failing health' The effect of having the negative report from the House of Lords Select committee and other criticisms of him had a deleterious effect on his children, especially those that had chosen to follow him into Osteopathy, and must have had an equally negative effect on his wife and friends.[cxvi] Despite Littlejohn's assertion that "these insinuations and lies do not move me"[cxvii] it must have had an impact on him and his health, as would be expected of any person. He was at heart an educator, Osteopath and family man, but above all these was his Christianity and devotion to God that we find in his writings and set out so clearly in his letter to his son, James, when he says:

"in my last word to you my devoted children and wife and my brothers beyond the sea my only wish is that the example I set of hard work and devotion to God and his cause may be an inspiration to you to follow my example as I pass into the presence of God and into the fellowship of Jesus my saviour.[cxviii]"

---

[i] El Paso herald March 9-10 1918), page 12

[ii] Letter from J Martin Littlejohn to Dr Mitchell, February 26th, 1935; National Osteopathic Archive, now held at the Wellcome Library.

[iii] Report from the Select Committee of the House of Lords appointed to consider the Registration and Regulation of Osteopaths Bill, together with the Proceedings of the Committee and Minutes of Evidence; 17th July 1935; His Majesty's Stationary Office; Paragraph 3645, Page 228.

[iv] Ibid paragraph 3461, page 228

[v] Ibid paragraph 3296, page 222

[vi] Ibid paragraph 3362, page 224

[vii] The Spectator 26th December 1925, page 13

[viii] Osteopathy; by John Wernham, an autobiography, page 59; Published by The Maidstone College of Osteopathy

[ix] Ibid, page 59

[x] "We have to go over all the ground and I myself have to supply the information. I have handed over 94 typed foolscap pages of material to Counsel. He says it is a pity I can't present it myself. But this committee is court procedure." Letter to Dr Mitchell February 26th, 1935; National Osteopathic Archives.

[xi] Taped interview with Ralph Hardy D.O.; 10th January 1993

[xii] Letter sent to graduates of the BSO, copy held in the National Osteopathic Archives at the Wellcome Library

[xiii] Letter sent to graduates of the BSO, copy held in the National Osteopathic Archives at the Wellcome Library

[xiv] Report from the Select Committee of the House of Lords appointed to consider the Registration and Regulation of Osteopaths Bill, together with the Proceedings of the Committee and Minutes of Evidence; 17th July 1935; His Majesty's Stationary Office Paragraph 3461, page 228

[xv] Unqualified Practice Correspondence and BMA briefing documents; Wellcome Library reference SA/BMA/C.390-7

[xvi] Wellcome Library, BMA briefing documents, May 5th, 1925; SA/BMA/C.390-7

[xvii] Report from the Select Committee of the House of Lords appointed to consider the Registration and Regulation of Osteopaths Bill, together with the Proceedings of the Committee and Minutes of Evidence; 17th July 1935; His Majesty's Stationary Office; Paragraph 1382, Page 99.

[xviii] Ibid paragraph 1685, page 127

[xix] Ibid paragraph 1681, page 127.

[xx] The Osteopathic Technique and Philosophy of John Wernham; DVD section 9 'a brief biography of J. M. Littlejohn'; 1996 C Campbell and The Institute of Classical Osteopathy; Original from a letter by Dr. Streeter in the Pacific Journal of Osteopathy in unknown year – Taped interview with Dr. Stoddard 1993, at 9 minutes 37 seconds

[xxi] Osteopathy in Britain – the First Hundred years; Dr. Martin Collins, ISBN:1-4196-0784-7: 2005, PAGES 21-3

[xxii] Email correspondence with Dr. Martin Collins; He sourced John O'Brien on this.

[xxiii] Letter from T. D. Michell, to Mitchell Fox, Dean of the Western School of Osteopathy, 29th June 1933. National Osteopathic Archives

[xxiv] Letter from Littlejohn to Dr. Michell dated July 9th, 1932, National Osteopathic Archives

[xxv] Letter to T. D. Michell from T. Mitchell-Fox dated 27th May 1933, National Osteopathic Archives

[xxvi] Letter, undated, from J. M. Littlejohn, to T. D. Michell, headed 'Anent Matriculation certificate' (note; Anent is old formal English for about or in reference to); National Osteopathic Archives

[xxvii] Email correspondence with Dr. Martin Collins re his upcoming book 'The British School of Osteopathy: The first hundred years'

[xxviii] Email correspondence with Dr. Martin Collins

[xxix] personal correspondence with Martin Collins re quote from his book 'The British School of Osteopathy: The first hundred years'

[xxx] Letters to the BSO from T. D. Michell's son; now held in the Wellcome archives, national osteopathic Archive. J martin Littlejohn Archive Box 1(code: NOA/JML/file box 1/0104

[xxxi] Wellcome Library Archives; BMA proof of evidence

[xxxii] Report from the Select Committee of the House of Lords appointed to consider the Registration and Regulation of Osteopaths Bill, together with the Proceedings

of the Committee and Minutes of Evidence; 17th July 1935; His Majesty's Stationary Office; Paragraph 1601, Page 120.

[xxxiii] Osteopathic Blue Book – The Origin and Development of Osteopathy in Great Britain; Compiled and issued by the General Council and Register of Osteopaths Ltd. page 12; (1964?)

[xxxiv] Report from the Select Committee of the House of Lords appointed to consider the Registration and Regulation of Osteopaths Bill, together with the Proceedings of the Committee and Minutes of Evidence; 17th July 1935; His Majesty's Stationary Office; Paragraph 1680, Page 127

[xxxv] Report from the Select Committee of the House of Lords appointed to consider the Registration and Regulation of Osteopaths Bill, together with the Proceedings of the Committee and Minutes of Evidence; 17th July 1935; His Majesty's Stationary Office; Paragraph 1681, Page 127

[xxxvi] Ibid paragraph 2456-2457, page 171

[xxxvii] Ibid paragraph 2458, page 171

[xxxviii] Wellcome Library, BMA proof of evidence

[xxxix] The Osteopathic Technique and Philosophy of John Wernham; DVD section 9 'a brief biography of J. M. Littlejohn'; 1996 C Campbell and The Institute of Classical Osteopathy; Original from a letter by Dr. Streeter in the Pacific Journal of Osteopathy in unknown year – Taped interview with Dr. Stoddard 1993, at 9 minutes 37 seconds

[xl] Report from the Select Committee of the House of Lords appointed to consider the Registration and Regulation of Osteopaths Bill, together with the Proceedings of the Committee and Minutes of Evidence; 17th July 1935; His Majesty's Stationary Office; Paragraph 4712-9, page 326.

[xli] Personal interviews and private conversation with John Wernham, at the Maidstone College of Osteopathy.

[xlii] John Martin LittleJohn biography by John Wernham, page 60, Private publication by The Maidstone Osteopathic Clinic;
Also, Journal of Osteopathy, British School of Osteopathy; July-August 1935, page 2

[xliii] Report from the Select Committee of the House of Lords appointed to consider the Registration and Regulation of Osteopaths Bill, together with the Proceedings of the Committee and Minutes of Evidence; 17th July 1935; His Majesty's Stationary Office; Paragraph 3059, Page 210.

[xliv] Ibid paragraph 3221, Page 219

[xlv] Ibid paragraph 322 page 219

[xlvi] The Cap and gown. Chicago 1898, Page 8: Hathi Trust; http://hdl.handle.net/2027/uiuo.ark:/13960/t1zc95t2r

[xlvii] Report from the Select Committee of the House of Lords appointed to consider the Registration and Regulation of Osteopaths Bill, together with the Proceedings of the Committee and Minutes of Evidence; 17th July 1935; His Majesty's Stationary Office, paragraph 3266, page 221

[xlviii] Ibid paragraph 3411, page 227

[xlix] Ibid paragraph 3389, page 225

[l] Ibid paragraph 3393-4, page 226
[li] Private conversations and in Lectures
[lii] Ibid paragraph 3372-81, page 224
[liii] Ibid paragraph 3054-8, page 230
[liv] Report from the Select Committee of the House of Lords appointed to consider the Registration and Regulation of Osteopaths Bill, together with the Proceedings of the Committee and Minutes of Evidence; 17th July 1935; His Majesty's Stationary Office, paragraph 2468, page 172
[lv] Ibid, paragraphs 4708-4719, page 325-6
[lvi] Journal of Osteopathy, (British School of Osteopathy) Vol 6 No's 3&4, June-August 1935
[lvii] Personal unrecorded interview with Mrs. Wernham in 1993
[lviii] The Christian Nation Oct 19th, 1892, page 6
[lix] The AAO Journal Spring 2003, Page 10; The Contribution of John Martin Littlejohn to Osteopathy; T. Edward Hall and John Wernham
[lx] Letter to Dr Mitchell, August 6th, 1935; National Osteopathic Archives, now held in the Wellcome Library.
[lxi] This Thy Body; Mrs. Cecil Chesterton; Stanley Paul & Co., Ltd. Paternoster house, London E.C.4; Introduction
[lxii] Ibid page 134
[lxiii] Ibid page 134
[lxiv] The Osteopaths Bill; a report of the proceedings before a select committee of the House of Lords, 1935; Reprinted from the British Medical Journal; London, office of the British Medical Association, Tavistock Square W. C. 1; page 65
[lxv] This Thy Body; Mrs. Cecil Chesterton; Stanley Paul & Co., Ltd. Paternoster house, London E.C.4; Page 134-5
[lxvi] Ibid page 135
[lxvii] Letter to graduates of the BSO by Hall and Canning, after the report of the Select Committee of the House of Lords 1935
[lxviii] Ibid paragraph 3484
[lxix] Ibid paragraph 3483
[lxx] Morning Post England- Monday 30 August 1897, page 6
[lxxi] Littlejohn's letters to Hall, 1926 1940; courtesy of the European School of Osteopathy
[lxxii] Osteopathy in Britain – the First Hundred years; Dr. Martin Collins, ISBN:1-4196-0784-7: 2005, page 145-6
[lxxiii] Osteopathy in Britain – the First Hundred years; Dr. Martin Collins, ISBN:1-4196-0784-7: 2005, PAGES 14
[lxxiv] Letter from G. Anderson to Dr. Olin West of the American Medical Association, 19th December 1934; Wellcome Library archives ref. SA/BMA/C.397
[lxxv] Ibid, Letter from Dr. G. C. Anderson, Medical Secretary, The British Medical Association, to Dr. Olin West Secretary and General Manager, The American Medical Association, 8th March 1935; Wellcome Library archives ref. SA/BMA/C.397

[lxxvi] Wellcome Library archives ref; Bertrand Edward Dawson, Viscount Dawson of Penn PP/BED/F. 1. Box 2; Handwritten notes concerning the House of Lords Select Committee on which he sat.
[lxxvii] Report from the Select Committee of the House of Lords appointed to consider the Registration and Regulation of Osteopaths Bill, together with the Proceedings of the Committee and Minutes of Evidence; 17th July 1935; His Majesty's Stationary Office, pages xiv and xvi.
[lxxviii] https://en.wikipedia.org/wiki/Mitford_family
[lxxix] Spartacus Educational: Lord Redesdale: https://spartacus-educational.com/SSredesdale.htm
[lxxx] Report from the Select Committee of the House of Lords appointed to consider the Registration and Regulation of Osteopaths Bill, together with the Proceedings of the Committee and Minutes of Evidence; 17th July 1935; His Majesty's Stationary Office, page 271.
[lxxxi] Report from the Select Committee of the House of Lords appointed to consider the Registration and Regulation of Osteopaths Bill, together with the Proceedings of the Committee and Minutes of Evidence; 17th July 1935; His Majesty's Stationary Office, page 237-9.
[lxxxii] Taped interview with Douglas Mann Jan 1993, minutes 11.43; Ralph Hardy taped interview; 7.56 – 8.27 minutes; 10th January 1993
[lxxxiii] Osteopathy in Britain – the First Hundred years; Dr. Martin Collins, ISBN:1-4196-0784-7: 2005, Page 17; Journal of Osteopathy, British School of Osteopathy, October 1932, page 2 column 3
[lxxxiv] Report from the Select Committee of the House of Lords appointed to consider the Registration and Regulation of Osteopaths Bill, together with the Proceedings of the Committee and Minutes of Evidence; 17th July 1935; His Majesty's Stationary Office, paragraph 3192-3, page 217
[lxxxv] Shields Daily news June 11th, 1925
[lxxxvi] HISTORY OF OSTEOPATHY AND TWENTIETH-CENTURY MEDICAL PRACTICE; E. R. BOOTH; 1924; page 311-2
[lxxxvii] Ibid page 314
[lxxxviii] Wernham; Osteopathy, an historical and autobiographical account, page 46
[lxxxix] Report from the Select Committee of the House of Lords appointed to consider the Registration and Regulation of Osteopaths Bill, together with the Proceedings of the Committee and Minutes of Evidence; 17th July 1935; His Majesty's Stationary Office, page iii; and page 437.
[xc] Ibid paragraph 1681, Page 127.
[xci] The Lancashire Daily Post November 20th, 1930
[xcii] John Martin Littlejohn An Enigma of Osteopathy; John O'Brien; 2019 Anshan ltd. ISBN 978 1 848291 386;
[xciii] John Martin Littlejohn An Enigma of Osteopathy; John O'Brien; 2019 Anshan ltd. ISBN 978 1 848291 386; page 97 and 98
[xciv] The British School of Osteopathy, 1927 announcement
[xcv] Death Certificate HC 1 9 6 8 6 1 district of Benfleet, County of Essex;

[xcvi] Osteopathy in Britain – the First Hundred years; Dr. Martin Collins, ISBN:1-4196-0784-7: 2005, Page 44; Letter to Webster Jones, June 16th 1940, NOA, now held in the Wellcome Library archives

[xcvii] Letter to Mrs Littlejohn from Edgar Littlejohn's Commanding Officer, 13th April 1934.; NOA, now held in Wellcome library archives.

[xcviii] J. Wernham, the Life and Times of J. Martin Littlejohn, page 58

[xcix] J. Wernham, personal communications in private and lecture

[c] Letter to Dr Mitchell, August 6th, 1935; NOA, now held in Wellcome library archives.

[ci] John Martin Littlejohn An Enigma of Osteopathy; John O'Brien; 2019 Anshan ltd. ISBN 978 1 848291 386; page 109

[cii] Letter to Dr Mitchell, arch 10th Wellcome library archives

[ciii] J Wernham, the Life and Times of J. Martin Littlejohn, page 65

[civ] Littlejohn's letters to T. E. Hall courtesy of the European School of Osteopathy; Copies held in the Archives of the A. T. Still Museum in Kirksville.

[cv] J Wernham, the Life and Times of J. Martin Littlejohn, page 77

[cvi] Osteopathy in Britain – the First Hundred years; Dr. Martin Collins, ISBN:1-4196-0784-7: 2005, Page 209

[cvii] Wernham expressed these ideas and opinions in his lectures and in private conversation, and wanted to put them 'on the record'

[cviii] Osteopathy in Britain – the First Hundred years; Dr. Martin Collins, ISBN:1-4196-0784-7: 2005, Page 209

[cix] Littlejohn's letters to T. E. Hall, 22 April 1940; courtesy of the European School of Osteopathy; Copies held in the Archives of the A. T. Still Museum in Kirksville.

[cx] Osteopathy in Britain – the First Hundred years; Dr. Martin Collins, ISBN:1-4196-0784-7: 2005, Page 209

[cxi] John Martin Littlejohn An Enigma of Osteopathy; John O'Brien; 2019 Anshan ltd. ISBN 978 1 848291 386; page 96-97

[cxii] 23rd March 1949 REF; NOA documents, now held at the Wellcome Library archives.

[cxiii] Littlejohn's letters to T. E. Hall courtesy of the European School of Osteopathy; Copies held in the Archives of the A. T. Still Museum in Kirksville. April 11th, 1932

[cxiv] ; His Majesty's Stationary Office, page iii; and page
THE OSTEOPATHS BILL- A REPORT OF THE PROCEEDINGS BEFORE A SELECT COMMITTEE OF THE HOUSE OF LORDS; 1935
Reprinted from the British Medical Journal; Office of the British Medical Association, Tavistock Square, W.C.l; page 154 : See also - Report from the Select Committee of the House of Lords appointed to consider the Registration and Regulation of Osteopaths Bill, together with the Proceedings of the Committee and Minutes of Evidence; page xiv and xvi; 17th July 1935

[cxv] John Martin Littlejohn An Enigma of Osteopathy; John O'Brien; 2019 Anshan ltd. ISBN 978 1 848291 386; page 110

[cxvi] Talks, both recorded and personal with Osteopaths who had studied under Littlejohn and knew him personally, and Anne Kennard, his granddaughter.

[cxvii] Letter to Trenear Michell, August 6th 1935; National Osteopathic Archive, now held in the Wellcome Library.

[cxviii] Letter by Littlejohn to his son James re his will and funeral arrangements; National Osteopathic archive, now held in the Wellcome archives (courtesy of conversations with John Wernham)

A Footnote on the B.S.O.

On the founding of the British Scholl of Osteopathy Littlejohn, giving credit to his friend and colleague, says *"Several attempts have been made to secure recognition for our science. The last attempt before the Board of Trade brought forward this question from the officials: you tell us what you have done in research in American –but what have you done here? This stimulated Dr. Horne and myself (Littlejohn) to apply for a charter for a school of Osteopathy, which was granted to us March 7,1917. The British School of Osteopathy thus founded by us…. From a small beginning, like your own school* (The Chicago College of Osteopathy), *we hope to develop this first school founded in the British Empire to a large institution in the future. It is dedicated to OSTEOPATHY as a science, and is pledged to maintain unadulterated manipulative science as the foundation of therapeutics*[i]*"*

The B.S.O continues to do much good work having changed its name to 'University College Osteopathy' to reflect its new status.

During the forties when Littlejohn was ill and towards the end of his life and after he passed away in 1947 there was a great deal of strife within the B.S.O.[1]. Not least of it regarding Hall and his efforts to maintain the teaching of spinal mechanics and Littlejohn's principles and philosophy and contributed to by the lack of available teachers and the diminishing number of students in the school. According to Wernham[2], who was demobbed after the end of the second world war and arrived back in England in 1946 the year before his mentor, J.M. Littlejohn, passed away, there was a move at the time for Joselyn Proby to become the head of the B.S.O. with Hall and Jackson as the principle teachers and Wernham himself supporting this manoeuvre[ii]. However, as Wernham simply put it,

---

[1] Collins in his book 'Osteopathy in Britain the First Hundred Years' gives a detailed account of the struggles of the BSO at this time and of the problems Hall had with the rest of the faculty during the 1940's.

[2] Much of the material attributed to Wernham in this section is from private conversations, unrecorded lectures and notes taken by the Author during his association with him from 1984 to 2007 and is expressed as a personal memory when no other reference is given.

Proby did not want the job, Jackson was not at all interested and turned it down flat for no other reason than not being interested and Hall was too enamoured with alcohol at the time; so the 'fight for osteopathy within the B.S.O. was lost'.[iii]

Wernham was often accused of making derogatory remarks about the B.S.O. and others who did not teach osteopathy as he thought it should be taught, Viz. in line with Littlejohns and Stills teachings.

When he read an article entitled 'The Post War History of the B.S.O'. and saw his name attached to it, he was rather amused. It described him as being bitter about the changes in the B.S.O. and that he and his followers were the only true osteopaths: *Reading from the article he said:*

"john Wernham was befriend by the Littlejohn family in 1915.... Graduated in 1946[3], disheartened by the changes brought about by Webster-Jones he founded the Institute of applied technique (now the Institute of classical osteopathy) in 1953... and later the Maidstone college of osteopathy....John Wernham considers that he and his college represent the last vestige of true (i.e. Littlejohn) Osteopathy and that osteopathy is no longer taught at the BSO for which he has considerable bitterness"

He countered this by saying:

"when I went up to Manchester to lecture the people up there were saying things about the BSO that I wouldn't say and have never said, wouldn't dare say. you talk about bitterness, my word they hated the sound of the place, these were their own graduates. So, my considerable bitterness is outweighed by the very considerable bitterness of these other people. I would like that to go on record"

He then goes on to say:

"I have never criticised the schools organisation, I criticise its teaching and I am justified in saying that....I dislike the BSO because they don't teach

---

[3] There is much confusion about the graduation of those whose studies were interrupted by the war. Christian Fossum, in personal communication, says he saw Wernham's diploma and it was dated 29th September 1949. Collins mentions Wernham passing a postgraduate course at the BSO in 1948. (Osteopathy in Great Britain, page 247)

osteopathy and they don't and it must be said ....they have thrown it overboard and instituted medicine" [iv]

In essence he said he was not bitter and that bitterness had no place in it; but that he would state quite categorically the 'truth', as he saw it, and that was that osteopathy was no longer taught in the B.S.O.

Douglas Mann who graduated in 1936 and was another student of Littlejohn put it rather more delicately. He attributed the bitterness and fighting to the great divide between the north and the south in England which has been there since time immemorial[v], attributing the bitterness more to personalities.

According to Wernham[vi] the BSO had stopped teaching from the practice notes of Littlejohn which detailed the osteopathic approach to the treatment of diseases, stopped teaching general treatment and stopped teaching the spinal mechanics. He would recall going to Manchester and hearing the Manchester and northern group of osteopaths being more vocal and more bitter about the B.S.O. than he ever was. And in this conversation, he insisted that he wanted this put on the record.

Littlejohn himself had a high opinion of some of the osteopaths in the North, some of which originated in the Looker School. In correspondence with Hall he described Haycock and Milne as **"the best Osteopathic idealists in the north and they have the best method of expressing their ideas"**[vii]

So, for whatever the reason whether it was due to personalities, financial reasons, a dedicated move to save the B.S.O. from extinction or otherwise, the net effect was a significant change in direction in the teachings. The notes of Littlejohn's 'Principles and Practice of Osteopathy' and other older material was no longer taught. The general osteopathic approach to disease processes was not taught. The osteopathic lesion has been reduced to 'somatic disfunction' or best 'facilitated segment'.

It's unfortunate that after the war the school decided to change its approach to Osteopathic teaching. The opinion of Littlejohn's ideas has been summed up by O'Brien as follows, *"Professor Stephen Tyreman notes, the golden nuggets are there among the residue. In the end, using a slight ecclesiastical notion, his life, like the curate's egg, was good in parts"*[viii]

"The whole course had been dominated by J. Martin Littlejohn, and that on reflection his contribution, although influential, was too verbose with little substance underneath"...it was hardly a modus operandi that Webber or Middleton could adopt when planning a four year course in the post war years"[ix]

It is true now and it was then as Littlejohn stated[x] that the problem with osteopathy is that osteopaths do not **'understand the principle of osteopathy**[xi]**'** it. Or as Wernham[4] would have put it 'they don't want to understand it they want to walk with doctors, talk with doctors and have the privileges of doctors. All of this driven now as it was then as Littlejohn states:

"Drug vendors oppose it because it strikes at the root of the great medical evil of America – patent medicine and drug nostrums – and relies slowly upon the chemical and anatomical and physiological supplies of human nature. We have no kindred with any form of faith cure or charm cure but rely wholly on nature and the resources of nature which are inexhaustible."[xii]

One of the things that impressed me very much in talking to old osteopaths who were taught directly by Littlejohn was that they all agreed on one thing and that was that in the demonstrations that Littlejohn gave to the students on a weekly basis he never ever gave a medical diagnosis he always gave an **osteopathic diagnosis**. Some, like Wernham and Mann would say this in a complimentary manner. Others like Hardy would give it in a less flattering manner stating that he did not seem to know what he was doing because he did not give a medical diagnosis. Stoddard, being the true gentleman that he always was, would put it in a more mannerly manner saying that he was greatly impressed by Littlejohn's ability and diagnostic manner from the osteopathic point of view but would complain that he never gave a medical diagnosis. And following this, his treatment was always directed towards the osteopathic lesion and its effect on the body physiology and subsequent pathology. He tended to teach the general treatment, but this would have been in relation to his own philosophy as he outlined in his address to students in Kirksville in 1898,

---

[4] Much of the material attributed to Wernham in this section is from private conversations, unrecorded lectures and notes taken by the Author during his association with him and is expressed as a personal memory when no other reference is given.

not as an engine wiping process nor in the hope that you might hit something of use during your treatment but as a specific approach to the body as a whole.

"Do not be content to go out and give a general treatment. Remember that here is the danger of osteopathy as it has been the danger point of drugs"[xiii].

"you are sent out with principles and a correct knowledge of anatomy and physiology to apply these in the correction of diseases and disordered conditions"[xiv]

Wernham later changed the term to **"Body Adjustment"** as opposed to 'general treatment' in order to emphasise the **specific nature** of each so-called general treatment

"Littlejohn was largely written out of history in America and subsequently almost forgotten in England after his death"[xv]. Fortunately, John Wernham was obstinate enough not to be influenced by others and to stick to the principles as taught by Littlejohn and to pass them on and leaving behind the legacy of the **Institute of Classical Osteopathy** as a vehicle for continuing adherence to osteopathy – the osteopathy of A.T. Still as taught by Littlejohn, osteopathy without the influence of drugs but not reduced to a mere manipulative science.

Littlejohn and his family

Another aspect we find in his letters is Littlejohn's continuing communication with his brother James Buchan in America and their family. He says:

"we had a letter from Ellen saying my brother J.B. has been having severe haemorrhages and was very weak but a little better. I wrote him Tuesday myself for Wednesday's mail." - April 2nd, 1936

And this together with Littlejohn quoting James Buchan's attitude towards osteopathy in the Journal of the British School of Osteopathy gives further insight to his respect for James Buchan, and that both men were working towards the same outcome for osteopathy itself. In the April 1930 edition of the Journal of Osteopathy he quotes his brother as follows:

"Dr James B. Littlejohn, M.D., C.M., D.O., our brother clinches the matter in these potent words 'the answer to this, on behalf of the organisation here (Chicago College) is that they will show,
1. *'That osteopathy as a system of healing is worthwhile and should be perpetuated.*
2. *'That it can be taught, practised and exist as an independent principle.*
3. *'That incontrovertible methods can be adopted to demonstrate and prove its principle.*
4. *'Need we say more'.*

This is the spirit of the B.S.O. and we reciprocate the challenge to support, defend and prove the principle underlying the charter of both the B.S.O. and the C.C.O."[xvi]

This illustrates Littlejohn's continuing respect for his brother and his brother's opinion throughout the latter half of his life.

It may be the case that parents underestimate or are not aware of how much they influence their children by their own behaviour. This does not mean that they 'dictate' to them, but simply the children will look up and admire what their parents are doing. He goes on to say *that "another awkward subject that was discussed by his (Littlejohns) children and their* descendants was church going family attendance. During their time at Badger Hall Littlejohn would preach occasionally at the local congregational chapel and the neighbouring parish church. The whole family were made to attend under sufferings. In his later years, even though J.M.L. stopped attending church, his Christian message in limited osteopathic articles and letters was as strong as ever".[xvii] Littlejohn's own words in his letter to his son James, concerning arrangements for his own funeral puts a totally different perspective on it. When he says:

"in my last word to you my devoted children and wife and my brothers beyond the sea my only wish is that the example I set of hard work and devotion to God and his cause may be an inspiration to you to follow my example as I pass into the presence of God and into the fellowship of Jesus my saviour."[xviii]

This sentiment is in line with his attitude, shown throughout his life. Rather than telling people what to do, he would endeavour to lead them by example. In his own words He says July 19th, 1893 edition of the Christian Nation:

"Bringing up a child in the way he should go, and when he is old, he will not deviate from it. Such is the design of parentage and the influence of the home upon the young and rising generation.......the life of the child is like a force that stands unengaged looking for some groove along which to move; it stands waiting for direction and if the childhood influences that are brought to bear on its young life are such as made for God the issue rests with him for the best." ...."*we often see the children of sainted parents falling into devious paths. Why? Are the children wholly to blame? Yonder is a child that plods on from day to day preforming small tasks of its childish life; it searches into the parent's eye, aye, into the parent's heart, for a smile of approval. Does it meet with such a glance as would cheer its heart? The parent is engrossed with business, perplexed by harassing troubles of life; instead of a smile and an encouraging word, the child receives a cold glance and its tender heart is chilled. Coldness leads to carelessness, carelessness to indifference, indifference to open dislike and open dislike to separation. Does the blame rest with the child? We think not. The child may have done some trivial wrong. For this it has suffered chastisement the chastisement of an alienation and not of love.......... Parents should not repress their children, unless they can take them into their confidence and lead them by the hand into their bosom and point them in their own heart and life the way in which to walk.... Parental influence that reigns supreme in the Christian home in which Jesus resides,*

tempers discipline with kindness and confidence in leading, not driving from paths that are dangerous to better and holier ways".

Perhaps his own words could be applied to his own family life. Given the dedication he had to osteopathy and the trials that he suffered particularly in later years through illness and external anxieties with the school and osteopathy in general, he may have been guilty of the failings that he describes in these paragraphs.

In his Will of 1912, he gave specific instructions about what he would like his family to do after his death. He said it was his desire that his children receive a suitable education and that is was his *"wish that some or all of them qualify themselves in Osteopathic Science so as to take up and continue the work to which my own life was devoted. It was my purpose to establish a Sanitorium in England for the maintenance of this method of treatment and if my wife and children can see their way to devote the home that I have made provision for to his purpose it would be a fitting memorial of my life and work."* He goes on to say it is his *"desire and wish that they stick together as brothers and sisters in love and remembrance of him who lived only for their service and good"*

The context if one of expressing a desire without being dictatorial. One aspect of this will that maybe controversial if read outside of the times that he was writing. That his is about the custody of his children. He goes to lengths to explain who should look after them if his wife should remarry. In the times he was writing the husband would have been the 'head of the household' and without having any knowledge of who that might be, Littlejohn would have to fulfil his obligations, even after his death, to see his children were brought up in a manner consistent with his faith. So far from being disrespectful to his wife, it freed her up to remarrying without being disloyal.[xix]

---

[i] The Reflex, The Chicago College of Osteopathy, 1923; Osteopathy in Great Britain by J M Littlejohn
[ii] Taped personal interview with J Wernham; 1st November 1993
[iii] Taped personal interview with J Wernham; 1st November 1993
[iv] Taped personal interview with J Wernham 1st November 1993
[v] Taped interview with Douglas Mann 11 January 1993
[vi] courtesy of conversations with John Wernham
[vii] Littlejohn's letters to T. E. Hall courtesy of the European School of Osteopathy; Copies held in the Archives of the A. T. Still Museum in Kirksville. May 22nd ,1935

[viii] John Martin Littlejohn An Enigma of Osteopathy; John O'Brien; 2019 Anshan ltd. ISBN 978 1 848291 386; page 111

[ix] John Martin Littlejohn An Enigma of Osteopathy; John O'Brien; 2019 Anshan ltd. ISBN 978 1 848291 386; page 105

[x] J M Littlejohn; Principles of Osteopathy page 13

[xi] Principles of Osteopathy, by Littlejohn (being a collection of his papers collated and published by L Meyran) Page 13

[xii] The Scotsman, August 24th, 1899; Letter by J. Martin Littlejohn re Osteopathy in America, page 6: quoted in Journal of Osteopathy, British School of Osteopathy, June – August 1935

[xiii] Journal of Osteopathy, Vol 5, No 3, August 1898, page 119

[xiv] Journal of Osteopathy, Vol 5, No 7 December 1898, page 329

[xv] Personal recollection of statements by J Wernham given in lectures and discussions

[xvi] Journal of Osteopathy, British School of Osteopathy, Vol 1 Number 4, April 1930; page 1.

[xvii] John Martin Littlejohn An Enigma of Osteopathy; John O'Brien; 2019 Anshan ltd. ISBN 978 1 848291 386; page 110; quoting conversations with Kennard, Anne and Sarah Littlejohn family interview

[xviii] Letter by Littlejohn to his son James re his will and funeral arrangements; National Osteopathic archive, now held in the Wellcome archives

[xix] Last will and testament of J. Martin Littlejohn, written but unsigned, in 1912: National Osteopathic archive, now held in the Wellcome archives

J M LITTLEJOHN'S LEGACY

It's always possible to take episodes or events in a person's life out of context, to read events with a bias view, to leave out certain aspects so that the negative always seems to come to the fore. This does a great disservice to John Martin Littlejohn who devoted his life and gave his health in many ways to osteopathy. It is true that he got his health back as a result of Still's ministrations and in a sense was repaying his debt to Still and osteopathy by promoting and preserving the teachings of osteopathy. However, this may have been his true calling in life and certainly by his actions, in particular how he has stuck to his osteopathic principles throughout his whole life. He seemed to believe so himself.

> *My slogan is 'OSTEOPATHY'*
>
> *and*
>
> *I don't care who says yea or nay –*
>
> *it is the Osteopathy of A. T. Still*
>
> *and like him, we will win –*
>
> *The keynote is adjustment*
>
> (The Osteopath, No. 192. November 1931, page 8)
>
> *Personally, I have ever been loyal to osteopathy.*
>
> *Its principle is an abiding truth,*
>
> *the comprehensiveness of which we have not yet begun to realize*
>
> (Journal of the American Osteopathic Association October 1911, Page 727)
>
> **John Martin Littlejohn**

He left a considerable body of work including

- ❖ His articles and essays on Osteopathic Principles collected by Lawrence Meyran in 'Principles of Osteopathy'; many of these articles were first published in 'The Journal of the Science of Osteopath' or 'The Osteopathic World', journals of which Littlejohn was editor.
- ❖ His 'Practice of Osteopathy' and 'Osteopathic Therapeutics'
- ❖ His research in the field of Cancer and Toxicosis, first published in the Journal of the American Osteopathic Association in 1907.[1]
- ❖ Osteopathy a Biological Science; Published in the Journal of Osteopathy, BSO, in 1935 to much acclaim

Apart from his writing, we also inherit the Colleges of Osteopathy that he founded; 'The Chicago College of Osteopathy', since incorporated in "The Midwestern university"; The British School of Osteopathy' since renamed 'University College of Osteopathy' – in recognition of its degree awarding status-an achievement Littlejohn would surely be proud of.

The other institution Littlejohn would surely have pride in, was founded by his pupils Thomas Edward Hall and S. G. John Wernham, in 1956 as the 'Osteopathic Institute of Applied Technique' and in 1993 renamed 'The Institute of Classical Osteopathy' and registered as a charity,

---

[1] His thesis on the treatment of cancer which should have revolutionised the treatment of cancer but for the criticisms that were unfairly pointed at him when it was published in 1907. That and the failure of osteopaths of that day to take on board the principle of anti-doting banished this great work and insight into the treatment of the scourge of cancer to an after note in the early journals of osteopathy rather than finding its place in the history of the treatment of these diseases.

Its aims are to:

'Preserve, explore and develop the osteopathic concept and philosophy as formulated by A.T. Still and further interpreted by J.M. Littlejohn.

'Help the postgraduate osteopath gain a deeper understanding of the anatomical and physiological relationship of body mechanics to health and disease and how that knowledge may be applied clinically to enable a precise diagnosis and safe treatment.

'Provide mentored postgraduate training in classical osteopathy in the UK and throughout the world.

'Bring together and support members of the osteopathic profession worldwide who follow a classical approach.

'The Institute maintains its role by running postgraduate courses, workshops and conferences to help osteopaths interpret and apply classical osteopathic concepts. It also offers a unique mentored clinical training programme at the London Clinic of Classical Osteopathy - a community-based clinic in North London and has numerous affiliations with educational groups throughout Europe, Canada and Japan.

'The Institute has over the years published a series of academic books, Yearbooks and DVDs – all of which are available for purchase on-line'.

In Littlejohn's life certain patterns emerge quite clearly. He put his heart and soul into everything that he undertook even to the detriment of his health

Like his father he never deviated from this plan. (*His father's last words to John Martin and his brothers was that he had upset people because he had never changed, he had stayed the same.*) He was dedicated to his chosen cause and not flinching or holding back on the energy that he put into it.

> "In all the twenty years that T. E. H spent with John Martin as a student, colleague and personal assistant he became increasingly aware of his great scholarship, unstinting generosity to his students and his absolute dedication to osteopathy. As a teacher he was unsurpassed"
>
> J Wernham

His foresight, forward thinking and application of the osteopathic principle is an example to everyone who comes to this great noble career in the healing art of osteopathy. To paraphrase his last word his children, wife and brothers it could be said that his Osteopathic heritage is

'that the example he set of hard work and devotion to Osteopathy and its cause may be an inspiration to you, student of osteopathy, to follow his example so that you may go out guided by the Principles of Osteopathy and a Correct Knowledge of Anatomy and Physiology to apply these in the Correction of diseases and disordered conditions'

Another aspect that should be remembered was that while he was a family man, and educator and an osteopathy, he was primarily a 'Practical Covenanter' who tried to live his life according to the abiding principles of hard work and devotion to God, holding to the truth as he saw it without becoming dogmatic. To paraphrase Dobbyn *'his beliefs have not made a bigot of him. The truth has made him free'*. In this it is well to remember that Having and trying to live by lofty ideals and principles does not mean that he had lost the frailties of being human.

> *"The new idea of the body as a, mechanism, consisting of units so fitly framed together in the formation of the organism of the body, that if these units are displaced or their organic relations disturbed, then a doorway is opened for disturbed functioning which is called disease. With this fundamental conception of the origin of disease it sets to work to frame its own therapeutic plans to correct the abnormalities and restore the irregularities of the structures and the structural relations of the body parts, so as to make the body what it was intended to be, a perfect and perfectly articulating mechanism in which the vitality of the body and its vital processes can function a natural life"*
>
> British School of Osteopathy
> prospectus 1927

APPENDICES

National University of Chicago.

Littlejohn's association with the National University of Chicago(also known as the Chicago National University) began in about 1893 when he was a student in the post graduate school of theology gaining one of his Doctor of Divinity degrees in 1893, and subsequently a Fellow (F.N.U.[2]) gaining a Ph.D. in 1895,[i] and LL.D. in 1895[ii]

Confusion between the National University of Chicago and the University of Chicago can be traced back to the beginning of both colleges. Another confusion seems to have arisen from Flexner's report where he says, regarding the **National Medical University,** that it is *"A night school, organized in 1891 as "homeopathic, which word was subsequently dropped. Ostensibly the medical department of the "Chicago Night University," which claims departments of arts, law, dentistry, pharmacy, etc."*[iii]. There was no connection between the 'National university' and the 'National Medical university'. Both were registered separately with no overlap of their officers or directors according to the registration papers filed at the State of Illinois department of State.[iv]

Nor was there an entity such as the "National Night University", the 'Chicago Night University', with L D. Rodgers of the National Medical University as a director, only coming into existence in 1906, again with no overlap in Directors with the National University[v].

The name 'national Night University'[vi], while having no existence in fact or reality, seems to have evolved from Flexner's description of the association between the National Medical University and the Chicago Night University both having R. D. Rodgers as a Director

---

[2] Post nominal letters that appeared on the copy of Littlejohn's thesis which came into possession of T. E. Hall. It would seem that this copy was Littlejohn's personal copy printer by the Current Press in Amity as a textbook and not as a thesis for submission to Columbia University.

The National University of Chicago was associated with or an off shoot of the Chicago Polytechnique both organisations being run by Professor Harkins. Its listed in the July 1900 – June 1902 Superintendent of public instruction for the state of Illinois report[vii] as being founded in 1889[viii] (that's one year prior to the new University of Chicago) with 192 pupils and a library consisting of over 1000 volumes. The value of its real estate is estimated at about $1,000 with a further $2,000 in terms of equipment, books etc.

The 'Old University of Chicago' never really got off the ground having many financial difficulties partly due to the politics of the founding donor, the financial crisis in 1873 and the fires in Chicago in 1871 and 1874. It also suffered from poor administration, leading to a court case for foreclosure in 1885. The American Baptist Educational society thought that Chicago might be the ideal location for a new 'Baptist University, the outcome of which was that John D. Rockefeller, and William Rainey Harper joined forces to found the new University of Chicago 1890 – the previous entity changing its name to the 'old university of Chicago' so that the new one could start a new as the 'University of Chicago'[ix]

William Rainey Harper was list as "president of the new Baptist university of Chicago" and express his educational plan to be one for college extension, to bring the higher education within reach of the common people , operating through a system of branch schools or academics scattered through the country[x]. This sounds very similar to the plan of the national University.

In the advertisements[xi] for the National University of Chicago it says *"grants all college degrees without residence but vigorously guards them by examination at the student's home under local examiners or assistant professors. Tuition is carried on by correspondence under large core of professors who teach almost every subject. Those who have left college without graduating should write us for requisite conditions and graduate as soon as possible. Post-graduate courses all higher degrees[xii]."*

An idea of why Littlejohn would be attracted to the National University can be gleaned from the following announcements in 1889 and 1890.

"The National magazine (Published at 147 Throop Street, Chicago) for January announces two new and valuable departments "Biblical Literature" and "Pedagogy" with Rev. J. C. Quinn, Ph. D., and J. S. Mills, A. M., President of Western College, as editors. Agricultural readers will be especially interested in the new "Institute of Agriculture," described in this number - a part of the University Extension System of the National University of Chicago, whose non-resident or correspondence undergraduate and post-graduate courses have met with such favor. Other articles are by Prof. E. A. Birge, of the University of Wisconsin, and eminent specialists[xiii]."

"A Very Great Compliment to Prof. Blair.: Prof. Wm. A. Blair, A. M., Superintendent of Schools of Winston. N. C, who has an enviable record as a scholar and teacher, has lately been honored by the National University of Chicago by an election as Associate Professor of Pedagogy[3]. Prof. Blair will inaugurate the famous English University Extension system in the South, having charge of the Institute of Pedagogy and perhaps of the Institute for Bible study. Prof. Blair will conduct his Institute by correspondence. He is one of many distinguished educators who compose the faculty of this great University, which gives instruction to thousands of students all over the United States. Nothing better illustrates the progressive spirit of the South than the ready instruction of the best modern educational methods, and we believe our teachers will heartily second Prof. Blair's efforts in their behalf".[xiv]

These two announcements give an idea of the workings of the National University. With its background of being supposedly planned along the lines of the university extension scheme, modelled after the University of London and making education and recognition for educational qualifications available to those who for one reason or another had not been able to follow full-time university course, and its association with Bible studies, it is easy to see why Littlejohn would have been attracted to it.

---

[3] the art, science, or profession of teaching and education

It fulfilled his ideals, that education should be made available to all people and not exclusively to those who had privilege, and that of promoting Bible studies.

The college ran into some difficulty when it was charged with selling diplomas and degrees and this even crossed the water to and made quite a bit of publicity in England. One of its agents a Prof. Van Angelbek was found guilty of fraudulent use of the mail in the sale of bogus diplomas in May 1893.

Van Angelbek was found to have enticed people to purchase a diploma from the National University of Chicago, *"giving a fictitious name of the person from whom to obtain diplomas thus raking in money for the same."*[xv]

Harkins, the chancellor of the National University, was never charged with any offence.[xvi] He gave a stalwart defence of his college in the Morning Post of August 1897.

Harkins defence of the National University

"AMERICAN DEGREES. Sib, - Great public interest having been excited by the discussion raised by a question in the House of Commons. "Whether there was any such institution in the United States as the National University of Chicago, and whether the Government would consider whether any steps could be taken to stop this alien interference with the duties and prerogatives of our authorised Universities," permit me space in your paper to meet the points involved, and also to protest against the charge made that this University has been granting degrees to *"worthy but impecunious persons for five dollars. "I enclose a printed circular which shows that this University is a regularly chartered institution, and, so far as that goes, has, in the absence of any law to the contrary, as much right to grant degrees as the Universities of Oxford or Cambridge, or any in this country. But I assure the friends of these institutions, whose mistaken kindness caused so much publicity to our supposed efforts to benefit the poor man, that they really have nothing to fear, for instead of antagonising their interests our design is to supplement in a humble way the great good which they do and to reach worthy persons they would never reach. What possible objection can the graduate of*

Oxford have to a "worthy but impecunious" student bearing an American degree from the National University? Such an objection does us "too much honour", I fear. Again, is it not ridiculous to suppose that anything we do can affect the "prerogatives of our authorised Universities?" But "you grant degrees in absentia" they say. Well, what of that? Does not that distinguish our degrees sufficiently? In the United States 'every year hundreds of honorary degrees are given as sops to rich or successful men – bribes to purchase influence or awards for services, irrespective of education. Forsooth, we grant degrees to "worthy but impecunious persons". Now, as to the $5.00 charge, although its absurdity is its own refutation, we never granted a degree for that sum during our entire existence. Would it not be absurd to offer degrees for less than the cost of the engraved diplomas issued by us? But so prone are the simple-minded to believe a newspaper charge that we have been with their application since its publication. Nor do we employ agents in any proper sense. The whole trouble, I believe, arose from our efforts to stop the fraudulent advertisements of the man Horne, who without authority was falsely using our name for swindling purposes, concerning whom we wrote to the Chief of Police of London and Edinburgh, as well as to London journals, and to the Consul-General of the United States, by whom the latter was referred to Scotland Yard. Now, if I may be allowed a word as to our work, we have never knowingly granted a degree to an unworthy applicant at any price, and no one has ever charged that one of our graduates (who are generally already graduates of some college) was unworthy. We grant degrees in absentia – a questionable method possibly – but we try to hedge them about by all the means in our power, requiring a history of the candidate's education at the outset before rendering a decision of our Council, and only when satisfactory allowing him to sit for an examination and submit his required thesis. Many will question this method, no doubt, but our work has been done frankly and above board and is deemed a boon by the many who otherwise would never have known a college course or would have missed the enjoyment of its higher honours. Confident that with your usual courtesy you will grant my request – I am, yours, Ac, F.W. HARKINS, Chancellor. The National University, Chicago, August 19.[xvii]

While many negative references can be found to this University, there are also many positive ones. Littlejohn would undoubtedly have become aware of the controversy surrounding it especially when details of the scandal in England were published in the Christian Nation in 1897.

"..Mr. F. W. Harkins, the ' Chancellor ' of the National University of Chicago, has lately been receiving an amount of attention from the English press such as has perhaps fallen to the lot of no other university dignitary in the United States. I need not point out that the National University of Chicago, or the Universitas Nationalis Illinoiensis, as is its academical title for solemn occasions, exists for the sole purpose of selling degrees and diplomas to those who have been unable to obtain the coveted honors in any more reputable fashion". (Christian Nation Vol 27 Oct 6th, 1897)

There are many stories about Dr. Harkins including one in which he set off by train to a place he didn't know and cold called on a gentleman and, in the afternoon,, talked that gentleman into donating a large track of land to his college[xviii]. The excesses of this story make its veracity hard to accept, but it may be based upon a grain of truth. Whether this is true or not the story does illustrate that Dr. Harkins had a gift of convincing people about his project. It's also reported that of the first directors or promoters of the college one resigned very quickly when he found out or thought that some of the practices were not legitimate, others could not get their names removed from the list of promoters without taking court action[xix]. With this in mind and given Dr. Harkins eloquent defence of his college given above and how it would have fitted neatly with Littlejohn's approach to education and life in general it's hardly surprising that Littlejohn if approached by the college would have given his time and energy to it at least until he became aware of its shortcomings.[4]

---

[4] "Being unable to continue his work in the Eastern climate of America, after spending some months under hospital treatment in Philadelphia, he migrated west to a sanatorium in Waukesha. Wisconsin, from which he started research work on Psychology in Chicago, first in connection with the National University, founded and Modelled after London University, as a research Fellow: later he continued in the University of Chicago where his special work in the Seminar department was 'The Fee system of payment of officials in

Chicago being a major center of learning within striking distance of the famous Waukesha Springs, it would hardly have been surprising that Littlejohn would have found some employment in the city. That he started with the National University and *"later continued in the University of Chicago*[5],[xx] again should be no surprise. The university of Chicago was in formation at the time and his research into the fee system verse the salaried was current. It also represents his journey from 'Political Science' per se into the realms of education itself. In 1895 he presented his first paper to the Society of Science, Letters and Art, London. It was the first of three papers on Education. On reflecting on his tour of Europe in 1903 Littlejohn remarked *"In that hall (the hall and offices of the Society of Science) our papers on "Education" were read in 1895, 1896, and 1897. In 1898"*[xxi] it is quite probable that it was for his work on education that he received his Ph.D. from the National university in 1895.

---

contrast with salaried service.' Having recuperated to some extent he received the position of President of Amity College, Iowa". (Journal of osteopathy -BSO- June-august 1935)

[5] The debate around the Fee system as against Salaries was the subject of his research "The Fee system of payment of officials in contrast with salaried service." This debate is adequately summed up in the" **Report of the commissioners appointed to inquire concerning the mode of Appointing and remunerating certain provincial officials now paid by fees And the extent of the remuneration they should receive.**" (Warwick bros. & Rutter, printers, sec., 68 and 70 front St. west Toronto, 1895) *"The advantage of the fee system consists in the fact that the salary or compensation is paid under it by those persons who make use of the office to which the fees are attached. Its disadvantage is to be found in the fact that on account of the smallness «rf the fee usually required; extortion is not infrequently practiced by the officers, and submitted to by the public, notwithstanding the most stringent penal provisions that may be passed to prevent it. The compensation actually received is out of all proportion Lo the work done and comes to be regarded rather as a reward for political service, than as a compensation for work done. On this account the tendency at present is to replace fees by fixed salaries."* (Page 57);..." In this state (New York) the trend of affairs has been to change from payment by fees into payment by salaries. This was brought about because of the excessive fees received in urban localities. (Page 83) ...This state (New Jersey) stands upon the old ways, unmoved in the midst of change. All officers are paid by fees; no accounts are kept, and no returns are required page 83).

While I have found no other evidence of this employment the associate Dean of University of Chicago wrote in answer to Halls inquiry in 1952 *"I regret to say that the records of the University for the first ten years of its operation are not immediately available to me, and I am unable to supply any comment on Dr .Littlejohn's relation to the University. None of us recall the existence at the university of Chicago of a "Seminar Department*[xxii]*."* This is no surprise as the University was in formation at that time and It would seem Littlejohn took a short-term position researching the fee system in preparation for a seminar within the University or as part of a larger project which the University had undertaken.

The magazine of the National University of Chicago, in 1889[xxiii], carried an article by Professor Raymond Mayo Smith of Columbia College on 'Political Science'. While this was before Littlejohn's time at Columbia it does show some connection in his chosen field of Political Science. Professor Mayo was still a Professor during Littlejohn's time at Columbia.[xxiv]

The National Medical College.

Littlejohn's connection with the national Medical College was as Professor of Physiology for the years 1904-1906[xxv]

"The National Medical University of Chicago was incorporated August 22, 1891, as the National Homeopathic Medical College. It dropped the word "Homeopathic" from its name in 1895 and in 1900 took the above title. The first of its classes was graduated in 1892 and a class graduated each subsequent year until the school was declared not in good standing by the Illinois State Board of Health in 1909" .... In 1898, the Board of Directors of the college *"were compelled, because of its phenomenal growth, to seek larger and better quarters, now at No. 531-533 Wells Street, with an ideal amphitheatre capable of seating more than 500 students." In the same year, night classes were formed, presaging the medical department of the "Chicago Night University," with which it affiliated in 1906"*[xxvi].

The following is the entry for the National Medical College in Chicago in the Association of American Medical Colleges proceedings of June 5th, 1899 vol. 4 no. 1 and no. 3 of the bulletin of the American Academy of Medicine.

National. Medical, College CHICAGO, homeopathic, coeducational, Chicago, pop. 1,099,850, Dean, Thomas C. Duncan, M.D., LL.D., 100 State St.
Session opens 12 S, '98; closes 30 Mr, '99; length, 61 mos.; matriculates, 1897-98, 114; graduates, 1897-98, 15; matriculates, 1898-99, 136.
Admission: certificate of good moral character signed by two physicians; graduation from high school, college, matriculation college or equivalent certificate of having passed in English grammar, arithmetic, geography, algebra, physics, U. S. history, Latin; diploma from normal school, academy, military training school or other institution giving instruction in above subjects; to advanced standing: work of recognized schools or preparatory courses covering work of first year; college graduates having studied biology, botany, inorganic chemistry, anatomy and physiology; credit given for special work; one year credit given graduates of recognized schools.
Graduation: age 21; good moral character; attendance on lecture courses the required time, the last at this college; four years' study; attendance on six cases of labor; service in hospital, dispensary, or preceptor's office; examinations. Course: four years for all graduating after 1900.
Fees: matriculation, 15; one course, 165; two courses, 1110; three courses 1150; full course, 1200; partial course, $10; demonstrators, $5; laboratories, $5 each; examination, $25; graduates of other colleges, $50.
Subjects: anatomy, histology, physiology, chemistry, biology, materia medica, physics, and electricity, sanitation, pathology, bacteriology, physical diagnosis, hygiene, pharmacology, toxicology, obstetrics, embryology, medicine, neurology, etiology, laryngology, rhinology. ophthalmology, otology. gynecology, pedology. mental science, jurisprudence. electro-therapeutics, psychiatry. brain diseases. diseases of the chest, abdomen, of the skin. urinary, venereal diseases.
Faculty: professors, 39; lecturers, 22: instructors. 2; demonstrators, 3.

Total property. $-----; receipts, $----; expenditures. $---- (1898). Organized 1891; first class graduated 1892, and in each subsequent year.

> "What school of practice shall I study?" is another question that confronts the young man or woman who is contemplating the study of medicine. Shall I be a "regular", a homeopath or eclectic or an osteopath? If it is your ambition to make the most wonderful cures and to get the most money for your services be a homeopath, but if you want office, popularity and a great name when you die, join the crowd, be a "regular"
>
> L. D. Rogers, M.D., in the Chicago Night University Bulletin
> The Clinique Vol. xxix 1908, Page 621

Despite its name it had no association with the National University of Chicago[6] and was initially set up as a homeopathic college changing its name from the National Homeopathic Medical College at Chicago to the National Medical College in 1895 and was run by a Dr. L. D. Rogers. In Its 1896 annual announcement it lists Prof.

---

[6]One possible, but rather tenuous connection comes form The annual report of the State Board of Health of Illinois for 1898 which states that the traffic *in 'legally chartered medical college diplomas ... is principally in the hands of one Harkins, on whose card appear the titles A. B., A. M., M. D., D. C. L., LL. D. and Ph. D., (degrees all conferred by himself) the name of his alma mater being legion"(Page CLX).* It gives no further information, nor does it give the initials of the said Harkins.

The F. W. Harkins being listed in State registration and annual reports for 1903 as president and treasurer of the National University is not listed anywhere in the announcements nor registration papers of the National Medial University. This similarity in names only adds to the confusion.

William R. Harper, the President of the University of Chicago as one of its Board of Advisers. It attracted people of the quality of Julia Holmes Smith who was its Dean from 1898 – 1900.

She *"graduated with the Boston University School of Medicine tickets after one term in the Chicago Homoeopathic College, in 1877, taking her degree of M. D. from the latter institute, in which she afterward held a lectureship until women were debarred from the student corps. Subsequently she did no college work, except post-graduate study, until 1898, when she became dean of the National Medical College, Chicago, resigning that office in 1900"*[xxvii].

She was regarded as one of the leading lights of homeopathy and was the first women to be elected Dean of a co-educational medical school that is the National Medical College in Chicago and dedicated to the suffragist movement. She was active outside of medical practice and was appointed by the Governor of Illinois as a Trustee of the University of Illinois[xxviii].

This give some indication of the reasons some of the lesser colleges existed and why people like Littlejohn and others may have been attracted to them. Littlejohn was Professor of Physiology during the middle part of the first decade of the twentieth century[xxix].

"Before the opening of the session of 1900-1 an arrangement was made by which a part of the faculty and a good portion of the student body was transferred to the Dunham from what was then known as the National Medical College of Chicago"[xxx]. [7]

The college itself had a rather chequered history and a number of run-ins with the State Board of Health being deprived of it being in good standing on more than one occasion. Much could be written about this college and its history but suffice to say that it attracted a number of prominent physicians, ran a four-year course

---

[7] King's four volume History of Homeopathy does not give any detail on the National Medical College, Chicago, formerly known as the National Homeopathic Medical College.

for all graduating after 1899 (including a John Maxwell Auld M.D. who was on the staff of the Temperance hospital, the Chicago Baptist Hospital, the National Emergency Hospital and for eight years served as professor of rectal and intestinal diseases at the Harvey Medical Hospital and at the Chicago Night University.) The National Medical College was associated with the Baptist Hospital, which was originally set up as a homeopathic institution and its constitution was made to provide that the medical staff shall be comprised of homeopathic physicians. But early on the hospital became a separate institution and started to employ physicians of all schools and became eclectic on the basis that not all Baptist were homeopaths. The association of the college with a night school has been the cause of some ridicule by some people, however, we find that even within the orthodox medical profession at the time the idea of a night school was being actively promoted.

The Chicago Clinic and Pure Water Journal 1905 reported on a discussion on night schools. *"At a recent meeting of the physician's club of Chicago the place of night schools in medical education was discussed by representatives of day schools and night schools and by members of the state board of health. While there were a few who were radically opposed to evening schools, the general trend of opinion was quite uniform, that there is a place in medical education which the night school fills which cannot be satisfactorily filled by the day school. It seemed to be the consensus of opinion that the night school, to be equal to the day school, should cover an additional year. In fact, the conservative medical men who talked at this meeting held quite to the views of this journal recently published and commented by the New York and Philadelphia Medical Journals"*.[xxxi] Later in the same article, they comment on the circuit court in Wisconsin administering a *"scading arraignment to the board (state board of health of Wisconsin) and stated that it had acted upon such trifling evidence as to be guilty of an abuse of its discretionary power"*. This is in relation to not allowing a graduate of the Harvey Medical College of Chicago to be admitted to examination on the ground solely that the college was a night school. The date of this magazine is January 1905. Even in the medical profession night schools were allowed and indeed the objective of them was held in regard.

The night school aspect was run on the basis that three months in the evening school was counted as two months in the day school.

The work of both day and evening schools were so arranged that students be changed from one to the other without inconvenience or disadvantage on the ratio of time just stated. In other words, it wasn't a quick and easy way to attain and education just a method of making education available to those who could not afford full time education. In the same way we find today that many colleges like the open university or some osteopathic colleges are run, at least for part of the course, on a "part-time, home study basis".

In the session 1897-8 it is listed as having 18 students[8] in the annual report of the State Board of Health of Illinois for 1898[xxxii], while Dunham College is listed at having 37 students: both of which are listed as adopting a four-year course.

O'Brien in his book on Littlejohn says that: *"The good dean (of the National Night University, Chicago) informed J.M.L. that a number of his staff and most of his students of his National Medical College were transferring to Dunham Medical School for the academic year 1900-1."* Littlejohn is not mentioned as a matriculant in the National Medical University[xxxiii] for the years 1896/7, 1897/8, 1900/1[9] but is listed as matriculating at Dunham Medical College for the year 1901/2.[xxxiv]

In connection with the National Medical College, Dr. L. D. Rodgers set up 'The Chicago Night University' on the 22nd August 1906., prior to that The National Medical School did have both night and day courses, but was not referred to as the 'National Night University'. Flexner's report which was published in around 1910. It gives the following description,

---

[8] The Annual announcement for the National Medical College for 1897/8 lists over 100 matriculants which seem to include most previous matriculants and not just those for 1897/8. There is no mention of any Littlejohn. It also lists 12 graduates for 1897.
[9] No data has been found for the year 1899/1900 but the 1902 announcement lists matriculants for the years 1899, 1900 and 1901 with no Littlejohn listed.

"National Medical University. A night school, organized in 1891 as "homeopathic," which word was subsequently dropped. Ostensibly the medical department of the "Chicago Night University," which claims departments of arts, law, dentistry, pharmacy, etc. The school appears to be owned by the "dean[xxxv]."

The term 'National Night University' appears to be a misnomer, born out of Flexner's description. The registration papers, with the Secretary of State for Illinois never used the term 'National Night University' for either the National University (of Chicago) or the National Medical University.

The National Medical University seemed always to be in a state of flux. Not only changing its name, dropping the word 'Homeopathic' and then in 1901/2 changing from the National Medical College' to 'National Medical University'.

The Dean of the College also changed frequently during this time, in 1896/7 was J. J. THOMPSON, A. M., M. D.; In 1897/8 was C. C. BERNARD, B. S., M. D. and in 1900/1 was JULIA HOLMES SMITH, A. B., M. D. Dr L. D. Thompson had left the National Medical College after or during the 1896/7 year to join the Hering College with a number of other lectures and some students [xxxvi]– so 1900 was not the first time students left the National Medical University. I would have been unlikely that Littlejohn would have chosen to go to this College in 1897 when the Dean and a number of lectures and students had just left to join another college; even so he is not listed as a matriculant nor as a student during this perion.

A Chicago paper is a authority for the statement that Chicago is to have the first night university in the world. All the details of organisation are perfected, the land purchased, the plans for the building drawn and the preliminary work done. The Chicago Night University will be open to everybody, young and old, rich and poor, male and female. It will offer special advantages to those who are employed during the day and who wish to gain an education either in the liberal arts, medicine, the law, electrical engineering, dentistry, pharmacy or any other branches taught in universities. It will also have a preparatory school.

The Teachers Journal
August 1906: page 238

Illinois Medical Journal
Vol XVIII July -December 1910

Some time ago the Illinois State Board of Health declared the National Medical University, one of the Chicago 'Night' medical schools, not in good standing. The Dean of the school now charges that he paid a fee to a Chicago lawyer-legislator for the apparent purpose of influencing the State Board to reinstate the school. The Dean further charges that five or six other medical colleges in Chicago are paying money to keep in the good graces of the State Board of Health. All of the charges are denied, both generally and specifically, by the Board and the Governor and State's Attorney have each started investigations of the whole matter

Dunham and Herring Colleges

Dunham Medical College of Chicago was founded in the summer of 1895 with a particular emphasis on trying to get back to the original doctrines as promulgated by Samuel Hahnemann particularly in his "organon of the art of healing". Then in 1900 the college secured the services of James Tyler Kent. It was no wonder that Littlejohn was attracted[10] to this college not only from its homeopathic point of view but also from the fact that it stood by the original principles of homeopathy and particularly from the anti-doting side of things which was taught primarily in Dunham compared to other places.

"Early in the year 1900 negotiations were matured by which the post-graduate school of homeopathy in Philadelphia which had being operated for a number of years by James Tyler Kent M.D. and a few earnest supporters was brought to Chicago and affiliated with Dunham Medical College. Dr Kent became Dean of the combined institutions and Harvey Farrington M.D. who came with the post-graduate school was given a professorship in the Department of Materia Medica. During the same year and before the opening of the session 1900/1901 an arrangement was made by which part of the faculty and a good portion of the student body was transferred to Dunham from what was then known as the National Medical College of Chicago. This change added to the teaching force Thomas C. Dunham M.D., Edwin R. McEntyre M.D., George E. Dienst M.D., Francis C. Ford M.D., A. Sylvester Fish M.D., and several others who had been associated previously with them in college work[xxxvii]*"*

The Dean in 1896/7, J. J. Thompson left the National Medical College after or during the 1896/7 year to join the Hering College with a number of other lectures and some students. 1900 was not the only time The National Medical College was in difficulty. 1896/7 was just prior to Littlejohn choosing Dunham for his medical studies in 1897.[xxxviii] This would have been another factor in Littlejohn not choosing The National Medical College.

Dunham and Herring were united in the early part of the first decade of the twentieth century. His two brothers are listed as members of the teaching staff of Dunham College in 1900/1901 and it was during this time that Littlejohn completed his studies in that

---

[10] Cf. the chapter on 'Chicago prior to Kirksville' and the story of Theresa K Jennings.

[xxviii] HISTORY OF HOMOEOPATHY AND ITS INSTITUTIONS IN AMERICA; EDITED BY WILLIAM HARVEY KING, M. D., LL. D.; THE LEWIS PUBLISHING COMPANY 1905 Volume 4; page 229

[xxix] Report from the Select Committee of the House of Lords appointed to consider the Registration and Regulation of Osteopaths Bill, together with the Proceedings of the Committee and Minutes of Evidence; 17th July 1935; pages 210 and 229

[xxx] History of Homeopathy and its institutions in America; WILLIAM HARVEY KING, M. D., LL. D.; THE LEWIS PUBLISHING COMPANY 1905 Volume 3 page 120-1

[xxxi] Chicago Clinic and Pure Water Journal volume 18, 1905 page 21

[xxxii] Appendix to The Twentieth Annual Report Of The Illinois State Board Of Health. Springfield, Illinois, Phillips Bros., State Printers, 1898. page cl

[xxxiii] National Medical College (Chicago, I. Annual announcement. Chicago: Calumet Books & Eng. Co.; viewable on Hathi Trust digital library

[xxxiv] Eighth annual announcement of the Dunham Medical College and Twelfth annual announcement of the Post-Graduate School of Homeopathics: 1902-1903; Held in the Center for Research Libraries, Chicago

[xxxv] Medical education in the United States and Canada: a report to the Carnegie foundation for the advancement of teaching by Abraham Flexner, with an introduction by henry s. Pritchett president of the foundation; BULLETIN NUMBER FOUR (1910), page 212

[xxxvi] History of Homeopathy and its institutions in America; WILLIAM HARVEY KING, M. D., LL. D.; THE LEWIS PUBLISHING COMPANY 1905 Volume 2 page 431

[xxxvii] History of Homeopathy and its institutions in America; WILLIAM HARVEY KING, M. D., LL. D.; THE LEWIS PUBLISHING COMPANY 1905 Volume 3 page 120-1

[xxxviii] History of Homeopathy and its institutions in America; WILLIAM HARVEY KING, M. D., LL. D.; THE LEWIS PUBLISHING COMPANY 1905 Volume 2 page 431

[xxxix] Eighth annual announcement of the Dunham Medical College and Twelfth annual announcement of the Post-Graduate School of Homeopathics: 1902-1903; Held in the Center for Research Libraries, Chicago

[xl] Eighth annual announcement of the Dunham Medical College and Twelfth annual announcement of the Post-Graduate School of Homeopathics: 1902-1903; Held in the Center for Research Libraries, Chicago.

THE SOCIETY OF SCIENCE, LETTERS AND ART[1]

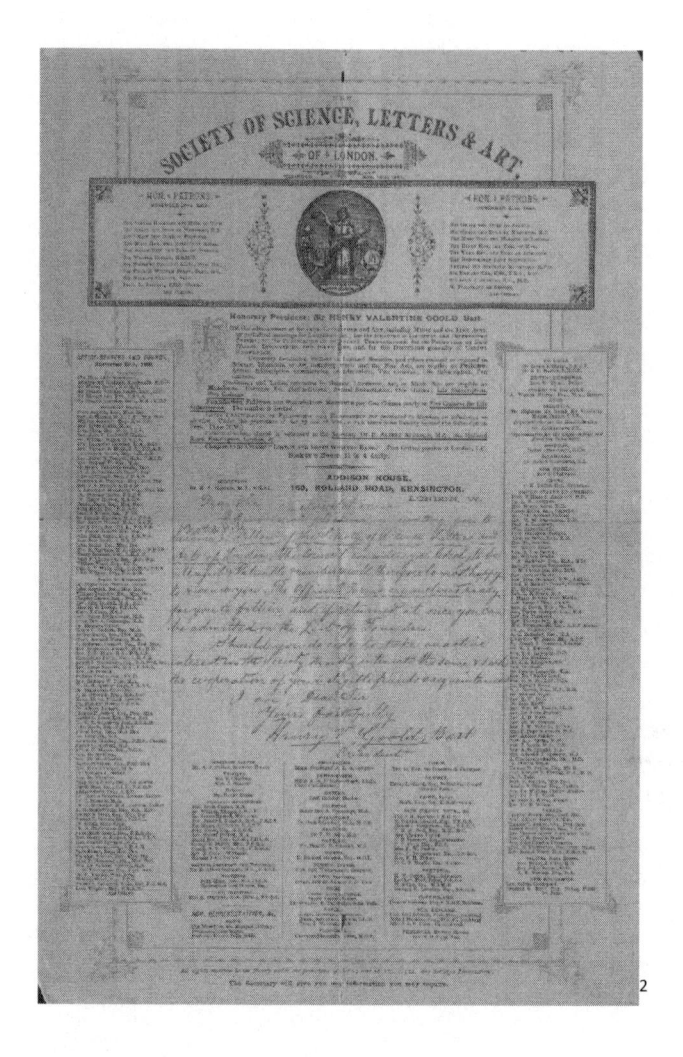

---

[1] The official short designation of the Society of Science, Letters and Art was 'The Society of Science' with post nominal letters as FSSc
[2] Source unknown

Littlejohn's association with this society started in 1895 when he became a Fellow[i]. He presented papers on education to the society in 1895 and 1896 and 1897 and in 1898 his first paper on osteopathy was read in his absence. The substance of it being an address delivered to the graduating class of the American School of Osteopathy in June 1898. In 1899, he was invited to deliver an address before the Society, just after being elected a Fellow of the Royal Society of Literature. However, due to the sudden death of the secretary, that was presented to the Society to be read in absence at a later meeting and published as an in memoriam to the deceased secretary.

Then, in August 1900, he was present at the annual meeting of the society and delivered in person the address on "Osteopathy-- a New View of Therapeutics," which was published in the Journal of the Science of Osteopathy[ii]

The Littlejohn association with the Society of Science, Letters and Art goes back to 1895 when he was elected a Fellow, shortly after his appointment as President of Amity College.

It is possible that he had heard of the Society much earlier than this and may even have confused it with a British Government department of Education. His brother William presented prizes at the Garvagh Science Academy in connection with the **'Science and Arts department South Kensington'** in 1889[3]. With the name of the official Government department being 'Science and Arts department South Kensington', it would be easy to confuse it with the Society of Science, Letters and Art as this society had its headquarters in Kensington and was also involved in school examinations. Littlejohn himself had attended and won prizes the Garvagh Science Academy, so he may also have been influenced by this confusion.

---

[3] A report in the Belfast Telegraph of 10th Jan 1889 mentions the distribution of prizes gained at the examination the previous May in connection with the "Science and Art Department, South Kensington" took place at the upper school in Garvagh. The Rev. William Littlejohn was present in connection with the school committee.

Littlejohn presented three papers on Osteopathy to the Society of Science, Letters and Art, 1898,1899 and 1900, and received their gold medal in 1899. The controversy around his association with this society started during 1899, the year he was specifically invited to give a lecture and was elected a Fellow of the Royal Society of Literature. This controversy was fuelled by correspondence between Charles Still and a Dr. Ernst Roberts in England. The essence of this correspondence was that the lecture did not happen and that Littlejohn *"received a great deal of free advertising for his supposed lecture or address. Some have suggested that maybe he did write this address, and then presented it in the way that some political speeches or addresses are mailed out over the country*[4].

Some of the controversy concerned the labelling of his talk as being given 'to the Royal Society of Literature' or 'Royal Society'. Littlejohn never pretended that the lecture was to the Royal Society and it was published in the Journal of the Science of Osteopathy February 1900 as The Science of Osteopathy Its Value in Preventing and in Curing Diseases by J. Martin Littlejohn Ph.D., L.L.D., F.S.Sc, F.R.S.L (London). In that journal, it was given as an address delivered before the Royal Society of Literature. It had always puzzled me why if he had thought it was going to be given to the Royal Society of Literature that when he arrived and gave the lecture he did not see that it was not to that society but to the Society of Science, Letters and Art. This evident mistake can be put into perspective by the fact that he arrived in England to find that his friend and colleague Dr. Sturman, secretary of the Society of Science, had passed away suddenly and his talk was then cancelled only to be *"read in absence at a later meeting and published as an in memoriam to the deceased secretary"*[iii]. He was notified of his election as a Fellow of the Royal Society of Literature in January 1899[iv] and the announcement of this talk at around the same time, thus leading to confusion as to which society it was to be given.

On his return to America Littlejohn walked into the controversy over Hildreth. The sequence of events can be outlined as

---

[4] As detailed earlier, Littlejohn set the record straight and was probably the source of the information that Charles Still refers to in his letter when he says, "It was again brought to our notice this fall that such a thing (the Lecture) did not happen.".

follows: having lost his father early in the year (1899), survived the tornado in Kirksville, his brother then joined the Masons in contradiction to Littlejohn's own beliefs about oath bound societies, on his way then to England having had his request for graduating with the June class turned down, his friend and colleague in the Society of Science passes away and then on his return he ran into the controversy within the college.

It is no wonder that this confusion was never fully corrected and that while others seemed to take the line in the address where he states *"your charter rights as Royal Society give you privilege and honour of branding any scientific truth as genuine"* ….. as meaning that it was towards a Royal Society instead of the Royal Society of Literature. It's clear that in writing in the journal of the Science of Osteopath, August 15th, 1900 and again in the Osteopathic World concerning his European tour, in 1903 that he sets the record straight without any fuss or pomp or circumstance. His statement *"The editor was privileged to present in printed form his previous address (due in 1899) as an 'In memoriam' of Dr. E. A. Sturman"*,[v] printed in August 1900, makes it quite clear that the talk itself did not take place.

Given this 'history' it is important to understand what the Society was and its standing.

What was the Society of Science, Letters and Art?

A common source of information is Wikipedia. Their article on the society starts with the following:

"The Society of Science, Letters and Art, also known as the Society of Science or SSLA was a soi-disant[5] learned society which flourished between 1882 and 1902. Dr Edward Albert Sturman M.A., F.R.S.L. owned and ran the society for his own financial benefit from his house at Holland Road, in Kensington, London." It goes on to say *"the society sold the privilege of wearing academic dress and using the post nominal letters F.S.Sc. to both eminent and ordinary people around the world without the obligation to sit an examination or submit*

---

[5] soi-disant = self-styled; so-called.

papers. Many members of legitimate learned societies were duped into thinking that they were being offered fellowships by a department of their own respected institutions. *"The society also sold diplomas and masqueraded as an examining board for schools although it merely provided exam papers and did not examine candidates."*

The article also gave some information on the society as providing school examinations and acting as school boards for certain schools. But also lends the criticism *"notwithstanding the above information from schools via respectable press* **the society's honorary secretary Dr. Sturman admitted in 1892 that he only sent out exam papers and did not examine candidates; he accepted that this was 'a little bit wrong'.** *He said the society 'examined some fifty schools a year charging a fee from 2 shillings and 6 pence to 7 shillings and 6 pence per head for each pupil but sometimes quoting wholesale rates and giving certificates. It is significant that the press only records each school using the society as an exam board once."* [vi]

Wikipedia's open editing policy means that it may contain inaccuracies', but does give an overview of how the Society, which is now defunct, is viewed today. Most of the accusations are taken from an article published in 'Truth' magazine in April 21st 1892[6]

In this article Henry Labouchère published his interview with Dr. Sturman, who had voluntarily come to his offices to clear up any misunderstanding that *the Society of Science, Letters and Art had no affiliation with the "International Society of Literature, Science, and Art"* [7]

If we look at the text of the interview the most damning accusation was that **"the society's honorary secretary Dr. Sturman admitted in 1892 that he only sent out exam papers and did not examine candidates; he accepted that this was 'a little bit wrong'."** This statement is not accurate. What Dr. Sturman actually said was that

---

[6] The Wikipedia article gives the date incorrectly as 21st August 1892

[7] The principals of the International Society of Literature, Science and art were tried for fraud and imprisoned. (Wikipedia)

(Labouchère[8]) *"The examiner, as I understand it, certifies as to the education and knowledge of the pupils, and you grant them certificate accordingly? —(Sturman)* **Not quite that. There is a regular form of instructions for examiners to carry out. Candidates' papers are all printed and given to the pupils, and it is the work of the local representatives to send them back to me…We don't always send men down to the schools. It is not the usual thing…we have local representatives who attend to the local work.[vii]**

Later in the interview, Labouchère stated that he had *"evidence., very strong evidence"* that Dr. Sturman was selling certificates without checking if the pupils were up to standard, citing one specific case. Dr. Sturman stated that he knew of the case and that he had *"proved the people were liars"* Labouchère didn't pursue it or produce the evidence but changed the subject[9]. He then finished his 'quotes' from the interview with

"you draw the fees, and the pupils get the certificates, so that nobody can complain. Isn't that so?! (Pause). – **Well, I admit the exams are a little bit wrong**"[viii]

Putting the quote '**Well, I admit the exams are a little bit wrong**' in context gives a different impression than the one given above Wikipedia text, especially as Labouchère had plied Sturman with strong alcohol.

It is worth noting who Labouchère was and what his credentials were as an exposer of the truth. Quoting from Wikipedia:

He inherited a large fortune and had a number of occupations including member of parliament, editing and funding his own magazine (Truth) and theatre owner. *"He is remembered for the Labouchère Amendment to British law, which for the first time made all male homosexual activity a crime*[ix]*"*

---

[8] Editor of the magazine Truth.
[9] This apparently concerned a certificate given to "a girl of eleven…testifying that she had passed 'with honours' and examination in anatomy and physiology" (New Zealand evening post June 7, 1893). I don't know if the writer was more incredulous that a 'girl' or someone of 'eleven' could possibly pass an exam in 'anatomy and physiology'

Educated at Eton and Cambridge he *"was accused of cheating in an examination and his degree was withheld"* and *"In 1897, Labouchère was accused in the press of share-rigging, using Truth to disparage companies, advising shareholders to dispose of their shares and, when the share prices fell as a result, buying them himself at a low price. When he failed to reply to the accusations, his reputation suffered accordingly."*[x]

Even given that this is taken from Wikipedia he does not sound like the sort of person whose word you would take at face value. Add to this the fact he admits during the article, that he plied Dr. Sturman with alcohol during the interview, makes his accusations seem less reliable. In 1916 he is quoted by the American Medical Association as saying *"Sturman, who was a stupid and illiterate man, came here to see us, and we published the interview, which made very funny reading. After this the concern went downhill and Sturman himself died six or seven years ago"*

This again shows the cultural bias that existed between 'Eton and Cambridge' educated and those from a less privileged background. Sturman was a schoolmaster from an early age and hardly illiterate, but Labouchère's word was taken as 'gospel' without question.

How the Society recruited Members and Fellows

An idea of how and why Littlejohn might have been approach by Sturman to become a Fellow of the Society can be gleaned by the following letter published in the London Evening Post in 1883:

"During the Colonial and Indian Exhibition, 1886, I, in common, I believe, with many other colonial Commissioners, received about the same time invitation to join the Society of Arts (an old – established and important body) and the Society of Science, Letters and Art, on the usual term as to fellowship. As I had ceased to join other Societies after being elected FRS., I wrote at once declining both offers From the Society of Arts I heard nothing more ; but a few days later I received a letter from Dr. Sturman, informing me that the Council of the Society of Science, Letters and Art had elected me an

'Honorary Fellow,' and forwarding a list of. Men, more or less distinguished, who had already accepted that honour. ...

"It is only fair to add that since posting my letter to you of 5th August, I have received a long communication from Dr. Sturman, in which ho repudiates the allegation in Truth, stating that the matter is now in his solicitor's hands, and urging that 'the Society has a right to be judged by its work, and not by the misleading statements of persons connected with other institutions and jealous of its success' He a asks me to suspend my judgment till I have attended the 143rd meeting of the Society in November next. . I have replied, confirming my withdrawal, and stating that a public refutation of the allegation in question would be far more satisfactory to me than a long explanatory letter marked ; 'private and confidential.' If the solicitor is vindicating the honor of the Society, he seems to be a long time about it, for the first article in Truth appeared 16 months ago. 11th August. 1893. 11th August. 1893. W.L.B. [xi]"

Since Littlejohn was elected a Fellow in 1895, it would seem reasonable to assume his name was drawn to the attention of Sturman when he was elected president of Amity College and an invitation similar to the one in the letter above was sent to him. Littlejohn, when he received an invitation to join a learned society he was not one to just taken it just as an 'Honour'. He entered into the societies affairs wholeheartedly, presenting three papers on his subject of Education. However it would not be until his visit in 1900, one year after the death of Dr. Sturman, that he would see the difficulties within the society. That was. In August, 1900, when he was "present at the annual meeting of the society and delivered in person the address on "Osteopathy-- a New View of Therapeutics," which was published in the Journal of the Science of Osteopathy, on our return."[xii] All his previous Osteopathic and most, if not all of his papers on Education, of his previous papers presented at the Society were "in abstensia". This experience of being present at the annual meeting after the death of Sturman would have exposed all the problems and difficulties within the society. Littlejohn's next visit to England was in 1903 when "They were making preparations for the annual meeting in September and gave us a very pressing invitation to remain to that meeting and meet the friends of science, literature and art that we have known for the last nine years"[xiii] He was unable to stay and never presented another paper nor, as far as we know, attended another meeting. The implication is that he started to withdraw from his association with the Society after the death of Sturman.

> Kindly send an Outline of your Educational Career. Give Names and Addresses of three Referees.

THE SOCIETY OF
Science, Letters, and Art, of London.

ADDISON HOUSE,
160, HOLLAND ROAD,

KENSINGTON,
LONDON, W.

HONORARY PRESIDENT — SIR HENRY VALENTINE GOOLD, BART.

Formal Certificate of a Candidate for Admission as Fellow.

Name_____
Residence_____
Qualification_____

being desirous of becoming a **FELLOW OF THE SOCIETY OF SCIENCE, LETTERS, AND ART, OF LONDON**, We, the undersigned propose and recommend him as likely to be a useful and valuable Member thereof.

Dated this_____ day of_____ 189

Henry V. Goold, Bart.

Proposed_____ 189
Admitted_____ 189

University Graduates, Fellows of Learned Societies, and others, eminent or engaged in Science, Literature, or Art, including Music and the Fine Art, are eligible as **Fellows**. Annual Subscription (commencing on admission), Two Guineas; Life Subscription, Ten Guineas.
Gentlemen and Ladies interested in Science, Literature, Art, or Music, &c., are eligible as **Members**. Annual Subscription, One Guinea. Life Subscription, Five Guineas. Entrance Fee, Half-a-Guinea.
Foundation Fellows and **Foundation Members** pay One Guinea yearly or Five Guineas for Life Subscription. The number is limited.
Life Fellows are eligible for admission as Fellows by Examination.
LATIN CERTIFICATES OF FELLOWSHIP OR MEMBERSHIP are presented to Members on admission or election.

[10]

---

[10] Original Source unknown

Criticisms of the Society of Science, Letters and Art

It was involved in a controversy with the Royal Society of Arts leading to the Royal Society of Arts, in December 1879 making known to its members that they had nothing to do with the Society of Science, Letters and Art while acknowledging that some newly elected members of the Royal Society of Arts had been solicited by the Society of Science, Letters and Art for membership of that organisation. Some of these members complained and wanted to know from the Royal Society of Arts if it was a legitimate sister organisation' to which the Royal Society replied it was not[xiv]

This gives some indication of how the Society solicited new members. This was not much different from other societies at the time, for example the Royal Society of Arts; Walter L Buller wrote to the London Evening Post,

"During the Colonial and Indian Exhibition, 1886, I, in common, I believe, with many other colonial Commissioners, received about the same time invitation to join the Society of Arts (an old – established and important body) and the " Society of Science, Letters, and Art," on the usual term as to fellowship. As I had ceased to join other Societies after being elected FRS., I wrote at once declining both offers"[xv]

Sturman was using the same methods used by other societies and universities of the time, and even today, in offering 'Honorary Fellowship' to persons he wanted to be associated with his society. He wrote to Buller repudiating the allegations in Truth and saying " *the Society has a right to be judged by its work, and not by the misleading statements of persons connected with other institutions and jealous of its success*", and asking Buller to not judge the society until he had attended a meeting, inviting him to the next one (the 143rd meeting) in November 1893.- a reasonable offer by any means but one that was declined[xvi]

Wikipedia gives another example of the method used by Sturman to gain new members:

"In October 1886 the society received strong criticism from New Zealand. The complaint was that 'the society favours (i.e. the offering of scientific fellowships) appears to be sown broadcast.' The complaint was prompted by the following note sent speculatively from London to likely candidates in the colonies by the society.

'We shall be pleased to add your name to the list of fellows of the Society of Science, Letters and Art of London. We are admitting the principle men of science, letters and art from all parts of the world. With Sir H.V. Goold's complements.[xvii]'

The complaint, like most others, quoted the article in Truth Magazine. While Dr. Sturman's methods, and the underlying aim, and those of Goold may have been questionable, in essence they were no different from those of the so-called respectable societies.

Buller puts the culture at the time well when he says, "*I had ceased to join other Societies after being elected FRS*[11]". The meaning of which is clear. Having reached the pinnacle of societies, i.e. The Royal Society, there was no need to be a member of any others, worthy or not.

The other criticism leveled at Sturman was that *"persons 'eminent or engaged in science, literature, or arts are eligible as Fellows, that gentlemen and ladies **interested**[12] in the science, literature, or art, or music .&c.(delightfully comprehensive this) are eligible as Members"*[xviii]

These complaints, which may have some legitimacy, came from the 'privileged' elements of society, who had been sought out by the Society and usually quoted the article by Labouchère, in Truth.

When he was dealing with Minifie's Cuban adventure Labouchère showed his bias around philanthropy and religion.

---

[11] FRS = Fellow of the Royal Society
[12] Emphasis in original newspaper article

"I instinctively dislike any business proposition emanating from a minister or ex-minister of the Gospel".[xix]

He made his position clear on the use of post-nominal letters in the following exchange:

If I were a Vicar engaging a Curate, and a young man with an Oxford RA- degree came after the place I would have at once a certain security that if I asked him to dine at the vicarage with a few select parishioners, he would not drop his h's or dip his knife into the salt-cellars, or otherwise offend the weaker brethren. If I am the editor of a newspaper in want of a leader writer, and a man comes to me with Sturman's diploma and the degree of F.S.S., I need not belong in sending him about his business. In these and almost all other cases, the degree —bogus or otherwise—does signify something and so far, saves trouble to all parties. The mischief of the present state of things, however, is that the something which is signified is not sufficiently definite. If the only M.A.'s and B.A.'s and LL.D.'s among us were graduates of the old-established Universities everybody would know exactly what the letters imply,[xx]

The main criticism seemed to centre on the fact that the society solicited members[13] and offered memberships of different grades to people who were either 'qualified' or' engaged in' or' interested in' promoting science, letters or arts'. and that this was done without any examination. This really wasn't any different from many other so-called learned societies at this time including the Royal Society of Literature of which Littlejohn was a member, and the Royal Society of Arts; the membership criteria of which were to be proposed by two members and pay an annual subscription.

---

[13] Labouchère also attacked the Academy of Political and Social Science of Philadelphia, a well-founded academy for the promotion of political and social science for the same reasons. It was, as is today, associated with universities in the Pennsylvania region. Littlejohn was associated with the similarly named Academy of Political Science as part of his studies at Columbia College, New York.

An Interpretation and possible explanation

The basic question is how do we interpret all of this? One interpretation that has being put forward is that Littlejohn joined a bogus society and hoodwinked people into thinking it was something other than what it was. This argument is supported by the references in some publications to his proposed lecture in 1899 being held before the 'Royal Society', 'Royal society of Science' and sometimes the misuse of letters.

Another view would be that he was duped into joining this society thinking it was something else as other members of the Royal Society, Royal Society of Literature, and Royal Society of Art had been and didn't realise this mistake until later.

However, a third possibility exists. Littlejohn was a Reformed Presbyterian and a reformer and educator by nature and thus would have had an affinity for an organisation which was or could be seen as reforming and having aims broader than the conventional at the time, viz. trying to encourage an interest in science and the arts among the general public and women. If we quote Littlejohn from the prospectus of the British School of Osteopathy 1927 and he says:

"In modern times colleges of physicians and surgeons have been set apart for medicine and surgery after the pattern of the apostolic college, and these colleges have been incorporated for the purpose of educating those who should be considered 'qualified' to engage in the profession and thus certifying the 'qualified'. These colleges have in recent years debarred all others not possessing their qualification as 'unqualified' just as the conformist in religion branded the unbeliever as a heretic and non-conformist. It's only in comparatively recent years that such qualifications have been limited, the 'qualified' healer claiming the prescriptive right to exercise the gift of healing. Hence there has sprung up in the healing profession a body of dissenters or non-conformists just in the same way as there arose in the history of religion dissenters from the predominant established religions. This became necessary because of the discovery of new ideas and ideals in healing as in religion since the new has always being branded as a heresy."

This paragraph gives an idea of how the man thought and how he would have had affinity for an organisation such as the Society of Science, Letters and Art in that it was non-conformist in the sense that it was open to everybody and that it allowed the expression of free and new ideas and promoted these in its meetings.

This view is supported by the fact that he did not just join the Society of Science, Letters and Art and sit back and use the Post-nominal letters to promote himself. He presented six papers, three on education and three on Osteopathy to the Society and only disengaged himself after the Society lost its leader, Dr. Sturman and its short comings became evident. Even then he withdrew in a dignified manner and without fuss or condemnation.

On reading the article in Wikipedia it would be easy to come away with the idea that this was a bogus society. However, when the original letters in The Times and the reply by the secretary of the society and the newspapers clippings on the society are read, there is evidence that it was doing at least some good work. It may have been misused by some people while others, like Littlejohn, give the Society support to advance peoples interest in the Society of Science, Letters and Art.

The Society of Science, Letters and Art had what seems to be two faces. One as an illegitimate society handing out 'bogus' certificates for a price. The producing a journal and organising meetings to favour the advancement of Science and Arts particularly providing a means for those with no formal background to meet and converse with those working in the field and thus advancing their interest and knowledge.

As an interesting aside to this we see, in Littlejohn's reply to enquiries from the Committee to Establish the University of the United States, the same professional response to an idea that he would support. In this case a National University of the United States, in the case of the Society of Science, Letters and Art the promotion of the interest in Science and Arts amongst the general public. Not only did he endorse the idea but was prepared to give time and energy to it, as is seen by his response.[xxi]

"My Dear Sir:

"Your letters and enclosed papers have been received. I have read with much interest your statements and am rejoiced to hear of the increasing interest manifested in the scheme to establish a national university. I think there can only be one candid position on this matter, namely, that of favor toward the plan. I am satisfied no denominational institution, such as Bishop Hursts university, can ever occupy the field, and no State institution is competent to supply the lacuna. Only a national university can fill the place at the very top of our national educational system. I have nothing to add to or take away from the expression I sent you almost two years ago, the lapse of time having served to increase my sympathetic interest in this movement.

"In answer to your queries I will say (I) I- do believe that the most effective work should be and ought to be done in the States. I think that State committee ought to be organized and to act in this matter. I think President Schaeffer of State University, or President Gates of Iowa College, Grinnell, would be good for the position. (2) I think that such a national rally in Washington would be a good thing.

"About the holidays would be convenient because advantage could be taken of college recess to attend in larger numbers. (3) I do think that friends of the cause should begin to think of plans for endowments. I think that fellowships open to professors in the colleges of the United States, tenable, say for one or two years, and periodical lectureships, tenable for a number of years, would be a fine form of endowment. It would be a means of commanding a wide field of scholarship for specialisms and would arouse an interest among those who would prospectively be interested.

"I shall be pleased to aid you in any way I can at any time. You may count upon my increased interest and sympathy.
"Yours, for the success of this movement in behalf of the higher national education.

J. Martin Littlejohn, Amity College, College Springs, Iowa, November 10, 1897

[i] British School of Osteopathy announcement 1927/8
[ii] The Osteopathic World October 1903, page 472
[iii] The Osteopathic World October 1903, page 472
[iv] Kansas City journal January 23rd, 1899
[v] The Journal of the Science of Osteopathy, Volume 1, Number 4 first page, first paragraph
[vi] Wikipedia; Society of Science, Letters and Art
[vii] Truth; April 21st, 1893, page 817; Courtesy of the British Library
[viii] Truth; April 21st, 1892, page 818; Courtesy of the British Library
[ix] Wikipedia; Henry Labouchère
[x] Wikipedia; Henry Labouchère
[xi] Evening Post, Volume XLVI, Issue 80, 2 October 1893, Page 3
[xii] The Osteopathic World October 1903, page 472 etc
[xiii] The Osteopathic World October 1903, page 472 etc.
[xiv] Journal of The Royal Society of Arts; No. 1,412. VOL XXVIII Friday, December 12 1879.; Courtesy of the Royal Society of Arts
[xv] Evening Post, Volume XLVI, Issue 80, 2 October 1893, Page 3
[xvi] Ibid
[xvii] *Auckland Star, 18th October 1885*
[xviii] New Zealand evening post, June 7th, 1893
[xix] Truth, March 10th, 1915, page 371; British Library Holdings
[xx] Truth; September 28th, 1893, page 638; Courtesy of the British Library
[xxi] IN THE SENATE OF THE UNITED STATES.
UNIVERSITY OF THE UNITED STATES.
April 1, 1902. Submitted by Mr. DEBOE from the Committee to Establish the University of the United States and ordered to be printed. WASHINGTON: GOVERNMENT PRINTING OFFICE.1902. Page 142

Hymns and Psalms for Littlejohn's Funeral

Psalm 100
From Scottish Metrical Psalms 1650
Meter: 8,8,8,8

1 All people that on earth do dwell,

   Sing to the Lord with cheerful voice.

2 Him serve with mirth, his praise forth tell,

   Come ye before him and rejoice.

3 Know that the Lord is God indeed;

   Without our aid he did us make:

   We are his flock, he doth us feed,

   And for his sheep he doth us take.

4 O enter then his gates with praise,

   Approach with joy his courts unto:

   Praise, laud, and bless his name always,

   For it is seemly so to do.

5 For why? the Lord our God is good,

   His mercy is for ever sure;

   His truth at all times firmly stood,

   And shall from age to age endure

Psalm 23

From Scottish Metrical Psalms 1650

Meter: 8,6,8,6

1   The Lord's my shepherd, I'll not want.
2   He makes me down to lie
    In pastures green: he leadeth me
        the quiet waters by.
3   My soul he doth restore again;
        and me to walk doth make
    Within the paths of righteousness,
        ev'n for his own name's sake.
4   Yea, though I walk in death's dark vale,
        yet will I fear none ill:
    For thou art with me; and thy rod
        and staff me comfort still.
5   My table thou hast furnished
        in presence of my foes;
    My head thou dost with oil anoint,
        and my cup overflows.
6   Goodness and mercy all my life
        shall surely follow me:
    And in God's house for evermore
        my dwelling-place shall be.

Lead, Kindly Light

Lead, kindly Light, amid th' encircling gloom,
Lead Thou me on;
The night is dark, and I am far from home,
Lead Thou me on;
Keep Thou my feet; I do not ask to see
The distant scene; one step enough for me.

I was not ever thus, nor prayed that Thou
Shouldst lead me on;
I loved to choose and see my path, but now
Lead Thou me on;
I loved the garish day, and spite of fears,
Pride ruled my will; remember not past years.

So long Thy pow'r has blest me, sure it still
Wilt lead me on,
O'er moor and fen, o'er crag and torrent, till
The night is gone,
And with the morn those angel faces smile,
Which I have loved long since, and lost awhile.

The story behind the hymn

The poem, originally called "the Pillar of the Cloud[1]," was written by, the Anglican theologian and vicar, John Henry Newman (1801-90), after he had recovered from a severe fever. He is said to have been "displeased when the poem was turned into a hymn in 1845 – by which time he had converted to Catholicism, where congregational hymn-singing formed no part of divine service".[2]

---

[1] Exodus 13: 21-22:
[2] The story behind the hymn; by Rupert Christiansen, The Telegraph, 22 Sep 2007

The osteopaths of the Twin cities celebrated the arrival of Dr. J. Martin Littlejohn in the northwest by a picnic at Minnehaha Falls this afternoon. A large number of the physicians and their friends tendered a reception to Dr. Littlejohn at 5 o'clock and then enjoyed a park dinner.

Dr. Littlejohn is recognised as the greatest scholar and writer in osteopathy. He is a graduate of several medical schools, holds a number of literary and scientific degrees, has written several books and is Fellow of the Royal Society of Science, London, Eng.

He came to Minneapolis primarily for a half month's rest and is the guest of the Dobbyns at Minnehaha Falls

The Minneapolis Journal, August 27th, 1904

Some final words about the man
John Martin Littlejohn

"Man drinks in the pleasures of life because he has a natural appetite for whatever nature furnishes to his life. Man delights in employment for his hands. How do we regard our avocations in life? Sacred gifts from God. "Idle men tempt the devil." "He that works not, cannot pray, cannot see the sun." What a life of dreary monotony and dull desolateness would be man's if he lay down upon the face of nature and said to God, *I cannot use the physical strength of my manhood; I refuse to employ the faculties of my mind; I will close in the leaden casket the love and sympathy of my heart.*

"No man comes nearer to God than does he whose time is fully occupied in the work of life. We can serve God with our hands, our minds and our hearts. The talents we possess, whatever they be, must be in active exercise, if we are to appreciate the high place we fill very near our Maker.

" Carlyle says he honors two classes of men above all others - the hard worker whose hands are pinched and furrowed by love's labor of necessity; and the hard laborer for the spiritual daily food of the suffering and sinful, - these he says are the realizers of the life-principles of Jesus of Nazareth. When we think of this great continent opened up four hundred years ago by the pioneers of progress, of its broad acres, un-numbered treasures, unpainted beauties and brilliant opportunities for work and employment in the service of God and of humanity, we ask, What could God have done more for man than he has done, in giving him a physical sphere of life and avocations in life to occupy time and attention?"
(Devine Gifts to Man; Prof. J. M. Littlejohn, D. D.
The Christian Nation, Vol. 19, July 12, 1893, page 5)

"Osteopathy has not made the advance which its system guarantees, and its equality with other systems demands. This is we believe the reason within ourselves why we have not made success this year that were made in former years. We need organisations. We do not believe in the curtain-lecture about dues, duties etc as a means of promoting organisations. We do not believe that the profession is steeped in selfishness, nor do we believe as the ordinary osteopathic physician, that the osteopath is financially embarrassed. His expenses are great, his work is constant, and he is buried to a large extent in his work. Our principle failure is a failure to appreciate the true position of osteopathy in the field of science, healing or medicine and in the field of law. Osteopathy is in the line of succession, apostolically to all that is good and true and scientific in medicine. It is a system of medicine. By special legislation, we have tried to legislate ourselves out of the field of medicine, while the law, both common and statuary places medicine in the field of healing, recognising different systems, complete, independent and all sufficient in themselves to deal with disease, ill health, accident etc....We seem to be afraid that anyone thinks we practice medicine or surgery, while as a matter of fact, we are practising the primitive medicine and surgery that existed before drug adulterations were admitted into the fold of healing."

    (The Osteopathic World, The Editor's Own, J. Martin Littlejohn
    April 1903, page 164-5)

Wm. R. Dobbyn describing J. Martin Littlejohn

    He is a scholar in the best sense of the word, and a man of great intellectual honesty and courage. Fortunately for Osteopathy his scholarly attainments have not made a bigot of him. The truth has made him free. His power of co-ordinating and co-relating enables him to become a safe interpreter of the meaning of events and these characteristics give authority to his utterances on the printed page before his class and upon the platform. We doubt if there is a man in America to-day who is as well read in the history of medicine as he. His acute memory summoned into action by a singularly alert mind, gives him possession of the fields over which he traverses for information, and he is assisted to his dogmas by an imagination and a judgment quite as wonderful as his memory.

One bright day last Summer it was our pleasure to be with him the whole day. He and the writer were guests of Dr. Herron whose sketch and halftone appear in this issue of The Osteopathic World. Between Herron's sallies of wit, we had Littlejohn at his best. The day was one of the most enchanting of Minnesota's delightful climate, and what with the entrancing features of Minnehaha, Como, Wildwood, and Lake Harriet, Herron's chief guest became loquacious. We felt fortunate in being able to direct his conversation. We were curious to know the sources of the man's strength.

He had browsed through our whole library in a week. That was nothing very wonderful for we had met men before him who could do that. But we had never met a man, save and except Andrew D. White, who appreciated men and human events so keenly as he. For the fabled age of Aesculapius to the present time, in measure of years, is a long period. Greece and Rome had risen upon the world's horizon, swept across its zenith, and, barring their legacy of art and intellect, had gone down behind the visual skyline beyond which rest the hills – the tombs of the ages. Yet this modest Scotch-Huguenot, Littlejohn, was as familiar with the great characters of the great periods of this great span of time as if he had in some ante-natal capacity, lived with them and through it all, sharing the triumphs or the defeats of intellect, luxuriating in courtly arrogance with brilliant favorites, or suffering in exile or in ghastly prisons with the excommunicated and the damned. An age to him was as a book to be read.

As we talked of the history of medicine our curiosity was increased, for we yet were unable to understand how he reached his convictions upon questions intimately illustrative of the life and times of men and peoples. Shifting him to a field more familiar to us, and noting the way he drafted his historical formulae, we think we satisfied our curiosity and learned of the secret of the man's wonderful versatility. Besides having a good memory, an unusual power of co-ordinating and co-relating, he is gifted with an imagination which enables him to transplant himself to any age and associate himself intimately with the characters whom he chooses.

This power of invoking the historical sense is his most striking intellectual characteristic. It is this, fortified by those other intellectual qualities, which makes of him an inspiring teacher. It is this quality which more completely differentiates him from other men, than anything else about him. He is an admirable combination of the student, teacher and philosopher, and is an ideal College professor. It is too early to fully appreciate him."

(The Osteopathic World, August 1905, Pages 19-20)

'A wish is life, a life is Love
Love hateth strife, love leads above;
Love fills a heart, a heart makes true;
Truth is a part of God and you

J. M. Littlejohn; Columbia College, New York Jan 11 1893

"The bride...wore a white silk dress, and carried a handsome shower bouquet, the gift of the bridegroom."